Paris Metro

• The stations Liège and Rennes are closed after 8pm and on Sundays and holidays.

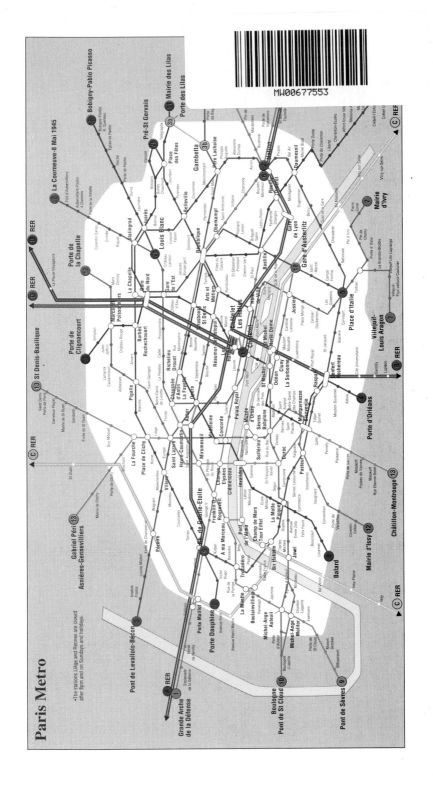

Paris: Overview and Arrondissements

1 Cimetière de Montmartre
2 Sacré Coeur Basilica
3 Parc La Villette
4 Parc des Buttes Chaumont
5 Jardins du Trocadero
6 Palais Chaillot
7 Cimetière de Passy
8 American Embassy
9 British Embassy
10 Petit Palais
11 Grand Palais
12 Arc de Triomphe
13 Madeleine
14 Gare St-Lazare
15 Parc Monceau
16 Palais de la Découverte
17 Opéra Garnier
18 Galeries Lafayette
19 Printemps
20 Gare du Nord
21 Gare de l'Est
22 Opéra Bastille
23 Palais Omnisports de Bercy
24 Ministère des Finances
25 Gare de Lyon
26 Parc de Montsouris
27 Cité Universitaire
28 Cimetière Montparnasse
29 Gare Montparnasse

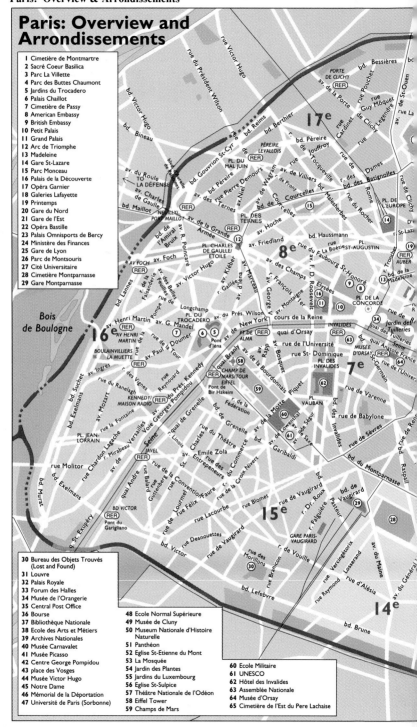

30 Bureau des Objets Trouvés
(Lost and Found)
31 Louvre
32 Palais Royale
33 Forum des Halles
34 Musée de l'Orangerie
35 Central Post Office
36 Bourse
37 Bibliothèque Nationale
38 Ecole des Arts et Métiers
39 Archives Nationales
40 Musée Carnavalet
41 Musée Picasso
42 Centre George Pompidou
43 place des Vosges
44 Musée Victor Hugo
45 Notre Dame
46 Mémorial de la Déportation
47 Université de Paris (Sorbonne)

48 Ecole Normal Supérieure
49 Musée de Cluny
50 Museum Nationale d'Histoire
Naturelle
51 Panthéon
52 Eglise St-Etienne du Mont
53 La Mosquée
54 Jardin des Plantes
55 Jardins du Luxembourg
56 Eglise St-Sulpice
57 Théâtre Nationale de l'Odéon
58 Eiffel Tower
59 Champs de Mars

60 Ecole Militaire
61 UNESCO
62 Hôtel des Invalides
63 Assemblée Nationale
64 Musée d'Orsay
65 Cimetière de l'Est du Pere Lachaise

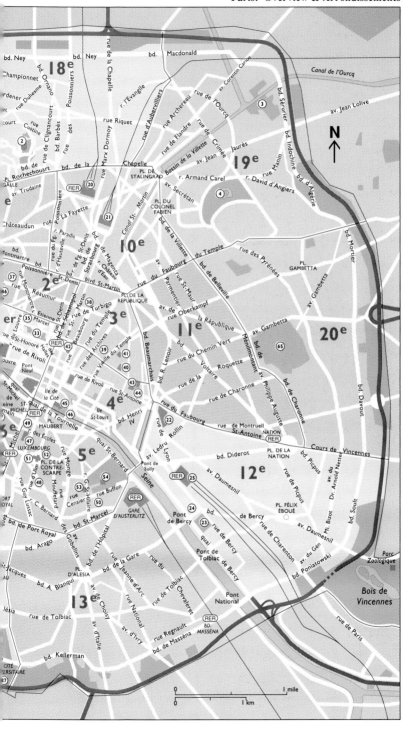

Paris: 1er and 2e

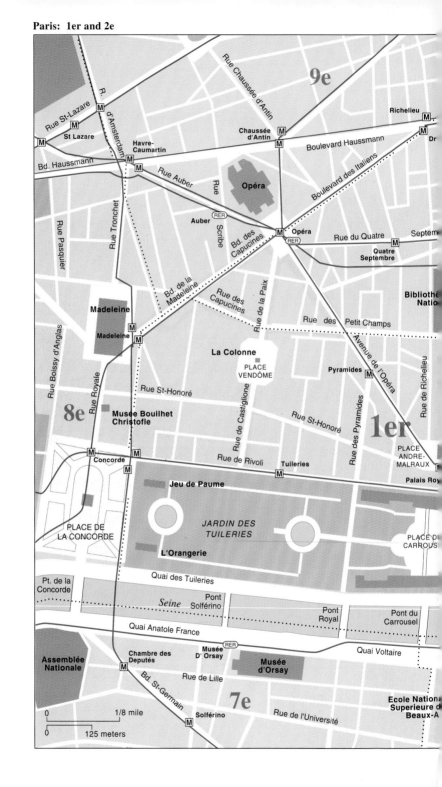

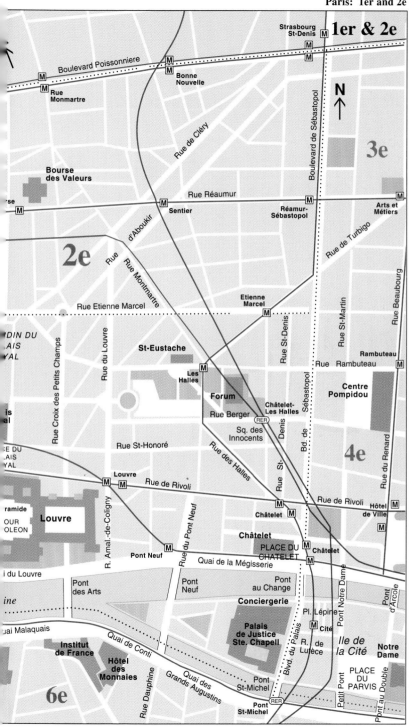

Palais du Louvre

Pont Neuf

Châtelet

Quai du Louvre

Pont des Arts

1er

Pont au Change

Cité

Pont du Carrousel

Pont Neuf

Conciergerie

Ste-Chapelle

Hôte Dieu

Quai Malaquais

Quai de Conti

Palais du Justice

Ile de la Cité

Rue de la Cité

Ecole Nationale Superieure des Beaux Arts

R. Bonaparte

Institut de France

Hôtel des Monnaies

Quai des Grands Augustins

Pont St-Michel

Rue des Sts-Pères

Rue Jacob

Rue de Seine

Rue Mazarine

Rue Dauphine

Pont St-Michel

St-Michel RER

M

M

St-Michel

Rue St-Jaques

R. de l'Abbaye

PLACE ST-GERMAIN-DES-PRÉS

St-Germain Des Prés

Rue St-André des Arts

Pl. St-Michel

Rue Danton

M

Bd. St-Germain

Bd. St-Germain

St-Germain des Prés

M

Mabillon

Odéon

Bd. St-Germain

Musée du Cluny

7e

R. du Four

Rue de l'Odéon

Boulevard

St-Michel

Sorbonne

R. de Sèvres

R. du Vieux Colombier

R. du Saint Sulpice

Rue de Tournon

Rue Racine

PLACE DE LA SORBONNE

R. du Cherche Midi

M

St-Sulpice

PLACE ST-SULPICE

St-Sulpice

PLACE DE L'ODÉON

Rue Soufflot

R. d'Assas

R. de Rennes

Palais du Luxembourg

M

Luxembourg

Bd. Raspail

R. de Vaugirard

6e

Boulevard St-Michel

Rue Gay-Lussac

Rennes

JARDIN DU LUXEMBOURG

St Placide

M

Rue du Montparnasse

Notre-Dame des Champs

M

Rue Vavin

Rue Notre-Dame des Champs

Rue d'Assas

Rue St-Jaques

Montparnasse Bienvenüe

M

Vavin

M

Boulevard du Montparnasse

Avenue de la Observatoire

Port Royal

M

R. du Depart

Edgar Quinet

M

Boulevard Edgar Quinet

14e

Boulevard Raspail

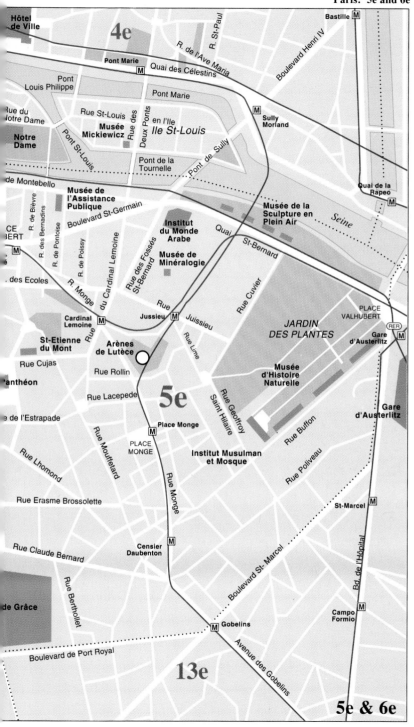

Hôtel
de Ville

4e

R. St-Paul

R. de l'Ave Maria

Bastille

Pont Marie

Quai des Célestins

Boulevard Henri IV

Pont
Louis Philippe

Pont Marie

Rue du
Notre Dame

Rue St-Louis

Rue des
Deux Ponts

en l'Île
Île St-Louis

Sully
Morland

Musée
Mickiewicz

Notre
Dame

Pont St-Louis

Pont de Sully

Pont de la
Tournelle

Quai de la
Rapeo

de Montebello

Musée de
l'Assistance
Publique

Musée de la
Sculpture en
Plein Air

Seine

CE
BERT

R. de Bièvre

R. des Bernadins

R. de Pontoise

R. de Poissy

Boulevard St-Germain

Rue des Fossés
St-Bernard

Institut
du Monde
Arabe

Musée de
Minéralogie

Quai

St-Bernard

Rue Cuvier

PLACE
VALHUBERT

Gare
d'Austerlitz

. des Ecoles

R. Monge

Rue du Cardinal Lemoine

Rue
Jussieu

Juissieu

*JARDIN
DES PLANTES*

Cardinal
Lemoine

St-Etienne
du Mont

Arènes
de Lutèce

Rue Lime

Musée
d'Histoire
Naturelle

Gare
d'Austerlitz

Rue Cujas

Rue Rollin

5e

'anthéon

Rue Lacepede

Rue Mouffetard

Rue Geoffroy
Saint Hilaire

Rue Buffon

Place Monge

PLACE
MONGE

Institut Musulman
et Mosque

Rue Poliveau

Rue Lhomond

Rue Erasme Brossolette

Rue Monge

St-Marcel

Rue Claude Bernard

Censier
Daubenton

Rue Berthollet

Boulevard St. Marcel

Bd. de l'Hôpital

Campo
Formio

de Grâce

Gobelins

13e

Boulevard de Port Royal

Avenue des Gobelins

Paris: RER

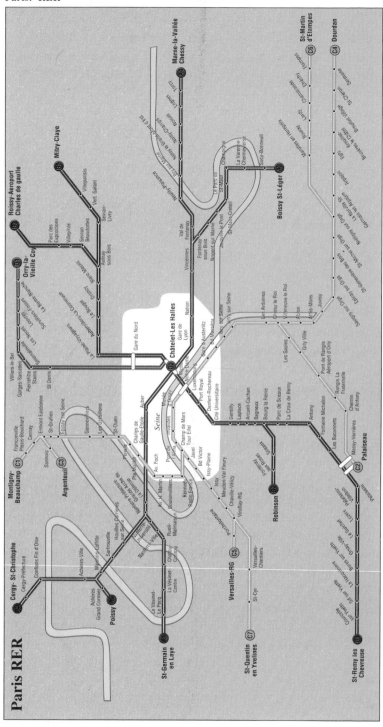

Paris RER

Let's Go

PARIS

is the best book for anyone traveling on a budget. Here's why:

▨ No other guidebook has as many budget listings.

In Paris, we list over 2,500 budget travel bargains. We tell you the cheapest way to get around, and where to get an inexpensive and satisfying meal once you've arrived. We give hundreds of money-saving tips that anyone can use, plus invaluable advice on discounts and deals for students, children, families, and senior travelers.

▨ Let's Go researchers have to make it on their own.

Our Harvard-Radcliffe researcher-writers travel on budgets as tight as your own—no expense accounts, no free hotel rooms.

▨ Let's Go is completely revised each year.

We don't just update the prices, we go back to the place. If a charming café has become an overpriced tourist trap, we'll replace the listing with a new and better one.

▨ No other guidebook includes all this:

Honest, engaging coverage of the cities and beyond; up-to-the-minute prices, directions, addresses, phone numbers, and opening hours; in-depth essays on local culture, history, and politics; comprehensive listings on transportation; straight advice on work and study, budget accommodations, sights, nightlife, and food; detailed maps; and much more.

▨ Let's Go is for anyone who wants to see Paris on a budget.

Books by Let's Go, Inc.

EUROPE

Let's Go: Europe

Let's Go: Austria & Switzerland

Let's Go: Britain & Ireland

Let's Go: Eastern Europe

Let's Go: France

Let's Go: Germany

Let's Go: Greece & Turkey

Let's Go: Ireland

Let's Go: Italy

Let's Go: London

Let's Go: Paris

Let's Go: Rome

Let's Go: Spain & Portugal

NORTH & CENTRAL AMERICA

Let's Go: USA & Canada

Let's Go: Alaska & The Pacific Northwest

Let's Go: California

Let's Go: New York City

Let's Go: Washington, D.C.

Let's Go: Mexico

MIDDLE EAST & ASIA

Let's Go: Israel & Egypt

Let's Go: Thailand

Let's Go

The Budget Guide to

PARIS

1995

Miranda Frances Spieler
Editor

Written by
Let's Go, Inc.
A subsidiary of
Harvard Student Agencies, Inc.

St. Martin's Press ■ New York

HELPING LET'S GO

If you have suggestions or corrections, or just want to share your discoveries, drop us a line. We read every piece of correspondence, whether a 10-page e-mail letter, a velveteen Elvis postcard, or, as in one case, a collage. All suggestions are passed along to our researcher-writers. Please note that mail received after May 5, 1995 will probably be too late for the 1996 book, but will be retained for the following edition.
Address mail to:

> **Let's Go: Paris**
> **Let's Go, Inc.**
> **1 Story Street**
> **Cambridge, MA 02138**
> **USA**

Or send e-mail (please include in the subject header the titles of the *Let's Go* guides you discuss in your message) to:
> **letsgo@delphi.com**

In addition to the invaluable travel advice our readers share with us, many are kind enough to offer their services as researchers or editors. Unfortunately, the charter of Let's Go, Inc. and Harvard Student Agencies, Inc. enables us to employ only currently enrolled Harvard students.

About Let's Go

Back in 1960, a few students at Harvard University got together to produce a 20-page pamphlet offering a collection of tips on budget travel in Europe. For three years, Harvard Student Agencies, a student-run nonprofit corporation, had been doing a brisk business booking charter flights to Europe; this modest, mimeographed packet was offered to passengers as an extra. The following year, students traveling to Europe researched the first full-fledged edition of *Let's Go: Europe*, a pocket-sized book featuring advice on shoestring travel, irreverent write-ups of sights, and a decidedly youthful slant.

Throughout the 60s, the guides reflected the times: one section of the 1968 *Let's Go: Europe* talked about "Street Singing in Europe on No Dollars a Day." During the 70s, *Let's Go* gradually became a large-scale operation, adding regional European guides and expanding coverage into North Africa and Asia. The '80s saw the arrival of *Let's Go: USA & Canada* and *Let's Go: Mexico*, as well as regional North American guides; in the '90s we introduced five in-depth city guides to Paris, London, Rome, New York City, and Washington, DC. And as the budget travel world expands, so do we; the first edition of *Let's Go: Thailand* hit the shelves last year, and this year's edition adds coverage of Malaysia, Singapore, Tokyo, and Hong Kong.

This year we're proud to announce the birth of *Let's Go: Eastern Europe*—the most comprehensive guide to this renascent region, with more practical information and insider tips than any other. *Let's Go: Eastern Europe* brings our total number of titles, with their spirit of adventure and reputation for honesty, accuracy, and editorial integrity, to 21.

We've seen a lot in 35 years. *Let's Go: Europe* is now the world's #1 best selling international guide, translated into seven languages. And our guides are still researched, written, and produced entirely by students who know first-hand how to see the world on the cheap.

Every spring, we recruit over 100 researchers and 50 editors to write our books anew. Come summertime, after several months of training, researchers hit the road for seven weeks of exploration, from Bangkok to Budapest, Anchorage to Ankara. With pen and notebook in hand, a few changes of underwear stuffed in our backpacks, and a budget as tight as yours, we visit every *pensione*, *palapa*, pizzeria, café, club, campground, or castle we can find to make sure you'll get the most out of *your* trip.

We've put the best of our discoveries into the book you're now holding. A brand-new edition of each guide hits the shelves every year, only months after it is researched, so you know you're getting the most reliable, up-to-date, and comprehensive information available. The budget travel world is constantly changing, and where other guides quickly become obsolete, our annual research keeps you abreast of the very latest travel insights. And even as you read this, work on next year's editions is well underway.

At *Let's Go*, we think of budget travel not only as a means of cutting down on costs, but as a way of breaking down a few walls as well. Living cheap and simple on the road brings you closer to the real people and places you've been saving up to visit. This book will ease your anxieties and answer your questions about the basics—to help *you* get off the beaten track and explore. We encourage you to put *Let's Go* away now and then and strike out on your own. As any seasoned traveler will tell you, the best discoveries are often those you make yourself. If you find something worth sharing, drop us a line. We're at Let's Go, Inc., 1 Story Street, Cambridge, MA, 02138, USA (e-mail: letsgo@delphi.com).

Happy travels!

Don't forget to write.

Now that you've said, "Let's go," it's time to say "Let's get American Express® Travelers Cheques." If they are lost or stolen, you can get a fast and full refund virtually anywhere you travel. So before you leave be sure and write.

Table of Contents

■ Maps

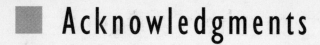 Acknowledgments

An editor couldn't ask for a more sympathetic publisher than Pete Keith; his steadfast support and judicious management is gratefully appreciated. Alexis Averbuck and Liz Stein were more than generous with their computer expertise. Marc Zelanko's insouciance ill hides the sympathy that saw me through many an editorial crisis. Anne Chisholm's professionalism is the backbone of this office, and is too rarely recognized as such. The summer's work was made bearable by Olivia's quiet intelligence, Joe's chivalry, Maria's graceful charm, and by Yael, Liz, and Natalie's camaraderie. Declan—European, ironic, and confident—kept the office and this job in perspective. Nicholas Peterson's agile eye and deft red pen will not be easily replaced.

The unflappable Laurent helped make *Let's Go: Paris* a book with a happy, though flustered, ending. Steadfast Julie was helpmeet in the final hours. Last minute thanks also to my amanuensis Alp, to Maia, and to Haneen. Steve, there are no better friends. Thanks to Bubbi, to Mommy, to Abby, to Cassie, to Ben, and to Daddy as always.—M.F.S.

STAFF

Editor	Miranda Frances Spieler
Managing Editor	Joseph E. Mullin III
Publishing Director	Pete Keith
Production Manager	Alexis G. Averbuck
Production Assistant	Elizabeth J. Stein
Financial Manager	Matt Heid
Assistant General Manager	Anne E. Chisholm
Sales Group Manager	Sherice R. Guillory
Sales Department Coordinator	Andrea N. Taylor
Sales Group Representatives	Eli K. Aheto
	Timur Okay Harry Hiçyılmaz
	Arzhang Kamerei
	Hollister Jane Leopold
	David L. Yuan
President	Lucienne D. Lester
General Manager	Richard M. Olken

Researcher-Writers

Bruce McKinnon *Paris*

With all of Bruce's enthusiasm for the saxophone-soaked, rain-slick streets of the Parisian Jazz Age, one could be forgiven for not realizing that his real instrument is the piano. Facing down muggers, he bravely sallied forth, never losing his keen eye for adventure. Night and day, he was the one for the eclectic and puzzling Marais; he guided readers deftly to the top of the Louvre museum—and still found time to remember to play in the Fête de la Musique.

Karen E. Todd *Paris*

With her lightning fast-talk and masterful asides, Karen excavated brand-new gems from the mines of Parisian museums and nightlife, then soared through EuroDisney®; her compelling research has left its mark on every ride.

Julianna Tymoczko *Paris*

If we could hand every new researcher Julianna's work ethic, staying-power, and courageous wit—along with the customary set of maps'n'notepads—these guidebooks would be in near-perfect shape. From the Latin Quarter to Flaubert's Rouen to Monet's lily-choked Giverny, Julianna's copy revealed her industriousness and her sparkling pen. Next year's editors will thank her for her work (she may even be thanking herself). And Paris-bound runners can thank their advance-woman Julianna for finding the best routes among the cobblestones.

Krzysztof Owerkowicz *Normandy*

Tripler Pell *The Loire Valley*

Important METRO stops:

ST-MICHEL

In the heart of the Student Quarter. Lots of interesting side streets and shops/restaurants/people. Also near Notre Dame cathedral.

TROCADERO

Best view of Eiffel Tower is from nearby Palais Chaillot plaza.

CONCORDE

US Embassy and bottom of Champs Elysees

LES HALLES

Nice outdoor restaurants between here and Centre Pompidou art museum

How To Use This Book

Paris has been the subject of thousands of books about aspects of its varied life, from its Roman past, to the cafés of the 1880s, to today's bustling nightlife and art and architecture. We give you a sense of the city's history and where to find its traces, and we help you budget time and money. This book is designed to give both first-time visitors and long-time friends an introduction to Paris's (budget) riches.

Paris: An Introduction fills you in on Paris's history, politics, architecture, art, and literary life. **Essentials** offers practical advice for before you go and after you arrive. **Planning Your Trip,** with its helpful information on necessary documents, useful maps, and currency will help you think ahead. **Getting There** gives tips about budget travel to Paris. **Once There** provides information on useful organizations in Paris, emergency services, and the layout of the city. We cover *métro,* bus, and other services that will help you get around. We offer special tips and resources for students, seniors, families, women, and other travelers with specific needs.

In the **Accommodations** section, hotels, hostels, and *foyers* are listed in the order of value, based on price, location, safety, and comfort, as determined by our researcher-writers. **Food and Drink** includes restaurant reviews organized by *arrondissement* and accompanied by a full list cross-referenced by type of food, price, hours, and atmosphere. We also list cafés, wine bars, sweet shops, and groceries. Organized by *arrondissement,* the **Sights** section gives a sense of the hidden and not-so-hidden treasures in Paris's different neighborhoods. **Museums** get a section of their own, with detailed descriptions of the large museums—the Louvre, Musée d'Orsay, and more—and informative listings of smaller collections for every taste. **Entertainment** is chock full of film, theater, music, and dance. It includes listings of both participatory and spectator sports, and for the less *sportif,* a sampling of Paris's finest bars. **Shopping**—entertainment for some—includes the city's major department stores as well as harder to find specialty shops, book stores, and street markets. For those who want to see another part of France, our many **Daytrips** include châteaux, cathedrals, and even theme park fun. We feature **Weekend trips** to châteaux of the Loire, and to Rouen and the Normandy coast. Check our **Appendices** for useful phrases and an extensive menu reader.

A NOTE TO OUR READERS

The information for this book is gathered by *Let's Go*'s researchers during the late spring and summer months. Each listing is derived from the assigned researcher's opinion based upon his or her visit at a particular time. The opinions are expressed in a candid and forthright manner. Other travelers might disagree. Those traveling at a different time may have different experiences since prices, dates, hours, and conditions are always subject to change. You are urged to check beforehand to avoid inconvenience and surprises. Travel always involves a certain degree of risk, especially in low-cost areas. When traveling, especially on a budget, you should always take particular care to ensure your safety.

Paris:
An Introduction

A Paris on peut s'amuser, s'ennuyer, rire, pleurer, faire tout ce qui vous plaît; nul ne vous jette un regard car il y a des milliers qui y font la même chose et chacun à sa manière.
(In Paris you can enjoy yourself, bore yourself, laugh, cry, do all that pleases you, and no one casts a glance at you because there are thousands who do the same thing and each one in her own way.)
—Frédéric Chopin, 1831

■ HISTORY AND POLITICS

To have been Lutèce and to have become Paris—what could be a more magnificent symbol! To have been mud and to have become spirit!
—Victor Hugo

In the beginning, there was a crossroads and an island, the Ile de la Cité, home to a tribe called the Parisii. The Parisii's *Loutonheze,* "a dwelling in the midst of the waters," became the Roman *Lutetia* (Lutèce), and in the Middle Ages, the ruling Franks shortened *Lutetia Parisiorum* to a simple *Paris.* Its regional power dates to 987 when Hugh Capet, count of Paris, became King of France and brought prestige to the tiny medieval town by making it his capital. Over the years, prestige has had its price; as the capital of France, Paris has borne the brunt of fighting between monarchs, the citizens of Paris, and lords and, during the Hundred Years War (1337-1453), with England. During this war, the now mythic Jeanne d'Arc, who allied with the French King Charles VII against Henry V of England, was wounded on the streets of Paris.

Religion was at the center of daily life in the Middle Ages and the Renaissance. Nascent Protestantism fomented strife across France in the late 16th century. During this period, Cathérine de Médicis, Henri II's wife, then his widow, ruled France through her sons. Concerned by a rising Huguenot (French Protestant) power, she married her daughter to the Protestant Henri of Navarre. When all of the leading Protestants in France had assembled in Paris for the wedding, she signaled the start of the St-Bartholomew's Day Massacre. A wild Parisian mob slaughtered some 2000 Huguenots. When that same Henri became King Henri IV in 1589, he converted to Catholicism, waving off the magnitude of his decision with *"Paris vaut bien une Messe"* (Paris is well worth a mass).

During the 17th century Cardinal Richelieu, first minister to Louis XIII, began to fashion the greatest absolutist state Europe has ever seen, a nation where sovereignty rested solely and entirely with the monarch. The power of the king reached its height during the reign of Louis XIV, the *Roi Soleil* (the Sun King), who rose to the throne as a five-year-old in 1642 and ruled for 72 years. In 1648, fines on Parisian homeowners drove the city to the barricades in a revolt known as the Fronde. In retreat from the rebellious city, Louis XIV moved his capital to Versailles. The palace became a showcase for regal opulence and noble privilege as the king surrounded himself with exquisite luxuries and submissive nobles. Marie-Antoinette, Louis XIV's equally extravagant queen, lives on in paintings and in popular legend—"let them eat cake" is her infamous line. The Sun King's great-grandson, Louis XV, continued the tradition of expensive wars and lavish consumption into the late 18th century. His mistresses, including Madame de Pompadour and Madame du Barry, were notorious for their "power behind the throne."

Paris: Map of Maps

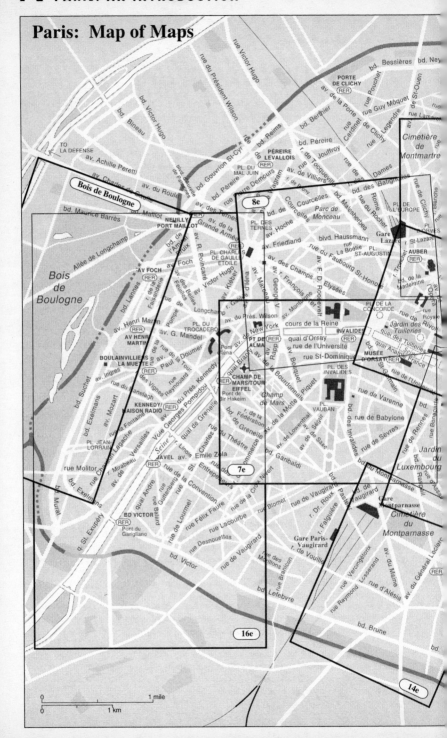

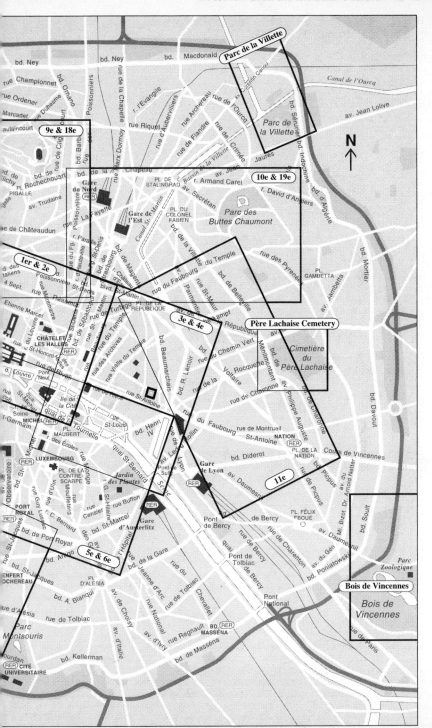

HISTORY

Discontent with the monarchy, its policies, and its excesses contributed to the French Revolution. The Revolution's declared goal was twofold, at once destructive and constructive: to tear down the vestiges of feudalism and to erect in its place a new society built on the tripartite ideal of *liberté, égalité,* and *fraternité.* On July 14, 1789, an impatient mob stormed the Bastille to seize its gunpowder. The French now celebrate July 14 (*le quatorze juillet*) as the *Fête Nationale,* Bastille Day. In September 1792, efforts at revolt were successful and the French republic was declared. Major reforms, such as the abolition of guilds and the dismantling of the Church, transformed the nation, but could not bring lasting peace to Paris. In 1793, the radical Jacobin faction, led by Maximilien Robespierre and his Committee of Public Safety, took over the Convention and began a period of suppression and mass execution known as the Terror. The Jacobins guillotined the king and queen, their enemies, and eventually one another. The place de la Concorde, now a glorified traffic circle, was once the site for more than 1300 beheadings. Thankfully, such a system did not last, and the leading Jacobins were arrested in the revolutionary month of Thermidor (August 1793).

An exhausted French people yearned for stability and welcomed the rise of a man they felt could achieve it: Napoleon Bonaparte. This famed military commander and megalomaniac took power in a coup in 1799 and by 1804 had declared himself emperor. Napoleon established a strong central bureaucracy and a system of law that still lies at the foundation of legal systems around the world. He was not satisfied with ruling France alone, and soon initiated a series of military campaigns that nearly yielded him hegemony over the entire European continent. Napoleon ruled until his ultimate defeat at Waterloo in 1815. But the combined power of the Royal Navy, the Russian winter, and various opposing armies proved too much, and on March 30, 1814 the Prussians occupied an undefended Paris. A short period of monarchical government followed. Napoleon would bring an end to the short-lived reign of Louis XVIII when he returned to Paris from his exile on Elba. His ultimate defeat at Waterloo came, however, that same year. The Restoration of the monarchy folllowed, and Louis XVIII resumed his throne. His repressive successor Charles X was France's last Bourbon king, to be overthrone in 1830 by violent, armed protests that once againg employed Revolutionary slogans crying for liberty and equality. Power passed to Louis-Philippe, the "citizen-king." His July (constitutional) Monarchy was seen as a compromise between the Bourbon kings' autocracy and the Republic's excess. He was king not of France, but of the French; in a symbolic gesture, he kept the Revolutionary tricolor as his flag.

Revolution hit again in 1848 when veterans of a 1830 revolt joined students in a march on the Chambre des Députés, demanding a republic. Louis-Philippe abdicated peacefully, and the Second Republic was declared. Even more than in 1792, the change in regime had been determined solely by events in the capital. Despite Paris's power, in 1851 an anti-Parisian, conservative peasantry elected to the presidency an ambitious man named Louis-Napoleon Bonaparte. Aided by his popular slogan *"l'Empire c'est la paix"* (the Empire means peace), he successfully proclaimed himself Emperor Napoleon III. His downfall came soon after he launched the Franco-Prussian War in July 1870; he was captured by the Prussians and deposed.

Paris's revolutionary tradition continued into the Third Republic with the establishment of the Paris Commune in 1871. For four months a committee of leftist politicians held power, temporarily replacing the conservative regime led by Adolphe Thiers. The Commune threw up barricades to defend against the inroads of the expelled government, but the wide boulevards designed by Baron Haussmann enabled the regulars to outflank the defenders. The crushing of the Commune broke both the power of Paris over the provinces and of the Parisian proletariat over the city. Into the beginning of the next century France ambled along, through both conservative and liberal regimes, under the republican tricolor.

The Third Republic, which began in 1871, introduced modern politics and political parties to France; modern formations of a nationalist, religious "blood and soil"

Right emerged behind Barrès and Maurras, while the labor-oriented Left crystallized behind Jaurès, as a new political culture took shape around the turn of the century over the Dreyfus Affair. Alfred Dreyfus, a Jewish captain in the French Army, was framed for treason in 1894; when novelist Emile Zola's 1898 article "J'accuse" declared Dreyfus innocent (and the French military establishment venal and corrupt), all of France agonized over, and took sides in, the "Dreyfus affair." Dreyfusards invoked, with Zola, the Rights of Man and the weight of the facts; anti-Dreyfusards (generally antisemiticconservatives of the Old and New Right) wanted to preserve the honor of the state and the army by preserving Dreyfus' conviction.

World War I devastated the youth of Europe, but its specific effects on Paris weren't much to see: the German army never made it into the French capital, and by 1916, despite occasional air raids, the theaters, cinemas, and galleries of Paris were humming once again. After the war, delegates from around the world arrived to redraw the map of Europe at the Paris Peace Conference, which eventually produced the flawed Treaty of Versailles.

The Great Depression inaugurated a decade of disorder in French politics, as government after government rose and fell. For a brief period (1936-37), power was held by the Popular Front, a leftist coalition formed in response to the rise of the Nazis in Germany. French generals were ill-prepared for the German attack when it came, and Paris was occupied easily on June 14, 1940. The French government, pushed south to the small town of Vichy, signed a treaty that ceded the northern third of the country to the Nazis. This put Paris at the heart of occupied France; for four years it swarmed with German officials, diplomats, and the occasional Resistance spy. Well-attended exhibits purported to show the evils of Freemasonry, Bolshevism, and international Jewry, and a detention center was set up just outside Paris in Compiègne. The future leader of the Resistance, General Charles de Gaulle, was in England when France surrendered to the Germans; from London he delivered his now famed appeal for French patriots to resist, and declared his Comité National Français to be the legitimate government-in-exile. While the Nazi presence in Paris made it unsuitable as a Resistance center for most of the war, some heroes did emerge: Albert Camus, for example, who directed the inspiring underground newspaper *Combat*.

Paris narrowly avoided destruction in the waning months of World War II. With Allied troops approaching from Normandy in the summer of 1944, Hitler ordered that occupying troops lay waste to the city. Fortunately, his garrison commander disobeyed the order. By August, Allied armies had swept east to liberate Paris. Even if the physical results of the occupation were not catastrophic, this period certainly left its mark on Paris and the Parisians. Vichy collaboration with the Nazis has left scars that are still tender. Today's government has attempted to bring to trial high-ranking officials of the Vichy government, including Vichy police chief Réné Bousquet, who was murdered in June 1993 before he could be tried. 1993 saw the much publicized case of Paul Touvier, who collaborated in Lyons with the Gestapo. For nearly forty years, he was harbored by laymen and priests within France's Catholic church.

Soon after the war, the Fourth Republic was declared, with de Gaulle as its first-president (although he resigned out of frustration within months). Its twelve years (1946-58) saw the reconstruction of French transport and industry, the formation of the European Economic Community (EEC) in 1957, and the faltering of French colonial rule in Indochina, Tunisia, and Morocco. But problems with the colonies continued to plague the Fourth Republic, and a 1958 revolution in Algeria triggered its final collapse. De Gaulle returned in triumph to inaugurate the Fifth (and current) Republic in 1958. He allowed Algeria to become independent by referendum in 1962, and focused on building a strong, independent France.

The French political system under the Fifth Republic blends the traditional European parliamentary system with the American concept of an independent executive. Parliament—made up of the 317-member *sénat* and the 491-member Assemblée Nationale, both elected by universal suffrage—holds legislative power.

The Assemblée is housed in the Palais Bourbon in the 7ème *arrondissement*; the *sénat* meets in the Palais du Luxembourg in the 6ème. The prime minister is elected by popular vote for a seven-year term, holds executive power. He or she appoints a Council of Ministers, headed by the Prime Minister, which manages the country and is responsible to Parliament. The majority in the Assemblée need not be of the President's party; when it isn't, the President is obliged to appoint a Prime Minister from a rival party and share power.

The Fifth Republic came close to collapse in May 1968. Frustrated by racism and sexism, by capitalism's failure to collapse, by an outdated curriculum, and by the threat of a reduction in the number of students allowed to matriculate, university students seized the Sorbonne. Barricades were erected in the *quartier latin*, and an all-out student revolt had begun. The situation escalated for several weeks; police used tear gas and clubs to storm the barricades, while students fought back by throwing Molotov cocktails and lighting cars on fire. Though no one was killed, hundreds of students and police officers were wounded in the fighting. Workers in state industries went on strike in support of the students, paralyzing the country. The government, planning for the worst, arranged for tanks and commando units to be brought into the city in the event of a Communist insurrection. But a march of hundreds of thousands of de Gaulle's supporters down the Champs-Elysées confirmed public support of the government, and helped to extinguish the crisis. By then, de GHe resigned for the last time after losing a referendum in 1969. Ironically, the Paris revolt— settled, in part, by concessions over university textbooks and curriculum committees— became a model for radical "student uprisings" in Mexico and many other nations in the next few years.

Three parties and their leaders have dominated the French political scene since de Gaulle's exit. Two are parties of the center-right which formed when de Gaulle's old allies split in 1974: the Union pour la Démocracie Française (UDF), led by Valery Giscard d'Estaing; and the Rassemblement pour la République (RPR), led by Jacques Chirac, who doubles as Paris's mayor. On the left is the Socialist Party, led by the aging François Mitterrand, France's President since 1981. Although they retain some support in the so-called "red belt" that crosses the 12ème and the 20ème *arrondissements*, the Communists are a minor player today.

The neo-Gaullists on the center-right reigned during the 1970s. De Gaulle's former Prime Minster Georges Pompidou won the presidency in 1969, followed after his death in 1974 by the UDF's Giscard d'Estaing. The elections of 1981 swept the Socialists into a majority in the Assemblée and Mitterrand into the presidency; within weeks they had raised the minimum wage and added a fifth week to the French worker's annual vacation. The Socialists' popularity began to wane, however, as the 1983 recession hit, and the party met with serious losses in the 1986 parliamentary elections. Mitterand was forced to appoint Chirac as Prime Minister, ushering in two years of uncomfortable *cohabitation* with a conservative cabinet. But the Socialists made a timely recovery for the 1988 elections, giving Mitterand another seven-year term and allowing him to appoint a new Socialist government.

The 1986 parliamentary elections marked the emergence of an ugly new force in French politics—the ultra-right, racist Front National, led by Jean-Marie Le Pen, which picked up 10% of the vote by blaming France's woes (unemployment in particular) on immigrants and foreigners. Since World War II, much of France's immigration has come from its former colonies in Asia and Africa; today, almost half of the immigrants in France live in or around Paris—particularly in the 13ème, 19ème, and 20ème *arrondissements,* as well as in the suburbs—making up 13% of the city's population. Only the second generation born in France can gain French citizenship, but non-citizens are eligible for many state-provided benefits. With economic hardship increasingly widespread, the Le Pen's slogan of "*La France pour les français*" ("France for the French") has apparently struck a chord with some. Le Pen's popularity has grown only slightly since his debut on the national stage. But his mere presence has pulled the entire political spectrum a bit to the right.

After the electoral success of 1988, Mitterand ran through a series of Socialist governments, including one led by Edith Cresson, who became France's first woman Prime Minister in 1992. Yet popularity remained elusive for the Socialists. One problem was the issue of European integration, a trend spearheaded by France since World War II. In the wake of 1991's Maastricht treaty, which pulled the 12-nation European Community into an even more tightly-knit European Union, the French people have manifested a profound unease about the prospect of further integration. President Mitterand led the campaign for a "oui" vote in France's September 1992 referendum on the treaty. He escaped defeat by the slimmest of margins—while allowing the opposition to paint the Socialists as unthinking Europhiles.

In the parliamentary elections of March 1993, the Socialists suffered their worst defeat in 25 years. Outgoing Prime Minister Pierre Bérégovoy, a broken man, committed suicide weeks later. Another period of *cohabitation* began, with Chirac's former finance minister Edouard Balladur becoming Prime Minister. Balladur's approval ratings have been high, and Mitterand has seemed increasingly like a spent force. Yet the Prime Minister has made little progress in solving France's chronically high unemployment. Balladur looks to be the strongest contender for the presidency in 1995, much to the chagrin of his nominal superior in the RPR, Chirac. On the left, current polls show the demoralized Socialists as having only one viable candidate—the respected Jacques Delors, who has just finished 10 years atop the growing Eurobureaucracy in Brussels as the Chairman of the European Commission.

As the end of the century approaches, the French people are uncertain about their future. For decades France has pushed doggedly to bring Europe together, under the premise that cooperation and inter-dependence was the best guarantee of the continent's security and prosperity. But Bosnia and 11% unemployment have called these assumptions into question. Culturally, France is at the same time haughty and insecure: witness the recent attempts by the government to ban the use of Anglicisms in the French language (a quest that has earned culture minister Jacques Toubon the nickname of "Mr. All-Good"). Tensions over immigration seem destined to worsen: if Algeria's descent into gunfire and chaos continues, France can expect a tide of refugees— and a racist backlash against North Africans and for the Front National. French politics may be headed for dark waters, but they won't be boring anytime soon.

■ ARCHITECTURE AND URBAN DESIGN

The Romans transformed Paris from a collection of fishing huts into a place of civilization, a title the city has prided itself on ever since. They rebuilt the city in their own image, with vineyards, an arena, and a perpendicular street plan. Traces of the Romans' Greek-inspired pristine forms and simple geometry exist in such diverse buildings as the 17th-century **Cour Carrée** of the Louvre and Napoleon's **triumphal arches**. An early type of architecture modeled after Roman basilicas blossomed into the massive Romanesque cathedrals of the 11th century. The oldest parts of **St-Germain-des-Prés** show the immense walls and semicircular arches characteristic of this style. The prosperity of the 12th century allowed the invention of a new, far more ornate architectural style—the Gothic. From this period Paris boasts **St-Denis,** Europe's first Gothic cathedral, as well as the jewel-like **Sainte-Chapelle.**

The 12th century also saw the basic segregation of functions that still characterizes the city. King Philippe-Auguste established political and ecclesiastical institutions on Ile de la Cité, academic on the Left Bank, and commercial on the Right. By the 14th century, Paris's 80,000 inhabitants made it one of the great cities of Europe. To cope with this growth, Charles V replaced an earlier wall with a new, larger wall on the Right Bank. Though it was destroyed in the 17th century, its outline defines the northern and eastern borders of the third *arrondissement.* The color of present day Paris dates back to the 16th century when fire regulations decreed that wooden exteriors had to be plastered over, creating a gray city. The late 16th and early 17th century saw the construction of the **Pont Neuf,** the **Palais du Luxembourg,** and the

Palais Royal, as well as the widening of Paris's streets. Meanwhile the city's population skyrocketed, reaching almost 400,000 by the mid-17th century.

The 17th century—reign of the Sun King, **Versailles,** and the Absolute Monarchy— ushered in the age of the Baroque. In place of the Gothic architecture banned by Louis XIV, Italianate domes popped up across the city. Le Nôtre, Le Brun, and Le Vau reigned as the triumvirate of French art, designing respectively the gardens, architecture, and all-important interior paintings of Versailles and château Vaux-le-Vicomte. Paris had become the largest city in Europe. Earlier walls became wide streets to accommodate the growing population. This process continued into the following centuries: a wall constructed in the late 18th century was replaced by the "exterior boulevards" in the 19th. The outer borders of the 8ème, 9ème, te 10ème, and 11ème *arrondissements* as well as the bd. St-Jacques, bd. de Grenelle, and other streets on the Left Bank have their origins in this replacement.

Not too surprisingly, destruction outweighed construction during the French Revolution. Most of its impressive architectural achievements were temporary: an artificial mountain on the Champ de Mars, a cardboard Neoclassical interior for Notre-Dame, and various plaster statues of Liberty. More lasting were the various defacements, especially of kings' statues and churches. At the same time, the Jacobins were not too busy beheading people to open up to development parts of the city center previously owned by the Church and nobility. Napoleon made further improvements in the early 19th century; he planned cemeteries, dug sewers, numbered houses, widened the streets, and brought back the plunder of a continent to the Louvre.

Despite two bloody revolutions, the early 19th century was a prosperous time for Paris. The government's decision that France's major railroads would all terminate in the capital guaranteed Paris's position at the center of the French economy in the new industrial age. Paris thrived as the center of manufacture, a magnet attracting thousands of migrants from the provinces. It continued to be innovative in architecture, adopting the (now ubiquitous) apartment building, a form which was imitated throughout the world. The products of industrialization made many living quarters more pleasant—glass became cheaper and windows proliferated. But unchecked growth continued to swamp improvements, and many of Paris's one million people lived in congested slums.

Though traces of the past abound, parts of pre-19th century Paris would be virtually unrecognizable to a modern visitor. Today's city is the Paris remade under the (somewhat dictatorial) direction of Baron Georges-Eugène **Haussmann.** From 1852 to 1870, Haussmann transformed Paris from an intimate medieval city to a centralized modern metropolis. Commissioned by the government to modernize the city, Haussmann tore long, straight boulevards through the tangled clutter and narrow alleys of old Paris, creating a unified network of *grands boulevards*. These avenues were designed not only to increase circulation of goods and people, but to make Paris a work of art, a splendid capital worthy of France. Not incidently, the wide avenues and oblique intersections also impeded insurrection, limiting once and for all the effectiveness of street barricades.

The changes during this period were momentous. The city doubled its area and Haussmann shifted the boundaries of the 20 existing *quartiers,* establishing Paris's present organization into 20 *arrondissements*. Five of Paris's seven hills were leveled; only Montmartre and the Montagne Ste-Geneviève remain. Twelve thousand structures were destroyed and 136km of straight avenues created. Wide sidewalks (demolished in the next century to make room for automobiles) encouraged strollers, sidewalk cafés, kiosks, and general crowds, giving birth to Paris's famed street culture. But the transformation was not without its costs. Intimate neighborhoods were destroyed by the avenue de l'Opéra and the boulevard St-Michel. Their homes demolished to make room for boulevards and luxury apartments, the workers of Paris were forced eastward to Belleville and beyond.

The transformation of Paris continued along the same lines into the early 20th century. Traffic circles, varied façades, electrical lamps, and elevators became important elements in the development of the city's appearance. Paris continued to establish itself as an international center of innovation with the Exhibitions of 1889 and 1900. Both left several quintessentially Parisian landmarks in their wake: the **Métropolitain**, the **Grand** and **Petit Palais,** and of course, the **Eiffel Tower,** a celebration of steel construction.

Paris's cityscape and its architectural styles survived two world wars fundamentally unchanged. In the interwar period, a few radical architects began to focus on new building materials. **Le Corbusier,** a Swiss citizen who lived and built in Paris, was a pioneer in the new material of reinforced concrete. During the postwar years, architects began to make buildings that would stand out, rather than blend in. Most of the changes were made in the outer *arrondissements,* like the 13ème and the 17ème, leaving the historic core relatively intact. The old market place of Les Halles, now a subterranean shopping mall, was torn down, and the *quais* of the Left Bank, like those of the Right, were almost converted into expressways—acts that inspired calls for conservation.

Paris's growth was not restricted to its center. Its history of expansion into the surrounding territory dates back to the emergence of working-class districts (*faubourgs*) in the late 18th century. In the 19th century, rail lines and trolleys made the suburbs more inviting by enabling workers to commute from the outer districts and suburbs. During the 1950s and 60s, the government sponsored housing developments and a plan for a ring of "new towns" surrounding Paris. Five of these towns have been built, including Marne-la-Vallée, now the home of Euro Disneyland® Park. Parisian suburbs, often the only source of affordable housing, are home mainly to the working class and immigrants. As high rents have pushed the working class out to the suburbs, Paris's middle class has gentrified the old workers' quarters, making them tidy but, some would say, dull.

The last two decades may go down in history as one of the greatest periods of building in Paris. Presidents Giscard d'Estaing and Mitterrand have been enthusiasts of dramatic architectural endeavors. Mitterrand initiated the famous (some say infamous) 15 billion franc Grands Projets program to provide a series of modern monuments symbolic of France's role at the center of art, politics, and the world economy. From **La Défense** to **La Villette,** these government offices, museums, and public buildings constitute some of the boldest and most controversial additions to the city. I.M. Pei's 1989 modernist glass pyramid, part of the program, was planted smack in the middle of the courtyard of the Louvre. One of the most recent Mitterrand-sponsored projects is construction of the **Bibliothèque Nationale,** part of a massive urban renewal project called ZAC (zone d'aménagement concerte) Seine-Rive Gauche. The library's design by architect Dominique Perrault has prompted ongoing debate. Whether Paris should be preserved as a city of another era (or eras) or be host to sometimes jarringly innovative projects, and who should make these aesthetic and economic decisions remain the subjects of a lively public dialogue.

■ VISUAL ARTS & MUSIC

Paris' surviving medieval art is religious in purpose and public in tone: stunning stained glass at Chartres, Sainte-Chapelle, and Notre-Dame cathedrals retells Bible stories for the benefit of the (usually illiterate) medieval churchgoer, and the churches' intricate stone facades show off the complexity of God's creation. When human achievement (and Greek and Roman influence) became the center of attention in the Renaissance, France imported its styles fromItaly; even François I imported Italian artists to decorate his palace at Fontainebleau in the latest Mannerist style.

Later, under Louis XIV, an indigenous French art flourished. The center of Western painting and sculpture shifted decisively from Rome to Paris. Nicolas Poussin elaborated the theory of the "grand manner," with its huge canvases and panoramic subjects taken from mythology and history. The French Académie Royale, founded in 1648, came to value this style above all others and all subsequent French painters

THE ARTS

had to contend with these weighty "academic" precepts. Claude Lorraine's idyllic landscapes defined the Académie's landscape tradition. In 1725, the Académie inaugurated annual Salons, held in the vacant halls of the Louvre.

A sober 18th-century bourgeoisie admired scenes of everyday life by Chardin and Greuze before turning its attention to Jacques-Louis David, whose historical scenes frequently had political or moral "meanings." The more playful French aristocracy hired Rococo artists like Boucher and Fragonard to decorate its gold-embossed salons and bedrooms with flying cherubs and mischievous escapades. Watteau painted the *fêtes* and secret *rendez-vous* of the aristocracy as a magnificently theatrical display. Elisabeth Vigée-Lebrun painted the French nobility with a charm that many years later earned her a great success with the court of Russia.

Art during the Revolution, with its emphasis on classical style and public display, was a far cry from the Rococo. Ceremonies, with elaborate Neoclassical props and costumes planned by David, fêted such state occasions as the transfer of Voltaire's body to the Panthéon. David himself joined the Jacobin party, painting such striking works as *The Oath in the Tennis Court* and *The Dead Marat*. In 1793—the year of the Terror—the Louvre opened the Royal collection to the public, providing the beginnings of what would become the world's most famous art museum. After being imprisoned (and then released) by the Directory in 1794, David changed allegiance, moving to the camp of the Corsican Emperor-to-be and painting the monumental *Coronation of Napoleon*. Napoleon encouraged painters and carpet-makers alike to use Egyptian and Greek motifs, which expressed his notion of himself as the heir of the Roman emperors; the result, in the decorative arts, is now called the Empire style.

The period of the Restoration and July Monarchy marked the division that would define the rest of the century: the Classical school led by Jean-Auguste Dominique Ingres, a student of David, and the Romantic school led by Eugène Delacroix. Ingres's sinuous lines and sensual surfaces sharply contrasted with Delacroix's emphasis on brilliant colors, dramatic movement, and emotional excess. Meanwhile the invention of photography by Parisians Nièpce and Daguerre provided a new artistic medium, sparking an intense debate over the relative merits of painting and photography.

Paris had become, too, a capital of classical music. Frederic Chopin, arriving from Poland, brought Romanticism to piano music with his sensitive, highly personal works; Hector Berlioz– who grew up in the mountains without a piano– brought strong feeling and original instrumentation to French orchestral music. The concerts of Hungarian-born pianist and composer Franz Liszt drew swooning crowds any modern rock star might envy.

Napoleon III's declaration of the Second Empire spawned a generation of artists utterly disillusioned with a government that no longer represented their ideals. Like the itinerant gypsies after which they were named, the Bohemians proclaimed for themselves a life free from normal conventions. This "race of obstinate dreamers for whom art has remained a faith and not a career" gathered in the cafés of the *quartier latin* and starved proudly in the garrets of Paris. Poet (and art critic!) Charles Baudelaire, Champfleury, Nadar, and Rodolphe Bresdin were but a few of the famous characters whose way of life was made famous in Henry Murger's bestselling *Scènes de la Vie de Bohème* (later turned into Puccini's opera, *La Bohème)*.

While urban Bohemians starved in the attics of Paris, artists like Millet and Rousseau followed the Romantics' urge to escape from nature, retreating to Barbizon to paint the forêt de Fontainebleau and the French peasantry. Influenced by the social-Utopian theories of Charles Fourier, Gustave Courbet rejected Academic historical painting in favor of a "living art" that would portray what he saw around him. As Europe spread its tentacles across the globe in the 19th century, the East became an inspiration for fashion, painting, and the decorative arts. Academic artists like Jean-Léon Gérôme created lush scenes of Turkish baths and snake-charmers. Japanese *ukiyoe* prints inundated the market from 1853 on, inspiring nascent Impressionists.

Claude Monet, Pierre-Auguste Renoir, and Frédéric Bazille met during the 1860s in Paris and began to develop their now-famous technique. Used to the smooth surfaces and clear-cut lines of Academic painting, critics objected to the "mess"—the rough brushwork and the sketchy quality—the soon-to-be Impressionists produced. Edouard Manet's *Déjeuner sur l'Herbe* was refused by the Salon of 1863; in defiance he exhibited his painting just outside in a separate *"Salon des Refusés* (Salon of the Rejected), with a 50 centimes entrance fee.

The Third Republic (1870-1940) is seen by many as the age of Impressionism. Monet, increasingly the head of this group of young radicals, and Camille Pissaro established their own exhibition in 1874, sick of juries, official competition, and establishment taste. Housed in the former photographic studio of Nadar, the exhibit consisted of 165 canvases of which one was Monet's *Impression: Sunrise.* A snide critic made fun of this canvas, labeling its creator an "Impressionist." Monet and his colleagues gleefully adopted this name, and the show became an annual event. The newly dubbed Impressionists set about playing with light and color to capture perceived reality. For the first time, the crowd—already so aptly described by Hugo and in Baudelaire's *Les Fleurs du Mal*—became a subject worthy of painting. Impressionist paintings, like Manet's *A Bar at the Folies-Bergères* (1882) and Degas's *The Glass of Absinthe* (1876), focused on cafés, balls, cabarets, and ballets. At the same time, a new interest in the countryside created an ideal arena for the Impressionists' credo of *plein air* (open-air) painting.

The next generation– the "Post-Impressionists"– took painting farther and farther from mere depiction: Paul Cézanne's overlapping planes of color evoked sculpture and geometry, and gave viewers the sense of touching or even of being apples, bowls and mountains. Vincent Van Gogh's now-beloved thick lines, odd colors and risky emotions left the viewers of his own time cold. Paul Gauguin, to whom Van Gogh mailed his severed ear, left a family and a highly successful career as a stockbroker to paint the peasants of Brittany and the "natives" of Tahiti. Meanwhile, Pointillists like Seurat explored a highly scientific type of painting, with works made up of tiny dots in primary colors. In sculpture, Rodin, with the aid of Camille Claudel, focused on a highly energetic, muscular shaping of bronze and stone.

During the last decades of the 19th century, Bohemia had moved outside Haussmann's city to the cabarets and cafés of Montmartre—an oasis for artists and bourgeois alike from the sterility of the modern city below. Offenbach composed his celebrated cancan; Toulouse-Lautrec captured the spirit and flashy theatricality of the Belle Epoque in the vibrant silkscreen posters that covered Paris, as well as in his starkly linear paintings of brothels, circuses, and cabarets. "Impressionist" composers like Debussy and Ravel in turn evoked the sounds of the ocean, the winds, and the rising sun. At the same time, Nietzsche's philosophy, rooted in a belief in artifice, in surface, and in the rejection of decayed traditions, formed the basis of a new, decorative style—Art Nouveau. Art Nouveau quickly embraced architecture, furniture, lamps, jewelry, fashion, and book illustration in its search for an all-conclusive aesthetic in which style was more important than function.

The 20th century brought a deeply self-conscious, chaotic art world, following the generation just before in its search for a new and *modern* art. Erik Satie, a wandering Bohemian of Montmartre, composed his pensive, ponderous *Gymnopèdes*. A young group of artists led by Henri Matisse and inspired by Gauguin painted with increasingly brilliant colors and decorative surfaces. Critics labeled them the *fauves* (wild beasts), yet their "wildness" barely hinted at the extreme to which Pablo Picasso and George Braque would carry art with their Cubist experiments of 1907 to 1914. Together with Braque and a poet friend—Guillaume Apollinaire—Picasso formulated rigid precepts for the movement: Cubist painting sought to represent the idea of an object, rather than the object itself. In order to represent a three-dimensional "idea" on a flat canvas, Picasso presented his subjects from several angles at once. Marcel Duchamp added an element of dynamic movement to Cubism with *Nude Descending a Staircase.* Utrillo and Man Ray formed part of the same set, while Eugène Atget, a photographer who documented the streets and shop fronts of Paris, provided Picasso and his friends with photographic "sketches" to use as a basis for their art. Marc Chagall and Giorgio de Chirico immigrated to Paris from Russia and Italy and brought with them their own visions; Chagall created his Cubist fairy-tale pictures of Russian villages and Jewish legends, while de Chirico's dark-green skies and spilt statuary anticipated Surrealism.

On the eve of World War I, Paris argued over ballets: Debussy's *L'Après-midi d'un faune* (1912), for example, danced and choreographed by the famous Nijinsky. Debussy's symphonic setting of Mallarmé's poem, with the flute taking the role of Pan, provided perhaps the era's most perfect expression of the union between musical sound and words, while Nijinsky's highly erotic choreography caused a truly magnificent scandal. Yet no one was prepared for the 1913 opening of Stravinsky's *Rites of Spring*: the plot (a maiden dances herself to death in a tribal ritual in order to make spring come) was disturbing enough, but the music erupted with violent passages and scandalous atonalities. The opening show on May 29, 1913 at the Théâtre des Champs-Elysées erupted almost immediately into an uproar; to Stravinsky's amazement, the conductor kept going and was able (amid catcalls, fights, whistles, and applause) to finish the show.

In 1917 came the *ballet russes*'s final great triumph—*Parade*, written by the poet Jean Cocteau, inspired by the audience "participation" at the opening of *Rites of Spring*, with music by Satie, Cubist costumes and set by Picasso, and choreography by Nijinsky. As the war continued, however, the Cubists and their circle dispersed, and Apollinaire died at the front. Horrified by the slaughter of the war, Duchamp switched from painting his futurist machine-worshiping images to leading the Dadäists, a group of artists who focused on nonsense and non-art—drawing a mustache on a picture of the Mona Lisa and exhibiting a urinal titled *La Fontaine*.

In 1924, André Breton published his *Surrealist Manifesto*. The Surrealists claimed to create an art of the subconscious, seeking out the dream world that was more real than the rational world around them. René Magritte, Salvador Dalí, Yves Tanguy, and Max Ernst painted and etched their playful images of top hats, castles, angels, misplaced nude bodies, and melting clocks. Many constructed Surrealist "objects"—modifications of ready-made things. Meret Oppenheim's *Furred Teacup* and Man Ray's nail-studded iron, *The Gift*, were both playful and menacing. Cocteau, now a full-fledged Surrealist, wrote *Les Enfants Terribles* and produced such dreamily evocative films as *La Belle et la Bête*.

During the 30s, photographers like Brassaï and Kertész, both emigrants from Hungary, recorded the streets and *quartiers* of Paris, especially Montmartre, in black and white. Jean Renoir (son of the painter) made his poetic, witty films which investigated the state of culture in the 20th century; *Boudu is Saved from Drowning* (the original version of *Down and Out in Beverly Hills*) tells the story of a beggar saved from the Seine and taken in by a book-seller. *La Grande Illusion*, on a more serious level, presents the interactions of three French prisoners of war, each from radically different social backgrounds, with the aristocratic German head of their World War I camp. In 1937, Picasso exhibited the huge and violent mural *Guernica* at the Paris International Exposition, in the pavilion of the Spanish Republic. Based on the bombing of a Basque town during the Spanish Civil War, *Guernica* provided the century's most conclusive condemnation of the horrors of the war—three years before the Germans invaded Paris, bringing on the brutality of World War II.

As the Germans advanced on Paris, the masterpieces of the Louvre (except for the *Nike*, which was too heavy) were evacuated to the provinces. Within days of the German entry into Paris, the invaders filled the Opéra and the theaters, which staged uncontroversial farces to avoid offense. Braque and Picasso kept painting, and musicians pulled out their Wagner and Beethoven scores. Jacques Prévert and Marcel Carné teamed up to create two films, *The Devil's Envoy* (1942) and the epic *Children of Paradise* (1945). Edith Piaf and Maurice Chevalier sang in the music halls. In May 27, 1943, hundreds of "degenerate" paintings by Miró, Picasso, Ernst, Klee, and Léger were destroyed in a bonfire in the garden of the Jeu de Paume. Tens of thousands more "respectable" masterpieces belonging to Jewish collectors were appropriated and shipped to Germany, but were returned after the war.

After World War II, painting and sculpture more or less moved their worldwide HQ to New York, but Jean Dubuffet's gravelly grotesques still brought collectors to Paris. In classical music, Olivier Messiaen's wrenching "Quartet for the End of Time" (written partly in a prison camp) and his ambitious, mystical operas and organ-pieces have been justly well-received.

Post-war Paris responded to American dominance by making the USA's newer art forms in its own image: the New Wave of French cinema, inspired by gangster films and Alfred Hitchcock, burst into the cinematic scene in the 50s, using black and white to capture the fragmented, hurried quality of life on the edge. François Truffaut's *The 400 Blows,* Alain Resnais's *Hiroshima mon Amour,* and Jean-Luc Godard's *A bout de souffle,* all made in 1959 are examples of this style. More recently, Eric Rohmer's skillful movies– *A Tale of Winter,* for example– show off character and not technique. Krzysztof Kieslowski, a transplant (like Chopin) from Poland, has made an international splash with his trilogy *Blue, White,* and *Red.*

A Parisian jazz tradition began almost as soon as recorded jazz from the United States reached French shops: as the 1930s opened, French musicians (some classically trained) copied and varied the swing they'd found in early Louis Armstrong wax. Pioneering jazz violinist Stéphane Grapelli and heartbreakingly stylish Belgian-Romany guitarist Django Reinhardt were among the players at the 1934 Club Hot, at 14, rue Chaptal. New Orleans saxophonist Sidney Bechet found a royal reception when he fled America's Depression for the Right Bank's clubs; renowned French clarinettists Claude Luter and Maxim Saury made Bechet the basis for their own styles.

It wasn't until after World War II that Parisian clubs began to fill with first-rank American players, and the city's proverbial rain-slick streets took on their inevitable saxophonic gloss. When Duke Ellington dropped by to play the new Club St-Germain in 1948, he was greeted at the train station by a plaid-clad mob of trendy young jazz fans nicknamed *cavistes,* or *rats du cave,* after the Left Bank jazz hotspot the Caveau de la Huchette (see Entertainment—Jazz). A year later, a jazz festival drew Kenny Dorham, Al Haig, Charlie Parker and Max Roach across the waters. Miles Davis' standard "April in Paris" supposedly "describes" his two-week stay here (at the age of 22) and infatuation with Parisian actress Juliette Greco; legend has it that Sartre tried to convince Miles to marry her, and that subsequent interest in jazz among the intellectuals of St-Germain-des-Pres grew out of Miles' visit.

Bird, Duke and Miles may have passed through, but other American players were happy to stick around. It's hard to say if the American émigrés were more drawn by the low cost of living in postwar France, the city's reputation as a haven for other arts, the relative lack of racism in continental Europe, the romance of drinking in Paris, heroin, or simply French love for the American music. But drawn they were: between 1948 and 1963, the roster of transplanted jazz greats included Bud Powell, Kenny Clark, and Dexter Gordon (about whose stay in the capital the movie "Round Midnight" was made).

Now more than ever before, the jazz that gets attention in Paris is played by people who grew up in France. Native son Michel Petrucciani sells out big halls with his pianism. Another pianist, Jacky Terrason, won last year's Thelonious Monk competition; he now resides in the US, but Laurent Wilde continues to appear in his hometown. Jazz stars you're more likely to *see* are Eddy Louiss, a master of old-guard blues on the Hammond-organ, and funk-flavored guitarist/bandleader Hervé Krief.

Yes, France lacks a rock-and-roll tradition in the manner of England, America, or even Germany and Australia. But Paris did have its own clique of aggressive punk-rock oddballs around 1977: the *modernes,* as they were dubbed, affected surgical cleanliness and white-on-white uniforms, and among them was one of the great rock bands of any decade: Metal Urbain, whose snarled lyrics (in French!) and choppy guitar hammerings indicted mechanization'n'modernity even as their sped-up, clunky drum machines seemed to mimic it. Every English-speaking "industrial" band of the 80s and 90s is a pale echo of what Metal Urbain (and their spinoffs the Metal Boys and Dr. Mix and the Remix) accomplished.

If Paris isn't a world-class centre for rock and roll, it has sheltered another, very French tradition, the witty, worldly cabaret songwriter, as exemplified by Jacques Brel and , more recently, Boris Vian. English expatriate and adoptive Parisian Wreckless Eric fits neatly into this category while extending a hand to punk; he's found a fitting home with the Paris-based label New Rose Records, whose thriving store is a must for loudness-minded visitors. And Paris's greatest effect on pop music elsewhere may have been through a few twentysomething malcontents called Situationists: Guy Debord, Raoul Vaneigem, and their embittered friends roamed the city in the 50s and 60s, made angry collages, and tried to overturn work, consumption and capitalism by turning everyday life into a ragged new art form. It didn't work, of course, but it very well may have inspired some of the student rebels of May '68, and it most definitely had a hand in what became the ideals behind punk rock.

■ LITERARY PARIS

During the Middle Ages, the Sorbonne (recognized by the pope in 1209) and other academies attracted such intellectual giants as Pierre Abélard (of the celebrated romance with Héloïse), St-Thomas d'Aquin, and Roger Bacon to a city that had become Europe's most prestigious center for theological study. The Humanism of 15th-century Renaissance, coupled with the invention of the printing press in about 1450, resulted in a widely circulated literature addressing the foundations of human nature. These concerns continued into the 16th century in Rabelais's social satire, Calvin's reformist works, and Montaigne's personal essays. The *Très Riches Heures du Duc de Berry,* an illuminated prayer book now in the collection of the Chantilly museum, ushered in the Northern Renaissance with its naturalistic portrayal of the labors of the months.

Within the walls of the aristocracy's elaborate palaces, a system of patronage tied the age's most respected literati to the whim of their ruler. The rigidly rhythmed tragedies of Corneille and Racine explored the issues of love, honor, and duty. Molière's brilliant satires were performed in the gardens of Vaux-le-Vicomte and Versailles and sponsored by the king's cousin at the Comédie Française. La Fontaine read his highly moralistic fables in the salons of the immoral aristocracy, who were in turn serenaded by the operas of Jean-Baptiste Lully. Pascal, in his pessimistic *Pensées,* wrote "the heart has its reasons of which reason knows nothing," while his colleague Descartes ushered in the Enlightenment with a more intellectual "I think, therefore I am." Commentary on the leading intellectuals of the day is provided by *salon* hostess Mme. de Sévigné, who recorded her reflections in hundreds of letters to her daughter. All this was regulated by the newly formed Académie Française (1635), which gathered 40 men to regulate and codify French literature, grammar, spelling, and rhetoric. The rules and standards they set loosely at this time would soon solidify into rigid regulations, launching the "Classical" age of French literature. The *académie* has ever since righteously preserved the tradition of classical French letters, with Racine's *Phèdre* as its Bible and the crystal clear poetry of Malherbe as its *Book of Songs.*

In 1666, Colbert founded the Académie des Sciences to argue over such important issues as whether a dead fish weighs more than a live fish (actually weighing two such fish was *not* considered conclusive evidence). The publication of Newton's *Principia* in 1687 ushered in the era of faith in reason known as the Enlightenmen, in which Voltaire declared that "if God did not exist, we would have to invent Him." A generation later, Diderot gathered around him a group of young intellectuals, intent on creating the *Encyclopédie,* a multi-volume work that sought to catalogue, systematize, and rationalize the whole of human knowledge. Rousseau's *Social Contract* and autobiographical *Confessions* rejected this rationality entirely, claiming that a return to nature alone could save human nature, long corrupted by modern society.

Beaumarchais's *Marriage of Figaro,* produced in 1784, was hugely popular with nobility and working class alike, yet its sharp wit and eloquent dialogues held an open condemnation of the aristocracy. Louis XVI, when he first heard the play, exclaimed prophetically "the Bastille would have to be destroyed if the performance of the play is not to have dangerous consequences;" the playwright was imprisoned, not in the Bastille as protocol dictated, but in the St-Lazare prison for delinquent boys. Choderlos de Laclos illuminated the same world, part sparkling wit, part licentiousness, part emptiness, in his controversial *Dangerous Liaisons.*

The Romantic movement came to a focus in the essays of Mme. de Staël and the novels of Chateaubriand. Chateaubriand's isolated, melancholy young hero in *René* provided perhaps the first example of the *mal du siècle*—a feeling of disillusionment and alienation among 19th-century literati, rooted in the conviction that their century was a dying age. The *petit cénacle,* a group of poets led by Victor Hugo and including Gérard de Nerval and Théophile Gautier, espoused an emotional, lyrical style. Alfred de Vigny's *Chatterton* blamed society for the tragic suicide of a young, idealistic poet. Alfred de Musset eloquently expressed the gloomy outlook of his contemporaries when he declared that "I came too late in a century that is too old."

The prolific Honoré de Balzac rejected the Romanticism of his peers, focusing on the harsh realities of bourgeois society under Louis-Philippe, the "citizen-king." His *Comédie Humaine*—a series of novels that attempted to describe all of Parisian society—covered everyone from the melancholy poet to the bejeweled courtesan and the *nouveau riche* noble. At the same time, George Sand, the preeminent female literary figure of the 19th century, was celebrated for her *romans champêtres* (pastoral novels) and for her scandalous habit of wearing trousers and smoking cigars. She kept equally well-known company, spending nine years as Chopin's on-again-off-again lover. A second affair, between Sand and de Musset, ended unhappily—in the best of romantic traditions, both used the failed romance as a subject for their next books.

In the Second Republic, Hugo himself served in the Assemblée Nationale, eloquently defending the cause of *"liberté."* After Louis-Napoleon Bonaparte's coup d'état, Hugo was exiled and spent the next 19 years on the isle of Guernsey, where he penned *Les Châtiments,* a book of vehemently anti-Bonaparte poems.

Hugo's exile became the clarion-call for a new generation of artists utterly disillusioned with a government that no longer represented their ideals. Their world, together with that of the bourgeois society they rejected, was described by Emile Zola in his *Rougon-Macquart* series. Inspired by Balzac's *Comédie Humaine,* Zola added a newly "scientific" element of detail and called his movement Naturalism. Flaubert's *Madame Bovary,* published in 1857 and charged with "offense to public and religious morality and to good morals," caused a sensational trial.

At the same time, Charles Baudelaire led the way to modernism with his perverse, disturbingly beautiful *Fleurs du Mal* (Flowers of Evil), a collection of poems that focused on the sordid world of modern Paris, seen through the eyes of the elderly, the poor, the prostitutes, and, amid all these, the poet. With this alternative guidebook to Paris, the *flâneur* (wanderer) came into being—the Bohemian ideal of someone who wanders endlessly without direction, roaming among the crowds, yet standing apart from them. In August 1857, half a year after the *Madame Bovary* trial, *Les Fleurs du Mal* was put on trial for the same charge; the same prosecutor this time succeeded. Baudelaire was fined and six poems were censored from his book, not to be reinstated until a second trial in 1949.

As the century closed, a circle of Symbolist poets—Verlaine, Rimbaud, and, later, Mallarmé—followed Baudelaire to create a "musical" poetry, founded in sounds and images *(vers libérés)* rather than in meaning, reaching its epitome in Mallarmé's *l'Après-midi d'un faune.* Rimbaud's career as a poet was precocious and short; he began writing at fifteen only to abandon it later for life as a gunrunner and explorer in the depths of Abysinnia. Rimbaud's involvement with the Parisian poetry scene included a stormy relationship with fellow poet Verlaine; the relationship ended violently when Verlaine wounded Rimbaud in a drunken quarrel. Rimbaud's work (and his life) had a strong and lasting influence on modern French poetry.

Politics and the artistic and literary worlds overlapped as Paris erupted into the controversy of the Dreyfus Affair in 1898. The affair set the Rightists and anti-Semites, who believed Jewish army captain Alfred Dreyfus a traitor, against Leftists of various types. Emile Zola published *J'accuse*—a letter that accused the government of a huge cover-up that had made Dreyfus into a national scapegoat. Artists and writers took sides in a public dialogue that swept Paris. Manet, Pissaro, Signac, and Mary Cassatt joined Zola in the *dreyfusard* camp; Cézanne, Renoir, Rodin, and the anti-Semitic Degas joined the *anti-dreyfusards*.

In 1909, André Gide, whose own novels and journals reflected a pure, classical detachment, founded the *Nouvelle Revue Française,* a journal which would become *the* grounding board for up-and-coming writers in the inter-war period. In the years between 1913 and 1927, Marcel Proust wrote his monumental *Remembrance of Things Past,* a semi-autobiographical summation of the Belle Epoque and its complex social undercurrents. Proust sent his first chapter to the *Nouvelle Revue;* in one of history's great miscalculations, Gide refused the piece without even unwrapping the package, claiming that the aristocratic Proust—"a snob, a dilettante, and a man-about-town"—was incapable of producing good literature. The journal's history was not always illustrious: under a collaborationist editor during World War II, the journal promoted fascism as an alternative to communism.

Colette's multi-layered descriptions of the sensual world of Paris in the 20s were unique in their focus on issues of love and sexuality, especially between women. Besides her, the 1920s and 30s were the decades of the expatriates. Even before the war, much of the cutting edge had belonged to foreigners, such as Stravinsky and Picasso. After the Armistice, a "lost generation" of literati streamed in from America and western Europe—James Joyce, Ernest Hemingway, Ford Madox Ford, Ezra Pound, Gertrude Stein, and F. Scott Fitzgerald among them. The Americans, above all, sought a freedom in Paris they could not find at home—and enjoyed the power of the American dollar against the highly devalued French franc. Gertrude Stein expressed the feelings of her fellow expatriates: "America is my country, but Paris is my home town." Soon they were joined by a different kind of migrant: refugees from the tyrannical states that were sprouting up around Europe. Walter Benjamin, for example, fled to Paris from Nazi Germany, only to flee again (unsuccessfully) after the fall of France. Robert Capa, a Hungarian Jew who grew up in Germany, escaped to Paris before beginning his twenty years as a war photographer.

The years before World War II were marked by the beginnings of Existentialism, led by Jean-Paul Sartre. Sartre's *Being and Nothingness,* written at Café de Flore in the midst of the Occupation, became the veritable encyclopedia of Existentialism. Albert Camus published *The Stranger* in 1942, telling the story of the young Meursault who is fundamentally incapable of relating to his fellow human beings. After the war Paris was still the city of the Existentialists, who met at the cafés of Montparnasse to discuss the absurdity and meaninglessness of the world around them. Sartre published *Huis Clos* in 1945, with its telling assertion that *"L'Enfer, c'est les autres"* (Hell is other people). Simone de Beauvoir, his lifetime companion, wrote the significant feminist work *The Second Sex,* as well as existentialist novels. Camus's *The Plague* (1947) provided the spiritual summation of the movement, with its description of a town quarantined by a renewed epidemic of the bubonic plague. Paris moved into the 1950s with the absurdist plays of Eugène Ionesco and expatriate Samuel Beckett. Ionesco's plays *The Bald Soprano* and *The Lesson* have been running for 34 years in the *quartier latin's* Théâtre de la Huchette.

Despite philosophies which deemphasized the meaning of political events, politics and the arts and letters mixed as the Fourth Republic (1947-58) witnessed the collapse of the French Empire in Indochina, Tunisia, and Morocco. By 1958, France, reluctant to give up control, was embroiled in a war in Algeria. Writers of the political left in Paris, such as Sartre, made an outcry, torn between loyalty to the French government and their desire to condemn imperialism.

While Sartre and Camus preserved somewhat traditional literary styles, experimental writing in the 50s and 60s produced the *nouveau roman* (the new novel), which abandoned conventional narrative techniques, embracing subject matter previously considered trivial and mundane. Among its best known exponents are Alain Robbe-Grillet, Nathalie Sarraute, and Marguerite Duras. Sarraute presents character dialogue with an emphasis on *sous conversation* (what people think as they converse) as opposed to spoken dialogue. Marguerite Duras's novels and her script for the haunting film *Hiroshima Mon Amour* claim to present the abstract painting of literature. In a less abstract vein, Georges Simenon has described the streets of Paris relentlessly perused by his detective hero, Inspector Maigret. France is also home to many of the great names in modern philosophy—Lacan, Foucault, Saussure, Barthes, Baudrillard, and Derrida have been at the center of such movements as Cultural Criticism, Semiology, Structuralism, and Deconstructionism. For more on the latest in French writing (in French), check the list of best sellers in the weekly magazine *Livre,* or look for reviews in the literary section of a French newspaper.

∎ LA POLITESSE AND OTHER NECESSITIES

MANNERS

Many visitors from abroad or even from the French provinces have returned with stories of the Parisians' xenophobia and snobbery. These tall tales of Parisian discourtesy may come true if you address people in English without the prefatory *"Parlez-vous anglais, Madame/Monsieur?"* Although some Parisians have the somewhat annoying habit of answering all queries in English, even the simplest of efforts to speak French will be appreciated. Be lavish with your *Monsieurs, Madames,* and *Mademoiselles*—unlike English, French demands use of titles when addressing strangers—and greet everyone with a friendly *bonjour* or *bonsoir*. When you do encounter rude locals, consider their point of view. Every summer, tourists more than double the city's population. Many do not speak French and are unwilling to accept the challenge of dealing with people who do not understand them. Parisians have a soft spot for those who wish to share their love of French language and culture, but Paris is not about to pamper you.

LANGUAGE

> *Il n'est bon bec que dans Paris (There is no good speech except from Paris)*
>
> —*François Villon, 1461*

For centuries, France has been a country obsessed with language. Spelling changes proposed by the state in the 1980s brought die-hard purists to the brink of riot. All such changes occur under the watchful eye of the Académie Française, which compiles the French dictionary and oversees the language. In the summer of 1992, the Assemblée Nationale added a line to the constitution: French is now the undisputable official language of France. Parisian French, although full of anglicisms, remains the "official" dialect. Like the city itself, the language of Paris was instrumental in forging the political unity of the nation and in creating its national culture. The Jules Ferry laws of the Third Republic sent state-employed instructors to spread the Parisian lingo and culture through the provinces. While a regional twang still lingers in the southwest, the Parisian pronunciation, like the BBC accent among the British, endures as the standard of excellence.

While English-speaking visitors may find themselves occasional targets of ridicule, don't despair. Paris is also a city for tourists, highly adapted to the needs of the multilingual crowds it receives each year. You will find a wide variety of English-language signs, tours, and brochures, and should have no trouble finding your way around and making yourself understood. Most major sites offer guided tours in English, or at least printed English translations.

■ Essentials

PLANNING YOUR TRIP

Note: In Paris addresses "M." indicates the nearest metro stop. All *arrondisse-ment* names have been abbreviated using the French contraction for ordinal numbers. Thus the eighth *arrondissement* contracts to 8ème, which is an abbreviated form of *huitième*. The postal code of Paris addresses is formed by affixing the two-digit *arrondissement* number to 750. Thus, the postal code of an address in the 8ème is 75008. An international telephone call to Paris requires dialing 33 (France code) plus 1 (Paris code) before the 8-digit number.

■■■ USEFUL ADDRESSES AND PUBLICATIONS

Research your trip early. The government and private agencies listed below will provide useful information.

FRENCH GOVERNMENT SERVICES

The French government is well aware of the benefits of tourism for the country's economy, and will gladly provide prospective visitors with sundry brochures.

French Government Tourist Office: Write for information on any region of France, festival dates, and tips for travelers with disabilities. **U.S.,** 610 Fifth Ave., New York, NY 10020 (tel. nationwide (900) 990-0040, 50¢/min.). **Canada,** 1981, av. McGill College, #490, Montréal, Qué. H3A 2W9 (tel. (514) 288-4264). **U.K.,** 178 Piccadilly, London W1V OAL (tel. (071) 629 12 72). In **Ireland,** citizens should consult the Consular Section within the French Embassy at 36 Ailesbury Rd., Ballsbridge, Dublin 4 (tel. (353) 1 77 18 71). **Australia,** BNP Building, 12th Fl., 12 Castlereagh St., Sydney, NSW 2000 (tel. (02) 231 52 44). For information and visas **New Zealanders** should contact this branch or the Consular Section within the French Embassy at 1 Willeston St., Wellington (tel. (64) 4 4720 200).
Cultural Services of the French Embassy: U.S., 972 Fifth Ave., New York, NY 10021 (tel. (212) 439-1400). **U.K.,** 23 Cromwell Rd., London SW7 2EL (tel. (071) 581 52 92). General information about France including culture, student employment, and educational possibilities.

FRENCH CONSULATES

The French consulate in your home country can supply you with important legal information concerning your trip, arrange for necessary visas, and direct you toward a wealth of other information about tourism, education, and employment in France. Write or call for more information.

U.S., Consulate General: 3 Commonwealth Ave., Boston, MA 02116 (tel. (617) 266-1680); Visa Section, 20 Park Plaza, Statler Bldg., 11th Fl., Boston, MA 02116 (tel. (617) 482-3650 for a recording of general information, (617) 482-2864 for specific inquiries; open 8am-noon). There are 12 branch offices across the U.S.; contact the Consulate General to locate the branch nearest you. **Canada,** 2, Elysée, Place Bonaventure, BP 202 Montréal, Qué. H5A 1B1 (tel. (514) 878-4381); other consulates in Moncton, Québec City, Toronto, Edmonton, and Vancouver; French Embassy in Ottawa. **U.K.,** 21 Cromwell Rd., London SW7 2DQ (tel. (071) 581 52 92); Visa Section, 6A Cromwell Pl., London SW7 2EW (tel. (089) 820 02

89). **Irish** residents in the U.K. should address inquiries to this consulate. In Ireland, citizens should consult the Consular Section within the French Embassy at 36 Ailesbury Rd., Ballsbridge, Dublin 4 (tel. (353) 1 77 18 71), or the antenna office at 35 Lower Abbey St., Dublin 1 (tel. (353) 1 77 18 71). **Australia,** 31 Market St., 26th Fl., Sydney, NSW 2000 (tel. (02) 261 5931 or (02) 261 5779). **New Zealand,** 1 Willeston St., Wellington (tel. (64) 4 4720 200).

USEFUL TRAVEL ORGANIZATIONS

Campus Travel. A new travel service, it offers special student and youth fares on travel by plane, train, boat, and bus, as well as flexible airline tickets. Also provides discount and ID cards for youths, special travel insurance for students and those under 35, and maps and guides. Office at 52 Grosvenor Gardens, London SW1W 0AG (tel. (071) 730 88 32; fax (071) 730 57 39).

Council on International Educational Exchange (CIEE/Council Travel). Provides low-cost travel arrangements, books (including *Let's Go)*, and gear. Operates 43 offices throughout the U.S., including those listed below and branches in Chicago, IL; Dallas, TX; Portland, OR; Seattle, WA; Providence, RI; Cambridge, MA; San Diego, San Francisco, Berkeley, La Jolla, and Long Beach, CA. **Boston,** 729 Boylston St., #201, MA 02116 (tel. (617) 266-1926; fax (617) 266 7168); **Los Angeles,** 1093 Broxton Ave., #220, CA 90024 (tel. (310) 208-3551). **New York,** 205 E. 42nd St., NY 10017 (tel. (212) 661-1450).

Council on International Educational Exchange (CIEE) has **affiliates** abroad that charter airline tickets, arrange homestays, and sell international student ID cards, travel literature, insurance, and hostel cards. CIEE also helps students secure work visas and find employment through its work-exchange programs. In **Australia,** contact SSA Swap Program, P.O. Box 399 or 220 Faraday St. (1st Fl.), Carlton South, Melbourne, Victoria 3053 (tel. (03) 348 17 77). In the **U.K.,** contact London Student Travel, 52 Grosvenor Gardens, London WC1 (tel. (071) 730 34 02). In **Canada,** write to Travel CUTS (Canadian University Travel Services Ltd.), 187 College St., Toronto, Ont. M5T 1P7 (tel. (416) 979-2406). If you can't locate an affiliated office in your country, contact CIEE's main office: 205 E. 42nd St., New York, NY 10017 (tel. (212) 661-1450, (800) 223-7402 for charter flight tickets only), or the **International Student Travel Confederation,** listed below.

Council Travel and **Council Charter.** 2 budget subsidiaries of CIEE. Council Travel sells Eurail and BritRail passes, guidebooks, travel gear, discounted flights, ISIC, FIYTO, and ITIC cards, and HI memberships. Publishes Council Travel's Budget Traveler newsletter. In the **U.S., branch offices** are located in New York, Boston, Los Angeles, Chicago, San Francisco, and Austin. Also in **U.K.,** at 28A Poland St., London W1V 3DB (tel. (071) 437 77 67).

Educational Travel Centre (ETC), 438 North Frances St., Madison, WI 53703 (tel. (608) 256-5551). Flight information, HI/AYH cards, Eurail and regional rail passes.

International Student Exchange Flights (ISE), 5010 E. Shea Blvd., #A104, Scottsdale, AZ 85254 (tel. (602) 951-1177). Budget student flights, BritRail and Eurail passes, traveler's checks, and travel guides. Free catalogue.

International Student Travel Confederation (ISTC), Store Kongensgade 40H, 1264 Copenhagen K, Denmark (tel. 45 33 93 93 03). Applications includes many procedural requirements US$14. Cards are valid Sept.-Dec. of the next year.

Let's Go Travel, Harvard Student Agencies, Inc., 53 Church St., Cambridge, MA 02138 (tel. (617) 495-9649 or (800) 553-8746). They sell plane tickets, railpasses, HI/AYH memberships, ISIC, ITIC, and IYC cards, traveling gear, and travel guides.

London Student Travel, 52 Grosvenor Gardens, London WC1 (tel. (071) 730 34 02); in Ireland, **USIT Ltd.,** Aston Quay, O'Connell Bridge, Dublin 2 (tel. (01) 679 88 33; fax (01) 677 88 43).

SSA Swap Program, P.O. Box 399 or 220 Faraday St. (1 fl.), Carlton South, Melbourne, Victoria, 3053 Australia (tel. (03) 348 17 77).

STA Travel, a worldwide youth travel organization. Offers bargain flights, railpasses, accommodations, tours, insurance, and ISICs. 10 offices in the **U.S.,** including 17 E. 45th St., New York, NY 10017 (tel. (212) 986-9643 or (800) 777-

TOP 5 Ways to Save Money While Traveling

5. Ship yourself in a crate marked "Livestock." Remember to poke holes in the crate.

4. Board a train dressed as Elvis and sneer and say "The King rides for free."

3. Ask if you can walk through the Channel Tunnel.

2. Board the plane dressed as an airline pilot, nod to the flight attendants, and hide in the rest room until the plane lands.

1. Bring a balloon to the airline ticket counter, kneel, breathe in the helium, and ask for the kiddie fare.

But if you're serious about saving money while you're traveling abroad, just get an ISIC--the International Student Identity Card. Discounts for students on international airfares, hotels and motels, car rentals, international phone calls, financial services, and more.

For more information:

In the United States:

0112), and 7202 Melrose Ave., Los Angeles, CA 90046 (tel. (213) 934-8722). In the **U.K.,** STA's main office is at 86 Old Brompton Rd., London SW7 3LQ.

Travel CUTS (Canadian University Travel Services Ltd.), 187 College St., Toronto, Ont. M5T 1P7 (tel. (416) 979-2406). In the **U.K.,** 295-A Regent St., London W1R 7YA (tel. (071) 637 31 61). Does many wonderful things including offering discounted transatlantic flights with special student fares and discount rail passes. Sells ISIC, FIYTO, and HI hostel cards. *The Student Traveller* is available free at all 35 offices across Canada.

HOSTEL ASSOCIATIONS

Hostelling International (HI) is the new and universal trademark name adopted by the International Youth Hostel Federation (IYHF). The 6000 official youth hostels worldwide will normally display the new HI logo (a blue triangle) alongside the symbol of one of the 70 national hostel association.

A one-year Hostelling International (HI) membership permits you to stay at youth hostels in Paris at reasonable prices. Despite the name, you need not be a youth; travelers over 25 pay only a slight surcharge for a bed. You can save yourself potential trouble by procuring a membership card before you leave home; some hostels do not sell them on the spot. (For more details on youth hostels, see Accommodations.)

The guide *Budget Accommodation Vol. 1: Europe and the Mediterranean* (US$13.95, including postage and handling) lists up-to-date information on HI hostels.

One-year hostel membership cards are available from some travel agencies, including Council Travel, Let's Go Travel, and STA Travel, and from the following organizations:

Hostelling International (HI), headquarters, 9 Guessens Rd., Welwyn Garden City, Hertfordshire AL8 6QW, England (tel. (44) (0707) 33 24 87).

American Youth Hostels (AYH), 733 15th St. N.W., #840, Washington, DC 20005 (tel. (202) 783-6161; fax (202) 783-6171); also dozens of regional offices across the U.S. (call above number for information). AYH is the U.S. member of HI. Cards cost US$25 (renewals US$20, under 18 US$10, over 54 US$15, family cards US$35). 200 hostels in U.S. Contact AYH for ISICs, student and charter flights, travel equipment, and literature on budget travel.

Hostelling International—Canada (HIC), National Office, 1600 James Naismith Dr., #608, Gloucester, Ottawa, Ont. K1B 5N4 (tel. (613) 748 56 38). 1-yr. membership fee CDN$26.75, under 18 CDN$12.84, 2-yr. CDN$37.45.

Fédération Unie des Auberges de Jeunesse (FUAJ), 27, rue Pajol, 75018 Paris (tel. 46 07 00 01; M. La Chapelle).

Youth Hostels Association of England and Wales (YHA), Trevelyan House, 8 St. Stephen's Hill, St. Albans, Herts AL1 2DY (tel. (0727) 85 52 15), or 14 Southampton St., Covent Garden, London WC2E 7HY (tel. (071) 83 610 36). Fee £9, under 18 £3.

Scottish Youth Hostel Association (SYHA), 7 Glebe Crescent, Sterling FK8 2JA (tel. (0786) 511 81).

An Oíge (Irish Youth Hostel Association), 61 Mountjoy St., Dublin 7 (tel. (01) 30 45 55; fax (01) 30 58 08). Fee IR£9, under 18 IR£3.

Youth Hostel Association of Northern Ireland (YHANI), 56 Bradbury Pl., Belfast BT7 1RU (tel. (0232) 32 47 33).

Australian Youth Hostels Association (AYHA), Level 3, 10 Mallett St., Camperdown, NSW 2050 Australia (tel. (02) 565 16 99; fax (02) 565 13 25). Cards AUS$40.

Youth Hostels Association of New Zealand (YHANZ), P.O. Box 436, 173 Gloucester St., Christchurch 1, New Zealand (tel. (64) 3 379 99 70; fax (64) 3 365 44 76).

LET'S USE CTS

THE YOUTH & STUDENT TRAVEL SPECIALISTS

FROM PARIS

in USD$ one way	✈	🚢
Amsterdam	55	57
Athens	171	195
Barcelona	121	76
Berlin	125	125
Copenhagen	125	170
Dublin	136	162
Lisbon	125	111
London	67	77
Madrid	132	90
Milan	125	65
Munich	102	
Nice	74	71
Palma	140	
Pisa (Florence)	139	79
Prague	127	
Rome	89	86
Tel Aviv	258	
Venice	137	92

Accommodation • budget hotels, family accommodations and youth hostels in the main tourist destinations. **Rent a car or a van** for 3, 6 or even more days, with chance of a drop-off in a different country. **Ferry boat** • discounted tickets for Greece, Sardinia and Corse. **Eurotrain Explorer Pass** • to use as you like the rail network of Hungary, Poland, Check and Slovakian Republic, Baltic countries, Portugal. **And also** • sightseeings and excursions to the most important European tourist highlights, tours all over Europe, seaside resorts in Greece and all possible budget tourist services.

ONE WAY BUDGET FLIGHT TICKETS FOR THE UNITED STATES AND LONG HAUL AVAILABLE
PUBLISHED PRICES ARE SUBJECT TO CHANGE

YOUTH & STUDENT TRAVEL CENTRE

Paris ■ 20, rue des Carmes • tel. (01) 43250076 • *Underground station: Maubert Mutualité*

Rome ■ via Genova, 16 (*off via Nazionale*) tel. (06) 46791 • *Underground station: Repubblica* ■ Corso Vittorio Emanuele II, 297 • tel. (06) 6872672/3/4

Florence ■ via dei Ginori, 25/R • tel. (055) 289721/289570

Milan ■ via S. Antonio, 2 tel. (02) 58304121

Naples ■ via Mezzocannone, 25 • tel. (081) 5527975/5527960

Venice ■ Dorso Duro Ca' Foscari, 3252, tel. (041) 5205660/5205655

London ■ 44 Goodge Street W1P 2AD • tel. (071) 5804554/6375601 *Underground station: Goodge Street*

London ■ 220 Kensington High Street, W8 7RA • tel. (071) 9373265 • *Underground st.ation High Street Kensington*

Other 80 CTS offices are to be found in all major italian cities

BOOKS, GUIDES, MAPS, ETC.

The European Association of Music Festivals, 122, rue de Lausanne, 1202 Geneva, Switzerland (tel. (22) 732 28 03; fax (22) 738 40 12), publishes the booklet *Festivals,* which lists dates and programs of major European music and theater events.

Forsyth Travel Library, P.O. Box 2975, Shawnee Mission, KS 66201 (tel. (800) 367-7984). Call or write for their catalogue of maps, railpasses, and timetables.

Hippocrene Books, Inc., 171 Madison Ave., New York NY 10016 (tel. (212) 685-4371; orders (718) 454-2360; fax (718) 454-1391). Free catalogue. Publishes travel reference books, travel guides, maps, and foreign language dictionaries.

Press and Information Division of the French Embassy, 4101 Reservoir Rd. N.W., Washington, DC 20007 (tel. (202) 944-6048). Write for information about political, social, and economic aspects of France. Publishes a biweekly newsletter, *News from France,* as well as *France Magazine.*

Superintendent of Documents, U.S. Government Printing Office, Washington, DC 20402 (tel. (202) 783-3238), prints another helpful, regionally specific publication, *Tips for Travelers* (US$1).

Travelling Books, P.O. Box 77114, Seattle, WA 98177 (tel. (206) 367-5848), publishes a catalogue of guides which will make the traveler weep with wanderlust.

Wide World Books and Maps, 1911 N. 45th St., Seattle, WA 98103 (tel. (206) 634-3453). Write them for hard-to-find maps. Open Mon.-Fri. 10am-7pm, Sat. 10am-6pm, Sun. noon-5pm.

■■■ DOCUMENTS AND FORMALITIES

Remember to file all visa and passport applications at least a month before your departure date. Most offices suggest that you apply in the winter off-season (Aug.-Dec.) for speedier service. When you travel, always carry on your person two or more forms of identification, including at least one photo ID. Currency exchanges, especially banks, require several IDs before cashing traveler's checks. It is useful to carry extra passport-size photos for transit and other IDs you'll acquire while abroad.

PASSPORTS

You need a valid passport to enter France and to re-enter your own country. Photocopy the page of your passport that contains your photograph and identifying information; your passport number is especially important. Consulates recommend that you carry an expired passport or an official copy of your birth certificate in your baggage separate from other documents. If you do lose your passport, it may take weeks to process a replacement, though immediate temporary traveling papers will permit you to return to your home country. On the brighter side, some consulates can issue new passports within two days if you give them proof of citizenship.

Applying for a passport is complicated, so make sure your questions are answered in advance. The countries listed below require various forms of identification, two recent and identical passport-sized photographs, the application form, and a processing fee; for more specific information, contact your local passport office.

U.S. citizens may apply for a passport at a U.S. Passport Agency or at one of several thousand federal or state **courthouses** or **post offices** authorized to accept passport applications. Refer to the "U.S. Government, State Department" section of the telephone directory or call your local post office for addresses.

Applications take three to four weeks to process, though the process is quicker at a U.S. Passport Agency. Passports are processed according to the departure date indicated on the application form. During peak travel season (March-Aug.) processing may take even longer. Passport agencies also offer **rush service:** if you have proof (e.g. an airplane ticket) that you are departing within five working days, a Passport Agency will issue a passport while you wait.

U.S. embassies and consulates in Paris can usually issue new passports, given proof of citizenship. For more **information,** contact the U.S. Passport Information's helpful 24-hour recorded message (tel. (202) 647-0518) or call the recorded message of the passport agency nearest you.

Canadian application forms in English and French are available at all passport offices, post offices, and most travel agencies. Citizens may apply in person at any one of 29 regional passport offices across Canada. You can also apply by mail to the Passport Office, External Affairs, Ottawa, Ont. K1A OG3. The processing time is approximately five business days for in-person applications and three weeks for mailed ones. If a passport is lost abroad, Canadians must prove citizenship with another document in order to get a replacement. For additional **information,** call the 24-hour number (tel. (800) 567-6868). Refer to the booklet *Bon Voyage, But...* for further help and a list of Canadian embassies and consulates abroad. It is available free of charge from any passport office or from: Info-Export (BPTE), External Affairs, Ottawa, Ont. K1A OG2.

British citizens, British Dependant Territories citizens, and British Overseas citizens may apply for a full 10-year passport. Residents of the U.K., the Channel Islands, and the Isle of Man can also apply for the more restricted British Visitor's Passport. For a full 10-year passport, apply in person or by mail to one of six passport offices, located in London, Newport, Liverpool, Peterborough, Glasgow, and Belfast. Application forms are also available from main post offices (in Northern Ireland from any local office of the DSS). The fee is £18. The one-year British Visitor's Passport covers travel only to western Europe and Bermuda. It is not valid for the purpose of employment, nor for visits lasting more than three months in any one country. The Visitor's Passport may be obtained at main post offices in England, Scotland, and Wales, and from passport offices in Northern Irelend, the Channel Islands, and the Isle of Man. The fee is £12.

Irish citizens can apply for a passport by mail to one of the following two passport offices: Department of Foreign Affairs, Passport Office, Setanta Centre, Molesworth St., Dublin 2 (tel. (01) 671 16 33), or Passport Office, 1A South Mall, Cork (tel. (021) 27 25 25). Obtain an application form at a local Garda station or request one from a passport office. Passports cost £45 and are valid for 10 years. Citizens younger than 18 and older than 65 can request a three-year passport that costs £10.

Australian citizens must apply for a passport in person at a local post office, a passport office, or an Australian diplomatic mission overseas. An appointment may be necessary. Passport offices are located in Adelaide, Brisbane, Canberra, Darwin, Hobart, Melbourne, Newcastle, Perth, and Sydney. Application fees are adjusted every three months.

Applicants for **New Zealand passports** must contact their local Link Center, travel agent, or New Zealand Representative for an application form, which they must complete and mail to the New Zealand Passport Office, Documents of National Identity Division, Department of Internal Affairs, Box 10-526, Wellington (tel. (04) 474 81 00). The standard processing time is 10 working days from receipt of an application; urgent applications receive priority. The application fee is NZ$80 for an application lodged in New Zealand and NZ$130 for one lodged overseas (if under 16, NZ$40 and NZ$65, respectively).

South African citizens can apply for a passport at any Home Affairs Office. Two photos, either a birth certificate or an identity book, and the R30 fee must accompany a completed application. For further information, contact the Home Affairs Office nearest you.

VISAS

A visa is an endorsement or stamp placed in your passport by a foreign government allowing you to visit their country for a specified purpose and period of time. Visas are not required of visitors to France from EU member countries, from the U.S., Canada, New Zealand, Scandinavia, Poland, or Switzerland among others. Visas are required of Australian citizens and *anyone* planning to stay more than three months (see below). It must be obtained from the French consulate *in your home country.* For more details write to R. Woods, Consumer Information Center, Dept. 454V, Pueblo, CO 81002, for *Foreign Visa Requirements* (US50¢), or contact **Center for International Business and Travel,** 25 West 43rd St., Suite 1420, New York, NY 10036 (tel. (800) 925-2428 or (212) 575-2811 from NYC. This company secures visas for travel to and from all possible countries. The service charge varies, but the average cost for a U.S. citizen is US$15-20 per visa.

Requirements for a long-stay visa vary with the nature of the stay: work, study, or *au pair.* Apply to the nearest French Consulate at least three months in advance. For a **student visa,** you must present a passport valid until at least 60 days after the date you plan to leave France, an application with references, a passport photo, a letter of admission from a French university or a study abroad program, a notarized guarantee of financial support for $600 per month, and a fee which fluctuates according to the exchange rate (currently US$57). To obtain a **work visa,** you must first obtain a work permit. After securing a job and a work contract from your French employer, your employer will obtain this permit for you and will forward it with a copy of your work contract to the consulate nearest you. After a medical checkup and completion of the application, the visa will be issued on your valid passport. Note, however, that it is illegal for foreign students to work during the school year, although they can receive permission from a *Direction départementale du travail et de la main-d'oeuvre étrangère* to work in summer (see below). For an *au pair* stay of more than three months, an **au pair's visa** is required and can be obtained by submission of a valid passport, two completed application forms, two passport photos, a fee (varies between US$15-25), a medical certificate of good health completed by a Consulate-approved doctor, two copies of the *au pair's* work contract signed by the *au pair,* and proof of admission to a language school or university program. (See Au Pair Positions, below, for more information.)

In addition to securing a visa, if you are staying longer than 90 days in France for any reason, you must obtain a **carte de séjour** (residency permit) once in France. Report to the local *préfecture* of the *département* in which you are residing. You must present a valid passport stamped with a long-stay visa, a medical certificate, six (yes, six) application forms completed in French, six passport photos, a letter of financial guarantee, and, if you're under 18, proof of parental authorization. Be prepared to jump through hoops, bark like a dog, and stand in line, perhaps repeatedly. Bring your Proust.

For more information, send for the U.S. government pamphlet *Foreign Visa Requirements.* Mail a check for 50¢ to Consumer Information Center, Dept. 454V, Pueblo, CO 81009 (tel. (719) 948-3334). The company **Visa Center, Inc.,** 507 Fifth Ave., #904, New York, NY 10017 (tel. (212) 986-0924), secures visas for travel to and from all possible countries. Average cost for a U.S. citizen is US$15-20 per visa.

STUDENT, TEACHER, AND YOUTH IDENTIFICATION

In the world of budget travel, youth has its privileges. Two main forms of student and youth identification are accepted worldwide; they are extremely useful, especially for the insurance packages that accompany them.

The **International Student Identity Card (ISIC)** (US$16) is an internationally recognized proof of student status. If you have a student ID from a school in France or from your home country, it will usually qualify you for the same discounts on train and theater tickets and on admission to museums, historical sites, and festivals—you probably won't need an ISIC card. The ISIC offers other benefits including lower fares on many forms of local and international transportation—it's essential if you plan to use student charter flights or clubs. The card incorporates the International Union of Students card. If you purchase the card in the U.S., it also provides you with US$3000 medical and accident insurance and US$100 per day for up to 60 days of hospitalization. The **International Teacher Identity Card (ITIC)** (US$17) offers identical discounts to teachers.

To apply for either, contact one of the student travel services listed above (see Useful Addresses: Budget Travel Services). Applicants must be at least 12 years old. Because of the proliferation of phony and improperly issued ISIC cards, many airlines and some other services now require double proof of student or teacher identity. It is wise to have a signed letter from a school registrar attesting to your student or teacher status and stamped with the school seal, or to carry your school ID card.

If you're not a student but are under age 26, inquire about other youth discounts. The **Federation of International Youth Travel Organizations (FIYTO)** issues the **International Youth Travel Card** to anyone under age 26; it is also available from a number of the travel services listed above. Also known as the **GO 25 Card,** this one-year card (US$16) is internationally recognized and gives you access to over 8000 discounts on international and intra-European transport, accommodations, restaurants, cultural activities, and tours. For more information, contact FIYTO at Bredgade 25H, DK-1260, Copenhagen K, Denmark. Or, call your local Council Travel office.

INTERNATIONAL DRIVER'S LICENSE

An International Driving Permit (a translation of your driver's license into nine languages) is required to drive in France. A valid driver's license from your home country must always accompany the IDP. Most car rental agencies do not require the IDP, and many foreigners drive without it. This is risky, however, since the permit comes in handy in sticky situations like accidents—especially when they occur in areas in which most citizens and police officers do not speak English.

Your IDP must be issued in your own country before you depart. U.S. license holders can obtain an International Driving Permit (US$10), valid for one year, at any **American Automobile Association (AAA)** office or by writing to its main office, AAA Florida, Travel Agency Services Department, 1000 AAA Drive (mail stop 28), Heathrow, FL 32746-5080 (tel. (800) 222-4357, (407) 444-4245; fax (407) 444-7380). For further information, contact a local AAA office. You may also procure an IDP from the **American Automobile Touring Alliance,** Bayside Plaza, 188 The Embarcadero, San Francisco, CA 94105 (tel. (415) 777-4000; fax (415) 882-2141.

Canadian license holders can obtain an IDP (CDN$10) through any **Canadian Automobile Association (CAA)** branch office in Canada, or by writing to CAA Toronto, 60 Commerce Valley Dr. East, Thornhill, Ont., L3T 7P9 (tel. (905) 771-3000; fax (905) 771-3046).

You will also need a **green card,** or **International Insurance Certificate,** to prove that you have liability insurance. The application forms are available at any AAA or CAA office. Or, you can get one through the car rental agency; most of them include coverage in their prices. If you lease a car, you can obtain a green card from the dealer. Some travel agents offer the card, and it may be available at the border. Even if your auto insurance applies abroad, you will need a green card to prove this to foreign officials.

CUSTOMS

Don't be alarmed by customs procedures. The many regulations of customs and duties pose nary a threat to the budget traveler. Most countries prohibit or restrict the importation of firearms, explosives, ammunition, fireworks, controlled drugs, most plants and animals, lottery tickets, and obscene literature and films. To avoid problems when you transport prescription drugs, ensure that the bottles are clearly marked, and carry a copy of the prescription to show the customs officer.

Anything exceeding the allowance of what a visitor can bring into France is charged a duty. Among other things, if you are bringing in more than 200 cigarettes, 2L of wine, 1L of alcohol over 38.8 proof, or 50g of perfume, you must declare such items.

Upon returning home, you must declare all articles you acquired abroad and must pay a duty on the value of those articles that exceeds the allowance established by your country's customs service. Holding onto receipts for purchases made abroad will help establish values when you return. Make a list of any valuables that you carry with you from home; if you register this list with customs before your departure, you will avoid import duty charges and ensure an easy passage upon your return.

Keep in mind that goods and gifts purchased at duty-free shops abroad are not exempt from duty or sales tax at your point of return; you must declare these items along with other purchases. For a complete and specific list of what can and cannot be brought back home, contact your local customs service. Before leaving, **U.S. citizens** should record the serial numbers of expensive (especially foreign-made) items that will accompany them abroad. Have this list stamped by the Customs Office before you leave; this will prevent you from being taxed on items you already own. U.S. citizens may bring in US$400 worth of goods free of U.S. taxes every 30 days; the next US$1000 is subject to a 10% tax. You must be 21 or older to bring liquor into the U.S. Non-prescription drugs and narcotics, and many food, plant, and animal products may not be imported into the U.S. Write for the brochure, *Know Before You Go* (50¢), U.S. Customs Service, Box 7407, Washington, D.C. 20044, or call (202) 927-6724. *Travelers' Tips on Bringing Food, Plant, and Animal Products into the United States* is available from the Animal and Plant Health Inspection Service, U.S. Department of Agriculture, 6505 Belcrest Rd., Attn: Public Information, Washington, DC 20250.

For more information on mailing gifts from France contact the U.S. Customs Service, P.O. Box 7407, Washington, DC 20044 (tel. (202) 927-6724).

Canadian citizens who remain abroad for at least one week may bring back up to CDN$300 worth of goods duty-free once every calendar year; goods that exceed the allowance will be taxed at 12%. You are permitted to ship goods home under this exemption as long as you declare them when you arrive. For more information, contact Canadian customs, 2265 St. Laurent Blvd., Ottawa, Ontario, K1G 4K3 or call (800) 461-9999.

European Union nationals who travel between EU countries no longer need to declare the goods they purchase abroad. Goods for personal use are not taxed or dutied beyond the V.A.T., provided that duty and tax are paid at the time of purchase. Members of the EU are: Belgium, Denmark, France, Germany, Greece, Ireland, Italy, Luxembourg, the Netherlands, Portugal, Spain, and the U.K.

British citizens are allowed an exemption of up to £136 of goods purchased outside the EU, and are also exempt from paying taxes on limited quantities of tobacco products, wine, and perfume. Citizens must be over 17 to import liquor or tobacco. For more information about U.K. customs, contact Her Majesty's Customs and Excise, Custom House, Heathrow Airport North, Hounslow, Middlesex, TW6 2LA (tel. (081) 910 37 44; fax (081) 910 37 65).

Irish citizens may return home with the equivalent of IR£34 of goods purchased outside the EU, in addition to small quantities of cigarettes, alcoholic beverages, and fragrances. Citizens under 17 are not entitled to any allowance for tobacco or alcoholic products but may bring back IR £17 of regular goods plus small quantities of perfume and toilet water. For more information, contact the Revenue Commissioners, Dublin Castle (tel. (01) 679 27 77; fax (01) 671 20 21).

Australian citizens over 18 may import 1 liter of liquor and 250 cigarettes or 250 grams of tobacco products duty-free. Travelers may import AUS$400 (under 18 AUS$200) of other goods duty-free—if they are intended as gifts. When AUS$5000 (or the equivalent in foreign currency) is brought into or out of the country, travelers must report it. For further information contact the Australian Customs Service, 5 Constitution Ave., Canberra ACT 2601 (tel. (6) 275 62 55; fax (6) 275 69 89).

Each **New Zealand citizen** may bring home up to NZ$700 worth of goods duty-free if they are intended for personal use or are unsolicited gifts. Only travelers over 17 may bring tobacco or alcoholic beverages into the country. For more information, consult the *New Zealand Customs Guide for Travelers,* available from customs offices, or contact New Zealand Customs, 50 Anzac Avenue, Box 29, Auckland (tel. 0 (9) 377 35 20; fax 0 (9) 309 29 78).

MONEY

Each **South African citizen** may import limited quantities of tobacco and liquor duty-free. You may import other items up to a value of R500. You may not export or import South African Bank notes in excess of R500. Persons who require specific information or advice concerning customs and excise duties can address their inquiries to: The Commissioner for Customs and Excise, Private Bag X47, Pretoria, 0001. This agency distributes the pamphlet, *South African Customs Information,* for visitors and residents who travel abroad. South Africans residing in the U.S. should contact: South African Mission to the IMF/World Bank, 3201 New Mexico Ave. #380 NW, Suite 390, Washington, DC 20016 (tel. (202) 364 8320/1; fax (202) 364-6008).

Value-Added Tax

Value-Added Tax (called TVA in France) is a varying sales tax levied especially in the EU. The French rate is 18.6% on all goods except books, food, and medicine. There is a 33% luxury tax on such items as videocassettes, watches, jewelry, and cameras.

If you spend more than 2000F (4200F for EU members) in a particular store, you can participate in a complex over-the-counter export program for foreign shoppers that exempts you from paying TVA. Ask the store for an official **formulaire de détaxe pour l'exportation** (detax invoice) and a stamped envelope. At the border, show the invoices and your purchases to the French customs officials, who will stamp the invoices. (Make sure you leave all the articles you have purchased near the top of your suitcase.) If you're at an airport, look for the window labeled **douane de détaxe,** and be sure to budget at least an hour for the intricacies of the French bureaucracy. On a train, find an official (they won't find you) or get off at a station close to the border. Then send a copy back to the vendor. With this official TVA-exempt proof, they will refund the agreed amount. The refunds are sent to your bank account and not to your address, a process which may take as much as six months. Upon returning to your country, you may have to pay customs charges if your purchases amount to more than the allotted amount (US$400), but this often falls short of the TVA refund.

■■■ MONEY

CURRENCY AND EXCHANGE

US$1 = 5.33F	1F = US$0.19
CDN$1 = 3.87F	1F = CDN$0.26
UK£1 = 8.22F	1F = UK£0.12
IR£1 = 8.11F	1F = IR£.12
AUS$1 = 3.96F	1F = AUS$0.25
NZ$1 = 3.20F	1F = NZ$0.31
SAR1 = 1.49F	1F = SAR0.67

> Note on Prices and Currency: The information in this book was researched in the summer of 1994. Since then, inflation will have raised most prices at least 10%. The exchange rates listed were compiled on August 17, 1994. Since rates fluctuate considerably, confirm them before you go by checking a national newspaper.

The basic unit of currency in France is the franc, divided into 100 centimes, and issued in both coins and paper notes. The smallest unit of French currency is the five-centime piece. The new franc, equal to 100 old francs, was issued in 1960. Those travelers who save unused foreign currencies for future trips, take note: the old (large) French 10F coin is no longer in circulation; only the two-toned, smaller, newer version is accepted.

Remember that it is usually more expensive to buy foreign currency than it is to buy domestic; therefore francs will be less costly in France than at home. Converting a small amount of money before you go, however, will allow you to breeze through the airport while others languish in exchange counter lines. This is also a good practice in case you find yourself stuck with no money after banking hours or on a holiday.

When looking to change money in Paris, try to approach the event with the spirit of competition. Not every *bureau de change* offers the same rates and most do not charge commission. Don't be fooled by what seem like fantastic rates. Make sure that no strings (like having to exchange at least 15,000F worth of currency) apply. The best rates in town are found at the Banque de France (1er) and around the Opéra, on rue Scribe, rue Auber, and rue de la Paix (8ème). Many post offices will change cash and American Express Traveler's Cheques at competitive rates and without commission; bureaus at train stations and airports offer less favorable rates. Most banks are open 9am-noon and 2-4:30pm, but not all exchange money. Check before you get in line.

American Express: 11, rue Scribe, 9ème (tel. 47 77 77 07). M. Opéra or Auber. Across from the back of the Opéra. Unastounding exchange rates and long lines in summer, especially Mon. and Fri.-Sat. No commission. Cardholders can cash personal checks from a U.S. bank account every 21 days; bring your passport. The office receives moneygrams and will hold mail for cardholders or for those with AmEx Traveler's Cheques; otherwise 5F per inquiry. English spoken. Open Mon.-Fri. 9am-5:30pm, Sat. 9am-5pm.

At Train Stations: Remember these offices offer less-than-attractive rates intended for impatient travelers. **Gare d'Austerlitz,** 13ème (tel. 45 84 91 40). Open daily 7am-9pm. **Gare de Lyon,** 12ème (tel. 43 41 52 70). Open daily 6:30am-11pm. **Gare de l'Est,** 10ème (tel. 46 07 66 84). Open Mon.-Fri. 9am-6:30pm, Sat. 9:30am-5:00pm. **Gare du Nord,** 10ème (tel. 42 80 11 50). Open daily 6:15am-10:30pm. **Gare St-Lazare,** 8ème (tel. 43 87 72 51). Open daily 7am-9pm.

At Airports: Also not the best place to change your currency. Exchange just enough to get to Paris and change the rest within the city. **Orly-Sud:** open daily 6am-11:30pm. **Roissy-Charles de Gaulle:** open daily 6am-11:30pm.

TRAVELER'S CHECKS

Traveler's checks are the safest and least troublesome means of carrying funds. Several agencies and many banks sell them, usually for face value plus a 1% commission. (Members of the American Automobile Association can get their checks commission-free through AAA.) American Express and Visa are the most widely recognized, though other major checks are sold, exchanged, cashed, and refunded with almost equal ease. Keep in mind that in small towns, traveler's checks are less readily accepted than in cities with large tourist industries.

Each agency provides refunds if your checks are lost or stolen, and many provide additional services. (Note that you may need a police report verifying the loss or theft.) Inquire about toll-free refund hotlines, emergency message relay services, and stolen credit card assistance when you purchase your checks.

You should expect a fair amount of red tape and delay in the event of theft or loss of traveler's checks. To expedite the refund process, keep your check receipts separate from your checks and store them in a safe place, or with a traveling companion; record check numbers when you cash them and leave a list of check numbers with someone at home; and ask for a list of refund centers when you buy your checks. American Express and Bank of America have over 40,000 centers worldwide. Keep a separate supply of cash or traveler's checks for emergencies.

While U.S. citizens can easily exchange dollars for francs in France, New Zealanders and Australians may have difficulty exchanging their currencies. Buying **French franc traveler's checks** eliminates the need for expensive multiple transactions (such as Canadian to U.S. dollars and then U.S. dollars to francs). In smaller French cities and towns, as in stores and restaurants, it is often easier to exchange checks in francs. Most banks will cash French franc traveler's checks commission-free (be sure to ask, however, *before* you give them your money). Depending on

fluctuations in the value of the French franc, you may either gain or lose money by
buying them in francs in advance.

American Express, tel. in the U.S. and Canada (800) 221-7282; in the U.K. (0800)
52 13 13; in Ireland, (1800) 62 60 00; in New Zealand, call (0800) 44 10 68; in
Australia, (008) 2519 02 (except Sydney; from there, call (612) 886 06 89; in
France, call toll-free (19) 05 90 86 00). Or, from anywhere in Europe, the Middle
East, and Africa, call the England office collect at 44 273 57 16 00; from Asia, Australia, and the Far East call the Sydney office (listed above). Available in 9 currencies, commission-free for members of AAA. American Express has more than 20
offices in France, each of which will cash their cheques commission-free. Provides a mail-holding service (see Keeping in Touch), assistance with lost travel
documents, temporary IDs, and airline, hotel, and car rental reservations. Call and
ask for their cute booklet, *Traveler's Companion,* which gives full addresses for
all their travel offices, as well as stolen checque hotlines for each European country. AmEx maintains a Global Assist hotline for travel emergencies (tel. from overseas collect (202) 783-7474 or in the US (800) 554-2639). Buy the cheques at
participating banks, AmEx travel service offices, and AAA offices.
Barclay's Bank sells Visa traveler's checks in U.S. and Canadian dollars, British
pounds, and German marks. For lost or stolen checks, in the U.S. call Visa (tel.
(800) 227-6811); when the checks are issued, you will receive the number to call
from outside the U.S. For Barclay's information specifically, call (800) 221-2426 in
the U.S. and Canada, (202) 67 12 12 in the U.K; from elsewhere call New York
collect (212) 858-8500. Many branches throughout Britain. 1-3% commission. Barclay's branches cash Barclay's-Visa and any other Visa brand traveler's checks for
free.
Citicorp (tel. in the U.S. and Canada (800) 645-6556, in the U.K. (071) 982 40 40,
or collect from elsewhere (813) 623-1709) sells both Citicorp and Citicorp Visa
traveler's checks. Commission is 1-2% on check purchases. Checks available in
U.S. dollars, British pounds, German marks, and Japanese yen at banks throughout the U.S. Checkholders are automatically enrolled for 45 days in Travel Assist
Hotline (tel. (800) 523-1199) which provides travelers with English speaking doctor, lawyer, and interpreter referrals as well as check refund assistance. Also has a
World Courier Service which guarantees hand-delivery of traveler's checks anywhere in the world.
MasterCard International (tel. in the U.S., Canada, and Mexico (800) 223-9920,
collect from anywhere else in the world 44 733 50 29 95. Commission 1-2% for
purchases depending on the bank. Issued in U.S. dollars only.
Thomas Cook also sells Mastercard traveler's checks. Call (800) 223-7373 for
refunds in the Americas, (800) 223-4030 for orders. From elsewhere call collect
44 733 50 29 95. Thomas Cook Currency Services offices (located in major cities
around the globe) charge no commission. You can buy Mastercard traveler's
checks from Thomas Cook at any bank displaying a Mastercard sign.
Visa (tel. in the U.S. and Canada (800) 227-6811, in the U.K. (071) 937 8091; collect to the U.S. from anywhere else in the world (212) 858-8500) sells its traveler's
checks by mail; call (800) 235 7366 to order them.

CREDIT CARDS

Credit cards in Europe do everything they do in America. The easist way to reserve
a hotel room before you leave is to send a confirming fax with your card number
after requesting a room by phone. **Mastercard** and **Visa** are the most welcomed in
shops and hotels; heavy surcharges keep small businesses and hotels out of the
American Express loop. All three major credit cards offer instant cash advances
from banks and teller machines throughout Western Europe, in local currency.
Nearly 800 banks in France, indicated by the sticker CB/VISA or EC, will allow you
to withdraw money at a teller with a Visa or Mastercard, the equivalent of the British
Access and Barclay cards. Keep in mind that Mastercard and Visa have aliases here,
Eurocard and **Carte Bleue.** Cashiers are more familiar with the French equivalents.
In the event of confusion, show your card.

You can't buy beans without francs.

You'll probably find that the country that gave us the words "gourmet," "couture" and "champagne" isn't cheap. And it's très likely you might find yourself a little short on francs. Which is why there's Western Union Money Transfer.

With Western Union you can receive money from the States within minutes. Simply call 161 43 54 46 12 in Paris or 1-800-325-6000* in the United States for the locations nearest you.

And relax, we'll send your francs as far as you need, in case yours don't go far enough.

WESTERN UNION | MONEY TRANSFER

*The fastest way to send money worldwide.*SM

Credit cards are also invaluable in an emergency—an unexpected hospital bill or the more prosaic loss of traveler's checks—that would otherwise leave you temporarily without other resources. Try to pay for large purchases abroad by credit card; the credit card company gets a better exchange rate than you would have. In the Paris office, **American Express** cardholders can cash up to US$1000 in personal checks (US$5000 for gold card holders) every three weeks. With someone feeding money into your account back home, this can be one of the easiest and cheapest ways to send money overseas. **Global Assist,** a 24-hour hotline offering information and legal assistance in emergencies, is also available to cardholders (tel. (800) 333-2639 in U.S. and Canada; from abroad call collect (202) 554-2639). Call **American Express Travel Service** (tel. (800) 221-7282) for more information on services, or consult their *Traveler's Companion* booklet which lists full-service offices worldwide.

Mastercard: For lost cards call 45 67 84 84. For customer service call 43 23 41 52. **Visa:** For lost cards or for customer service call 42 77 11 90. **American Express:** For lost cards call 47 77 72 00. Call 05 20 12 02 for a free English-language information line on Paris and AmEx, available May-Oct. 8:30am-8pm.

CASH CARDS

Automatic Teller Machines—popularly called ATMs—are widespread within Paris, and in the last years huge advances have been made in the extension of the **Cirrus** network (tel. (800) 4-CIRRUS (424-7787)) to European countries. Depending on the system that your bank at home uses, you will probably be able to access your own personal bank account whenever you're in need of funds. Keep in mind that the ATM machines get the wholesale exchange rate which is generally 5% better than the retail rate most banks use (which is better than the rate most *bureaux de change* use). **American Express** card holders can sign up for AmEx's Express Cash service through which you can access cash from your account at any ATM with the AmEx trademark. American Express cards work in ATMs at **Credit Lyonnais** banks, as well as at AmEx offices and major airports. Each transaction costs a minimum US$2.50 (max. US$10) plus conversion fees and interest. For a list of ATMs where you can use your card, call AmEx at (800) CASH-NOW (227-4669) and they'll send you a list of participating machines. Make sure to set up your Express Cash account a few weeks before you plan to travel. **Visa** cards can access ATM networks in 40 countries around the world (usually Cirrus, but it varies according to the issuing bank). **Mastercard** functions in essentially the same way as Visa. Be sure to contact your issuer before you travel in order to get the **Personal Identification Number (PIN)** essential for ATM use. There are no letters on European bank machines, so persons with words for passwords should figure out the corresponding numbers before leaving home. Don't rely too heavily on automation. There is often a limit on the amount of money you can withdraw per day, and computer network failures are not uncommon.

In Paris, **Crédit Mutuel's Minibanque/24** and **Crédit Agricole** teller machines are on the Cirrus network. See Essentials—Other Services for a short list of ATMs on this network and consult Crédit Agricole's brochure *Rencontrez un specialiste* for an extensive list of that bank's ATM locations. In France, most ATMs are outdoors; don't let anyone distract you while at the machine and, as always, use discretion with regard to safety and money storage as you walk away from the machine.

SENDING MONEY ABROAD

Money can be wired abroad through international money transfer services operated by **Western Union** or **American Express**. **American Express** offers a Money-Gram service by which US$100-10,000 may be sent abroad. MoneyGrams sent from the US to France arrive in 10 minutes at the designated AmEx office. It costs US$35 to send US$250 and US$70 to send US$1000. For more information, call the American Express MoneyGram Customer Service toll-free number: (800) 543-4080; in

Canada (800) 933-3278. Money can also be cabled from England, Ireland, New Zealand, and Australia.

Western Union offers a convenient service for cabling money abroad to any of 7 cities in France. In the U.S., call Western Union any time at (800) 325-6000 to cable money with your **Visa** or **MasterCard.** The money will be available in France within an hour. (US$40 to send US$500, US$50 for US$1000).

If you're staying in France long enough to have a personal bank account, a cheaper alternative may be to **cable money** from bank to bank. Find a local bank big enough to have an international department, tell your home bank by mail or telegram the amount you need and the name and address of the receiving bank, together with the destination account number, and follow instructions from there. Transfer can take several days; the fee is usually US$20-30.

In emergencies, U.S. citizens can have money sent via the State Department's **Citizens Emergency Center,** Department of State, 2201 C St. NW, Washington, DC 20520 (tel. (202) 647-5225; at night and on Sundays and holidays (202) 647-4000). For a fee of US$15, the State Department will forward money within hours to the nearest consular office, which will then disburse it according to instructions. The center serves only Americans in the direst of straits abroad and prefers not to send sums greater than US$500. The quickest way to have the money sent is to cable the State Department through Western Union or to leave cash, a certified check, a bank draft, or a money order at the department itself.

OPENING A BANK ACCOUNT

If you are planning a long-term stay in Paris and have fairly liquid assets, consider opening a bank account. Foreigners can open non-resident bank accounts, but banks expect that these will be long-term (a few years) and often require a hefty opening deposit, and the maintenance of a high minimum balance (30,000F). Go to main bank offices near the Opéra to inquire about such accounts—neighborhood branches without a foreign affairs department are not equipped to provide such services.

■■■ HEALTH AND INSURANCE

Common sense is the simplest prescription for good health while you travel: eat well, drink enough, get enough sleep, and don't overexert yourself. All food, including seafood, dairy products, and fresh produce, is normally safe in Paris. The water is chlorinated and also quite safe; to avoid the infamous traveler's diarrhea, you may want to drink mineral water for the first day or two while your body adjusts to new bacteria.

Although no special immunizations are necessary for travel to France, be sure that your **inoculations** are up-to-date. Typhoid shots remain good for three years, tetanus for 10.

Always go prepared with any **medication** you may need while away. Carry up-to-date prescriptions and/or a statement (with a translated version) from your doctor, especially if you use insulin, syringes, or any narcotic drug. Keep all medicines in your carry-on luggage. Matching prescriptions with foreign equivalents may be difficult.

If you wear **glasses** or **contact lenses,** take an extra prescription with you. Bring along adequate supplies of your cleaning solutions. For heat disinfection you'll need outlet and low-watt voltage adapters. In general, use chemicals if you can while you're traveling; even with a converter, heat-disinfecting units don't always work the same way in Europe. Many, for example, will not shut off automatically.

Any traveler with a medical condition that cannot be easily recognized (i.e. diabetes, epilepsy, heart conditions, allergies to antibiotics) may want to obtain a **Medic Alert Identification Tag.** In an emergency, their internationally recognized tag indicates the nature of the bearer's problem and provides the number of Medic Alert's 24-hour hotline. Lifetime membership (tag, annually-updated wallet card, and hotline access) begins at US$35. Contact Medic Alert Foundation, P.O. Box 1009, Turlock, CA 95381-1009 (tel. (800) 432-5378). The **American Diabetes Association**, 1660 Duke St., Alexandria, VA 22314 (tel. (800) 232-3472), provides copies of an article "Travel and Diabetes" and diabetic ID cards.

All travelers should be concerned about **Acquired Immune Deficiency Syndrome (AIDS),** called le SIDA in French. The Center for Disease Control's **AIDS Hotline** provides information on AIDS in the U.S. and can refer you to other organizations with information on France (tel. (800) 342-2437; TTD (800) 243-7889). Call the **U.S. State Department** for country-specific restrictions for HIV-positive travelers (tel. (202) 647-1488; fax (202) 647-3000) or write Bureau of Consular Affairs, #5807, Dept. of State, Washington, DC 20520. The **World Health Organization** provides written material on AIDS internationally (tel. (202) 861-3200).

Contraception is readily available in most pharmacies. Condoms, called *préservatifs* (pray-zehr-vah-TEEF) can be bought at most pharmacies, but you have to ask at the counter. The French branch of the International Planned Parenthood Federation, the **Mouvement Français pour le Planning Familiale (MFPF)** (tel. 48 07 29 10; fax 47 00 79 77), can provide more information.

Abortion is legal in France, and is performed on request. The controversial abortion pill RU486 is both legal and practiced. The **National Abortion Federation's hotline** (tel. (800) 772-9100, Mon.-Fri. 9:30am-5:30pm) can direct you to organizations which provide information on abortion in France.

For additional information before you go, you may wish to contact the **International Association for Medical Assistance to Travelers (IAMAT).** IAMAT provides brochures on health for travelers, an ID card, a chart detailing advisable immunizations for 200 countries, and a directory of English-speaking physicians who have had medical training in Europe or North America. Membership to the organization is free (although donations are welcome) and doctors are on call 24 hours. Contact chapters in the **U.S.,** 417 Center St., Lewiston, NY, 14092, (tel. (716) 754-4883); in **Canada,** 40 Regal Rd. Guelph, Ont. N1K 1B5, (tel. (519) 836-0102), and 1287 St. Clair Ave. West, Toronto, M6E 1B8 (tel. (416) 652-0137); in **New Zealand,** P.O. Box 5049, 438 Pananui Rd., Christchurch 5 (tel. (03) 352 9053; fax (03) 352 4630).

For more information, write the **Superintendent of Documents.** Their publication Health Information for International Travel (US$5) details immunization requirements and other health precautions for travelers.

Beware of unnecessary insurance coverage—your current policies might well extend to many travel-related accidents. **Medical insurance** often covers costs incurred abroad. **Medicare** does not cover travel to Paris. Canadians are protected by their home province's health insurance plan: check with the provincial Ministry of Health or Health Plan Headquarters. Your **homeowners' insurance** may cover theft during travel. Homeowners are generally covered against loss of travel documents up to about US$500. ISIC, CIEE, STA and AmEx provide varying levels of insurance (see Useful Travel Organizations above).

Remember that insurance companies usually require a copy of the police report for thefts, or evidence of having paid medical expenses before they will honor a claim, and may have time limits on filing for reimbursement. Have all documents written in English to avoid possible translating fees. Always carry policy numbers and proof of insurance. Note that some of the plans listed below offer cash advances or guaranteed bills; check with each insurance carrier for specific restrictions.

■■■ SAFETY AND SECURITY

Paris has much less violent crime than its American big-city equivalents, but crime on the whole is disturbingly on the rise. A few precautions will see you safely through your travels more effectively than constant paranoia. Take as few valuables as possible; flashy jewelry and big cameras will draw unwanted attention. Keep all valuables with you whenever you leave your room, even if it has a lock, as others may have a pass-key. At night, sleep with valuables on your person. Carry all your valuables (including your passport, railpass, traveler's checks, and airline ticket) either in a **money belt** or **neckpouch** stashed securely inside your clothing. These will protect you from thieves who use razors to slash open backpacks and fanny packs.

Like so much else, **pickpocketing** has been brought to a fine art in Paris. Parisian pickpockets are fast, practiced, and professional. Pros can unzip a bag in just a few seconds, so wear yours with the opening against your body. Threading a safety pin or keyring through both zippers on a pack makes it difficult to open quickly. Thieves often work in pairs, one providing a distraction and the other grabbing your wallet or purse. Some street children will do anything to distract you. In busy areas, walk quickly and purposefully. Thieves in metro stations may try to grab your bag as you walk through the turnstile or as you board the subway, just before the doors close.

Photocopy all important documents such as your passport, identification, credit cards, and traveler's checks' serial numbers. If you are robbed, check your surroundings carefully. Thieves may throw away your wallet after taking the cash, and you might be able to retrieve non-cash items such as credit cards. Report the theft to the police station in the area where it occurred. Be insistent; a police report may be necessary to claim stolen traveler's checks.

Especially if you are traveling alone, be sure that someone knows your itinerary. Never say that you're traveling alone. Steer clear of empty train compartments, and avoid large metro stations after dark. Ask the managers of your hotel, hostel, or foyer for advice on specific areas, and consider staying in places with a curfew or night attendant. Some cheap accommodations may entail more risks than savings; when traveling alone, you may want to forego dives and city outskirts.

There is no sure-fire set of precautions that will protect you from all situations you might encounter when you travel. A good self-defense course will give you more concrete ways to react to different types of aggression, but it might cost you more money than your trip. **Model Mugging** (East Coast tel. (617) 232-2900; Midwest tel. (312) 338-4545; West Coast tel. (415) 592-7300), a U.S. organization with offices in several major cities, teaches a comprehensive course on self-defense (course prices US$400-500). Women's and men's courses offered. Community colleges frequently offer self-defense courses at more affordable prices. **U.S. Department of State's** (tel. (202) 783-3238) pamphlet A Safe Trip Abroad (US$1) summarizes safety information for travelers. It is available by calling the above number or by writing the Superintendent of Documents, U.S. Government Printing Office, Washington, DC 20402. For an official Department of State travel advisory on France call their 24-hour hotline at (202) 647-5225. Pamphlets on traveling to specific areas are also available. More complete information may be found in Travel Safety: Security and Safeguards at Home and Abroad, published by **Hippocrene Books, Inc.,** 171 Madison Ave., New York, NY 10016 (tel. (212) 685-4371; orders tel. (718) 454-2360; fax (718) 454-1391).

■■■ WHEN TO GO

Traveling during the off-season is a great way to minimize damage to your bank account. Airfares drop and domestic travel becomes less congested. What's more, the off-season includes the world-famous "Paris in the Springtime." In spite of the rain, spring is the time to visit. In summer, tourists move in and Parisians move out—on vacation. On the other hand, if you stay away from the Champs-Elysées, Versailles, and the Eiffel Tower, August can be pleasingly calm. On August 15, a national holiday, all of Paris (except the tourist areas) is eerily deserted. For the most authentic Paris, try the city in autumn and winter—it's just as beautiful, and free of the tourists that flood in during the warmer months. Traveling in winter may be tougher on your wallet than you planned; taking refuge from the cold in cafés helps soak up your budget. Paris is a city best appreciated outdoors, wandering through its narrow streets and along the banks of the Seine. Off-season visitors with strong constitutions will, however, reap their share of rewards—pop corks with Parisians on New Year's Eve, avoid long museum lines, and take in a dynamic city that rises above bad weather.

CLIMATE

Nobody goes to Paris for the climate. No matter when you go, expect it to be cold and rainy. Early and late summer are often quite cool. Evenings can be windy and cold throughout the summer, and hot days (in the 80s, 30°C) don't hit Paris until mid-July. Then you'll discover Paris in the summer, with its high humidity and persistent pollution. Keep the weather in mind when renting rooms in your hotel. Top floors become unbearable in real heat. Air-conditioning is not as widespread as in America, so the entire city escapes to Deauville in the north when the days begin to swelter. For the tourist, hottest days are best spent in the city's parks and air-conditioned museums. Consider a daytrip to the Bois de Boulogne or the Bois de Vincennes, both parks on the outskirts of the city. Otherwise, leave the city entirely; several short day- and overnight trips are suggested in the back of this book. Winters are mild, averaging about 40°F (5°C) during the day, but the ever-present dampness makes them feel much colder.

PACKING

Pack light, lay out everything you think you'll need, pack only half of it, and take more money. Remember that you can buy almost anything you'll need in Paris, and the more luggage you carry, the more alien you'll feel. Avoid taking electrical appliances, but if you must, remember that electricity in most European countries is 220 volts AC, twice as much as in North America. In France, as in most of Europe, sockets accommodate two-pin round plugs; get an **adapter.** If the appliance is not dual voltage, you'll also need a **converter** (US$15-18). Both adapters and converters can be purchases in most hardware stores. Otherwise wait until you arrive. For more information, contact **Franzus,** Murtha Industrial Park, P.O. Box 142, Railroad Ave., Beacon Falls, CT 06403 (tel. (203) 723-6664; fax (203) 723-6666), for their free pamphlet, *Foreign Electricity is No Deep Dark Secret.*

If you take expensive **cameras** or equipment abroad, it's best to register everything with customs at the airport before departure. Buy a supply of film before you leave; it's more expensive in France. Unless you're shooting with 1000 ASA or more, airport security X-rays should not harm your pictures. It never hurts, however, to buy a lead pouch, available at any camera store. Either way, pack film in your carry-on, since the X-rays employed on checked baggage are much stronger. If you're bringing a laptop or notebook **computer,** be sure to have both computer and floppy discs hand-inspected, lest stray x-rays wipe out your as-yet-unpublished *chef-d'oeuvre.* Officials will ask you to turn it on, so be sure the batteries are fully loaded. A warning: Lost baggage is common, and not always retrieved. Keep all valuables in your carry-on.

NATIONAL HOLIDAYS

Banks, museums, and other public buildings are closed on the following **public holidays:** January 1, Easter Monday, May 1 (Labor Day), May 8 (Victory in Europe Day), Ascension Day (the 40th day after Easter, a Thursday), Whit Monday (the 7th Monday after Easter), July 14 (Bastille Day), August 15 (Assumption Day), November 1 (All Saints' Day), November 11 (Armistice Day), and December 25 (Christmas). When a holiday falls on a Tuesday or Thursday, the French often also take off the Monday or Friday, a practice known as *faire le pont* (to make a bridge). Note that banks close at noon on the day, or the nearest working day, before a public holiday.

■■■ SPECIFIC CONCERNS

WOMEN AND TRAVEL

Women on their own inevitably face additional safety concerns. In all situations, trust your instincts: if you'd feel safer elsewhere, move on. You might want to consider staying in women's hostels or foyers, often run by religious organizations. Stick to centrally located accommodations and avoid late-night treks or metro rides. Remember that hitching is safe neither for lone women, nor for women in pairs.

Foreign women in Paris are frequently beset by unwanted and tenacious followers; try to exercise reasonable caution, although you need not conclude that all French men are best avoided. To escape unwanted attention, walk with assurance, look straight ahead, and try not to look anyone directly in the eye. Sunglasses are helpful, since they prevent unwanted suitors from catching your glance. While all of this might seem constraining at first, remember that Americans are known for their friendliness and are often approached because of it. The less approachable you seem, the fewer advances you'll have to rebuff. Try to ask women or couples for directions if you're lost or if you feel uncomfortable. The best answer to verbal harassment may be no answer at all. Seek out a police officer or a female passerby before a crisis erupts, and don't hesitate to scream for help (*"Au secours"*: oh suh-KOOR). Always carry a *télécarte,* change for the phone, and enough extra money for a bus or taxi. Carry a whistle on your keychain, and don't hesitate to use it in an emergency.

SOS Viol, the national **rape hotline,** answers calls (in French) from Monday through Friday, 10am to 6pm (tel. 05 05 95 95). A **model mugging** course will not only prepare you for a potential mugging, but will also raise your level of awareness of your surroundings (see Safety and Security). All of these warnings and suggestions should not discourage women from traveling alone. Keep your spirit of adventure, but don't tempt fate.

For general information, contact the **National Organization for Women (NOW),** whose branches across the country refer women travelers to rape crisis centers and counselors. They also provide lists of feminist events in your area. Main offices include: 22 W. 21st St., 7th Fl., **New York,** NY 10010 (tel. (212) 807-0721), 425 13th St., NW, **Washington,** DC 20004 (tel. (202) 234-4558) and 3543 18th St., San Francisco, CA 94110 (tel. (415) 861-8880). The following publications provide tips to women travelers, from women travelers:

The Handbook for Women Travelers (UK£9), by Maggie and Gemma Moss. Encyclopedic and well-written. From Piatkus Books, 5 Windmill St., London W1P 1HF England (tel. (44) (071) 631 07 10).

Women Going Places (US$14). A travel and resource guide of women-owned enterprises. Though geared towards lesbians, it offers advice appropriate to all women. Available from Inland Book Company, P.O. Box 120261, East Haven, CT 06512 (tel. (203) 467-4257).

Wander Women, a travel networking organization for women over 40, publishes the newsletter Journal 'n Footnotes. Write to the organization at 136 N. Grand Ave., #237, West Covina, CA 91791.

The Virago Women's Travel Guides: Paris, Catherine Cullen. Provides information specific to Paris for women travelers. From Virago Press/Ulysses Press (US$13.95).

OLDER TRAVELERS AND SENIOR CITIZENS

Cut-rate tours and transportation discounts have made travel abroad convenient and affordable for those over 65. Proof of age is required for most discounts. Write the Superintendent of Documents (see Useful Addresses and Publications above) for a copy of *Travel Tips for Older Americans* (US$1). See below (Once There—Older Travelers and Senior Citizens) for publications and organizations in Paris. The following foundations provide information, assistance, and discounts to seniors.

AARP (American Association of Retired Persons), 601 E. St. N.W., Washington, DC 20049 (tel. (202) 434-2277 or (800) 927-0111). U.S. residents over 50 and their spouses receive benefits which include travel programs and discounts for groups and individuals, as well as discounts on lodging, car and RV rental, air arrangements, and sightseeing. US$8 annual fee per couple.

Elderhostel, 75 Federal St., 3rd fl., Boston, MA 02110 (tel. (617) 426-8056). You must be 60 or over, and may bring a spouse who is over 50. Programs at colleges and universities in over 40 countries focus on varied subjects and generally last 1 week.

Gateway Books, P.O. Box 10244, San Rafael, CA 94912 (tel. (510) 530-0299; fax 530-0497). Publishes Gene and Adele Malott's *Get Up and Go: A Guide for the Mature Traveler* (US$10.95, postage US$1.90). Offers recommendations and hints for the budget-conscious senior. For credit card orders call (800) 669-0773.

National Council of Senior Citizens, 1331 F St. N.W., Washington, DC 20004 (tel. (202) 347-8800). For US$12 a year, US$30 for three years, or US$150 for a lifetime, an individual or couple of any age can receive hotel and auto rental discounts, a senior citizen newspaper, use of a discount travel agency, and supplemental Medicare insurance.

Pilot Books, 103 Cooper St., Babylon, NY 11702 (tel. (516) 422-2225). Publishes *The International Health Guide for Senior Citizens* (US$5, postage US$1) and *The Senior Citizens' Guide to Budget Travel in Europe* (US$6, postage US$1).

TRAVELERS WITH DISABILITIES

The following provide general information and guides. For organizations and publications specific to Paris, see Once There—Disabled Travelers.

American Foundation for the Blind, 15 W. 16th St., New York, NY 10011 (tel. (212) 620-2147). ID cards (US$10); write for an application, or call the Product Center at (800) 829-0500. Also call this number to order AFB catalogs in braille, print, or on cassette or disk.

L'Association des Paralysées de France, Délégation de Paris, 22, rue de Père Guérion, 75013 Paris (tel. 44 16 83 87). Publishes *Où ferons nous étape?* (180F), which lists French hotels and motels accessible to persons with disabilities.

Mobility International, USA (MIUSA), P.O. Box 10767, Eugene, OR 97440 (tel. (503) 343-1284 for voice and TDD fax (503) 343-6812). International headquarters in Britain, 228 Borough High St., London SE1 1JX (tel. (071) 403 56 88). Info on travel programs, international work camps, accommodations, access guides, and organized tours. Membership costs US$20/year.

Tours are provided by the following organizations; call for further information:

Directions Unlimited, 720 North Bedford Rd., Bedford Hills, NY 10507 (tel. (800) 533-5343 or (914) 241-1700). Specializes in arranging individual and group vacations, tours, and cruises for those with disabilities.

Evergreen Travel Service, 4114 198th St. SW, Suite #13, Lynnwood, WA 98036 (tel. (800) 435-2288 or (206) 776-1184). Arranges wheelchair-accessible tours and individual travel worldwide, including tours for the visually and hearing impaired.

The Guided Tour, Elkins Park House, Suite 114B, 7900 Old York Road, Elkins Park, PA 19117-2339 (tel. (215) 635-2637 or (800) 738-5841). Year-round travel programs for persons with developmental and physical challenges as well as those geared to the needs of persons requiring renal dialysis.

Society for the Advancement of Travel for the Handicapped, 347 Fifth Ave., Suite 610, New York, NY 10016 (tel. (212) 447-7284; fax (212) 725-8253). Publishes quarterly travel newsletter *SATH News* and information booklets (free for members, US$3 each for non-members). Advice on trip planning for people with disabilities. Annual membership is US$45, students and seniors US$25.

BISEXUAL, GAY, AND LESBIAN TRAVELERS

Are You Two... Together?, published by Random House; available at bookstores (US$18). A gay and lesbian guide to bars, hotels, and restaurants in Europe that cater or are friendly to gays. Written by a lesbian couple; covers Western European capitals and gay resorts.

Ferrari Publications, P.O. Box 37887, Phoenix, AZ 85069 (tel. (602) 863-2408). Publishes *Ferrari's Places of Interest* (US$16), *Ferrari's Places for Men* (US$15), *Ferrari's Places for Women* (US$13), and *Inn Places: USA and Worldwide Gay Accommodations* (US$14.95).

Gay's the Word, 66 Marchmont St., London WC1N 1AB, England (tel. (0171) 278 76 54). Tube: Russel Sq. Open Mon.-Fri. 11am-7pm, Sat. 10am-6pm, Sun. and holidays 2-6pm. A gay and lesbian bookshop which also sells videos, jewelry, and postcards. Mail order service available. No catalogue of listings, but they will provide you with a list of titles germane to a given subject.

Giovanni's Room, 345 S. 12th St., Philadelphia, PA 19107 (tel. (215) 923-2960; fax 923-0813). International feminist, lesbian, and gay bookstore with mail-order service carrying many of the publications listed here. Call or write for free catalogue.

Inland Book Company, P.O. Box 120261, East Haven, CT 06512 (tel. (203) 467-4257). Publishes *Women Going Places* (US$14), an international travel and resource guide emphasizing women-owned enterprises. Though geared toward lesbians, it offers advice appropriate for all women. Available in bookstores. Direct sales only in bulk.

Renaissance House, P.O. Box 533, Village Station, New York, NY 10014 (tel. (212) 674-0120; fax 420-1126). A comprehensive gay bookstore which carries many of the titles listed in this section. Send self-addressed stamped envelope for a free catalogue.

Spartacus International Gay Guide, published by Bruno Gmnunder (US$29.95). Order from 100 East Biddle St., Baltimore, MD 21202 (tel. (410) 727-5677) or c/o Bruno Lützowstraße, P.O. Box 301345, D-1000 Berlin 30, Germany (tel. 49 (30) 25 49 82 00). List of gay bars, restaurants, hotels, bookstores and hotlines worldwide. For men.

KOSHER AND VEGETARIAN TRAVELERS

National tourist offices often publish lists of kosher and vegetarian restaurants. See the Food Intro and listings under "Kosher" and "Vegetarian" in the restaurant sections.

The European Vegetarian Guide: Restaurants and Hotels is available from the Vegetarian Times (tel. (800) 435-9610, orders only).

The International Vegetarian Travel Guide (UK£3) was last published in 1991, but copies are still available from the **Vegetarian Society of the UK,** Parkdale, Dunham Rd., Altringham, Cheshire WA14 4QG (tel. (61) 928 07 93). VSUK also publishes other titles; call or send a self-addressed, stamped envelope for a listing.

The Jewish Travel Guide (US$12, postage US$1.75) lists synagogues, kosher restaurants, and Jewish institutions in over 80 countries. Available in the U.K. from **Jewish Chronicle Publications,** 25 Furnival St., London EC4A 1JT (tel. (0171) 405 92 52; fax 831 51 88), and in the U.S. from **Sepher-Hermon Press,** 1265 46th St., Brooklyn, NY 11219 (tel. (718) 972-9010).

North American Vegetarian Society, P.O. Box 72, Dolgeville, NY 13329 (tel. (518) 568-7970) publishes several titles related to travel in the U.S. and Canada. Call or write for a free catalogue of titles available by mail order.

■■■ ALTERNATIVES TO TOURISM

If the often madcap, train-changing, site-switching pace of tourism loses its appeal, consider a longer stay in Paris. Study, work, or volunteering will help you get a better sense of parts of the city that are often hidden to the short-term visitor.

STUDY

If you choose your program well, study in Paris could be one of the most exciting and cosmopolitan experiences you'll ever have. You'll have to be stubborn about speaking French; it's far too easy to hang out exclusively with other English speakers. Research your options well, as programs vary in expense, academic quality, living conditions, and exposure to French culture and language. Many American undergraduates enroll in programs sponsored by domestic universities, and many colleges give advice and information on study abroad. Ask for the names of recent participants in the programs, and talk to them. Consider enrolling directly in the French universities—by far the cheapest and most authentic (if least organized) way to go.

American Field Service (AFS), 220 E. 42nd St., 3rd floor, New York, NY 10017 (tel. (800) 237-4636 or (212) 949-4242). Summer and year-long home stay exchange programs for high school students. Financial aid available.

American Institute for Foreign Study/American Council for International Studies, 102 Greenwich Ave., Greenwich, CT 06830 (tel. (800) 727-2437; for high school students, call (617) 421-9575). Organizes study in various European universities for high school and college students. Government loans recommended.

Institute of International Education Books (IIE Books), 809 United Nations Plaza, New York, NY 10017-3580 (tel. (212) 984-5412; fax (212) 984-5358) puts out several annual reference books on study abroad. *Academic Year Abroad* (US$42.95 plus US$4 postage) and *Vacation Study Abroad* (US$36.95 plus US$4 postage) detail over 3700 programs offered by U.S. colleges and universities overseas. Also offers the free pamphlet *Basic Facts on Foreign Study*.

World Learning, Inc., Summer Abroad, P.O. Box 676, Brattleboro, VT 05302 (tel. 802-257-7751, ext. 3452, or 800-345-2929) was founded in 1932 as **The Experiment in International Living.** Organizes language-training programs, followed by elective homestays, for international visitors of all ages. If you are over 24, you can apply to lead one of World Learning's summer programs for high school students.

Central Bureau for Educational Visits and Exchanges, Seymour Mews House, Seymour Mews, London W1H 9PE, England (tel. (071) 486 5101). Publishes Study Holidays (£7.75) which gives basic information on over 600 language study programs in 25 European countries. Distributed in North America by IIE Books.

French educational terminology and equivalencies are radically different from almost anyone else.For free pamphlets on various fields of study in France, contact the **Cultural Services of the French Embassy.** The **American Center for Students and Artists** is a student advisory service that provides information on housing, education, and *au pair* and small jobs. Contact the center at 51, rue de Bercy, 12*ème*, or at 75592, Paris Cedex 12 (tel. 44 73 77 77). Open Wed.-Mon. 11am-7pm.

Language Schools

Language instruction is a booming business in France; semester- and year-abroad programs are run by American universities, independent international or local organizations, and divisions of French universities. The **tourist office** in Paris maintains a list of member language schools.

Alliance Française, Ecole Internationale de Langue et de Civilisation Française, 101, bd. Raspail, 75006 or 75270 Paris Cedex 06 (tel. 45 44 38 28; fax 45 44 89 42). M. Notre-Dame-des-Champs, St-Placide, or Rennes. Offers French language courses at all levels, business French, French for the tourism industry, teacher training, and refresher courses for teachers of French.

Cours de Civilisation Française à la Sorbonne, 47, rue des Ecoles, 75005 Paris (tel. 40 46 22 11; fax 40 46 32 29). The Sorbonne has been giving its French civilization course since 1919. Academic-year course can be taken by the semester; four-, six- and eight-week summer programs with civilization lectures and language classes at all levels. The Sorbonne also offers a special course in commercial French during the academic year, and a 3-week session for high-level students during the summer. You can also take the Cours de Civilisation through the **American Institute for Foreign Study (AIFS),** 102 Greenwich Ave., Greenwich, CT 06830 (tel. (800) 727-2437), which also arranges accommodations and meals in Paris for its students.

Eurocentres, 101, N. Union St., Alexandria, VA 22314 (tel. (703) 684-1494; fax (703) 684-1495). Another of Council Travel's many associates, with centers worldwide. Long and short intensive courses, holiday courses, and teacher refresher courses. Center in Paris at 13, passage Dauphine, 6ème (tel. 43 25 81 40; fax 46 34 65 34).

Institut Catholique de Paris, 21, rue d'Assas, 6ème, 75270 Paris Cedex 06 (tel. 44 39 52 00). M. St-Placide. Semester-long and summer classes at all levels, taught during the school year by the institute's full-time professors.

French Universities

While it is tempting (and comforting) to meet and talk to other Americans, you might regret it later. If your French is already extremely competent, direct enrollment in a French university can be more rewarding than a language or civilization class filled with English-speakers . It can also be up to three or four times cheaper than an American university program, though it's harder to receive academic credit at your home university. After 1968, the **Université de Paris** split into ten isolated universities, each occupying different sites and offering a different range of fields. The century-old Sorbonne, now the Université de Paris IV, devotes itself to the humanities. For a more experimental approach, try one of the more modern universities. Each of them requires at least a *baccalauréat* degree or its equivalents (British A-levels or two years of college in the United States) for admission. For details contact the cultural services office at the nearest French consulate or embassy. Start this way ahead of time and expect to be confused—the bureaucracy of the French educational system is notorious.

As a student registered in a French university, you will be given a student card *(carte d'étudiant)* by your school upon presentation of your residency permit and a receipt for your university fees. In addition to the card's standard student benefits, many additional benefits available to students in Paris are administered by the **Centre Régional des Oeuvres Universitaires et Scolaires (CROUS) de Paris,** which has recently started accepting ISIC cards. Founded in 1955 to improve the living and working conditions of students of each academy, this division of the Oeuvres Universitaires welcomes foreign students and can be of great help in answering your (many) questions. The regional center for Paris is at 39, av. Georges-Bernanos, 5ème, 75231 Paris Cedex 05 (tel. 40 51 36 00; RER Port-Royal). CROUS also publishes the brochure Le CROUS et Moi, which lists addresses and information on every aspect of student life in Paris. Pick up the helpful guidebook *Je vais en France* (free), available in French or English, from any French embassy.

WORK

Permits

With the exception of *au pair* jobs, it is illegal for foreign students to hold full-time jobs during the school year. Students registered at French universities may get work permits for the summer with a valid visa, a student card from a French university, and proof of a job. After spending one academic year in France, Americans with a valid student *carte de séjour* can find part-time work if they will be enrolled at a French university again in the fall. Check the fact sheet Employment in France for Students, put out by **Cultural Services of the French Embassy,** which provides basic information about work in France and also lists the government-approved organizations through which foreign students must secure their jobs.

Work permit programs are run by **CIEE** and its member organizations (see Useful Travel Organizations above). For a US\$125 application fee, CIEE can procure three-to six-month work permits (and a handbook to help you find work and housing). You just hop on the plane, land, and start job-hunting. French positions require evidence of language skills. CIEE will provide information on accommodations and job-hunting, but will not place you in a job. Jobs available are mostly short-term, unskilled work in hotels, shops, restaurants, farms, and factories. Wages should cover food, lodging, and basic living expenses. Complete information and an application are enclosed in their Work Abroad brochure. Travel CUTS' Canadian program is similar.

Useful Publications

World Trade Academy Press, 50 East 42nd St., New York, NY 10017 (tel. (212) 697-4999), publishes *Looking for Employment in Foreign Countries* (US$16.50) which gives info on federal, commercial, and volunteer jobs abroad and advice on resumes and interviews. Other publications to check out are *Working Holidays*, an annual guide to short-term paid and voluntary work in Britain and worldwide, and *Home From Home*, a guide to international homestays, termstays, and exchanges, both available from the Central Bureau for Educational Visits and Exchanges or IIE Books (see Study above). **InterExchange,** 161 Sixth Avenue, New York, NY 10013 (tel. (212) 924-0446), provides information in pamphlet form on international work programs and au pair positions in a number of western European countries, including France.

Finding a Job

Once in Paris, start your job search at the **American Church in Paris,** 65, quai d'Orsay, 7ème (tel. 47 05 07 99), which posts a bulletin board full of job and housing opportunities targeting Americans abroad. Those with ambition and an up-to-date resume, in both French and English, should stop by the **American Chamber of Commerce in France,** 21, av. George V, 1st floor, 8ème (tel. 47 23 80 26; M. George V or Alma Marceau), an association of American businesses in France. Your resume will be kept on file for two months and placed at the disposal of French and American companies. Chamber of Commerce membership directories may be purchased at the Paris office for about US$100 (up to half-price for older editions). Otherwise, browse through the office's copy (library open Tues. and Thurs. 10am-12:30pm; admission 50F). The chamber also publishes a brochure (50F) describing paid and unpaid internships in France; filled with practical information on working as an American abroad, it is most useful to have it sent to you before your arrival in France. The **Agence Nationale Pour l'Emploi,** 4, impasse d'Antin, 8ème (tel. 43 59 62 63; M. Franklin D. Roosevelt), has specific information on employment. You should also visit the **Centre d'Information et de Documentation Jeunesse (CIDJ),** 101, quai Branly, 15ème (tel. 44 49 12 33; RER Champ de Mars/Tour Eiffel), a government-run information clearinghouse on every imaginable practical concern for young people, including education, resumes, employment, careers, long-term accommodations, camping, touring, and sports. (Open Mon.-Sat. 10am-6pm.) Part-time jobs and housing listings are posted at 9am on the bulletin boards outside. Of particular interest are pamphlets on university enrollment for foreign students (reference 1.63212 and 1.633), courses, jobs, and *au pair* positions for foreigners (ref. 5.5701-5.577), concerns and associations related to handicapped visitors (5.580-5.5883), and general tourism in France (7.51-7.53), all including extensive contact lists. You can consult these pamphlets for free in the reading room, and buy a copy of the pertinent ones for 10F each. First pick up a free brochure entitled *Les publications du CIDJ,* which lists the holdings and their reference numbers. To buy pamphlets, list their reference numbers on a ticket from the front desk and take it to the cashier. Also check help-wanted columns in newspapers, especially *Le Monde, Le Figaro,* and the English-language *International Herald Tribune,* as well as *France-USA Contacts,* a weekly circular filled with classifieds, which can be picked up at the American Church. Many of these jobs are "unofficial," and, thus, don't require work permits. For more under-the-table work, try giving English lessons. Because there are so many foreigners in Paris already offering lessons, don't expect to support yourself on this alone.

Several programs offer practical experience to people with technical and business skills. The **International Association for the Exchange of Students for Technical Experience (IAESTE)** program, a division of the Association for International Practical Training (AIPT), is an internship exchange program for science, architecture, engineering, agriculture, and math students who have completed at least two years at an accredited four-year institution. There is a non-refundable US$75 fee. Apply to the IAESTE Trainee Program, c/o AIPT, 10 Corporate Ctr., #250, 10400 Little Patuxent Parkway, Columbia, MD 21044 (tel. (410) 997-2200). Applications are due December 10 for summer placement.

Teaching English

Post a sign in markets or learning centers stating that you are a native speaker, and scan the classifieds of local newspapers, where residents often advertise for language instruction. Securing a position will require patience and legwork because teaching English abroad has become enormously popular in the past few years. Professional English-teaching positions are harder to get; most European schools require at least a bachelor's degree and most often training in teaching English as a foreign language.

> **Office of Overseas Schools,** A-OS, Room 245, SA-29, Department of State, Washington DC 20522 (tel. (703) 875-7800). Keeps a list of elementary and secondary schools abroad and agencies which arrange placement for Americans to teach abroad.
>
> **International Schools Services,** P.O. Box 5910, Princeton, NJ 08543 (tel. (609) 452-0990) publishes a free newsletter, *NewsLinks;* call or write to get on the mailing list. Its educational Staffing Department, which coordinates placement of teachers in international and American schools, publishes the free brochure *Your Passport to Teaching and Administrative Opportunities Abroad.* The *ISS Directory of Overseas Schools* (US$34.95) is distributed by **Peterson's, Inc.** (see listing above)

Au Pair Positions

Au pair positions are reserved primarily for single women aged 18 to 30 with some knowledge of French; a few men are also employed. The *au pair* cares for children and does light housework five or six hours each day for a French family while taking courses at a school for foreign students or at a French university. Talking with children can be a great way to improve your French, but looking after them (and ironing their jeans, underwear, etc.) may be extremely strenuous. Make sure you know in advance what the family expects of you. *Au pair* positions usually last six to 18 months; during the summer the contract can be as short as one to three months, but you may not be able to take courses. You'll receive room, board, and a small monthly stipend (around 1600F).

The **Cultural Services of the French Embassy** offers a detailed information sheet on *au pair* jobs. Organizations offering placement include **L'Accueil Familial des Jeunes Etrangers,** 23, rue du Cherche-Midi, 75006 Paris (tel. 42 22 50 34; fax 45 44 60 48; M. Sèvres-Babylone), which arranges 10-month *au pair* jobs beginning in September. They have a placement fee of 700F and will help you switch families if you are not happy at your initial location. **InterExchange Program,** 161 Sixth Ave., New York, NY 10013 (tel. (212) 924-0446), provides information in pamphlet form on international work programs and *au pair* positions throughout France and other western European countries. *Au pair* jobs can also be arranged through individual connections, but make sure you have a contract detailing hours per week, salary, and living accommodations.

Volunteering

Volunteer work can provide a wonderful opportunity to meet people and, in some cases, to receive free room and board in exchange for your work. Try international firms, museums, art galleries, and non-profit organizations like UNESCO; they may have unpaid internships available. The Council on International Educational Exchange (CIEE) and the Commission of Religious Volunteer Agencies publish the booklet *Volunteer! The Comprehensive Guide to Voluntary Service in the U.S. and Abroad*. It offers advice on choosing a voluntary service program and lists over 200 organizations in fields ranging from social work to construction. Write to CIEE (US$8.95, postage US$1.50). See Useful Travel Organizations for more information.

LONG-TERM ACCOMMODATIONS

If you plan to stay in Paris for a longer period of time, consider renting an apartment. Though rent is high and utilities are expensive, apartments offer convenience, privacy, and a kitchen. Call, fax, write, or visit **Allô Logement Temporaraire,** 4, pl. de la Chapelle, 18ème (tel. 42 09 00 07; fax 46 07 14 41; M. Chapelle). This helpful, English-speaking association charges a membership fee of 250F if they succeed in finding an apartment for you, which is followed by an additional charge of 150F per month beginning in the second month of your stay. Be sure to leave a phone or fax number where you can be reached easily; vacancies come and go very quickly (open Mon.-Sat. noon-8pm). Consult the French Department at your local university; it may be able to connect you with students abroad who want to sublet. Remember that short-term rentals, usually more expensive per month than longer rentals, can be difficult to procure, especially in winter months.

If possible, stay in a hotel your first week in Paris and find an apartment when you're there. This will allow you to see what you're getting. Try the bulletin boards in the **American Church.** Those upstairs tend to advertize for long-term lessors, while those downstairs list more short-term, often cheaper arrangements. Also check bulletin boards posted in the anglophone **Lindsay's Tea Shop,** 4, rue Yvonne Le Tac, 18ème (tel. 42 52 74 09), a Montmartre tea room with housing bulletin boards inside. Make sure to order something if you go there to look. Check listings in any of the English-French newsletters like **Free Voice** or **France-USA Contacts (FUSAC).** FUSAC is a free publication found in English bookstores throughout Paris. It is also distributed in the U.S. (write or fax to 104 W. 14th St., New York, NY 10011-7314; tel. (212) 989-8989; fax (212) 255-5555). It includes an extensive classifieds section, in which anglophones offer apartments for rent or sublet. Renting an apartment—negotiating rent, utilities, and leases—can be difficult for even the most linguistically proficient, but it is manageable with patience and persistence. Decide whether you want your apartment **meublé** (furnished) and negotiate accordingly. Most buildings in Paris don't have elevators. Student apartments sometimes have only kitchenettes, with range-tops but without ovens.

When you do rent an apartment, make sure to sign a contract with your lessor detailing the finances of the transaction. Note that subletting is technically illegal in France. Because of this unofficial status, a subletter cannot depend on the concierge to explain how to turn on the pilot light or how to unclog the bathroom sink.

GETTING THERE

■■■ FROM NORTH AMERICA

Finding a cheap airfare amid the confusion that the airlines deliberately create will be easier if you understand the system better than the airlines think you do. Call every toll-free number and don't be afraid to ask about discounts. Have a knowledgeable travel agent (or two) guide you through the options. Students and people under 26 should never need to pay full price for a ticket. Many airlines offer senior traveler club deals or airline passes and discounts for seniors' companions as well. Outfox airline reps with the phonebook-sized *Official Airline Guide* (at large libraries); this monthly guide lists every scheduled flight in the world (including prices). George Brown's *The Airline Passenger's Guerilla Handbook* (US$14.95; last published in 1990) is a more renegade resource.

Most airlines maintain a fare structure that peaks between mid-June and early September. Midweek (Mon.-Thurs.) flights run about US$30-40 cheaper each way than on weekends. Leaving from a travel hub such as New York, Atlanta, Dallas, Chicago, Los Angeles, San Francisco, Vancouver, Toronto, Melbourne, or Sydney will win you a more competitive fare than you'd get leaving from smaller cities; the gains are not as great when departing from travel hubs monopolized by one airline, so call around. Flying to London is usually the cheapest way across the Atlantic, though special fares to other cities—such as Amsterdam, Luxembourg, or Brussels—can cost even less. A New York-Paris round-trip summer student fare should cost $700 at most.

Except on youth fares purchased through the airlines, traveling with an "open return" ticket can be pricier than fixing a return date and paying to change it. Avoid one-way tickets, too: the flight to Europe may be economical, but the return fares can be outrageous. Whenever flying internationally, pick up your ticket in advance of the departure date and arrive at the airport several hours before your flight.

COMMERCIAL AIRLINES

The commercial airlines' lowest regular offer is the **APEX** (Advance Purchase Excursion Fare); specials advertised in newspapers may be cheaper, but have more restrictions and fewer available seats. APEX fares provide you with confirmed reservations and allow "open-jaw" tickets (landing in and returning from different cities). Reservations must usually be made at least 21 days in advance, with 7- to 14-day minimum and 60- to 90-day maximum stay limitations, and hefty cancellation and change-of-reservation penalties. For summer travel, book APEX fares early. Call **Air France** (tel. (800) 237-2747) and ask for student discounts; be sure to inquire about restrictions.

Most airlines no longer offer standby fares, once a staple of the budget traveler. Standby has given way to the **three-day-advance-purchase youth fare.** It's available only to those under 25 (sometimes 24) and only within three days of departure—a gamble that could backfire if the airline's all booked up. Return dates are open, but you must come back within a year, and once again can book your return seat no more than three days ahead. Youth fares in summer aren't really cheaper than APEX, but off-season prices drop precipitously. **Icelandair** (tel. (800) 223-5500) is one of the few airlines which still offer this 3-day fare.

Look into flights to relatively less popular destinations or on smaller carriers. Call **Icelandair** (tel. (800) 223-5500) or **Virgin Atlantic Airways** (tel. (800) 862-8621) for information on their last-minute offers. Icelandair offers a Supergrouper plan that transports travelers to Luxembourg and back without requiring a specified return date (US$699). Virgin Atlantic offers a "Visit Europe" plan to European cities—including Paris and Nice—for $109 one-way.

STUDENT TRAVEL AGENCIES

Students and people under 26 with proper ID qualify for deliciously reduced airfares. These are rarely available from airlines or travel agents, but instead from student travel agencies like CIEE's **Council Travel, STA, Travel CUTS,** and **University Travel Network** (see under Budget Travel Services at the beginning of the book). These agencies negotiate special reduced-rate bulk purchases with the airlines, then resell them to the youth market; in 1994, peak season round-trip rates from the east coast of North America to even the offbeat corners of Europe rarely topped US$700 (though flights to Russia on Western carriers were higher), and off-season fares were considerably lower. Return date change fees also tend to be low (around US$50).

Most of their flights are on major scheduled airlines, though in peak season some seats may be on less reliable chartered aircraft. Student travel agencies can also help non-students and people over 26, but may not be able to get the same low fares.

CHARTER FLIGHTS AND TICKET CONSOLIDATORS

Ticket consolidators resell unsold tickets on commercial and charter airlines that might otherwise have gone begging. Look for their tiny ads in weekend papers (in the U.S., the Sunday *New York Times* travel section is best). There is rarely a maximum age; tickets are also heavily discounted, and may offer extra flexibility or bypass advance purchase requirements. Unlike tickets bought through an airline, however, you won't be able to use your tickets on another flight if you miss yours, and you will have to go back to the consolidator—not the airline—to get a refund. Pay with a credit card; you can't stop a cash payment if you never receive your tickets. Find out everything you can about the agency you're considering, and get a copy of their refund policy *in writing.* Ask also about accommodations and car rental discounts; some consolidators have their fingers in many pies. Insist on a **receipt** that gives full details about the tickets, refunds, and restrictions, and if they don't want to give you one or just generally seem clueless, use a different company.

Consolidators sell a mixture of tickets; some are on scheduled airlines, some on **charter flights.** Once an entire system of its own, the charter business has shriveled and effectively merged with the ticket consolidator network. The theory behind a charter is that a tour operator contracts with an airline (usually a fairly obscure one that specializes in charters) to use their planes to fly extra loads of passengers to peak-season destinations. Charter flights thus fly less frequently than major airlines and have correspondingly more restrictions. They are also almost always fully booked. Schedules and itineraries may change at the last moment and flights may be cancelled suddenly. Shoot for a scheduled air ticket if you can, and pay with a credit card. You might also consider travelers insurance against trip interruption.

Council Charter, 205 E. 42nd St., New York, NY 10017 (tel. (800) 800-8222). CIEE-affiliated. Has experience in placing individuals on charter flights. Its flights can also be booked through Council Travel offices. One of the most reliable resellers of unsold tickets around.

Unitravel (tel. (800) 325-2222); they offer discounted airfares on major scheduled airlines from the U.S. to over 50 cities in Europe and will hold all payments in a bank escrow until completion of your trip. You should also try **Interworld** (tel. (800) 331-4456, and in Florida (305) 443-4929); **Rebel** (tel. (800) 227-3235); and **Travac** (tel. (800) 872-8800).

Airhitch, 2790 Broadway #100, New York, NY 10025 (tel. (212) 864-2000). Choose a five-day date range in which to travel and a list of preferred European destinations. Usually gets you *toward* where you want to go (for $169 from the East Coast of the U.S., $229 from the West), but it only guarantees that you'll end up in Europe. For your return ticket, call Airhitch's Paris office at 44 75 39 90. Be aware that the Better Business Bureau of New York received complaints about Airhitch a few years ago.

AirTech Unlimited, 584 Broadway, Suite 1007, New York, NY 10012 (tel. (212) 219-7000) or 2, rue Dussoubs, 75002 Paris (tel. (1) 42 36 02 34) is a discounter that flies to Europe and five other regions. Travelers choose a destination region but must be flexible about specific cities. They also must allow a two- to five-day window in which to travel. One-way rates to Europe are US$169 from the Northeastern U.S. and US$229 from the West Coast.

Discount clubs and **fare brokers** offer savings on European travel, including charters and tours. Research your options carefully. Try **Last Minute Travel Club,** 1249 Boylston St., Boston, MA 02215 (tel. (800) 527-8646 or (617) 267-9800); **Discount Travel International** (tel. (212) 362-3636). **Moment's Notice** (tel. (212) 486-0503; $25 annual fee); **Traveler's Advantage** (tel. (800) 835-8747; US$49 annual fee); or **Worldwide Discount Travel Club** (tel. (305) 534-2082; US$50 annual fee). **Travel**

FROM EUROPE

Avenue will search for the lowest international airfare available and then discount it 5-17% (tel. (800) 333-3335) for US$25, though the often labyrinthine contracts for all these organizations bear close study.

Another alternative is flying as a courier. This involves contacting a courier company that has a delivery to make to the destination you are trying to reach. Consult the *Courier Air Travel Handbook,* published by Thunderbird Press (5930-10 W. Greenway Blvd. #112H, Glendale, AZ 85306, USA. Tel. (800) 345-0096; fax (602) 978-7836.) Try **Now Voyager** (74 Varick St. #307, New York, NY 10013, USA; tel. (212) 431-1616). **Halbart Express,** 147-05 176th St., Jamaica, NY 11434 (tel. (718) 656-8279) flies to Paris and other European cities.

■■■ FROM EUROPE

BY PLANE

Unless you're under 25, flying across Europe on regularly scheduled flights will eat through your budget; nearly all airlines cater to business travelers and set prices accordingly. For continental travel, some of the lowest fares can be found on Eastern European airlines. Budget fares are also frequently available in the spring and summer on high-volume routes between northern Europe and resort areas in the Mediterranean. **Air France** (tel. (800) 237-2747) and its subsidiary **Air Inter** serve major cities and resorts in France. Student travel agencies in Europe and America also sell cheap tickets. **Council Travel** offers rates of around US$130-200 between London or Amsterdam and Paris. Also contact **STA Travel** or a **CIEE** office for information about inexpensive flights throughout Europe. The **Air Travel Advisory Bureau,** Strauss House 41-45, Goswell Road, London EC1V 7DN (tel. (071) 636 2908) can put you in touch with discount flights to worldwide destinations, for free.

BY FERRY

Many ferries link France with England and Ireland. **Sealink Stena Lines** and **P&O European Ferries** offer extensive service across the English Channel. Sealink ferries leave from Dover to Calais, take about 1½ hours, and are the most frequent (at peak times every ½hr.). Alternate routes between England and France include Southhampton to Cherbourg (6hr., night service 8hr.) and Newhaven to Dieppe (3-4 per day, 3hr.). **P&O European Ferries** cross in 1½ hours from Dover to Calais (every 45min.). Other convenient Channel crossings include Portsmouth to Le Havre and Cherbourg. Le Havre has the fastest road connections to Paris. **Brittany Ferries** run from Plymouth or Cork to Roscoff, from Portsmouth to St-Malo/Caen, and from Poole to Cherbourg. From any of these destinations in France, you should be able to catch a train to Paris. **Irish Ferries** offers service between Cherbourg or Le Havre to Rosslare in Ireland, and to Le Havre from Cork. Irish Ferries is rather expensive (372-870F, depending on season and discounts), but Eurailpass holders travel free after paying a small tax.

Traveling by **catamaran** is quicker (50min.), but you should book in advance. **Hoverspeed** departs for Calais or Boulogne from Dover. Service is suspended in rough weather, so you may find yourself waiting for a ferry instead. Hoverspeed also offers combination rail/bus and hovercraft service to and from London, Paris, Brussels, Amsterdam, and points in southwestern France. This is often the easiest and cheapest way to get to Paris. Students under 26 travel at youth rates. For information, write Travelloyd, 8 Berkeley Sq., London SW1, or the British Travel Centre, 2-12 Lower Regent St., London SW1Y 4PQ.

GETTING IN AND OUT OF PARIS

■■■ FROM THE AIRPORTS

ROISSY-CHARLES DE GAULLE

Most transatlantic flights land at **Aéroport Roissy-Charles de Gaulle,** 23km northeast of Paris. As a general rule, Terminal 2 serves Air France and its affiliates (arrivals: 43 20 12 55; departures: 43 20 13 5; real-live telephone operator: 44 08 24 24, 9am-9pm; 24-hr. recorded info in French: 43 20 14 55). Most other carriers operate from Terminal 1; for info call 48 62 22 80. The 24-hr. English-speaking passenger info center can be reached at tel. 48 62 22 80.

The two cheapest and fastest ways to get into the city from Roissy-Charles de Gaulle and vice versa make use of the RATP local transit system. The **Roissy Rail** (tel. 43 46 14 14) bus-train combination begins with a free shuttle bus from Aérogare 1 arrival level gate 28, Aérogare 2A gate 5, Aérogare 2B gate 6, or Aérogare 2D gate 6 to the Roissy train station. From there, the **RER B3** (one of the Parisian commuter rail lines) will transport you to central Paris. If you are going to transfer to the metro, be sure to buy an RER ticket that includes metro transfer, and get off at **Gare du Nord, Châtelet-Les Halles,** or **St-Michel,** which double as RER and metro stops. To go to Roissy-Charles de Gaulle from Paris, take the RER B3, any train with a name starting with the letter "E", to "Roissy," which is the end of the line. Then change to the free shuttle bus (RER daily 5am-12:30am, every 15 min., train 30–35min., bus 10min., 35F, 37F with metro transfer). For more direct service to the airport, the **Roissybus** (tel. 48 04 18 24) runs from in front of the American Express office on rue Scribe, near M. Opéra, to gate 10 of Terminal 2A (which also serves terminal 2C), to gate 12 of Terminal 2D (which also serves Terminal 2B), and to gate 30 of Terminal 1, arrivals level (every 15 min., to airport 5:45am-11pm, from airport 6am-11pm, 45min., 30F).

Alternatively, daily **Air France Buses** run to and from: the **Arc de Triomphe** (M. Charles de Gaulle-Etoile) at 1, av. Carnot (every 12 min. 5:40am-11pm, 40 min., 48F, group of 3 passengers 112F, group of 4 140F); to and from the **pl. de la Porte de Maillot/Palais des Congrès** (M. Porte de Maillot), near the Air France booking agency (same schedule and prices); and to and from 13, bd du Vaugirard near the **Gare Montparnasse** (M. Montparnasse-Bienvenue; to the airport hourly 7am-9pm; from the airport hourly 6:30am-7:30pm, 45 min., 64F, group of 3 passengers 144F, group of 4 170F). At Roissy, the shuttle stops between terminals 2A and 2C; between 2B and 2D; and at terminal 1 on the arrivals level, outside exit 34. Call 49 38 57 57 for recorded information, available in English, on all Air France airport shuttles.

Taxis take at least 50 minutes to the center of Paris and cost about 200F during the day, 280F at night.

ORLY

Aéroport d'Orly (tel. 49 75 15 15 for passenger info, available daily and in English 6am-11:45pm), 12km south of the city, is used by charters and many continental flights. From Orly Sud gate H or Orly Ouest arrival level gate F, take the shuttle bus (every 15 min. 5:40am-11:15pm) to the **Pont de Rungis/Aéroport d'Orly** train stop where you can board the **RER C2** for a number of destinations in Paris (daily 5:30am-11pm, every 15 min., 35min., 27F; call RATP at 43 46 14 14 for info).

Another option is the **RATP Orlyval** combination of metro, RER and Val rail shuttle. To get to Orly, buy a combined Orlyval ticket (45F, 22F child), take the metro to Gare du Nord, Châtelet-les-Halles, St-Michel, or Denfert-Rochereau, and change to the RER B. Make sure that the station Antony-Orly is lit up on the changing schedule panel next to the track (see RER section). Get off at Antony-Orly and transfer to the Val train. Reverse these instructions to enter the city from Orly, and remember that with the combined ticket, your subsequent transfers in the Paris metro are included. From the airport, buy a ticket at an RATP office (Ouest gate W level 1 or gate J level O; sud gate E or gate F, baggage area, tel. 43 46 14 14). Note that weekly or monthly yellow or orange cards are not valid for Orlyval. Val trains run from Antony to Orly Mon.-Sat. 6:30am-9:15pm and Sun. 7am-10:55pm; trains arrive at Orly Ouest 2 min-

utes after reaching Orly Sud. They run from Orly to Antony Mo.
9:15pm and Sun. 7am-10:57pm, every 7 min., 30 min. from Châtelet.

Air France Buses run between Orly Montparnasse, 36, rue de Maine,
Montparnasse-Bienvenue), and the downtown Invalides Air France agency
12 min., 30 min., 32F, group of 3 passengers 83F, group of 4 103F). Air France s.
tles stop at Orly Sud, gates C or D and Orly Ouest, Gate E, arrivals level. In additio.
the RATP runs **Orlybus** to and from metro and RER stop Denfert-Rochereau, 14ème.
Board at Orly Sud gate H, platform 4 or Orly Ouest level O, door D (Mon.-Fri. every
13 min., Sat.-Sun. every 16-20 min., 6am-11pm, 30min., 25F).

Taxis from Orly to the center cost at least 120F during the day, 160F at night.
Allow at least 45 minutes for the trip.

LE BOURGET

Paris's third airport, **Le Bourget** (tel. 48 62 12 12), is most remembered as Charles
Lindbergh' landing site after his historic transatlantic flight. In odd-numbered years,
it now hosts an internationally renowned air show, the **Salon International de
l'Aéronautique et de l'Espace.** For the most part, however, Le Bourget is used for
charter flights, generally within France. Should you land at Le Bourget, take **Bus
#350** (every 15 min. 6:10am-11:50pm, 2 metro tickets) to Gare du Nord or Gare de
l'Est. **Bus #152** also makes these stops and, for the same price, will take you to Porte
de la Villette, where you can catch the metro or another bus.

■■■ FROM THE TRAIN STATIONS

Each of Paris's six train stations is a veritable community of its own, with resident
street people and police, cafés, tabacs, and banks, plus stores selling perfume and
tacky Flashdance fashions. Locate the ticket counters (*guichets*), the platforms
(*quais*), and the tracks (*voies*), and you will be ready to roll. Each terminal has two
divisions: the *banlieue* and the *grandes lignes*. **Grandes lignes** depart for and arrive
from distant cities in France and other countries—each of the six stations serves destinations in a particular region of France or Europe. Trains to the **banlieue** serve the
suburbs of Paris and make frequent stops. Within a given station, each of these divisions has its own ticket counters, information booths, and timetables; distinguishing
between them before you get in line will save you hours of frustration. All train stations are reached by at least two metro lines; the metro station bears the same name
as the train station. For **train information** or to make reservations, call the SNCF at
45 82 50 50; for reservations call 45 65 60 60 or use the minitel 3615 SNCF (see
Communications; reservations and minitel both open daily 8am-8pm). The SNCF
line may seem perpetually busy—visiting a local travel agency will let you buy your
tickets or make your reservations with more personal attention and little to no fee.
There is a free telephone with direct access to the stations on the right-hand side of
the Champs-Elysées tourist office. In addition, there are yellow **automatic guichets**
at every train station; if you know you PIN you can use a Mastercard or Visa to buy
your own tickets. Mastercard and Visa are also accepted at the ticket booths.

A word on safety: though full of atmosphere, each terminal also shelters its share
of thieves and other undesirables. Gare du Nord, for example, becomes rough at
night, when drugs and prostitution take over; Gare d'Austerlitz can be similarly
unfriendly. Be cautious in and around stations. Naïve tourists are easily taken advantage of. In each train station metro stop, you will encounter friendly looking people
who will try to sell you a metro ticket at exorbitant prices. It is not advisable to buy
anything in the stations except at public counters.

Note: the following prices vary according to the time of year, day of the week,
and other bureaucratic criteria. Call ahead.

Gare du Nord: Trains to northern France, Britain, Belgium, the Netherlands, Scandinavia, the Commonwealth of Independent States, and northern Germany
(Cologne, Hamburg). To: Brussels (10/day, 3hr., 220F); Amsterdam (6/day., 6hr.,

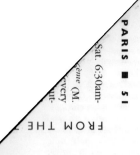

PARIS ■ 51

Sat. 6:30am-
...ème (M.
...very
...ut-

FROM THE

STATIONS

6 indirect/day, 5-6hr., 332F); Boulogne (11/day, 2½hr., ...rect, 2 indirect/day, 16hr., 1030F); London (by train and ...5 days 602F, within 2 months 502F).

...n France (Champagne, Alsace, Lorraine), Luxembourg, ...sel, Zürich, Lucerne), southern Germany (Frankfurt, ...ngary. To: Zürich (7/day, 6hr., 381F); Munich (4 direct, ...t, 613F); and Vienna (3-4/day, 15hr., 923F).

...rn and southeastern France (Lyon, Provence, Riviera), ...eva, Lausanne, Berne), Italy, and Greece. To: Geneva (4/...6-80F TGV reservation); Florence (4-5/day, 10-12hr., ...-16hr., 678F); Lyon (12/day, 2hr., 280F plus 16-80F TGV reservation); Nice (8/day, 7hr., 452F plus 16-48F TGV reservation); Marseille (8/day, 5-10hr., 374F plus 16-48F TGV reservation).

Gare d'Austerlitz: To the Loire Valley, southwestern France (Bordeaux, Pyrénées), Spain, and Portugal. TGV service to southwestern France leaves from Gare Montparnasse. To Barcelona (3/day, 11-14hr., 575F) and Madrid (5/day, 12-16hr., 561F).

Gare St-Lazare: To Normandy. To: Caen (10/day, 2½hr., 163F).

Gare Montparnasse: To Brittany, and the TGV to southwestern France. To: Rennes (15/day, 2-2½hr., 248F plus 32-80F TGV reservation).

■■■ FROM THE BUS STATIONS

Most buses to Paris arrive at **Gare Routière Internationale du Paris-Gallieni,** av. du Général de Gaulle, Bagnolet 93170 (tel. 49 72 51 51; M. Gallieni; formerly at Porte de la Villette). Some buses, however, have more bizarre ports of call. The **City Sprint** bus (tel. 42 85 44 55), operating in conjunction with Hoverspeed from England, drops its passengers in front of the Hoverspeed offices, three blocks from Gare du Nord at 135, rue Lafayette (M. Gare du Nord). For information about buses to other European countries, call **International Express Eurolines Coach Station** at 40 38 93 93.

■■■ HITCHHIKING AND RIDE SHARING

While *auto-stop* (hitchhiking) is more common in Europe than in the States, don't feel pressured to save money by putting yourself at risk. Women, even in a group, should never hitchhike. And anyone who values safety over penny-pinching will take a train or bus out of Paris. Hitchhikers ask around at youth hostels for tips on where to hitch. They don't wait at *portes* (city exits); traffic is too heavy for cars to stop safely. Because of decreased traffic, hitchers find summer a better time to hitchhike. A sign clearly stating the destination, with the letters "S.V.P." *(s'il vous plaît)* helps ingratiate hitchhikers. Hitchhikers sometimes ask customers at gas stations if they are going their way.

For a more formal "hitch," **Allostop-Provoya,** 84, passage Brady, 10ème (in Paris tel. 42 46 00 66; outside Paris 16 (1) 47 70 02 01; Minitel 3615 PROVOYA; M. Strasbourg-St-Denis), will try to match you with a driver going your way. An economical way to go; price varies according to destination.

ONCE THERE

■■■ TOURIST OFFICES

Though packed in the summer, the following offices are usually able to keep the wait down to an hour at most. Lines are worst in the afternoon. They all stock the

requisite reams of brochures, maps, and pamphlets, as well as information on special seasonal events. Tourist offices will help you find a room in a one-star hotel for
20F, two-star for 25F, three-star for 40F, and hostels for 8F. The Champs-Elysées
tourist office will also help you reserve rooms in other parts of the country, though
no more than seven days in advance, for a 30F minimum charge. All the offices
exchange at decent rates with no commission; they are a sensible option when
banks are closed.

Bureau d'Accueil Central: 127, av. des Champs-Elysées, 8ème (tel. 49 52 53 54).
M. Charles-de-Gaulle-Etoile. English-speaking staff. Mobbed in summer. Open
daily 9am-8pm. There are 5 smaller Bureaux d'Accueil, also operated by the *office
de tourisme,* located in the following train stations and at the Eiffel Tower:
Bureau Gare du Nord, 10ème (tel. 45 26 94 82). M. Gare du Nord. Open Mon.-
Sat. 8am-9pm; Nov.-Easter daily 8am-8pm. **Bureau Gare de L'Est,** 10ème (tel. 46
07 17 73). M. Gare de l'Est. Open Mon.-Sat. 8am-9pm; Nov.-April Mon.-Sat. 8am-
8pm. **Bureau Gare de Lyon,** 12ème (tel. 43 43 33 24). M. Gare de Lyon. Open
Mon.-Sat. 8am-9pm; Nov.-April Mon.-Sat. 8am-8pm. **Bureau Gare d'Austerlitz,**
13ème (tel. 45 84 91 70). M. Gare d'Austerlitz. Open Mon.-Sat. 8am-3pm. **Bureau
Tour Eiffel,** Champs de Mars, 7ème (tel. 45 51 22 15). M. Champs de Mars. Open
May-Sept. 11am-6pm. **Bureau Gare Montparnasse,** 15ème (tel. 43 22 19 19). M.
Montparnasse-Bienvenue. Open Mon.-Sat. 8am-9pm; Nov.-Easter daily 8am-8pm.

In addition, both international airports run tourist offices where you can make same-
day hotel reservations (with deposit equal to 12% of room rate) and receive information about Paris.

Orly, Sud: Near gate H. **Orly, Ouest:** Near gate F (tel. 49 75 01 36). Both open
daily 6am-11:45pm.
Roissy-Charles de Gaulle: Near gate 36 arrival level (tel. 48 62 27 29). Open daily
7:30am-9pm.
Also call **Tourist Information** (tel. 49 52 53 56) where a recorded message in
English (updated weekly) gives the major events in Paris—call 49 52 53 55 for
French.

■■■ BUDGET TRAVEL OFFICES

Accueil des Jeunes en France (AJF): 119, rue St-Martin, 4ème (tel. 42 77 87 80).
M. Rambuteau. Across from the pedestrian mall in front of the Pompidou Center.
Open Mon.-Sat. 9am-5:30pm; Oct.-May Mon.-Sat. 9am-6pm. Also 16, rue du Pont
Louis-Philippe, 4ème (tel. 42 78 04 82), near the Hôtel de Ville. M. Hôtel-de-Ville or
Pont-Marie. Open Mon.-Fri. 9:30am-6:30pm. Also 139, bd. St-Michel, 5ème (tel. 43
54 95 86), in the *quartier latin.* M. Port-Royal. Open Tues.-Sat. 10am-1pm and
1:30-6pm. Another in Gare du Nord arrival hall next to Agence de Voyages SNCF
(tel. 42 85 86 19). Open June-Sept. daily 7am-10pm; Oct. and March-May Mon.-Fri.
8:30am-5:15pm. The small Gare du Nord office only books accommodations. The
other offices will give you free maps, sell ISIC cards (60F), and make room reservations in hotels and youth hostels in Paris (10F) and in foyers (72-85F/night).
Reduced-price student train and bus tickets, budget weekend holidays, and meal
vouchers for Paris youth hostels. The office across from the Pompidou Center can
be used as a mailing address but is so ridiculously crowded that it pays to try one
of the other branches—all friendly, centrally located, English-speaking, and very
crowded.
Centre Régional des Oeuvres Universitaires (CROUS): 39, av. Georges Bernanos, 5ème (tel. 40 51 36 00). M. Port-Royal. Next door to the OTU, this helpful
university organization has information on student dormitory housing in Paris
(min. 2 days stay, max. 1 month) and on the many university restaurants that offer
simple but filling meals for rock bottom prices. The **Restaurant Universitaire
Bullier** next door is open all year (even during the summer when the university is

not in session) for lunch (12F70; 11:30am-2:15pm) and for dinner (12F70; 6-8pm).

Council on International Educational Exchange (CIEE): main office at 1, pl. de l'Odéon, 6ème (tel. 44 41 74 74; fax 43 26 97 45). M. Odéon. answer questions about work abroad. The branch at place d'Odéon has a comprehensive library with useful information about job offers, travel, and housing opportunities (library open 3-6pm). Open Mon.- Fri. 9am-6pm.

Council Travel, 16, rue de Vaugirard, 6ème (tel. 46 34 02 90). M. Odéon. 22, rue des Pyramides, 1er (tel. 44 55 55 44). M. Pyramides. English-speaking travel service for young people. Books international flights. Sells student train tickets, guidebooks, and ISIC cards (60F). BIJ/Eurotrain tickets. If you lose your CIEE charter flight ticket, one of the offices will telex the U.S. for a substitute; penalty fee for lost ticket varies by flight. All offices open Mon.-Fri. 9:30am-6:30pm; Vaugirard branch open Sat. 10am-5pm. Pyramides branch open Sat. 9:30am-5:30pm. MC, V.

Office de Tourisme Universitaire (OTU): 39, av. Georges Bernanos, 5ème (tel. 43 36 80 27). M. Port-Royal. A French student travel agency. English spoken. The same reduced train and plane tickets for students under 26 that are sold at any travel agent in Paris, but more crowded. Bring an official form of ID. Also sells ISIC (60F) and BIJ tickets. Open Mon.-Fri. 10am-1:45pm and 3-6:45pm.

■■■ EMBASSIES AND CONSULATES

If anything serious goes wrong, make your first inquiry to your country's consulate in Paris. The distinction between an embassy and a consulate is significant: an embassy houses the offices of the ambassador and his or her staff; you won't gain access unless you know someone inside. All facilities for dealing with nationals are in the consulate. If your passport gets lost or stolen, your status in France is immediately rendered illegal—go to the consulate as soon as possible to get a replacement. A consulate is also able to lend (not give) up to 100F per day (interest free), but you will be forced to prove you are truly desperate with no other source of money. The consulate can give you lists of local lawyers and doctors, notify family members of accidents, and give information on how to proceed with legal problems, but its functions end there. Don't ask the consulate to pay for your hotel or medical bills, investigate crimes, obtain work permits, post bail, or interfere with standard French legal proceedings. If you are arrested during your stay in France, there is little, if anything, that your own government can do to help you.

U.S.: 2, av. Gabriel, 8ème (tel. 42 96 12 02 or 42 61 80 75), off pl. de la Concorde. M. Concorde. **Consulate** at 2, rue St-Florentin (tel. 42 96 12 02), 3 blocks away. Passports replaced for 325F (under 18 200F). Open Mon.-Fri. 9am-3pm. Closed for both American and French holidays.

Canada: 35, av. Montaigne, 8ème (tel. 44 43 29 00). M. Franklin-Roosevelt or Alma-Marceau. **Consulate** at same tel. and address. Ask for "consular services." New passport 380F. Open Mon.-Fri. 9-10:30am and 2-3pm.

U.K.: 35, rue du Faubourg-St-Honoré, 8ème (tel. 42 66 91 42). M. Concorde or Madeleine. **Consulate** at 9, av. Hoche (tel. 42 66 91 42), near Parc Marceau. M. Charles de Gaulle-Etoile. Open Mon.-Fri. 9am-noon and 2-5pm. Visa bureau open Mon.-Fri. 9am-noon.

Australia: Embassy at 4, rue Jean-Rey, 15ème (tel. 40 59 33 00). M. Bir-Hakeim. **Consular services:** new passport 380F. Open Mon.-Fri. 9am-noon and 2-5pm.

New Zealand: Embassy at 7ter, rue Léonard-de-Vinci, 16ème (tel. 45 00 24 11). M. Victor-Hugo. New passport 400F. Open Mon.-Fri. 9am-1pm and 2-5:30pm.

Ireland: Embassy at 12, av. Foch, 16ème (tel. 45 00 20 87). M. Charles de Gaulle-Etoile. Open Mon.-Fri. 9:30am-5:45pm. **Consular Services** (tel. 45 00 22 16). New passport 380F. Open 9am-1pm.

South Africa: Embassy at 59, quai d'Orsay, 7ème (tel. 45 55 92 37).

■■■ COMMUNICATIONS

MAIL

Post offices are marked on most maps of Paris by their abstract flying-letter insignia; if you don't have a map, look for the yellow and blue PTT signs. Streets with post offices are usually marked by a cheerful sign at the corner. In general, post offices in Paris are open weekdays until 7pm (they stop changing money at 6pm) and on Saturday mornings. Avoid long lines by purchasing stamps at local tabacs or from the yellow coin-operated vending machines outside major post offices.

Air mail between Paris and North America takes five to 10 days and is fairly dependable. Send mail from the largest post office in the area. Surface (*par eau* or *par terre*) mail is by far the cheapest way to send mail, but takes one to three months to cross the Atlantic. It's adequate for getting rid of books or clothing you no longer need; a special book rate makes this option more economical. It is vital to distinguish your airmail from surface mail by labelling it clearly **par avion.** To airmail a 20g (about 1 oz.) letter or postcard from France to the U.S. or Canada costs 4F30, to Australia or New Zealand 5F10 . The **aerogramme,** a sheet of fold-up, pre-paid airmail paper, requires no envelope and costs more (5F). To airmail a package, you must complete a green customs slip. Registered mail is called **avec recommandation** and costs 23F. To be notified of a registered letter's receipt, ask for an **avis de réception** and pay an additional 7F70. In France there are two grades of express mail: letters mailed **exprès** costs an extra 28F and arrive within 5 days to North America; letters mailed **chronopost** arrive in 3 days at a soaring cost of 280F for a letter-sized package. Chronopost is only available until 6pm.

If you're writing from home to France and expect a reply (e.g., when making hotel reservations), enclose an **International Reply Coupon** (available at post offices for US$1) for a response by surface mail; send two for airmail.

Postcards and letters sent from the U.S. cost 40¢ and 50¢. The post office also sells aerograms for 45¢. Many U.S. city post offices offer Express Mail service, which sends packages under 8 oz. to major overseas cities in 40 to 72 hours (US$11.50-14). Private mail services provide the fastest, most reliable overseas delivery. **DHL** (US$30), **Federal Express** (US$32), and **Airborne Express** (US$34, max. 8 oz.) can get mail from North America to Paris in 2 days.

If you do not have a specific address in Paris, you can receive mail through the **Poste Restante** system, handled by the 24-hour post office at 52, rue du Louvre, 1er (tel. 40 28 20 00 for urgent telegrams and calls; 42 80 67 89 for postal information; M. Châtelet-les-Halles). To ensure the safe arrival of your letter, address it: LAST NAME (in capitals), first name; Poste Restante; R.P. (Recette Principale); 52, rue de Louvre, 75001 Paris, FRANCE. You will have to show your passport as identification and pay 2F50 for every letter received.

American Express also receives and holds mail for up to 30 days, after which they return it to the sender. If you want to have it held longer, just write "Hold for x days" on the envelope. The envelope should be addressed with your name in capital letters, with "Client Letter Service" printed below your name. In Paris, this service is free to cardholders.

TELEPHONES

Almost all French pay phones accept only **télécartes;** in outlying districts and cafés and bars, some phones are still coin-operated. You may purchase the card in two denominations: 40F for 50 unités, and 96F for 120 unités, each worth anywhere from six to 18 minutes of conversation, depending on the rate schedule. Local calls cost one unité each. The télécarte is available at post offices and most metro stations and tabacs. The best places to call from are phone booths and post offices. If you phone from a café, hotel, or restaurant, you risk paying up to 30% more. Emergency or collect calls do not require coins or a télécarte.

A brief **glossary:** A call is *un coup de téléphone* or *un appel;* to dial is *composer;* a collect call is made *en PCV (pay-say-vay);* a person-to-person call is *avec préavis.*

A small digital screen on the phone will issue a series of simple commands: *décrochez* means to pick up, *racrochez* to hang up. On some *télécarte* phones, you need to *ferme le volet;* pull down the lever directly above the card slot and wait for a dial tone.

You can make **intercontinental calls** from any phone booth, but it will cost less to have the other person call you back. Most European phones receive incoming calls. The number is posted on a sticker inside the booth, prefaced by *ici le.*

To call from the U.S., dial the **international access code** (011 from the U.S. and Canada, 00 from the U.K., 0011 from Australia, 00 from New Zealand, 09 from South Africa), 33 (France's country code), 1 (Paris's city code), and the eight-digit local number. Calling overseas can cost as little as 5F, and it's much cheaper this way (the French tax calls by as much as 30%). This technique is cheaper than calling collect or via credit card. Country codes are posted inside most telephone booths. If your credit isn't good at home, the 196 *unités télécarte* will serve you well (call to the U.K. 120 units for 20min.; call to the U.S. or Canada 120 units for 12min.).

Another alternative is AT&T **USA Direct** service, which allows you to be connected instantly to an operator in the U.S. Simply dial 19, wait for the tone, then dial 0011. USA-France rates are US $1.71 for the first minute and $1.06 for each additional minute. Another AT&T service is **World Connect,** which is for calling between two countries other than the United States. Calls must be made either collect (US$2.75 surcharge) or billed to an AT&T calling card (US$2.50); the people you are calling need not subscribe to AT&T service. For more information call AT&T at (800) 331-1140 or (800) 545-3117. To call **Canada Direct** from France, dial 19, wait for the tone, then dial 0016 and the number. It will be billed as a person-to-person call. **Australia Direct** and **New Zealand Direct** are similar, though not as extensive. For information in Canada, call (800) 561-8868; in Australia, dial 0102; and in New Zealand, dial 018. **MCI** has combined its **Call USA** and **WorldReach** programs to form a new service called **World Phone.** The service lets you call the U.S. using your MCI calling card and an access code, which you'll receive before you leave for France. For more information, call MCI at (800) 444-3333. **Telephone rates** from America to France are cheapest from 6pm-7am. Remember **time differences** when you call—Paris is one hour ahead of Greenwich mean time and six hours ahead of New York.

Telephone rates are reduced Monday through Friday 9:30pm-8am, Saturday 2pm-8am, and Sunday all day for calls to the European Community and Switzerland; Monday through Friday noon-2pm and 8pm-2am, and Sunday afternoon to the U.S. and Canada; Monday through Saturday 9:30pm-8am and Sunday all day to Israel.

A brief **directory:**

AT&T operator: tel. 19 00 11.
MCI operator: tel. 19 00 19
Direct international calls: tel. 19 + country code (listed above and in most phone booths) + area/city code + the number.
Direct long-distance calls within France: To call from the Paris region to elsewhere in France, dial 16 + the number. To call the Paris area from elsewhere in France, dial 1 + the number. Within the Paris area, just dial the number; do the same to make a call to a region outside of Paris from a region outside of Paris.
Directory information (Renseignements téléphoniques): tel. 12.
International information: 19 33 12 + country code (Australia 61; Ireland 353; New Zealand 64; U.K. 44; U.S. and Canada 1).
International Operator: tel. 19 33 11.
Operator (Téléphoniste): tel. 10.

TELEGRAMS AND MORE

To send a **telegram** to France from the U.S., Western Union (tel. (800) 325-6000) charges 76 cents per word plus a $9 international surcharge. Delivery is same-day. Major cities across Europe also have bureaus where you can pay to send and receive **faxes.**

Between May 2 and Octoberfest, EurAide (P.O. Box 2375, Naperville, IL 60567; tel. (708) 420-2343) offers **Overseas Access,** a service most useful to travelers in Europe without a set itinerary. It costs US$15 per week or US$40 per month for an electronic message box (plus a $15 registration fee).

MINITEL

Minitel is a computer system which provides telephone numbers, addresses, and professions of French telephone subscribers, as well as newspapers on screen (including the *International Herald Tribune*), shopping, the weather, train schedules, and lots of other information. There are several coin-operated minitels (2F/min.) for public use at the Bibliothèque Publique Information at the Centre Pompidou (directory information in English: 3614 ED). If you have a listed telephone number, you can lease your very own from the phone company. This is not advisable for anyone on a budget; at 2F a minute, minitel could break your budget before you're even aware of it. Minitel has a cheaper cousin found in post offices. Use the little yellow machines as phone books to find out numbers and services. There is no charge for use and they are workable with the most rudimentary knowledge of French. In requesting an address, save yourself some trouble and type PARIS for everything short of the name of the business or person you are inquiring about. On the whole, minitel may not be that useful to visitors: you may want to stick to *Pariscope, Let's Go,* and tourist offices.

■■■ SPECIFIC CONCERNS: PARIS

OLDER TRAVELERS AND SENIOR CITIZENS

Although the Tourist Office has no specific publications concerning seniors, most museums, concerts, and sights in Paris offer reduced prices for visitors over 60. Call ahead for *prix réduit* for senior visitors. For additional discounts on sights, special events, and transportation, you may want to invest in the **Carte Vermeille** (see Train Discounts and Railpasses above for details). For travel in Paris, the RATP (Régie Autonome des Transports Parisiens) publishes a free brochure which outlines metro and city bus service for senior travelers called *Circuler sans fatigue dans le metro et le RER;* pick one up at the main RATP office or order one by phone (in French only; RATP, 53ter. quai des Grands Augustins, 6ème or 75271 Paris Cédex 06; tel. 43 46 14 14; open Mon.-Tues. 9am-4pm and Wed.-Fri. 9am-5pm).

The Ministère des Anciens Combattants (Ministry of Veteran Affairs), 37, rue de Bellechasse, 7ème (tel. 45 56 50 00) can offer information for veterans abroad.

TRAVELERS WITH DISABILITIES

The Mairie de Paris provides a number of free publications of interest to travelers with disabilities. The extensive and comprehensive *Touristes Quand Même: Paris* (144 pages) provides useful information in English and French on wheelchair accessibility, closed-caption screenings, sign-language translation, and other services in Parisian hotels, museums, restaurants, and sights. The publication *Paris: Musées, Bibliothèques, Centres et Ateliers culturels... A l'Usage des Personnes Présentant un Handicap* (242 pages) provides information on services for those in wheelchairs or with vision or hearing disabilities. Both are published by the Comité National Français de Liaison pour la Réadaptation des Handicapés (see below) and are available from the publisher at 30F and 40F, respectively. The Office du Tourisme on the Champs-Elysées (tel. 49 52 53 54) sells the *Paris: Musées, Bibliothèques . . .* publication and keeps a copy available for free reference.

Very few metro stations are wheelchair-accessible, but most RER stations are. For a guide to metro accessibility, pick up a free copy of the RATP's brochure, *Circuler sans fatigue dans le metro et le RER* (in French), which provides a list of stations equipped with escalators, elevators, and moving walkways. Request the brochure at the RATP's main office, or order by phone (for the RATP address, see Older Travelers and Senior Citizens). The main office also distributes the brochure *Handicaps et déplacements en région Ile-de-France,* which provides transit info on the Ile-de-France region.

A free metro service called **Voyage Accompagné** (Accompanied Travel) allows vision-impaired visitors to be escorted to their destination by a designated guide. This service is offered by the RATP (tel. 49 59 60 00) and is available daily, 8am-8pm, on all 13 metro lines, RER lines A and B, and over 100 bus routes. Guide dogs are transported free. If transporting a seeing-eye dog to France, you will require a rabies vaccination certificate issued in your home country, or a certificate showing there have been no cases of rabies in your country for over three years.

Many museums and sights are fully accessible to wheelchairs and some provide guided tours in sign-language.

Unfortunately, budget hotels and restaurants are generally ill-equipped to handle the needs of handicapped visitors. Handicapped bathrooms are virtually non-existent among hotels in the 1-2 star range. Many hotel elevators could double as shoeboxes; even travelers with narrow wheelchairs will find it a tight squeeze. As a result, the hotels described in this book as **wheelchair-accessible** are those with reasonably wide (but not regulation size) elevators or with ground-floor rooms wide enough for wheelchair entry. Travelers are encouraged to ask restaurants, hotels, railways, and airlines about their facilities: *"Etes-vous accessibles aux chaises roulantes?"* In general, modern buildings in Paris are wheelchair-accessible, as are the more expensive hotels. Check with the following organizations for more information on accessibility and traveling with disabilities in Paris.

Association des Paralysés de France, Délégation de Paris, 22, rue du Père Guérin, 13ème (tel. 44 16 83 83). Publishes *O ferons-nous étape?* (100F), which lists French hotels and motels accessible to disabled persons.

Association Valentin-Hauy, 5, rue Duroc, 7ème (tel. 44 49 27 27). Houses a cassette and Braille library for vision-impaired tourists and residents of Paris (free admission). Also provides a free metro map in Braille.

Audio-Vision guides, at Parisian theaters like the Théâtre National de Chaillot, 1, pl. Trocadéro, 11 Novembre, 16ème (tel. 47 04 86 80), and the Théâtre National de la Colline, 15, rue Malte-Brun, 20ème (tel. 44 62 52 52). Service for the blind or vision-impaired, which describes the costumes, sets, and theater design of the plays that are currently running.

Auxiliaire des Aveugles (tel. 43 06 39 68). Bilingual staff provides information on services in Paris for people who are visually impaired.

Comité National Français de Liaison pour la Réadaption des Handicapés (CNFLRH), 38, bd. Raspail, 7ème (tel. 45 48 90 13). Provides a list of hotels with wheelchair access (25F).

Fédération de France, 40, av. Hoche, 8ème (tel. 42 25 66 66). Publishes the guide *Des Musées Ouvert à Tous les Sens* (in Braille, French only), a list of museums where visitors with visual disabilities may touch the sculptures in their collections.

Neuf Orthopedio: Orthopédie, Prothèse, Chaussures, 9, rue Léopold Bellan, 2ème (tel. 42 33 83 46). M. Sentier. This store sells wheelchairs, canes, and other important accessories.

TRAVELING WITH CHILDREN

Paris is a wonderful place to travel with children, as long as you don't drag them to every possible museum, historic monument, church, and nearby château. Try following them for a change; you'll see the city in a new and very different light. Parks, most of which have playgrounds, fountains, and lots of interesting people-watching, provide an excellent spot for a relaxed, fun, and very Parisian afternoon. Despite the fact that French schoolchildren may seem very well dressed in their miniature Izod shirts and Benetton pullovers, they like to get just as messy as their American counterparts. The **Jardin du Luxembourg** has a *guignol* (puppet show), pony rides, go-carts, a carousel, boats to rent and sail on the ornamental ponds, and swings with attendants who, for a tip, will push the swings while you vanish into a café. In the summer, the carnival at the **Tuileries** has a collection of rides suitable for all ages. Parents will enjoy the ferris wheel—with its outstanding view of central Paris—as much as their kids. **La Villette,** a huge science museum, aquarium, and Omnimax theater complex, offers an entire days worth of innovative entertainment. A climb up the tower of **Notre-Dame,** with its steep, winding stairs, its view of Paris at the top, and—most of all—its leering gargoyles, will liven up any child's tour of the cathedral. The **Jardin des Plantes** (with its new museum La Grande Galérie de l'Evolution) and the Paris **Zoo** are also fun, and even the most clichéd sights, such as the Eiffel Tower and the bateaux mouches (tour boats on the Seine), rejuvenate jaded travelers when seen with children. Remember that not all museums in Paris are devoted to traditional art; flip through our Museum section for some more unusual selections. For a surrender to international capitalist homogeneity and children's occasionally unrefined tastes, take the RER out to **Euro Disney® Resort.** You may not like the idea of shaking hands with Mickey on "Main Street USA" while you're in France, but remember that your child put up with you in the Louvre. The **Jardin d'Acclimatation** (tel. 45 01 88 91 or 40 67 97 66) in the **Bois de Boulogne** offers a children's zoo, a hall of mirrors, and a playground, for only 9F. Donkey rides and remote-control speed boats cost extra (7-10F).

In the culinary domain, don't fight the siren song of *le hot dog, le croque monsieur* (a grilled ham-and-cheese sandwich), *les frites* (french fries), or even the dreaded "McDonalds!" If your kids don't take to the subtleties of *haute cuisine*, they aren't any different from French kids, who dismay their parents by insisting on fast food. In general, it's not very common to see kids in restaurants. Head for the less formal cafeterias, café-restaurants, and brasseries. Not all restaurants have high chairs; you may want to ask first (*"Est-ce que vous avez une chaise haute?"*).

For bedtime stories before or during your trip, follow the 12 little girls around the sights of Paris in Hugo Bemelmans's *Madeleine* picture books. *Crin blanc* and *Le ballon rouge,* both by Albert La Morisse, are two stories that exemplify a peculiarly French sentimentality regarding early childhood. Kids will enjoy seeing scenes from them come to life on the streets of Paris. Goscinny and Sempé's *Le Petit Nicolas* and *Nicolas en Vacances* recount the antics of the mischievous little Nicolas and friends in rural France. The well-known Tintin and Astérix comics appeal to a wide range of ages, and the hardbound copies are both travel- and child-proof (well, almost).

For more hints on traveling with children (and on parent-survival) write to **Lonely Planet Publications,** Embarcadero West, Oakland, CA 94607 (tel. (510) 893-8555 or (800) 275-8555), or P.O. Box 617, Hawthorn, Victoria 3122, Australia, for Maureen *Wheeler's Travel with Children* (US$10.95, postage US$1.50 in the U.S.).

MINORITY TRAVELERS

In France, as in much of the world, xenophobia and hate-crimes seem to be on the rise. The blood and soil National Front party, led by Jean-Marie Le Pen, emerged in the 1986 legislative elections and has since remained a major force in French electoral politics. In France, anti-immigrant sentiments toward North Africans and others were taken to a higher register in 1993, when Interior Minister Charles Pasqua proposed there be "zero immigration" (later amended to "zero illegal immigration.") Non-white tourists should have few official problems. People of color might, however, find it particularly difficult to gain entry to Paris' nightclubs, where unofficially discriminatory door policies can exclude non-whites, particularly those of Arab descent. *Let's Go* welcomes letters from travelers who encounter such difficulties. In the event of a racist encounter, call the following organizations.

S.O.S. Racisme, 14, Cité Griset, 11*ème* (tel. 48 06 40 00). Occupied primarily with helping illegal immigrants and people whose official documentation is irregular. They provide legal services and are accustomed to negotiating with *préfectures de police.*

MRAP (Mouvement contre le racisme et pour l'amitié entre les peuples), 89, rue Oberkampf, 11ème (tel. 48 06 88 00). Handles immigration issues and monitors racist publications and propaganda.

Should you confront race-based exclusion or violence, you will be advised to make a formal complaint to the police. We encourage you to work through either SOS Racisme or MRAP in order to facilitate your progress through a confusing, foreign bureaucracy.

BISEXUAL, GAY, AND LESBIAN CONCERNS

Next to London, Amsterdam, and Berlin, Paris has one of the largest gay populations in Europe: an estimated 100,000 gay and lesbian people. The recent France-wide increase in right-wing intolerance, combined with the enormous toll taken by *le SIDA* (AIDS), has helped rally political consciousness and activism within Paris' gay community. In 1993, AIDS was reported the second largest killer of Parisian men 24-44 years old.

The gay and lesbian bookstore **Les Mots à la Bouche** is an excellent resource for travelers just arriving to the city (see Shopping—Bookstores). Consult the encyclopedic **Guide Gai 1995** (50F, at Paris newsstands and in most American gay bookstores), with almost 400 pages of information in French and English about gay hotels, restaurants, nightlife, organizations, and services throughout France. For information on HIV, AIDS, and safer sex, call the 24-hour free and anonymous AIDS information hotline, **SIDA Info Service** (tel. 05 36 66 36).

ACT-UP PARIS, BP231 Paris Cedex 17 (tel. 42 01 11 47). The Paris chapter of ACT-UP (the AIDS Coalition to Unleash Power) meets Tues. 7:30pm at Amphitheater 1, 106, bd. de l'Hôpital, 13ème, to discuss issues related to HIV, AIDS, and homophobia. Foreign members are welcome, but are not expected to take part in actions and protests that could lead to arrest.

Centre du Christ Libérateur, 3bis, rue Clairaut, 17ème (tel. 46 27 49 36). M. La Fourche. Founded by Pasteur Doucé, this center provides cultural, medical, legal, and personal advice and counseling for bisexual, gay, and lesbian people.

Ecoute Gaie (tel. 44 93 01 02). A gay hotline. Takes calls July-Aug. Tues.-Wed. 6-10pm; Sept.-June Mon.-Fri. 6-10pm.

Fréquence Gaie/Radio Orient, 94.3FM (tel. 45 02 12 12), 24-hr. gay and lesbian radio station providing news, music, and information in French and English.

Centre Gai et Lesbien, 3 rue Keller, 11ème (tel. 43 57 21 47). M. Ledru Rollin. A variety of documentation, fellowship, services and associations concerned with homosexuality, including AIDS information.

Maison des Femmes, 8, Cité Prost, 11ème. Information and cultural center for lesbians and bisexual women.

Maison des Homosexualités, 25, rue Michel-le-Compte, 3ème (tel. 42 77 72 77). M. Rambuteau. Cultural center which provides information on gay and lesbian activities as well as information on HIV, AIDS, and conferences on sexuality. Open Mon.-Sat. 3-8pm.

Le Projet Ornicar, 8, rue Auguste Blanqui, 93200 St-Denis (tel. 48 09 22 10). Political action group which organizes protests, lobbying, and the dissemination of information regarding homophobia, discrimination, and public policy on gay, bisexual, and lesbian issues. Some English spoken

EMERGENCY, HEALTH, AND HELP

Fire: tel. 18.

Emergency Medical Assistance: Ambulance (SAMU): tel. 15. Outside of Paris, call 45 67 50 50.

Poison Control: tel. 40 37 04 04.

Police Emergency: tel. 17.

Police: Each *arrondissement* of Paris has its own *gendarmerie* (police force) to which you should take all your non-emergency concerns. Call the operator (tel. 12) and ask where your local branch is.

Rape Crisis: SOS Viol, tel. 05 05 95 95. Call from anywhere in France for counseling, medical and legal advice, and referrals. Open Mon.-Fri. 10am-6pm.

Hospitals: Hospitals in Paris are numerous and efficient. They will generally treat you whether or not you can pay in advance. Settle with them afterward and don't let your financial concerns interfere with your health care. Unless your French is exceptionally good, you'll have the best luck at one of the anglophone hospitals. **Hôpital Franco-Britannique de Paris:** 3, rue Barbès, in the Parisian suburb of Levallois-Perret (tel. 46 39 22 22). M. Anatole-France. Considered a French hospital and bills like one. Has some English-speakers and a good reputation. **Hôpital Américain de Paris:** 63, bd. Victor Hugo, Neuilly (tel. 46 41 25 25). M. Port Maillot, then bus #82 to the end of the line. In a suburb of Paris. Employs English-speaking personnel, but much more expensive than French hospitals. You can pay in U.S. dollars. If you have Blue Cross, your hospitalization is covered as long as you fill out the appropriate forms first. They can also direct you to the nearest English-speaking doctor and provide dental services.

Late Night Pharmacies: Les Champs Elysées, in the Galerie des Champs, 84, av. des Champs-Elysées, 8ème (tel. 45 62 02 41). M. George V. Open 24 hrs. The only all-night pharmacy in Paris. **Drugstore St-Germain,** 149, bd. St-Germain, 6ème (tel. 42 22 80 00). M. St-Germain-des-Prés or Mabillon. Open Mon.-Sat. 8:30am-2am, Sun. 10am-2am. **Grande Pharmacie Daumesnil,** 6, pl. Félix-Eboué, 12ème (tel. 43 43 19 03). M. Daumesnil.Visible as you exit the metro. Open 24 hrs.

Every *arrondissement* should have a pharmacie de garde (pharmacy on call), which will open in case of emergencies. The locations change, but your local pharmacy can provide the name of the nearest one.

AIDS information: AIDES, Fédération Nationale, 247, rue de Belleville, 19ème (tel. 44 52 00 00). AIDES is one of the oldest and most prolific AIDS public service organizations in France. Roughly equivalent to the AIDS Action Committees found in most major American cities. AIDES runs a hotline that provides information in French and English (tel. 05 36 66 36; open 24 hrs.).

Alcoholics Anonymous: 3, rue Frédéric Sauton, 5ème (tel. 46 34 59 65). M. Maubert-Mutualité. A recorded message in English will refer you to several numbers you can call to talk to telephone counselors. Daily meetings. Open 24 hrs.

Birth Control: Mouvement Français pour le Planning Familial, 10, rue Vivienne, 2ème (tel. 42 60 93 20). M. Bourse. Open Mon. noon-4pm, Tues. 5-7pm, Thurs. noon-3pm. Answers questions and provides information on birth control, pregnancy, and STD prevention.

Drug Problems: Hôpital Marmottan, 17-19, rue d'Armaillé, 17ème (tel. 45 74 00 04). M. Charles de Gaulle-Etoile. You're not always guaranteed an English speaker. For consultations or treatments, open Mon.-Sat. 9:30am-7pm; Aug. Mon.-Fri. only.

Emotional Health: Services and aid for those in need in Paris are provided by a number of organizations. Try calling **SOS Crisis Help Line: Friendship** (tel. 47 23 80 80). English-speaking. Support and information for the depressed and lonely. Open daily 3-11pm. For personalized crisis-control and counseling (for anything from pregnancy to homesickness), the **American Church,** 65, quai d'Orsay, 7ème (M. Invalides or Alma-Marceau) offers the **International Counseling Service (ICS)** and the adjunct **American Student and Family Service (ASFS),** provide access to psychologists, psychiatrists, social workers, and a clerical counselor. Payment is nominal and negotiable. Open Mon.-Sat. 9:30am-1pm. The office is staffed irregularly July-Aug., but will respond if you leave a message on its answering machine. Call for an appointment (tel. 45 50 26 49 for both) at the American Church. The American Church also offers **Free Anglo-American Counseling Treatment and Support** (FAACTS) for people with and/or affected by HIV.

HIV Testing: 218, rue de Belleville, 20ème (tel. 47 97 40 49). M. Télégraphe. Free and anonymous. Mandatory counseling. Test results take 1 week. Some English spoken. Open Mon.-Fri.1-6:30pm, Sat. and Sun. 9:30am-noon. Also at 3-5, rue de Ridder, 14ème (tel. 45 43 83 78). M. Plaisance. Open Mon.-Fri. noon-6:30pm, Sat. 9:30am-noon. For more information and counseling, call **SIS (Sida Information Service)** (tel. 05 36 66 36).

STD Clinic: 43, rue de Valois, 1er (tel. 42 61 30 04). M. Palais-Royal. Testing and treatment for sexually transmitted diseases. Free consultations, blood tests, and injection treatments. Syphilis tests free. Plasma and chlamydia tests usually around 300F each, but free if you are in dire straits. Tests for HIV are free, anonymous, and include mandatory counseling. If you wish to see a doctor, call for a free appointment. Some English spoken. Open Mon.-Fri. 9am-7pm.

OTHER SERVICES

American Church in Paris: 65, quai d'Orsay, 7ème (tel. 47 05 07 99). M. Invalides or Alma-Marceau. As much a community center as a church. Bulletin boards with notices about jobs, rides, apartments, personals, etc., both in the lobby and downstairs. *Free Voice*, a free English-language monthly specializing in cultural events and classifieds, is published here; submit your ad (60F for 30 words by the 22nd of the month before). Inter-denominational services Sun. at 11am, followed by a ½-hr. coffee break and, during the school year, by a filling, friendly luncheon at 12:30pm (50F, children 40F). International counseling service (tel. 45 50 26 49). Church open Mon.-Sat. 9am-10pm, Sun. 9am-8pm. Free student concerts Oct.-June Sun. at 6pm. Hosts meetings for AA, AL-ANON, ACOA, and FAACTS (workshops for people affected by AIDS, ARC, or HIV-positive status). In October the church sponsors an orientation program for newcomers to Paris. There is a minimal fee (150F, call for more information). The church also holds a flea market on the 1st and 3rd Sat. of each month (2-5pm).

ATMs: A selected list of ATM machines on the CIRRUS network: 5, rue de la Feuillade, 1er (M. Bastille); corner of rue Monge and rue des Bernardins, 5ème (M. Maubert-Mutualité); 22, rue de Sèvres at Le Bon Marché, 7ème (M. Sèvres-Babylone, open during store hours); 24, bd. Malesherbes, 8^{ème}(M. Madeleine); 94-96 bd. Magenta, 10ème (M. Gare du Nord); 82, bd. Soult, 12ème (M. Porte Dorée); 53, av. des Gobelins, 13ème (M. Gobelins); 28, rue d'Auteuil, 16ème (M. Eglise d'Auteuil); 30. av. Niel, 17ème (M. Pereire-Levallois); 13, rue des Abbesses, 18ème (M. Abbesses); 7, pl. des Fêtes, 19ème (M. pl. des Fêtes); 167-171 av. Gambetta, 20ème (M. Porte des Lilas).

Catholic Information Center: 6, pl. du Parvis Notre-Dame, 4ème (tel. 46 33 01 01). Information about religious activities, prayer, and pilgrimages. Open Mon.-Fri. 9am-noon and 2-6pm.

Lost Property: Bureau des Objets Trouvés, 36, rue des Morillons, 15ème (tel. 45 31 98 11). M. Convention. When you visit or write , describe the object and when and where it was lost. No information given by phone. Open Mon. and Wed. 8:30am-5pm, Tues. and Thurs. 8:30am-8pm.

Public Baths: 8, rue des Deux Ponts, 4ème (tel. 43 54 47 40). M. Pont-Marie. Shower 6F, families 3F each person, with soap and towel roughly 18F. For the same price you can also rub-a-dub-dub at 42, rue du Rocher, 8ème (tel. 45 22 15 19; M. St-Lazare), and at 40, rue Oberkampf, 11ème (tel. 47 00 57 35; M. Oberkampf). They are clean, respectable, and quite popular in summer. All open Thurs. noon-7pm, Fri. 8am-7pm, Sat. 7am-7pm, Sun. 8am-noon.

Public Libraries: Bibliothèque Publique Information, in the Centre Pompidou, 4ème (tel. 44 78 12 33). M. Rambuteau, Hôtel-de-Ville, or Châtelet-Les-Halles. Many books in English. Record and video listening room. Novels are arranged alphabetically by century on the 1st floor (entrance to the library on the 2nd floor), so you'll have to hunt for those in translation. Guide books and books about France and Paris abound. Books cannot be checked out. Open Mon.-Fri. noon-10pm, Sat.-Sun. 10am-10pm. For a quiet place to read or write, the **Bibliothèque Mazarine,** 23, quai de Conti, 6ème (tel. 44 41 44 06; M. Pont-Neuf), provides old volumes and a tranquil desk to work at. You will need a passport to get in the first time. If you plan to visit frequently, bring two photos and apply for a *carte d'entrée*. Open Aug. 16-July 31 Mon.-Fri. 10am-6pm. Free.

Society of Friends (Quaker), 114bis, rue de Vaugirard, 6ème. M. St-Placide or Montparnasse-Bienvenüe. Enter through the garage door and walk down the courtyard stairs. The Paris Friends meeting is a small, intimate, and friendly community, with many seniors and a fair number of students during the school year.

Messages are delivered in French, but nearly everyone is fluent in English. Meeting Sun. 11am, preceded by a 10am discussion hour.

St. Michael's Church: 5, rue d'Aguesseau, 8ème (tel. 47 42 70 88). M. Concorde. Holds Anglican services in English Sun. at 11:35am and 6:30pm. On the 1st floor, outside the offices, bulletin boards list jobs offered and wanted, accommodations available and sought, as well as information on activities of interest. Office open Mon.-Tues. and Thurs.-Fri. 9:30am-12:30pm and 2-5:30pm. Even if the office is closed, boards and pamphlets should be accessible.

Synagogue: Union Libéral Israélite de France, 24, rue Copernic, 16ème (tel. 47 04 37 27). M. Victor-Hugo. 1-hr. services Fri. at 6pm and Sat. at 10:30am, mostly in Hebrew with a little French. English-speaking rabbi stays after the service to chat. Services also on the evenings and mornings of the High Holy Days; call for specifics, as well as info about religious groups. Secretariat open Mon.-Thurs. 9am-noon and 2-6pm, Fri. 9am-noon.

Weather: Allo Météo, 5-day recorded forecasts. Preferable to call from touch-tone phones. **Paris,** tel. 36 68 02 75; **Ile de France,** tel. 36 68 00 00; **France,** tel. 36 68 01 01; **mountain regions** (choice of northern Alps, southern Alps, Pyrénées, and Massifs), tel. 36 68 04 04; **marine conditions,** tel. 36 68 08 08. All in French. You can also check out a map of the day's predicted weather at the corner of Rapp and Université in the 7ème, posted by **Météorologie Nationale.**

■■■ PUBLICATIONS ABOUT PARIS

On those heartbreaking and rare occasions when *Let's Go* falls just short, consult the following guides. *Le Petit Futé* (65F), *Paris Pas Cher* (109F), and *Paris Combines* (95F) can guide you to the best and cheapest stores, services, restaurants, and a smorgasbord of options especially useful for the long-term traveler. *Connaissance de Vieux Paris* (100F) is a street-by-street guide to the history of Paris. Popular among the French is *Guide du Routard* (69F); basically a French *Let's Go,* complete with smart-alec comments, it provides useful information on how to live on a budget in Paris. *Gault Millau* is a well-respected guide to Parisian eateries. Patricia Wells's *The Food Lover's Guide to Paris* (US$15, about 100F in France) lists most of the city's greatest and most famous restaurants, cafés, bakeries, cheese shops, charcuteries, wine shops, etc. Gourmets may not share all of Wells's opinions (and budget travelers may not be able to verify them), but the guide is generally reliable. Both of the above are available at **Gibert Jeune** and other Parisian bookstores (see Shopping—Bookstores).

Your most important printed resource will invariably be a map (see Maps). The tourist office distributes a free monthly booklet entitled *Paris Sélection* that highlights exhibitions, concerts, suggested walking tours, and other useful information. Similarly, the **Mairie de Paris** publishes the monthly *Paris le Journal* (10F) with articles and listings about what's on, touristically and culturally, around the city. It is available at the Mairie's Salon d'Accueil, 29, rue de Rivoli, 4ème (tel. 42 76 42 42; M. Hôtel-de-Ville), and at most *mairies.* Some *arrondissements* (like the 16ème) publish their own magazines.

The weeklies *Pariscope* (3F) and *Officiel des Spectacles* (2F; published every Wed.) list current movies, plays, exhibits, festivals, clubs, and bars. Pariscope is the most comprehensive—buy one as soon as you arrive to get the rundown on Parisian life. *Pariscope* has recently (in cooperation with the British entertainment magazine *Time Out)* added a new English-language section called *Time Out Paris.* The Wednesday edition of *Le Figaro* includes *Figaroscope,* a supplement about what's on in Paris. *Free Voice,* a monthly newspaper published by the Cooperative for Better Living at the American Church is available there and at many student centers for free. *France-USA Contacts (FUSAC),* printed twice monthly and available free from English-speaking establishments (bookstores, restaurants, travel agencies) throughout Paris, lists job, housing, and service information for English speakers.

Although the newspapers in France do have political leanings, they do not necessarily determine who reads them. *Libération* (6F), a socialist newspaper, is carried everywhere by students in search of amusingly written but comprehensive news coverage of world events. Heavy on culture, including theater and concert listings, "*Libé*" (as it is known in France) has excellent controversial interviews and thought-provoking full-page editorials.

Readers with a penchant for politics will disappear behind a copy of *Le Monde* (6F), decidedly centrist in outlook with a tendency to wax socialist. The equally respectable, solid *Le Figaro* (6F)—a French attempt at The Wall Street Journal—leans to the right, with greater emphasis on the financial pages. *Le Parisien* (4F50), *François* (5F), *France-Soir* (5F), and *Quotidien* (6F) also write from the right, though their efforts tend toward the more-style-than-quality end of the journalistic spectrum. The Communist Party puts out *L'Humanité* (6F) to present its views. Militants and revolutionaries will want to buy *Lutte Ouvrière,* carried at few newsstands. Look for it in the streets and metro. Those homesick for the *Washington Post* and the *New York Times* can get the best of both in the *International Herald Tribune* (8F50). *L'Equipe* (6F), the sports and automobile daily, offers coverage and stats on most sports you can think of and some that you cannot. True hippofanatics will gallop to get *Paris-Turf* (6F50), the horse racing daily.

■■■ DETAILS

WEIGHTS AND MEASURES

I millimeter (mm) = 0.04 inch	I inch = 25mm
I meter (m) = 1.09 yards	I yard = 0.92m
I kilometer (km) = 0.62 mile	I mile = 1.61km
I gram (g) = 0.04 ounce	I ounce = 25g
I liter = 1.06 quarts	I quart = 0.94 liter

TIME

In general, Paris is six hours ahead of North America (Eastern Standard Time) and one hour ahead of the United Kingdom. France springs forward one hour on the last Sunday in March and falls back an hour on the last Saturday in September. Beware: these time changes occur on different weekends than in North America.

■■■ ORIENTATION

LAYOUT

Coursing languidly from east to west, the Seine River forms the heart of modern Paris. Perhaps single-handedly the basis of the city's legendary romance, the river played midwife to Paris's birth on an island some 2300 years ago. Today, the Ile de la Cité and neighboring Ile St-Louis remain the geographical center of the city, while the Seine splits Paris into two large expanses—the renowned *rive gauche* (Left Bank) to its south and the *rive droite* (Right Bank) to its north. By the time of Louis XIV, the city had grown to 20 *quartiers*; Haussmann's 19th-century reconstructions shifted their boundaries but kept the number, dividing Paris into 20 *arrondissements* (districts) which spiral clockwise around the Louvre.

The *arrondissement* system provides the organizational framework for this book. Note that each *arrondissement* contains a host of smaller neighborhoods, which are often the remains of old Parisian quartiers that survived Haussmann's restructuring of the city. See the Sights chapter for a detailed description of what each *arrondissement,* and its various neighborhoods, has to offer.

MAPS

A map of Paris is essential if you plan to do any serious strolling. By far the best guide to Paris is the **Plan de Paris par Arrondissement,** which includes a detailed map of each *arrondissement,* all the bus lines, a wealth of miscellany, and an essential index of streets and their nearest metro stops. You can pick up a copy of the red- or black-covered *plan* at FNAC or Gibert Jeune for 52F. Don't pay more unless you plan to drive in Paris. Before you buy, be sure to check that you've got one of the more expansive versions with maps of the *banlieue* (city outskirts). All such *plans,* marketed by several different companies, can be found at most bookstores, *papeteries* (stationery stores), and kiosks. Unfortunately, the metro map in these guides is sometimes out of date. Pick up a free, updated one in any metro station: it also includes bus lines and the RER suburban system. If you're lost, keep your eyes out for a metro station; every station has a map of the neighborhood, with a street index. **L'Astrolabe,** 46, rue de Provence, 9ème (tel. 42 85 42 95; M. Chaussée d'Antin), or 14, rue Serpente, 6ème (tel. 46 33 80 06; M. Odéon), stocks the most comprehensive collection of maps imaginable. Both locations sell guidebooks, magazines, and travel literature in almost every language. At the 9ème *arrondissement* location, an entire floor is dedicated just to France (both open Mon.-Sat. 9:30am-7pm).

GETTING AROUND

■■■ PUBLIC TRANSPORTATION

The **RATP (Régie Autonome des Transports Parisiens)** coordinates an efficient network of subways, buses, and commuter trains in and around Paris. For information on the services of RATP, contact their office at the **Bureau de Tourisme RATP,** pl. de la Madeleine, 8ème (tel. 40 06 71 45; M. Madeleine; open Mon.-Sat. 7:30am-7pm). An English-speaking representative is usually available. RATP can also be reached round the clock through Minitel: 3615 RATP (see Communications).

   If you're only staying in Paris for one day but expect to do a lot of traveling, consider buying a **metro pass.** At 90F for three days and 145F for five, you probably won't get your money's worth with the **Paris Visite** tourist tickets, which are valid for unlimited travel on bus, metro, and RER, and which facilitate discounts on sightseeing trips, bicycle rentals, and more. A more practical saver-pass is the **Formule 1;** for 27F per day, you get unlimited travel on buses, metro, and RER within Paris. If you're staying in Paris for more than a few days, get a weekly *(hebdomadaire)* **Coupon Vert** or a monthly *(mensuel)* **Coupon Orange,** which allow unlimited travel (starting on the first day of the week or month) on the metro and buses in Paris. Both of these must be accompanied by the ID-style **Carte Orange**. To get your carte orange, bring an ID photo (taken by machines in most major stations) to the ticket counter, ask for a carte orange with a plastic case, and then purchase your handsome coupon vert (59F) or equally swanky coupon orange (208F). Finally, the **Carte Hebdomadaire** is a weekly coupon that allows you two rides per day, six days out of seven, starting with the day it was purchased (40F). Write the number of your carte on your coupon before you use it. Also remember that these cards have specific start and end dates and may not be worthwhile if bought in the middle or at the end of the month or the week. All prices quoted here are for passes in zones 1 and 2 (the metro and RER in Paris and the immediate suburbs). If you intend to travel to the distant 'burbs, you'll need to buy RER passes for more zones (up to 5). Ask at the ticket windows for details.

METRO

Inaugurated in 1898, the *Paris Métropolitain* (metro) is one of the world's oldest and most efficient subway systems, able to whisk you within walking distance of nearly any spot in the city. Stations are marked with an "M" or the *"Métropolitain"* in lettering designed by Art Nouveau pioneer Hector Guimard. Trains run frequently and connections are easy. The first trains start running at 5am; they last leave the

Paris: Overview and Arrondissements

1 Cimetière de Montmartre
2 Sacré Coeur Basilica
3 Parc La Villette
4 Parc des Buttes Chaumont
5 Jardins du Trocadero
6 Palais Chaillot
7 Cimetière de Passy
8 American Embassy
9 British Embassy
10 Petit Palais
11 Grand Palais
12 Arc de Triomphe
13 Madeleine
14 Gare St-Lazare
15 Parc Monceau
16 Palais de la Découverte
17 Opéra Garnier
18 Galeries Lafayette
19 Printemps
20 Gare du Nord
21 Gare de l'Est
22 Opéra Bastille
23 Palais Omnisports de Bercy
24 Ministère des Finances
25 Gare de Lyon
26 Parc de Montsouris
27 Cité Universitaire
28 Cimetière Montparnasse
29 Gare Montparnasse

30 Bureau des Objets Trouvés (Lost and Found)
31 Louvre
32 Palais Royale
33 Forum des Halles
34 Musée de l'Orangerie
35 Central Post Office
36 Bourse
37 Bibliothèque Nationale
38 Ecole des Arts et Métiers
39 Archives Nationales
40 Musée Carnavalet
41 Musée Picasso
42 Centre George Pompidou
43 place des Vosges
44 Musée Victor Hugo
45 Notre Dame
46 Mémorial de la Déportation
47 Université de Paris (Sorbonne)

48 Ecole Normal Supérieure
49 Musée de Cluny
50 Museum Nationale d'Histoire Naturelle
51 Panthéon
52 Eglise St-Etienne du Mont
53 La Mosquée
54 Jardin des Plantes
55 Jardins du Luxembourg
56 Eglise St-Sulpice
57 Théâtre Nationale de l'Odéon
58 Eiffel Tower
59 Champs de Mars

60 Ecole Militaire
61 UNESCO
62 Hôtel des Invalides
63 Assemblée Nationale
64 Musée d'Orsay
65 Cimetière de l'Est du Pere Lachaise

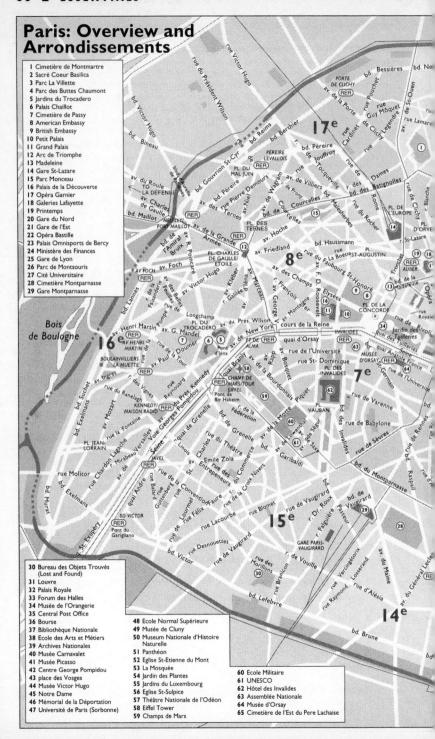

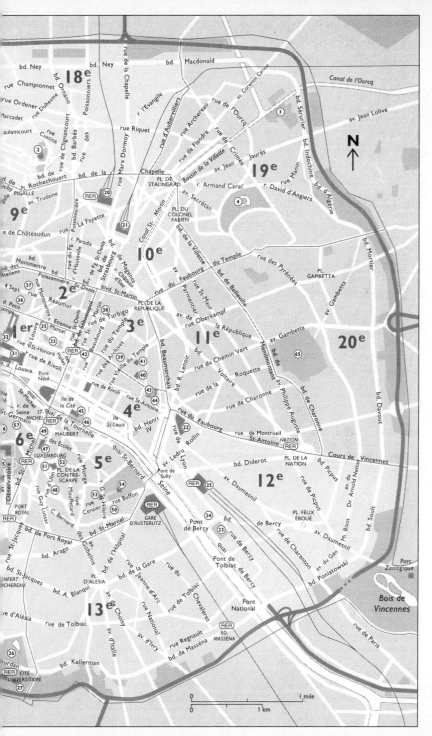

end-of-the-line stations (the *"portes de Paris"*) for the center of the city at 12:15am. One exception is the last train leaving from Porte de Balard; it does not travel the length of the line to Porte de Charenton but goes only as far as République. In the other direction the train runs the whole route from Porte de Charenton to Porte de Balard. For the exact departure times of the last trains from the *portes,* check the poster in the center of each station marked **Principes de Tarification** (fare guidelines).

Free, pocket-sized metro maps are available in most stations. Transportation maps are posted on train platforms and near turnstiles; all have a *plan du quartier* (map of the surrounding neighborhood). Connections to other lines are indicated by orange *"correspondance"* signs, and the exits by blue *"sortie"* signs. Metro lines are numbered (1 is the oldest), but referred to by their final destination. Transfers to other lines are free if made in the same station, but it is not always possible to reverse direction on the same line without exiting the station and using another ticket.

Each trip on the metro requires one ticket. Tickets can be bought individually (6F50), but a *carnet* of 10 (39F) is more practical. Don't buy tickets from anyone except the people in the ticket booths. To pass through the turnstiles, insert the ticket into the small slit in the metal divider just next to you as you approach the turnstile. It disappears for a moment, then pops out about a foot further along, and a little green or white circle lights, reminding you to retrieve the ticket. If a small electric whine sounds and a little red circle lights up, your ticket is not valid; take your ticket back and try another. **Hold onto your ticket** until you exit the metro, pass the point marked **Limite de Validité des Billets;** a uniformed RATP *contrôleur* (inspector) may request to see it on any train. If caught without one, you must pay a hefty fine. Also, any *correspondances* to the RER require you to put your validated (and uncrumpled) ticket into a turnstile. Otherwise you might need to buy a new ticket in order to exit. A word on being helpful to people who have "lost" their ticket and need to get through an entrance or exit; while it may seem a small matter to allow someone to follow you through the gate, be warned that **thieves** often use this strategy to insinuate their way into your bag or pocket. Keep in mind that a metro ticket is valid only within Paris. There is no longer first-class metro service; any cars still marked "1" are waiting to be repainted.

Most train lines are well traveled at night, and Parisian women often travel alone, though their familiarity with the city affords them a confidence you may lack. Violent crime in the metro is on the increase, so use common sense. Avoid empty cars and corridors. At night, many people ride in the first car, where the conductor is only a door away. Do not count on buying a metro ticket home late at night. Some ticket windows close as early as 10pm, and many close before the last train is due to arrive. Always have one ticket more than you need.

Stay away from the most dangerous stations (Barbès-Rochechouart, Pigalle, Châtelet, Trocadéro, and Anvers). Despite the good neighborhoods in which some of these stops are located, they are often frequented by thieves and other troublemakers looking to prey on the tourist or the wealthy.When in doubt, take a taxi. Should you choose to walk home, always follow buy, well-lit streets.

For information about metro services for people in wheelchairs or for people with impaired vision, see Once There—Travelers with Disabilities.

RER

The **RER** (Réseau Express Régional) is the RATP's local suburban train system, which passes through central Paris. Introduced in 1969, the RER runs through deeper tunnels at higher speeds. Within the city, the RER travels much faster than the metro, and for all intents can be regarded as a faster, though more confusing, set of metro lines. There are four RER lines, marked A-D, with different branches designated by a number, such as the C5 line to Versailles-Rive-Gauche. The principal stops within the city, which link the RER to the metro system, are Gare du Nord and Châtelet-les-Halles on the Right Bank and St-Michel on the Left Bank. To check for the right train, watch the electric signboards next to each track. These signs list all the possible stops for trains running on that track. Be sure that the little square next to your destination is lit up. There are two transit classes on RER trains. Unless you indicate otherwise, you'll be sold a second-class ticket. Every RER car is marked "1" or "2"; second-class ticket holders are excluded from first-class cars under penalty of fine. First-class seating caters to commuters with nicer seats and more leg-room. Second-class tickets cost 6F50 within the city, first-class tickets cost 3F more. To get to the suburbs, you'll need to buy special tickets, prorated to your particular destination's distance from the center city (9F50-35F one-way) Classier, faster, and more confusing, the RER differs from the metro on yet another count; you'll need your ticket to *exit* RER stations: Insert your ticket just as you did to enter, and pass through.

BUS

Because the metro is so efficient and convenient, the Parisian bus system is often neglected by both locals and visitors. Think of bus rides as cheap sight-seeing tours and helpful introductions to the city's layout. The free bus map *Autobus Paris-Plan du Réseau* is available at the tourist office and at some metro information booths. The routes of each line are also posted at each stop. The buses no longer take the same tickets as the metro; special bus tickets cost the same as metro tickets and are available in metro stations, tabacs, and from the bus drivers themselves. Most trips within the city and nearest suburbs cost one ticket. If your journey takes you out of the city you might need more than one ticket—ask the driver. Enter the bus through the front door and punch your ticket by pushing it into the machine by the driver's seat. If you have a *coupon orange,* flash it at the driver, but **do not** insert the ticket into the machine. Controllers may ask to see your ticket, so hold onto it until the end of the ride.

Most buses run 7am-8:30pm, although those marked **Autobus du Soir** continue until 12:30am. Still others, called **Noctambus,** run all night. Night buses (3 tickets, 4 if you use 2 buses) start their runs to the *portes* of the city from the "Châtelet" stop and leave every hour on the half hour from 1:30 to 5:30am. Buses departing from the suburbs to Châtelet run every hour on the hour 1 to 5am. Buses with three-digit numbers come from or are bound for the suburbs, while buses with two-digit numbers travel exclusively within Paris. Buses with numbers in the 20s come from or are bound for Gare St-Lazare, in the 30s Gare de l'Est, in the 40s Gare du Nord, in the 70s Châtelet/Hôtel de Ville (with exceptions), in the 80s Luxembourg (with exceptions), and in the 90s Gare Montparnasse.

For more detailed diagrams of all bus routes, consult the *Plan de Paris par Arrondissement* (see Maps). The RATP prints a number of useful brochures. Ask for their *Grand Plan de Paris* which includes legible maps off all Parisian bus routes and numbers. Their pamphlet *Paris Bus metro RER* lists several bus routes that pass through interesting neighborhoods and by the main sights of Paris (available at metro stops). It also lists directions to major museums, churches, and monuments. Some routes pass by enough sights to make them mini-tours in themselves. Buses worth riding from start to finish include:

Bus #20: From Gare St-Lazare to the Opéra, Montmartre-Poissonière, République, Bastille (50 min.). A trip down the grands boulevards. Open platform in back.

Bus #21: From Gare St-Lazare to the Opéra, Palais Royal, the Louvre, the Pont Neuf, St-Michel, Gare du Luxembourg, Porte de Gentilly (40 min.).

Bus #29: From Gare St-Lazare to Porte de Montempoivre (50 min.). Intrepid ride through narrow streets of the Marais. Open platform in back.

Bus #82: From Gare du Luxembourg to Gare Montparnasse, Ecole-Militaire, Champs-de-Mars, Tour Eiffel, Porte Maillot, Neuilly (45 min.).

Bus #83: From pl. d'Italie, along bd. Raspail, Gare des Invalides, pl. des Ternes (50 min.). Paris's finest real estate and views of the quais. Open platform in back.

Bus #95: From Tour Montparnasse past St-Germain-des-Prés, the Louvre, Palais Royal, the Opéra, and to Montmartre, near Sacré-Coeur (50 min.).

TAXI

Taxi trips within Paris represent the height of decadence for the budget traveler. Rates vary according to time of day and geographical area, but they're never cheap. **Tarif A,** the basic rate, is in effect in Paris proper 7am -7pm (3F23/km). **Tarif B** is in effect in Paris proper Mon.-Sat. 7pm- 7am, all day Sunday, and during the day from the airports (5F10/km). **Tarif C,** the highest, is in effect from the airports 7pm- 7am (6F88/km). In addition, there is a *prix en charge* (base fee) of about 11F. Should you call a taxi, rather than getting one at a taxi stand, the base fee will increase according to how far way you are and how long it takes the driver to get there. For all cabs, stationary time (at traffic lights and in traffic jams) costs 120F per hour. Additional charges (5F-10F) are added for luggage weighing over 5kg, a pet in the backseat, a fourth adult in the cab, or for taxis leaving from train stations and marked taxi stops. All taxis have lights on top indicating the rate being charged, so you can check to see that the driver is playing it straight. Make sure the meter is on when you start the ride. A 15% tip is customary (round up to the nearest 5F). If you must take a taxi, try picking one up at a train station or waiting at a stand, called *arrêt taxis,* usually found near bus stops. Calling a radio-cab **(Alpha Taxis,** tel. 42 41 50 50, **Taxis Radio Etoile** tel. 42 70 41 41, **Taxis G7** tel. 47 39 47 39, or **ARTAXI** tel. 42 41 50 50) is far more expensive, since you must pay for the distance the cab drives to pick you up. Technically, taxis cannot refuse to take a fare if their roof light is on, but can refuse to take more than three people. Illegal overcrowding of cabs can bring heavy fines upon the driver. If you have a complaint, write to **Service des Taxis de la Préfecture de Police,** 36, rue des Morillons, 75015 (tel. 45 31 14 80). If you expect to file a complaint, ask the driver for a receipt; make sure to accurately record and include in your complaint the driver's cab license number.

■■■ BICYCLE

Bicyclists in Paris may appear to the uninitiated observer as a horde of Mr. Magoos, pedaling obliviously through a chaos of pushy Fiats and bumpy cobblestone streets. If you have never ridden a bike in heavy traffic, don't use central Paris as a testing ground. The Bois de Boulogne and the Bois de Vincennes should be more your speed (see Sports). The metro cannot accommodate bikes, but local trains list specific times when they allow bicycles on board for free.

> **Mountain Bike Tours,** Three Ducks Hostel, 6, pl. Etienne Pernet, 15ème (tel. 48 42 57 87). M. Félix Faure. Runs popular 6-hr. guided bike tours (in English) past the Eiffel Tower, the Louvre, and the Tour Montparnasse, with a lunch stop in the *quartier latin.* Low impact, less strenuous than walking, and geared for the amateur cyclist 14-65. Tours make frequent stops for up-close sightseeing. Groups of 12-17 people. 118F per person. Or rent a mountain bike for 90F/day. Helmet and insurance included. Open daily 11am-7pm.
>
> **Bicyclub,** 8, pl. de la Porte-Champerret, 17ème (tel. 47 66 55 92; fax 43 80 35 68). M. Porte de Champerret. 6 locations, including the Bois de Boulogne (Pré Catelan), the Bois de Vincennes, the Canal de l'Ourcq, and the Forêt de Rambouillet. The telephone number gives a recorded message (in French) listing the bicyclub locations and how to find them from the metro. 3-speed bikes from 25F/hr., 100F/day. 1500F deposit includes insurance that covers you but not the bike. Locks, maps, and baby seats available. The main location at the Bois de Boulogne is open daily 9am-7pm; Oct.-June Mon.-Fri. 9am-7pm, Sat. 9am-1pm and 2-7pm.
>
> **Paris-Vélo,** 2, rue de Fer-à-Moulin, 5ème (tel. 43 37 59 22). M. Censier Daubenton. Bikes 90F for 8 hrs., 140F per day, 495F per week. Bike rental with 1000F deposit, which includes accident insurance. Open Mon.-Sat. 10am-12:30pm and 2-7pm.

For motorcycles or scooters, stop by **Agence Contact Location,** 24, rue Arc de Triomphe, 17ème (tel. 47 66 19 19; M. Etoile). Scooters 200F for 8 hrs., 230F per day,

850F per week. 7000F credit card deposit required. Motorcycles from 290F for 8 hrs., 320F per day, 1350F per week. 10,000F credit card deposit required.

C
A
R

■■■ CAR

"Somewhere you have heard a dark apocryphal statistic—that one driver out of every twelve in Paris has killed his man. On foot, the Parisian is as courteous as the citizen of any other city. But mounted, he is merciless." So wrote Irwin Shaw, and he liked Parisians. The infamous rotary at the Arc de Triomphe has trapped many an unwary tourist; at rush hour, cars move in any direction they want here. **Priorité à droite** gives the right of way to the car approaching from the right, regardless of the size of the streets, and Parisian drivers make it an affair of honor to take this right even in the face of grave danger. Drivers may not to honk their horns within city limits unless they are about to hit a pedestrian, but this rule is often broken. The legal way to show discontent is to flash the headlights, so you should be on the look-out in case a law-abiding driver refrains from honking until just before impact. If you don't have a map of Paris marked with one-way streets, the city will be impossible to navigate. Parking is hard to locate (although Parisians park on sidewalks, corners, etc.) and garages are expensive.

Possibly the best excuse for renting a car in Paris is to escape from the city into the provinces. Renting a car for a group of three or four may be even cheaper than buying train tickets. Foreigners need a passport, a license of at least one year (check with your rental agency), and a credit card to rent in Paris; an international license is not required. None of the agencies in Paris will rent to drivers under 21. The following prices represent quotes for the agency's smallest economy car available. Note that few of these agencies offer cars with automatic transmissions.

ACAR, 77, rue de Lagny, 20ème (tel. 43 79 54 54; fax 43 72 68 63). M. Porte de Vincennes. The best deal in town. Peugeot Sencif 228F per day. First 100km free plus 1F21 per additional km. Weekend with 700km and insurance included1342F. A week with unlimited mileage and insurance included 1620F. Additional insurance 35F. No cars with automatic transmission. Open Mon.-Fri. 8am–7pm, Sat. 9am-2:30pm and 3:30-6pm.

Inter Touring Service, 117, bd. Auguste Blanqui, 13ème (tel. 45 88 52 37; fax 45 80 89 30). M. Glacière. Fiat Pandas 267F per day with 200km and insurance included, or 1407F per week, distance and insurance included. Also provides vehicles equipped for **drivers with disabilities.** Open Mon.-Sat. 8:30am-6:15pm.

Autorent, 98, rue de la Convention, 15ème (tel. 45 54 22 45; fax 45 54 39 69). M. Boucicaut. Also at 3-5, av. Jean Moulin, 14ème (tel. 49 92 55 06). M. Alésia. Rents Fiat Pandas for 280F per day with 250km included; unlimited mileage for rentals of 3 days or more. 1500F for a week with 1000km; 1800F with unlimited mileage. Some cars with **automatic transmission.** Open Mon.-Fri. 8:30am-7pm, Sat. 8:30am-midnight. Rents to drivers who've had a license for at least one year.

Accommodations

Three basic types of Parisian accommodations are suitable for the budget traveler: hotels, hostels, and *foyers*. While hotels are comfortable and give you complete privacy and independence, hostels and *foyers* are the least expensive options especially for people traveling alone. According to the Office du Tourisme, high season in Paris falls around Easter, May-June, and September-October (when trade shows—*salons*—take over the city.) Indeed, many hotels in the 11ème and the 12ème consider July and August to be off-season. But for hostels and other truly budget accommodations the high season is invariably summer (June-August) and most places are perpetually full. Try to make a reservation in advance, but if you do arrive in Paris without one, don't panic. The **Office du Tourisme** on the Champs-Elysées or one of its other bureaus should be able to find you a room, although the lines may be long and the selections not necessarily among the cheapest in Paris. Unless otherwise noted, we list hostel prices per person; prices elsewhere are per room. Be aware that the city of Paris has a *Taxe de Séjour* of 1-5 per person per day within the city; this may be augmented in January of 1995. Most hotels and *foyers* include this *Taxe* in their listed prices, but hostels may or may not consider it part of the room's cost. It is also advisable to check the locks at the establishment where you choose to stay.

Should you arrive in Paris with no place to stay, stop by one of the following booking offices, located near train stations and major metro lines. Their English-speaking staff will arrange for stays in hostels and budget hotels throughout the city.

La Centrale de Réservations (FUAJ-HI), 4, bd. Jules Ferry, 11ème (tel. 43 57 02 60; fax 40 21 79 92). M. République. The best way to secure a bed in a hostel or to book any other budget accommodation in Paris. They find rooms for 90-130F per night per person. Two buildings down from the Jules Ferry hostel. Provides same-day reservations in one of their affiliated youth hostels or budget hotels—a total of 10,000 beds in and around the city. The earlier you show up the better, but they can usually help anyone any time. Supplementary hostels open in summer and can sometimes get you hotel rooms for hostel rates. Books beds throughout France and Europe and arranges excursions. Open Mon.-Sat. 9am-6pm.

Accueil des Jeunes en France (AJF), 119, rue St-Martin, 4ème (tel. 42 77 87 80). M. Rambuteau. Walk away from rue Rambuteau along side of Centre Pompidou; turn left down street opposite plaza in front of the museum; AJF is halfway down this street, facing the Pompidou. Even in the busiest months, AJF guarantees you "decent and low-cost lodging with immediate reservation" for the same day only. You must pay the full price of the foyer room when making your reservation, even before seeing the room. AJF can also help find a hotel room, though not always for the full duration of your stay. Bookings are regularly made for stays of up to two weeks, so you may have to use AJF more than once. Employees speak English and one other foreign language. Services at AJF incur a total fee of 10F. Open Mon.-Sat.; Oct.-May 9:30am-6pm; June-Sept. 9am-5:30pm. Other offices: 139, bd. St-Michel, 5ème (tel. 43 54 95 86; M. Port-Royal; open Mon.-Fri. 10am-12:30pm and 1:30-6:15pm) and Gare du Nord, 10ème (tel. 42 85 86 19; M. Gare du Nord; open June-Sept. daily 8:30am-5:15pm).

■ HOSTELS AND FOYERS

Paris's big-city hostels don't bother with many of the restrictions—sleepsheets, curfews, and the like—that characterize most hostels in the world, but they do have maximum stays, though even these are flexible. Accommodations usually consist of bunkbeds in single-sex dormitories. To stay in a **Hostelling International (HI)** hostel, you must be a member. Prospective hostelers should become members of the

HI affiliate in their country before they leave. If you show up at an HI hostel without membership, the hostel should issue you a blank membership card with space for six validation stamps. Each night you'll pay a nonmember supplement (19F) and earn one Guest Stamp; get six stamps and you're a member. Membership purchased this way costs 114F. Most student travel agencies sell HI cards on the spot or you can contact one of the national hostel organizations (see Essentials—Useful Addresses and Publications). In summer 1992, the **International Youth Hostel Federation (IYHF)** officially changed its name to **Hostelling International (HI),** with the result that all signs, membership cards, and other products relating to the association now bear the HI initials and logo, as well as the symbols of the relevant national hosteling association.

HI has recently instituted an **International Booking Network.** To reserve space in high season, obtain an International Booking Voucher from any national youth hostel association (in your home country or Paris) and send it to a participating hostel four to eight weeks in advance, along with US$2 in francs. Pre-booking is wise.

While there are only two official HI hostels in the city proper (the Jules Ferry and Le D'Artagnan), many other privately run hostels and *foyers* exist all over the city. Normally intended for university students during the academic year, *foyers* offer the security and privacy of a hotel, while providing the lower prices and camaraderie of a youth hostel. Residents live anywhere from one week to three months to an entire year in the *foyer.* Facilities tend to be better in foyers, but the presence of permanent residents might make the atmosphere a little less open than in hostels.

■ HOTELS

Of the three classes of Parisian budget accommodations, hotels may be the most practical for the majority of travelers. There is total privacy, no curfew, and often concerned managers. Most important, hotels routinely accept reservations. Budget hotels in Paris are not significantly more expensive than their hostel/*foyer* counterparts. Groups of 2, 3, and 4 may actually find it more economical to stay in a hotel. Unlike *foyers,* hotels rent doubles by the room and not by person.

The French government publishes a comprehensive guide that classifies hotels with a star system: 4L (luxury), 4, 3, 2, and 1, depending on the services offered, the percentage of rooms with bath, and other such indicators. Most hotels in *Let's Go* are one-star or unclassified establishments, though two-star establishments offering inexpensive rooms are sometimes included. Most rooms come with double beds. In our listings, double refers to rooms with one double bed; 2-bed double refers to the rare room with two separate single beds. Expect to pay at least 150F for singles. If your room has no shower, you'll usually have to pay extra (12-25F) to get the key to the hall shower. Showers in your room are included in the room charge.

Paris has a number of very nice hotels in the 150-200F range. These hotels are often small, simple, and do not offer the amenities of the Sheraton or the Hilton. But the hotels listed in *Let's Go: Paris* are clean, have well-furnished rooms, and have adequate toilet and shower facilities. Most newly renovated hotels have double-paned glass windows which provide for better insulation against cold and noise.

A few tips about Parisian hotels: Many North Americans are surprised to discover a strange toilet-like apparatus located in all wash-closets called a *bidet.* A *bidet* is a somewhat archaic device intended for the cleansing of the private body parts. Do not use your *bidet* as a toilet. Keep in mind that the French call the ground floor the *rez-de-chaussée,* and start numbering with the first floor *above* the ground floor *(premier étage).* Many hotels serve breakfast for 15-25F. Since local cafés often serve croissants and coffee for less, you may want to eat breakfast out. Remember that there are usually rules against bringing food into your rooms. Parisian law forbids hanging laundry from windows or over balconies to dry. Most hotels in Paris are not wheelchair accessible especially the budget hotels whose rooms and hallways are too small to accommodate the necessary modification. It is advisable to call ahead for more information.

A
L
T
E
R
N
A
T
I
V
E

A
C
C
O
M
M
O
D
A
T
I
O
N
S

RESERVATIONS

Do not reserve for more nights than you might possibly need and always call or fax in advance to inquire about the availability of rooms before depositing any money. If you decide to leave Paris before you intended, or if you want to switch hotels, don't expect to get back all your money. Every year, *Let's Go* receives letters from readers complaining that hotel managers would not refund the nights that went unused. If in doubt, reserve for just one night; you can usually extend your stay once you get to the hotel.

Although most tourists visit Paris in the summer, this is not necessarily the heaviest-booked time, since business travelers take up many rooms in May, June, September, and October. Since the high and low seasons are both complicated and counterintuitive, reserve as soon as you know when you will be in Paris. Make reservations at least two weeks in advance; a number of hotels claim that they are fully booked two months in advance for the summer. To guarantee that you have a room waiting when you arrive, the following process is advised:

1.) Call, write, or fax the hotel asking for a reservation for a specific date and kind of room (single, double, with bathroom, shower, etc.).

2.) If you write, enclose an International Reply Coupon (sold at post offices), so that the hotel need not bother with postage expenses.

3.) When you receive positive confirmation, send *la caution* (a deposit) for one night. Most hotels will confirm reservations only upon receipt of a check for the first night, although some will accept a credit card number instead. The easiest way to send this deposit is to mail a traveler's check in francs, double signed. This is the equivalent of sending a personal check, and you'll avoid the hefty US$25-30 charge for an international money order. Include an International Reply Coupon (two for air mail) for a prompt reply. Without a deposit, most hotels will not honor a reservation for more than an hour or so, the time it might take to arrive after calling from a pay phone somewhere in Paris.

4.) Call one or two days in advance to confirm (or cancel) and inform the manager of your intended arrival time.

Try your best to honor your reservation. Small budget hotels are of a nearly extinct breed. These small family-run hotels cannot afford to hold a room, turn away potential guests, and then swallow their losses if you decide you don't want it.

■ ALTERNATIVE ACCOMMODATIONS

STUDENT ACCOMMODATIONS

For travelers planning a summer visit to Paris, student housing is available in the dormitories of most French universities. Contact the **Centre Régional des Oeuvres Universitaires (CROUS)** at 39, av. Georges Bernanos, 5ème (tel. 40 51 36 00; 75231 Paris Cedex 05). Additional lodging is available on a month-to-month basis at the **Cité Universitaire** (15, bd. Jourdan, 14ème; tel. 45 89 35 79; M. Cité Universitaire). Over 30 different nations maintain dormitories at the Cité Universitaire, where they board their citizens studying in Paris. In summer, dorms lodge anyone on a first-come, first-serve basis. Reserve a bed months in advance—at least by April for June and July. To stay in the American House write to Fondation des Etats-Unis, 15, bd. Jourdan, 75690 Paris Cedex 14 (tel. 45 89 35 79). Room rates vary according to demand in summer: 3200F/month June-July; 2850F/month Aug.-Sept. (when there is often space, so call or show up in person). Office open Mon.-Fri. 10-11:30am and 4-6pm. For info about other dorms, write to M. le Délégué Général de Cité Universitaire de Paris, 19 bd. Jourdan, 75690 Paris Cedex 14. No kitchen facilities, but the restaurant in the Maison Internationale offers decent institutional fare at rock-bottom prices. Open Mon.-Fri. 11:45am-1:50pm and 5:45-8:20pm. Meal ticket 12F.

HOTELS, HOSTELS, AND FOYERS

■ FIRST ARRONDISSEMENT

In the shadow of the Louvre, much of the 1er remains true to its kingly past. Cartier, Chanel, and the Banque de France set an intimidating mood on the street for the budget traveler. Yet while financiers and ladies-who-lunch may whisk past you, don't let them scare you away. Single travelers who stay near Châtelet-les-Halles should revel in their central, generally safe location, but should consider using a different metro station at night.

Henri IV, 25, place Dauphine (tel. 43 54 44 53). M. Cité. Walk toward the Conciergerie, turn right on bd. du Palais, and left on quai de l'Horloge; turn left at the front of the Conciergerie onto pl. Dauphine. Last outpost of cheap accommodations on Ile de la Cité; one of the best-located hotels in the city. Somewhat dilapidated, average-sized rooms with squishy beds. To reach the quirky first floor toilet, follow the staircase that curls around the building. All other toilets located (inside) on each floor. Singles 105-135F. Doubles 140-195F. Triples 190-220F. Quads 250F. Reserve 2 months in advance; send a check in francs for 1 night.

Hôtel de Lille, 8, rue du Pélican (tel. 42 33 33 42). M. Palais-Royal. Walk toward the Palais-Royal and turn right onto rue St-Honoré, left on rue Croix des Petits Champs, and take your first right on rue du Pélican. What it lacks in extras it makes up in calm and price. Functional rooms with slightly worn mattresses and decor. Located on a quiet street close to the Louvre. Coin-operated phone on 1st floor. Outside door locked at 9pm; arrive before 7pm to pick up your personal and main door keys. Singles 170F. Doubles 200F, with shower 250F. Showers 30F. Reserve 1 month in advance with check for one night's payment. No elevator, no breakfast, no English, no credit cards.

Hôtel Lion d'Or, 5, rue de la Sourdière (tel. 42 60 79 04; fax 42 60 09 14). M. Tuileries or Pyramides. From M. Tuileries walk down rue du 29 Juillet away from the park, turn right on rue St-Honoré; turn left on rue de la Sourdière. Carpeted, sparsely decorated rooms with colorful bedspreads and double-paned glass; You'll hear the bells toll from nearby Eglise St-Roch, but little else. Very small showers in rooms with showers. English-speaking staff. Singles 180F, with shower 250F. Doubles 250F, with shower 280F, with bath and toilet 380F. Extra bed 60F. Showers 20F. Breakfast 25F. Reserve 2 weeks ahead, 1 month ahead in summer. 5% discount if you plan to stay more than 3 days. MC, V, AmEx.

Hôtel du Palais, 2, quai de la Mégisserie (tel. 42 36 98 25; fax 42 21 41 67). M. Châtelet. Location by the Seine, at the corner of place du Châtelet and quai de la Mégisserie, gives all rooms (except those on top floor) splendid views. Double-glazing reduces street noise from animal market outside. High ceilings on first floor. Singles with shower 280F, with shower and toilet 320F, with bath and toilet 350F. Doubles with shower 320F, with shower and toilet 350F, with bath and toilet 380F. Triple 420F. Large quad (480F) and quint (550F) with 2-sink bathroom and huge windows. On garret-like top floor: singles 180F, doubles 230F. Extra bed 70F. Breakfast 30F. Shower included for top-floor, no-frill rooms. In summer, reserve 3 weeks in advance. MC, V.

Hôtel Richelieu-Mazarin, 51, rue de Richelieu (tel. 42 97 46 20). M. Palais-Royal. Walk left around the Palais Royal to rue de Richelieu. Industrial carpeting, plastic flowers, and Monet prints. Doubles in converted attic are an oasis of taste— muted flowered wallpaper, pine furniture, and skylight (but no view). Otherwise, smallish rooms have radios and a view of the bustling thoroughfare. Double-glazing. Little English spoken. Singles 190-210F, with shower or bath and toilet 280-310F. Doubles 230F, with shower or bath and toilet 300-330F. Extra bed 60F. Showers 10F. Breakfast 25F-30F. Reserve 3 weeks ahead in summer. MC, V.

Hôtel Montpensier, 12, rue de Richelieu (tel. 42 96 28 50; fax 42 86 02 70). M. Palais-Royal. Walk left around the the Palais Royal to rue de Richelieu. Clean, hospitable atmosphere. Elevator. Choose between sunny rooms that face the street or quieter ones with dingy courtyard views. Spruced-up lounge with cheery, stained-glass ceiling. TVs in rooms with shower or bath. Singles 240F. Doubles 250F. Singles or doubles with toilet 285F, with shower and toilet 365F, with bath and toilet 420F. Extra bed 75F. Shower 25F. Breakfast 30F. MC, V, AmEx.

Hôtel de Rouen, 42, rue Croix des Petits Champs (tel. and fax 42 61 38 21). M. Palais-Royal or Louvre. Walk toward the Palais-Royal, turn right on rue St-Honoré and left on rue Croix des Petits Champs; across from the Banque de France. Steep, narrow staircase leads to small rooms with postage stamp-sized bathrooms. Warm proprietors seek to please their mostly young clientele; ask to use the refrigerator. To avoid street noise, also ask for a room on a higher floor. English spoken weekdays 8am-6pm. Triple on the courtyard priced as a double. Singles or doubles 180F, with shower 240F, with shower, toilet, and TV 290F. Triple with shower and toilet 290F. Quads with shower, toilet, and TV 350F. Free shower on 5th floor. Breakfast 20F. MC, V.

Hôtel Saint-Honoré, 85, rue St-Honoré (tel. 42 36 20 38 or 42 21 46 96; fax 42 21 44 08). M. Louvre, Châtelet, or Les Halles. From M. Louvre, cross rue de Rivoli onto rue du Louvre and turn right on rue St-Honoré. Renovations currently underway should conclude April '95. As of now, tired and peeling orange rooms have sleek modern lights, double-paned windows, colorful bedspreads and sparkling bathrooms with decorative tile. Once fully renovated, the hotel will no longer offer plain singles and doubles. Friendly, English-speaking staff, and young clientele. Guests have access to fridge. Until April '95, singles or doubles 180-200F, with shower and toilet 280F. Triples or quads with shower and toilet 380-450F. Showers 15F. Breakfast 24F. In summer, reserve 2 weeks ahead and confirm the night before or upon arrival. MC, V.

Hôtel du Centre, 20, rue du Roule (tel. 42 33 05 18; fax 42 33 74 02). M. Pont Neuf, Louvre, Châtelet, or Les Halles. Take rue de la Monnaie toward les Halles straight onto rue du Roule. Recently renovated rooms with slick modern plumbing and double-glazing. Rudimentary English spoken. Relatively spacious singles or doubles with shower and toilet 330F. Extra double bed, available only for a few rooms 30% extra. Breakfast 28F. Reserve 2 weeks in advance. If arriving after 7pm on 1st night, send 1 night's deposit. MC, V, AmEx.

Hostels and Foyers

Centre International de Paris (BVJ). Relatively luxurious chain of youth hostels; they polish the floors, water the plants, and offer stylish common areas to offset bunkbed uniformity. All meals except breakfast at Paris Louvre. All open 6-2am. No families. Rooms available at 2:30pm. Singles, doubles, triples, and quads 120F per person, breakfast and showers included. No singles in Paris Louvre. Weekend reservations up to 1 week in advance; reserve 1 day ahead for weekday bookings. Rooms held 1 hr. after your expected check-in time; call if you'll be late.

Paris Louvre, 20, rue J.-J. Rousseau, (tel. 42 36 88 18; fax 42 33 40 53). M. Louvre. 200 beds. 214 high-ceilinged, bright dorm-style rooms. Courtyard hung with brass lanterns and strewn with *brasserie* chairs. 2-10 beds/room. Lunch or dinner 50F. Groups must pay for 1 meal/day, lunch or dinner.

Paris Opéra, 11, rue Thérèse (tel. 42 60 77 23; fax 42 33 40 53). M. Pyramides. 68 beds. Bigger rooms with fewer beds; more subdued than Paris Louvre. Open Mar.-Sept.

Paris Les Halles, 5, rue du Pélican, (tel. 40 26 92 45; fax 42 33 40 53). M. Palais Royal. 55 beds. Low-ceiling, somewhat cramped rooms. Toilets and showers on alternate floors. Less common space than other BVJ hostels. Open Mar.-Sept.

Maisons des Jeunes Rufz de l'Avison, 18, rue J.-J. Rousseau (tel. 45 08 02 10). M. Louvre (not "Musée du Louvre") or Palais-Royal. From M. Louvre take rue du Louvre away from river, turn left on rue St.-Honoré and right on rue J.-J. Rousseau. During the academic year, it's a private residence for male college students. In summer it's a coed *foyer.* (Some coed rooms open during school year as well.) Stunning open-air courtyard. Doubles, triples, and quads 95F per person. Beds in quads are close together, so it's better to come in a group or book long in advance. 3-day min. stay. Reception open 7am-7pm. No curfew. Shower and breakfast included. Reserve by mail with 1 night's payment or arrive early.

■ SECOND ARRONDISSEMENT

Though blessed with few major sights of its own, the 2ème is within easy walking distance of the Marais, the Centre Pompidou, and the Louvre. Its safe, animated southern half includes the cobbled market street rue Montorgueil, and the pedestrian rues Tiquetonne and Léopold Bellan. In general, try to avoid the the seedy area further north, particularly on or near rue St-Denis.

Hôtel La Marmotte, 6, rue Léopold Bellan (tel. 40 26 26 51). M. Sentier. On a quiet, cobbled pedestrian street close to Marché Montorgueil, with double-glazing. Well-kept rooms with firm beds and high ceilings. Reception located in ground-floor bar. (Bar frequented mainly by hotel guests.) TV and small safe in every room. Singles 180F-200F, with shower and toilet 260F. Doubles 200F-240F, with shower and toilet 290F. Twins with shower and toilet 300F. Extra bed 80F. Breakfast 20F. Shower 15F. Reserve 2-3 weeks in advance. MC, V, AmEx.

Hôtel Sainte-Marie, 6, rue de la Ville Neuve (tel. 42 33 21 61; fax 42 33 29 24). M. Bonne Nouvelle. This bright little hotel is simple, clean and distinctly superior to many other hotels in its price range. New mattresses on all beds. Some English spoken. No elevator. Singles 160F, shower and toilet 220F. Doubles 180F, shower and toilet 240F. Triples with shower and toilet 300F. Shower 10F. Breakfast 20F.

Hôtel Vivienne, 40, rue Vivienne (tel. 42 33 13 26; fax 40 41 98 19). M. Bourse or Richelieu-Drouot. From M. Bourse, turn right on rue Vivienne. Hotel successfully reconciles gracious living with budget accommodations. The ungainly, tiled hallway leads to large rooms with armoires, TVs, full-length mirrors, and double-glazing. Elevator. Singles with shower 280F. Doubles with shower 345F, shower and toilet 410F, bath and toilet 435F. 2-bed doubles with bath and toilet 450F. 3rd person under 10 yrs. free, over 10 yrs. 30% extra. Breakfast 40F. MC, V.

Hôtel Tiquetonne, 6, rue Tiquetonne (tel. 42 36 94 58). M. Etienne-Marcel or Réaumur-Sébastopol. Near intersection of rue St-Denis with rue de Turbigo, and close to Marché Montorgueil. No open-arms reception, but clean and affordable. Elevator. Singles 120F, with shower and toilet 190F. Doubles with shower and toilet 220F. Showers 25F. Breakfast 22F served in your room. Open Sept.-July.

Hôtel Chénier, 1, rue Chénier (tel. 42 33 92 32; fax 45 08 57 73). M. Strasbourg-St-Denis. Look for the bright yellow entrance. Newly renovated, quiet rooms all with automated telephone wake-up service. Toilet in every room. No elevator. No English spoken. If returning after 1am, get key to the front door. Singles with shower 230F, with bath 300F. Doubles with shower 250F, with bath 300F, with bath and TV 330F. Triples with shower or bath 450F. Quads with bath 500F, with bath and TV 530F. MC, V.

Hôtel Bonne Nouvelle, 17, rue Beauregard (tel. 40 08 42 42, for reservations 45 08 87 71; fax 40 26 05 81). M. Strasbourg-St-Denis or Bonne Nouvelle. Somber, mens'-club feel to lobby and hallways. Sound-proofed, sizeable rooms with TVs. Spotless, modern bathrooms. Safe box at reception. Singles and doubles with toilet and bath or shower 260-360F. Triples with bath and toilet 390F. One triple/quad with toilet and bath 510F. Breakfast 30F, in room 35F. Reserve with 1 night's deposit. MC, V.

Hôtel Zora, 4, rue Léopold Bellan (tel. 45 08 18 75). M. Sentier. Family-run hotel on a quiet, cobblestoned street. Dim, adequate rooms are a little frayed around the edges. No elevator. Good English spoken during the day. No deposit required for reservations. Singles 130F, with shower and toilet 200F. Doubles 180F, with shower and toilet 250F. Showers 25F.

■ THIRD ARRONDISSEMENT

Once the address of Paris' noblest families, the southern portion of the 3ème *arrondissement* has reclaimed its former elegance. Galleries, boutiques, and museums now hole up in its restored 17th-century mansions. Meanwhile, budget hotels cluster in the 3ème's noisy, commercial northwest—particularly on and north of rue Turbigo. There, budget hotels sidle up to Paris' garment district.

Grand Hôtel des Arts et Métiers, 4, rue Borda (tel. 48 87 73 89; fax 48 87 66 58). M. Arts-et-Métiers. Walk opposite traffic on rue Turbigo and turn left across the pedestrian island on rue Borda. Blistering wallpaper and bumpy rugs are compensated for by decent location, clean linen, clean bathrooms, and mostly clean rooms. Size varies considerably. Double-paned windows reduce street noise. 10-20% discount for mentioning *Let's Go* ensures you'll bump into other student budget travelers. Minimal English spoken. No elevator. Fridge on the main floor. Singles with toilet 130-160F. Doubles with toilet 200F. Singles or doubles with shower 250F, with toilet and shower 270F. Showers 20F. Breakfast 20F. MC, V.

Hôtel Picard, 26, rue de Picardie (tel. 48 87 53 82; fax 48 87 02 56). M. République or Filles-du-Calvaire. From M. République descend bd. du Temple and turn right on rue de Franche-Comté; turn left on rue de Picardie (before the Carreau du Temple). Near the sq. du Temple and specialty stores on rue de Bretagne. Cheerful, smallish rooms. Twin doubles are bunk-bed style. Mention *Let's Go* for a 10% discount if you stay more than 1 night. Singles 200F, with shower 250F, with bath and toilet 320F. Doubles 240-260F, with shower 320F, with bath and toilet 390F. Triples 510F. Extra bed 120F. Showers 20F. Breakfast 30F. MC, V.

Hôtel de Roubaix, 6, rue Greneta (tel. 42 72 89 91; fax 42 72 58 79). M. Réaumur-Sébastopol or Arts-et-Métiers. From M. Réaumur-Sébastopol, walk opposite traffic on bd. de Sébastopol and turn left on rue Greneta. Flowered wallpapersome balconied rooms. Double-paned glass windows minimize street noise. Affable management. Basic English understood. Recently refurbished breakfast room on the first floor. 2 other lounges, 1 with TV, plus meeting room with minitel (1F50/min.). Elevator not wheelchair-accessible. All rooms have shower and toilet. Singles 300-330F. Doubles 400F. Triples 500F. Extra bed 40F, only with double. Breakfast 25F. MC, V.

Hôtel Bretagne, 87, rue des Archives (tel. 48 87 83 14). M. Temple or Arts-et-Métiers. From M. Temple walk opposite traffic down rue du Temple, turn left on rue de Bretagne and right on rue des Archives. Pleasantly located across from square du Temple. The glitz of the mirrored entryway quickly disappears as you climb the stairs. Light sleepers should ask for rooms on higher floors to avoid street noise. Two small lounges. Wide price range reflects range in room quality. Cheaper rooms are simple, while more expensive ones have TVs and snazzy new bathroom fixtures. The one shower is free for those (on any of the 5 floors) without one. Reception open 24 hrs., but the receptionist before 7pm doesn't speak English. Singles 155F, with bath, toilet, and TV 300F. Doubles 195F, with bath, toilet, and TV 350F; 2-bed double 210F. Triples 330F, with bath, toilet, and TV 500F. Quad 440F, with bath, toilet and TV 600. Breakfast 30F. No credit cards.

Hôtel Paris France, 72, rue de Turbigo (tel. 42 78 00 04, reservations 42 78 64 92; fax 42 71 99 43). M. République or Temple. From M. République take rue de Turbigo and hotel is on left. The lobby, and to a lesser extent the rooms, are feebly lit at night. Windows provide inadequate protection from the very noisy rue de Turbigo, though higher rooms are somewhat quieter. Tiny showers, but roomy tiled baths. Thinking of taking a room with no shower? Be warned: no other showers at all. Toilets on every floor. English spoken passably during the day, less well at night. Elevator not wheelchair-accessible. Singles or doubles 220F, with shower 280F, with bath, toilet, and TV 350F. Extra bed 100F. Breakfast 25F. MC, V, AmEx.

■ FOURTH ARRONDISSEMENT

Limned by Les Halles to the west and the Bastille to the east, the 4ème *arrondissement* has emerged in recent years as a pivot for often upscale, alternative nightlife. Meanwhile, small cobblestoned squares and medieval aristocratic residences flavor the byways of this *quartier*. This portion of the city, referred to as the Marais, served as trotting ground for the Parisian nobility until well into the 17th century. Since then it has been a centerpiece for the city's Jewish community. On either side of the rue de Rivoli, a web of narrow streets and alleyways harbor galleries, boutiques, and overflow crowds from local bars; the 4ème is a great place to get lost. Hotels and hostels here provide travelers with an ideal base to explore the Pompidou and Seine islands.

Castex Hôtel, 5, rue Castex (tel. 42 72 31 52; fax 42 72 57 91). M. Bastille or Sully-Morland. Exit M. Bastille on bd. Henri IV and take the third right on rue Castex. Affable family management tends to these tidy, streamlined rooms. TV room on main floor. English spoken. Check-in 1pm. Singles with shower 215F, with shower and toilet 235-265F. Doubles with shower 280F, with shower and toilet 300-330F. 2-bed doubles with shower and toilet 310-320F, with bath and toilet 340F. One triple with bath and toilet 440F. Extra bed for adolescent 70F, for baby 30F. Breakfast 25F. Reserve 7-8 weeks in advance. Reserve with 1 night's deposit by check in francs or by credit card. MC, V.

Hôtel de la Herse d'Or, 20, rue St-Antoine (tel. 48 87 84 09). M. Bastille or St-Paul. Exit M. Bastille on rue St-Antoine and continue for about two blocks. Built around an enclosed courtyard, hotel offers refurbished rooms off taxi-yellow hallways. Expect pared-down decor and only rudimentary English from the desk clerk. Singles and doubles 150F, with toilet 190F, with toilet and shower 250F, with toilet and bath 270F. Triples with toilet and shower 375F, with toilet and bath 405F. Room rates fall 10% Nov.-May. Breakfast 25F. Reserve 1-3 days in advance.

Hôtel Practic, 9, rue d'Ormesson (tel. 48 87 80 47; fax 48 87 40 04). M. St-Paul or Bastille. From M. St-Paul cross to the opposite side of rue de Rivoli and walk opposite traffic; turn left on rue de Sévigné and right on rue d'Ormesson. Clean, practical little rooms make good on the hotel's name. Travelers should opt for those with views of the quaint, cobblestoned pl. du Marché-Ste-Catherine. If the petulant pink spreads don't thrill, the location and price will. No elevator. Basic English spoken. Singles with toilet 150F. Doubles with toilet 230F, with shower 275F, with toilet, shower, and bath 340F. Free showers for guests in rooms without them. Breakfast 25F, served 7-11am. No credit cards.

Hôtel Sansonnet, 48, rue de la Verrerie (tel. 48 87 96 14; fax 48 87 30 46). M. Hôtel-de-Ville or Châtelet. Walk down rue du Temple with your back to the Hôtel de Ville and turn left on rue de la Verrerie. Clean, breezy rooms close to the Centre Pompidou. No elevator. English spoken. Singles 240-250F, with shower 280F, with shower and toilet 335F, with bath and toilet 360F. Doubles with toilet and shower 345F, with toilet and bath 370F. Showers 20F. Breakfast 32F. Reserve 3 weeks in advance. MC, V.

Hôtel Andréa, 3, rue St-Bon (tel. 42 78 43 93). M. Châtelet or Hôtel-de-Ville. Exit M. Châtelet on rue de Rivoli, cross bd. Sébastopol and take your third left on rue St-Bon. It's just as well they have an elevator, since travelers in cheaper rooms must descend to use the common shower on the 1st floor. TV in rooms with shower or bath. Rooms face Pizza Hut or a gray wall. Located on a quiet side street near sights. Singles 190-200F, with toilet and shower or bath 250-290F. Doubles with toilet and shower 310-330F. Extra bed 60F. Showers 15F. Breakfast 30F. Reserve 1 night in advance with check in FF. Cheaper doubles without bathrooms can't be reserved by phone.

Hôtel de la Place des Vosges, 12, rue de Birague (tel. 42 72 60 46; fax 42 72 02 64). M. Bastille. From the metro take the third right off rue St. Antoine. Trip through the medieval throw-back lobby and head upstairs for rooms with modern-day cleanliness and comfort. English spoken. TV in all rooms. During summer months rooms on higher floors are steam baths. Elevator. Singles with toilet and shower 305F, with toilet and bath 415F. Doubles with toilet and bath 420F. 2-bed doubles with toilet and bath 440F. One quad on top floor 680F. Extra beds for children under 12 110F. Breakfast 40F. Reserve 2-6 months ahead. MC, V, AmEx.

Grand Hôtel Jeanne d'Arc, 3, rue de Jarente (tel. 48 87 62 11; fax 48 87 37 31). M. St-Paul or Bastille. From M. St-Paul cross to the left side of rue de Rivoli and walk opposite traffic; turn left on rue de Sévigné and right on rue de Jarente. Elegant, newly redecorated rooms (all with double beds) offer solace to those travelers who can afford them. Quads are an attractive, affordable option for groups of 4-5. Passable English spoken. Elevator. 2 rooms on ground floor handicapped-accessible. Cable TV. Singles or doubles with toilet and bath or shower 360-425F. Triples with toilet and bath or shower 500F. Quads with toilet and bath or shower 550F. Extra bed 75F. Breakfast 35F. Reserve at least 6 weeks in advance. MC, V.

Hôtel de Nice, 42bis, rue de Rivoli (tel. 42 78 55 29; fax 42 78 36 07). M. Hôtel-de-Ville. From the metro walk opposite traffic on rue de Rivoli for about four blocks;

the hotel is on the left. Recently, lavishly refurbished. Decorative flamboyance cuts between cute and kitsch: dancing cupids, a swish of crimson, a dab of mauve. Sparkling bathrooms and lots of light. Singles and doubles with toilet 340F, with shower or bath 360-380F, depending upon the view. Pricier rooms face rue de Rivoli. Triples with toilet and bath 450F. Breakfast 30F. Extra bed 80F. Reserve a month in advance for summer. Reserve with 1 night's deposit. MC, V.

Hôtel du 7ème Art, 20, rue St-Paul (tel. 42 77 04 03; fax 42 77 69 10). M. St-Paul. From the metro walk opposite traffic on rue du Prévôt, turn left on rue Charlemagne and right on rue St-Paul. For the French, the "7th art" is film-making; this hotel is a theme-park for golden-era film buffs. Stills from Hollywood classics plaster the walls. Sculpted red couches in the lobby. Otherwise, the hotel borrowed its color scheme from a black-and-white movie. Smallish rooms, all with phone, safe-deposit box and cable TV. Singles 295F, with toilet and shower or bath 395-450F. Doubles with toilet and shower or bath 395-450F. Extra bed 100F. Breakfast 35F. Reserve with deposit 1-2 months in advance. MC, V, AmEx.

Hostels

Hôtel des Jeunes (MIJE) (tel. 42 74 23 45; fax 42 74 08 93) books stays in "Le Fourcy," "Le Fauconnier," and "Maubuisson." All 3 are first-rate *foyers* located in former aristocratic residences of the Marais, close to sights and to one another. All give priority to groups of 10 or more (but no group discounts), and help organize educational tours; call well ahead. No smoking. All three have with public phones, although only those in le Fourcy permit international calls. For groups, no age specifications or limits on length of stay. Individuals must be 18-30 and have a 7-day maximum. Reception open 7am. English spoken. Check out by noon. Lockout noon-4pm. Silence after 10pm. No entry to hostels after 1am. 115F per person. Shower in room, toilet down the hall, breakfast served 7:30-10am—all included. The budget **Restaurant la Table d'Hôtes,** entered through le Fourcy, offers a 1-course meal (25F) and 3-course "hosteler special" (50F). Open 11:30am-1:30pm and 6:30-8:30pm. Lockers 2F in each hostel. Individuals may reserve rooms only in person and by paying in full in advance. Rebooking must be requested before 10pm the day before. Groups may reserve 1 year in advance.

Le Fourcy, 6, rue de Fourcy. M. St-Paul. From the metro walk opposite traffic for a few meters down rue François-Miron and turn left on rue de Fourcy. Hostel surrounds a large courtyard ideal for meeting travelers or for open-air picnics. In summer, school groups raise Cain under evening skies; light sleepers beware of rooms on the courtyard. Elevator makes 3 floors accessible to slim wheelchairs.

Le Fauconnier, 11, rue du Fauconnier. M. St-Paul or Pont Marie. From M. St-Paul walk opposite traffic on rue du Prevôt, turn left on rue Charlemagne and take the first right on rue du Fauconnier. A luxury in modern hostelry, with spacious rooms of 3, 4, and 8 beds.

Maubuisson, 12, rue des Barres. M. Hôtel-de-Ville or Pont Marie. Exit M. Hôtel-de-Ville on rue de Lobau. Walk away from rue de Rivoli and take the first left through pl. St-Gervais (in front of the church); keep left on rue François-Miron and take the first right on rue des Barres. A former girls' convent, lively Maubuisson offers smaller rooms of 2- 7 beds. Faces St-Gervais monastery.

■ FIFTH ARRONDISSEMENT

With the Sorbonne as its focal point, the 5ème *arrondissement* is a bookish neighborhood with the feel of a bustling village. Wander its café-filled squares and outdoor markets, take in a movie, and then launch yourself on its unparalleled nightlife. Most hotels fill up for August far in advance. Try to reserve rooms at least a month ahead.

Hôtel d'Esmeralda, 4, rue St-Julien-le-Pauvre (tel. 43 54 19 20; fax 40 51 00 68). M. St-Michel. Walk along the Seine on quai St-Michel and turn right at the park. Romantic hotel with homey, traditionally furnished rooms and the best view of Notre-Dame on the Left Bank. Right next to the bookstore Shakespeare and Co. English spoken. Singles 160F, with shower 320F. Doubles with shower 420-490F.

Triples with shower and toilet 550F. Quads with shower and toilet 600F. Breakfast 40F. Shower 10F.

Hôtel St-Jacques, 35, rue des Ecoles (tel. 43 26 82 53; fax 43 25 65 50). M. Maubert-Mutualité. Walk up rue des Carmes and turn right on rue des Ecoles. Clean, quiet hotel, with a bit of peeling paint on the ceilings. Impressive lobby with a glass chandelier and red carpet. English spoken. Elevator. Singles 220F, with shower or bath and toilet 405F. Doubles with shower 300F. Twins with shower 465F. Triples with shower 535F. Shower 25F. Breakfast 30F. MC, V, Amex.

Hôtel des Médicis, 214, rue St-Jacques (tel. 43 54 14 66). M. Luxembourg. From the metro take rue Royer-Collard and turn right on rue St-Jacques. Rooms are in better repair than the lobby, but luxury is not bought this cheaply in Paris. Young, energetic clientele. Located near cafés and groceries. Singles and doubles 75-150F, with toilet 160F. Showers 10F. Reception open 9am-10pm.

Hôtel des Grandes Ecoles, 75, rue Cardinal Lemoine (tel. 43 26 79 23; fax 43 25 28 15). M. Cardinal Lemoine. From the metro take a left on rue Cardinal Lemoine in the direction of the Panthéon. The place to go all-out on a hotel in Paris. Built around a flower garden where guests breakfast in warm weather, this ivy-covered establishment maintains impeccably clean, tasteful rooms to the great pleasure of its faithful guests. Singles 450F, with shower 480F. Doubles 530F, with shower 550F. Several smaller, less well-equipped rooms available as singles or doubles 320-350F. Breakfast 40F. Reserve well ahead. MC, V.

Hôtel des Alliés, 20, rue Berthollet (tel. 43 31 47 52; fax 45 35 13 92), off bd. Port Royal. M. Censier-Daubenton. Walk down rue Monge in the direction of bd. Port-Royal, turn right on rue Claude Bernard and left on rue Berthollet. Not as scenic or well-located as other hotels in the 5ème, but offers very cheap, clean, comfortable rooms. Street tends to be a little noisy. Singles 135-145F. Doubles 180-220F, with shower and toilet 295F. Showers 15F. Breakfast 28F. MC, V.

Hôtel Gay Lussac, 29, rue Gay-Lussac (tel. 43 54 23 96). M. Luxembourg. From the metro walk down rue Gay-Lussac to rue St-Jacques; hotel is across the street at the intersection. Clean, sunny rooms with sculpted plaster ceilings. An old but well-preserved hotel on a noisy street. Renovations now in progress will furnish all rooms with showers. Brand-new elevator. Tour groups limit available space. Doubles and singles 150-230F, with shower 250-350F. Triples or quads with shower and toilet 500F. Breakfast 25F. Reserve by phone; no deposit required.

Grand Hôtel du Progrès, 50, rue Gay-Lussac (tel. 43 54 53 18). M. Luxembourg. Multilingual proprietors provide a warm welcome. Clean, bright rooms with great windows and simple decor. Charming annexes on the top floor overlook the Panthéon. Plant-filled breakfast room has a piano and a small library (for your travel literature needs). Singles 148-170F, with shower and toilet 310F. Doubles 240F, with shower and toilet 330F. Triples 285F. Shower 15F. Breakfast included.

Hôtel de Nevers, 3, rue de l'Abbé-de-l'Epée (tel. 43 26 81 83). M. Luxembourg. From the metro walk down rue Gay-Lussac and turn right on rue de l'Abbé-de-l'Epée. Run by a spritely retired couple, this 6-story hotel on a quiet street offers clean rooms, renovated bathrooms, and a view of the Panthéon. Some saggy beds. Singles 140-150F. Doubles 200-240F, with shower 270-280F. Triples with shower and toilet 350F. Showers 15F. Breakfast 20F. Reserve with 1 night's deposit.

Hôtel Marignan, 13, rue du Sommerard (tel. 43 54 63 81). M. Maubert-Mutualité. Turn left on rue des Carmes and right on rue du Sommerand. Quiet, spacious rooms, many recently renovated with fresh paint and handmade cabinets. Laundry room and a breakfast room where residents can bring their own food for meals during the day. Singles 180F. Doubles 270-310F. Triples 360-390F. Quads 430-460F. Breakfast included. Reserve far in advance, though the Californian proprietress saves some rooms for unexpected arrivals. Group discounts in winter.

Hôtel le Central, 6, rue Descartes (tel. 46 33 57 93). M. Maubert-Mutualité. Walk up rue Cardinal Lemoine and take a right on rue Clovis, then another right on rue Descartes. Small hotel on a café-rich *place* that's party-central at night. Some bright rooms face the street. Some low, squishy beds. Singles 150-195F. Doubles with shower 210-240F. Triples with folding bed for same price as doubles.

Hôtel Gerson, 14, rue de la Sorbonne (tel. 43 54 28 49). M. Cluny-Sorbonne. Left on bd. St-Michel, then left on rue des Ecoles and right on rue de la Sorbonne.

Location across from the Sorbonne and bright, clean rooms more than compensate for lackluster, mismatched furnishings. Singles 210F, with bathroom and shower 280F. Doubles 250F, with bathroom and shower 310-360F. Shower 20F. Breakfast 25F. MC, V.

Hostels and Foyers

Young and Happy (Y&H) Hostel, 80, rue Mouffetard (tel. 45 35 09 53; fax 47 07 22 24). M. Monge. Cross rue Gracieuse and take rue Ortolan to rue Mouffetard. Clean, cramped rooms. Lively hostel in the heart of the raucous student quarter on rue Mouffetard. Claustrophobes beware the serpentine staircase and tight hallways. Rooms with 2-6 beds (mostly bunks). Lockout 11am-5pm. Curfew 1am. 95F per night, 600F per week. Breakfast and shower included. Sheets 12F. Towels 20F. Reserve with 1 night's deposit; otherwise show up at 8am.

Centre International de Paris (BVJ): Paris Quartier Latin, 44, rue des Bernardins (tel. 43 29 34 80; fax 42 33 40 53). M. Maubert-Mutualité. Walk down bd. St-Germain to rue Monge and turn right on rue des Bernardins. 137 beds. Spacious, spotless ultra-modern hostel with tile and chrome decor. Filled with a friendly, boisterous crowd. Photocopier, typewriter, and kitchen available to guests. No families. Rooms available at 2:30pm. Reception open 6am-2am. Doubles, triples, and quads 120F per person. Breakfast and showers included. Singles 130F. Lockers 10F. Reservations made through the **Centrale de Réservation** of the **Bureau des Voyages de la Jeunesse,** 20, rue J.-J.-Rousseau, 1er (tel. 42 36 88 18; fax 42 33 40 53). Students may stay from one month to a year; call for info and prices.

Laundromats

Lavabo, 214bis rue St-Jacques. Detergent 2F, wash 20F per 6kg, dry 60F. **Laverie,** 36 rue des Bernardins. Detergent 2F, wash 20F per 6kg, dry 2F per 5 min. Open daily 7am-10pm. **Laverie,** 8 rue l'Arrey. Detergent 2F, wash 20F per 6kg, dry 2F per 5 min. Open daily 8am-9pm.

■ SIXTH ARRONDISSEMENT

Marked by the art galleries centered around the Ecole des Beaux Arts, by the scholars from the *quartier latin,* and by the trafficked boulevards that border and cross it, the *6ème arrondissement* is lively, central, and often expensive. Budget hotels are sparse in this chic neighborhood, stretching from the Seine to bd. Montparnasse, but the following exceptions provide surprising bargains. Residential pockets and small side-streets mean that you can find a tranquil hotel one block away from a part of the city that never sleeps.

Hôtel Nesle, 7, rue du Nesle (tel. 43 54 62 41). M. Odéon. From the metro walk up rue de l'Ancienne Comédie and onto rue Dauphine; take a left on rue du Nesle. The Egyptianesque frescoes, ducks in the rose garden, warm, outgoing management and outrageously low price make for a whimsical departure from the monotony of Paris' like-seeming budget hotels. Many of the quiet, clean rooms display murals depicting the history of Paris. One of the best hotels on the Left Bank. Laundry. Singles with breakfast and shower 200F. Doubles 160F, with breakfast and shower 260-350F. Toilets in the hall if not in your room. Shower 25F. Breakfast 25F. No reservations; arrive around 10am.

Hôtel Stella, 41, rue Monsieur-le-Prince (tel 43 26 43 49; fax 43 54 97 28). M. Odéon or Luxembourg. From M. Odéon walk down rue Dupuytren and take a left on rue Monsieur-le-Prince. While the office can be a steam bath in summer, wood-trimmed bedrooms are pleasant and breezy. Singles with toilet and shower 198F. Doubles with toilet and shower 274F. Reserve by fax or telephone.

Hôtel St-Michel, 17, rue Git-le-Coeur (tel. 43 26 98 70). M. St-Michel. From pl. St-Michel walk one block on rue St-André-des-Arts and turn right on rue Git-le-Coeur. Comfortable (if bland) rooms just steps away from the Seine on a quiet street. Friendly staff. Curfew 1am. Singles 205F, with shower 305F, with shower and toilet 345F. Doubles 230F, with shower 330F, with shower and toilet 370F. 2-bed doubles with shower 380F, with shower and toilet 410F. Shower 12F. Breakfast included. Reserve with 1 night's deposit.

Hôtel St-André des Arts, 66, rue St-André-des-Arts (tel. 43 26 96 16; fax 43 29 73 34). M. Odéon. From the metro take rue de l'Ancienne Comédie, walk one block, and take first right on rue St-André-des-Arts. Beautiful, unusual fabric on walls, curtains, and bedding. Charming rooms and central location. Singles 220F, with shower 285-320F. Doubles with shower 410F, with 2 beds and shower 430F. Triples with double bed, single bed, and shower 500F, with 2 double beds and shower 520F. All rooms have toilets. Breakfast included. MC, V.

Hôtel de la Faculté, 1, rue Racine (tel. 43 26 87 13; fax 46 34 73 88). M. Cluny-Sorbonne. Walk down bd. St-Michel away from the Seine until you find rue Racine on your right. Small, clean rooms, each with balcony, private shower and toilet. Elevator. Singles or doubles 325-360F. Extra bed 85F. Breakfast 28F. MC, V.

Hôtel Petit Trianon, 2, rue de l'Ancienne Comédie (tel. 43 54 94 64). M. Odéon. Tiny, clean, whitewashed rooms on a sometimes noisy *place.* Singles 170F. Doubles with shower 300-320F, with shower and toilet 370F. Showers 25F. Breakfast 30F. Reserve at least 1 week in advance with 1 night's deposit.

Dhely's Hotel, 22, rue de l'Hirlondelle (tel. 43 26 58 25). M. St-Michel. On the west side of pl. St-Michel, through the archway and down the stairs, just steps from the Seine. Wood panelling, flower boxes, modern facilities, and a quiet location make for a pleasant stay. Singles 210F. Doubles 320F, with shower 410F. Triples 440F, with shower and toilet 550F. Showers 25F. Breakfast included except in high season when it costs 30F. Extra bed 100F. Reserve with deposit. MC, V, AmEx.

Hôtel du Dragon, 36, rue Dragon (tel. 45 48 51 05; fax 42 22 51 62). M. St-Germain-des-Prés. The justifiably proud owner of this hotel in the chic-er part of the 6ème has appointed all rooms with Victorian bird-and-flower wallpaper and with presumably antique furniture. Singles with shower 275F. Doubles with shower and toilet 390F. 2-bed doubles with shower and toilet 450F. Breakfast 28F. Open Sept.-July. MC, V. (AmEx only accepted for stays costing 2000F or more.)

Hôtel des Balcons, 3, rue Casimir Delavigne (tel. 46 34 78 50; fax 46 34 06 27). M. Odéon. Find rue Dupuytren off pl. Odéon and walk to the end; take a left on rue Monsieur-le-Prince and the first right on rue Casimir Delavigne. Classy façade and lobby, redone in 1993. Many clean, airy rooms renovated as well, some updated with unsettling color schemes. All rooms have toilet and a shower or bath. Singles 320-360F. Doubles 410-465F. Triples 535F. Elevator not wheelchair-accessible. Breakfast 40F. English spoken. Reservations welcome. MC, V.

Hostels

Foyer International des Etudiantes, 93, bd. St-Michel (tel. 43 54 49 63). M. Luxembourg. Across from Jardin du Luxembourg. Marbled reception area library, TV lounge, kitchenettes, and laundry facilities are all fit with elegant wood panelling. Spacious and comfortable. Some rooms have balconies. Oct.-June women only; singles 133F, doubles 82F per person, breakfast and shower included; *foyer* open Sun.-Fri. 6am-1:30am, Sat. all night. July-Sept.: men and women; singles 155F, doubles 105F per person, breakfast and shower included; *foyer* open 24 hrs. Reserve in writing 2 months in advance, 200F deposit if confirmed. Call ahead or arrive around 9:30am to check for no-shows.

Laundromats

Julice Laverie, 24, rue Monsieur le Prince. M. Cluny-Sorbonne or Odéon. Wash 20F per 6kg, 40F per 12kg. Dry 5F per 5min. Open daily 7:30am-9:30pm.

■ SEVENTH ARRONDISSEMENT

Budget hotels cluster around the western edge of the 7ème *arrondissement,* all advertising (though not all providing) rooms with views of the Eiffel Tower. Frequented by business travelers and older couples, hotels in this quarter are quieter and more expensive. Pay a little more and enjoy telephones and TVs in most rooms, breakfast in bed, bathtubs, and the convenience of paying by credit card.

Hôtel de la Paix, 19, rue du Gros Caillou (tel. 45 51 86 17). M. Ecole Militaire, up av. Bosquet and left on rue de Grenelle. The only true budget hotel in the 7ème, and it shows. Worn carpets, soft mattresses, peeling paint, but fairly clean and quiet. English spoken. Reception open 9am-10pm. Get key if returning after 10pm. Check-out at noon. Singles 145F, with shower 210F. Doubles with shower 270, with shower and toilet 300-340F. Triples with shower and toilet 440F. Shower 15F. Breakfast 32F. Reservations recommended. Deposit required if you plan to arrive after 3pm, payable by travelers check in francs or dollars. Call ahead to make sure someone is at reception to greet you upon arrival.

Grand Hôtel Lévêque, 29, rue Cler (tel. 47 05 49 15; fax 45 50 49 36). M. Ecole Militaire. On festive rue Cler, amid *boucheries, charcuteries,* and fruit grocers. Small rooms with tiled bathrooms and wake-up-call service. Reception open 24 hrs. Singles and doubles 195-220F, with shower 285F, with shower and toilet 310F, with shower, toilet, and a view onto rue Cler 355F. Triples 420F. Extra bed 80F. Showers included. Breakfast 25F, served 7-11am. MC, V.

Hôtel Kensington, 79, av. de la Bourdonnais (tel. 47 05 74 00; fax 47 05 25 81). M. Ecole Militaire. Classy but not as expensive as other 7ème hotels. Bright, compact rooms all have TVs, shower or bath, and toilet. Beds with firm mattresses, classy spreads, and mirrored tile. Ground-floor rooms wheelchair-accessible. Singles 295F. Doubles 370F-400F. Two-bed doubles 370-470F. Breakfast 28F, served 7:30-11am in dining room or bedroom. Reservations recommended. MC, V, AmEx.

Royal Phare Hotel, 40, av. de la Motte-Picquet (tel. 47 05 57 30; fax 45 51 64 41). M. Ecole Militaire. Next to metro. Rainbow curtains and water-drop tile make these small rooms even more cheerful. TV in each room (hair dryer in some). Reception open 24 hrs. English spoken. Singles with shower and toilet 300F. Doubles with shower or bathtub and toilet 320-380F. Breakfast 30F, served 7-10am in room or in lobby. Reserve with 1-night's deposit. MC, V, AmEx.

Hôtel du Centre, 24bis, rue Cler (tel. 47 05 52 33; fax 40 62 95 66). M. Ecole Militaire. Across from the Grand Hôtel Lévêque on rue Cler. Dining room full of shiny copper pots is reminiscent of a farmhouse. Dark, small rooms are clean, if not new. Check-out noon. Elevator. Singles 220F, with shower 280F. Doubles with toilet 220-240F, with shower, toilet, and TV 350-380F. Triples with shower, TV, and toilet 450F. Breakfast 30F. Shower 10F. AmEx, MC, V.

Hôtel du Palais Bourbon, 49, rue de Bourgogne (tel. 45 51 63 32 or 47 05 29 26; fax 45 55 20 21). M. Varenne or Invalides. Near Musée Rodin down the road from Palais Bourbon. Familial atmosphere. Ultra-modern, ultra-slick bathrooms. Prices as high as the ceilings, but doubles are more affordable. English spoken. Reception open 24 hrs. Singles with shower 267F, with toilet and shower 310F, with toilet, shower, and TV 380. Doubles with shower 310F, with toilet, TV, and shower 380F. Singles with toilet, tub, TV, minibar, and double bed 448F. Doubles with all of the above 482F. 2-bed doubles with the works 510F. Triples with the works 636F. Quads with the works 720F. Showers 12F. Breakfast included. Reservations recommended. MC, V.

Hôtel du Champs de Mars, 7, rue du Champ de Mars (tel. 45 51 52 30). M. Ecole Militaire, off av. Bosquet. Wheelchair-accessible once you clear the 1st step. Attractive stock furnishings. Singles with toilet and shower 350F, with toilet, shower, and tub 380F. 2-bed doubles with tub and toilet 410F. Triples with tub and toilet 490F. Breakfast 35F, served in rooms or salon 7-10am. Reserve by phone and confirm in writing with 1 night's deposit. Closed for 15 days (roughly Aug. 10-25). MC, V.

■ EIGHTH ARRONDISSEMENT

The 8ème is more for jetsetters than for budget travelers. While you might spot a film-star at Fouquet's, or as she hops in a car outside Christian Dior, you'll be hard-pressed to find comfortable, affordable lodging nearby. The accommodations we list here are within budget, if without the service extras found in less exclusive neighborhoods.

Hôtel d'Artois, 94, rue La Boétie (tel. 43 59 84 12 or 42 25 76 65; fax
a stone's throw from the Champs-Elysées. M. St-Philippe de Roule;
metro take a left on rue la Boetie; the hotel is down the street on your righ
rug, has-been mattresses, but impeccable bathrooms. Plant-filled lobby
incense-scented breakfast room. English spoken. Someone always at desk. Sing
235F, with shower and toilet 385-405F. Doubles with shower 365F, with shower
and toilet 410-430F. Showers 20F. Breakfast 25F. Reservations recommended,
with deposit for late-night arrivals. MC, V.

Hôtel Wilson, 10, rue de Stockholm (tel. 45 22 10 85). M. St-Lazare. Walk up rue
de Rome; turn left on rue de Stockholm. No-frills hotel near Gare St-Lazare. Soft
mattresses, aged carpet, cracks in wallpaper—but at this price, what did you
expect? Bathrooms within rooms are newer. The occasional velvet chair offsets
drabness. Relatively spacious rooms. Singles 150-160F, with shower and toilet
220F. Doubles 170-220F, with shower and toilet 240F. Breakfast included.

Hostels and Foyers

UCJF (Union Chrétienne de Jeunes Filles) or **YWCA,** 22, rue Naples (tel. 45 22
23 49). M. Europe. From metro take Rue de Constantinople and turn left onto Rue
de Naples. Extremely organized, well-kept, homey environment. This *foyer*
accepts women for 3-day min. stay June-Sept. Spacious, airy rooms, hard wood
floors, large beds. Large oak-panelled common room with fireplace, VCR, theater
performance space, and family-style dining room with varied daily *menu*. Conge-
nial staff. In summer, singles 150 per day and 130F per person to share a double.
Sept.-May, the *foyer* caters to longer stays by women 18-24, breakfast and dinner
included in price. 1 week: singles 670F, doubles 572F. 1 month: doubles 2135-
2600F. All guests must pay 30F YWCA membership fee and 100F processing fee
to stay in YWCA *foyers* and *pensiones* worldwide. 200F key deposit returned to
you when you leave. Reception open Mon.-Fri. 9am-6:30pm, Sat.-Sun. 9:30am-
4:30pm. Curfew 12:30am, negotiable. Reserve space if you can (500F deposit
required). Other locations: 65 rue Orfila, 20ème (tel. 46 36 82 80; M. Gambetta),
and 168, rue Blomet, 15ème (tel. 45 33 48 21; M. Convention). Men should contact
the YMCA *foyer* **Union Chrétienne de Jeunes Gens,** 14 rue de Trévise, 9ème
(tel. 47 70 90 94).

■ NINTH ARRONDISSEMENT

The 9ème bridges some of Paris' wealthiest and most heavily touristic quarters—the
2ème and the 8ème—to the less tantalizing and less affluent 10ème and 18ème. There
are plenty of hotels here, but many in the northern half of the area are used by prostitutes and their customers. Avoid the M. Anvers, M. Pigalle, and M. Barbès-Rochechouart; use the Abbesses stop instead. Just a few streets south of bd. de Clichy and
rue Pigalle, the neighborhood shifts from red-light district to a quiet, diverse residential quarter. Pricier hotels line side streets near bd. des Italiens and bd. Montmartre.

Hôtel des Trois Poussins, 15, rue Clauzel (tel. 48 74 38 20). M. St-Georges. Uphill
on rue Notre-Dame-de-Lorette, right on rue H. Monnier, and right on rue Clauzel.
Quiet, family-owned hotel with lovely courtyard and clean rooms. No kids under
10. Singles 140-150F. Doubles with shower 220-240F, with shower and toilet
260F. Basic English. Showers 15F. Breakfast 25F. Reserve 2-4 weeks ahead.

Hôtel Beauharnais, 51, rue de la Victoire (tel. 48 74 71 13). M. le Peletier. Follow
traffic on rue de la Victoire; hotel is on left. Elegant array of beds, *armoires,* and
mirrors span the centuries and showcase owner's passion for antiques; no two
rooms are alike. Lots of calm, sun, and fresh flowers. Your mother would love it,
as you will. Singles and doubles with shower 300F, with shower and toilet 350F.
Triples with shower and toilet 465F. Breakfast 25F.

Hôtel des Arts, 7, cité Bergère (tel. 42 46 73 30; fax 48 00 94 42). M. Montmartre.
Walk uphill on rue du Faubourg Montmartre; turn right at no. 6 onto Cité Bergère.
Two rooms on ground floor decorated with owner's antiques. Recently renovated, sunny, and neat. While somewhat smaller than those on lower floor, top-
floor rooms have attic charm. All rooms have showers, TV, cable, and hair dryer.

...histle at you, it's probably the parrot out front. Elevator ...air. Singles with shower 345F, with bath 325F. Doubles ...h bath 380F. Triple 500F. Breakfast 28F. MC, V, AmEx.

...en, 21, rue Notre-Dame-de-Lorette (tel. 48 78 60 47; fax 42 ...ame-de-Lorette. Identically renovated pastel rooms, all very ...rooms; TVs in rooms. Automated wake-up calls. Rooms on ...evator. Lovely breakfast salon, a faithful variation on peach- ...glish spoken. Doubles with shower and toilet 350F-360F. ...ads 480F. Reserve 1-2 weeks ahead. Breakfast 25F. MC, V.

..., cité Bergère (tel. 42 46 73 30; fax 48 00 95 69). M. Rue ...phill on rue du Faubourg Montmartre and turn right at no. 6 onto cité ... Not elegant, but clean, with high ceilings and decent beds. Rooms are a definite improvement over fraying green hallway runners. Some English spoken. TVs in some rooms. Singles and doubles 180-200F. Singles and doubles with shower and toilet 300F, with bath and toilet 320F. Triples with shower and toilet 420F. Quads 510F. 1 common shower, 10F. Breakfast 28F. Reserve 2 weeks in advance. Accepts foreign traveler's checks. MC, V, AmEx.

■ TENTH ARRONDISSEMENT

In response to the voluminous traffic that pours through the Gare de l'Est and the Gare du Nord, quite a few inexpensive hotels have set up shop in the 10ème. In fact, the supply often exceeds demand, making this a good place to look if you've struck out elsewhere. Some portions of this multi-ethnic residential quarter have been hard hit by France's current recession. The most gloomy and depressed areas are found north of the Gare du Nord, particularly along bd. de Magenta heading toward M. Barbès. These hotels are far from sights and nightlife, so you'll have to use taxis once the metro stops running.

Palace Hôtel, 3, rue Bouchardon (tel. 42 06 59 32). M. Strasbourg/St-Denis. Follow bd. St-Denis away from the large arch, past the smaller arch at the top of rue St-Martin, turn left on rue René Boulanger and left on rue Bouchardon. A friendly family business, with lots of young students passing through. Small, cheerful rooms off a dark hallway, many of which face a plant-filled courtyard. Lots of sunny doubles and triples. Safe back-street location close to a laundromat and a supermarket. English spoken. Singles 100F. Doubles 140F, with shower and toilet 230F, with bath and toilet 250F. Triples 180F, with shower and toilet 280F. Quad 230F, with shower and toilet 350F. Breakfast 20F. Reserve two weeks in advance in summer. V.

Cambrai Hôtel, 129bis, bd. de Magenta (tel. 48 78 32 13; fax 48 78 43 55). M. Gare du Nord. Follow traffic on rue de Dunkerque to pl. de Roubaix and turn right on bd. de Magenta. Just steps away from the *gare*. Clean, airy rooms with high ceilings. Beds are wide and firm. Large clean showers. Some English spoken. Singles 133F, with shower 204F. Doubles 181F, with shower 227F, with shower and toilet 228-251F. Triples 344F, with shower 367F. 2-room suite for 4 with shower 367F. Showers 20F. Breakfast included.

Hôtel Sibour, 4, rue Sibour (tel. 46 07 20 74; fax 46 07 37 17). M. Gare de l'Est. Walk straight from the *gare* on bd. de Strasbourg and turn left on rue de Sibour before church. Small, well-lit rooms. TVs in rooms with shower or bath. Reasonably clean with new wallpaper and stream-lined fixtures ordered from the stockhouse of budget accommodations. Refurbished breakfast salon. Some ground-floor rooms are wheelchair-accessible. Some English spoken. Singles and doubles 190F, with toilet 210F, with shower and toilet 280F. Triples 275F, with shower and toilet 355F. Quads 375F. Showers 15F. Breakfast 25F. MC, V.

Hôtel Métropole Lafayette, 204, rue Lafayette (tel. 46 07 72 69). M. Louis Blanc. On the far side of the triangular island near metro. Quite loud unless you get one of the few rooms with double glazing. Labyrinthine staircase. Some bedspreads have holes, and not all bedside lamps work. Make sure to see your room before taking it. Otherwise clean, with friendly reception. Some English spoken. Singles 110F, with shower 150F. Doubles 130F, with shower 180F, shower and toilet

200F. Triples with shower 230F, shower and toilet 250F. Showers 25F. Breakfast 15F. MC, V, AmEx.

Hôtel des Familles, 216, rue du Faubourg St-Denis (tel. 46 07 76 56). M. Gare du Nord. From the *gare* walk opposite traffic parallel to its main entrance, go left at the corner on rue du Faubourg St-Denis, and walk a while. Dark lobby and spare, well-lit rooms; big beds and hot showers. Shutters on ground-level rooms are locked shut for safety. Singles 130-150F, with shower 270-320F. Doubles 180-220F, with shower 270-320F. Triples 270F, with shower and toilet 350F. Quad 320F, with shower and toilet 350F. Showers 20F.

■ ELEVENTH ARRONDISSEMENT

The 11ème is a crazyquilt of alterno-chic, urban decay, family businesses, and final sales. Inexpensive hotels cluster around the Opéra Bastille, providing travelers with easy access to nightclubs, bars, record stores, and other signs of misspent youth. Other budget hotels rim the place de la République, a touristed transportation hub; watch your wallet. The area north of av. de la République near M. St-Maur, M. Couronnes, and M. Belleville can be quite dangerous.

A few metro stops away from major museums and sights, hotels here tend to have vacancies in July and August. The *arrondissement's* large-sized youth hostels are generally well-equipped and popular year-round.

Hôtel Rhetia, 3, rue du Général Blaise (tel. 47 00 47 18; fax 42 61 23 17). M. St-Ambroise, St-Maur, or Voltaire. From M. Voltaire, walk north on av. Parmentier, turn right on rue Rochebrune and take the next left onto rue du Général Blaise. Well-lit, tastefully decorated rooms overlook the square Maurice Gardette, a peaceful and child-filled park. The hotel is calm and the neighborhood is quiet, though not too far from the Opéra Bastille. Reception open Mon.-Fri. 7:30am-10pm, Sat.-Sun. and holidays 8am-10pm. Singles 170F, with shower or bath and toilet 210F. Doubles 190F, with shower or bath and toilet 230F. Triples 240F, with shower or bath and toilet 280F. Showers 10F. Breakfast 10F.

Hôtel de Nevers, 53, rue de Malte (tel. 47 00 56 18; fax 43 57 77 39). M. Oberkampf or République. From M. République, walk down the av. de la République and take a right on rue de Malte. Expect large, bright rooms, some recently redecorated with lace curtains and flowered wallpaper. The owners have lived in the U.S., love Americans, and speak English. Elevator! Singles 140F, with shower 210F, with shower and toilet 235F. Doubles 160F, with shower 210F, with shower and toilet 235F. 2-bed doubles with shower and toilet 250F. Triples 300F. Quads 350F. Showers 20F. Breakfast 22F, served in the rooms. Reserve by credit card or by check for one night's deposit. MC, V.

Plessis Hôtel, 25, rue du Grand Prieuré (tel. 47 00 13 38; fax 43 57 97 87), off av. de la République. M. Oberkampf or République. From M. Oberkampf, walk north on rue du Grand Prieuré; from M. République, walk south on av. République and turn right on rue du Grand Prieuré. Enthusiastic, English-speaking proprietors. Many of the hotel's 49 room are newly renovated, equipped with cable TV and modern bathrooms. Guests are invited to play the hotel's piano, located in one of its two lounges. If you stay more than three nights, you get 10% or more off the cost of your room. Singles 195F, with shower, toilet, and TV 265F. Doubles 195F, with shower, toilet, and TV 295F-350F. Triples with shower, toilet, and TV 350F. Showers included. Elevator. Continental breakfast 30F. Bigger, "American-style" breakfast 35F. Open Sept.- July. MC, V, AmEx.

Hôtel de Belfort, 37, rue Servan (tel. 47 00 67 33; fax 43 57 97 98). M. Père Lachaise, St-Maur, or Voltaire. From M. Père-Lachaise, walk west on rue du Chemin Vert and turn left on rue Servan. Especially attractive for its *Let's Go* backpacker special: only 100F per person per night in doubles, triples, and quads. All rooms with shower, toilet, phone, and TV. English spoken. Breakfast served in downstairs salon. Lizard King's tomb is a stone's throw away. Breakfast 15F with *Let's Go* special, served 7:30-9:30am. MC, V.

Hôtel de l'Europe, 74, rue Sedaine (tel. 47 00 54 38; fax 47 00 75 31). M. Voltaire. Walk north on bd. Voltaire and take a left on rue Sedaine. Clean, spacious rooms have suffered some wear. A very popular hotel among German tourists. Doubles 185F, with shower or bath 210F, with shower and toilet 230F, with bath and toilet 250F. Breakfast 20F. Shower 10F.

Hôtel Baudin, 113, av. Ledru-Rollin (tel. 47 00 18 91; fax 48 07 04 66). M. Ledru-Rollin. A clean and quiescent hotel with 20 big, recently renovated rooms. Only a few blocks from the Bastille. Check-out noon. Singles 160-200F, with shower 220F, with bath and toilet 250F. Doubles 200-220F, with shower 250F, with bath and toilet 300F. Extra bed 100F. Showers 20F. Breakfast 25F, served 7-11am. MC, V, AmEx.

Hôtel de Vienne, 43, rue de Malte (tel. 48 05 44 42). M. Oberkampf or République. From M. Oberkampf, exit at Crussol and turn left on rue de Malte; from M. République, walk down av. de la République and turn right on rue de Malte. Peaceful, pastel rooms with flowered curtains. Hotel has a familial atmosphere. No hall shower for those without one in their room. Singles 108F, bigger bed 133F. Doubles 161F, with shower 221F. Breakfast 30F. Open Sept.-July.

Hôtel Notre-Dame, 51, rue de Malte (tel. 47 00 78 76; fax 43 55 32 31). M. République. Walk down av. de la République and take a right on rue de Malte. 51 sunny rooms are quite clean and modern-like, if not brand-new. TV in more expensive rooms. English spoken. Check-out noon. Elevator. Singles 190F, with shower 230-280F, with shower or bath and toilet 330F. Doubles 190F, with shower 280F, with shower or bath and toilet 330F. Twins 360F. Extra bed 70F. Showers 20F. Breakfast 32F. MC, V.

Pax Hotel, 12, rue de Charonne (tel. 47 00 40 98; fax 43 38 57 81). M. Bastille or Ledru-Rollin. From M. Bastille walk east on rue du Faubourg St-Antoine and turn on rue de Charonne; from M. Ledru-Rollin, walk west on rue du Faubourg St-Antoine and turn onto rue de Charonne. Remember that Best Western in Kansas? Long hallways and immaculate, generic-looking rooms with TVs and hair dryers. All but three rooms come with bathrooms. Within steps of the nightlife, galleries, and budget restaurants that ring the opera house. Singles 200F, with shower 230F, with shower and toilet 250F. Doubles with shower and toilet 250F. Triples 300-360F. Quads 400F. Breakfast 30F in the breakfast room, 40F in bedrooms. Reserve by credit card or check a few days in advance. MC, V, AmEx.

Hôtel Beaumarchais, 3, rue Oberkampf (tel. 43 38 16 16; fax 43 38 32 86). M. Oberkampf or Filles du Calvaire. From M. Oberkampf exit on rue de Malte and turn right on rue Oberkampf; from M. Filles du Calvaire, walk one block south on bd. des Filles du Calvaire and turn left at rue Oberkampf. Newly refurbished interior with TV, shower or bath, and toilet in each room. Fluent English and German spoken. One room is wheelchair-accessible—call ahead. Singles 280F. Doubles 320-330F. 2-bed doubles 320F. Extra bed 120F. Breakfast 30F, free if you plan to stay more than 3 nights. MC, V, AmEx.

Hôtel de France, 159, av. Ledru-Rollin (tel. 43 79 53 22). M. Voltaire. Walk west on rue de la Roquette and then turn left on av. Ledru-Rollin. Good location near the opera house. Aged furnishings, decrepit plumbing, and moulting plaster help explain the cheap room-rates. Singles with shower 150F. Doubles with shower 200F, with bath 220F. Triples (with extra bed) with shower or toilet 280F. Breakfast 25F, served 7-9am. Call and confirm reservations in writing. MC, V.

Hostels

Auberge de Jeunesse "Jules Ferry" (HI), 8, bd. Jules Ferry (tel. 43 57 55 60). M. République. Walk east on rue du Faubourg du Temple and turn right on the far side of bd. Jules Ferry. About 100 beds. Wonderfully located. Clean, large rooms. Slightly crowded, friendly party atmosphere. Jovial, multilingual staff. Most spaces full by 10am. If they are full, they'll help you find other city lodgings; they work with the **Centrale de Réservations,** located at 4, bd. Jules Ferry. 3-night max. stay (sometimes extended during the winter). Reception open 24 hours. Cleaning lockout noon-2pm but reception staff always present to answer questions or accept membership cards for reservations. No curfew. Single-sex lodging, but can accommodate male/female couples; all members of a room are asked before it becomes coed. 4-6 bed rooms 105F per person. Doubles 115F per person. Showers and breakfast (self-serve 7-9:30am) included. Lockers 5F. Sheets 14F (paper as of summer 1994; by the winter of 1994-1995, they may have 25F cotton sheets). Wash 20F, dry 10F; no laundry soap available in the hostel. Basement bike storage.

Résidence Bastille (AJF), 151, av. Ledru-Rollin (tel. 43 79 53 86). M.Voltaire. Walk across the pl. Léon Blum and head south onto av. Ledru-Rollin. Slowly renovating, with 2-4 wooden bunks per room. About 170 beds. Recently redone triples and quads have bathrooms in the room. Older rooms use hall bathrooms. Less crowded and more subdued, but attractive rooms and a friendly multilingual staff. Ages 18-35 only, though not strictly enforced if you can climb up and down a bunk safely. Male/female couples can be accommodated in doubles (though only with the beds super-imposed). Reception open 7am-1am. Curfew 1am. Lockout noon-4pm. 113F. Showers, breakfast, and sheets included. No reservations, so arrive early in the morning. A welcoming station at the Gare du Nord, inside the suburban station (tel. 42 85 86 19) can make same-day reservations.

Maison Internationale des Jeunes, 4, rue Titon (tel. 43 71 99 21; fax 43 71 78 58). M. Faidherbe-Chaligny. Walk one block north on rue Faidherbe, turn right on rue de Montreuil, and then take your second left onto rue Titon. Well-located, exceptionally clean, airy, and tranquil, with a garden in back whose bushes hide a pair of pet bunnies. Except for 1st floor, not a bunkbed in sight. Big, bright, clean rooms with 2-8 beds for ages 18-30 (flexible). Especially beautiful new doubles, all in a relaxed atmosphere. Single-sex rooms, but exceptions made for traveling buddies, couples, and consenting groups who are 18 or over. Coed bathrooms. Family housing. Handicapped access. 3- or 4-day max. stay is fairly flexible. If full, they'll find you another place. Reception open 8am-2am. Lockout 10am-5pm. Curfew 2am. Quiet hours 10pm-8am. 110F. Showers and breakfast included. Sheets 15F for entire stay, or bring your own.

Auberge Internationale des Jeunes, 10, rue Trousseau (tel. 47 00 62 00; fax 47 00 33 16). M. Ledru-Rollin. Walk east on rue du Faubourg St-Antoine and turn left on rue Trousseau. Until recently the Hôtel Ste-Marguerite. None of the bathrooms have toilet seats. All are located off the hall unless you have a 6-bed room. Most rooms have 4 beds, though a few have 2 or 6. Safebox for valuables. Common rooms downstairs. Lockout 10am-3pm. 91F per person; Nov.-Feb. 81F per person. Breakfast and shower included. Sheets 5F. Show up at 8am to get a room. MC, V.

■ TWELFTH ARRONDISSEMENT

A shock of budget hotels ring the Gare de Lyon in the northwest corner of the 12ème; apart from train station riff-raff, this neighborhood is mostly safe. In the *arrondissement's* southeast corner, hotels are far enough from central Paris to be both cheap and quite comfortable. They also provide easy access to the Bois de Vincennes, a lovely park with jogging paths and an artificial lake.

Hôtel de Reims, 26, rue Hector Malot (tel. 43 07 46 18). M. Gare de Lyon. Walk east on bd. Diderot (away from the river) and take a left onto rue Hector Malot. Charming proprietress tends to the immaculate hotel and tree-filled courtyard. Breakfast in a familial, am-I-really-away-from-home dining room. Singles 170F. Doubles 200F, with shower 250F, with shower and 2 beds 320F, with shower and toilet 270F. Triples with shower 350-360F. Showers 25F. Breakfast 30F. Reserve by phone and confirm in writing. A good bet should you arrive in the city without reservations, but look respectable when you show up. Open Sept.-July.

Nièvre-Hôtel, 18, rue d'Austerlitz (tel. 43 43 81 51). M. Gare de Lyon or Quai de la Rapée. Walk away from the train station (and tracks) on rue de Bercy and take a right on rue d'Austerlitz. Slow-moving renovations, currently under way, promise youth to already pleasant, cheerful rooms. Resident cat presides at the entrance. High-ceilinged, often down-right big rooms. No large groups, please. Singles 160-180F. Doubles 200-220F, with shower 260F, with shower and toilet 300F. Showers 20F. Breakfast 20F. Call for reservations and confirm in writing, but space frequently available in summer.

Mistral Hôtel, 3, rue Chaligny (tel. 46 28 10 20). M. Reuilly-Diderot. Walk west on bd. Diderot and take a left onto rue Chaligny. A spectacularly clean, family-run hotel with a comfortable, homespun decor. Singles and doubles 200F, with shower 250F, with shower and toilet 250F. 2-bed doubles with shower 280F. Triples 295F. Quads 320-340F. Showers included. Breakfast 35F, served in rooms 7-10am. Call 7am-11pm to make reservations and confirm in writing. Often has space July-Aug.

Hôtel de l'Aveyron, 5, rue d'Austerlitz (tel. 43 07 86 86). M. Gare de Lyon, Quai de la Rapée, or Bastille. From Gare de Lyon, walk away from the train station (and tracks) on rue de Bercy and take a right on rue d'Austerlitz. Small, clean, and unpretentious rooms. Capacious bathrooms come stocked with towels. TV lounge downstairs in leather and chrome. English spoken. Singles and doubles 170F, with shower and toilet 245F. Triples 210F, with shower and toilet 290F. Quads with shower and toilet 320F. Hall showers included, making this a very good deal. Breakfast 15F. Reservations recommended. MC, V.

Hôtel du Stade, 111, bd. Poniatowski (tel. 43 43 30 38). M. Porte Dorée. 39 American-style, French-size rooms; bright, modern, and uniform, they leave nothing to be desired except a bit of space. Just a block from the Bois de Vincennes. Elevator. Singles and doubles with TV 180F, with shower 230F, with shower and toilet 260F. 2-bed doubles 190F. Extra bed 70F. Showers 20F. Breakfast 26F, served in rooms 6:45-9:30am. Best to reserve by phone 7am-8pm, though rooms are frequently available. MC, V.

Hôtel Printania, 91, av. du Dr. Netter (tel. 43 07 65 13). M. Porte de Vincennes. Walk west on the cours de Vincennes and turn left on av. du Dr. Netter. 25 spotless, sedate, modern rooms. Elevator after the first floor. Doubles 160F, with shower and toilet 210F, with shower, toilet, and TV 250F. Extra bed 40F. Showers 25F. Breakfast 25F, served 7-9am in rooms. Call for reservations. MC, V.

Grand Hôtel Chaligny, 5, rue Chaligny (tel. 43 43 87 04; fax 43 43 18 47). M. Reuilly-Diderot. Walk west on bd. Diderot and take a left onto rue Chaligny. Snazzy purple-and-blue designer bedspreads, TVs, telephones, and hair dryers in each of 43 rooms. While some rooms are dingy and some bedspreads patched, the whole is a respectable deal. Attracts tourists the world over. Coffee dispenser in lobby. Elevator. Singles and doubles 200F, with shower and toilet 280F, with bath and toilet 290F. 2-bed doubles with shower and toilet 300F, with bath and toilet 310F. Triples 350F. Quads 450F. Extra bed (matching the other bedspreads) 50F. Showers 25F. Breakfast 25-30F, served 7-10am. MC, V.

Modern's Hôtel, 11, rue d'Austerlitz (tel. 43 43 41 17 or 43 44 51 16). M. Gare de Lyon or Quai de la Rapée. From Gare de Lyon, walk away from the train station (and tracks) on rue de Bercy and take a right on rue d'Austerlitz. Cheap enough, clean enough, eclectically-decorated enough, but no great shakes. English spoken. Singles 130-140F, with shower 196F, with shower and toilet 210F. Doubles 140F, with shower 196F, with shower and toilet 210F. Extra bed 40F. Showers 15F. Breakfast 17F. Usually 10 rooms available per day.

Hôtel Jules-Cesar, 52, av. Ledru-Rollin (tel. 43 43 15 88; fax 43 43 53 60). M. Ledru-Rollin or Gare de Lyon. From M. Ledru-Rollin, exit onto av. Ledru-Rollin. Fancy bedspreads, nice mirrors, and bright, tiled bathrooms—and you pay for them. All rooms have toilets and shower or bath, but there is a wide range in bathroom size and quality, particularly among doubles; try to see one before settling in. Singles with shower and toilet 330-350F. Doubles with shower and toilet 350F. Extra bed 80F. Breakfast 30F. MC, V.

Hostels and Foyers

Centre International du Séjour de Paris: CISP "Ravel," 6, av. Maurice Ravel (tel. 44 75 60 06; fax 43 44 45 30). M. Porte de Vincennes. Walk east on cours de Vincennes, turn right on bd. Soult, left on rue Jules Lemaître, and right on av. Maurice Ravel. Large, institutional-looking, efficient hostel on the edge of the city. With 216 beds, it caters mostly to groups. Large rooms (most with 4 or fewer beds), bar, restaurant, and access to municipal pool next door (50% discount for guests, 15F). Flexible 3-day max. stay. Reception open daily 6:30am-1:30am. Singles 145F, rooms with 2 beds 122F. Breakfast included. Reserve a few days in advance. Self-serve restaurant open 7:30-9:30am, noon-1:30pm, and 7-8:30pm.

■ THIRTEENTH ARRONDISSEMENT

Hostels and Foyers

Association des Foyers de Jeunes: Foyer des Jeunes Filles, 234, rue de Tolbiac (tel. 44 16 22 22; fax 45 65 46 20). M. Glacière. From the metro walk 100m east on bd. Auguste Blanqui, turn right on rue de Glacière, then a left on rue de Tolbiac. Large, modern foyer for young women (ages 18-30) with excellent facilities—including kitchens on all floors, cable TV, washers, dryers, piano, exercise room, library, cafeteria, and garden. Run by exceptionally friendly, helpful staff. Sunny singles with a sink, desk, chairs, and closet space; their brick walls, however, connote either Alcatraz or the inside of a chimney. Excellent security. Reception open 24 hrs. July-Aug. 110F per night. Showers and breakfast (served 6:30-8:30am) included. Dinner 46F. Sept.-June 100F per night and 2950F per month; breakfast and dinner included. 30F registration fee (good for one year) required of all first-time visitors. There are usually vacancies in summer.

CISP "Kellerman," 17, bd. Kellerman. M. Porte d'Italie. From the metro turn right on bd. Kellerman. Institutional-looking hostel complex, affiliated with CISP Ravel in the 12ème. 248 beds. Rooms with 2-4 beds 127F per person; with 8 beds 101F per person. Singles with shower and toilet 173F. Doubles with shower and toilet 143F. Breakfast included, served 7-9:30am. Restaurant open 6:30-9:30pm. Some handicapped rooms; call for details.

Maison des Clubs UNESCO, 43, rue de Glacière (tel. 43 36 00 63; fax 45 35 05 96). M. Glacière. From the metro walk 100m east on bd. Auguste Blanqui and take a left on rue de la Glacière. Enter through garden on right. Small, no-extras rooms, some newly renovated. Run by helpful, multilingual management. Caters to tour groups. Reception open 7am-1:30am. Curfew 1:30am. Singles 151F. Doubles 131F per person. Triples 111F per person. Showers and breakfast included. Breakfast served 7:45-9am. No individual reservations.

■ FOURTEENTH ARRONDISSEMENT

Renowned for its nightlife, this commercial district just south of the *quartier latin* lured Picasso and his artistic circle from Montmartre. (What would Modigliani, Zadkine, Braque, Chagall, and Klee have said of the 200m giant the Tour de Montparnasse?) Today, areas closest to bd. du Montparnasse glimmer with vitality while adjoining neighborhoods, especially those around rue d'Alésia and rue Raymond Losserand, are residential and sedate. Sex-shops prosper at the northern end of av. du Maine (M. Gaîté). On the bright side, there are also an abundance of laundromats in this area.

Hôtel de Blois, 5, rue des Plantes (tel. 45 40 99 48; fax 45 40 45 62). M. Mouton-Duvernet. From metro take a left onto rue Mouton Duvernet and another left onto rue des Plantes. Unquestionably one of the best deals in Paris; these rooms, decked-out with full bathrooms, TVs, telephones, and pseudo-Laura Ashley décor, would go for twice the price if there were an elevator. Laundromat across the street. Doubles 220F, with bath or shower 250F, with shower and toilet 270F. Triples 350F. Shower 15F. Breakfast 25F. AmEx, MC, V.

Hôtel du Midi, 4, av. René-Coty (tel. 43 27 23 25; fax 43 21 24 58), off pl. Denfert-Rochereau. M. Denfert-Rochereau. A large, professionally run hotel that recalls a Holiday Inn. The lobby's fake wood veneer and cold tiles suggest a conference hotel. Antique headboards on queen-sized beds. Each rooms has TV and spotless bathroom. Doubles with shower and toilet 228-328F. Breakfast 30F. MC, V.

Hôtel Plaisance, 53, rue de Gergovie (tel. 45 42 11 39 or 45 42 20 33; fax 41 13 74 42). M. Pernety. Walk down rue Raymond Losserand and turn left on rue de Gergovie. On a quiet street in a dull neighborhood. The cheapest hotel in the 14ème. Institutional-looking, though clean and comfortable. Some fraying drapes and bedspreads. Singles 135F, with shower 190F, with shower and toilet 210F. Doubles 170F, with shower 210F, with shower and toilet 250F. Showers 20F. Breakfast 25F. MC, V, AmEx.

Hôtel du Parc, 6, rue Jolivet (tel. 43 20 95 54; fax 42 79 82 62). M. Montparnasse-Bienvenue. Take rue d'Odessa to rue de la Gaité and turn right on to rue Jolivet. Clean, spacious, and bright rooms. Some rooms overlook a tranquil courtyard, others a lively park. Singles 240F. Doubles with shower and toilet 350F. Shower 20F. Breakfast 20F. MC, V.

Ouest Hôtel, 27, rue de Gergovie (tel. 45 42 64 99; fax 45 42 46 65). M. Pernety. Turn right onto rue de Gergovie from rue Raymond Losserand. Mirrored, disco-like lobby gives way to paneled, gray carpeted rooms. Spotless bathrooms. Singles 120F. Doubles 160F, with shower 220F. 2-bed doubles 200F, with shower 230F. Showers 20F. Breakfast 20F. MC, V, AmEx.

Central Hôtel, 1bis, rue du Maine (tel. 43 20 69 15). M. Montparnasse-Bienvenue. Across from the Hotel du Parc. Modern, impeccably clean rooms, some with views of the adjacent park. TV in all rooms. Singles with bath 330F. Doubles with bath 365F, 2-bed doubles with bath 400F. Triples 430F. Breakfast 30F. MC, V.

Hostels and Foyers

FIAP Jean-Monet, 30, rue Cabanis (tel. 45 89 89 15; fax 45 81 63 91). M. Glacière. From métro, go down bd. St-Jacques, turn left at the 1st street (rue Ferrus), then right onto rue Cabanis. An international student center with 507 beds, mostly full of visiting American tour groups in summer. Comfortable, well-furnished rooms are impeccably maintained and equipped with toilet and shower. Offers disco and jazz concerts at night (free), French language classes, and stacks of tourist info, as well as 12 conference rooms, game room, laundry room, and cheap cafeteria (full meal 57F). Some rooms wheelchair accessible. 3-day max. stay. Singles 250F. Doubles 165F per person. Quads 145F per person. 8-bed rooms 120F per person. Open April-Sept. MC, V.

■ FIFTEENTH ARRONDISSEMENT

Because of the nearby Parc des Expositions, hotels of the 15ème fill with business-people who arrive in the tourist off-season for conventions and trade shows. During the summer, when the hall is closed, these hotels have many vacancies, and offer a quality of service found in few budget hotels of the central *arrondissements.*

Mondial Hôtel, 136, bd. de Grenelle (tel. 45 79 73 57 or 45 79 08 09; fax 45 79 58 65). M. La Motte-Grenelle. Near cafés, shops, and the metro. Bright and spacious, with saggy beds, modern showers, and great view of bd. de Grenelle. Singles with toilet 200F, with shower 220F. Doubles with toilet 240F, with shower 270F. Triple with toilet 280F, with shower 300F. Breakfast 20F. Shower 10F. MC, V.

Practic Hôtel, 20, rue de l'Ingénieur Keller (tel. 45 77 70 58; fax 40 59 43 75). M. Charles Michels. From pl. Charles Michels walk up rue Linois, take the next left and turn right on rue de l'Ingenieur Keller. The most elegant budget hotel in the 15ème. Modern, clean rooms with bedspreads worthy of a Sheraton, comfortable mattresses, vanities, and TVs. Doubles with toilet 250F, with shower 315F. Triples with shower and TV 420F. Breakfast 34F. Free showers. MC, V, AmEx.

Hôtel de l'Ain, 60, rue Olivier de Serres (tel. 45 32 44 33 or 45 32 49 36; fax 45 32 58 95). M. Convention. Walk down rue de la Convention and take the first right onto rue Oliver de Serres. On a quiet residential street. Clean, smallish rooms with whitewashed walls and plaid bedspreads. Pleasantly furnished breakfast room. Singles 140F. Doubles 200F, with shower 240F, with shower and toilet 260F. Twins with bath and toilet 320F. Triples with bath 360F. Breakfast 25F. MC, V.

Hôtel Printania, 142, bd. de Grenelle (tel. 45 79 23 97; fax 45 78 02 66). M. La Motte-Picquet-Grenelle. Located next to the metro. Friendly management greets you with fresh flowers in marbled lobby. Follow red-carpeted hallway up the winding staircase to rooms with red bedspreads and modern bathrooms. Singles with toilet 195F, with shower 230F, with shower and toilet 310F, with bath and toilet 350F. Doubles with toilet 240F, with shower 260F, with shower and toilet 350F, with bath and toilet 370F. Breakfast 30F. MC, V, AmEx.

Hostels and Foyers

Aloha Hostel, 1, rue Borromée (tel. 42 73 03 03), on a tiny side street across from 243, rue de Vaugirard. M. Volontaires. Despite the cheesy name, one of the best in the city. Newly renovated, quiet, and centrally located. Young but experienced management full of advice about Paris. Bright rooms with new beds, new mattresses, and freshly painted interiors have space for 2-4 guests. Top floor rooms have slanted roofs and good view of the *quartier*. Brand new kitchen facilities, communal refrigerator, café-style common room. Lockout 11am-5pm. 85F per person. 537F per person per week. Arrive at 9am or send 1 night's deposit for reservations.

Three Ducks Hostel, 6, pl. Etienne Pernet (tel. 48 42 04 05). M. Commerce. On the street to the right of the church. Without a doubt one of the most rowdy and fun hangouts in the city for young vacationing backpackers during the summer months. Has all the amenities (clean, though slightly run-down dorm-style rooms with bunkbeds for 2-8 people). Green, ivy-covered central courtyard becomes a loud, fun café hangout on summer nights when a young, mostly Anglo crowd drinks cheap beer from the hostel's watering hole, **Richie's Bar.** Flexible 1-week max. stay. Small kitchen. Lockout 11am-5pm. Curfew 1am. Nightly rate 93F. Weekly rate 630F. Reservations accepted with 1 night's deposit. Fabulous **Mountain Bike Trip** (tel. 48 42 57 87) tours of Paris begin here (see Getting Around). Mountain bike rental 90F per day.

■ SIXTEENTH ARRONDISSEMENT

Wealthy and residential, the 16ème may inconvenience budget tourists on several counts; though a short walk from the Eiffel Tower, accommodations require a 20-minute metro ride to the more renowned museums and traditional axes of Parisian nightlife. The area also has few of the groceries, open-air markets, and cheap restaurants abundant elsewhere. Nonetheless, hotels here are comparatively luxurious and apt to have vacancies in high season.

Hôtel Ribera, 66, rue La Fontaine (tel. 42 88 29 50; fax 42 24 91 33). M. Jasmin. Walk down rue Ribera to its intersection with rue La Fontaine. Various shades of pink complement various shades of brown in spacious, immaculate rooms. Safe, quiet, even sleepy neighborhood. Rooms with shower and toilet have TVs. Singles 200F, with shower 230F, with shower and toilet 270F. Doubles 230F, with shower 260F, with shower and toilet 310F. 2-bed doubles 250F, with shower 280F, with shower and toilet 330F. Breakfast 28F. MC, V, AmEx.

Villa d'Auteuil, 28, rue Poussin (tel. 42 88 30 37; fax 45 20 74 70). M. Michel-Ange-Auteuil. Walk up rue Girodet and take a left on rue Poussin. High-ceilinged, large rooms crammed with 2-star amenities (TV, shower, toilet, and telephone). Singles 280F. Doubles 310F. Triples 395F. Breakfast 30F. Reservations advised. MC, V.

Hôtel Résidence Chalgrin, 10, rue Chalgrin (tel. 45 00 19 91; fax 45 00 95 41). M. Argentine or Charles-de-Gaulle-Etoile. From M. Argentine walk down av. de la Grande Armée toward the Arc de Triomphe, take a right on rue Argentine and another right onto rue Chalgrin. Entryway and some rooms with tapestries and lovely antiques. Most rooms are dim, small, and quiet. Those with shower or bath and toilet have TVs. Dogs receive a warm welcome. Rooms with toilet 210F, with toilet and shower 320F, with toilet and bath 360F. Suite 430F. for April and Sept. Breakfast 30F. MC, V.

■ SEVENTEENTH ARRONDISSEMENT

The 17ème combines the elegance of its western neighbor Neuilly with the sordidness of its eastern neighbor pl. Pigalle; some of its hotels cater to prostitutes, others to visiting businesspeople and tourists. Safety is a concern where it bounds the 18ème, especially on bd. des Batignolles and near pl. de Clichy. Most of the hotels listed are found in safer enclaves of this district, near its southern border with the 16ème. Though far from the center city, they can be wonderful bargains.

Hôtel Belidor, 5, rue Belidor (tel. 45 74 49 91; fax 45 72 54 22). M. Porte Maillot. Go north on bd. G. St-Cyr; turn right on rue Belidor. Rooms face a peaceful, tiled courtyard. Modern and clean, with floral wallpaper and personality. Singles 150F, with shower 220F, with shower and toilet 270F. Doubles 180F, with shower 253F, with shower and toilet 303F. Two-bed doubles 280F, with shower 340F, with shower and toilet 410F. Breakfast included. Shower 20F. Open Sept.-July.

Hôtel Avenir-Jonquière, 23, rue de la Jonquière (tel. 46 27 83 41). M. Guy Moquet. A friendly hotel with attractive, clean, bright rooms. The neighborhood is fairly safe, though not wealthy. Singles 105F, with shower 145F, with shower and toilet 165F. Doubles 170F, with shower 220F, with shower and toilet 250F. Breakfast 25F. Shower 10F. Renovations may cause prices to increase in 1995.

Hôtel Riviera, 55, rue des Acacias (tel. 43 80 45 31; fax 40 54 84 08). M. Charles de Gaulle-Etoile. Walk north on av. MacMahon; turn left on rue des Acacias. Close to the Arc de Triomphe and Champs-Elysées. Don't be alarmed by the spareness of the lobby. Well-furnished, blue and pink rooms face patios and courtyards. All with large, comfortable beds and TVs. One of the best-located, most agreeable hotels in Paris. Singles 230F, with shower 270F, with shower and toilet 320-350F. Doubles with shower and toilet 340-400F. Triples with shower and toilet 400F. Elevator. Breakfast 25F. Reservations encouraged, by phone or fax. MC, V.

Hôtel des Batignolles, 26, rue des Batignolles (tel. 43 87 70 40; fax 44 70 01 04). M. pl. Clichy. From the metro walk 2 blocks north on rue Boursault, turn right on rue de la Condaminé, and take the next right on rue des Batignolles. Lovely courtyard, brass railings, and fresh flowers in lobby. A luxurious, reasonably priced hotel. Free maps and info in lobby. English spoken. Singles 190F. Singles and doubles with shower and toilet 310-350F. Triples with shower and toilet 370-420F. Breakfast 25F in salon or 35F in room. Reservations recommended. MC, V.

Hôtel des Deux Avenues, 38, rue Poncelet (tel. 42 27 44 35; fax 47 63 95 48). M. Ternes. Walk 1 block west on av. des Ternes and turn right on rue Poncelet. A bargain for its location only 10 min. from the Champs-Elysées and Arc de Triomphe. Clean, tidy rooms. The lobby is a blue, mirrored fantasy. English spoken. Singles and doubles 210F, with shower 280F, with shower and bath 350F. Quads with 2 large beds, bath, and toilet 430F. Showers 20F. Breakfast 25F. MC, V.

Hôtel des Deux Acacias, 28, rue l'Arc de Triomphe (tel. 43 80 01 85; fax 40 53 94 62). M. Charles de Gaulle-Etoile. Only seconds from the Arc de Triomphe. Professional management. You have the privilege of paying slightly more than usual for the spotless but nonetheless run-of-the-mill brown wallpaper, brown bedspread combo. Dogs allowed. Singles 225F. Doubles 310-350F with shower and toilet, depending on size of the room. Breakfast 25F. MC, V.

■ EIGHTEENTH ARRONDISSEMENT

The area known as Montmartre owes its reputation to the fame of artists who lived there. Now, keep in mind that artists are rarely reputable folk. By day, the 18ème crawls with tourists; by night, it can be dangerous, especially for those easily lost in its winding streets. Hotel rates rise with the northern, uphill approach to Sacré-Coeur. The higher you go, the higher the prices. Downhill and south at seedy pl. Pigalle, hotels tend to rent by the hour. Avoid M. Anvers, M. Pigalle, and M. Barbès-Rochechouart; use the Abbesses metro stop instead. Do not walk unaccompanied through the 18ème at night.

Hôtel Tholozé, 24, rue Tholozé (tel. 46 06 74 83). M. Abbesses. From rue des Abbesses take a right onto rue Durantin, go straight on rue Garreau, and take a right on rue Tholozé. Small, family-run hotel on a quiet street, away from the "action" of Pigalle. Just a few steps from the Moulin de la Galette. Reasonably sized rooms are spare but clean and well-lit. Singles 150F, with shower 200F. Doubles 180F, with shower and toilet 240F. Triples with shower and toilet 300F. Showers 20F. Breakfast 20F.

Hôtel André Gill, 4, rue André Gill (tel. 42 62 48 48; fax 42 62 77 92). M. Abbesses. From the metro walk downhill on rue des Abbesses, turn right on rue des Martyrs and left on rue André Gill. Found on a quiet, dead-end street. Note the sign, "No guests allowed in rooms." Liberace-style decor with glittery, pastel walls and sateen bedspreads. Go crazy. Elevator. English spoken. Singles 210F, with shower 300F. Doubles 240F, with shower and toilet 300F, with bath and toilet 330F. Triples with bath and toilet 440F. Showers 25F. Breakfast 25F. MC, V.

Ideal Hotel, 3, rue des Trois Frères (tel. 46 06 63 63). M. Abbesses. Walk down rue Yvonne le Tac and turn right on rue des Trois Frères. Respectable hotel on a lively, reasonably safe street lined with shops and restaurants. Small, clean sparsely decorated rooms are in good repair. Singles 125-135F, with shower 255F. Doubles 170F, with shower 290F. Showers 20F. No breakfast. Reservations accepted by telephone.

Hôtel Sofia, 21, rue de Sofia (tel. 42 64 55 37; fax 46 06 33 30). M. Anvers. Walk up rue de Steinkerque, turn right at place St-Pierre onto rue Pierre Picard; cross rue de Clignancourt, and take your first left on rue de Sofia. Oak-timbered lobby leads to bright white rooms with modern bathrooms, new beds, and views of street below. Neat and pleasant, though less than spotless. All have shower and toilet. Singles 190F. Doubles 220F. Triples 270F. Quads 360F. Breakfast 20F. Call ahead or fax for reservations.

■ NINETEENTH ARRONDISSEMENT

The 19ème is far from central; apart from a visit to Parc de la Villette, you'll have to commute to do your sight-seeing. Less hectic than more central Parisian neighborhoods, a stay here can provide needed respite from the tourist hordes along the Seine. The hilly Parc des Buttes-Chaumont is a worthy, romantic picnic area. Safety is a concern, however, along rue de Belleville, which can be quite dangerous.

Rhin et Danube, 3, place Rhin et Danube (tel. 42 45 10 13; fax 42 06 88 82). M. Danube. Steps from metro. Facing what looks like a village square, this hotel feels like a country inn. Not that it's without modern amenities—TV and kitchenette in every room. Doubles can accommodate up to 2 extra people. Singles with bath and toilet 300F. Doubles with bath and toilet 330F. Extra bed 50F. Triples with bath and toilet 380F. Quads with bath and shower 430F. MC, V, AmEx.

La Perdrix Rouge, 5, rue Lassus (tel. 42 06 09 53; fax 42 06 88 70). M. Jourdain. Quite plush, though some carpets have been worn a little by the tour groups that often stay here. All rooms have TV and toilet. Good location next to a pretty church and a metro stop. No English spoken. Singles with shower 260F. Doubles with shower 290F, with bath 310F. Triples with bath 340F. No extra beds. Breakfast 26F. Dog 20F. Reserve by fax 2-3 weeks ahead in summer. MC, V, AmEx.

Hôtel Polonia, 3, rue de Chaumont (tel. 42 49 87 15; fax 42 06 32 91). M. Jaurès. Walk down avenue Secretan and turn left on rue de Chaumont. Friendly Polish immigrants run this modest but clean hotel. Singles 108F. Doubles 161-176F, with shower 241F. Extra bed 75F. Showers 25F. Breakfast 27F. Reserve 1 month ahead.

Hôtel du Parc, 1, pl. Armand Carrel (tel. 42 08 08 37, 42 08 86 89, or 42 08 55 12; fax 42 45 66 91). M. Laumière. Good location next to metro and the Parc des Buttes Chaumont. Spacious, clean, and well-lit rooms—most with views of the park. Range in decor from garish yellows to lovely pastels. Elevator. Singles with shower 225F. Doubles with shower 260F. 2-bed doubles with shower 300F. Triples with shower 350F. Breakfast 30F, served in your room for an extra 5F. Nov.-Feb. prices fall roughly 10%. Reserve 2 weeks ahead. MC, V, AmEx.

Atlas Hôtel, 12, rue de l'Atlas (tel. 42 08 50 12; fax 40 36 29 57), off bd. de la Villette. M. Belleville. Continuing renovations have yielded new fixtures and much-needed paint jobs. Clean, simple rooms. UCLA-educated proprietor. Singles 140F, with shower and toilet 200F. Doubles 170F, with shower and toilet 210F. Twins 180F, with shower and toilet 230F. No elevator. Free showers. Breakfast 25F.

Crimée Hôtel, 188, rue de Crimée (tel. 40 35 19 57 or 40 36 75 29; fax 40 36 29 57). M. Crimée. Near lots of restaurants. Rather upscale, modern rooms with soundproofing, hair dryer, TV, radio, and alarm clock. Singles with shower and toilet 280F, with bath and toilet 300-310F. Doubles with shower and toilet 310F, with bath and toilet 320-340F. Triples with shower and toilet 380F. Quads with shower and toilet 420F. Extra bed 50F. Breakfast 30F. MC, V, AmEx.

Hôtel des Sciences, 219, rue de Crimée (tel. 40 38 91 00; fax 40 38 44 23). M. Crimée. Near metro. Clean, comfortable rooms with minibars and TVs. Narrow hallways and bathrooms. Double-glazing deflects street noise. Elevator. Singles with toilet and shower 330F, with toilet and bath 370F. Doubles with toilet and shower 380F, with toilet and bath 400F. Breakfast 35F. MC, V, AmEx.

■ TWENTIETH ARRONDISSEMENT

The 20ème often gets a bad rap from Parisians—generally from those who have never been there. While cheap high-rises dot the hillsides and seem to grow at breakneck speed (for Paris), charming streets and open-air markets are no strangers to this quarter. In summer, the slowdown in commercial activity leaves the two-star hotels of this *arrondissement* half empty, which makes them a good bet if you're having trouble finding a place to stay. This quarter is on the periphery of the city, so expect a half-hour metro ride to the Louvre.

Hôtel Eden, 7, rue Jean-Baptiste Dumay (tel. 46 36 64 22). M. Pyrénées or Jourdain. Good value. Recently renovated, clean, and equipped with wonderfully firm beds. All rooms have TV, shutters, and double-glazed glass. Some double rooms fairly small, however—it's worth paying the extra 20F for more elbow room. Salon downstairs stocked with plants and fresh flowers. Elevator, but not wheelchair accessible. Singles 180F. Doubles 220F, with shower and toilet 260-280F. Prices 20F higher Sept.-July. Breakfast 25F. Dogs 30F. MC, V.

Hôtel Printana, 355, rue des Pyrénées (tel. 46 36 76 62). M. Jourdain. Devoted proprietors, refurbished rooms, and a clientele that always comes back. Nice, clean little rooms at very reasonable prices. Elevator. Singles with toilet 120F. Doubles with toilet 180F, with shower and toilet 220F. Triples with shower and toilet 260F. Showers 10F. Breakfast 25F. MC, V.

Hôtel Dauphine, 236, rue des Pyrénées (tel. 43 49 47 66; fax 43 36 05 79). M. Gambetta. Homey, pastel rooms, though not luxurious on the 2-star hotel spectrum. Sparsely furnished with TV, and sometimes a minibar. Double-glazing keeps out most noise from bustling vendors on the rue des Pyrénées. Elevator. Singles with shower 200F. Doubles with shower 240-260F, with bath 300F. Extra bed 70F. Breakfast 25F. MC, V, AmEx.

Hôtel Palma, 77, av. Gambetta (tel. 46 36 13 65; fax 46 36 03 27). M. Gambetta. plush rooms with cable TV and hair dryer. Hallways narrow and a bit dark. Lounge downstairs, replete with oriental rug, chintz, and artsy photos. Singles with shower and toilet 330F, with bath and toilet 350F. Doubles with shower and toilet 330-360F, with bath and toilet 350-380F. Triples with bath and shower 435-455F. Breakfast 30F.

Hôtel Pyrénées-Gambetta, 12, av. du Père-Lachaise (tel. 47 97 76 57; fax 47 97 17 61). M. Gambetta. Modern, well-lit, tastefully decorated. Elevator fits narrow wheelchairs. Some rooms have big, airy bathrooms. Singles with shower and toilet 311F, with shower, toilet, TV, and fridge 324F, with bath, toilet, TV, and fridge 337-350F. Doubles with shower and toilet 337F, with shower, toilet, TV, and fridge 350-376F, with bath, toilet, TV, and fridge 376-402F. Breakfast 26F.

Hostels and Foyers

Auberge de Jeunesse "Le d'Artagnan" (HI), 80, rue Vitruve (tel. 43 61 08 75; fax 43 61 75 40). M. Porte de Bagnolet or Porte de Montreuil. A cross between a hostel and a mall. 411 beds. 7-floor compound with restaurant, bar, and even a small movie theater. Vending machines and free microwaves downstairs. Mostly triples; a few doubles; some 8-bed rooms. English spoken. Wheelchair access. Flexible 3-day max. stay. Open 24 hrs. Lockout 10am-2pm. Triples and dorms 100F per person. Breakfast and sheets included. Doubles 115-125F per person. Lockers 15F. Laundry 15F/wash, 5F/dry; soap 3F. Reservations a must; hostel is packed Feb.-Oct.

Food and Drink

> At daybreak he woke us again to drink the early morning soups; and
> after that we ate only one meal, which lasted all day. We did not know
> whether it was dinner or supper, luncheon or bed-time snacks.
> —*Rabelais*, Gargantua and Pantagruel

Neither budget travelers nor most Parisians have the time, appetite, or cash for the Rabelaisian stupor that six-course meals require. Both affordable and eminently French are the breads, cheeses, and pastries that appear as standard fare, with regional modifications, throughout the hexagon and its capital. With a bakery on every corner and dozens of open-air markets, food is a high-profile, high-quality affair. The soup and salad the Parisian makes at home for dinner may not be fancy, but they are made from fresh ingredients carefully selected from specialized food stores, and prepared with love, respect, and creativity.

FRENCH CUISINE

For a list of French food terms and descriptions of some classic dishes, please consult the Menu Reader at the back of the book.

The aristocratic tradition of extreme richness and elaborate presentation known as **haute cuisine** is actually not French at all; Cathérine de Médicis brought it from Italy along with her cooks, who taught the French to appreciate the finer aspects of sauces and seasonings. In their work and writings, great 19th-century chefs made fine food an essential art of civilized life. To learn about the skills involved—such as preparing base sauces, which are in turn combined with other ingredients to make the classic sauces—leaf through the *Larousse Gastronomique,* a standard reference for chefs, first compiled in the 19th century.

The style made famous in the U.S. by Julia Child is **cuisine bourgeoise,** quality French home-cooking. Both *haute cuisine* and *cuisine bourgeoise* rely heavily on the **cuisine de province** (provincial cooking, also called *cuisine campagnarde,* or country cooking), by creating sophisticated versions of traditional French regional cuisine. The trendy **nouvelle cuisine,** consisting of tiny portions of delicately cooked, artfully arranged ingredients with light sauces, became popular in the 1970s and is now little more than a source of country-wide amusement. Simple meals such as *steak-frites* (steak and fries) or *poulet rôti* (roasted chicken) can be found for quite reasonable prices on just about every corner in Paris.

French **meat** is not all frogs and snails, though those tasty morsels both make great first courses (frog is reminiscent of both chicken and crab; snails taste like succulent shellfish). It is true that the French tend to eat a wider variety of creatures than do most Anglo-Saxons. *Tripes* (stomach lining of a cow) cooked in herbs is well-loved by many; the sausage version is called *andouille* or *andouillette.* Rabbit is fairly common; pigeon shows up in casseroles and pastry shells. Though not all steaks are *tartare* (raw), most red meat is served quite rare unless you request otherwise. **Fish**-lovers should celebrate seafood specialties of the French southwest and be adept with a blade. Unless clearly marked *filet,* the fish will arrive eyes, tail, and all. Smoked salmon is a popular summertime entrée, served with *crème fraîche* and, sometimes, crushed peppercorns. *Tarama,* made with cheap salmon roe and *crème fraîche*, is a Greek import which has become popular of late. Skate is an unusual fish that is sometimes bland and tough but can be delectable *au beurre noir.* Mostly, though, fine French food consists of less exotic fare: saltwater fishes from the Atlantic or Mediterranean, freshwater fish from the Loire, and grilled or sautéed meats, topped with unforgettable sauces—*bordelais, béchamel,* and their kin—and accompanied by potatoes. **Sauce** is a never-ending story, the chef's trademark that makes or breaks evenings. Most are variations on a small family of French classics (for information on specific sauces, consult the Menu Reader).

Vegetables may be overcooked by some standards. French asparagus (often served in vinaigrette) is a pale, stumpy version of the matchstick you've come to love. *Haricots verts* (green beans) are a svelte and tastier cousin of the ones your mother made you eat. Americans may be taken aback by the cost of produce. With no immigrant, under-paid, non-unionized sharecroppers to work the land, the farmer, his wife, and their friends charge what they need to and think you can swallow. Restaurants often serve *pommes frites* (french fries) or potato *gratins,* potatoes sliced, doused with cream, butter, and cheese, and baked in an oven. Other starches, such as rice, are pretty good, but stay away from the noodles, which are more of a hellish *al Dante* than a nice and firm *al dente.*

Bread is served with every meal. It is perfectly polite to use a piece of bread to wipe your plate. The *baguette* is the long, crisp, archetypal French loaf which, at about 4F, has kept many a budgeteer afloat on treks through Paris. The *bâtard* has a softer crust, the smaller *ficelle* a thicker, harder crust. *Pain de campagne,* made with whole wheat flour, is heavier inside than the baguette. The *pain complet* is a whole grain loaf, and the *pain à six céréales* is made with six grains. Finally, some argue that the best bread in Paris is the *pain Poilâne,* a sourdough blend baked in a wood-burning oven and available from only a few *boulangeries*—ask around. The cheap, government-subsidized bread you buy from a nameless bakery in Paris may well be the best you have ever eaten; don't hesitate to make it your staple.

Tremendously bountiful and various, French **cheeses** fall into three main categories. Cooked cheeses include *beaufort* and *gruyère.* Veined cheeses, such as *bleu* and *roquefort,* gain their sharp taste from the molds that are encouraged to grow on them. Soft cheeses, like brie (the king of cheeses) and Camembert, round out a basic cheese tray. Tangy *fromages de chèvre* (goat cheeses) come in two forms: the soft, fresh *frais* and crumbly, sharp *sec* (dry). Within these broad categories there is much variation. Generally speaking, the criteria by which one judges cheese are the inverse of those for other foods. Runny, moldy, smelly cheeses are the prize of every Parisian; if your wedge of brie appears a near-liquid mass oozing out of its shell, it is probably the best money can buy. Americans have really never had French cheese until they come here; exported versions must be sterilized, killing the bacteria that many believe make the flavor.

Among **charcuterie** (cold meat products), the most renowned is *pâté,* a spread of finely minced liver and meat. Often a house specialty, it comes in hundreds of varieties, some highly seasoned with herbs. *Pâté de campagne* (from pork) is chunky, while *pâté de foie* (liver) is soft and silky. (Technically, a *pâté* is baked in a pastry crust, and the variety without a crust is a *terrine.* In practice, *pâtés* with crusts are rare, and the terms are used interchangeably.) *Rillettes,* rich minced pork, is similar to *pâté,* but more greasy. Both *pâté* and *rillettes* are eaten on or with bread, and often garnished with *cornichons* (gherkins). Though the sausages of France are not as famous as the *Wursts* of Germany or the salamis of Italy, dozens of varieties are quite worth sampling, either as a cold appetizer, or hot, as a main course.

French **pastry** is one of the major arguments in favor of civilization. Breakfast pastries include the delectable *pain au chocolat* (chocolate croissant) and *croissant aux amandes* (almond croissant). More elaborate choices are fruit tarts and *flans* (open tarts), including the *chausson aux pommes,* a light pastry with apple filling. Many *gâteaux* (cakes) were invented in the 19th century, such as the chocolate-and-espresso *opéra,* the cream-filled, many-layered *mille-feuilles,* and the *forêt-noire,* a rich slice of fudge with a cherry topping. The Paris-Brest cake, another filo dough and cream delight, is the only dessert named for a round-trip on the SNCF. All of these can be eaten in the afternoon with tea, or after dinner as a dessert—eat pastry whenever you want to. Also good with tea are crumbly cookies like macaroons and *madeleines.*

And of course, **wine.** In France, wine is not a luxury; it is a necessity. During World War I, French infantry pinned down by heavy shellfire had only iron rations brought to them: bread and wine. And when France sent its first citizen into orbit on a Soviet spacecraft, he took the fruit of the vine with him. Wines are distinguished first by color—white wines are produced by the fermentation of the juice of red grapes. Rosés allow some of the red color from the skin to seep in before the skins are removed, and reds come from the fermentation of the juice, skins, and sometimes stems of black grapes. In general, white wine is served with fish and red wine with everything else, but it is the color of the sauce, not the color of the meat, that really matters. Red wine is preferred with cheese. The wines of Bordeaux break down into three broad categories: *rouge* (red), *blanc sec* (dry white), and *moelleux,* a sweeter white very easy to drink. Different regions, due to soil, climate, types of grapes, and aging processes, produce widely different wines. Connoisseurs know that French wine is best one to three years after an armistice; the years 1921, 1945, and 1947 are celebrated vintages. When buying wine look for the words *Appellation Controlée* surrounding the name of a region. Don't get too self-conscious about not knowing anything about wine. Waiters can give recommendations, and wine bars (see below) let you sample expensive wines by the glass. Or fall back on the *vin ordinaire* (house wine) of the restaurant—it's usually pretty good.

The French frown on hard liquor before meals; it dulls the palate. Lighter *apéritifs* (before-dinner drinks) are preferred. Among the major *apéritifs* are *kir,* made from white wine and *cassis,* a black currant liqueur *(kir royale* substitutes champagne for the wine). *Pastis,* otherwise known as "51" *(cinquante-et-un),* a licorice liqueur diluted with water, is popular with *tabac* owners, gamblers, and the Bastille crowd. *Suze,* fermented *gentiane,* a sweet-smelling mountain flower, yields a wickedly bitter brew; *picon-bière* is beer mixed with a sweet liqueur. It is fairly rare for Parisians to drink these in restaurants; they prefer them at home or, if they are going out, in a bar or café (this is a good way to kill time before restaurants start serving around 7:30pm). Popular *digestifs* (after-dinner drinks) are cognac and various brandies, such as Norman *Calvados.*

Paris's cosmopolitan atmosphere and its colonialist past have provided it with restaurants serving **ethnic cuisine** from all over the globe. Particularly common are North African restaurants, specializing in *couscous. Indo-chinoise* restaurants serve Cambodian and Vietnamese specialties. Caribbean and West African restaurants are in large supply in many of Paris' outlying arrondissements, like the 10ème and the 20ème. Paris has attracted cooks from India, China, Japan, Italy, and the United States. You can often eat their cuisines for much less than what you'd pay for a comparable French dinner, perhaps because ethnic restaurants are in general less accepted than French restaurants and have to make their food better and cheaper to attract customers. Ethnic food is adapted to the local palate and you may find that certain foods are less spiced then you expect.

The number of **vegetarian restaurants** in Paris has increased dramatically over the past few years. Yet for the most part, vegetables here are prepared with salt, butter, sugar, or meat stock. Vegetarians will further have trouble eating cheaply in most restaurants, since *menus à prix fixe* almost always feature meat or fish. Ordering a salad may prove cheaper (be careful, however, of green salads with eggs, ham, tuna, or chicken in them). A *salade verte* is a green salad with lettuce only; a *salade de tomates* is a delicious tomato topped with vinaigrette. Served with a healthy basket of French bread, both make an inexpensive and surprisingly satisfying meal at a café or *brasserie. Viande* refers only to red meat. If you don't eat pork, chicken, fish, eggs, or dairy products, you should make this clear to the server. Ethnic cuisine, especially Vietnamese and North African, often provides excellent vegetarian options. Look for health food stores *(diététiques* or *maisons de régime).* Health food products are sometimes referred to as *produits à santé* and are often available in supermarkets. *Biologique* refers to organically grown food (see Essentials—Specific Concerns for more information).

Kosher travelers and anyone else looking for a good deli should stroll through the Jewish neighborhood around rue des Rosiers, in the 4ᵉᵐᵉ *arrondissement,* where you'll find an assortment of delicious bakeries, groceries, and kosher restaurants. There are a number of kosher butcher stores in both the ninth and eleventh *arrondissements.* You might also ask at a synagogue for tips. Given the large North African community that has settled in Paris, **halal** food should also be readily available, particularly in the 5ᵉᵐᵉ, 19ᵉᵐᵉ, and 20ᵉᵐᵉ *arrondissements.*

Breakfast *(petit déjeuner)* is usually light, consisting of bread and sometimes *croissants* or *brioches* and *café crème* (espresso with hot milk) or hot chocolate. Many people still return home for **lunch** *(déjeuner)*, the largest meal of the day, between noon and 2pm. Most shops, businesses, and government agencies close for two hours during this time; Paris has four rush hours—morning, evening, and two in the middle of the day as people hurry home and back. But this tradition is slowly giving way as more working Parisians choose to take their two-hour lunches in restaurants with friends and colleagues.

Dinner *(dîner)* begins quite late, and goes on for hours as revelers extend their meals into the early morning. Traditionally, the complete French dinner includes an *apéritif, entrée* (appetizer), *plat* (main course), salad, cheese, desserts, fruit, coffee, and a *digestif.* The French generally take wine with their meals, but mineral water is an almost acceptable substitute. Order sparkling water *(eau pétillante* or *gazeuse)* or flat mineral water *(eau plate).* Ice cubes *(glaçons)* are rare. To order tap water, ask for *une carafe d'eau.* Finish the meal with espresso, which comes in lethal little cups. Of course, few Parisians indulge in the entire ritual frequently (or even sometimes); most eat an abbreviated version in a restaurant.

French etiquette dictates keeping the hands above the table, not in the lap. As many a high school French teacher will attest, if you put your hands out of view, your companions may ask what you're doing with them. Elbows shouldn't rest on the table, but they often do. If you want to try eating in true French manner, hold your fork in your left hand, your knife in the right, and scoop food onto your fork with the sharp edge of the knife. A last word: don't say *"Je suis plein,"* meaning "I'm full." This phrase is used for cows, and means they're pregnant. A more polite way of refusing food: *"Je n'ai plus faim."* (I'm not hungry anymore.)

Cheap eats in Paris abound for the wily strategist. At breakfast-time, head to the nearest *boulangerie* (bakery) for croissants of all varieties, often still warm from the oven. Bakeries also sell delicious sandwiches (12-25F) throughout the day, an excellent option for a cheap lunch; ham and cheese *(jambon et gruyère)* is a Parisian mainstay; if you're starved for vegetables, the *crudités* sandwich is a delectable lettuce, tomato, and hard-boiled egg concoction. Most sandwiches are made with fresh-baked *demi-baguette.*

Though its possible to subsist on Paris' sundry breads and pastries, plan to spring for one real sit-down meal per day, for the sake of your health and sanity. Many elegant restaurants offer 60-80F lunch *menus* (about one-third the cost of dinner a la carte).

GROCERIES

When cooking or assembling a picnic, buy supplies at the specialty shops found in most neighborhoods. *Crémeries* (selling dairy products), *fromageries* (cheese shops), *charcuteries* (meats, sausages, *pâtés,* and *plats cuisinés*—prepared meals by the kilo), and *épiceries* (groceries, with cold salads by the kilo) are open in the morning until noon and then again from 2 or 3 to 7 or 8pm. *Epiceries* also carry staples, wine, produce, and a bit of everything else. *Boulangeries* sell several varieties of bread; get there in the morning, when the goods are still hot. *Pâtisseries* sell pastries, and a *confiserie* stocks candy and ice cream (though the border between these two kinds of stores is often unclear). You can buy your produce at a *primeur.*

Boucheries sell all kinds of meat and poultry, as well as roast chicken. Look for small neighborhood stores to unearth some truly incredible deals. Your hotel manager or any local can point you to the neighborhood *fromagerie, charcuterie, boucherie,* and *boulangerie.* Warning: French store owners are incredibly touchy about people touching their fruits and vegetables; unless there's a sign outside your corner store that says *"libre service,"* ask inside before you start grabbing stuff outside.

Supermarkets *(supermarchés)* are found in every neighborhood. Avoid the evening scramble, lest you be trampled by homemakers trying to get the last loaf of bread. Also take note that in many *supermarchés* it is up to you to weigh your produce, bag it, and label it. If you're in the mood for a five-and-dime complete with a supermarket, go to any of the **Monoprix, Prisunics, Franprix** or **Uniprix** that litter the city. Also look for the small foodstore chains such as **Casino** and **Félix Potin.** Starving students and travelers-in-the-know swear by the ubiquitous **Ed l'Epicier.** Buy in bulk and watch the pile of francs you save grow; it's possible to end up paying 30-50% less than you would at other stores. Two of Ed's drawbacks: you can't find some brand names (alas, no Nutella) and some stores do not carry produce. **Picard Surgelés,** with 50 locations throughout the city, stocks every imaginable frozen food—from *crêpes* to calamari. Most branches offer free delivery.

Open-air markets, held at least once a week in most *arrondissements,* remain the best places to buy fresh fruit, cheese, vegetables, fish, and meat. Competition here is fierce, and prices can be low (see Markets). The **Nicolas** chain sells wines at inexpensive prices, but doesn't always carry the widest selections. No luck finding that special ingredient? Try the following:

Alleosse, 13, rue Poncelet, 17ème (tel. 46 22 50 45). M. Ternes. An immense and exquisite selection of cheeses, perfect for classy evenings and extravagant sandwiches. Open Tues.-Sat. 9am-1pm and 4-7:15pm, Sun 9am-1pm. MC, V.

Bon Marché, 3, rue de Babylone, 7ème (tel. 45 49 21 22). M. Sèvres-Babylone. Visit Bon Marché's food annex, La Grande Epicerie, to purchase high-priced ingredients for fancy French food. Also a lot of "gourmet" American fare. English aisle stocks ever-elusive Lee and Perkins Worcestershire sauce and a large selection of Twinings tea (12F50). Well-wrapped chocolates and *bonbons* make great souvenirs. Open Mon.-Sat. 9:30am-7pm.

Charcuterie Coesnon, 30, rue Dauphine, 6ème (tel. 43 54 35 80). M. Odéon. Homemade sausages, pâtés, and salads line the walls of this tiny store. Purchase sandwiches here at lunchtime. Open Tues.-Sat. 8:30am-8pm. MC, V.

Fauchon, 26, pl. de la Madeleine, 8ème (tel. 47 42 60 11). M. Madeleine. The supermarket to end all supermarkets. You can savor the scent from the *pâtisserie* at least a block away. But do not dare to pick your expensive tea off the shelf yourself—turn to the brown-clad salespeople with the ornate F on their breast to do the dirty work for you. Indulge. Open Mon.-Sat. 9:40am-7pm. V, MC.

Finkelsztajn's, 27, rue des Rosiers, 4ème (tel. 42 72 78 91). 24, rue des Ecouffes, 4ème (tel. 48 87 92 85). M. St-Paul. Grab a bagel or *pirogbi* on your gambol through the Marais. Serving East European Jewish delicacies since 1946, this is the place to go for everything to-go from strudel to chopped liver. Baked sweets around 13F. Gargantuan meat sandwiches 30-40F. Store on rue des Rosiers open Wed.-Sun. 10am-2pm and 3-7pm; store on rue des Ecouffes open Mon. and Thurs.-Sun. 10am-2pm and 3-7pm. No credit cards.

Hédiard, 21, pl. de la Madeleine, 8ème (tel. 42 66 44 36). M. Madeleine. A store of spices and exotic products, founded in 1854. Their neighboring *cave* offers a fine selection of wines. Open Mon.-Sat. 9:30am-9pm. MC, V, AmEx.

Paul, 4, rue Poncelet, 17ème (tel. 42 27 80 25). M. Ternes. Parisians from all over the 17ème come to purchase this bakery's mystically aromatic crusty loaves, baked in wood-fired ovens. Open Tues.-Sat. 7:30am-7:30pm, Sun. 7:30am-1pm.

Poilâne, 8, rue Cherche-Midi, 6ème (tel. 45 48 42 59), off bd. Raspail. M. Sèvres Babylone. This tiny, rather sparse shop services the huge bakery responsible for Paris' most famous bread. Fragrant, crusty, sourdough loaves are baked throughout the day in wood-fired ovens. Menus in the city's finest restaurants declare that they serve only *pain Poilâne.* Unlike the *baguette,* these circular loaves don't come cheap; priced according to weight, a whole loaf usually costs 38-40F. For just a taste, ask for a *quart* (a quarter-loaf), about 10F. It's probably enough since they're extraordinarily filling. Bread can also be bought by the slice. Open Mon.-Sat. 7:15am-8:15pm.

Tang Frères, 48, av. d'Ivry, 13ème (tel. 45 70 80 00). M. Porte d'Ivry. In the heart of Chinatown, this grocery is huge, gigantic, and very big; come to buy rices, spices, soups and noodles in bulk. Also stocks canned goods and high-quality, often hard-to-find Eastern and Western produce. If you don't read French, don't worry; the signs are in Chinese, too. Open Tues.-Fri. 9am-7:30pm, Sat.-Sun. 8:30am-7:30pm.

Thanksgiving, 20, rue St-Paul, 4ème (tel. 42 77 68 29). M. St-Paul or Pont Marie. Homemade American delicacies like cheesecake and pecan pie, plus nacho chips, brownie mix, peanut butter, and ketchup. Prices are pretty high. Brownies 10F, cookies 5F, bagel with cream cheese 18F. Take-out dishes also available: chili 100F per kg, barbecue ribs 40F for 5 pieces. Restaurant upstairs serves brunch on weekends for around 80F. Store open Mon.-Sat. 11am-8pm, Sun. 11am-6pm. Restaurant open Tues.-Fri. noon-3:30pm, Sat.-Sun. 11am-4pm.

MARKETS AND NOTEWORTHY STREETS

In the 5th century, the ancient Roman settlement of Lutèce held the first market on what is now Ile de la Cité. More than a millennium later, markets are not a novelty but an integral part of daily life. Both open-air and covered markets can be found around almost every corner, in every *arrondissement*. For a complete list of food and other markets, along with hours and days open, pick up *Les Marchés de Paris* at the tourist office or your local *mairie*.

Marché Montorgeuil, 2ème. M. Etienne Marcel. Market extending from rue Réaumur to rue Etienne Marcel, along rue des Petits Carreaux and rue Montorgeuil. Superabundance of fishmongers, butcher stores, bakeries, and fruit stands. Start at the end of rue Montorgeuil nearest M. Etienne Marcel and eat as you go. Purchase salads (59-129F/kg) at the *traiteur de produits grecs.* At the nearby *fromagerie* (cheese shop), fresh *chèvre* fills half the store April-September. *Charolais* is a moderately moist goat cheese. Also sample cheap, exotic cow cheeses like the garlic and pepper-flavored *gaperon,* or more pungent *boulettes d'avesnes,* both around 18F/100g. Market's cheapest produce at the **Halles Montorgeuil Codec** supermarket at 69, rue Montorgeuil (near the other end of the street) open Mon. 8:30am-8pm, Tues.-Thurs. 9am-1pm and 3:30-8pm, Fri.-Sat. 9am-7:30pm. Independent wine merchant at the **Repaire de Bacchus,** 88, rue Montorgueil (tel. 42 36 17 49) carries dependable, inexpensive table wines. 12F for the cheapest red, 16F for the cheapest white.

Rue Mouffetard, towards the intersection of bd. du Port-Royal, 5ème. M. Censier-Daubenton. Chaotic narrow streets crammed with wonderful produce, fish, cheese, and meats. Tables loaded down with shoes, cheap chic, and housewares. Open daily 9am-1pm and 4-7pm.

Marché Biologique, on bd. Raspail between rue Cherche-Midi and rue de Rennes, 6ème. M. Rennes. French hippies peddle everything from organic produce to 7-grain bread to tofu patties. A great place to buy natural beauty supplies, to stock up on homeopathic drugs, or just to people-watch. Open Sun. 7am-1:30pm.

Rue Cler, between rue de Grenelle and av. de la Motte-Picquet, 7ème. M. Ecole Militaire. A bustling market filled with produce, meat, cheese, and bread stands.

Marché Europe, 1, rue Corvetto, 8ème. Covered food-market. Open Mon.-Sat. 8am-1:30pm and 4-7pm, Sun. 8am-1pm.

Marché Raspail, on bd. Raspail between rue Cherche-Midi and rue de Rennes, 6ème. M. Rennes. A small open-air market with fresh fruits and vegetables, meats and cheeses, nuts and dried fruits, and a few household appliances (lampshades and the like). Check several stalls to find the best prices and the best quality food. Open Tues. and Fri. 7am-1:30pm.

Marché Saint-Germain, at 3ter, rue Mabillon, 6ème. M. Mabillon. Walk down rue du Four until you find rue Mabillon. Open Tues.-Sat. 8am-1pm and 4-7:30pm, Sun. 8am-1pm.

Marché St-Quentin, 85bis, bd. de Magenta, 10ème. M. Gare de l'Est. This market is a massive, elegant construction of iron and glass, built in 1866 with a glorious glass ceiling. Inside you'll find an enormous variety of goods, including flowers and fresh produce. Open Tues.-Sat. 8am-1pm and 3:30-7:30pm, Sun. 8am-1pm.

Rue du Convention, at the intersection of rue de Vaugirard, 15ème. M. Convention. A bewildering array of fruits, vegetables, meat, fish, cheese, and pastries every Tues. and Sun. 7am-1pm.

Marché Bastille, on bd. Richard-Lenoir from pl. de la Bastille north to rue St-Sabin, 11ème. M. Bastille. Fruit, cheese, potato, exotic mushroom stalls, bread, meat, and cheap housewares stretch from M. Richard Lenoir to M. Bastille. Expect to spend at least an hour here. Popular as a Sunday morning family outing for area residents. Thurs. and Sun. 7am-1:30pm.

Marché Popincourt, on bd. Richard-Lenoir between rue Oberkampf and rue de Crussol. M. Oberkampf. An open-air market close to hotels in the 11ème. The street fills with fresh, well-priced perishables (fruit, cheese, groceries, bread). Open Tues. and Fri. 7am-1:30pm.

Marché Beauvau St-Antoine, on rue d'Aligre between rue de Charenton and rue Crozatier, 12ème. M. Ledru-Rollin. One of the largest Parisian markets, with the cheapest produce in the city. Make sure to brouse before buying, given the wide range in fruit and vegetable quality. Also visit the market's large tag sale, with scattered old clothing, fabrics, and household remnants. Produce market open Tues.-Sun. 7:30am-1pm and Tues.-Sat. 3:30-7:30pm. Tag sale open daily 7:30am-12:30pm.

Marché Président-Wilson, on av. Président-Wilson between rue Debrousse and pl. d'Iéna, 16ème. M. Iéna or Alma-Marceau. An excellent alternative to the 16ème's exorbitant restaurants. Competitively priced produce, meats, and cheeses. Clothing, table linen, and other household goods available. Open Wed. and Sat. 7am-1:30pm.

Marché Saint-Didier, at the corner of rue Mesnil and rue St-Didier, 16ème. M. Victor-Hugo. Walk all the way down rue Mesnil. This small market offers a good selection of produce. Many hard-to-find herbs and (inside) dry goods. Wide selection of grains and rice (including Thai, Japanese, and whole-grain). Covered market open Mon.-Sat. 7am-1:30pm and. 4:30-7:30pm, Sun. 7am-1:30pm. Open-air market open Tues. and Thurs.-Sat. 8am-2pm.

UNIVERSITY RESTAURANTS

For travelers or long-term visitors truly strapped for cash, university restaurants provide cheap and dependable meals. Meal tickets can be purchased at each restaurant location while food is being served (tickets 24F60; 19F60 with ISIC or *Carte Jeunes*). The following university restaurants are most convenient, but the list is not nearly exhaustive. For more information—summer and weekend schedules, a list of other restaurant locations—visit **CROUS (Centre Regional des Oeuvres Universitaires et Scolaires),** 30, av. Georges Bernanos, 5ème (tel. 40 51 36 00; M. Port-Royal). Open 11:30am-1:30pm and 6-8pm. All of the following, except Citeaux, Grand Palais, and C.H.U. Necker, are open between lunch and dinner for sandwiches and drinks: **Bullier,** 39, av. Georges Bernanos, 5ème (M. Port-Royal); **Cuvier-Jussieu,** 8bis, rue Cuvier, 5ème (M. Cuvier-Jussieu); **Censier,** 31, rue Geoffroy St-Hilaire, 5ème (M. Censier-Daubenton; closed for dinner); **Châtelet,** 10, rue Jean Calvin, 5ème (M. Censier-Daubenton); **Mazet,** 5, rue Mazet, 6ème (M. Odéon); **Assas,** 92, rue d'Assas, 6ème (M. Port-Royal or Notre-Dame-des-Champs; closed for dinner); **Mabillon,** 3, rue Mabillon, 6ème (M. Mabillon); **Grand Palais,** cours la Reine, 8ème (M. Champs-Elysées Clemenceau); **Citeaux,** 45, bd. Diderot, 12ème (M. Gare de Lyon); **C.H.U. Pitie-Salpetrière,** 105, bd. de l'Hôpital, 13ème (M. St-Marcel); **Dareau,** 13-17, rue

Dareau, 14ème (M. St-Jacques); **C.H.U. Necker,** 156, rue de Vaugirard, 15ème (M. Pasteur); **Dauphine,** av. de Pologne, 16ème (M. Porte Dauphine).

RESTAURANTS

The world's first restaurant was born in Paris over 200 years ago. Ironically, its purpose was not to indulge its clientele with delicious foods and wines, but rather to restore (from the French verb *restaurer)* over-fed party-goers to physical health. Restaurants were a social respite from the high-calorie world of soirées, balls, and private dinner parties. Here one could be in society and eat nothing.

Do not approach French dining with the equation that chic equals *cher.* Recent economic hard times have led to the return of the bistro, a more informal, less expensive, often family-run restaurant. Even more casual are *brasseries,* usually oriented towards beer and Alsatian specialties—lots of *choucroute,* a sauerkraut and sausage. Usually crowded and lively, *brasseries* are best for large groups and high spirits. The least expensive option is usually a *crêperie,* a restaurant specializing in the thin Breton pancakes filled with various meats, cheeses, chocolates, fruits, and condiments; surprisingly, you can often eat at one for the price of McDonald's.

There are several gastronomic cautions. Dinner is generally served later than in the U.S. (7pm on) and is composed of smaller, multiple courses. An *entrée* is an appetizer, the *plât* is the main course. Service or the tip is usually *compris,* included in the price. The check *(l'addition)* may be a long time in coming—spending two hours in a restaurant is not unusual. If you are particularly pleased with the service, feel free to leave a small cash tip as a sign of your gratitude (anywhere from a few francs to 5% of the check) but don't feel obligated. The initials BC mean *boisson compris,* drink included; BNC, or *boisson non-compris,* means the opposite.

If you are on a tight budget, be sure to ask for a *carafe d'eau* (a pitcher of tap water). If you simply order "water" (*de l'eau*), you will end up paying for a 25F bottle of Evian. Although wine can be lovely with your meal, you might consider skipping it because unless it is included (*vin compris*) you will pay too much. To enjoy wine inexpensively, buy it for lunch at any supermarket. You will have an extensive choice for 8-35F, and most fine vintages will cost no more that 15-20F. Also, consider ordering the fixed *menu* or *formule,* a *prix fixe* lunch or dinner usually composed of three or four courses and a choice of several appetizers, main courses, and desserts. Ordering a la carte can be much more expensive, especially at dinner.

The restaurants are arranged both by type and by location. Restaurants—By Type provides a list of restaurants cross-referenced by food and features (including price, hours, and ambience). The "Splurge" category consists of restaurants where the dinner *prix fixe menu* costs over 100F. Every restaurant listed in this section is followed by an *arrondissement* label; turn to Restaurants—By Location for the full write-up. Restaurants—By Location segregates eateries by *arrondissement,* then lists them within their location in order of *value:* the top entry may not be the cheapest, but it won't be dear, and it will be the best in its price range and area.

■■■ RESTAURANTS—BY TYPE

All-You-Can-Eat
Restaurant L'Escapade, 5ème
Sangria Restaurant, 17ème

American
Elliott Restaurant, 8ème
The Front Page, 1er
Hard Rock Café, 9ème

Hayne's Bar, 9ème
Hollywood Canteen, chains
The Rib Joint, 5ème
Slice, 6ème
Le Taxi Jaune, 3ème

Beer and Wine
Le Château Poivre, 14ème

Léon de Bruxelles, chains
La Taverne, 3ème
Le Temps des Cérises, 4ème

Belgian

Léon de Bruxelles, chains
La Taverne, 3ème

Bistro

Au Lyonnais, 2ème
Au Petit Keller, 11ème
Les Bacchantes, 9ème
Bistro Bourdelle, 15ème
Bistro Romain, chains
Le Mazet, 6ème
Le Passage, 11ème
La Poule au Pot, 7ème
Restaurant Perraudin, 5ème
La Route du Château, 14ème

Cambodian, Thai, and Vietnamese

Cap St-Jacques, 13ème
Dynastie Thai, 8ème
Hien Vuong, 13ème
Lao Thai, 13ème
Phetburi, 15ème
Thien Co, 13ème
Tricotin, 13ème

Caribbean

Babylone, 2ème
La Papaye, 20ème
Le Rocher du Diamant, 12ème

Chinese

Aux Délices de Széchuen, 7ème
Château de Choisy, 13ème
Man Lung, 16ème
Le Palais de l'Est, 10ème
Tai-Yien, 19ème

Crêperie

Le Bouquet de Grenelle, 15ème
Crêperie Le Biniou, 14ème
Crêperie Saint Germain, 6ème
Crêperie St-Malo, 14ème
La Pie Gourmande, 7ème

Deli

Chez Jo Goldenberg, 4ème
Finkelsztajn's, 4ème

Eastern European

Chez Marianne, 4ème
Finkelsztajn's, 4ème
Restaurant Le Beautrellis, 4ème
Restaurant Maroussia, 6ème

French (Traditional)

See any *arrondissement* for one of Paris's abundant French restaurants.

Greek

Café Le Volcan, 5ème
Donys, 2ème
Le Tahar, 15ème
Orestias, 6ème

Indian

Anarkali, 9ème
Kamathenu, 10ème
La Rose du Kashmir, 10ème

Italian

Il Fiorentino Angelo, 5ème
Le Carpaccio, 1er
Le Jardin des Pâtes, 5ème

Japanese

Japanese Barbecue, 2ème
Kiotori, 6ème
Restaurant Japonais Robata, 2ème

Kosher

L'as du Fallafel, 4ème
Pizzería King Salomon, 9ème
(also see Vegetarian, below)

Lebanese

Byblos Café, 16ème
Café le Volcan, 5ème
Samaya, 15ème
Sannine, 9ème

Marxist

Sampiere Corsu, 15ème

Middle Eastern

Chez Marianne, 4ème
L'as du Fallafel, 4ème
Restaurant Olympia II, 17ème

North African

Au Clair de Lune, 2ème
Le Dogon, 10ème
L'Ebouillanté, 4ème
Paris-Dakar, 10ème
Restaurant Le Berbère, 14ème

Nouvelle Cuisine

Au Petit Prince, 6ème

Open Late

Au Paradis du Fruit, chains
Babylone, 2ème
Les Bacchantes, 9ème

Le Bouquet de Grenelle, 15ème
Brasserie Flo, 10ème
Café Aux Artistes 15ème
Chez Gladines, 13ème
Chez Paul, 11ème
Crêperie Saint Germain, 6ème
Donys, 2ème
Il Fiorentino Angelo, 5ème
L'Epi d'Or, 1er
Le Mazet, 6ème
Le Palais de l'Est, 10ème
Pizza Pino, 6ème
Refuge des Fondues, 18ème

Organic
Aquarius Café, 14ème
Crêperie Saint Germain, 6ème
Grand Appetit, 4ème
Le Grenier de Notre Dame, 5ème
Le Jardin des Pâtes, 5ème

Outdoor Dining
A la Courtille, 20ème
Anarkali, 9ème
Aux Délices de Széchuen, 7ème
Le Chartier, 9ème
Chez Lena et Mimille, 5ème
La Dame Tartine, 3ème
L'Ebouillanté, 4ème
Fontaine de Mars, 7ème
L'Incroyable, 1er
La Poule au Pot, 7ème

Pizza
Pizza Pino, 6ème
Pizzeria King Salomon, 9ème
Slice, 6ème

Provençale
Au Boeuf Bourgignon, 9ème
Le Divin, 4ème
Fontaine de Mars, 7ème

Regional Cuisines
Aquarius, 4ème
Au Limonaire, 12ème
Au Sancerrois, 20ème
Aux Arts et Sciences Réunis, 19ème
Chez Francis, 18ème
Chez Gladines 13ème
La Croque au Sel, 7ème
La Franche-Comté, 9ème
Joël's, 12ème
Occitanie, 11ème
Le Petit Chose, 18ème

Sandwich Shops
Antoine's: Les Sandwichs des 5 Continents, 8ème
Le Boulanger, 1er

Le Bouquet de Grenelle, 15ème
Così, 6ème
CROQ 100WICH, 7ème
Donys, 2ème
Le Monsegur, 5ème

Seafood
Brasserie Flo, 10ème
La Criée, chains
Léon de Bruxelles, chains

Spanish
Casa Tina, 16ème

Splurge
L'Auberge Nicolas Flamel, 3ème
Auberge de Jarente, 15ème
Auberge de la Reine Blanche, St-Louis
Au Gourmet de l'Isle, St-Louis
Au Grain de Folie, 18ème
Au Lyonnais, 2ème
Au Pierre de la Butte, 18ème
Aux Délices de Széchuen, 7ème
Brasserie Flo, 10ème
Café du Commerce, 15ème
Chez Claude et Claudine, 18ème
Chez Francis, 18ème
Chez Lena et Mimille, 5ème
Le Club des Poètes, 7ème
Le Colvert, 14ème
Crémerie Restaurant Polidor, 6ème
La Criée, chains
Dynastie Thai, 8ème
La France-Comté, 9ème
Le Hangar, 3ème
Joël's, 12ème
La Maison du Valais, 8ème
Le Perdrix, 2ème
Le Petit Chose, 18ème
Le Vieil Ecu, 1er
Restaurant Les Listines, 15ème
Restaurant Montecristo, St-Louis
Restaurant Natacha, 17ème
Le Rocher du Diamant, 12ème

Swiss
La Maison du Valais, 8ème
La Taverne Suisse, 8ème
Refuge des Fondues, 1er

Take-Out
Le Boulanger, 1er
Chez Jo Goldenberg, 4ème
Finkelsztajn's, 4ème
Hollywood Canteen, chains
Le Palais de l'Est, 10ème

Tex-Mex
Ay, Caramba!, 19ème

Grill Churrasco, 17ème
Texas Blues, 10ème

Vegetarian

Aquarius, 4ème
Aquarius Café, 14ème
Au Grain de Folie, 18ème
Au Paradis du Fruit, chains
Le Chant de la Terre, 10ème
Country Life, 2ème

L'Epicerie Verte, 17ème
Le Grenier de Notre Dame, 5ème
Joy in Food, 17ème
Naturesto, 8ème
Piccolo Teatro, 4ème

West African

A la Banane Ivoirienne, 11ème
N'Zadette-M'foua, 14ème

■■■ RESTAURANT CHAINS

Au Paradis du Fruit, 1, rue des Tournelles, 4ème (tel. 40 27 94 79). M. Bastille. Exit metro on rue St-Antoine and turn right on rue des Tournelles. Paradis St-Michel, 27-29, quai des Grands Augustins, 6ème (tel. 43 54 51 42). M. St-Michel. Cross pl. St-Michel onto quai des Grands Augustins. Paradis Wagram, 32, av. de Wagram, 8ème (tel. 44 09 02 02). M. Ternes or Ch. de Gaulle Etoile. From M. Ternes, walk down av. de Wagram toward l'Arc de Triomphe. A whimsical chain of health-food cafés, all papered with orientalist murals color-coded to match the sorbet. Parisians gather for late-night sundaes and fresh-squeezed fruit juices (20F). Salads 58-74F. Hearty *marmite* stews 59-69F, winter only. Open daily 11:30am-2am; last service at 1am.

Bistro Romain has over 40 locations around Paris including 103, bd. Montparnasse, 6ème (tel. 43 25 25 25); 9, bd. des Italiens, 2ème (tel. 42 97 49 55); and 6, av. Jean Moulin, 14ème (tel. 40 44 03 63). Chain or no, the combination of plush benches, tapestry-covered walls, and affordable, reliable food is tough to beat if not exceptional. At lunch, their 60F *menu* gives a choice of filling dishes; the *menu* at 76F is appropriate for dinner. Lighter *menu* at 89F, full of fruit and fish, provides a pleasing summer meal. Dinner a la carte 130-150F. Desserts are a house specialty; choose from a selection of 35. Usually open daily 11:30am-1am, but times vary from location to location. MC, V.

La Criée, 15, rue Lagrange, 5ème (tel. 43 54 23 57). M. Maubert-Mutualité. 31, bd. Bonne Nouvelle, 2ème (tel. 42 33 32 99). M. Bonne Nouvelle. 54, bd. Montparnasse, 15ème (tel. 42 22 01 81). M. Montparnasse-Bienvenüe. One of the few places in Paris with affordable seafood. All branches suited with a cute nautical theme. Reasonably priced given the quality of the food. 3-course *menu* 85F. 119F version includes wine. Open daily noon-2:30pm and 7-11:30pm. MC, V, AmEx.

Hollywood Canteen, 4, rue Pierre Lescot, 1er (tel. 42 33 66 30). M. Châtelet-Les-Halles. 8, rue de Berri, 8ème (tel. 45 62 35 97). M. Georges V or Etoile. 53, rue de la Harpe, 5ème (tel. 46 33 89 33). M. St-Michel. 18, bd Montmartre, 9ème (tel. 42 46 46 45). M. Montmartre. 25, rue de la Roquette, 11ème (tel. 47 00 18 28). M. Bastille. They also have their own *boutique traiteur* (food shop) at 29, rue de Charenton, 12ème (tel. 40 02 09 42). M. Bastille. More American than America. Neon-illuminated 1950s-style diner grills decent burgers named after American movie stars (22-45F) pinned with tiny stars-and-stripes instead of deli toothpicks. 59F *menu* features salad, steak, and a choice of wine or Coke. Huge brownies drowned in ice cream and chocolate sauce 25F. Open daily 8:30am-1am.

Léon de Bruxelles, 8, pl. de la République, 11ème (tel. 43 38 28 69). M. République. Also at 63, av. des Champs Elysées, 8ème (tel. 42 25 96 16), in Les Halles at 120, rue Rambuteau, 1er (tel. 42 36 18 50), at the Bastille, on 3, bd. Beaumarchais, 11ème (tel. 42 71 75 55), and at 1-3, pl. Pigalle, 18ème (tel. 42 80 28 33). Once a seafood stand, now a restaurant chain, Léon's has served *moules-frites* (mussels and fries) since 1893. *Moules-frites* from 59F; with a beer 65F; with appetizer and a beer 98F. Many locations throughout Paris. Safety is a concern at locations in pl. Pigalle and in pl. République. Open daily 11:45am-12:30am. MC, V, AmEx.

Oh! Poivrier, 143, bd. Raspail, 6ème (tel. 43 26 98 27). M. Notre-Dame des Champs. 25, quai des Grands Augustins, 6ème (tel. 43 29 41 77). M. St-Michel. This chain's *grandes assiettes gourmandes* make a great light lunch, snack, or quick dinner. Snazzy gray, black, and glass interior. Plates come with an assortment of salads, smoked fish, duck, roast beef, fresh fruit, coleslaw, and cheese (48-70F). All accompanied by toasted *pain levain* (a sourdough bread). Open daily 11:30am-midnight. MC, V.

Pizza Pino, 57, bd. Montparnasse, 6*ème* (tel. 45 48 46 89). M. Montparnasse. Also at 33, Champs-Elysées, 8*ème* (tel. 43 59 23 89); 38, rue Severin, 5*ème* (tel. 43 29 60 69). All pizzeria branches bake pies in wood-burning ovens. Late-night hours are their strongest appeal. Open daily 11am-4am (Champs-Elysées location stays open until 4:30am). MC, V, AmEx.

■■■ RESTAURANTS —BY LOCATION

■ ILE ST-LOUIS

The restaurants on Ile-St-Louis are everything you'd expect: expensive, romantic, and charming to a fault. In summer, rue St-Louis en l'Ile, which traverses the island, becomes a pedestrian mall of just-showered Americans looking for the little restaurant they remember from last year. For the most part, budget travelers in search of bargain *menus* had better look elsewhere. The following establishments are, however, good bets for a dinner-date:

Les Fous de l'Isle, 33, rue des Deux-Ponts (tel. 43 25 76 67). M. Pont Marie. From the metro walk straight over the bridge. A cantina for the year-round neighborhood crowd, this artsy tearoom-cum-restaurant provides comfort without an attitude. An ideal place to read. Hosts occasional evening concerts. Appetizers 25-35F; check the blackboards for daily specials. Salads 28-85F, starting with *cabreze* (the cheapest) and ending with the *scandinave* mixed platter of smoked salmon and trout, tarama, and toast (the most expensive). Hot main courses 70-85F, featuring pastas and steak. Our compliments to whomever baked the brownies, cheesecake, and carrot cake (30-35F). Open Tues.-Fri. noon-3pm and 7-11pm, Sat. 7:30-11pm, Sun. noon-3pm for brunch; *salon de thé* open Tues.-Sun. 3-7pm. MC, V.

Restaurant Montecristo, 81, rue St-Louis-en-l'Ile (tel. 46 33 35 46). M. Pont Marie. Cross the Pont Marie and continue on rue des Deux-Ponts until it intersects rue St-Louis-en-l'Ile. An elegant gourmet Italian restaurant appointed with plants and Art Nouveau lamps. The specialties are pasta, veal, and sorbets. 2-course dinner *menus* at 98F and 128F include an appetizer and main course. Reservations are essential. Open daily noon-2:30pm and 7-11:30pm. MC, V, AmEx.

Au Gourmet de l'Isle, 42, rue St-Louis-en-l'Ile (tel. 43 26 79 27). M. Pont Marie. Cross the Pont Marie and continue on rue des Deux-Ponts until it intersects rue St-Louis-en-l'Ile. Lattice-covered walls and decorative wine bottles furnish the snug setting for traditional French food. The house specialty is *pavé de saumon à l'estragon* (salmon steak with tarragon). 130F menu proffers an appetizer, main dish, salad or cheese, and dessert. Dinner a la carte is expensive: appetizers 30-50F, main courses 65-85F, and desserts 40F. Open Wed.-Sun. noon-2pm and 7-10pm. Dinner reservations recommended. MC, V.

Auberge de la Reine Blanche, 30, rue St-Louis-en-l'Ile (tel. 46 33 07 87). M. Pont Marie. Cross the Pont Marie and continue on rue des Deux Ponts until it intersects rue St-Louis-en-l'Ile. Small, cute, and full of doll-house miniatures and fetching French food aromas. Lots of veal, lamb, and beef in heavy sauces. Draws families and middle-aged couples—mostly tourists. *Menus* at 110F and 140F. Open Fri.-Tues. noon-11:30pm, Wed.-Thurs. 6-11:30pm. Reservations recommended for dinner. MC, V, AmEx.

■ FIRST ARRONDISSEMENT

The small streets around the Palais-Royal teem with small, traditional restaurants, each worth a special visit. Cheaper, louder eateries constellate Les Halles, offering everything from fast food to 4-course Italian feasts. The disreputable delights of rue St-Denis may put off first-time visitors. Sex shops and thoroughly respectable restaurants coexist *face à face* down the portion of this street near Les Halles. During day-light hours, travelers should consider these eateries welcome bargains, despite being part of a street scene that might be unwelcome.

L'Incroyable, 26, rue de Richelieu or 23, rue de Montpensier (tel. 42 96 24 64). M. Palais-Royal. Walk along the right side of the Palais Royal and turn right on rue de Montpensier; look for passage Potier on your left. An intimate restaurant with an incredibly cheap 3-course *menu* (60F, 70F in the evening). Steak and grilled pork are among its simple, good-tasting main courses; 10F extra for veal or chicken cut-let, and 8F extra for a slice of the delectable tartes maison. *Foie de veau* (calf's liver) 55F. Terrace and quaintly decorated interior. Open Tues.-Fri. noon-2:15pm and 6:30-9pm, Sat. and Mon. noon-2:15pm. Closed late Dec. and for the first 2 weeks of Jan.

Au Petit Ramoneur, 74, rue St-Denis (tel. 42 36 39 24). M. Les Halles. Walk down Rambuteau toward the Pompidou and turn on rue St-Denis. Crammed during lunch hour, this is a place to eat—and eat well—but not to relax. You'll also have to get over the restaurant's proximity to sex shops. 64F *menu* includes appetizer, main course, and ½L of wine; as the menu declares, "Not bad!" Open Mon.-Fri. 11:30am-2:30pm and 6:30-9:30pm.

Le Vieil Ecu, 166, rue St-Honoré (tel. 42 60 20 14). M. Palais-Royal. Walk toward the Palais Royal (away from the Louvre) and turn right on rue St-Honoré. Look for the restaurant on your left. Checkered tablecloths, lace-draped lamps, and the exposed beams of a 300-year-old building set a hospitable tone. 63F lunch *menu* of traditional French food, drink included. Dinner *menu* 114F. Main courses 79-83F. Feast upon dishes like *confit de canard* and *onglet à l'échalottes* (flank steak with shallots) along with a glass of Beaujolais (20F). Finish with a *tarte tatin* (38F). Vegetarian entrees available. Most Saturdays, live piano and folk guitar play upstairs. Open Mon.-Sat. 11:30am-3pm and 6:30-11pm. MC, V.

L'Emile, 76, rue J.J.-Rousseau (tel. 42 36 58 58). M. Les Halles. Walk toward the church St-Eustache and bend right onto rue Coquillère; turn right on rue J.-J. Rousseau. Slightly over-slick decor made up for by sophisticated cuisine and friendly staff. 3-course lunch *menu* 82F. A la carte, beef with onion preserves 78F, saffron filet of salmon 82F. The menu changes with the season. Open Mon.-Fri. noon-2:30pm and 8pm-midnight, Sat. 8pm-midnight. MC, V.

Le Carpaccio, 6, rue Pierre Lescot (tel. 45 08 44 80). M. Les Halles. Near the Pompidou. Waiters maneuver 4-foot pepper grinders over this restaurant's outstanding Italian food. Large terrace on a pedestrian street in Les Halles. Real pizza 37-66F. A variety of 2-course *menus* (49-92F), coffee included. Try the namesake beef (58F), duck (60F), or salmon (87F) carpaccio. Memorable pastries (29-37F). Open daily noon-12:30am.

L'Epi d'Or, 25, rue J.-J. Rousseau (tel. 42 36 38 12). M. Les Halles. The elegant interior adds zing to simple French food. Antique-strewn dining room filled with copper pots, majolica, and fresh-cut flowers. Frequented by journalists from the nearby *Figaro* offices. 2-course *menu* 105F. Main courses from 90F. Try *entrecôte bordelaise* (102F). *Menu* served till 9pm. Open Mon.-Fri. noon-2:30pm and 7:30pm-2am, Sat. 7:30pm-2am; last order at midnight. Closed Aug. and 1 week in Feb. MC, V.

La Mangerie, 17, rue des Petits Champs, not to be confused with rue Croix des Petits Champs (tel. 42 97 51 01). M. Bourse. Offers casual, understated refinement and a view of the Palais Royal and its gardens. Daily special 60F. A second cheaper one (40F) is offered June-July. *Entrecôte* 65F. Save room for home-baked pastry. Fruit tart 22F, *crème caramel* 18F. Only the room in the back has the view; it's worth reserving a table there. Otherwise, sit in the undistinctive front room. Open Mon.-Fri. noon-2pm. MC, V.

Lescure, 7, rue de Mondovi (tel. 42 60 18 91). M. Concorde. A lively, popular restaurant, serving hearty French food for over 70 years. 3-course *menu* (98F) includes wine. Wide selection and huge servings. Open Mon.-Fri. noon-2:15pm and 7-10:15pm, Sat. noon-2:15pm. Closed Aug. MC, V.

The Front Page, 56-58, rue St-Denis. M. Châtelet-Les Halles. The menu states: "I must be suffering from a mental disease" to choose American over French food.

Similarly afflicted tourists and Parisians should head here. Choose from 3 *menus* featuring hamburger with chili and fries, grilled chicken with BBQ sauce or *entrecôte*. 3-course *menu* 59F. Elaborate burgers 56F50 and up. Lunch special of burger and dessert 49F. Open daily 11:30am-5am; serves tea and pastries 2:30-6:30pm. MC, V.

Le Boulanger, 80, rue St-Denis (tel. 42 36 53 58). M. Les Halles. A cafeteria-like bakery and café. What's special about it? The prices. Take out a salad (15-30F) or sit and eat for a few francs more (24-34F). *Plats du jour* hover around 40F. Quiche 17F. *Café crème* 5F50-7F50. Open daily 7am-8pm.

■ SECOND ARRONDISSEMENT

Wedged between the wide, touristed boulevards of the 9ème, the affluence of the 1er near the Louvre, and the bohemian grunge of Les Halles, the 2ème provides inexpensive meals to tourists exploring this and neighboring *quartiers*. Graze along rue Montorgueil, a market street lined with excellent bakeries, fruit stands, and prepared specialty stores. (The Codec supermarket at no. 69 caters to the impatient among you.) For Japanese, Thai and Vietnamese food, visit the passage des Panoramas, a food court off rue St-Marc (M. Bourse).

Au Clair de Lune, 27, rue Tiquetonne (tel. 42 33 59 10). M. Etienne-Marcel. Small corner restaurant offering huge plates of well-priced French and Algerian food. Couscous (52-68F) for ravenous (though discriminating) eaters. *Entrecôte* 58F. 3-course lunch *menu* 62F. Sample Algerian wines like *Royal Smabah* or *Sidi Brahim* (60F). *Paella,* Fri. only, 70F. Open daily noon-2:30pm and 7:30-11pm. MC, V.

Au Lyonnais, 32, rue St-Marc (tel. 42 96 65 04; fax 42 97 42 95). M. Richelieu-Drouot or Bourse. Copious, traditional French food set with floral tile and Victorian lamps. Dine upstairs or downstairs on *caille rôtie* (roast quail) or *lapin aux échalotes* (rabbit with shallots, 70F). 2-course *menu* 87F. Open Mon.-Fri. noon-2:30pm and 7pm-midnight, Sat. 7pm-midnight. Reserve a table for dinner. AmEx, MC, V.

Japanese Barbecue, 60, rue Montorgueil (tel. 42 33 49 61). M. Sentier. A Western clientele gathers in the modest dining room for delicious Japanese food. Sit at the bar and watch the Japanese chef tend the charcoal grill. All *menus* come with broth and rice. 64F *menu* includes 7 shishkebabs. The 80F *chiraci menu* features a variety of raw fish. Lunchtime *menus* around 54F. Open Mon.-Sat. noon-2:30pm and 7-10:45pm.

La Perdrix, 6, rue Mandar (tel. 42 36 83 21). M. Sentier. Lunchtime business crowd gathers affordable French cuisine. The long, paneled interior's occasional hunting trophies make it resemble a medieval banquet hall. 59F *menu* includes 3 courses and a drink. 80F *menu* spotlights *canard à l'orange* (duck with orange zest). More sumptuous 100F *menu* as well. A la carte: *entrecôte* 58F, *cassoulet au confit de canard* (kidney bean and duck stew, 79F). Excellent homemade desserts. Open Mon.-Fri. 11:30am-3pm and 6:30-10pm, Sat. 11:30am-3pm.

Country Life, 6, rue Daunou (tel. 42 97 48 51). M. Opéra. Often fancy vegetarian cuisine served in a charming, wood-accented health food store. 62F buffet (the only way to eat here) includes soups and salads as well as hot main courses and wide selection of *crudités* (raw veggies). Fresh carrot juice 10F, *infusions* (herbal tea) 5F. No smoking. Open Mon.-Fri. 11:30am-2:30pm. Store open Mon.-Thurs. 10am-6:30pm, Fri. 10am-3pm.

Donys, 8, rue Etienne Marcel (tel. 42 36 28 30). M. Etienne-Marcel. On the corner of rue St-Denis mixed in with like-minded Greek sandwich places. Great-tasting meat (22F), tuna (12F), or chicken (20F) sandwiches. Take-out available. Open daily 10am-2pm and 4pm-7am.

Babylone, 34, rue Tiquetonne (tel. 42 33 48 35). M. Etienne-Marcel. Late-night revelers stream in from discos for Antillean specialties like like *gombo* and *maffé.* Zebra skins and African carvings on the walls, banana leaves on the ceiling, zouk and reggae on the stereo. Sardis-like display of photos, featuring Black celebrities who've eaten here, like Stevie Wonder and Jesse Jackson. Prices are quite high. Main courses 80-100F. Tantalizing desserts like *aloko* (flamed bananas in liqueur,

35F) and *saisai* (*aloko* with raisins and *crème fraîche* 45F). *Apéritifs* 30-50F, plantation punch 40F, cocktails 50F. Open nightly 8pm-8am.

■ THIRD ARRONDISSEMENT

Close to both the 3ème's museums and to the big-city clamor of its whole-sale stores, the restaurants listed here are as varied in personality as the *arrondissement* in which they reside. For the most part, expect sit-down meals of classic Parisian fare. Dinner a la carte can be pricey, but lunchtime *menus* make even the glamorous affordable.

Vue du Parc, 4, rue du Parc Royal (tel. 48 04 90 50). M. Chemin-Vert. Take rue St-Gilles off bd. Beaumarchais; the restaurant is opposite the park just past rue de Sévigné. Light, Brazilian-inflected cuisine in a sunny restaurant. Tasty salads, like the "exotique" with avocado and *roquefort*, are reasonably priced (40-50F, half that for *entrée* size). Try to get a window seat overlooking the square Léopold Achille. Brazilian fare includes *boulettes*, rolled and grilled balls of cheese, corn or ground meat (32-36F). *Assiettes* such as grilled lemon chicken 55-59F. Desserts 21-28F. Open Tues.-Sat. noon-3:30pm and 7:30-11pm, Sun. noon-3:30pm. MC, V.

L'Auberge Nicolas Flamel, 51, rue de Montmorency (tel. 42 71 77 78). M. Rambuteau. Walk opposite traffic on rue Beaubourg and turn left on rue de Montmorency. Occupying what is believed to be the second oldest residential building in Paris, this *auberge* has a history spanning 5 centuries. In the 15th century, Nicolas Flamel, alchemist and idealist, used this address as a soup kitchen and shelter for transients. In its current state, the *auberge* feeds a less needy crowd. Slick, un-upholstered Louis XVI chairs, gilt mirrors, and whimsical Chagallian wall and window decorations serve as backdrop for adventurous regional cuisine. A la carte prices will send penny-pinchers reeling, but the 2-course midday *menu* (69F) recalls the *auberge's* charitable origins. Rationalize the 3-course midday *menu* (98F) as the cost of both a meal and a museum visit. Only another 40F for a *demi-pichet* of Haut-Médoc. The menu changes with the seasons, but usually includes Lyon sausage prepared with lentils, *chicken fricassée à l'ancienne,* and chocolate cake. Dinner *menu* 170F without wine. Open Mon.-Fri. 12:15-2:15pm and 8:15-11:30pm, Sat.-Sun. 8:15-11:30pm. MC, V.

Le Hangar, impasse Berthaud (tel. 42 74 55 44). M. Rambuteau. Exit on the even-numbered side of rue Beaubourg, walk away from the Pompidou, and the *impasse* is soon to the right. Tucked up an alley near the Centre Pompidou, Le Hangar cloisters wine-sipping people-who-lunch from the nearby rush of traffic. Amiable and unpretentious atmosphere as its name, *le hangar* (lean-to), would suggest. Appetizers 28-58F and many main dishes at 78F, such as the vast asparagus salad with green beans, *jambon de pomme,* and fresh *chèvre,* or *foie gras de canard poêlé.* Open Mon. 7pm-midnight, Tues.-Sat. noon-midnight. Tea and cakes served 3:30-7pm.

Chez Alexandre, 75, rue des Archives (tel. 42 78 82 18). M. Arts-et-Métiers. Walk away from the two churches on rue Réaumur (which becomes rue de Bretagne) and turn right on rue des Archives; watch for the small awning on the right, before the post office. While the busy modern lights, watercolors and light French pop might dash hopes of a romantic Italian dinner, the dozen varieties of pasta (40-50F) here will convince you to stay. Perfect for frugal backpackers on whirlwind treks through the Marais.

Les Arquebusiers, 10, rue des Arquebusiers (tel. 48 87 94 12). M. St-Sébastien Froissart. Walk south toward Bastille along bd. Beaumarchais, turn right on rue St-Claude, and les Arquebusiers is on the corner to the left. A Marais cross-section of artists, merchants, and young plain-folk dodges tourist hordes for the wood paneling and soft lighting of this corner bar. The upright piano in the corner caters to a young crowd that has had a few drinks. Temporary art expositions rotate monthly. Dinner *assiettes* (70-98F) change daily. Past options have included lamb chops (75F) and grilled salmon and seafood (80F). 3-course set lunch *menu* 77F. Desserts 30-38F, beer on tap 20F. Open Mon.-Fri. 11:30am-3:30pm and 7:30pm-1:30am, Sat. 7:30pm-2am. MC, V.

FOURTH ARRONDISSEMENT

Le Taxi Jaune, 13, rue Chapon (tel. 42 78 92 24). M. Arts-et-Métiers or Rambuteau. From M. Arts-et-Métiers walk with traffic along rue Beaubourg and turn left on rue Chapon. Cheerfully decorated in kitsch Americana, with piped-in Beach Boys and Dick Tracy-esque cartoons. The 68F 3-course lunch *menu* includes a drink. Try the *brochette d'agneau* and *oeuf à la neige*. At 89F, the dinner *menu* offers an economical chance to try duck, served in raspberry vinegar, and *profiterolles*. Open Mon. 11:30am-2:30pm, Tues.-Fri. 11:30am-2:30pm and 8-11pm, Sat. 8-11pm. MC, V.

La Taverne, 5, place de la République (tel. 42 78 50 86). Also at 155 boulevard St-Germain, 6ème (tel. 45 48 22 66). M. République. For beer fans in search of the exotic but familiar; menu features mussels cooked in beer (45-66F, plus 21F for a side order of *pommes frites*) and beer *fondue*. Beer 16-40F a pint. This is not a frat-party joke; the Tavern is deadly serious about providing Belgian cuisine, which happens to rely heavily on Belgium's distinctive beers, *gueuze* and *kriek*. The prices are fairly high (set *menu* 105F), but portions are generous. Seating in back and in the basement, should you choose to avoid the noise and pollution on the terrace. Open daily 9am-2am. MC, V, AmEx.

■ FOURTH ARRONDISSEMENT

Be warned: the 4ème *arrondissement* is fast becoming a museum. A landmark on every corner, a gallery for every *tabac*, the lower half of the Marais is not the humble quarter it once was. Even with prices on the rise, however, budget restaurants are holding their ground. Filling, inexpensive meals are easily culled from the delis and falafel stands on rue des Rosiers, pulse of the Marais' Jewish quarter. Avoid the pricey *croque-monsieurs* on the rue de Rivoli.

Chez Marianne, 2, rue des Hôspitalières-St-Gervais (tel. 42 72 18 86). M. St-Paul. From the metro cross to the left side of rue de Rivoli and continue up rue Pavée; turn left on rue des Rosiers and right on rue des Hôspitalières-St-Gervais. Sample Israeli and Eastern European specialties in this folksy canteen and specialty store. Wine bottles and bins of pickled delicacies, stacked floor to ceiling, provide a cheerfully cluttered backdrop. Here the Marais' Jewish community converges *en famille* or with friends for falafel (30F), blini (10F), and *vatrouchka*, a *gâteau de fromage* rather different from American cheesecake. Sample 4, 5, or 6 specialties (55F, 65F, or 75F). Choose from such options as *zaziki*, tabouli, *méchouia* and hummus. Arrive before 7:45pm to avoid the dinner crowd. Take-out available. Open Sat.-Thurs. 11am-midnight.

L'Ebouillanté, 6, rue des Barres (tel. 42 78 48 62). M. St-Paul or Pont Marie. From M. St-Paul walk opposite traffic down rue François-Miron and turn left on rue des Barres. A casual restaurant and tearoom, l'Ebouillanté offers light snacks and meals in ambiant calm just steps from the bustle of cars and *bouquinistes* along the Seine. In summer months, sit on the quiet cobblestone terrace and watch arty passers-by from local galleries cross paths with the monks from adjacent Eglise St-Gervais. House specialities include *bricks*—filled Tunisian *crêpes* (41-56F); try them with salmon and *fromage blanc* or with cheese, eggs, and tomatoes. Open Tues.-Sun. noon-9pm.

La Dame Tartine, 2, rue Brisemiche (tel. 42 77 32 22). M. Rambuteau. Next to the Stravinsky fountain. Also at 69, rue de Lyon, 12ème (tel. 44 68 96 95). The fountain-side terrace fills with a mostly young, dressed-down crowd. Just a stone's throw from the Pompidou's album-cover street life. The restaurant itself is almost as lively as the fountain. Main courses 25-40F. Open daily noon-11:30pm. MC, V.

Piccolo Teatro, 6, rue des Ecouffes (tel. 42 72 17 79). M. St-Paul. From the metro walk in the direction of traffic down rue de Rivoli and take a right on rue des Ecouffes. Vegetarian cuisine served in the heart of the Jewish quarter. A romantic hideout for the health-conscious. Come for a candle-lit tryst over bulghur wheat. Midday menu at 53F includes soup or appetizer (try the miso soup), a *gratin de légumes,* and dessert of *fromage blanc.* Various platters (all about 60F) offer a savory, filling combination of grains and vegetables. Nighttime *menu* hovers around 74F. Open Wed.-Sun. noon-3pm and 7-11pm. MC, V, AmEx.

Auberge de Jarente, 7, rue de Jarente (tel. 42 77 49 35). M. St-Paul. From the metro cross to the left side of rue de Rivoli and walk opposite traffic; walk two blocks and turn left on rue de Sévigné and right on rue de Jarente. Disappear into this dreamy cottage-like restaurant to feast on Basque specialties like *cailles* (quail) and *cuisses de grenouilles* (frogs' legs). 115F *menu* includes *entrée, plat,* salad or cheese, and dessert. 130F *menu* includes a quarter-*pichet* of wine. Finish your meal with or with *oeufs à la neige.* 75F lunch *menu.* Open Tues.-Sat. noon-2:30pm and 7:30-10:30pm. MC, V, AmEx.

L'as du Fallafel, 34, rue des Rosiers (tel. 48 87 63 60). M. St-Paul. From the metro cross to the left side of rue de Rivoli and continue up rue Pavée; turn left on rue des Rosiers. In the vitrine of this kosher falafel stand and grocery hang portaits of Rebbe Schneerson and, surprise, Lenny Kravitz. In *Rolling Stone,* Kravitz credited this unlikely little eatery with "the best falafel in the world, particularly the special eggplant falafel with hot sauce." Gonna go his way with the falafel (20F)? Otherwise, wander slowly through the Marais with hummus (18F) or schwarma (32F).

Le Temps des Cérises, 31, rue de la Cerisaie (tel. 42 72 08 63). M. Bastille or Sully-Morland. From M. Bastille exit on bd. Henri IV and turn left onto rue de la Cerisaie. Yellowing snapshots of yesteryear's Paris and a young, neighborhood crowd make this restaurant/bar a relaxed hangout with elbow-to-elbow familiarity. Hearty 3-course lunch *menu* (62F) usually includes veal sauté or ratatouille with fries. Beer 9F20-13F50. Open for lunch Mon.-Fri. 11:30am-2:30pm; bar closes at 8pm.

Chez Jo Goldenberg, 7, rue des Rosiers. M. St-Paul. From the metro cross rue de Rivoli and walk up rue Pavée; turn left on rue des Rosiers. In the heart of the Marais' Jewish quarter, Goldenberg's has become something of a landmark. A deli and restaurant since 1920, it suffered a 1982 terrorist attack which took the life of the owner's son. A pilgrimage site for tourists and celebrities (from Moshe Dayan to Harry Belafonte), prices are somewhat high. A slice of the old world almost, but not quite. Not quite kosher, either. *Plat du jour* (70F), soups (50F), and pastries galore. Take-out section where you can buy borscht, sauerkraut, pickles, pastries, bagels (6F), and other traditional foods. Deli open daily 8:30am-11pm; dining room open daily noon-midnight.

Le Divin, 41, rue Ste-Croix-de-la-Bretonnerie (tel. 42 77 10 20). M. Hôtel-de-Ville or Rambuteau. Walk away from the Hôtel de Ville on rue du Temple and turn right on rue Ste-Croix-de-la-Bretonnerie. A taste of Provence in a countrified stucco-and-beam setting. 3-course lunch *menu* 62F. Lighter fare includes *assiettes* with salads, blini, and cheeses all for around 70F. In the evening couples 30-45 commingle here, drawn by the sophisticated decor and 89F, 3-course dinner. Open Tues.-Sun. noon-2pm and 7:30-11pm. MC, V.

Restaurant le Beautreillis, 18 rue Beautreillis (tel. 42 72 36 04). M. Bastille. Exit the metro on rue St-Antoine and take the fifth left onto rue Beautreillis. Jim Morrison fans will want to stop by this restaurant, located across from the address where he died. Vieran, the proprietor, dons a leather vest and chains during daylight hours to blend with the groupies. 7 volumes of comment books are a fascinating read over goulash (house specialty). 60F lunch *menu* highlights Slavic cuisine. This year we must report that the lack of a cabaret licence has brought dinner music with the accordionist who may have once played for Ceaucescu to a lamentable end. Now tapes of *tsigane* music fill the silences between Monday *Doors* nights. Open Sept.-July noon-11pm. MC, V, AmEx.

Aquarius, 54, rue Ste-Croix-de-la-Bretonnerie (tel. 48 87 48 71). M. Hôtel-de-Ville. Walk away from the Hôtel de Ville on rue du Temple and turn right on rue Ste-Croix-de-la-Bretonnerie. Also at 40, rue de Gergovie 14ème (tel. 45 41 36 88). Potted plants, straight-backed wooden chairs, and clean, smoke-free air make dinner or lunch here seem like a stint in a new-age terrarium. Between courses, you might or might not want to browse through the small occult library. Fresh, wholesome vegetarian dishes borrow from rural regions of France. A simple rainy day snack is "bread and butter and something warm to drink" (22F). *Menu* at 53F includes delicious homemade yogurt and veggie daily special. Try the *assiette paysanne* (54F), a combo platter of *chèvre chaud,* garlic bread, roasted mushrooms and potatoes (dinner only). Open Mon.-Sat. noon-10pm. *Plats du jour,* cereals, and hot vegetable dishes served noon-2pm and 7-10pm. Closed last three weeks of August.

Grand Appetit, 9, rue de la Cerisaie (tel. 40 27 04 95). M. Bastille. Exit the metro on bd. Bourdon and turn right on rue de la Cerisaie. This organic food store houses a small, nourishing, and inexpensive vegetarian restaurant with a Southeast Asian bent. Miso soup (18F) will fortify those on even the tightest of budgets; a bowl of rice topped with grains and veggies makes a fine lunch (32F). Those with larger appetites should opt for the *assiette composée* (57F). Japanese tea is free for bowl and *assiette* meals. *Café* and *infusions* 10F, juices 12-20F. Restaurant open Mon.-Thurs. noon-8pm, Fri. and Sun. noon-2pm. Store open Mon.-Thurs. 10am-8pm, Fri. and Sun. 10am-4pm. MC, V.

L'Arbre Aux Sabots, 3, rue Simon-le-Franc (tel. 42 71 10 24). M. Rambuteau. Walk along rue Beaubourg for half the length of the Centre Pompidou (rear-side) and turn left on rue Simon-le-Franc. The decoration (a lot of Klimt, some temporary art exhibits) and good location near the Centre Pompidou may explain why this restaurant attracts such an artsy crowd. The 65F midday *menu* includes *foie de veau* (calf's liver). The 95F evening *menu* features *cuisse de canard à l'orange* and a choice of sorbet, chocolate mousse, or vanilla cream. Salads 45-60F, *plats du jour* 65-75F. Open Mon.-Fri. noon-2pm and 7:30pm-midnight. MC, V, AmEx.

Finkelsztajn's, 27, rue des Rosiers (tel. 42 72 78 91). 24, rue des Ecouffes (tel. 48 87 92 85). M. St-Paul. This delicatessen offers huge meat sandwiches (30-40F). (See Groceries.) Store on rue des Rosiers open Wed.-Sun. 10am-2pm and 3-7pm; store on rue des Ecouffes open Mon. and Thurs.-Sun. 10am-2pm and 3-7pm.

■ FIFTH ARRONDISSEMENT

Foraging for food in the 5*ème* requires no special skills. Rue Mouffetard is the undisputed main culinary artery of this lively *arrondissement.* Traditional French, Greek, and Lebanese restaurants dovetail along the "Mouff," extending down rue Descartes all the way to bd. St-Germain. The highest density of cheap eateries are found along the pedestrian rue de Pot-de-Fer. To assemble your own lunch or dinner, spend a morning at one of the 5*ème*'s open-air markets, on rue Mouffetard or on pl. Maubert (See Markets).

L'Apostrophe, 34, rue de la Montagne Ste-Geneviève (tel. 43 54 10 93). M. Maubert-Mutualité. From the metro walk down bd. St-Germain toward the Institut du Monde Arabe and turn right on rue de la Montagne Ste-Geneviève. Tiny, unpretentious French restaurant on a lovely street that winds down the hill from the Panthéon. Somewhat garishly decorated with huge candles. This restaurant offers 3 well-priced *menus:* at 49F, served until 8pm; at 65F, served until 9pm; at 85F, served all night. The first two *menus* include an appetizer and main course (10F supplement for dessert or cheese course). The third offers 3 courses, with an all-you-can-eat buffet as an appetizer choice. Open daily 6pm-2am.

Café Le Volcan, 10, rue Thouin (tel. 46 33 38 33). M. Cardinal Lemoine. Turn left on rue Cardinal Lemoine and take a right on rue Thouin. Boisterous restaurant heats up at night with a youthful crowd of regulars. Posters of Bogart, Chaplin, and Dexter Gordon punctuate the otherwise plain, brick-floored interior. Specializes in *mousaka* and other Greek dishes. The 55F *menu* (served until 9pm) includes appetizer, main course, and dessert; at lunch it includes a glass of wine as well. Dinner *menus* 80-100F. Open daily noon-2pm and 7-11:30pm. MC, V.

Chez Lena et Mimille, 32, rue Tournefort (tel. 47 07 72 47). M. Censier-Daubenton. From the metro walk across pl. Bernard-Halfern to rue Arbalète; turn right on rue Lhomond and continue to pl. Lucien-Herr. Everything you imagine a classic French restaurant to be, and more. Truly traditional cuisine served in an elegant pink and burgundy setting. In summer, dine on the terrace overlooking a leafy *place.* 2-course lunch *menu* at 98F. Dinner with complimentary cocktail, *entrée,* *plat,* dessert, wine, and coffee 185F. Open Mon.-Fri. noon-2pm and 7:30-11pm, closed for lunch Sat.-Sun. Reservations accepted. MC, V.

L' Estrapade, 15, rue de l'Estrapade (tel. 43 25 72 58). M. Luxembourg. From pl. du Panthéon turn right on rue Clotaire and left on rue de l'Estrapade. This tiny, salmon and green bistro specializes in modest, exquisitely prepared French cuisine like *poulet de pot* and *soupe à l'oignon.* Antique caricatures of French celebrities and statesmen dot the wall. Excellent location near the Panthéon. 89F lunch *menu* includes appetizer, main course, dessert, and coffee. Dinner ala carte 62-89F. Open Wed.-Mon. noon-2:30pm and 7-11pm. MC, V.

Le Grenier de Notre Dame, 18, rue de la Bûcherie (tel. 43 29 98 29). M. St-Michel. Walk along quai St-Michel to quai de Montebello; turn right on rue Lagrange and immediately left on rue de la Bûcherie. Macrobiotics' and soybean-freaks' delight. A restaurant that ladles up vegetarian *cassoulet*—a stew of beans, tofu, and soy sausages—along with an appetizer and dessert, all for 75F. Delicious *polenta* with stir-fried vegetables 70F. Open daily noon-2:30 and 7:30-11pm. MC, V, AmEx.

Le Jardin des Pâtes, 4, rue Lacépède (tel. 43 31 50 71). M. Jussieu. From the metro walk up rue Linné and turn right on rue Lacépède. Organic, whole-grain gourmet pasta accompanies a host of farm-fresh sauces—from sesame butter to duck and *crème fraîche.* Locals suggest the *pâtes de seigle* (54F), with ham, white wine, and *comté* cheese. Many vegetarian offerings. 8 tables unassumingly set with woven placemats. Main courses 48-70F. Open Tues.-Sun. noon-2:30pm and 7-10:30pm.

Restaurant L'Escapade, 11, rue de la Montagne Ste-Geneviève (tel. 46 33 23 85). M. Maubert-Mutualité. From bd. St-Germain turn right on rue de la Montagne Ste-Geneviève. All-you-can-eat meets Paris chic. 85F *menu* includes an hors d'oeuvre, a buffet of cold salads and pâté, a main course, dessert, and wine (serve yourself from the keg). For atmosphere, eat in the cool, dark *cave* downstairs. Reservations accepted. Open 6:30pm-2am.

Restaurant Perraudin, 157, rue St-Jacques (tel. 46 33 15 75). M. Luxembourg. From the metro take rue Royer Collard to rue St-Jacques. At this family-style bistro, locals gather to relax in the burgundy and dark wood interior. Gamble on *le plat du jour selon l'humeur du chef* (daily special according to the chef's mood), or try old favorites like *sautée d'agneau aux flageolets* (sautéed lamb with white beans) 58F. Come early to avoid crowds. 3-course lunch *menu* 60F. Appetizers from 26F. Main dishes 58F. Open Tues.-Fri. noon-2:15pm and 7:30-10:15pm, Mon. and Sat. 7:30-10:15pm.

The Rib Joint, 14, rue Thouin (tel. 43 26 37 09). M. Cardinal Lemoine. From the metro walk up rue Cardinal Lemoine and turn right onto rue Thouin. An American BBQ pit abroad. The filling 95F *menu* includes a choice of Southern BBQ pork ribs or Louisiana-style chicken, macaroni salad, potato salad, coleslaw, beans, and a brownie with *crème fraîche.* Some vegetarian plates. Open 7:30pm-2am.

Il Fiorentino Angelo, 26, rue de la Montagne Ste-Geneviève (tel. 46 34 71 61). M. Maubert-Mutualité. From bd. St-Germain take a right on rue de la Montagne Ste-Geneviève. Neat little Italian restaurant with a breadth of pasta offerings (45-65F) and a friendly, relaxed ambiance. 69F *menu* includes appetizer, main course, and coffee. 80F *menu* includes appetizer, main course, dessert, coffee, and wine. Open daily 7pm-1am. MC, V, AmEx.

■ SIXTH ARRONDISSEMENT

Tiny restaurants with rock-bottom *menus* jostle each other for space and customers in the area bounded by bd. St-Germain, bd. St-Michel, and the Seine, making this an excellent quadrangle to wander in search of a filling meal. The rue de Buci harbors bargain restaurants and a rambling daily street market, while the nearby rue Gregoire de Tours has the highest density of cheap restaurants, making it a great place to browse. Toward the boundaries of the 6ème restaurants tend to get more expensive. Nonetheless, bargains can still be found along the streets near M. Odéon.

Le Petit Vatel, 5, rue Lobineau (tel. 43 54 28 49). M. Odéon or Mabillon. This tiny restaurant offers little in spaciousness—three tables fill the room completely—

but provides delicious, inexpensive meals. At lunch and on weekdays, choose a main dish plus an appetizer or dessert from the 59F *menu* scribbled on the chalkboard, including rotating daily specialties like *poivrons farcis* (stuffed peppers), *gratin de courgettes au jambon, mousaka,* and vegetarian stews. A vegetarian plate is always offered. Take-out available. Open Mon.-Sat. noon-3pm and 7pm-midnight, Sun. 7pm-midnight. Closed 1 week in Aug. MC, V, AmEx.

Orestias, 4, rue Grégoire-de-Tours (tel. 43 54 62 01). M. Odéon or Mabillon. Off bd. St-Germain. Stuffed heads of mammals and birds line the walls of what remains nonetheless an airy restaurant. The food here is French with a heavy Greek influence—*dolmata,* Greek wine, and *baklava* are offered alongside more traditional French foods. Fries and green beans accompany each meal. Offered at both lunch and dinner, their 44F *menu* is an inspired bargain with copious first and second courses and a choice of cheese or dessert. You can't eat more for the price anywhere in the area. Open Mon.-Sat. noon-2:30pm and 6-11:30pm. MC, V.

Kiotori, 61, rue Monsieur-le-Prince (tel. 43 54 48 44). M. Odéon or Luxembourg. From M. Odéon walk all the way down rue Dupuytren, where it intersects rue Monsieur-le-Prince. A youthful international crowd packs this Japanese restaurant for succulent skewers of grilled beef, chicken, and shrimp, and picture-perfect plates of sushi and maki. A large variety of amazingly cheap *menus* 40-90F. All *menus* include a bowl of soup, *salade de crudités,* a main course and a saki *digestif.* Unbelievably fast service. Open Mon.-Sat. noon-2:30pm and 7-11pm. MC, V.

Crémerie Restaurant Polidor, 41, rue Monsieur-le-Prince (tel. 43 26 95 34). M. Cluny-Sorbonne or Luxembourg. From M. Cluny-Sorbonne walk down bd. St-Michel away from the river, take a right on rue Racine and your first left on rue Monsieur-le-Prince. Always crowded, the Polidor gleams with the mirrors, brass, and polished wood of over a century's worth of history. Neighborhood residents have always frequented this restaurant; when Rimbaud lived on rue Monsieur-le-Prince, he ate here with Verlaine. The Polidor offers traditional French cuisine cooked perfectly; the *escargots* are an excellent introduction to snails for nervous first-timers, the *boeuf bourguignon* is wonderful, and the *bavarois au cassis* (a cake soaked in blackberry liqueur) is famous. The *menu* offers an appetizer, a main dish, and a dessert for 100F. 3-course dining a la carte 120-130F. Open Mon.-Sat. noon-2:30pm and 7pm-12:30am, Sun. noon-2:30pm and 7-10pm. No credit cards.

Così, 54, rue de Seine (tel. 46 33 35 36). M. Odéon. Walk up rue de l'Ancienne Comédie one block, take a left on rue de Buci and your next right on rue de Seine. It would be a sandwich shop were it slightly less vain; let's call it a sandwich atelier. Sandwiches made to order with a choice of ingredients like curried turkey, goat cheese, and tomato and basil salad, served between slices of warm *focaccia* fresh from the oven. These gargantuan sandwiches (33-48F) will seem more refined with a glass of wine (12-16F). Open daily noon-midnight. Another branch at 53, avenue des Ternes, 17*ème* (tel. 43 80 86 70).

Crêperie Saint Germain, 33, rue St-André-des-Arts (tel. 43 54 24 41). M. St-Michel. From the metro find pl. St-André-des-Arts and proceed down rue St-Andre-des-Arts; the crêperie is on your left. The Flintstones go Euro-trash in this clublike crêperie. Faux boulders serve as chairs and mosaics as tabletops; mirrored disco balls dangle from the ceiling. House specializes in *crêpes noirs,* made from all-natural wheat flour. Try a *rasta* (cucumbers, red beans, and corn) and as many dessert *crêpes* as you can eat or afford; fillings like chocolate, whipped cream, berries, and coconut appear in every imaginable combination. Most *crêpes* (30-45F) are unusually filling, for *crêpes.* For the uninitiated, *cidre* (13F50) is a mildly alcoholic drink more like beer than its American version. A 52F *formule* includes a fairly simple dinner *crêpe,* an equally simple dessert *crêpe,* and a glass of *cidre.* Open Sun.-Thurs. noon-1am, Fri.-Sat. until 2am. MC, V, AmEx.

La Cambeuse, 8, rue Casimir Delavigne (tel. 43 26 48 84), off pl. Odéon. M. Odéon. Specializing in traditional French cuisine, this simple restaurant will satisfy your craving for *soupe à l'oignon, boeuf bourgignon,* or *coq au vin.* Expect hearty servings. 3-course *menu* 80F. Open Mon.-Sat. noon-2:30pm and 7-10:15pm (roughly). MC, V.

Le Mazet, 61, rue St-André-des-Arts (tel. 43 54 68 81). M. Odéon. Walk up rue de l'Ancienne Comédie one block and take a right on rue St-André-des-Arts. Talk to Pierrot and Paulette, the friendly owners of this café/bar, as you nurse a drink and wait (briefly) for a meal of *saucisse frites, poulet frites,* or *steak frites* (35-40F). The jukebox has everything from Elvis to Nirvana and the pinball machine is calling your name. 14 varieties of beer on tap at 14F per glass. Open daily 10am-2am.

Restaurant Maroussia, 9, rue de l'Eperon (tel. 43 54 87 50). M. Odéon. This tiny restaurant specializes in hearty Russian and Ukrainian fare. Red tablecloths, red drapes, red napkins, and red paint either make a political statement or complement the pink flowers in the courtyard. Come at lunch for the affordable 75F *menu,* which includes 2 courses and wine. Dinner specialties like chicken kiev or blini with smoked salmon and herring go for about 70F. Dinner *menu* 150F. Open Mon.-Fri. noon-2:30pm and 7:30-11pm, Sat. 7:30-11pm. Musical entertainment Friday and Saturday nights. MC, V.

Restaurant des Beaux Arts, 11, rue Bonaparte (tel. 43 26 92 64). M. St-Germain-des-Prés. Just across from the Ecole des Beaux Arts. Smiling service and the sound of English spoken all around you make this feel almost like home, if not a little like Epcot Center. The 72F *menu* includes wine, appetizers like *maquereau aux pommes à l'huile* (mackerel with potatoes in oil) and a daily vegetarian dish. Generous salads 25-35F. Open daily noon-3pm and 7-11pm.

Au Petit Prince, 3, rue Monsieur-le-Prince (tel. 43 29 74 92). M. Odéon. From M. Odéon, walk down rue Dupuytren and take a right on ruc Monsieur-le-Prince. St-Exupéry fans will love this sophisticated restaurant, offering delicate but rarely filling *nouvelle cuisine.* Try the grilled sole in orange butter. Subtly decorated with a tiny airplane in the window and watercolors of Le Petit Prince himself. The 125F *menu* includes 3 courses but no wine. Open Mon.-Sat. noon-2:15pm and 7:30-11pm. MC, V, AmEx.

Slice, 62, rue Monsieur-le-Prince (tel. 43 54 18 18). M. Odéon or Luxembourg. Bakes huge New York-style pizzas dripping with toppings of your choice. Whole pie (serves 4) 90-130F, half-pie (serves 2) 60-85F, slices 14-20F. Finish off with a brownie (9-10F) or chocolate chip cookies (6F each, 15F for 3). Open daily 11am-11:30pm. Delivery service noon-4pm and 7-11:30pm.

■ SEVENTH ARRONDISSEMENT

Restaurants are perhaps the only touristed spots in the militaristic 7ème not consecrated to the memory of Napoleon. The emperor himself never allowed more than 20 minutes to dine. Visitors here, however, must commit a few hours and a good deal of cash for a fancy meal they'll certainly remember but probably can't afford. As for low-budget options, expect dependable, generally unremarkable food.

Au Babylone, 13, rue de Babylone (tel. 45 48 72 13). M. Sèvres-Babylone. The pince-nezed proprietor has been serving simple, affordable dishes for over 30 years. 90F menu includes appetizer, steak or *plat du jour,* and cheese course. A la carte appetizers 12-40F. Main dishes 48-80F. Desserts 15-20F. Open Mon.-Sat. 11:30am-2:30pm.

Aux Délices de Széchuen, 40, av. Duquesne. M. St-François-Xavier. On the corner of av. Duquesne and av. Breteuil behind the Eglise St-François-Xavier. A family-run, elegant Chinese restaurant serving both French and Szechuan cuisine. Highlights include the *salade de méduse* (jellyfish salad) and *poulet sauté aux champignons noirs* (chicken sauteed with black mushrooms). Large, shaded outdoor terrace in summer. 96F 3-course *menu.* Open Tues.-Sun. noon-2:30pm and 7-10:30pm. MC, V, AmEx.

Le Club des Poètes, 30, rue de Bourgogne (tel. 47 05 06 03). M. Varenne. Take rue de Varenne and turn left onto rue de Bourgogne. Small, timbered dining room hosts lunch, dinner, and nightly poetry readings. Dinner (after 8pm) includes a 96F *menu* of veal, beef, or lamb, appetizer and cheese course. At lunch, same-priced *menu* also includes a dessert. Nightly readings at 10:15pm. V, AmEx. Proprietor Jean-Pierre Rosnay also directs the 24-hr. poetry hotline called **Allô Poésie** (tel. 45 50 32 33). (See Entertainment: Literary Life.)

EIGHTH ARRONDISSEMENT

CROQ 100WICH, 23bis, av. de la Motte Picquet. This deli/sandwich shop offers lunch counter service and take-out. Repertoire of filling sandwiches with fancy names, like the *"Méditeranée"* tuna sandwich (21F) and the *"Parisien,"* with ham and cheese (16F). *Salade paysanne* of potatoes, chicken, bacon, and olives 27F. Vegetarian options. Open Mon.-Fri. 9am-8pm, Sat. 9am-5pm.

La Croque au Sel, 131, rue St-Dominique (tel. 47 05 23 53), off av. Bosquet next to the Fontaine de Mars. M. Ecole Militaire. Painted windows and ceramic lamps furnish a cheerful, rustic setting for provincial cuisine. 2-course 56F *menu* includes dishes like *pavé de boeuf émincé* smothered in *sauce croque au sel* (the house specialty) and *quart de poule rôti aux herbes de Provence* (quarter chicken roasted with thyme and other herbs). 3-course 98F *menu* as well. Open Mon.-Fri. noon-2pm and 7-10:30pm, Sat. 7-10:30pm.

Fontaine de Mars, 129, rue St-Dominique (tel. 47 05 46 44), off av. Bosquet. M. Ecole Militaire. Picture-perfect restaurant with lace curtains, pine interior, and red checkered tablecloths. Terrace overlooks the fountain after which the restaurant is named. One of the best places in the 7ème for a generous sampling of hearty French fare. House specialties include tomatoes and basil with fresh *chèvre* (50F) or *salade canard* (duck salad, 70F). Unadventurous but filling 85F *menu* includes *steak tartare, pommes de terre* (potatoes), green salad, and dessert. *Andouillette au Chardonnay* (Southwestern sausage cooked with wine) 80F. Open Mon.-Sat. noon-2:30pm and 7:30-11pm.

La Pie Gourmande, 30, rue de Bourgogne (tel. 45 51 32 48). M. Varenne. Families and denim-clad friends mingle in this comfortable *crêperie.* Sit at the oak and brass counter or find a table. *Galettes* 14-42F. Dessert *crêpes* 14-32F. Open Mon.-Fri. 11:30am-3pm.

La Poule au Pot, 121, rue de l'Université (tel. 47 05 16 36), near the corner of rue Surcouf. M. Invalides or Pont de l'Alma. Join the suits on the small terrace under the faded striped awning or eat inside. Decorated like a 1930s bistro from a George Brassaï photograph. Try the *poule au pot farcie* (stuffed chicken stew, 85F), the signature dish. Appetizers 28-46F. Main dishes 72-106F. Dessert 22-36F. Open Mon.-Sat. 12:30-3pm and 7-11pm. MC, V, AmEx.

■ EIGHTH ARRONDISSEMENT

Despite the large concentration of deluxe restaurants and couture boutiques around the Madéleine and other salons of *haute couture* in the 8ème, there are a number of affordable restaurants. Swiss restaurants cluster on the side streets around the rue La Boétie just off the Champs-Elysées.

Restaurant de Paris, 38, rue de Ponthieu (tel. 42 56 50 86). Walk up av. Matignon and turn left onto Rue de Ponthieu. M. Franklin D. Roosevelt. Chaos may reign a few steps away on rue La Boétie, but you'll find peace through the stained-glass doors. Enticing lacy tablecloths, arched mirrors, piano music, and luscious dessert table. Several menus built around the all-you-can-eat buffet table with 50 kinds of entrees. 63F lunch *menu:* buffet table and meat or fish dish. Old leather-bound menu (in English and French) offers more elaborate *menus* at 75F and 120F. Open Mon.-Fri. noon-3pm and 7pm-midnight, Sat. 7pm-midnight.

Dynastie Thai, 101, rue La Boétie (tel. 43 59 69 57). M. St-Philippe du Roule. Swing a left onto rue la Boetie from the metro stop. Acknowledged top choice among Paris' Asian restaurants. One of the most elegant and appetizing places in the city. Bargain weekday *menu* (90F) lists exquisitely prepared Thai cuisine in an ambience *de luxe.* Chicken sautéed in basil, Thai beef sautéed in pepper, and chicken Thai lemon soup. Selection of Dim Sum, 46F. Open daily noon-2:30pm and 7-11:30pm, may be closed on Sundays in July and August—call to confirm. AmEx, MC, V.

La Maison du Valais, 20, rue Royale (tel. 42 60 22 72). M. Madeleine. Rue Royale is located just off Place de la Madelaine. This Swiss restaurant has great view of the Madeleine, but you might prefer to eat inside the wooden-beamed chalet interior with cowhide-upholstered chairs. Fondue, salmon tartare, and raclette from 95F. Open Mon.-Sat. 12:15-10pm.

Naturesto, 66, av. des Champs-Elysées, in the Galerie Point Show, no. 67 (tel. 42 56 49 01). M. Franklin D. Roosevelt. *"Mangez juste!"* is this vegetarian eatery's motto. Vitamin and protein shakes and fruity cocktails will "pump you up" without deflating your pocket, as will the tasty dishes (37-47F). Try the "Caroline"— lettuce, carrots, sprouts, apples, raisins, tomatoes, cheese, and sunflower seeds. Green salads 22F. "Salade Capri" with tomatoes, celery, mushrooms, and carrots 25F. Fruit tartes (apple and berries) 23F. Open Mon.-Fri. noon-3pm.

Le Roi de Pot-au-Feu, 40, rue de Ponthieu (tel. 43 59 41 62), off rue de la Boétie. M. Franklin D. Roosevelt. Small restaurant with red and white checkered tablecloths, dark wood interior, and black and white silver screen photos. Filling *pot-au-feu* (beef and vegetable stew 85F). Open Mon.-Sat. noon-3pm and 7-11pm.

La Taverne Suisse, 48, rue de Ponthieu (tel. 42 56 01 67) near restaurant le Roi de Pot-au-Feu. M. Franklin D. Roosevelt. Intimate Swiss restaurant with a central oak and brass bar. 68F buys *entrecote* and salad. 75F three-course *menu* features French and Swiss specialties like *fondue savoyard* and *raclette du valais.* Open Mon.-Fri. noon-2:30pm and 7-11pm, Sat.-Sun. 7-11:30pm. MC, V.

Antoine's: Les Sandwichs des 5 Continents, 31, rue de Ponthieu (tel. 42 89 44 20). M. Franklin D. Roosevelt. Before giving into temptation and buying a fast-food lunch on the Champs-Elysees, hop down rue de Ponthieu to this hip and modern sandwhich shop. Specialities include the Buffalo sandwich composed of barbecued chicken and melted cheese on hearty bread. American desserts and Haagen Daz ice-cream bars fill out the menu for a cheap, but appetizing meal. Beer 2-18F. Open Mon.-Sat. 8:30am-6pm.

Elliott Restaurant, 166, bd. Haussmann (tel. 42 89 30 50). M. Miromesnil. Walk up avenue Percier and turn left on boulevard Haussmann. A taste of home in the arrondisement that makes you feel like a stranger. Bistro-style restaurant with slick decor and food that's all American. Buffalo wings (30F), hamburgers (60F) and selected American beers (28-35F). Sunday brunch with eggs benedict (68F) and freshly squeezed orange juice. Open Mon.-Sat. noon-3pm and 8pm-midnight, Sun. noon-3pm. MC, V.

■ NINTH ARRONDISSEMENT

Except for a few gems, meals close to the heavily touristed Opéra area can be quite expensive; for truly cheap deals, head farther north. Displaced by the projectile force of the city's skyrocketing prices, much of ethnic Paris has found itself here, providing visitors to the ninth with wondrous delicacies from former French colonies. Non-French cuisine goes for lower prices, reflecting its lack of acceptance.

Anarkali, 4, place Gustave Toudouze (tel. 48 78 39 84). M. St-Georges. Walk uphill on rue Notre-Dame-de-Lorette and branch right onto rue H. Monnier. On a lovely secluded square. Serves up a familiar assortment of spicy South Indian fare. Relax on the terrace under wide, colorful umbrellas, cut from the cloth of the owner's native land. Meat dishes 55-60F, veggie dishes 30-40F. Chutneys cost an extra 6-8F. 3-course lunch *menu* 61F. Open Tues.-Sat. noon-2:30pm and 7pm-12:30am. Open Sun. 7pm-12:30am in summer. MC, V, AmEx.

Au Boeuf Bourguignon, 21, rue de Douai (tel. 42 82 08 79). M. Pigalle. Walk away from pl. Pigalle on rue Duperré to its corner with rue de Douai. Pearl of the neighborhood, sharing only a metro stop with the sleazy hangouts that line streets nearby. Checkered tablecloths and movie posters conjure a subdued bohemian atmosphere. 3-course 60F and 92F *menus.* The 92F *menu* offers more variety and a complimentary *kir.* The *boeuf bourguignon* comes highly recommended. Open Mon.-Sat. noon-3pm and 6:30-10:30pm. MC, V.

Hayne's Bar, 3, rue Clauzel (tel. 48 78 40 63). M. St-Georges. Head uphill on rue Notre-Dame-de-Lorette, branch right on rue H. Monnier, and right again on rue Clauzel. Bedecked with photos of jazz and blues greats, this restaurant/bar specializes in down-home New Orleans cooking. Come here for fried or BBQ chicken, New Orleans-style red beans, and fresh-baked cornbread. Portions are very generous and dinner comes out to less than 100F. On Fri. nights, a pianist plays New Orleans jazz. Hot tamales 40F. Gumbo with shrimp, chicken, okra, and rice 90F. Sister Lena's BBQ spare ribs 70F. Open Tues.-Sat. 7:30pm-1am.

Le Chartier, 7, rue du Faubourg-Montmartre (tel. 47 70 86 29). M. Rue Montmartre. Walk uphill on rue du Faubourg Montmartre; the small passage to your left harbors the restaurant. A huge restaurant in grand old French style, with chandeliers and wooden booths. The waiters here are older and very jovial; the clientele is mainly an older, local crowd. Specialties include beef in a house tomato sauce, *pot au feu* (stew), and roast veal. Portions are huge. A full meal will cost about 80F. Open daily 11am-3pm and 6-9:30pm. MC, V.

La Franche-Comté, 2, bd. de la Madeleine (tel. 47 42 86 52; reservations 49 24 99 09). M. Madeleine. On the left side of bd. de la Madeleine. Half restaurant, half tourist office about this eastern French province, this place offers tantalizing regional specialties. Wild mushrooms, trout, and pâté make frequent appearances, keeping prices a little high. *Menus* at 82F (2-course), 110F (3-course), and 175F. Brochures free. Open Mon.-Sat. noon-3pm and 7-10:30pm. AmEx, MC, V.

Sannine, 32, rue du Faubourg Montmartre (tel. 48 24 01 32). M. Montmartre. Walk uphill on ruc du Faubourg Montmartre to its corner with rue Richer. A small, family affair specializing in Middle Eastern basics: kebabs, marinated beef, felafel, and tabouli. Red tablecloths and painted murals of the Lebanon that once was. Dinner a la carte for around 90F; *menu* for 49F (lunch) and 62F (dinner). Open Mon.-Sat. noon-3pm and 6-11:30pm, Sun. 6-11:30pm. Take-out available. MC, V, AmEx.

Les Bacchantes, 21, rue de Caumartin (tel. 42 65 25 35). M. Havre-Caumartin. Hearty portions of perennial French favorites and wine. Nylon baseball caps wreathe the bar area. *Assiette de campagne* (40F) is a sampler of *rillette,* pâté, and sausage. Salads 40F. Wine 13-30F by the glass. Open Sept.-July Mon.-Sat. 11:30am-6am, Sun. 11:30am-10pm; Aug. Mon.-Sat. 11:30am-6am.

Hard Rock Café, 14, bd. Montmartre (tel. 42 46 10 00). M. Richelieu Drouot or Rue Montmartre. Loud music, burgers, and guitars on the wall. Seen it all before? Burgers, ribs, steaks—you know, American stuff. 69F lunch *menu* includes guacamole, cheesesteak, and beer or California wine. Happy hour 4-6:30pm. Good gig on July 4. You can buy t-shirts next door (100F). Please don't. Open daily 11:30am-2am. MC, V, AmEx.

Le Palmier de Lorette, 19, ruc de Châteaudun (tel. 48 78 34 41). M. Notre-Dame-de-Lorette. Across from the church. *Brasserie* style, plush interior owned by a couple who take pride in their food and hospitality. Monsieur does the cooking. Lunch and evening menu (74F50) offers farm-fresh French classics. Open Mon.-Fri. 7am-1am; open for meals noon-3pm and 7-11:30pm. MC, V.

Pizzéria King Salomon, 46, rue Richer (tel. 42 46 31 22). M. Cadet or Bonne Nouvelle. From M. Cadet descend rue Saulner and turn left on rue Richer. A kosher pizzeria in the heart of the 9*ème*'s Jewish community. Individual pizzas 42F. Take-out available.

■ TENTH ARRONDISSEMENT

While many tourists may see no more of the 10*ème* than their two-hour layover at the Gare du Nord allows, those who venture out will find enough French, Indian, and African food to make any gourmand smile. Catering to locals rather than tourists, these restaurants permit short and long-term visitors alike the chance to soak up a Paris that doesn't revolve around the Eiffel Tower or the Louvre. Passage Brady, filled with Indian eateries, offers a festival of the palate for rock-bottom prices.

Paris-Dakar, 95, rue du Faubourg St-Martin (tel. 42 08 16 64). M. Gare de l'Est. African masks and batiks decorate this popular, family-run restaurant. Try *Yassa* (chicken with lime and onions, 70F), *Maffé* (chicken or beef sauteed in peanut sauce, 69F) and *Tiep Bou Dieone,* the "national dish of Senegal" (fish with rice and veggies, 92F). Feast and explore, but use caution; the red chili and oil concoction will cauturize your stomach. Weekday lunch *menu* 59F, dinner *menu* 99F. Open Tues.-Sun. noon-3pm and 7pm-midnight. MC, V.

Kamathenu, 69, passage Brady (tel. 42 46 47 90). M. Château d'Eau or Strasbourg St-Denis. From M. Château d'Eau walk opposite traffic on bd. de Strasbourg and enter passage Brady at no. 33. One of the most affordable of restaurants found in this South Asian neighborhood. Lunch or dinner 25F, with many vegetarian options. Portions are not huge, so order some soft *Nan* bread (5F). Tandoori plate 35F. Curries 43-63F. Cool off with a mango or pineapple *Lassi*, a yogurt and rosewater drink (carafe 23-25F). Take-out available. Open daily noon-midnight.

Restaurant de Bourgogne, 26, rue des Vinaigriers (tel. 46 07 07 91). M. Château d'Eau. From the metro follow rue du Château d'Eau, turn left on rue du Faubourg St-Martin, and turn right on rue des Vinaigriers. Calico curtains, hearty traditional food, and service with a smile. 3-course lunch or dinner *menu* 59F includes old reliables: roast pork, ham omelettes, and grilled *andouillette*. 75cl house red 32F. Open Sept.-July Mon.-Fri. noon-2:30pm and 7-10:30pm, Sat. noon-1:30pm.

Brasserie Flo, 7, cour des Petites-Ecuries (tel. 47 70 13 59). M. Château d'Eau. Walk against traffic on rue du Château d'Eau, turn left on rue du Faubourg St-Denis; the entrance to the cour des Petites Ecuries is on the right. Elegant dining room with dark wood paneling and tuxedoed waiters. A chic chain, specializing in seafood, with every imaginable type of oyster; 6 of the cheapest for 60-84F. Dinner a la carte is exorbitant (200F), but the 109F, 2-course *menu* provides a superb, delicate meal. Reservations recommended. Open 7pm-2am. Credit cards accepted.

Le Chant de la Terre, 29, rue du Château d'Eau (tel. 42 49 39 08). M. Château d'Eau or J. Bonsergent. A vegetarian, smoke-free restaurant, located in a courtyard. Lunchtime self-service is a good bet for the healthful budgeteer fleeing from the bustle of the *gare* or place de la République. Daily specials 37F. 3-course *menu* 56F. Open Sept.-July Mon.-Fri. noon-2pm.

La Rose du Kashmir, 64-66, passage Brady (tel. 42 46 23 75). M. Château d'Eau or Strasbourg St-Denis. Walk opposite traffic on bd. de Strasbourg and enter passage Brady at no. 33. Two large, golden urns flank the entrance to this razzle-dazzle Indian eatery. Serves large portions of wide-ranging Tandoori specialties. Curries (with chicken, beef, lamb, or vegetables) 47-58F. Sit on the terrace or inside. Open noon-3pm and 6-11:30pm. MC, V.

Le Dogon, 30, rue René Boulanger (tel. 42 41 95 85). M. République. Elegant African (mainly Senegalese) restaurant steps away from pl. de la République. White walls, batiks, and animal pelts serve as the backdrop for sumptuous curries, couscous, and Mafé, made affordable by a 2-course, 55F lunch *menu*. Go easy on the chili sauce here. Delicious tropical fruit cup for dessert (25F). Open Mon.-Fri. 11:30am-2:30pm and 7pm-1am, Sat.-Sun 11:30am-2:30pm. MC, V.

Le Palais de l'Est, 186, rue du Faubourg St-Martin (tel. 46 07 09 99). M. Château Landon. Walk toward Gare de l'Est on rue du Faubourg St-Martin. Specializing in Chinese and Vietnamese cuisine, it's a good late-night option for hungry itinerants, located one metro stop north of Gare de l'Est. Karaoke gets the crowd on its feet. More expensive than many of its counterparts. Come for *dim sum*. Dinner a la carte around 170F. Lunch *menu* 48F, dinner 68F and 78F. Open daily noon-3pm and 7pm-5am. Take-out available. AmEx.

■ ELEVENTH ARRONDISSEMENT

The 11ème's restaurants fill to capacity with young and chic regulars who stay through the night. Low rents have made for low meal prices near and beyond the new Opéra-Bastille. Try to reserve tables ahead of time, or expect to wait at the restaurant bar.

Au Trou Normand, 9, rue Jean-Pierre Timbaud (tel. 48 05 80 23). M. Oberkampf. Walk north on rue de Malte until it intersects rue Jean-Pierre Timbaud. Not the hole in the wall its name would suggest, this restaurant is a neighborhood institution. Unbelievably low-priced, no-fuss French food. Youthful lunch crowd of regulars. The *onglet rocquefort* and *frites* (30F) is a favorite. Have one of the homemade tarts or madame might take offense. Appetizers 10-13F, *plats du jour* 29-39F, tasty desserts 9-13F. Open Sept.-July Mon.-Fri. noon-2:30pm and 7:30-11pm, Sat. 7:30-11pm.

Au Petit Keller, 13, rue Keller (tel. 47 00 12 97). M. Ledru-Rollin. Walk north on av. Ledru Rollin and turn left on rue Keller. Traditional bistro in the heart of the vibrant Bastille district. The filling, wholesome food has something of a neighborhood fanclub. 69F *menu* includes beer, wine, or mineral water. *Gâteau de riz* (rice cake) is a house specialty. Open Mon.-Fri. noon-2:30pm and 7pm-12:30am, Sun. 7pm-12:30am.

Chez Paul, 13, rue de Charonne (tel. 47 00 34 57). M. Ledru-Rollin, or Bastille. From M. Bastille, go east on rue du Faubourg St-Antoine and turn left on rue de Charonne. Late-night crowds laugh and eat until closing time. Friendly staff serves bounteous traditional food. Don't come for intimacy. Appetizers 30-50F. Entrees 60-80F. Open Sept.-July Mon.-Sat. noon-2:30pm and 7:15pm-2am, food served until 12:30am. MC, V, AmEx.

A la Banane Ivoirienne, 10, rue de la Forge-Royale (tel. 43 70 49 90). M. Faidherbe-Chaligny. Walk west on rue du Faubourg St-Antoine and turn right on rue de la Forge-Royale. Run by a gregarious Ivoirian emigré who wrote his doctoral thesis on his country's banana industry. Come for delicious West African specialties, such as *attieke,* made from cassava, and *aloko,* from bananas. Appetizers, like stuffed crabs à l'Abgidinaise, 25-30F. Main courses 49-80F. *Menu* 89F. Open Tues.-Sat. 7pm-midnight.

Le Bistro St-Ambroise, 5, rue Guillaume Bertrand (tel. 47 00 43 50). M. St-Maur. Walk southeast on av. de la République and turn right on rue Guillaume Bertrand. 1930s ads from French magazines paper the walls of the otherwise no-frills dining room. Skip dinner and set upon the expert wine *carte* and unrivaled repertoire of desserts (20-40F). Try the white chocolate mousse, the dark chocolate and coconut tart, and/or the more elegant *coupe normande* (apple ice cream and Calvados). 3-course lunch *menu* 68F. MC, V.

Le Passage, 18, passage de la Bonne-Graine (tel. 47 00 73 30). M. Ledru-Rollin. From the metro, walk 20m east on rue du Faubourg St-Antoine and take a near-hidden left on passage de la Bonne-Graine. A sequestered Bastille bistro for wine connoisseurs. Assorted *andouillettes* and hitherto-unknown dishes; dare to try the *pieds Janet* (pigs feet cooked in fois gras). Daily specials on chalkboard are cheaper than main dishes on *menu;* specials 60F, main courses otherwise about 70F. Wine by the glass of the week's chosen vintage. Inquire about regular wine-tasting events. Open Mon.-Fri. noon-3:30pm and 7:30-11:30pm, Sat. 7:30-11:30pm. MC, V, AmEx.

La Courtille, 16, rue Guillaume Bertrand (tel. 48 06 48 34). M. St-Maur. Walk southeast on av. de la République and turn right on rue Guillaume Bertrand. Peach interior for chic yuppie crowd. Lunch *menu* 72F; 121F at night. A la carte appetizers 36-45F, main courses 68-84F, desserts 34F. Open Mon.-Fri. noon-2pm and 7:45-10pm, Sat. 7:45-10pm. MC, V.

La Palette Bastille, 116, av. Ledru-Rollin (tel. 47 00 34 39). M. Ledru-Rollin. Walk north on av. Ledru-Rollin. A neighborhood haunt and Art Nouveau period piece. The original 1900 interior is preserved as a landmark. Locals and tourists convene under fleshy murals for unspectacular, honest-tasting food. Omelettes 20-32F. Appetizers 20-35F, main courses 59-69F, desserts 18-33F. The house specialty is *confit de canard* with sauteed potatoes (69F). Open Mon.-Sat. noon-2am, food served until midnight, Sun. noon-9:30pm. MC, V.

Occitanie, 96, rue Oberkampf (tel. 48 06 46 98). M. St-Maur. Go northwest on av. de la République, take your first right onto rue St.-Maur, and then turn right on rue Oberkampf. Burlap-covered refectory tables provide a rustic setting for southwestern French cuisine. 3-course midday *formule* at 50F includes a drink and a wide selection of salads and meats. Dinner *menus* are bargains at 62F (for 3 courses and wine) and 87F (for 4 courses). Appetizers 30-50F, main courses 48-98F. Open Sept.-July Mon.-Fri. noon-2pm and 7-11pm, Sat. 7-11pm. MC, V, AmEx.

Le Val de Loire, 149, rue Amelot (tel. 47 00 34 11). M. Filles du Calvaire or Oberkampf. From M. Filles du Calvaire, walk towards the Cirque d'Hiver and turn left on rue Amelot; from M. Oberkampf, walk west on rue de Crussol and turn right on rue Amelot. Locals share tables with tourists from nearby hotels. Traditional decor—red plaid tablecloths and a small wooden cask by the window—frames standard French fare. 2-course 48F *menu* includes a main course and choice of appetizer or dessert. 57F *menu* includes a phenomenal buffet of appetizers, a main course, and a dessert. 105F *menu* adds an opening *terrine*. Open Sept.-July Mon.-Sat. noon-2:30pm and 6:45-10pm. MC, V, AmEx.

■ TWELFTH ARRONDISSEMENT

With the Gare de Lyon as its gravitational center, the12^{ème} provides a monotony of goods and services for the no-frills tourist on a train layover; restaurants, however, are in short supply. Of those scattered through this sprawling *arrondissement,* only a handful merit special trips from the center city. Below we list some of the area's few finds. In ambiance and food quality, the following restaurants far upstage their neighborhoods.

Au Limonaire, 88, rue de Charenton (tel. 43 43 49 14). M. Ledru-Rollin or Gare de Lyon. From M. Ledru-Rollin walk south on av. Ledru-Rollin and take a left on rue de Prague, which terminates at the corner of the restaurant. Founded in 1890 as Au Pissenlair, this bistro/folk music venue preserves the feel of a Parisian institution. Comfortable and informal, the dining room's tables are arrayed around an antique zinc bar. Tasty regional cuisine and fine wines from the Rhône Valley. Two-course lunch *menu* 65F. 125F dinner *menu* provides an appetizer, main course, cheese, and dessert. A la carte appetizers 30-40F, main courses 60-75F, desserts 25-35F. Wed.-Sat. at 10pm, folk musicians perform live on accordion, violin, and guitar; repertoire runs from Brel to burlesque. Reservations encouraged. Drop by to pick up monthly schedule. Open Tues.-Sat. noon-3pm and 6pm-midnight, Sun. 6pm-midnight. MC, V.

Joël's, 22, rue de Cotte (tel. 43 43 88 20). M. Ledru-Rollin. Walk east on rue du Faubourg St-Antoine and take a left on rue de Cotte. Decorated in blue and yellow, restaurant's interior bears a certain resemblance to a soccer jersey. Young Parisians gather for specialties from the southwestern province of Tarn; all the foie gras you could want. 60F lunch menu includes appetizer, main course, and dessert picked from the *ardoise* (chalkboard). 3-course 86F dinner *menu* features pâté, trout, and crème caramel. For those long on funds and appetite, the 4-course 155F *menu gastronomique* stars a fabulous *pavé de boeuf à la mousse de foie gras.* Open Mon.-Thurs. noon-2:30pm and 7-11pm, Fri. noon-2:30pm and 7pm-midnight, Sat. 7pm-midnight. MC, V.

Le Parrot, 5, rue Parrot (tel. 43 43 05 64). M. Gare de Lyon. Walk north on rue de Lyon and take a right on rue Parrot. A cheap, friendly place to go for a meal should you live near the train station. 54F menu includes appetizer, main course, and dessert. 3-course 80F menu offers more selection. Open Mon.-Sat. 11:30am-2:45pm and 7-10pm, Sun. 7-10pm.

Le Rocher du Diamant, 284, rue de Charenton (tel. 40 19 08 78). M. Dugommier or Daumesnil. From M. Dugommier walk south on rue Charenton; from M. Daumesnil, walk down rue Claude Decaen, take your first right on rue de la Brèche-aux-Loups and walk until it intersects rue de Charenton. Silver candlesticks on the tables and stuffed turtles in the windows embellish the tropical, palm-and-sea decor. An outpost of chic on the Paris outskirts. Specialties include fondues and cuisine from the Antilles. 3-course lunch *menus* at 54F and 89F. Additional 2-course lunch *menu* with main course and choice of an appetizer or dessert. Dinner *menu* 115F. A la carte, split the 2-person *marmites des Caraïbes* (seafood stew, 240F) with a friend. Colombos around 80F. A la carte: appetizers 35-50F, main courses 80-100F, desserts 40-45F. Open daily 11am-3pm and 7pm-1am.

■ THIRTEENTH ARRONDISSEMENT

Avenue de Choisy

Scores of Vietnamese, Thai, Cambodian, Laotian, and Chinese restaurants cluster south of pl. d'Italie on av. de Choisy. There, Paris' answer to Chinatown caches some of the city's cheapest eats. Note, however, that rice and tea aren't included in the price of your meal. Save room for dessert; some of Paris' best pastries await discovery here. Early eaters should note that many restaurants in this neighborhood are open all day.

Hien Vuong, 12bis, rue Caillaux (tel. 53 79 17 23). M. Maison Blanche. Walk north on av. d'Italie and take your first right onto rue Caillaux. If you eat at one Asian restaurant in Paris, eat here. Restrained and sophisticated decor with more tables than floor space would seem to allow. Outstanding Vietnamese and Laotian specialties; mostly soup and grilled meats. 52F lunch *menu* (Tues.-Fri.) includes an appetizer, main meal, and dessert. A la carte, main dishes 35-40F, desserts 15-17F. Open Tues.-Sun. noon-11:30pm.

Thiên Co, 41, av. de Choisy (tel. 45 85 55 00). M. Porte de Choisy. North on av. de Choisy. Walk through the green-trimmed, glassed-in patio to the small dining room for good, homestyle Vietnamese food. Reasonably priced, perfect-sized servings of soup or rice dishes with grilled meat (30-45F). Limited, though adequate, menu selection. Desserts 15-17F. Open Wed.-Mon. 10am-11pm.

Tricotin, 15, av. de Choisy (tel. 45 84 74 44), in the building labeled "le Kiosque de Choisy." M. Porte de Choisy. Whatever you want, they've got. The two, facing branches of this restaurant serve Cambodian, Vietnamese, Thai, and Chinese cuisine between them. The interior looks like an Asian Denny's, but you won't care a dime. Customers sit at long tables for noodles (30-40F) or dim sum (starting at 30F). One side open Wed.-Mon. 11am-3pm and 6:30-11:30pm, the other 9am-11:30pm. AmEx, MC, V.

Cap St-Jacques, 105, av. d'Ivry (tel. 45 86 06 72). M. Tolbiac. Walk east on rue de Tolbiac and take a right on av. d'Ivry. Large with a correspondingly large menu, this salmon-and-gray restaurant serves respectable Vietnamese meals. Spicy soup specialties, like their well-prepared rice noodles with beef and vegetables (32F). Open Tues.-Sun. 11am-3:30pm and 7-11:30pm. MC, V accepted over 100F; AmEx accepted with an added surcharge.

Lao Thai, 128, rue de Tolbiac (tel. 43 31 98 10). M. Tolbiac. Asian and French regulars convene for comparatively expensive Thai food. The 47F lunch *menu*, however, is a steal; it includes an appetizer, main dish, rice, and dessert or coffee. Dinner menus 184-198F (for 2 people). A la carte main courses 30-50F. Open Thurs.-Tues. noon-2:30pm and 7-11:15pm. MC, V.

Château de Choisy, 44-46, av. de Choisy (tel. 45 82 40 60). M. Porte de Choisy. North on av. de Choisy. A mainly Western crowd gathers for all-you-can-eat Chinese buffet (59F lunch, 65F dinner). On the whole, an astoundingly cheap and bounteous meal. The Chinese go elsewhere. Wide selection of dishes offered. Open daily 11:45am-2:45pm and 7-11:45pm; buffet not available Sat. evening. MC, V.

Butte aux Cailles

The Butte aux Cailles district encompasses a handful of streets stretching south of pl. d'Italie. Yet another haven for artists and intellectuals thrown from the Latin Quarter by soaring prices, the neighborhood's restaurants and bars fill with young, high-spirited locals.

Le Temps des Cérises, 18-20, rue de la Butte-aux-Cailles (tel. 45 89 69 48). M. pl. d'Italie. Walk south on rue Bobillot and turn right on rue de la Butte-aux-Cailles. A restaurant cooperative and venerated neighborhood institution. Locals meet over long tables to discuss everything from art (usually their own) to (liberal) politics, often with live music in the background. You wouldn't be able to afford the satisfying French food, were it not for the 3-course *menu* (58F), served until 9pm. Open Mon.-Fri. noon-2:15pm and 7:30-11:30pm, Sat. 7:30-11:30pm. MC, V, AmEx.

Le Samson, 9, rue Jean-Marie Jégo (tel. 45 89 09 23). M. pl. d'Italie. Walk south on rue Bobillot, turn right on rue de la Butte-aux-Cailles, and then turn right again on rue Jean-Marie Jégo. Spray-painted tables and red, sponge-painted walls flag artsy hipsters to this small restaurant. Daily menu on chalkboards around the room. Reasonably priced, very French food. 60F *menu* includes appetizer, main course, and dessert. A la carte, appetizers 20-35F and main courses 45-60F. Open Mon.-Fri. noon-3pm and 7:30pm-1am, Sat. 7:30pm-1am.

Chez Gladines, 30, rue des Cinq Diamants. M. pl. d'Italie. Walk west on bd. Auguste Blanqui and turn left onto rue des Cinq Diamants. A bar/restaurant and a café during non-dinner hours. Sit at long wooden tables for snails and other Basque specialties. Main courses 40-60F, salads 28-50F, *escargots* 35-50F. Despite Gladine's multiple rooms, crowds inevitably gather on the sidewalk, waiting for tables. Don't be discouraged; the turnover is quick. Open Sept.-July daily 9am-2am; dinner served 7:30pm-12:30am.

■ FOURTEENTH ARRONDISSEMENT

The budget traveler is forever indebted to the Bretons, the French from the northwest who flooded Paris at the turn of the century and settled in Montparnasse. The *crêpes* and *galettes* (a larger, buckwheat version) which they brought with them are easy to find, easy to eat, and even easier on the wallet. Don't be tempted to settle for an overcooked *biftek* and limp *frites* at one of the hundreds of utterly forgettable restaurants that cluster around the Tour de Montparnasse.

Aquarius Café, 40, rue de Gergovie (tel. 45 41 36 88). M. Pernety. Off rue mond Losserand. Serene, slightly hip vegetarian restaurant, where wood tables and an exceptionally friendly staff enhance a politically correct meal. The famous "mixed grill" includes tofu sausages, cereal sausages, wheat pancakes, wheat germ, brown rice and vegetables in a mushroom sauce for 65F. Or get your vitamins via an Aquarius salad (55F) with *chèvre*, avocado, egg, vegetable pâté, potato salad, *crudités,* and vinaigrette. 3-course lunch *menu* 60F. Open Mon.-Sat. noon-2:30pm and 7-10:30pm. AmEx, MC, V.

Le Château Poivre, 145, rue du Château (tel. 43 22 03 68). M. Pernety. Take rue Raymond Losserand in the direction of avenue du Maine and turn right onto rue du Chateau. The proud owner takes his food very seriously, and the generous portions, enhanced by 80 varieties of wine, will encourage you to do the same. 89F *menu* (lunch and dinner, but not served after 10pm) features *escargots, truite belle manière, gigot d'agneau, crème caramel,* and *mousse au chocolat.* Open Mon.-Sat. noon-2:30pm and 7-10:30pm. AmEx, MC, V.

Le Colvert, 129, rue du Château (tel. 43 27 95 19). M. Penerty. This tiny peach colored restaurant, frequented by locals in the know, is covered with ducks—they're on the walls, on the plates, and sitting (ceramic, of course) on the shelves. Even a quacking duck telephone. Beautifully presented, large portions of classic French fare. You will waddle out of here satisfied. Lunch *menu* 60F (wine included). Dinner *menus* 90-143F. Open Mon.-Fri. 11:30am-2:30pm and 7-11pm, Sat. 7-11pm. MC, V.

Crêperie Le Biniou, 3, av. du Général Leclerc (tel. 43 27 20 40). M. Denfert-Rochereau. To your right and across the street from the metro stop. Decorated in the starkest tones of yellow, blue, and white, but its twin on the traditional *crêpe* is far from minimalist. Unusual combinations of calamari or mussels with curry, or more mainstream cheese, egg, and ham. Top off your dinner with a killer pear, chocolate, and chantilly *crêpe.* Main course and dessert *crêpes* at 15-40F. Open Mon.-Sat. 11:45am-2:30pm and 6:45-10pm.

Crêperie St-Malo, 53, rue de Montparnasse (tel. 43 20 87 19). M. Edgar Quinet. Your mouth will water as you head down this street which boasts perhaps a higher concentration of *crêpes* and *galettes* than in all of Brittany. This restaurant offers the most promising *menu—galette,* dessert *crêpe,* hard cider and coffee 49F. Open Mon.-Fri. noon-3pm and 6pm-1am, Sat.-Sun. noon-midnight.

Le Jerobam, 72, rue Didot (tel. 45 39 39 13), off rue d'Alésia. M. Plaisance. Authentic, comfortable French restaurant serving superb traditional fare at unbeatable prices. Frescoed pastoral scenes on the ceiling give this place a homey touch. Three-course lunch *menu* at 65F includes delectable dishes such as *tarine de poisson aux olives et citron confit* (a fish stew with preserved lemons and olives). Two-course dinner *menu* 95F. Open Tues.-Sat. noon-2pm and 7-10pm, Mon. noon-2pm. MC, V.

N'Zadette-M'foua, 152, route du Château (tel. 43 22 00 16). M. Pernety. A well-received break from traditional French fare can be had at this lively restaurant specializing in Congolese cuisine. You'll be smiling after a "Sourire Congolais," a fish, tomato, pineapple, and cucumber concoction (42F). The daring will want to sample a *maboke,* meat or fish cooked in a wrapper of banana leaves. African relics and woven wall hangings will take your mind to sunnier climates, far from that infernal Parisian drizzle. *Menu* at 85F. Open daily noon-3pm and 7pm-2am.

Restaurant Le Berbère, 50, rue de Gergovie (tel. 45 42 10 29). M. Pernety. Left off of rue Raymond Losserand. A serious selection of Moroccan specialties, including hearty couscous with chicken or beef for just 48F. Save room to attack the glorious dessert tray, which supports an amazing array of fantastic sugar creations, such as the honey-laden baklava (19F). Open Mon.-Sat. noon-2:30pm and 7-10:30pm. AmEx, MC, V.

Restaurant au Rendez-Vous des Camionneurs, 34, rue des Plantes (tel. 45 40 43 36), off rue d'Alésia. M. Alésia. A low-key establishment with more emphasis on food than on décor (plain chairs and checkered tablecloths), but honest traditional fare at unbeatable prices. The 65F *menu* includes stuffed grape leaves, sausage in garlic, leg of lamb, and *civet de lapin* (rabbit stew). House wine starts at 5F50 a glass. Open Mon.-Fri. 11:30am-2pm and 6-9pm.

La Route du Château, 123, rue du Château (tel. 43 20 09 59). M. Pernety. This tiny bistro more than makes up for what its location lacks in ambience. Classy, authentic décor with food to match. Specialties include *langue de boeuf* and rabbit sautéed with cider. Three-course *menu* 82F, and definitely worth it. Open Mon. 7:30pm-2am., Tues.-Sat. noon-2pm and 7:30pm-2am. AmEx, MC, V.

■FIFTEENTH ARRONDISSEMENT

Eateries in this *arrondissement* remain treasured local establishments, where owners personally welcome their regulars to their usual tables and then lovingly detail the specials of the day. Traditional bistros, complete with oak and brass bars and mirrored walls, dot the area around bd. de Grenelle and the rue du Commerce. The food tends to be rich, heavy chicken and beef dishes in thick gravy sauces.

Bistro Bourdelle, 12, rue Bourdelle (tel. 45 48 57 01). M. Montparnasse-Bienvenue. From metro walk up Rue de l'Arrive, take a right onto Avenue de Maine and then a left onto Rue Bourdelle. A traditional small, dark bistro where many dignified old men come to pass lunch hour drinking decent house wine and feasting on the impeccably prepared dishes of meat and fish. 88F *menu* includes such house specialties as *salade de choux et champignons* (warm salad with cabbage and mushrooms) and *quenelles de brochet* (*crêpe* with fish). Open Mon.-Fri. noon-2:30pm and 7-10:30pm. MC, V.

Le Bouquet de Grenelle, 78, av. de la Motte-Picquet (tel. 47 34 30 01). M. La Motte-Picquet-Grenelle. This corner *brasserie* is one of the best places to hang out and watch the bustle of provincial life in the 15ème. It also has an affordable *brasserie* menu of *crêpes* (18-36F), omelettes (28-48F), and sandwiches (18-32F). Coffee 10F. *Café au lait* 25F. Open daily 8am-2am.

Café Aux Artistes, 63, rue Falguière (tel. 43 22 05 39). M. Falguière. Cheap restaurant with an extensive menu, where you can eat with your compatriots (whether they be Canadian, Australian, British, German, or American), while perusing posters of Ronald Reagan in his younger, better days. The low prices and late hours attract less discriminating palates; gourmets may want to keep looking. 2-course lunch menu 55F, 3-course dinner 75F. Open Mon.-Fri. noon-2:30pm and 7pm-1am, Sat. 7pm-1am. MC, V.

Café du Commerce, 51, rue du Commerce (tel. 45 75 03 27). M. La Motte-Picquet-Grenelle. Cross boulevard de Grenelle and walk straight. This venerable Paris institution has been around since 1921, offering great food at decent prices. The 3-level interior surrounds a central atrium courtyard with overflowing vines and flowers. Bright, airy, and surprisingly full, this café-restaurant has an 85F formule commerce *menu* (2 courses) and a 110F *menu* (3 courses) which feature *éscalope de saumon, cuisse du porc à l'ancienne,* and *mousse au chocolat.* Open daily noon-midnight. AmEx, MC, V.

Phetburi, 31, bd. de Grenelle (tel. 48 58 14 88). M. Dupleix. The place to go if you're suffering from Thai food withdrawal. Not the place to go if you're averse to lemon grass—specialties include lemon grass fish soup, lemon grass squid salad, lemon grass beef.... Lunch *menu* (68F), dinner *menu* (89F). Both menus include three courses and a portion of rice, the dinner menu simply offers more choices. Open Mon.-Sat. noon-2:30pm and 7-10:45pm. AmEx, MC, V.

Restaurant Les Listines, 24, rue Falguière (tel. 45 38 57 40). M. Falguière. A pink and green interior and a delicious menu of *saumon aux herbes, cuisses de canard, boeuf à la moutarde ancienne,* and other French delights. Both the 79 and the 130F *menus* offer all 3 courses. Open Mon.-Sat. noon-2:30pm and 7-10:30pm.

Samaya, 31, bd. de Grenelle (tel. 45 77 44 44). M. Dupleix. A small eatery/store specializing in Lebanese cuisine. Tasteful peach interior with dried flowers. 62F *menu* and 90F *menu* feature *taboulé, labaa concombre* (yogurt with cucumber), hummus, and lamb delicacies. Mint tea (10F) and a wide range of Middle Eastern desserts such as *baklava* (24F) and *Maihalabien* (a flan flavored with orange, 20F). Open daily noon-midnight. MC, V.

Sampieru Corsu, 12, rue de l'Amiral Roussin. M. Cambronne. Take a left onto rue de la Croix Nivert then another left onto rue de l'Amiral Roussin. Run by a Marxist Corsican separatist, as you can see from articles and posters on the walls. Simple tables which you might share with other visitors. Pay according to your means, though the suggested price for the simple, but copious, 3-course *menu* is 40F (beer or wine included). Don't expect translations, the management does not speak English. Do not fear, however, they will categorically refuse to serve you *boudin* (blood sausage) for your own good. Open Mon.-Fri. 11:45am-1:45pm and 6:45-9:45pm.

Le Tahar, 166, bd. de Grenelle (tel. 43 06 44 65). M. La Motte-Picquet-Grenelle. The simple décor and print curtains of this Mediterranean restaurant belie the wonderful menu. The 69F *formule méditerranéenne* features *carpaccio, sardine grillées, tomates basilic,* and *chèvre* with *escalope de volaille roquefort, brochette de boeuf* and *poêle de gigot d'agneau aux poivres et olives.* Daily specials around 72F. Open daily noon-3pm and 7pm-1am. MC, V.

■ SIXTEENTH ARRONDISSEMENT

If you are staying in the 16*ème*, eat elsewhere. If you are visiting the 16*ème*, bring a picnic. Hard-hitting sight-seers should explore one of the area's two markets—the marchés Président Wilson and St-Didier—while en route to yet another of the area's myriad museums. Here are some of the (few) inexpensive restaurants in this otherwise upscale, residential neighborhood:

Casa Tina, 18, rue Lauriston (tel. 40 67 19 24). M. Charles-de-Gaulle-Etoile. Walk up av. Victor Hugo 1 block and take a left on rue Lauriston. Favorably reviewed by both *Elle* and *Vogue,* this tiny Spanish restaurant provides excellent, affordable food. Terra cotta tiles and Spanish prints furnish an ambiant setting for *tapas* (light Spanish appetizers). The Andalusian chef turns out a range of traditional dishes, like *paella* (80F). Check the chalkboards for rotating daily specials. Appetizers 30-40F, main dishes 45-60F. 50F *menu* includes a plate of *tapas,* a glass of wine, and a cup of coffee—a light meal for a tired tourist. 100F *menu* includes a plate of *tapas,* the daily special, and a cup of coffee. Reserve a table in advance on weekends. Open daily noon-2:30pm and 7pm-1am, Sat.-Sun. 7pm-2am.

Byblos Café, 6, rue Guichard (tel. 42 30 54 54 or 42 30 90 90). M. La Muette. Walk down rue Passy one block and take a left on rue Guichard. A simply furnished Lebanese café-restaurant, with red tiles and terra cotta vases. Order a few hors d'oeuvres (30-45F) from a selection which includes *taboule, moutabal* (puréed eggplant with sesame paste), and a variety of hummus plates. 2-person dinner *menu* (190F) is a 7-dish sampler. Grilled meats 80-90F. Lunch *menu* 89F. Open daily 11am-11pm. Lunch served after noon, dinner served 7-11pm. MC, V, AmEx.

S E V E N T E E N T H   A R R O N D I S S E M E N T

Relais de l'Amazone, 93, rue de Passy (tel. 45 25 30 04). M. La Muette. Hardwood floors and velvet upholstery provide a distinctive setting for often nondescript food. Specialties include *mousseline de courgettes au saumon fumé* (smoked salmon with zucchini) and *lapin à la créme d'échalottes* (rabbit in shallot cream sauce). Appetizers 30-40F, main dishes 75-90F. 64F *menu* includes appetizer and main dish. 64F summer *menu* includes an immense salad and dessert. 3-course *menu* 130F. Open daily noon-2:30pm and 7-9:30pm. MC, V.

Le Victor Hugo, 4, pl. Victor Hugo (tel. 45 00 87 55). M. Victor Hugo. Spare, neighborhood *brasserie* executes affordable, if predictable, meals. Salads 42-52F, sandwiches 58-60F, sundaes 32-48F. Specialties include *coquilles St-Jacques provençale* (shellfish in provençale sauce, 88F) and *magret de canard à la lie de vin* (breast of duck in wine sauce, 90F). Open Mon.-Sat. 7am-10:30pm. MC and Visa accepted for checks over 100F.

Man Lung, 10, bd. Delessert (tel. 45 20 47 17). M. Passy. Walk up rue de Alboni to pl. de Costa Rica. Large portions of cheap, cheap-tasting Chinese food. The 69F *menu* includes an appetizer, main dish, dessert, and drink. Stick to duck. English spoken. Open daily noon-3pm and 7-11pm. MC, V, AmEx.

■ SEVENTEENTH ARRONDISSEMENT

You probably won't have your cheapest meal in the 17ème, especially where it abuts the staid, ritzy 16ème at pl. de la Porte Maillot. Cheaper and livelier establishments are found near its border with the animated 18ème, which can be dangerous at night. Use caution in this fun-though-seedy section of town, and avoid pl. de Clichy.

L'Epicerie Verte, 5, rue Saussier Leroy (tel. 47 64 19 68). M. Ternes. Walk north an av. des Ternes, take your first right on rue Poncelet, and turn left on rue Saussier-Leroy. This literally green grocery sells vegetarian food and runs an excellent lunch counter. Even unyielding carnivores may want to try their salads (25-35F) and quiche (45F). 2 warm dishes served daily. Order to go or grab one of the 9 spots at the long table. Open Sept.-July Mon.-Sat. 9:45am-8pm; food served Mon.-Sat noon-7pm. MC, V.

Grill Churrasco, 277, bd. Pereire (tel. 40 55 92 00), across from the Palais des Congrès. M. Porte Maillot. A companionable Argentinian restaurant specializing in beef. The 79F50 *menu* "Idée Churrasco" consists of gazpacho soup and *noix d'entrecôte grillé*; the 91F "Idée Cavaliero" serves *moules churrasco* and *brochette de rumsteack;* and the 102F "Idée Gringo" offers *empanada de queso* with *bife de chorizo grillé*. Bar serves sangria (21F), piña coladas (31F), and margueritas (32F). Desserts, mostly sundaes, 25-44F. Open daily 11:45am-midnight. MC, V, AmEx.

Joy in Food, 2, rue Truffaut (tel. 43 87 96 79), on the corner of rue des Dames. M. Rome. Walk one block up rue Boursault and turn right on rue des Dames. A vegetarian restaurant dedicated to not only taking care of your body, both with quiches and brown rice (30-50F) and with a non-smoking, relaxed atmosphere. The small interior and open kitchen put the chef in plain view of the customers.Restaurant specialties include omelettes, milkshakes, and fruit tarts. Two-course *menu* 59F. 3-course *menu* 69F. Open Mon.-Sat. noon-3pm, Tues. and Fri.-Sat. 7-10:30pm.

Restaurant Natacha, 35, rue Guersant (tel. 45 74 23 86). M. Porte Maillot. Another restaurant offering an extraordinary lunch *menu* with an hors d'œuvres buffet (mostly raw vegetables) or a standard appetizer, a filling second course of fish or a *grillade*, as well as dessert for only 80F. Dinner 100F. A *formule* at lunch includes either the buffet or a main dish, followed by cheese or dessert (60F). Open Mon. 7-11:30pm, Tues.-Fri. noon-2:30pm and 7:30-11:30pm, Sat. 7:30-11:30pm. Call ahead for reservations.

Sangria Restaurant, 13bis, rue Vernier (tel. 45 74 78 74). M. Porte de Champerret. A budget traveler's dream of a restaurant. Fabulous *formule* (80F at lunch, 95F at dinner) includes self-serve hors d'œuvres buffet, mouth-watering dishes like steak or char-grilled salmon, as much wine as you want, and desserts like chocolate mousse. Open Mon.-Fri. noon-2pm and 7-11pm, Sat. 7-11pm. MC, V.

Restaurant Olympia II, 76, av. Clichy (tel. 45 22 79 28). M. La Fourche. Two stores up av. de Clichy from the metro. *Spécialités Turques* isn't the name of the place, but this tiny Middle Eastern food stand is best identified by what's emblazoned on the awning. Oversized, specially baked pita is used for these enormous *shwarma* subs, served with fries (20F). Open Mon.-Sat. 11am-10pm.

■ EIGHTEENTH ARRONDISSEMENT

The touristed cafés and restaurants of the place du Tertre are pricey for dinner but perfect for coffee breaks. Otherwise, descend the *butte* toward cheaper eateries that circuit the lower hillside. Remember that safety is always a concern in the 18ème.

Le Petit Chose, 41, rue des Trois Frères (tel. 42 64 49 15). M. Abbesses. Walk down rue Yvonne le Tac and take a left on rue des Trois Frères. Tchatchke-filled restaurant, suitably named "trinket." Antiques and ephemera in the display case, Doisneau on the walls, silver candlesticks, and linen tablecloths. The phonograph plays hits from the 1920s. Bring a date and you'll be engaged by dessert. 90F and 160F *menus* (with 3 and 4 courses, respectively) include choices like melon with minted anise and rabbit in mustard sauce. Dinner a la carte runs 200F. Reservations recommended for dinner. Open Mon.-Sat. 7-11:30pm. MC, V.

Refuge des Fondues, 17, rue des Trois Frères (tel. 42 55 22 65). M. Abbesses. From the metro stop, walk down rue Yvonne le Tac and take a left on rue des Trois Frères. A small, finger-food restaurant with only two main dishes: *fondue bourguignonne* (meat fondue) and *fondue savoyarde* (cheese fondue). Wine served in baby bottles; Freudian revulsion/American puritanism drive many to remove the nipples. Fun and crowded at night. The 85F *menu* includes a kir *apéritif,* half a *pichet* (jug) of wine, appetizer, fondue, and dessert. Open daily 5pm-2am, dinner after 7pm.

Au Pierre de la Butte, 41, rue Caulaincourt (tel. 46 06 06 97). M. Lamarck-Caulaincourt. Popular with locals, offering excellent, affordable French food. Overlooking a peaceful garden, the dining room displays reproductions of famous Montmartrois paintings. 3-course dinner *menus* for 98F and 160F include favorites like the *huie de raie à la menthe fraîche* (ray fish pâté with fresh mint) and *eventail de veau aux tagliatelles et aux cèpes* (veal with tagliatelle and wild mushrooms). Also a 69F lunch *menu.* Reservations recommended. Open Mon.-Sat. noon-2pm and 7:30-11:30pm. MC, V.

Au Grain de Folie, 24, rue la Vieuville. M. Abbesses. A vegetarian restaurant for one and all, with a vast array of dishes from couscous to salads to every kind of cheese. On a quiet street. Dinner a la carte about 100F; also 65F and 100F *menus.* Open Tues.-Sun. noon-3pm and 7:30p-1:30am, Mon 7:30-11:30pm.

Chez Francis, 122, rue Caulaincourt (tel. 42 64 60 62). M. Lamarck-Caulaincourt. Sit on the terrace or inside this pleasant, homey restaurant. Specialties from the Pays Basques (in southwestern France), like *filet mignon,* filet of sole, lamb, *jambon de Bayonne* (ham), and *salade landaise* (a green salad with chunks of foie gras in it). 110F *menu.* Dinner a la carte runs about 190F. Reservations for dinner recommended. Open Thurs.-Mon. noon-2pm and 7-10:30pm, Wed. 7-10:30pm. MC, V, AmEx.

Chez Claude et Claudine, 94, rue des Martyrs (tel. 46 06 50 73). M. Abbesses. From the metro walk down rue Yvonne le Tac to rue des Martyrs. A tiny, plant-filled restaurant with large portions of good but not spectacular food. 3-course 59F *menu* includes choices like onion soup, *boeuf bourgignon,* and *poulet à l'éstragon* (chicken with tarragon). 3-course 100F *menu* offers more of a selection. 150F *menu* brings an *apéritif,* salad, appetizer, main course, and dessert. Expect to stagger out. Open daily noon-2:30pm and 6-11:30pm. MC, V.

■ NINETEENTH ARRONDISSEMENT

Despite the ethnic diversity in the 19ème, it has not translated into an abundance of notable restaurants. In fact, due to the proliferation of high-rise housing and office buildings, eateries are few and far between. Along main drags such as rue de Crimée, corner cafés do abound. The eastern half of rue de Belleville harbors a string of *pâtisseries, épiceries,* and *boucheries,* while the western end leads into an Asian enclave with Chinese, Vietnamese, Thai, and Malaysian restaurants and groceries.

Aux Arts et Sciences Réunis, 161, av. Jean-Jaurès (tel. 42 40 53 18). M. Ourcq. The neighborhood clientele provides a refreshing escape from the norm of tired tourists in restaurants in more frequented arrondissements. The food comes quickly and is outstanding, traditional fare from southwestern France (try foie gras or *canard*). 3-course *menu* with wine only 58F. Open Mon.-Fri. noon-2:!5pm and 7-9:15pm as well.

Ay, Caramba!, 59, rue de Mouzaïa (tel. 42 41 23 80). M. Botzaris. Tex-Mex food has become quite fashionable among young Parisians, with the unfortunate consequence that it is almost always overpriced. Not so at this lively restaurant, located on one of the most beautiful streets in the 19th, whose brightly colored walls make it visible from a mile away. Good food, fiesta atmosphere in a building which also houses a small Tex-Mex grocery and alcohol store. Margueritas 39F. *Nachos caramba* (chips, cheese, *pico de gallo,* guacamole, and choice of beef, chicken, or *chile con carne*) 43F. Fajitas 79F. *Menus* 120-140F. Open Mon.-Thurs. 7:30-11pm, Fri.-Sun. noon-2:30pm and 7:30-11pm. AmEx, MC, V.

Tai-Yien, 5, rue de Belleville (tel. 42 41 44 16). M. Belleville. The large size and simple decoration of this Chinese restaurant give it the atmosphere of an eating factory, but the excellent food compensates. Often packed, with a high proportion of Asian customers. Sautéed crab claws 60F. Rice is an extra 7F. 3-course *menu* 63F. Take-out available. Open daily 10am-2am. AmEx, MC, V.

■ TWENTIETH ARRONDISSEMENT

A la Courtille, 1, rue des Envierges (tel. 46 36 51 59). M. Pyrénées. Traditional French cuisine (with a yuppie flavor) served on a charming terrace on a cobblestone square. From the edge of the square, look past the uninspiring modern architecture to the lovely slopes of the Parc de Belleville. Lunch *menus* at 70F and 100F available Mon.-Sat. A la carte appetizers 35-40F, main courses 75-85F, desserts 35-40F. Open daily 11am-11pm, although lunch service doesn't begin until noon. MC, V.

La Papaye, 71, rue des Rigoles (tel. 43 66 65 24). M. Jourdain. Owner/chef has traveled the world over, serving an adventurous mix of Caribbean and South American specialties. Lunch *menu* (59F) and dinner *menus* (100F, and 149F) feature *colombos* (Caribbean curry dishes), grilled fish, and a delicious and light coconut cake, which hails from Brazil. A la carte main courses about 70F. Open Mon-Tues. and Thurs.-Fri. noon-2pm and 7pm until last customer, Sat.-Sun. open at 7pm. Groups of 10 or more may reserve for lunch on weekends. MC, V.

CAFÉS

The French café has long been suffused with a glamor absent from its rough American counterpart, the coffee shop. We suspect it has something to do with the unhurriedness of its waitstaff; since the café's invention in the 17th century, a few customers have written whole novels there. Visitors to Paris who don't drink coffee should still think of cafés as a worthwhile haunts. Take inspiration from the example of the Surrealists, themselves partially responsible for the café's global prestige; at the Café Deux Magots, where André Breton held court, the Communist poet Pierre de Massot drank his morning bottle of Coke.

Now on a practical note: café prices are two-tiered; it's cheaper at the counter (*comptoir* or *zinc*) than in the seating area, whether inside (*salle*) or on the *terrasse* (terrace). Both these prices should be posted. Aside from coffee and wine, other popular drinks include *citron pressé,* freshly squeezed lemon juice (with sugar and water on the side). Cafés also offer Coke, but charge twice what you would pay in the U.S. You can also order a wide range of spring, mineral, and soda waters.

Travelers seeking to save money should learn to drink coffee without milk. If you simply order "café," you will receive a demitasse of espresso with a few cubes of sugar, for which you'll pay about 15F. Coffee with milk, always steamed, costs twice as much, is called *café crème*, and is the loose equivalent of a caffe latte or cappuccino. To order a large cup of coffee with milk and sugar (about the size of what's ordinarily served in the U.S.) order a *grand crème*. You'll pay more, but you may be more satisfied.

If you order a *demi* or a *pression* of beer, you'll get a pale lager on tap. You can also order bottled imported beer: Heineken and Tuborg are popular in Paris. A glass of red is the cheapest wine in a café (4-6F), and Côte de Rhone is the cheapest red. White tends to cost more, from 12-20F depending on the clientele and the neighborhood.

Cafés, if not too famous and tourist-ridden, can have affordable light lunches and snacks. A *croque monsieur* (grilled ham-and-cheese sandwich), a *croque madame* (the same with a fried egg), and assorted omelettes cost about 15-20F. A more popular choice is a salad. Try the *salade niçoise*, the French version of a chef's salad, or a *chèvre chaud*, a salad with warm goat cheese. Cheaper and smaller varieties are the *salade verte* (read: lettuce) and *salade de tomates* (sliced tomatoes with a vinaigrette). Check the posted menu before you sit down; some cafés (particularly the ones near the big monuments) will charge you up to 50F for a salad.

One last point: Contrary to popular belief, it is *not* appropriate to call a waiter *garçon*. Café waiters in Paris, unlike part-time teenage waiters and waitresses in the U.S., are in professional, career positions and take their job very seriously. They should be politely addressed as Monsieur or Madame.

Listed here are some of the most historically important and currently fashionable cafés. By no means is this a list of budget establishments. Think of these cafés as museums, since the price of coffee or soda here is comparable to the average admission fee.

Café Beaubourg, 100, rue St-Martin, 4ème (tel. 48 87 63 96). M. Rambuteau. An indoor-outdoor showcase for alternative chic, designed by Phillip Starck. Visit its lookist neighbor Café Costes. Super-svelte granite tables, sculpted leather chairs, and lots of mirrors make this café look something like a spaceship's mess-hall. Order whatever you can afford and linger. By all means check out the bat-cave-like bathrooms. Coffee 17F, *café crème* or tea 25F, desserts 30F. The mezzanine provides a panoramic view of the outdoor musicians, dancers, and performers in front of the Centre Pompidou. Open Sun.-Thurs. 8am-1am, Fri.-Sat. 8am-2am. MC, V.

La Closerie des Lilas, 171, bd. du Montparnasse, 6ème (tel. 43 26 70 50). M. Port-Royal. Exit the metro and walk one block up bd. du Montparnasse. This lovely flower-ridden café was the one-time favorite of Hemingway (a scene in *The Sun Also Rises* takes place here), and of the Dadaists and Surrealists before him. Picasso came here weekly to hear Paul Fort recite poetry. If the gorgeous dark interior (see the baby grand?) suggests a culinary opulence that you can't afford, don't eat here. Drink prices are still manageable, though. In summer, luxuriate among the plants on the terrace. Coffee 15F, house wine 26F, *marquise au chocolat* 65F. Open daily noon-1am. MC, V, AmEx.

Café Cosmos, 101, bd. du Montparnasse, 6ème (tel. 43 26 74 36). M. Vavin. While newer and less famous than its neighbors, Café Cosmos is fast becoming this generation's Procope or Séléct. Its ultra-modern interior features neon-blue recessed lighting, black tables, and slick black leather chairs. Slide down the elegant cabaret staircase from the second floor. Sit under the huge yellow awning and umbrellas on the terrace and eavesdrop on French film moguls. Coffee 11F, *café crème* 23F, tea 22F, hot chocolate 23F. *Menus* at 69F for lunch and at 89F for dinner feature options like smoked salmon with toast and Viennese scallops. Open daily 24 hrs. MC, V.

CAFÉS

Café Costes, 4-6, rue Berger, pl. des Innocents, 1er (tel. 45 08 54 39). M. Les Halles. In front of the Fontaine des Innocents. Come to people-watch at Philippe Starck's strikingly modern café, located between Les Halles and Beaubourg. Gray marble tables and futuristic steel chairs. Desserts 30F. Espresso 16F, *grand crème* 24F, sandwiches 24-40F. Open daily 8am-2am.

La Coupole, 102, bd. du Montparnasse, 14ème (tel. 43 20 14 20). M. Vavin. This enormous Art Deco café decorated in mirrors, modern sculpture, wooden chairs, and elegantly tiled floor is part café and part 1930s emporia restaurant. This café has seen the likes of Lenin, Stravinsky, Hemingway, and Einstein at its tables. The *menus* are outrageously expensive, but you can still afford a coffee (10F). *Café crème* 20F, beer 20-27F, sandwiches 15-25F. Open daily noon-2am.

Les Deux Magots, 6, pl. St-Germain-des-Prés, 6ème (tel. 45 48 55 25). M. St-Germain-des-Prés. Sartre's second choice and Simone de Beauvoir's first, it was here that the couple first spotted each other. Home to Parisian literati since it opened in 1875, Les Deux Magots is now a favorite among Left Bank Parisian youth. Named after two Chinese porcelain figures (*magots*), this café has beautiful high ceilings, gilt mirrors, and 1930s Art Deco café decor. *Café des Deux Magots* 21F, *café-crème* 24F, *chocolat des Deux Magots* (a house specialty) 28F, beer 26-38F, ham sandwich 34F. Desserts such as *gâteau au chocolat amer* (bittersweet chocolate cake) 40F, *tarte tatin chaude* (similar to an apple turnover) 40F, assorted pastries 38F. Café open daily 7am-1:30am. MC, V. AmEx for purchases of 100F or more.

Le Dôme, 108, bd. du Montparnasse, 14ème (tel. 43 35 25 81). M. Vavin. This illustrious café shares all the literati history and fame of its neighbors, but its smaller interior and elegant 1920s décor make it the best café on the boulevard. The swank interior boasts yellow marble tables, black and white photos from the 1920s and 30s, gilded mirrors with engravings of 1920s flappers, and stained-glass Victorian windows behind the bar. Hanging lamps are draped in bohemian sheer cloth and weighted with glass amulets. Coffee 12F, beer 18-28F, Vittel 18F, ham and cheese sandwiches 18F. Open Tues.-Sun. 8am-1:30am. Closed Sun. in Aug.

Le Flore, 172, bd. St-Germain, 6ème, next door to Deux Magots (tel. 45 48 55 26). It was here, in his favorite hangout, that Jean-Paul Sartre composed *L'être et le néant* (Being and Nothingness). Apollinaire, Picasso, André Breton, and even James Thurber also sipped their brew in this friendly, relaxed atmosphere. *Café espresso spécial Flore* 21F, *café crème* 25F, beer 38-40F, sandwiches 34-62F. Open daily 7am-2am. AmEx.

Le Fouquet's, 99, av. des Champs-Elysées (tel. 47 23 70 60). M. George V. "Created" in 1899 and located in the shadow of the Arc de Triomphe, this is the premier gathering place for Parisian *vedettes* (stars) of radio, television, and cinema. Tourists, oblivious to celebrities drinking inside, bask on the *terrasse.* James Joyce dined here with relish. Bank-breaking coffee and a chance to be seen 25F. Entrees from 85F. Open daily 8am-midnight; food served noon-3pm and 7pm-midnight.

Café de la Paix, 2ème (tel. 40 07 30 12). M. Opéra. At the corner of av. de l'Opéra and rue de la Paix. This institution on rue de la Paix (the most expensive property on French Monopoly) has drawn a well-heeled crowd since it opened in 1862. The café is located on the terrace only. The two restaurants inside are well beyond your means, with *menus* around 300F. Friendly waiters appear to walk several inches above the ground. Coffee 22F, *café crème* 28F, ice cream desserts 43-58F. Open daily 10am-1am. No credit cards.

Le Procope, 13, rue de l'Ancienne Comédie, 6ème (tel. 43 26 99 20). M. Odéon. Founded in 1686, the first café in the world. Le Procope has often served as stage to weighty, historic moments: Voltaire came here for the 40 cups of coffee per day he needed to finish *Candide;* the young Marat stopped in regularly, to plot the Revolution and dodge the police. Figurines of other famous regulars line the café's back wall. Not unexpectedly, history has its price—a 299F *menu.* Frugal diners should choose the café, whose 72F *menu* includes a main course and a choice of appetizer or dessert. 3-course 99F *menu* offers a choice of entrées such as *coquille de crevettes* or *steak tartare,* and desserts like *panache de sorbets.* Coffee 14F, beer 21-28F. Open daily 11am-2am.

Le Séléct, 99, bd. du Montparnasse, 6ème (tel. 45 48 38 24). M. Vavin. Across the street from Le Coupole. Trotsky, Satie, Breton, Cocteau, and Picasso all frequented this swank bistro-like café. Coffee 12F (before 3pm), 15F (after 3pm), *café au lait* 22F, teas 22-25F, beer 24-50F, lemonade 24F, iced coffee 32F. Open Sun.-Thurs. 8am-2:30am, Fri.-Sat. 8am-3:30am. MC, V.

SALONS DE THÉ

It was T'ien Yi Heng who said, "one drinks tea to forget the sound of the world." Paris' *salons de thé* (tea rooms) provide low-key refinement and light meals. Long a preferred afternoon meeting spot for women of all ages, tea rooms now draw alterno-youth for Sunday brunch. Relax and regroup over an *infusion* (herbal tea); try an invigorating *menthe* (mint) or *verveine* (vervain).

Angelina's, 226, rue de Rivoli, 1er (tel. 42 96 47 10). M. Concorde or Tuileries. Two floors of mirrored luxury. Praised for its fine chocolate, Angelina's reputation extends to its pastry (20-35F). Take tea (22-30F) in this holdover from the era when everyone knew how to hold a demitasse and remembered who poured. Now it's popular among well-behaved tourists. Try the *millefeuille* or the *Opéra* (28F). Open Mon.-Fri. 9:30am-7pm, Sat.-Sun. 9:30am-7:30pm. MC, V.

A Priori Thé, 35-37, Galerie Vivienne, 2ème (tel. 42 97 48 75). M. Bourse or Palais-Royal. Classy place for lunch, a snack, or high tea. Shielded from the city noise in Paris' most elegant pleasant *galerie* (shopping atrium, see Sights—2ème). Enter from 6, rue Vivienne, 4, rue des Petits Champs, or 5, rue de la Banque. Best to visit on weekdays. Desserts nod to both Europe and the U.S. Brownies are a favorite. 1-course meals 75-85F. Tea 22F. Open Mon.-Sat. noon-6pm, Sun. 1-6pm. Tea service starts at 3pm during the week, 4pm on weekends.

L'Arbre à Canelle, 57, Passage de Panoramas, 2ème (tel. 45 08 55 87). M. Rue Montmartre or Bourse. Faded, turn-of-the-century paintings of plants and herbs decorate the tea room's exterior. From the lovely terrace, sample one the of house's 14 varieties of tea (20F). Fruit tart 26F, 2 scoops of Berthillon ice cream 32F, apple crumble 28F. A range of *assiettes gourmandes* (mixed platters, 56-108F), including the *suprême*, with smoked goose and *mousse de foie gras* (goose liver, 64F). Salads 39-56F. Open Mon.-Sat. noon-6pm; tea service only after 3:30pm. MC, V.

Dalloyau, 2, pl. Edmond Rostand, 6ème (tel. 43 29 31 10). M. Luxembourg. Also at 99-101, Faubourg Saint-Honoré, 8ème, and other locations. This chic *pâtisserie* serves light salads and lunches, but is best known for its tantalizing array of home-made pastries (18-20F). Purchase them to-go and bring them to the Jardin du Luxembourg. Young crowd on the terrace, 30+ upstairs. Open Mon.-Fri. 8:30am-7:30pm, Sat.-Sun. 8:30am-8pm.

L'Ebouillanté, 6, rue des Barres, 4ème (tel. 42 78 48 62). M. Pont Marie or St-Paul. A restaurant and *salon de thé* located on a cobblestone alleyway facing Eglise St-Gervais-St-Protais. Come here in good weather for pictoresque mid-afternoon grazing on the terrace. Salads (55F), *crêpes,* and blini are a cut above. Tea 22F, flavored coffees 35F. Homemade tarts and cakes 30F. Open Tues.-Sun. noon-9pm. No credit cards.

Les Enfants Gâtés, 43, rue des Francs-Bourgeois, 4ème (tel. 42 77 07 63). M. St-Paul or Chemin Vert. A *salon de thé* reinterpreted by the Marais' hip twenty-somethings. Help yourself to the latest cinema or animation review. Champagne brunch, served every day, is an event not to be missed if you have the cash (100-200F). Tea 25F, *café crème* 22F, salads 24-50F, pastry 40F. Reservations recommended. Open Mon.-Fri. 12:30-8pm, Sat.-Sun. noon-7:30pm. MC, V.

Ladurée, 16, rue Royale, 8ème (tel. 42 60 21 79). M. Concorde. The perfect spot for a sandwich (11F50-13F80) or an éclair (17F25), under the painted ceiling in this bustling tea room. Famous for its macaroons (20F) and almond croissants (9F20), Ladurée endures as *the* chic *salon de thé* near La Madeleine. You will pay less if you carry your goodies away with you and settle for the less-chic atmosphere of a park bench. Lunch served Mon.-Sat. 11:30am-3pm. Open Mon.-Sat. 8:30am-7pm.

Le Loir Dans la Théière, 3, rue des Rosiers, 4ème (tel. 42 72 90 61). M. St-Paul. Named "The doormouse in the teapot" after *Alice in Wonderland,* "Le Loir" offers a smorgasbord of home-baked *tartes* and crumbles in a setting reminiscent of bohemian student lodgings. The single open room is furnished with 1930s arm-chairs and tables assembled at flea markets. Tea 20F, coffee 10-16F, homemade cakes and tarts 35-45F. Sunday breakfast includes fresh-squeezed juice, tea, hot chocolate or coffee, croissants, and toast (60F). Sunday brunch includes all the above plus a savory tart (100F). Open Mon.-Sat. noon-6pm, Sun. 11am-7pm. No credit cards.

Lindsay's Tea Shop, 4, rue Yvonne Le Tac, 18ème (tel. 42 52 74 09). M. Abbesses. From the metro walk down rue Yvonne le Tac. As the sign says, "We don't just speak English, we are English." Lindsay, a native of Liverpool, presides over an easy-going, Anglo-American hot-spot. Inside, bulletin boards advertize employ-ment and housing opportunities. Homemade scones, pies, pastries, and vegetar-ian food. Teas 19F, espresso 9F, American-style coffee (black or with milk) 14F, café au lait 20F. Scones 11-15F, cakes and shortbreads 15-32F. Lunch served all day; dinner available on weekends only. *Menus* at 70F and 73F offer salads, pies, pastries, and beverages in different combinations. Open Mon., Wed., and Thurs. noon-7pm, Fri.-Sun. 11:30am-10:30pm.

Marriage Frères, 30, rue du Bourg-Tibourg, 4ème (tel. 42 72 28 11). M. Hôtel-de-Ville. Also at 13, rue des Grands Augustins, 6ème (tel. 40 51 82 50). An elegant rat-tan salon which takes tea oh-so-seriously; non-smoking tearoom fragrantly show-cases the 400 varieties of teas sold in the boutique. Try homemade desserts and lunch plates (85F), which include meals made with tea as an ingredient. Applaud house appreciation for "art of tea". Scoff at house's undisguised colonialist nostal-gia; *musée de thé* upstairs chronicles Marriage Frères' forays into the Orient from then to now. Open daily 10:30am-7:30pm.

Pény, 3, pl. de la Madeleine, 8ème (tel. 42 65 06 75). M. Madeleine. For afternoon tea, *chocolat,* or *café viennois* (26-30F), sit with the older couples and feel *très raffiné* (and pretend you're rich). Stay on the covered terrace to watch the wait-resses surveying the comings and goings in the *place.* Open daily 8am-8pm.

La Tarte Tempion, 195, bd. Voltaire, 11ème (tel. 43 70 75 97). M. Boulets-Mon-treuil. Beautiful pastries and chocolates. American-style sandwiches made with sliced bread. Try the *Voltaire,* a layered chocolate cake with candied fruit filling and powdered chocolate on top. The terrace projects into the pedestrian traffic outfront. Open Fri.-Wed. 8am-7:45pm. MC, V.

Thé-Troc, 46, rue Jean-Pierre Timbaud, 11ème (tel. 43 55 54 80). M. Parmentier. A non-smoking, alternative tearoom with display windows full of teas, spices, Asian figurines, records, comics, and t-shirts—all on sale inside. Natural and perfumed teas 13-18F. Open Mon.-Fri. 9am-noon and 2-8pm, Sat. 10am-1pm and 4-8pm.

WINE BARS

Although wine bistros have existed since the early 19th century, the modern wine bar emerged only a few years ago with the invention of a machine that pumps nitro-gen into the open bottle, protecting wine from oxidation. Rare, expensive wines, exorbitant by the bottle, have become somewhat affordable by the glass, but this is still not the place for pinching pennies. Expect to pay 20-80F for a glass of high-qual-ity wine. Add to that the requisite *tartine* and several more glasses of wine, and you'll find yourself on the streets, drunk and penniless. Keep in mind that Parisians frequent these places to socialize and sample with the intention to buy; wine bars are *not* the destination to do any serious partying. In the afternoon you will see groups of men and women in work attire doing a business lunch or relaxing before heading back to the office, as well as people taking a break from shopping, loaded down with bags from chic boutiques. In the evening the crowd mellows to couples staring soulfully into each other's eyes, or small groups of friends having a drink before a night on the town.

Try to go with a friend who knows wine, a helpful guide book, or an open mind and inquisitive tongue. The owners personally and carefully select the wines which constitute their *caves* (cellars) and are usually available to help out less knowledgeable patrons. Over 100-strong, the wine shops in the **Nicolas** chain are reputed for having the world's most inexpensive cellars, though Nicolas himself owns the fashionable and expensive wine bar **Jeroboam,** 8, rue Monsigny, 2ème (tel. 42 61 21 71; M. Opéra). Enjoy your bottle or glass with a full meal or a *tartine* (cheese and/or *charcuteries*—French equivalent of cold cuts—served on *pain Poilâne* or *pain de campagne)*. Don't hesitate to ask the waiters for advice on which wine best complements your order; most are more than happy to oblige.

Au Sauvignon, 80, rue des Sts-Pères, 7ème (tel. 45 48 49 02). M. Sèvres-Babylone. Come in early Nov. to sample the newest Beaujolais. Also specializes in Alsatian wines. Articles and caricatures paper the walls, attesting to the national recognition received by the owner for wines sold here. Wine from 25F a glass. Open Mon.-Sat. 8:30am-10pm.

Le Bar du Caveau, 17, pl. Dauphine, 1er (tel. 43 26 81 84), facing the front steps of the Palais de Justice. M. Cité. Turned-out Parisians turn up for lunch at this traditional brass and wood saloon. Sample glasses from the vast selection of heavenly wines (15-36F) over plates of grilled goat cheese on *Poilâne* bread (40F). Open Mon.-Fri. 10am-8pm.

Chez Bailly, 174 rue St-Jacques, 5ème (tel. 43 26 80 74). RER Luxembourg. This neighborhood favorite has served as a *cave* for 65 years, and in mid-1991 started serving wine by the glass. Proprietors Jean (a Frenchman) and Gary (an American/Irishman) will be happy to direct you to the perfect accompaniment to your *salade, fromage,* or *charcuterie* (42-65F), served in a casual, intimate setting, surrounded by wall-to-wall wines from all over France. Their wines by the glass are quite affordable (from 22F) because they do much of their own bottling. Walk away with a bottle of the house *cuvée bailly* (22F) or an 1873 cognac (25,000F). Open Tues.-Sat. 8pm-midnight. Wine sold 11:30am-2:30pm and 6pm-midnight.

L'Ecluse, 5, rue Mondétour, 1er (tel. 40 41 08 73). M. Les Halles. 13, rue de la Roquette, 11ème. M. Bastille. 15, quai des Grand-Augustins, 6ème. M. St-Michel. 15, pl. de la Madeleine, 8ème. M. Madeleine. 64, rue Francois 1er, 8ème. M. Georges V. The best and certainly the most famous of Parisian wine bar chains. Appetizers 46-95F, cheese plate 54F, seafood stew 57F, *foie gras* 95F. At Les Halles, 3-course *menu* 89F. L'Ecluse specializes in wine from Bordeaux, starting at a healthy 85F per bottle. Desserts 40-45F. Open Mon.-Sat. noon-midnight, no food service 3:30-7pm and after 11:30pm. MC, V, AmEx.

Le Franc Pinot, 1, Quai de Bourbon, 4ème (tel. 43 29 46 98). M. Pont Marie. A fixture on Ile St-Louis since the island became habitable; notorious in the 17th and 18th centuries as a meeting place for enemies of the state. The exterior's metal grillwork was installed as a security measure in 1642, to prevent criminals from escaping once trapped inside. Two guards stationed at the door kept track of all who entered and exited. To evade them, bar habitués dug a secret passage from the wine cellar to the Seine. The labyrinthine *caves* have been wonderfully preserved, now the upscale dining room of this restaurant/wine bar. The wine bar occupies the main floor only. Explore the lower levels on your way to the W.C. Burgundy wines are a specialty, by the glass 16-36F and up. Check chalkboards for house recommendations and specials. Selection of light hors d'oeuvres includes a 5-cheese platter (45F) and smoked filet of duck on toast (35F). Open Tues.-Sat. noon-2am. MC, V, AmEx.

Jacques Mélac, 42, rue Léon Frot, 11ème (tel. 43 70 59 27). M. Charonne. *The* Parisian family-owned wine bar and bistro. In Sept., Mélac (and friends) harvest, tread upon, and extract wine from grapes from his own vineyard. Wine from 12F a glass. Open Sept.-July Mon. 9am-7pm, Tues.-Fri. 9am-10:30pm. MC, V.

Le Relais du Vin, 85, rue St-Denis, 1er (45 08 41 08). M. Châtelet-les-Halles or Etienne-Marcel. Sit terrace-side for a glass of Bordeaux (12-26F), and watch male pedestrians saunter down sometimes-seedy St-Denis. 3-course *menus* of copious

French food at 65F and 83F, available all day. A la carte, beef bourgignon (65F) and *bavette aux échalottes* (83F). Extensive dessert selection includes *crème brulée* and *profiterolles* (20-39F). Wines by the glass 12-32F. English spoken. Open Mon.-Sat. 10am-1am; food served 'til midnight. Closed two weeks in August. Credit card minimum 120F. MC, V.

SWEETS

Unleash your foreign sweet-teeth on Paris' *glaces* (ice creams), which are lighter, wetter, and less creamy than their American counterparts. The city's pastries and chocolates, fail-safe cure-alls for the weary traveler, are generally made where you buy them. Recently, American desserts—like *brownies* and *cookies* (pronounced kookeys)—have gained a strong following among Parisians young and old.

The Baker's Dozen, 3, pl. de la Sorbonne, 5ème (tel. 44 07 08 09). M. Luxembourg. Fudge brownies (11F), chocolate chip cookies (5F or 3 for 13F), and muffins (9F) are the specialty of this micro-bakery. Indulge on the miniscule terrace facing pl. de la Sorbonne. Open Mon.-Fri. 8am-6:30pm.

Berthillon, 31, rue St-Louis-en-l'Ile, 4ème (tel. 43 54 31 61), on Ile-St-Louis. M. Cité or Pont Marie. The best ice cream and sorbet in Paris. Choose from dozens of *parfums* (flavors), ranging from chocolate to *tiramisu* to *cassis* (black currant). Since lines are quite long in summer, look for nearby Berthillon take-out windows; the wait is shorter and they're open in August, when the main Berthillon is closed. Open Sept.-July Wed.-Sun. 10am-8pm.

Christian Constant, 26, rue du Bac, 7ème (tel. 47 03 30 00). M. Rue du Bac. On one of the tastiest streets in Paris, Christian Constant stocks 30 flavors of tea, 5 varieties of sugar, and homemade jams and jellies. Bruited chocolates and desserts include the o*péra* (19F), a popular favorite. Open Mon.-Sat. 8am-8pm.

Debauve et Gallais, 33, rue Vivienne, 2ème (tel. 40 39 05 50). M. Bourse. Also at 30, rue des Sts-Pères, 7ème (tel. 45 48 54 67). M. St-Germain-des-Prés. A purported "chocolate pharmacy," founded in 1800 by confectioner and quack Sulpice Debauve. Need something for your nerves? Follow the house prescription of two almond milk chocolates. 40 different kinds of chocolate sold here, including the largest single piece in Paris. Chocolates 4F each. Come to brouse or buy. Open Mon.-Sat. 10am-7pm.

Gérard Mulot, 76, rue de Seine, 6ème (tel. 43 26 85 77). M. Odéon or St-Sulpice. An outrageous selection of handmade pastries, from *clafoutis* with virtually any kind of fruit, to flan and *millefeuilles,* to marzipan. Pastries 10-12F. Open Thurs.-Tues. 6:45am-8pm.

Maison du Chocolat, 4, bd. de la Madeleine, 9ème (tel. 47 42 86 52). M. Madeleine. Every imaginable kind of chocolate: bonbons, blocks, milk chocolate, dark chocolate. Plus delicious ice cream and sorbets. Chocolates 3-4F each. Open Mon.-Sat. 9:30am-7pm. MC, V.

Le Nôtre hawks wonderful pastries all around the city. Join the local children pointing out their chosen treat to *maman* at one of the counters. Place your order, pay your bill at the *caisse*, and then return to the same counter to pick it up. Quiche 16-19F, buttery croissants 4F70. Open daily 9am-9pm.

Peltier, 66, rue de Sèvres, 7ème (tel. 47 83 66 12 or 47 34 06 62). M. Vaneau or Duroc. Also at 6, rue St-Dominique, 7ème (tel. 47 05 50 02). M. Solférino. A famous and famously self-congratulatory chocolatier. Nonetheless, we love their desserts. The house specialty, a *tarte au chocolat,* is more gooey than rich (16F). Melt into a chair in the *salon de thé*. Take-out available. Open Mon.-Sat. 8:15am-7:45pm, Sun. 8:15am-7pm.

Pierre Mauduit, 54, rue du Faubourg St-Denis, 10ème (tel. 42 46 43 64). M. Château d'Eau. Mauduit catered a party for Madonna in 1992 and now her photo hangs in the shop. Its expensive but worth it. Wolf down an Opéra or millefeuille (19-23F). Liqueur chocolates 4-5F each. Open Mon.-Fri. 10am-6pm. MC, V.

Sights

You're not the first person to be fascinated by Paris. Over the centuries people have sung her praises, painted her portrait, and immortalized her in film and photographs. What is it about this city that creates such mystique and evokes such attraction? With map in hand, comfortable shoes on feet, and adventurous spirit, you are ready to discover what makes Paris tick.

Sights in Paris, however impressive by day, achieve new glamor once dark falls. At night, spotlights go up over everything from the Panthéon to the Eiffel Tower, Notre Dame, and Obélisque; then, Paris' monuments transform into glittering chandeliers. The lights go off at midnight. For a complete list of illuminations, pick up the pamphlet *Paris Illuminé* at the tourist office or your local *mairie*.

For a tour of Paris' sights from a distance, take a riverboat down the Seine. **Bateaux-mouches** (tel. 42 25 96 10) provide a classic, if goofy, tour of Seine-side Paris. Be prepared to laugh at the one-and-a-half hours of continuous sight-commentary in five languages and dozens of tourists straining their necks to peer over the next person. The ride is particularly worthwhile if taken at night. (Departures every ½hr. 10am-10:30pm from the Right Bank pier near Pont d'Alma. M. Alma-Marceau. 30F, under 14 15F.) **Vert Galant** boats (tel. 46 33 98 38) are another option. (Departures every ½hr. 10am-noon, 1:30-6:30pm and 9-10:30pm from the Pont Neuf landing. M. Pont-Neuf or Louvre. 40F, under 10 20F.) The **Canauxrama** (tel. 42 39 15 00) boat tours of Paris get excellent reviews for their 3-hour tour down the Canal St-Martin. The tour leaves at 9:30am from Bassin de la Villette, 5bis, quai de la Loire, 19*ème* (M. Jaurès) and at 2:30pm from Port de l'Arsenal facing 50, quai de la Bastille, 12*ème* (M. Bastille). In summer, tours also leave at 2:45pm from Bassin de la Villette and at 9:45am from Port de l'Arsenal (75F, students 60F, under 12 45F, under 6 free, weekend afternoons and holidays 75F).

For more armchair sightseeing, attend a screening of **Paristoric: "Paris...le Film,"** 78bis, bd. des Batignolles (tel. 42 93 93 46; M. Villiers or Rome). This 45-minute multi-media spectacle combines a montage of superimposed photos and artwork of Paris with classical music and modern French tunes. The narration (headsets provide simultaneous translation in 7 languages) traces the 2000-year history of Paris with painstaking accuracy, thanks to consultants from the Musée Carnavalet. Watch Paris' boundaries change and expand, roads widen, and landscape evolve, monument by monument, according to the whims, political leanings, and unabashed egoism of its rulers. The technique is innovative, and the quotes and poetry sprinkled throughout are entertaining. (Shows daily on the hour 9am-9pm; Nov.-Mar. Sun.-Thurs. 9am-6pm, Fri-Sat. 9am-9pm. 70F. Families or holders of weekly and monthly metro passes 50F, students and under 18 40F, under 16 free. Handicapped-accessible; room for 12 wheelchairs per show.)

■■■ SEINE ISLANDS

■ ILE DE LA CITÉ

If any one location could be called the sentimental and physical heart of Paris, it is this slip in the river. Ile de la Cité sits in the very center of Paris, and indeed at the very center of the Ile de France; all distance points in France are measured from the *kilomètre zéro*, a circular sundial on the ground in front of Notre-Dame. The island was first inhabited by a Gallic tribe of hunters, sailors, and fisherfolk called the Parisii, who immigrated to the island in the 3rd century BC in search of an easily fortifiable outpost to defend themselves against the Romans. The first certifiable record left by this tribe was, sadly, their defeat by Caesar's legions in the year 52 BC. The island became the center of the Lutèce colony, languishing for four centuries under the crumbling Roman empire. In the early 6th century, Clovis crowned himself king of the Franks and adopted the embattled island as the center of his domain. No kingdom being complete without an adequately glorious church, work was begun on St-Etienne, the island's first Christian church. The basilica, built into the wall which still surrounded the island-fortress, was finished in the late 6th century under Clovis's son, Childebert I, but completely destroyed only two centuries later by Norman invaders. It was rebuilt, but razed again to make room for Notre-Dame.

During the Middle Ages, the island began to acquire the features for which it is best known and loved today. In the 12th century work commenced on Notre-Dame and Ste-Chapelle under the direction of Bishop Maurice Sully. The cathedral, completed in the 14th century, was the product of five generations, 200 years, and millions of hours of work and is one of the most beautiful, and most famous, examples of medieval architecture.

NOTRE-DAME

In 1163, Pope Alexander III laid the cornerstone for the **Cathédrale de Notre-Dame-de-Paris** (tel. 43 26 07 39; M. Cité) over the remains of a Roman temple. The most famous and most trafficked of the Cité's sights, this massive structure was not completed until 1361. The exterior was gaily painted, making the now-somber cathedral as showy as any Italian church. During the Revolution, it was renamed the *Temple du Raison* and dedicated to the Cult of Reason. The Gothic arches were hidden behind plaster façades of virtuous, Neoclassical design. Although reconsecrated after the Revolution, the building fell into disrepair and was even used to shelter livestock. But Victor Hugo's 1831 novel, *Notre-Dame-de-Paris (The Hunchback of Notre Dame),* inspired King Louis-Philippe and thousands of citizens to push for restoration. The modifications by Eugène Viollet-le-Duc (including the addition of the spire, the gargoyles, and a statue of himself admiring his own work) remain highly controversial. Is Notre-Dame as we see it today a medieval building, or a product of the 19th century? After the restoration, the cathedral became a valued symbol of civic unity. In 1870 and 1940 thousands of Parisians attended masses to pray for deliverance from the invading Germans—both times without immediate success. But the faithful do not demand results; on August 26, 1944, Charles de Gaulle braved sniper fire to give thanks for his victory. All of this turmoil seems to have left the cathedral unmarked; as do the hordes of tourists who invade its sacred portals every day. In the words of e.e. cummings: "The Cathedral of Notre-Dame does not budge an inch for all the idiocies of this world." Victor Hugo expressed the same sentiment 100 years earlier: "Time is blind, humanity stupid."

Today, thousands of visitors float in torrents past the doors of the cathedral, depriving themselves of one the most glorious aspects of the structure: the **façade.** "Few architectural pages," Hugo proclaimed, "are as beautiful as this façade...a vast symphony in stone." Although it was begun in the 12th century, the façade was not completed even in the 17th, when artists were still adding Baroque statues of dubious artistic value. Highly symbolic, the carvings were designed to instill a fear of God and desire for righteousness in a population of which less than 10% were literate. Revolutionaries, not exactly your regular churchgoers, wreaked havoc on the façade of the church during the ecstasies of the 1790s; not content to decapitate Louis XVI, they attacked the stone images of his ancestors above the doors. The heads were found in the basement of the Banque Française du Commerce in 1977, and were installed in the Musée de Cluny (see Museums). Chips of paint on the heads led to a surprising discovery: Notre-Dame was once painted in bright and garish colors. Replicas of the heads (unpainted) now crown the royal bodies.

The cathedral's interior focuses on soaring light and the seeming weightlessness of the walls. Spidery flying buttresses support the vaults of the ceiling from outside, allowing the walls to be opened up to stained glass. The effect is increased by a series of subtle optical illusions, including the use of smaller pillars to surround the bigger ones, diminishing their apparent size. The most spectacular feature of the interior are the enormous stained-glass **rose windows** that dominate the transept's north and south ends. Originally, similarly masterful artistry adorned the windows on the ground level. But "Sun King" Louis XIV, trying to live up to his nickname, ordered all the windows on the ground level to be smashed. Louis's clear windows have since been replaced by mediocre stained glass.

Free **guided tours** of the cathedral are an excellent way to discover its history and architecture; inquire at the information booth to the right as you enter. A rousing tour in English is led by Irving Levine, "the only non-Roman Catholic to give tours at Notre-Dame." A 60-year-old psychiatric social worker from Atlantic City and Washington, D.C., he has been living in Paris for the last 28 years (tours in English Wed. and Thurs. noon, in French daily noon; free). The cathedral's **treasury,** south of the choir, contains a rather humdrum assortment of robes and sacramental cutlery from the stately period of 1949 (open Mon.-Sat. 10am-6pm, closed Sat. 12:30-2pm. Sun. 2-6pm; admission 15F, students 10F, under 17 5F).

Outside again, don't miss the opportunity to visit the haunt of the cathedral's most famous fictional resident, the Hunchback of Notre-Dame, with a hair-raising climb into the two **towers.** The perilous and claustrophobic staircase emerges onto a spectacular perch, where a bevy of gargoyles survey a stunning view of the heart of the city. The climb generally deters the bus-load tourists, and you may even have the towers relatively to yourself if you come early. Although this is not the highest view of Paris, it affords you a detailed view of both the festive *quartier latin* on the Left Bank in the 6ème, and the Marais on the Right Bank in the 4ème. Continue on to the south tower, where a tiny door gives access to the 13-ton bell, which even Quasimodo couldn't ring, since it requires the force of eight full-grown men to move. (Towers open daily 9:30am-6pm. Admission 31F, seniors and students 20F, under 17 7F. Cathedral open Mon.–Sat.8am-7pm, Sun. 8am-8pm. Confession can be heard in English.) Roman Catholic masses are celebrated here daily; high mass with music is celebrated on Sunday at 11am.

For a striking view of the cathedral, cross **Pont St-Louis** (behind the cathedral) to **Ile St-Louis** and turn right on quai d'Orléans. At night, the buttresses are lit up, and the view from here is breathtaking. The Pont de Sully, at the far side of Ile St-Louis, allows for a more distant, though equally thrilling aperture.

OTHER SIGHTS

The **Mémorial de la Déportation,** behind the cathedral, across from pl. Jean XXIII and down a narrow flight of steps, is a haunting memorial erected for the French victims of Nazi concentration camps. 200,000 flickering lights represent the dead, and an eternal flame burns over the tomb of an unknown deportee. The names of all the concentration camps glow in gold triangles which recall the design of the patch that French prisoners were forced to wear for identification purposes. A series of quotations is engraved into the stone walls—most striking of these is the motto *"Pardonne; N'Oublie Pas"* (Forgive; Do Not Forget) engraved over the exit. The old men who frequently visit the museum may act as voluntary guides. You may hear one of these men chanting the chillingly beautiful *kaddish,* the Jewish prayer for the dead (square and monument open daily 9am-9:45pm; free).

Far below the cathedral towers, in a cool and dark excavation beneath the pavement of the square in front of the cathedral, the **Archeological Museum,** pl. du Parvis du Notre-Dame (tel. 43 29 83 51), houses a remarkably preserved archeological dig of the Roman village that once covered the island. The museum provides a self-guided tour through the dig, wandering through the old *quais,* baths, and houses, as well as an exhaustive display of the history of Ile de la Cité (open daily Apr.-Sept. 10am-6pm, Oct.-March 10am-5pm; admission 26F, seniors and students 17F, under 17 7F).

Buy a sandwich and wander into the garden of the **Hôtel Dieu,** a hospital built in the Middle Ages to provide aid to foundlings. It was more a place to confine the sick than to cure them; guards were posted at the doors to keep the patients from getting out and infecting the city Pasteur did much of his pioneering research inside. As at the Institut Pasteur, feel free to give blood. In 1871, the hospital's proximity to

Notre-Dame saved the cathedral; *communards* were dissuaded from burning the latter by the fear that the flames could engulf their hospitalized wounded. Across the street is the **Préfecture de Police,** where at 7am on August 19, 1944, members of the Paris police force began the insurrection against the Germans that lasted until the Allies liberated the city six days later.

The **Palais de Justice** (tel. 44 32 51 51), spanning the western side of the island, harbors the infamous **Conciergerie,** prison of the Revolution, and **Ste-Chapelle,** St. Louis's private chapel. Since the 13th century, the structures here have contained the district courts for Paris. All trials are open to the public, but don't expect a *France v. Dreyfus* every day. *Chambre 1* of the *Cour d'Appel* witnessed Pétain's convictions after WWII. Even if your French is not up to legalese, the theatrical sobriety of the interior, with lawyers dressed in archaic black robes, makes a quick visit worthwhile (trials usually Mon.-Fri. at 1:30pm to around 5pm; free). Criminal cases are the most interesting (criminal courtrooms open Mon.-Fri. 1:30-4pm).

At the heart of the *palais,* **Ste-Chapelle** (tel. 43 54 30 09) remains one of the foremost examples of 13th-century French architecture. Because the church is crowded into an interior courtyard, its beautiful exterior is lost to view; the random passerby sees no more than a 19th-century iron steeple. The church was begun in 1241 to house the most precious of King Louis IX's possessions, the crown of thorns from Christ's Passion. Bought from the Emperor of Constantinople in 1239 along with a section of the Cross for an ungodly sum of 135,000 livres, the crown required an equally princely chapel. Although the crown—minus a few thorns which St. Louis gave away as political favors—has been moved to Notre-Dame, Ste-Chapelle still remains a masterpiece—"the pearl among them all," as Marcel Proust called it. In the upstairs chapel, formerly reserved for royalty and their court, the brilliantly colored stained-glass windows have lace-like delicacy; their blues and reds combine to produce a claret-colored lighting, giving rise to the saying "wine the color of Sainte Chapelle's windows." The windows are the oldest stained glass in Paris, tastefully restored in 1845; the glass you see is for the most part the same under which St-Louis prayed to his holy relic. Check weekly publications for occasional concerts here, or ask at the information booth; tickets run 75-155F. (Open daily 9:30am-6:30pm, Oct.-March 10am-5pm. Admission 26F, students and seniors 17F, under 17 7F. Combined ticket for the Chapelle and the Conciergerie 40F.)

The **Conciergerie** (tel. 43 54 30 06), around the corner of the Palais from the entrance to the Chapelle, lurks ominously, brooding over the memories of the prisoners who died here during the Revolution. The northern façade is that of a gloomy medieval fortress. At the farthest corner on the right, a stepped parapet marks the oldest tower, the Tour Bonbec, which once housed the prison's torture chambers. The modern entrance lies between the Tour d'Argent, stronghold of the royal treasury, and the Tour de César, which housed the revolutionary tribunal. As you enter, notice the 16th-century face of Paris's first public clock.

While its former function seems to promise an exciting and morbid museum, the actual space open to visitors is not that large. Besides the beautifully restored stonework, the Conciergerie does not have very much to offer. If you do, however, decide to pay the hefty admission fee, you'll follow the *"rue de Paris,"* the corridor leading from the entrance, named for *"M. Paris,"* the executioner. Past the hall, stairs lead to facsimiles of prisoners cells, now inhabited by glum-looking mannequins, especially in the *pailleux* cell, where prisoners who weren't rich enough to bribe their jailers were forced to sleep on straw. Further down the hall is the cell where Maximilien de Robespierre awaited his death. It has been converted into a display of his letters. Engraved on the wall are Robespierre's famous last words: *"Je vous laisse ma Mémoire. Elle vous sera chère, et vous la défendrez"* (I leave you my memory. It will be dear to you, and you will defend it). The Conciergerie is still used as a temporary prison for those awaiting trial in the Palais de Justice which probably explains why the visit is so short. (Open daily 9:30am-6pm; Oct.-March 10am-5pm. Admission including guided tour in French 26F, seniors and students 17F, under 17 7F. Combined ticket to the Conciergerie and Ste-Chapelle 40F.)

The once beauteous **Place Dauphine,** behind the Conciergerie, lost its looks to 19th-century renovations. Now it's just a small dirt square. André Breton called it "one of the most profoundly withdrawn places that I know, one of the worst wastelands that exists in Paris. Every time I am there, I feel myself abandon little by little the wish to go anywhere else."

Leave Ile de la Cité from here by the oldest bridge in Paris, ironically named **Pont Neuf,** "New Bridge." Completed in 1607, the bridge's radical design lacked the usual domestic residences lining its sides. Before the construction of the Champs-Elysées, the bridge was the most popular thoroughfare, attracting peddlers, performers, thieves, and even street physicians. Although not of particular architectural interest, the bridge does have individual gargoyle capitals on its supports, which can be viewed by hanging your head over the edge, or better yet, from a *bateau-mouche* (see Entertainment). Christo, the Bulgarian performance artist, once wrapped the entire bridge in 44,000 square meters of nylon. After you have walked across the bridge, take a right up quai Conti and turn left on rue de Seine to explore some of the galleries on the Left Bank. **Applicat,** 16, rue de Seine (tel. 43 25 39 24), **Etienne de Causans,** 25, rue de Seine (tel. 43 26 54 48), **Berthet-Aittoures,** 29, rue de Seine (tel. 43 26 53 09), and **Vallois,** 36, rue de Seine (tel. 43 29 51 15), all host regular exhibits of 20th-century art and keep about the same hours (Mon.-Sat. 11am-1pm and 2:30-7pm). For information on recent openings or intelligent conversation) check out the *Officiel des Galleries* (see museums-galleries).

■ ILE ST-LOUIS

A short walk across the Pont St-Louis will take you to the elegant neighborhood of **Ile St-Louis.** Originally two small islands (the Ile aux Vâches and Ile de Notre-Dame), it was considered suitable for duels, cows, and little else throughout the Middle Ages. The eccentric king known as Saint Louis loved to sit and read in its seclusion, decked out in his preferred habit of white peacock feathers. In 1267, he departed for the Tunisian Crusade from the Ile aux Vâches, never to return; the island was later named in memoriam. It became habitable in the 17th century due to a contractual arrangement between Henri IV and the bridge entrepreneur Christophe Marie, after whom the Pont Marie is named. Virtually all of the construction on the island happened within a few short decades in the mid-17th century, giving Ile St-Louis an architectural unity lacking in most Parisian neighborhoods.

Today, the island looks much as it did 300 years ago, with only two small streets altered in any significant sense. Its *hôtels particuliers* and townhouses have attracted an elite that now includes Guy de Rothschild and Pompidou's widow; Voltaire, Mme. de Châtelet, Daumier, Ingres, Baudelaire, and Cézanne number among past residents. Floating somewhere between small village and chic address, the island retains a certain remoteness from the rest of Paris. Older residents say *"Je vais à Paris"* (I'm going to Paris) when leaving by one of the four bridges linking Ile St-Louis and the mainland. In a rare burst of activist vigor, inhabitants declared the island an independent republic in the 1930s.

While you may not be able to afford the rent, you can afford the view. Many a literary personage has watched the passage of *bateaux-mouches* down this stretch of the Seine, notably Jake Barnes in the *Sun Also Rises.* Leave Ile de la Cité by the Pont St-Louis and follow the **quai de Bourbon.** Camille Claudel lived and worked at no. 19 from 1899 until 1913, when her brother the poet Paul Claudel had her incarcerated in an asylum. Because she was the lover and protégée of sculptor Auguste Rodin, Claudel's most striking work is displayed in the Musée Rodin (see Sights—7ème). Catty-corner to the quai and rue des Deux Ponts sits the **Cabaret du Franc-Pinot,** whose wrought-iron and grilled façade is almost as old as the island. The grapes that punctuate the ironwork gave the cabaret its name; the *pinot* is a grape from Burgundy. Closed in 1716 after authorities found a basement stash of anti-government tracts, the cabaret reemerged as a treasonous address during the Revolution. Cécile Renault, daughter of the cabaret's proprietor, mounted an unsuccessful attempt on Robespierre's life in 1794. Cécile, a young admirer of Charlotte Corday, was guillotined the following year.

The island's most beautiful old *hôtels* line the **quai d'Anjou,** between Pont Marie and Pont de Sully. No. 29 once housed Ford Madox Ford's *Transatlantic Review, the* expatriate lit mag, to which Hemingway frequently contributed. At no. 17, the **Hôtel Lauzun,** built in 1657 by Le Vau, presents a simple façade but for the gold filigree on the iron balcony and on the fish-shaped structural supports. The interior may only be seen by guided tour; check the *"Conférences"* section of *Pariscope* or stop by the Caisse Nationale des Monuments Historiques, 62, rue St-Antoine (tel. 44 61 00 00). In the 1840s, the *hôtel* became the clubhouse for the Hachischins, a bohemian literary salon. Charles Baudelaire and Théophile Gautier reclined with houkahs at its evening gatherings. Jeanne Duval, Baudelaire's mulatto mistress—the famous "Black Venus"—lived nearby at 6, rue Legrattier. 9, quai d'Anjou marks the house where Honoré Daumier, realist painter and caricaturist, lived from 1846 to 1863.

Loop around the end of the quai and walk down **rue St-Louis-en-l'Ile.** This is the "main drag" of Ile St-Louis, harbors gift shops, art galleries, and traditional French restaurants, as well as the famous Berthillon *glacerie* (see Sweets, Restaurants, and Shopping). At the **Hôtel Lambert,** at no. 2, designed by Le Vau in 1640 for Lambert le Riche, once lived Voltaire and Mme. de Châtelet. **Eglise St-Louis-en-l'Ile,** at the corner of rue St-Louis-en-l' Ile and rue Poulletier, is another Le Vau creation built 1664-1726. Once beyond its sooty, humdrum façade, you'll find one of the airiest and lightest of Rococo interiors, decorated with gold leaf, marble, and statuettes. From inside, there appear many more windows than can be seen from the street. (Open to the public Mon.-Sat. 9am-noon and 3-7pm.) Legendary for its acoustics, the church holds a yearly music festival in July (check with FNAC for details). On either side of rue St-Louis-en-l'Ile, residential streets lead to the quais. Follow rue Budé to the **Musée Adam Mickiewicz,** 6, quai d'Orléans; the former home of the famous Polish poet now displays mementos relating to Mickiewicz and his circle of exiled Polish literati, including Chopin (see Museums). Marie Curie lived on the other side of the rue des Deux Ponts at 36, quai de Béthune, until she died of radiation poisoning in 1934. Proust fans should remember that Swann lived nearby on **quai d'Orléans.** And, though Marcel's Aunt Léonie found the island "a neighborhood most degrading," Parisians seem to have skipped that page.

■■■ FIRST ARRONDISSEMENT

The spectre of the Ancien Régime walks proudest through the first *arrondissement*. Hugging the Seine, the Louvre—world-famous art museum and former residence of kings—occupies about one seventh of the *arrondissement* (for a full description of the museum and its treasures, see Museums). The Jardin des Tuileries, a large formal garden attached to the Louvre, looks just as it did in the days of Catherine de' Medici. Next to the Louvre but on a smaller scale is the Palais-Royal, a palace that Cardinal Richelieu built for himself in 1632. This is the France of rising absolutism; sharp-cornered buildings and stone promenades built in the 16th and 17th centuries dwarf the passerby. The section of the 1er west of the rue du Louvre is one of elegance on a massive scale—a far cry from the cozy, meandering streets of the Marais which recall the village that was Paris. The projects mounted by Louis XIV (notably the place Vendôme) are grand, humbling, and seem to miss their king. To the other side of the rue du Louvre, the city takes on a more humble aspect and provides a patchwork of the medieval and here-and-now; Les Halles, a subterranean shopping mall, buzzes beneath a park which abuts the Eglise St-Eustache, the 16th-century church where Richelieu was baptized and the Sun King took his first communion. On the grounds of what was once the most feared and septic cemetery of Paris—la Cimetière des Sts-Innocents—skateboarders, bongo players, and guitar-strumming riff-raff entertain tourists heading to the Pompidou. To the east and to the west of the Louvre, the 1er moves to the beat of very different drums.

The **Jardin des Tuileries,** at the western foot of the Louvre, celebrates the victory of geometry over nature. The views from the elevated terrace by the river and along the central path of the park are spectacular. From the terrace you can see the Louvre, the gardens, the Eiffel Tower, and the Musée d'Orsay (right across the river). From the central path, gaze upon the obelisk of Luxor (in place de la Concorde), the Arc de Triomphe, and (on a clear day) the Arche de la Défense in the distance; turn around to see the Arc de Triomphe du Carrousel and the Cour Napoléon of the Louvre. Sculptures are sprinkled throughout the park, including 18 bronze nudes by Auguste Maillol. Catherine de' Medici, missing the public promenades of her native Italy, had the gardens built in 1564; in 1649 André Le Notre (designer of the gardens at Versailles) imposed his preference for straight lines and sculptured trees upon the landscape of the Tuileries. The gardens were made public and have since become one of the most popular open spaces in Paris. Flanking the pathway through the gardens are the Jeu de Paume (thus named because it was built on a tennis court in 1851) and the Musée de l'Orangerie (see Museums). Along with the gardens, Catherine ordered the **Palais des Tuileries,** which stretched along the west end of the Jardin du Carrousel, forming the western wall of the Louvre. Long after most of the Louvre had been converted into an art museum, the Tuileries remained the royal residence. Louis XVI and Marie-Antoinette attempted to flee the palace in 1791. Napoleon lived here prior to his exile; Louis XVIII was chased out upon Napoleon's return in 1814. Louis-Philippe fled in similar haste in 1848, and in 1870, the Empress Eugénie scrambled out as the mob crashed in the main entrance. She then successfully escaped Paris with the help of her American dentist. Nine months later, as forces streamed into the city to crush the Commune, a Communard official packed the palace with gunpowder, tar, and oil and the building erupted into flames. The burnt-out ruins of the Tuileries survived until 1882, when the Republican Municipal Council, unwilling to restore a symbol of the monarchy, had them flattened. Today, only the Pavillion de Flore and the Pavillion de Marsan remain.

In recent years, the government has allowed an amusement park to spring up seasonally. If you're with kids or simply want to nourish your inner child, come for the rides between the first weekend of December and the first weekend of January, or between the last Sunday of June and the first Sunday after August 15. At night, the huge Ferris wheel offers a magnificent view of nocturnal Paris. There are also some more traditional amusements for children, which operate year-round (except for a few weeks in winter). The park opens at 7am on weekdays, and on weekends and holidays at 7:30am. From the last Sunday of March to the Saturday preceding the last Sunday of September, closing time is 10pm; for the rest of the year it is 8pm.

The **place Vendôme,** three blocks north along the rue de Castiglione from the Tuileries, was begun in 1687 according to plans by Jules Hardouin-Mansart, who convinced Louis XIV and a group of five financiers to invest in the ensemble of private mansions and public institutions. The project ran out of funds almost immediately; for several decades before it was finished in 1720, the theatrical and ostentatious place Vendôme remained no more than a series of empty façades. Many of the buildings were gutted in the 1930s; again, their uniformly dignified façades were protected. Place Vendôme as it exists today is a series of 17th-century façades masking 20th-century offices. In 1972, a huge underground carpark was installed, another major change that did not vary the outside appearance of the square. The recently renovated *place* is one of the few in Paris safe for high heels, and looks today like the perfect spot to practice the box-step after dark under the iron lampposts past Chanel and Cartier. Waltz over to the Ritz (no. 15) where Hemingway drank, and drank, and is duly remembered: they named the bar after him. After riding into Paris with the U.S. Army, Hemingway gathered some Resistance troops and went off to liberate the Ritz. Greeted by his old chum, the assistant manager, Hemingway ordered 73 dry martinis. Raise a glass in his memory at **Hemingway,** 36, rue Cambon (tel. 42 60 38 30), and pay through the nose for a glimpse of this shrine to Papa (open daily 7pm-1am). Chopin died at no. 12; no. 11 and no. 13 house the **Ministry of Justice.** To the left of the entrance is **The Meter,** the mother of all rulers. Nowadays meters are defined using krypton 86 radiation, but this 1848 unit is a pretty reliable source. Today, the entire *place* shimmers with opulence. Well-known bankers, perfumers and jewelers sprinkle the area; savor the moment with a 50,000F watch from Cartier.

Napoleon presides over the square from atop the central **column,** looking down on the Ministry of Justice and the Bank of Spain. Originally, the square held a 7m statue of Louis XIV in Roman costume. The statue was destroyed on August 10, 1792, and the square was renamed place des Piques. *(Piques* were long spears used in the Revolution to carry guillotined heads.) In 1805, Napoleon erected a central column modeled after Trajan's column in Rome. Cast from Austrian and Russian bronze cannons captured in battle, surrounding a core of stone, the bas reliefs of the column showed a series of military heroes; the emperor at the top was represented in the Roman toga that once covered Louis XIV. Nine years later the statue of Napoleon was deposed—not without difficulty. (In order to remove it, the Royalist government had to arrest the maker of the statue and force him, on penalty of execution, to figure out how to get rid of it.) Soon after, the return of Napoleon from Elba brought the original statue back to its proud stance. Over the next 60 years it would be replaced by the white flag of the ancient monarchy, by a renewed Napoleon in military garb, and by a classical Napoleon modeled after the original. During the Commune, a group led by Gustave Courbet toppled the entire column, planning to replace it with a monument to the "Federation of Nations and the Universal Republic." Later, in Napoleon's final victory, the original column was recreated. New bronze reliefs were made from the original molds and the undamaged Emperor returned to the top where he still holds sway over the gracious square.

Nearby, at 328, rue St-Honoré, is the former site of the **Jacobin convent,** a Dominican convent which furnished a meeting-place for Robespierre, who lodged at no. 398-400. The **Feuillants Monastery** arranged for an apartment house to be built nearby between 229 and 235, rue St-Honoré, where the Feuillants club (a group of moderates such as Lavoisier) met in 1791, in close proximity to their opposition, the Jacobins. The monastery extended as far as the Tuileries riding school, known as the **Manége**. The National Assembly met here from 1789 to 1793, and in 1792 the Convention condemned Louis XVI to death here by a majority of only one vote.

The **Palais-Royal** lies across rue de Rivoli from the Louvre. Constructed in 1639 by Jacques Lemercier as Cardinal Richelieu's Palais Cardinal, it became a Palais Royal when Anne of Austria, regent for Louis XIV, set up house there, as did his mistress, Louise de Vallière. Louis-Philippe d'Orléans, the Duc de Chartres whose son became King Louis-Philippe, inherited the palace in 1780. Strapped for cash, in 1784 he built and rented out the elegant buildings that enclose the palace's formal garden, turning the complex into the 18th century's version of a shopping mall. It had boutiques, restaurants, prostitutes, and—in lieu of a multi-screen cinema—theaters, wax museums, and puppet shows. On July 12, 1789, 26-year-old Camille Desmoulins leaped onto a café table and urged his fellow citizens to arm themselves, shouting "I would rather die than submit to servitude." The crowd filed out, and was soon skirmishing with cavalry in the Tuileries garden. The revolutions of 1830 and 1848 also began with angry crowds in these gardens. In the second half of the 19th century, the Palais recovered as a center of luxury commerce, preserving a serene aristocracy amid the "commercialism" of Haussmann's boulevards and modern department stores.

Today, the galleries of the venerable buildings contain small shops and a few cafés with a splendid view of the palace fountain and flower beds, all of which were re-landscaped in 1992. The levels above the cafés and shops, as well as the older parts of the palace, are occupied by government offices (including the Ministry of Culture). A popular place for couples with a large height disparity to kiss isthe *colonnes de Buren*—a set of black and white striped pillars and stumps that completely fill the *cour d'honneur* (the main courtyard). Planted there in 1986, Daniel Buren's columns created a storm of controversy comparable to the one that greeted the Louvre pyramid. Separating this courtyard from the gardens are more staid columns, built in the early 19th century. On the southwestern corner of the Palais-Royal, facing the

Louvre, the **Comédie Française,** formerly the Théâtre Français, is home to France's leading dramatic group. The theater was built in 1790 by architect Victor Louis. The entrance displays a number of busts of famous actors, including Mirabeau by Rodin, Talma by David, d'Anges and Voltaire by Houdon. Molière, the company's founder, died here on stage; ironically, he was playing the role of the "Imaginary Invalid." The chair onto which he collapsed can still be seen. A monument to the great playwright rises not far from here at the corner of rue Molière and rue Richelieu, a few steps away from no. 40, where he died. The Fontaine de Molière, designed by Visconti, splashes nearby.

Stretching north from the Comédie into the second and ninth *arrondissements* is the glittering **Avenue de l'Opéra.** Haussmann leveled the *butte de Moulins* and many old homes to connect the old symbol of royalty, the Louvre, to the new symbol of imperial grandeur, the Opéra. The grand creation was intended to bear the mightiest name of all—avenue Napoléon—but the Franco-Prussian war interrupted this scheme, and when finished, the avenue was named for its terminus instead.

The **Bourse du Commerce** is the large round building between the rue du Louvre and the Forum des Halles. Not to be confused with the stock exchange (the "bourse des valeurs" or the "bourse"), the Bourse du Commerce is a commodities exchange where deals on agricultural produce are made. It's worth stepping inside to admire the iron-and-glass cupola and the paintings that surround it. (Open Mon.-Fri. 8:30am-7pm.) In the Middle Ages, a convent of repented sinners occupied the site. Catherine de' Medici threw out the penitent women in 1572, when a horoscope convinced her that she should abandon construction of the Tuileries and build her palace here instead. Cathérine's palace was demolished in 1748, leaving only the observation tower of her personal astrologer (a huge stone pillar that stands right next to the wall of the Bourse du Commerce) as a memorial to her superstition. Louis XV replaced the structure with a grain market on the site; it was transformed into a commodities market in 1889, when the current building was built.

St-Eustache (M. Les Halles, Châtelet-Les Halles) is the large Gothic/Renaissance church visible from all over Les Halles, right next to the Turbigo exit of the Les Halles *métro*. In front of the church is a large cobblestoned area with fountains and a distinctive sculpture of a huge human head and hand. Come to this area with a frisbee on a summer evening and you'll be sure to meet plenty of local youths and foreign backpackers who want to play. Eustatius was a Roman general who is said to have converted to Christianity upon seeing the sign of a cross between the antlers of a deer. As punishment, he and his family were locked into a brass bull which was then placed over a fire until it became white-hot. Construction of the church in his honor began in 1532, and dragged on for over a century. In 1754, the unfinished façade was knocked down and replaced with the Romanesque façade that it has today— incongruous with the rest of the building, but appropriate for the saint in question. You can get a good view of the older parts of the church if you go down the stairs of the Porte St-Eustache. To visit the interior you can just look around, or take a guided tour (in French only). See Colvert's tomb and Pigalle's exquisite statue of the Madonna. Perhaps the best way of taking in the architecture and the stained glass is to attend one of the **organ concerts** organized in June and July. The organ is one of the best in Paris; classical music lovers will not want to miss the experience of its thrilling baritone. Berlioz heard his *Te Deum* at St-Eustache for the first time; Liszt conducted his *Messiah* here in 1886. For information on the organ festival, check *Pariscope,* call 45 22 28 74, or read the posters in front of the church. (Organ festival tickets 120F, students 80F. Church open Mon.-Sat. 8:30am-7pm, Sun. 8:15am-12:30pm and 3-7pm. Guided tours 3pm on Sun.; June-July daily 2pm. Mass Mon.-Fri. 10am and 6pm, Sat. 6pm, Sun. 8:30am, 9:45am, 11am, and 6pm. On Sun., the 11am mass is with choir and organ; the 6pm mass is with organ.) The statue in front of the church was created in 1986 by sculptor Henri de Miller. Its apt title is *The Listener.*

Les Halles (M. Les Halles, Châtelet-Les Halles) was called *"le ventre de Paris"* (Paris's belly) by Emile Zola. Since 1135, when King Louis VI built two wooden buildings here to house a bazaar, Les Halles was the site of the largest food market in Paris. The Les Halles Zola described received a much-needed facelift in the 1850-60s with the construction of large iron and glass pavilions that sheltered the vendors stalls. Designed by Baltard, the pavilions resembled the one that still stands over the small market at the Carreau du Temple in the third *arrondissement*. In the 1960s, the market had again slipped into disrepair. This time, however, the authorities decided to solve the problem simply by sending the vendors to a suburb near Orly.

After moving the old market in 1970, politicians and city planners debated how to fill *le trou des Halles* (the gap at Les Halles), 106 open acres which presented Paris with the largest urban redesign opportunity since Hausmannization. Most of the city adored the elegant pavilions and wanted to see them preserved. But planners insisted that only by destroying the pavilions could they create a needed transfer point between the *métro* and the new RER; demolition began in 1971. The city retained architects Claude Vasconi and Georges Penreach to replace the pavilions with a subterranean shopping mall, the **Forum des Halles.** Two hundred boutiques (the most fashionable of which have floated to the uppermost levels) are crammed into the complex, along with a swimming pool and several museums: the Musée Grevin, the Musée d'Holographie, and the Les Martyrs de Paris/Rock 'n' Roll Hall of Fame complex (see Museums). A small Vidéothèque de Paris offers consultations on video and screenings of videos concerning Paris (tel. 40 26 34 30; open Tues.-Sun. 12:30-9pm; admission 20F). Putting the mall underground allowed the vast Les Halles quadrangle to be landscaped with greenery, statues, and fountains. Watch your wallet inside Les Halles, and stay above ground at night.

Getting around the Forum can be quite confusing; computerized maps scattered throughout the complex tell you what's available and how to get there. The computers will communicate with you in English—if you see a French screen, keep pressing the words *sommaire* or *fin* until you get to a display which features a button marked "change language." The Forum has wheelchair-accessible elevators.

South of the forum along the rue St-Honoré is the **rue de la Ferronnerie.** In 1610, as he passed no. 11, Henri IV met his death at the hands of a man named Ravaillac, who leapt into the king's carriage and stabbed him. Ravaillac, who was upset that Henri was not persecuting the Protestants, was later seared with red-hot pincers and scalded with boiling lead in an effort to uncover his accomplices; finally, the torturers concluded that Ravaillac acted alone. He was then torn to pieces and burned by an angry mob. Later, this street became the center of the metal trade in the city. The nearby **Fontaine des Innocents,** built in 1548, is the last trace of the church and cemetery that once stood there: **L'Eglise** and **Cimetière des Sts-Innocents,** which once bordered and overlapped with Les Halles. Until its demolition in the 1780s, the cemetery provided the macabre setting for many a merchant who sold his wares amidst tombstones and the smell of rotting corpses. The cemetery was closed during the era of Enlightenment hygienic reform; the corpses were relocated to the city's catacombs. The fountain, once attached to the church, now attracts punks and the overflow lunch-time crowd from McDonald's.

Tucked behind the Louvre near the Pont Neuf is the Gothic church **St-Germain l'Auxerrois.** On August 24, 1572, the church's bell functioned as the signal for the St. Bartholomew's Day Massacre. Huguenots were rounded up by the troops of the Duc de Guise and slaughtered in the streets, while King Charles IX shot at the survivors from the palace window. **Pont Neuf** itself, the oldest and most famous of the Seine bridges, connects the first *arrondissement* to the Ile de la Cité (see Sights—Seine Islands). At its left, **Samaritaine** is one of the oldest department stores in Paris. Founded in 1869, it ushered in the modern age of consumption. The building you see today began as a delicate iron and steel construction in 1906 and was revamped in the Art Deco style of 1928.

■■■ SECOND ARRONDISSEMENT

Since the 19th century, the 2ème has centered around barter and trade—in the *quartier*'s many indoor, glass-covered shopping arcades called *galeries* or *passages*, at the **Bourse des Valeurs** (national stock exchange), or among the prostitutes on rue St-Denis and rue d'Aboukir (see Shopping).

Galerie Colbert and **Galerie Vivienne,** near the Palais Royal, are the finest remaining examples of Parisian *galeries*—marbled, pedestrian walkways built within city blocks to house quaint, often exclusive boutiques (e.g. antique corkscrew stores, antiquarian print shoppes). Both arcades, recently restored, date from the early 19th century. These, like others of their kind, are the ur-past of modern shopping malls Enter Galerie Colbert at 4, rue des Petits Champs. Note the *trompe l'oeil* marble columns, actually made of wood. Follow the passage to the bronze statue (1822) within the rotunda. Making a U-turn from the rotunda into Galerie Vivienne, a similar, spectacular showcase of pastel, I-can't-believe-it's-not-marble luxury and little stores. Catch your reflection in the *vitrine* of Madonna's preferred designer, **Jean-Paul Gaultier,** 6, rue Vivienne (tel. 42 86 05 05). Other *galerie* windows display treasures (or copies thereof) belonging to the Bibliothèque Nationale, which uses portions of this building as a storage annex.

The **Passage des Panoramas,** off rue St-Marc, is less conspicuously posh but perhaps just as beautiful. It contains a fully intact 19th-century glass and tile roof and a more recently installed multicultural food-court. Other *galeries* in the 2ème include the **Passage du Grand-Cerf** (off rue St-Denis's lower end) and the **Passage des Princes** (off bd. des Italiens), closed for renovations until summer 1995.

The **Bibliothèque Nationale,** 58, rue de Richelieu (tel. 47 03 81 26), is the largest library in Continental Europe. Its collection of 12 million volumes includes two Gutenberg Bibles and assorted other first editions dating from the 15th century to the present. Since 1642, a year before Richelieu founded the Académie Française, every book published in France has been legally required to enter a national archive. The current library evolved out of the **Bibliothèque du Roi,** the royal book depository, and further expanded with sizeable donations from noted bibliophiles and authors, like Victor Hugo (1885) and Emile Zola (1904). To accommodate the ever-increasing volume of books, annexes have been purchased near the library, notably in the Galerie Vivienne. In the late 1980s, the French government eschewed annexes as a short-term solution and resolved to build the monstrously inadequate **Bibliothèque de France** (see 13ème). The Bibliothèque Nationale's collection will be relocated there, beginning in late 1994. When the move is complete, the old B.N. will become the Bibliothèque Nationale des Arts.

To enter the **Salle des lecteurs (main reading room),** scholars must pass through an often strict screening process. For the most part, only graduate students and professors qualify. To receive a **carte de lecteur,** bring a letter from your university, publisher, or publication that explains your research project in as much detail as possible; the library has a number of specialized departments to which individuals must be granted specific entry. Stop by the library's main office (tel. 47 03 81 02 ; open Mon.-Sat. 9am-4pm.) Non-scholars may peek into the main reading room from its semi-circular antechamber. In summer, the library fills to capacity soon after it opens at 9:00am. Those who arrive late must take a number from the clerk who sits at the entry to the reading room and wait for a seat to vacate. (Main reading room open Mon.-Fri. 9am-8pm, Sat. 9am-5:30pm.) A gallery within the building hosts temporary art exhibitions of prints and lithographs from the B.N. archives; call 47 03 81 10 for information; gallery hours vary with exhibit and season. Upstairs, the **Musée des Médailles** displays coins and medallions (open Mon.-Sat. 1-5pm, Sun. noon-6pm; admission 30F, reduced 20F).

Across from the B.N.'s main entrance is the **square Louvois.** The sculpted fountain at its center, completed by Visconti in 1839, depicts, among other things, the four great rivers of France. Represented as women are the Seine, the Saône, the

Loire, and the Garonne. At the fountain's base, cherubs ride sea creatures that spout water through their nostrils.

The Neoclassical exterior of the **Bourse des Valeurs** (stock exchange), 4, place de la Bourse (tel. 49 27 10 00; M. Bourse), is the architectural version of a poker face. Its massive Corinthian columns might, according to Victor Hugo, be those of "a royal palace, a house of commons, a town hall, a college, a riding school, an academy, a trade market, a tribunal, a museum, a barracks, a sepulchre, a temple, a theater." Founded in 1724, Paris' stock exchange opened well after those of Lyon, Toulouse, and Rouen. Bourbon kings soon began issuing worthless bonds there, which helped finance their expensive taste in palaces and wars. Jacobins closed the exchange during the Revolution in order to fend off war profiteers. It reopened under Napoleon. Construction of the present building began in 1808, proceeded slowly, and halted 1814-1821 for lack of funds. The left and right wings of the building were added 1902 -1907. Tours of the building (in French, 1-1¼ hrs., Mon.-Fri. 1:30-3pm on the ½-hour, 10F) will appeal either to those already passionate about foreign stock exchanges or to those caught outside in a sudden downpour. The trader's pit is tame compared to London or New York. Have your passport ready if you plan to take the tour.

To the east of the Bourse, rue de Cléry and parallel rue d'Aboukir mark the line of the old rampart of Charles V. The buildings between the two streets were constructed shortly after the wall's destruction in the 17th century. Their façades are modified versions of the fanciest Italianate forms, using lintels instead of arches and plaster instead of stone. These buildings currently serve as scrim to many of the city's prostitutes.

In the mid-1970s Paris' prostitutes demonstrated in churches, monuments, and public squares demanding unionization. They marched down **rue St-Denis,** the central artery of the city's prostitution district, to picket for equal rights and protection under the law. Their campaign was successful—prostitution is now legal in France. In recent years, rue St-Denis has resettled many of the sex workers who once plied their trade in the Bois de Boulogne; routed from the park by French police in 1993, many now work streets, like rue Blondel, just south of M. Strasbourg-St-Denis.

■■■ THIRD ARRONDISSEMENT: THE MARAIS

The 3ème *arrondissement*, together with the 4ème, is called the Marais ("the swamp") because of its distinguishing quality of dampness before 13th-century monks drained it. With Henri IV's construction of the place des Vosges (see Sights— 4ème) at the beginning of the 17th century, the area became the center of fashionable living. Leading architects and sculptors of the period designed the *hôtels particuliers* that still dot the Marais—elegant mansions with large front courtyards and rear gardens. Under Louis XV, the center of Paris life moved from the Marais to *faubourgs* St-Honoré and St-Germain, and construction of *hôtels* in the Marais lagged considerably.

The 19th and early 20th centuries were not kind to this old *quartier*. Many *hôtels* fell to ruin or disrepair. Narrow, medieval streets were widened at great architectural cost. New laws specified that any new building had to be built some meters back from the curb. This resulted in the saw-toothed or jagged appearance of curbs along streets with alternately old and new buildings. (Given the longevity of some buildings, widening a street in this manner would take several hundred years; the idea was abandoned 1964, part of the Marais was declared a historic neighborhood and protected from further destruction. As part of this effort to re-glamorize the neighborhood, museums such as the **Musée de la Chasse,** the **Musée Picasso,** and the **Musée Cognacq-Jay** moved into restored old *hôtels*.

In addition to the Marais' former aristocratic quarters, the district retains the stamp of a bustling medieval village whose storefronts have, over time, begun to sway with gravity. Some of Paris' oldest buildings are to be found here—on the rue de Montmorency and on the rue Volta, dating from the 14th and 13th centuries respectively. Look around; many of the attractions here don't charge admission.

The **square Emile-Chautemps** leads from **boulevard Sébastopol,** Haussmann's great central north-south thoroughfare to the **Conservatoire National des Arts et Métiers,** 292, rue St-Martin (tel. 40 27 20 00; M. Réaumur-Sébastopol or Arts-et-Métiers; general information office through archway to the left from main courtyard open Mon.-Fri. 10am-noon and 1:30-6pm, Sat. 9am-2pm.), a polytechnical institute housed in a compound about 13 centuries old. In 1060 Henri I built a church here over the ruins of an 8th-century parish church. The priory St-Martin des Champs, now restored and most visible from rue Réaumur, is a 12th-century addition to the complex. The school itself evolved out of a repository for technical inventions assembled at this site during the Revolution. Walk through the main gate toward the **Musée National des Techniques** (see Museums) in the former priory, with statues of Coulomb and Chaptal commanding its ornamented façade. Coulomb, the better known of the two scientists, established a law of electrical attraction; Chaptal was a chemist whose discoveries helped improve methods used to dye cotton and preserve wine.

Exit left out the main gate and turn left on rue Réaumur; keep left on rue Turbigo, continue a short way, and take a left on rue Volta. At no. 3 sits the oldest residential building in Paris, a four-story structure dating from 1300. Try to imagine away the hair salon and Cambodian restaurant now occupying the ground floor and imagine medieval artisans hard at work in the shops that once lined this stooping street.

Walk up rue de Nazareth and up rue du Temple to **place de la République,** (M. République), the meeting point of the 3*ème*, the 10*ème*, and the 11*ème* *arrondisse-ments.* In the center, a monument to the Republic of France celebrates the 23 years of intermittent republican rule between 1789 and the monument's inauguration in 1880. The statue of **la République** by Morice stands on a base by Dalou, with bronze reliefs representing various revolutions in French history. During the day, many *brasseries* and terraced restaurants offer a rather expensive resting place and view of this much-trafficked *place* and tourist hub; avoid this area at night, however, when prostitutes and swindlers abound.

Descend rue Béranger, turn left on rue du Franche-Comté, and head for the blue steel and glass structure of the market **Carreau du Temple** (see Shopping—Markets). In the morning, haggle over the price of a leather jacket or a pair of suit pants. In the afternoon, the building becomes a sports center. Head down rue de Picardie and cross rue de Bretagne to enter what will be either the 380-year old food market **Les Enfants Rouges** (see Food & Drink) or a parking lot under construction; the outcome is in the hands of local politicians. Should the market close, picnic lunches are easily assembled in the specialty food stores along the rue de Bretagne. Travelers should then head to park benches in the **square du Temple,** a public park in front of the 3*ème*'s impressive *mairie.* While you eat, consider the park's tumultuous past. Just beyond the playground was the **quartier du Temple,** the 12th-century headquarters for the Knights of the Templar. Under the direction of the Prince de Conti, the Grand Prior, the palace became the site for aristocratic social gatherings. Under the Revolution it became a state prison. The royal family lived here under house arrest while awaiting execution; Louis XVI was taken directly from this prison to the guillotine. The young Louis XVII died here in 1795. Napoleon destroyed most of the fortress in 1809, and the lot was replaced by the square during the Second Empire.

Walk to the far end of the park and turn left on rue du Temple. As you approach the landmark-packed section of the Marais, wade through a slough of mostly junky jewelry stores, button stores and vitrines filled with cheap handbags. Many of these wholesale dealers only sell in bulk (*en gros*), so bargain-hunters may be disappointed. Take a right on Montmorency and behold the **Auberge Nicolas Flamel,** at no. 51, built in 1407. The French alchemist Flamel ran a charity house here, providing medieval indigents with free food and lodging. An elegant restaurant now occupies this address (see Restaurants—3*ème*).

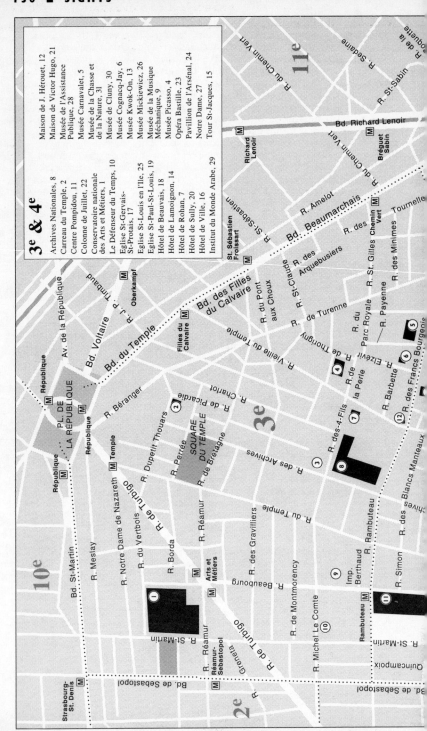

3e & 4e

Archives Nationales, 8
Carreau du Temple, 2
Centre Pompidou, 11
Colonne de Juillet, 22
Conservatoire nationale
  des Arts et Métiers, 1
Le Défenseur du Temps, 10
Eglise St-Gervais-
  St-Protais, 17
Eglise St-Louis en l'Ile, 25
Eglise St-Paul-St-Louis, 19
Hôtel de Beauvais, 18
Hôtel de Lamoignon, 14
Hôtel de Rohan, 7
Hôtel de Sully, 20
Hôtel de Ville, 16
Institut du Monde Arabe, 29

Maison de J. Hérouet, 12
Maison de Victor Hugo, 21
Musée de l'Assistance
  Publique, 28
Musée Carnavalet, 5
Musée de la Chasse et
  de la Nature, 31
Musée de Cluny, 30
Musée Cognacq-Jay, 6
Musée Kwok-On, 13
Musée Mickiewicz, 26
Musée de la Musique
  Mécanique, 9
Musée Picasso, 4
Opéra Bastille, 23
Pavillion de l'Arsénal, 24
Notre Dame, 27
Tour St-Jacques, 15

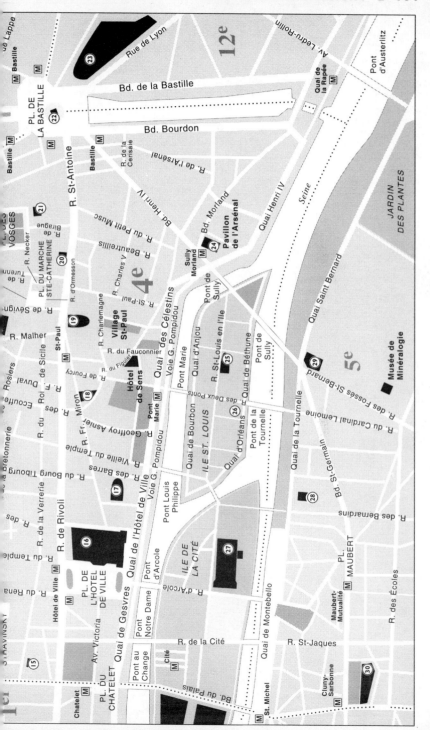

Pick up the trail on rue du Temple and turn left on rue des Haudriettes. One block down on the left side is the **Hôtel Guénégaud,** built by Mansart in the 17th century and the current address of the **Musée de la Chasse** (Hunting Museum—see Museums).

Return to rue des Archives and follow the high wall of the building to your left. Along the way, note the towered gate at no. 58, the only surviving portion of the Hôtel de Clisson, built in 1380. The unusual angle between the gate and the road was chosen to facilitate the entrance of litters and carriages. Turning left at the bottom on rue des Francs Bourgeois will reveal the entrance to the **Musée de l'Histoire de France** (see Museums), an exhibition space for the **Archives Nationales (National Archives)** housed at the **Hôtel de Soubise.** Some of the most famed French historical documents are stored in this *hôtel,* built between 1705 and 1709, and in the other old residences that occupy this block. The majestic courtyard of the Hôtel de Soubise is a classic example of 18th-century aristocratic architecture. The original, lavish interior decorations (executed between 1730 and 1745) are much as they had been. Located here is the Treaty of Westphalia, the Edict of Nantes and its Revocation, the first *Declaration of the Rights of Man,* a will from 627, the wills of Louis XVI and Napoleon, Marie-Antoinette's touching last letter, and correspondence between Benjamin Franklin and George Washington. Also cached here is Louis XVI's famous diary, with only the word *"rien"* (nothing) scrawled to describe the events of July 14, 1789 (Bastille Day); it had been a bad day for hunting. While the most intriguing of these documents would seem worthy of public display, access to them is limited to specialists. Scholars should apply to the **Centre d'Accueil et de Recherche des Archives Nationales,** 11, rue des Quatre-Fils (tel. 40 27 64 19 or 40 27 64 20).

Exit the museum to the left on rue des Francs-Bourgeois. In the opposite direction lies rue Rambuteau, which leads past the top of the Centre Pompidou and plaza to rue Quincampoix and its many one-room galleries. The rues des Francs-Bourgeois and Rambuteau divide the 3ème from the 4ème *arrondissements* and traverse the spiritual heart of the *quartier;* window-shop, stop at a *salon de thé,* and look out for corner *brasseries* selling famed Berthillon ice cream and sorbet (expect to pay about 12F for a small single scoop and 17F for a double). As you proceed to the intersection of rue des Francs-Bourgeois and rue Vieille du Temple, notice the crack between nos. 57 and 59. The stone base of the red brick building in the background is a vestige of Philippe-Auguste's city wall, built from 1180 to 1220. Also notice the tower on the corner, which belongs to the **Hôtel Hérouët,** built in 1528 for Louis XII's treasurer. Hérouët had to get special permission to add the bold angle turret to his home; normally such extravagances were reserved for royalty.

Turn left on rue Vieille-du-Temple, a street lined with stately residences. No. 75 marks the 18th-century **Hôtel de la Tour du Pin,** with an attractive private garden opposite the entrance. Consider stopping in the **Galerie Artis Flora,** a shop located within the *hôtel,* stocked with expensive replicas of famous tapestries on pillows, rugs and wall-hangings. The **Hôtel de Rohan,** one of the most famous *hôtels* in the Marais, stands at no. 87, rue Vieille-du-Temple (tel 40 27 60 00). Built between 1705 and 1708 for Armand-Gaston de Rohan, Bishop of Strasbourg, the *hôtel* has since housed many of his descendants. Cardinal Rohan was arrested here as a result of the infamous *affaire du collier* (the diamond necklace affair). One can only see the palace's sumptuous interior by visiting one of the frequent temporary exhibits, often held in the Cabinet des Singes (admission 10F); if there's no exhibit when you visit, just tour the impressive courtyard and rose garden (open Mon.-Fri. 9am-6pm; free).

Further along rue Vieille du Temple on the right is a pleasant park, the garden of the **Hôtel Salé,** once the Hôtel de Juigné and currently home of the **Musée Picasso** (see Museums). Built for a salt merchant and profiteer of the hated *gabelle* (salt tax), the *hôtel* has served many different functions in its transition from parvenu residence to Picasso museum. In 1793, it served as Dépôt Nationale Littéraire, a warehouse for books sequestered by Revolutionary censors. Honoré de Balzac lived there when it was a 19th-century pension for artists and students. Now the Picasso collection whimsically, even irreverently, fits the high-falutin, ornate interiors. His sculpture and paintings thumb jagged noses and raise one, long eyebrow at the cupids on the ceiling and the sphinxes which guard the building. Light fixtures by Giacometti share this incongruous setting.

On the other side of rue de Turenne lies **St-Denys du St-Sacrament.** The Neo-classical church features a large canvas by Delacroix of the deposition of the cross, the painting is located in the corner to the right as you enter. There's a light switch on the right of the dais; be sure to turn it off when you leave. (Vespers held Mon.-Fri. at 6:30pm.)

Turn right out of the Musée Picasso's courtyard and walk down rue de Thorigny. Straight ahead, at 1, rue de la Perle, is the five-room **Musée de la Serrure (Lock Museum),** located in the **Hôtel Libéral-Bruant.** The recently restored *hôtel* was built in the 17th century by Bruant, architect of the Invalides, as his private home.

Follow rue du Parc Royal to **square Léopold Achille.** The twin **square Georges Cain,** several yards down rue Payenne on the left, is quieter and shadier, but with-out the architectural scenery. Stop at the nearby Sévigné *brasserie*, a lively watering hole more fun at lunch than at dinner.

Winding around the corner down rue de Sévigné, an imposing gate is all that's left of the Hôtel de Flesselles at no. 52, built in the 18th century and demolished in 1908. No. 48 houses an elementary school; the woman doing the breast-feeding is Charity, as sculpted by Fortin in 1806. On the right side of the street (no. 23), in the former home of litterateur Mme. de Sévigné, the **Musée Carnavalet** contains paint-ings and knick-knacks relating to the city's changing appearance since prehistoric times (see Museums). Even if you don't visit the museum, it's worth looking at the building's gate and courtyard, built in the 1540s and 50s for Jacques des Ligneris, the ambitious president of the Parlement of Paris. The statue of Louis XIV in the middle of the courtyard was once in front of the **Hôtel de Ville** (see Sights—4ème). To main-tain architectural unity, the walls to your left and right, added in 1655, were given similar *bas-reliefs*; to the left are the Four Elements and to the right, the Four Winds. In the 1860s, architects tried to restore the building to its original appearance. Unfortunately, they mistook a 17th-century proposal to remodel the building for the original plans, and ended up carrying out the proposed remodeling two centuries late. From the Hôtel Carnavalet, continue your Marais tour by proceeding south to the 4ème.

■ ■ ■ FOURTH ARRONDISSEMENT: THE MARAIS (LOWER HALF)

Relatively undisturbed by Haussmann's reconstruction, the fourth *arrondissement* encourages visitors to wander past decaying edifices once inhabited by kings and their mistresses, through cobblestone streets lined with *galeries* and felafel stands, and into parks and *places* in which the well-heeled mix with the unshod. From place des Vosges on the north and Ile St-Louis on the south, to the Hôtel de Ville on the west and the boulevard Henri IV on the east, the 4ème offers a panoply of elegant historic monuments, market streets, and sudden, fanciful extravagance, bisected by the busy rue de Rivoli and rue St-Antoine. Royals and literary greats as well as a cen-turies-old and still thriving Jewish community have left their mark here.

The **Hôtel de Lamoignon,** 24, rue Pavée (M. St-Paul), directly south of the Hôtel Carnavalet (see 3ème), is one of the finest *hôtels particuliers* in the Marais, built in 1584 for Diane de France, daughter of Henri II. The noble façade, with its two-story Corinthian pilasters, is the first example in Paris of the "colossal" style of decoration later to appear in the Louvre. In the staid 16th century, these ground-to-roof pilas-ters were quite daring, but no one was going to tell that to the princess. The left wing, which blends rather clumsily into the original building, was added a genera-tion later by Diane's heir, Charles de Valois. The buildings of the small courtyard to the right date from 1968; added to make room for the library that moved here that year, they provide a surprisingly graceful counterpoint to the left wing. The unfortunate modern construction visible farther to the right dates from 1992. Through a door in the courtyard you can enter the **Bibliothèque Historique de la Ville de Paris** (tel. 42 74 44 44). This noncirculating library of Parisian history lends its 800,000 volumes to anyone, including foreigners with valid passports. This library is not a tourist attraction; visit only if you want information. (Open Mon.-Sat. 9:30am-6pm.) To see the gardens of the *hôtel*, which are closed to the public, exit onto rue Pavée (thus named because it was the first street in the city to be paved) and turn right on rue des Francs Bourgeois. Next door once stood the prison de la Force, where more than 150 citizens were massacred in 1792.

Place des Vosges (M. Chemin Vert or St-Paul), Paris's oldest remaining public square and perhaps its most charming, provides one of the city's most refreshing strolls. The central square, now the site of a park, is surrounded by 17th-century townhouses built at the height of French Renaissance style. Several kings lived in mansions on this site; the last was the Palais de Tournelles, which Catherine de' Medici ordered destroyed after her husband Henri II died there in a jousting tournament. The newly vacant space was the site of a horse market until 1605, when Henri IV expelled the market and decreed the construction of a new public square to be known as the place Royale. Wishing to promenade himself in courtly opulence, he wanted a *place* large and central enough to accommodate leisurely strolls. Each of the 36 buildings have arcades on the street level, topped by two stories decorated with pink brick capped by a steep, slate-covered roof. The "brick" on most of the façades is just a layer of mortar; this money-saving measure is most evident on the south side of the square (near the rue St-Antoine and the Seine), where the mortar has wrinkled and cracked. The largest townhouse, forming the *place*'s main entrance on the south side, was the majestic king's pavilion; directly opposite, a smaller but equally gracious exit, is the pavilion of the queen.

Assassinated in 1610, Henri IV died two years before the place Royale's completion. The marriage of his successor, Louis XIII, to Anne d'Autriche would inaugurate the square as a place of spectacle. The event drew a crowd of 10,000 spectators and 150 buglers. Although Henri intended the *place* as a home and workplace for merchants (hence the arcades), the king's design restrictions made the *place* an address only gentlefolk could afford. Mme. de Sévigné (born at 1bis) and Cardinal Richelieu number among the illustrious few. Another character who occupied and then got bounced from the *place* was Marion Délorme, renowned for her beauty and number of lovers. As a friend of Richelieu, Marion would visit his home in the guise of a man. Her house repossessed in 1648, Marion died at (and of) middle age, a pauper.

Molière, Racine, and Voltaire filled the grand parlors with their *bon mots*. Mozart played a concert here at the age of seven. Even when the majority of the city's nobility moved across the river to the faubourg St-Germain, the place Royale remained among the most elegant spots in Paris. Then, during the Revolution, the 1639 Louis XIII statue in the center of the park was destroyed (the statue there now is a copy erected by the restored monarchy in 1818) and the park renamed place des Vosges after the first department in France to pay its taxes (1800). Since then, successive liberal and right-wing regimes changed the name back and forth from "Vosges" to "Royale" until 1870 and the Third Republic, when "Vosges" finally won out.

Follow the arcades around the edge of place des Vosges for an elegant promenade and some delightful window-shopping. Look for plaques that mark the habitations of famous residents. Théophile Gautier and Alphonse Daudet lived at no. 8; Rachel, the 19th century's most famous actress for classical tragedy, lived at no. 9. Victor Hugo lived at no. 6, now an excellent museum with displays on his life, work, and contemporaries (see Museums). During summer weekends, these arcades fill with an array of talented musicians who play and sing mostly-classical music, from harp medleys to Mozart arias. For some first-class relaxation, stop at one of the many cafés for coffee. Or, if you can avoid the park *gardiens*, sit on the grass in the central park. Inside, under the shade of the tall trees and next to the fountains, visitors are entirely isolated from the traffic noises and fumes of central Paris. The most scenic way of escaping the place des Vosges is through the little corner door at the right of the south face (near no. 5), which leads into the garden of the Hôtel Sully.

The **Hôtel Sully,** 62, rue St-Antoine (M. St-Paul), is a restful enclave best appreciated on summer afternoons. The small inner courtyard offers the fatigued tourist several stone benches and an elegant formal garden. If you're lucky, you'll come upon one of their frequent concerts—either pre-scheduled, often free chamber music or the impromptu concerts of penniless students. The main building in the courtyard, adorned with allegorical statues of the four elements and the four seasons, was built in 1624 and acquired by the Duc de Sully, minister to Henri IV. Sully, often cuckolded by his young wife, would say when giving her money, *"voici tant pour la maison, tant pour vous, [et] tant pour vos amants"* (here's some for the house, some for you, and some for your lovers), asking only that she keep her paramours off the staircase.The **Caisse Nationale des Monuments Historiques** (tel. 44 61 20 00), a government agency dedicated to preserving historic monuments, occupies a few rooms in the *hôtel.* At the information office, you can pick up brochures about English-language guided tours of Paris monuments (40F, including the Hôtel de Sully). It you tire of relaxation, culture, and people-watching, cross through the gardens to the **rue St-Antoine,** the major thoroughfare of the *4ème arrondissement,* on the other side. Along this boulevard, you'll find cafés, fruit and vegetable stands, *fromageries,* and boutiques, together with the more prosaic Monoprix supermarket. Buy food here for a picnic lunch in the Hôtel Sully or place des Vosges.

The **Eglise St-Paul-St-Louis,** 99, rue St-Antoine (M. St-Paul),one of the earliest examples of the Jesuit style in Paris, dates from 1627 when Louis XIII placed its first stone. Its large dome—one of the trademarks of Jesuit architecture—is visible from afar, but hidden at close range by ornamentation on the façade. The royal origin of the church is recalled by paintings in the dome of four great French kings: Clovis, Charlemagne, Robert the Pious and St. Louis. The royal ties to the church were most shockingly solidified in the hanging of Louis XIII and Louis XIV's embalmed hearts , held in vermeil boxes carried by silver angels, from the arches on each side of the choir. Small wonder that the Revolutionary Convention sacked the church with particular vehemence, destroying the dynastic relics. The church, where the Jesuit Bossuet preached, retains a rich Baroque interior, complete with three 17th-century paintings representing the life of St. Louis. There used to be four, but one was lost and replaced by Eugène Delacroix's equally dramatic *Christ in the Garden of Olives* (1826). The two large holy water vessels were a gift from Victor Hugo. (Open Mon.-Sat. 9:30am-7:30pm, Sun. 9:30am-12:30pm. Masses Sat. 6pm, Sun. 10am and 11:15am and 7pm.)

The **Hôtel de Sens,** 1, rue du Figuier (M. Pont Marie), is one of the city's three surviving examples of medieval residential architecture. (The others are the Hôtel de Cluny in the *quartier latin* and Jacques Coeur's House in the 3*ème*.) Built in 1474 for Tristan de Salazar, the archbishop of Sens, its military features reflect both Salazar's life as a soldier and the violence of the day. The turrets on rue du Figuier and rue de l'Hôtel de Ville were designed to survey the streets outside, while the square tower at the far left corner of the courtyard served as a dungeon. An enormous Gothic arch for the entrance—complete with chutes for pouring boiling water on invaders— and steep chimneys and spires contribute to the mansion's intimidating air.

The former residence of Queen Margot, whom Henri IV divorced because of her infamous sexual appetite, Hôtel de Sens has witnessed some of Paris's most daring romantic escapades. One Sunday in 1606, the 55-year-old "Queen Venus" drove up to the door of her home, in front of which her two current lovers were arguing. One of them strode to open the lady's carriage door, and the other shot him dead. Unfazed, the queen demanded the execution of the other, which she watched from a window the next day. The same tempestuous queen had a fig tree that encumbered her carriage immediately removed from the street; this episode gave rue du Figuier its name. (One tour about every two months, usually on the second Friday of the month; call the Caisse Nationale des monuments Historiques (tel. 44 61 20 00)). The *hôtel* now houses the **Bibliothèque Forney** (tel. 42 78 14 60), a library that focuses on fine arts, decorative arts, graphic arts, and artisanry. The collection includes 200,000 books, 15,000 posters, and 1,000,000 postcards. Anyone with an ID can consult works in the library, but to check out books you must live in the Paris area. (Open Tues.-Fri. 1:30-8:30pm, Sat. 10am-8:30pm.)

Since the 13th century, when King Philippe-Auguste forced the Jewish population living in front of Notre-Dame to move to the Marais (then outside of city limits), this quarter has been the Jewish center of Paris. The area around rue des Rosiers and rue des Ecouffes still forms the spine of the Jewish community, with two synagogues (at 10, rue Pavée and 25, rue des Rosiers), one oratory (18, rue des Ecouffes), and dozens of kosher restaurants and delis. Down toward the river, at 17, rue Geoffroy de l'Asnier, the solemn 1956 **Mémorial du Martyr Juif Inconnu** (Memorial to the Unknown Jewish Martyr; M. St-Paul), commemorates European Jews who died at the hands of the Nazis and their French collaborators. Due to a 1983 terrorist shooting, the center now asks that visitors pass through a metal detector. The crypt downstairs contains ashes brought back from concentration camps and from the Warsaw ghetto. Comment books at the base of the stairwell provide a moving record of reflections and reactions by the survivors, partisans, and many others who have visited (open Mon.-Fri. 9am-1pm and 2-6pm, Sun. 2-6pm; June-Aug. Sun. 9am-6pm; free). Upstairs, the **Centre de Documentation Juive Contemporaine** (Jewish Contemporary Documentation Center; tel. 42 72 44 72) has a small Holocaust museum (admission 15F), a library (admission 30F/day) with more than 400,000 documents relating to the Nazi era, and frequent temporary exhibits (open Mon.-Fri. 2-5:30pm).

Two streets and centuries away at 68, rue François-Miron stands the **Hôtel de Beauvais,** built in 1655 for Pierre de Beauvais and his wife Catherine Bellier. The fortune used to build the *hôtel* was given to Catherine, Anne d'Autriche's chambermaid, because of Catherine's tryst with 15-year-old Louis XIV. As the story goes, Anne was actually overjoyed to learn that her son would please his future wife more than Anne's impotent husband Louis XIII had pleased her. From the balcony of the hôtel, Anne d'Autriche and Cardinal Mazarin watched the entry of Louis XIV and Marie-Thérèse into Paris. A century later, as a guest of the Bavarian ambassador, Mozart played his first piano recital here. Now the place appears cheapened and worn down, with crude iron banisters and visible lines of calking. The decline of the hotel began after the revolution, when its new owner tried to increase his profit from apartment rentals by adding another floor to the building.

The **Hôtel de Ville** (M. Hôtel de Ville), Paris's grandiose city hall, dominates a large square with refreshing fountains and Victorian-style lampposts. The present edifice is little more than a century old, a 19th-century creation which replaced the medieval structure built originally as a meeting hall for the *hause,* the cartel which controlled traffic on the Seine. In 1533, under King François I, the old building was destroyed; construction of a more spacious version, meant to house Paris's municipal government, began on the same spot. The newer building, designed by Boccadoro, recalled the Renaissance style of the châteaux along the Loire.

On May 24, 1871, *communards* doused the building with petrol and set it afire. Lasting a full eight days, the blaze spared nothing but the frame. The Third Republic built a virtually identical structure on the ruins—the few changes made are worthy of mention. The republican Gambetta regime integrated statues of its own heroes into the façade. Michelet, rhapsodic historian of the Revolution, flanks the right side of the building. Look for Eugène Sue, author of *Les Mystères de Paris,* a novel about the city's underbelly. This melodramatist of the boulevard can now be seen forever surveying the rue de Rivoli which he made (in)famous. In addition to updating the façade's cast of *Grands Hommes,* the Third Republic added a group of bronze knights to the roof. All dressed up and nowhere to go, the knights share much with the officials that commissioned them.

The Third Republic spared not a *centime* for the finest of crystal chandeliers and gilded every possible interior surface, even creating a Hall of Mirrors in conscious emulation of the one at Versailles. In choosing painters, the officials in charge were suspicious of the new-fangled Impressionists; when Manet, Monet, Renoir, and Cézanne offered their services, they were all turned down in favor of heavy, didactic art. Bare-breasted women act out *Philosophy* (in the Salon des Lettres), *The Triumph of Art* (in the Salon des Arts), and *Light Guiding the Sciences in the Heavens* (in the Salon des Sciences). To be fair, a few of the paintings are not so bad, and the opulent decoration can be quite impressive. Rodin's bronze bust of the Republic (in the Salon Laurens) is one work of note.

Foreign heads of state are welcomed with receptions at the Hôtel de Ville, but for most people the only way to visit the interior of the building is to take a guided tour (in French; Mon. at 10:30am except public holidays). Tours leave from the Information Office on 29, rue de Rivoli (tel. 42 76 40 40, open Mon.-Sat. 9am-6pm). Thanks to an elevator, these visits are entirely accessible to people in wheelchairs. The Information Office also holds temporary exhibits in its lobby.

In front of the Hôtel de Ville, the **place Hôtel de Ville** has entered the language under its former name, the place de Grève. The old name derived from the Right Bank's medieval topography. A marshy embankment (*grève*) of the Seine, the *place* would serve as a meeting ground for angry workers throughout the Middle Ages, giving France the phrase *en grève* (on strike). In the late 18th and 19th centuries, the place de Grève became a theater of political conflagration and metamorphosis. The first Paris Commune declared itself there in 1789; later the July Monarchy and Second Republic followed suit. Now, however, the only hordes demanding bread are the flocks of plump, swaggering, aggressive pigeons.

Cross quai de l'Hôtel de Ville to the backside of the city hall to the **Eglise St-Gervais-St-Protais,** one of the city's most beautiful examples of 16th- and 17th-century ecclesiastical architecture. The exterior is Neoclassical; the soaring interior, with its intricate vaulting and stained glass, is flamboyant Gothic. Look for the Baroque wooden Christ by Préault, the less dramatic 16th-century Flemish Passion painted on wood, the beautiful 16th-century stained glass in the choir, and the strange Boschian misericords in the 16th-century choir stalls of the nave. François Couperin (1688-1733), together with eight other members of his family (spanning two hundred years of the church's history), was the main organist here; the organ on which they played is the same used in services today. St-Gervais-St-Protais is part of a working monastery, and if you come at the right time (check posted services) you will hear the nave filled with Gregorian chant and sung passages of the Bible.

Two blocks west of this area, the **Tour St-Jacques** (between 39 and 41, rue de Rivoli) stands alone in the center of its own park. The flamboyant Gothic tower is the only remnant of the 16th-century Eglise St-Jacques-la-Boucherie which once stood here. (The rest of the church was destroyed in 1802.) The 52m tower has a meteorological station at its top, continuing a long, scientific tradition that began with Pascal's experiments on the weight of air performed here in 1648; the statue of Pascal at the base of the tower commemorates this event. The tower marks the grand intersection of the rue de Rivoli and the boulevard Sébastopol, Haussmann's treasured *grande croisée* (great crossing). Here was the intersection of the builder's new east-west and north-south axes for the city, only meters from where the Roman roads had crossed two thousand years earlier.

In the northwest corner of the fourth, the **Centre Pompidou** (also referred to as the **Palais Beaubourg**) looms like an oversized engine abandoned next to the Seine. An anti-Hôtel de Ville, the Palais Beaubourg's inside-out architecture has looked down on the surrounding buildings of the *quartier* since 1977: escalators, elevator shafts, and color-coded pipes (blue means air, green water, red electrical wires) pop out along the sides of the Centre. The center sits on the former site of a slum whose high rate of tuberculosis gained it the classification of an *îlot insalubre* (unhealthy block) and demolition in the 1930s. The lot remained vacant for many years, and two decades after the building's construction, some Parisians wish it still were. yet more people visit the Centre each year than step inside the Louvre (see Museums).

In afternoon and early evening, the vast cobblestone *place* in front of the center-gathers a mixture of caricature artists, street musicians, monologuists, mimes, grunge rebels and curious passersby. Pickpockets also frequent this area. In this chaotic scene, talent does not seem to matter; the police are quite tolerant just as long as you don't make too much noise. Consult the big numerical display that counts the seconds until the year 2000; if you want a precise record of your visit, buy a postcard which will tell you the date and time to the millisecond (30F). Late at night when the tourists have left, the square can get fairly dangerous due to the plethora of drunk men who hang around and occasionally pick fights.

The **Fontaine Stravinsky,** part of the museum complex, complements the Beaubourg crowd of minstrels and eccentrics with its cartoon-like kinetic sculptures. Its dancing g-clef, spinning bowlers, and multi-colored animals (elephant, birds) spit water on passing crowds. A collaborative effort between Jean Tinguely and Niki St-Phalle, the work does justice to the memory of Igor Stravinsky, whose atonal music shocked and dismayed audiences 80 years ago. Tinguely created the iron works, St-Phalle the animals.

Next to the fountain, the **Eglise St-Merri** conceals some impressive Renaissance painted-glass windows behind its flamboyant Gothic exterior. Ravaged during the Revolution, this church was known as the "Temple of Commerce" from 1796-1801, a sly reference to the flesh trade that has dominated this area since the 14th century. Free concerts are often held here (Sat. 9pm, Sun. 4pm, except Aug.). After the concert on the first and third Sunday of each month, there is a guided tour of the church (in French). Another clue to the widespread trade in this *arrondissement* can be found in the name of the rue du Petit Musc, which originated from *Pute y muse* (the prostitute idles here). One street away, in a house on the rue Beautreillis, pop culture icon Jim Morrison died, allegedly of a heart-attack, while in his bathtub. His grave can be found at Père Lachaise cemetery (see Sights—20ème).

■ ■ ■ FIFTH ARRONDISSEMENT: THE QUARTIER LATIN

Though the Romans built some of the 5ème's ancient streets, the latin in the *quartier*'s name refers to the language of scholarship and daily speech heard here until 1798. Home since the 13th century to the famed **Sorbonne,** the *quartier* has come to evoke bookish bohemians scribbling works-in-progress in attic apartments or corner cafés. Nonetheless, throughout most of the 19th century it was something of a slum, and students themselves spent as much time as possible on the more glamorous Right Bank.

Student dissent in the 1960s over outmoded educational and administrative practices within the French university system reached a boiling point in 1968; during the *jours de mai* (May days), violent protests spread from the Nanterre University campus, the anarchist and socialist hotbed of the day, to the Sorbonne. In partial result of his inability to comprehend or subdue the riots, then-President de Gaulle resigned; in a less sweeping response to the protests, the University of Paris was split into13 autonomous campuses.

With this decentralization, the *quartier latin* lost many of its youthful and scholarly inhabitants. In the 25 years since, tourist traffic has further displaced many of the small bookstores and cafés that were once the *quartier*'s hallmark. Much of the area now resembles any other Parisian commercial center, but for an occasional spate of used book and record shops and repertory cinemas, located for the most part along rue des Ecoles.

Bounded by the Seine to the north, the Jardin des Plantes to the east, bd. St-Michel to the west, and the bd. de Port Royal and bd. St-Marcel to the south, the 5ème *arrondissement* still swarms with students from the University of Paris at the Sorbonne and from the *grandes écoles,* prestigious exam-entry schools such as the Ecole Normale Supérieure. While artists and hipper intellectuals have migrated toward the Bastille, the *quartier latin* maintains an eternally youthful air. Intact medieval streets twist their way past cafés, restaurants, and neighborhood *pâtisser-*

ies and *charcuteries*. The many dead-end streets ending in walls testify to Hauss-mann's demolition of the hills that used to roll through the neighborhood. A few hills still remain; the tiny rue Rollin (M. Monge) drops down to rue Monge, a major thoroughfare.

The **boulevard St-Michel,** with its fashionable cafés, restaurants, bookstores, and movie theaters, is the pulsing center of tourist and, at certain hours of the day, student life in the *quartier*. **Place St-Michel,** at the northern tip of this *grand avenue,* stands as a medley of the surrounding neighborhood, attracting tourists, students, and drunken indigents. The majestic fountain dates from 1860, but includes a memorial to the liberation of France after World War II. (The *place* was the scene of student fighting against the Germans in August, 1944.) At the intersection of bd. St-Germain and bd. St-Michel at 6, pl. Paul-Painlevé, the **Hôtel de Cluny** (the city's second-oldest, extant residential building) is now home to the **Musée de Cluny,** one of the world's finest collections of medieval art, jewelry, architecture, and tapestry (see Museums).

Further south on bd. St-Michel, the **place de la Sorbonne** (M. Cluny-La Sorbonne, RER Luxembourg), a square lined with cafés, lounging students, and bookstores, is one of the many sites of student life in the *quartier latin*. **Librairie J. Vrin,** 6, pl. Sorbonne (tel. 43 54 03 47), is France's premier bookstore for philosophical dissertation. At the eastern end of the square stands the Sorbonne, 45-7, rue des Ecoles, which claims to be Europe's oldest university. (The other claimants are Oxford and Bologna.) Founded in 1253 by Robert de Sorbon as a dormitory for 17 theology students, the Sorbonne soon became the administrative base for the University of Paris. Its scholars were treated as nobility; they wore swords and were not subject to arrest while on campus. In 1469, Louis XI established the first printing house here. One of the Sorbonne's many famous students was the 15th-century poet and criminal François Villon. Later, Roger Bacon haltingly developed the scientific method, and Pierre Lombard assembled an early encyclopedia. As it grew in power and size, the Sorbonne often contradicted the authority of the French throne: during the Hundred Years War, it sided with England over France.

All the original buildings have been destroyed and rebuilt, the last time in 1885, except for **Ste-Ursule de la Sorbonne** (the main building), commissioned in 1642 by Cardinal Richelieu. The cardinal, himself a *sorbonnard*, lies buried inside, his hat suspended above him by a few threads hanging from the ceiling. Legend has it that when Richelieu is freed from Purgatory, the threads will snap and the hat will tumble down. The public is allowed only in the chapel, which occasionally hosts art exhibits (open Mon.-Fri. 9am-5pm). Behind the Sorbonne is the less exclusive **Collège de France,** an institution created by François I in 1530 to contest the university's supreme authority. The outstanding courses at the Collège, given over the years by such luminaries as Henri Bergson, Paul Valéry, and Milan Kundera, are free and open to all. Check the schedules that appear by the door in September. (Courses run Sept.-May. For more information, call 43 29 12 11.) Just south of the collège lies the **Lycée Louis-le-Grand,** where Molière, Robespierre, Victor Hugo, Baudelaire, and Pompidou spent part of their student years. Sartre taught there as well. If you're hooked on academic sight-seeing, the **Ecole Normale Supérieur,** France's leading liberal arts college and longtime home to deconstructionist Jacques Derrida, is located southeast of the Sorbonne on rue d'Ulm.

The **Panthéon,** its proud dome visible from any point in the *quartier latin,* towers over the highest point of the Left Bank (tel. 43 54 34 52; M. Cardinal Lemoine). The Panthéon began as only the latest church to be built on this hill, the Montagne Ste-Geneviève. The Romans used it for a temple to Mercury, and Clovis built a shrine to the saints Peter and Paul. The people of Paris, however, were faithful to their patron saint, Ste. Geneviève, whose prayers had deflected Atilla's hordes to Orléans; Parisians soon renamed the church and surrounding hill in her honor. (Oddly enough, the Orléannais prefer Jeanne d'Arc, as saints go.) After being destroyed by Norman invasions in the late 9th century, the church was rebuilt and remained basically untouched until 1754, when a new church was requisitioned by Louis XV. As a sign of his gratitude to Ste. Geneviève for helping him recover from a grave illness in 1744, the king commissioned the enormous, neo-classical structure we see today. Jacques-Germain Soufflot's design challenged the conventions of church architecture of the period, launching the Greek revival in France. The church took 40 years to build, reaching completion on the eve of the Revolution.

The Revolution converted the church into a mausoleum of heroes, designed to rival the royal crypt at St-Denis. On April 4, 1791, the great parliamentarian Mirabeau was interred, only to have his ashes expelled the next year when his correspondence with Louis XVI was revealed. Voltaire's body was moved here, amid great ceremony, to the new Temple of Reason and Science. Dubbed the Panthéon in this epoch, the building underwent minor alterations under the direction of Quatremere du Quincy, a renowned 18th-century design theorist. With nearly all its windows sealed to showcase light emanating from the dome, the necropolis took on the tomb-like aspect we see today. In addition, Quincy had a statue of liberty placed atop the dome to replace the cross. Over the next few centuries, the purpose of the Panthéon bounced between church and mausoleum, reflecting fluctuations in France's religio-political climate. In 1885, it became a national necropolis forever. Whoever the next trumpeted may be will enjoy immortality among an illustrious few: in the crypt you'll find Voltaire, Rousseau, Hugo, Zola, Jean Jaurès, Louis Braille, and Jean Moulin. At Hugo's interment here in 1885, two million mourners, and Chopin's *Marche funèbre,* followed the coffin to its resting place. Léon Daudet, in his *Souvenirs littéraires,* recalled the scene: "A cold crypt, where glory is represented by an echo which the *gardien* will make you admire. A room full of the leftovers of republican and revolutionary immortality. It's freezing in there, even in the summer, and the symbolic torch held up by a hand from Rousseau's tomb has the air of a cruel joke, as if the author of the *Confessions* could not even light a cigarette for the author of *Les Misérables."*

From the crypt, a twisting staircase winds upward to the roof and dome, where you can get an up-close view of garish Neoclassical frescoes proclaiming the glory and justice of France. While you can walk around the outside of the roof, the building is not high enough to afford anything but a view of nearby rooftops. The dome's interior is an extreme example of Neoclassical architecture, replete with grand, austere Corinthian columns and expansive heights (open daily 9:30am-6:30pm; admission 26F, students 17F, children 7F).

While you're at the Panthéon, don't miss the fanciful **Eglise St-Etienne du Mont** next door. St-Etienne was built between 1492 and 1626; the resulting edifice is a mix of flamboyant Gothic and gingerbread castle. Delicate rose windows are outlined by broken Renaissance pediments, topped off by a clock tower thatwould better suit a parish church in the Alps. Moving inside and feast your eyes on the huge 17th-century rood screen, a structure used in the abbey churches of Western Europe to separate the chancel occupied by monks from the nave where the congregation sat. On the right side of the nave, you will find epitaphs for Pascal and Racine, both of whom are buried further down at the opening of the choir. Also on your right is the sanctuary of Ste. Geneviève, a chapel and reliquary of gilt copper built in the 19th century. Ste. Geneviève's actual remains were burnt during the Revolution; the reliquary holds a piece of her original tombstone together with a few bones and other scraps. A blank book placed in front allows you to render homage to these fragments, as well as to ask for a few favors. Peer at the 16th- and 17th-century stained glass, particularly the cloister (accessible through the back of the choir).

From St-Etienne du Mont, head south on rue Descartes, past the Lycée Henri IV, to the picturesque **place de la Contrescarpe.** The geographical center of the 5*ème*, it has the feel of a tiny medieval village. The streets leading to it are even older; many, like rue Mouffetard, served as ancient Roman causeways. A festive atmosphere and cheap rent drew Hemingway here during his first years in Paris. He rented a studio at 39, rue Descartes and lived at 74, rue du Cardinal Lemoine with his wife Hadley. To the left of the latter's unassuming brown door once resided the Bal du Printemps, a dance hall that Hemingway used as a raucous setting for parts of *A Move-*

able Feast and *The Sun Also Rises.* At nº 67 on the same street Pascal died in 1662. John Dos Passos and Samuel Beckett were also former residents. Gone are those days; residents watch as the renovated buildings are snapped up by French yuppies.

If you get hungry, head down rue Mouffetard towards **boulevard de Port-Royal.** Here you'll find one of the liveliest street markets in Paris (daily 9am-1pm and 4-7pm). Wade through tables piled high with lingerie, shoes, and random housewares to reach the *charcuterie, fromagerie,* and vendors of fruits and vegetables that taste even better than they look. Also on rue Mouffetard, notice the old, picturesque houses; in 1938 3500 gold coins were discovered at nº 53, presumably hidden more than 150 years earlier by the Royal Counselor to Louis XV.

East of the Panthéon, at the intersection of rue de Navarre and rue des Arènes, rest the remains of the **Arènes de Lutèce,** a 100 by 130m oval Roman amphitheater, built to accommodate 15,000 spectators (far surpassing the needs of the still-tiny colony of Lutetia). The ruins were unearthed during the construction of rue Monge and were restored in the 1910s; all the seats are reconstructions. Benches that line the winding paths above the arena provide serene settings for a picnic supper.

However circuitous the streets, lively the outdoor markets, or atmospheric the cafés, much of the 5ème is a neighborhood-turned-tourist-attraction. Not so, however, for the **Jardin des Plantes,** where actual Parisians go for trysts or family outings (tel. 40 79 37 00 for information concerning the entire complex; M. Jussieu; main entrance at place Valhubert, off quai St-Bernard). The 45,000 square meter park, opened in 1640 by Guy de la Brosse, personal doctor to Louis XIII, was originally intended for the sole purpose of growing medicinal plants to promote His Majesty's health. Later it became a general garden for botanical research. Thomas Jefferson, an avid naturalist, loved this place. The garden has since been converted into a group of museums, including a three-part natural history museum, an insect gallery across the street, a hedge maze, an arboretum, greenhouses, and a full-fledged zoo. Watch the leopards, bears, and 4m pythons stalk and slither, then head over to admire 5cm-long diamonds and meter-high quartz formations. While attractions such as the arboretum—a series of rare trees labeled with metal nameplates, scattered throughout the park—and the hedge maze, located at the northeastern end of the park, are free, all of the museums have separate tickets and hours (see Museums). Ask at the entrance gate for a free park map. The Jardin des Plantes also has two botanical theme parks, the **Jardin Alpin** and **Serres Tropicales;** the first is full of rare flowers and plants from the Alpine domain and the second full of those from tropical and desert regions (Serres Tropicales open Wed.-Mon. 1-5:30pm, admission 12F, students 8F; Jardin Alpin open Mon.-Fri. 8-11 am and 1:30-5pm, free.) An interesting addition to the complex is the **Grande Galerie de l'Evolution,** newly opened in the summer of 1994. A renovation of the old Galerie de Zoologie which has been closed since 1965, this *galerie*—the first of its kind in the world—houses temporary exhibits, a cultural center, and a conference hall.

The **Ménagerie,** also found in the Jardin des Plantes, is a dejected-seeming zoo with an unhappy past. During the siege of Paris in 1871, the zoo was raided for meat; elephant became a great delicacy though no one dared try slaughtering the lions. The cages here are painfully small, the weather damp, and the countenance of the animals downtrodden. The great German poet Rainer Maria Rilke wrote a series of poems describing the animals lodged here. Of the panther he wrote: "His vision, from the constantly passing bars,/ has grown so weary that it cannot hold/ anything else. It seems to him there are/ a thousand bars; and behind the bars, no world." Meanwhile, in the Reptile House, pythons, cobras, rattlesnakes, and boa constrictors sleep peacefully in their tree displays. (Open in summer 9am-6pm, in winter 9am-5pm; admission 25F, students and ages 4-16 15F.)

Behind the Jardin des Plantes stands the **Mosquée de Paris,** a Muslim place of worship constructed in 1922 by French architects to honor the role played by the countries of North Africa in World War I. Admire the graceful ivory and aqua tower; enter the sculpted archways to tour the courtyard with its soothing fountain, carved wooden doors and ceilings, and ornate detailing. To really indulge, join flocks of

Parisians in the *hammam* for a wonderful steam bath (65F, bring your own towel and wear your underwear or a swimsuit) and enjoy a cup of mint tea (10F) in the *salon de repos* or the peaceful outdoor courtyard at 39, rue Geoffroy St-Hilaire (tel. 43 31 18 14; M. Jussieu). (Mosque open Sat.-Thurs. 10am-noon and 2-6pm. Guided tour 15F, students 10F. *Hammam* open to Mon.-Fri. 11am-8pm, Sun. 10am-8pm. Open to women Mon.-Tues.11am-8pm, Thurs. 11am-9pm, Sat. 10am-8pm.)

Walking west along the Seine back toward pl. St-Michel, stop to rest in the beautiful **Jardin des Sculptures en Plein Air,** quai St-Bernard, a lovely collection of modern sculpture on a long stretch of green along the Seine, with works by such artists as Zadkine, Brancusi, and Scheffer. Although a great place to read and sunbathe by day, this area should be avoided at night. Across the street and not to be missed is the **Institut du Monde Arabe** (see Museums). Just next door to the institute, **La Tour d'Argent,** 15, quai de la Tournelle (M. Maubert), is one of Paris's most prestigious, most expensive restaurants. Also in the area, on the small rue de Bièvre off the ancient **place Maubert,** note Mitterand's home; the president created quite a stir by preferring to reside here rather than at the Elysée.

Farther west along the Seine, **square René Viviani** (M. St-Michel) sequesters the oldest tree in Paris (a false acacia dating from 1693), one of the best views of Notre-Dame, and the **Eglise St-Julien-le-Pauvre.** The oldest though not the most beautiful Parisian church, it was completed in 1165 and thus predates Notre-Dame. (Some parts of St-Germain-des-Près are older, but were constructed back when St-Germain was a suburb of Paris.) The church now hosts musical concerts (check gates for upcoming events). Musical entertainment of a less lofty sort is available next door at the **Caveau des Oubliettes** (see Chansonniers).

■■■ SIXTH ARRONDISSEMENT: ST-GERMAIN-DES-PRÉS

Less frenzied and more sophisticated than its neighbors, the sixth *arrondissement* combines the youthful vibrancy of the *quartier latin* (Latin Quarter) to the east with the fashionable cafés, restaurants, and movie theaters of Montparnasse to the south. This area has long been the focus of literary and artistic Paris and remains less ravaged by tourists than other, more monumental quarters. Join the locals at one of the famous cafés on the bd. St-Germain, former haunts of Picasso, Sartre, de Beauvoir, Camus, Prévert, Apollinaire, and Hemingway, and watch well-dressed Parisians watch one another.

"There is nothing more charming, which invites one more enticingly to idleness, reverie, and young love, than a soft spring morning or a beautiful summer dusk at the **Jardin du Luxembourg"** wrote Léon Daudet in 1928 (RER: Luxembourg). Parisians are to be seen here sunbathing, writing, romancing, strolling, or just gazing at the beautiful rose gardens and into the central (simply decorative) pool. A mammoth task force of gardeners tends to this most beloved of Parisian gardens; each spring they plant or transplant 350,000 flowers and move the 150 palm and orange trees out of winter storage. Thanks to the 19th-century Parisians who defended this park against Haussmann's intentions to carve a street through it, you can still sail a toy boat, ride a pony, attend the *grand guignol* (a puppet show—see Entertainment), or play *boules* with a group of old men.

The **Palais du Luxembourg,** located within the park, was commissioned in 1615 by Marie de'Medici. Homesick for her native Tuscany, she commissioned its recreation in central Paris; the resulting Italianate palace was completed in a mere five years, marked by a symmetry and uniformity of design rare among Parisian buildings. Marie took occupancy in the palace in 1625. Her days there proved to be numbered, since she hated the powerful **Cardinal Richelieu.** Her son, Louis XIII, promised her he'd dismiss the cardinal, but revoked his promise the following day. In 1630 Richelieu took his revenge, banishing Marie to Cologne, where she died penniless. The palace would later house various members of the royal family and of the high nobility, including the Duchesse de Montpensier, known as La Grande Mademoiselle because of her girth. The palace served as a prison during the Terror, then as a prison for its Revolutionary perpetrators. Jacobin artist **Jacques-Louis David** used his time confined there to paint his haunting self-portrait, now displayed in the Louvre.

Future Empress Joséphine was imprisoned in the palace together with her republican husband, Beauharnais. Five years later, she took up official residence there with her second husband, the new Consul Bonaparte. The Chamber of Peers met there under the Restoration and July Monarchy, when it judged the trials of such traitors as Maréchal Ney and the young Louis-Napoleon Bonaparte. One of Napoleon's marshals, Ney rallied to support the ex-emperor in his unsuccessful attempt to escape Elba and return to power. The young Louis-Napoleon led several abortive rebellions against the July Monarchy, for which he was sentenced to life imprisonment; engineering his escape, he slipped past jailers disguised as a mason and fled abroad, only to return to France years later and become Napoleon III.

In 1852 the palace first served its current function as the meeting place for the *sénat,* the upper house of the French parliament. Despite its large and increasing membership,the *sénat* is a fairly ineffectual body that may be overruled by the Parliament. The president of the *sénat* lives in **Petit Luxembourg,** originialy a gift from Marie de'Medici to her nemesis, the Cardinal Richelieu. The **Musée du Luxembourg** (tel. 42 34 25 95), next to the palace on rue de Vaugirard, often shows free exhibitions of contemporary art.

The main entrance to the garden is from bd. St-Michel through lovely gold-leaved and wrought-iron gates. Bring a book and relax in one of the folding chairs in front of the palace, or saunter through the park's convolution of paths, past statues of the queens of France and through to one of the garden's secluded glens, each with monuments to poets and heroes of French history.

The **Fontaine Médicis** is a tranquil spot in the northeast corner, at the end of a long alleyway and reflecting pool. Tall shade trees line the alley, giving the spot the feel of an enchanted bower. A row of chairs along the reflecting pool provide a traditional spot for daydreaming. Unfortunately, the fountain tends to run dry in summer.

South of the park stretch its elegant, linear annexes, the Jardin R. Cavelier-de-la-Salle and the Jardin Marco Polo, both forming the northern half of the **avenue de l'Observatoire.** The elaborate **Fontaine de l'Observatoire** (1875) marks the half-way point between the Observatory and the Jardin du Luxembourg; its rearing horses provide a fittingly sumptuous perspective on the *grand avenue* that stretches at either side. At the extreme southeastern corner of the 6éme proudly stands Rude's statue of Maréchal Ney, whom Napoleon deemed "le plus brave des braves". After a lifetime as a soldier, the courageous marshal gave his last command to the firing squad arrayed before him; he asked that they punish his treason: "Comrades, fire on me, and aim well."

At the nearby **Closerie des Lilas** café, such notables as Baudelaire, Verlaine, Breton, Picasso, and Hemingway listened to poetry and discussed their latest works (see Cafés). Hemingway described it as "one of the best cafés in Paris. It was warm inside in the winter and in the spring and fall it was fine outside...." Other expatriate watering holes extend farther down the bd. Montparnasse: Le Sélect at n° 99, to which Jake Barnes and Brett Ashley taxied in *The Sun Also Rises,* and La Coupole at n°102-104. French artists sought refuge in this neighborhood as well. Picasso, along with Matisse, found encouragement and financial support at 27, rue de Fleurus, off bd. Raspail west of the *jardin,* where Gertrude Stein and her brother Leo patronized the century's greatest artists. Curving down from bd. Raspail toward Montparnasse is rue Notre-Dame-des-Champs. American artist James MacNeill Whistler had a studio at n° 86, and Ezra Pound lived in a rear garden apartment at n° 70.

At the end of rue Notre-Dame-des-Champs and running up one edge of the Jardin du Luxembourg, the **boulevard Saint-Michel**—central axis of the *quartier latin*— marks the eastern boundary of the 6ème. For a majestic view of the Panthèon

SIXTH ARRONDISSEMENT

(especially at night), walk up bd. St-Michel to pl. Edmond-Rostand, where a small fountain marks the end of the rue Soufflot (see Sights—5ème).

Follow the arcades of the rue de Médicis around the edge of the Jardin du Luxembourg to Paris's oldest and largest theater—the **Théâtre Odéon** (M. Odéon). Completed in 1782, the Odéon was built for the **Comédie-Française,** which, though Paris' only officially recognized actors' troupe since the 17th century, did not have a theater of its own. Beaumarchais' *Marriage of Figaro,* nearly banned by Louis XVI for its attacks upon the nobility, premiered here in 1784 before delighted aristocratic audiences. Outside the theater, people of other social castes clashed violently over rush tickets. Prior to the Revolution, the Odéon became a frequent stage for republican posturing. In 1789 the actor Talma staged a performance of Voltaire's *Brutus* in which he imitated the pose of the hero in David's painting (see Museums—Louvre), an act illustrating his liberal sympathies. As the Revolution approached, the Comédie-Française splintered over divided political loyalties. Republican members followed Talma to the Right Bank, settling into the company's current location near the Louvre (see Sights—1er *arrondissement*). Those actors who remained behind were jailed under the Terror, causing the theater to close. The Odéon would later earn the title of *théâtre maudit* (cursed theater) after a chain of failures left it nearly bankrupt. Destroyed twice by fire, its present Greco-Roman incarnation dates from 1818, when the painter David oversaw its renovation. The Odéon's fortunes changed after World War II, when it became a venue for contemporary, experimental theater. The theater would become the setting for a real-life, experimental drama on May 17, 1968, when student insurgents seized the building and destroyed much of its interior. The Odéon now enjoys a pensioned, middle-aged languor; it is currently run by the state. Nearby, off rue de Vaugirard at 5, rue de Tournon, resided Marie Lenormand, the *voyante* (fortune-teller) to Napoleon.

Two blocks west of the theater, the 17th-century **Eglise St-Sulpice** (M. St-Sulpice) is an under-admired marvel. Construction of the elegant façade, designed by Servadoni, began in 1733. Its Greco-Roman simplicity of line was found unbecoming in a Jesuit church, and the current building's obvious asymmetry is a consequence of failed attempts to make the structure more appropriate to the priests: in 1749, the architect Maclaurin was asked to redesign the towere. In 1777 a third architect, Chalgrin, was asked to revamp them; he replaced the north tower but never completed its southern counterpart. It remains unfinished. The church contains Delacroix frescoes in the first chapel on the right, a stunning *Virgin and Child* by Jean-Baptiste Pigalle in one of the rear chapels, and an enormous Chalgrin organ, among the world's largest and most famous, with 6588 pipes. In the transept of the church an inlaid copper band runs along the floor from north to south, crossing from a plaque in the south arm to an obelisk in the north arm. A ray of sunshine passes through a hole in the upper window of the south transept during the winter solstice, striking marked points on the obelisk at exactly mid-day. A beam of sunlight falls on the copper plaque during the summer solstice and behind the communion table during the spring and autumn equinox. In this way, the church tells its priest when to celebrate Easter mass. (Open daily 7:30am-7:30pm.) From St-Sulpice, move north to the boulevard St-Germain. This area, jam-packed with cafés, restaurants, cinemas, and expensive boutiques, is always crowded, noisy, and exciting.

Begin exploring this area with a stroll through the **Cour du Commerce St-André,** a historic pedestrian passageway one street west of rue de l'Ancienne Comédie off bd. St-Germain (look for the name of the *cour* arching over the entryway). As you pass under the arch, to your immediate right is a turn-of-the-century bistro, the **Relais Odéon.** Its stylishly painted exterior, decked with floral mosaics and an old-fashioned hanging sign, is a well-maintained period piece from the Belle Epoque. The proprietor of the Odéon swears that, during the Revolution, Jacobins placed a guillotine on the spot now occupied by his restaurant's terrace and killed some sheep there to test the sharpness of its blade. Others claim that the first guillotine was designed at nearby atelier no. 9 by Doctor Guillotin, intended as a more humane way of killing sheep. Dismayed at the subsequent misuse of his contraption, Dr. Guillotin is said to have ask the Assemblée to change its name. The Assemblée refused, in deference to the popular songs of the day; "guillotine" rhymed too well with "machine" to merit the change. In fact, the guillotine was developed as a less painful alternative to death-by-hanging; already present in other countries, it became associated with Dr. Guillotin only because he advocated its use in the interests of more humane capital deaths.

Further down this passageway, on the top floor of the building on your left, was the site of the Revolutionary-era clandestine press that published Marat's *L'Ami du Peuple*. Marat was assassinated in the bathtub of his home,which once stood where the courtyard meets the rue de l'Ancienne Comédie. The poet Baudelaire was born on another of the small streets off the place St. André-des-Arts, at 15, rue Hautefeuille.

Like bd. Montparnasse, bd. St-Germain has long been a gathering place for literary and artistic notables. **Les Deux Magots,** 6, pl. St-Germain des Prés, is named after a store that sold Chinese silk and imports at this spot in the 1800s. It was converted into a café in 1875 and by 1885 had become a favorite hangout of Verlaine, Rimbaud, and Mallarmé. Forty years later, it attracted Surrealists Breton, Desnos, and Artaud. Picasso and St-Exupéry (who wrote *The Little Prince*) were also regular patrons. Also worth a visit is **Café de Flore,** 172, bd. St-Germain. Established in 1890, this café was made famous in the 1940s and 50s by Sartre, Camus, and Jacques Prévert (see Cafés). Across from these cafés sits the **Brasserie Lipp,** a former haunt of the famous and well-dressed in search of a beer and *choucroute garnie*.

The nearby **Eglise St-Germain-des-Prés** (M. St-Germain-des-Prés) presides benevolently over all this name-dropping. King Childebert I commissioned the first church on this site to hold relics he had looted from the Holy Land. Completed in 558, it was consecrated by Saint Germain, Bishop of Paris, on the very day of King Childebert's death, and none too soon; the king was to be buried inside the church's walls. Sacked by the Normans and rebuilt three times, St-Germain-des-Prés remained for years a heavily fortified abbey outside of Paris. Parts of the modern-day church date from 1163, making it officially the oldest standing church in what is now Paris. The current building is a portmanteau of architectural styles, owing to renovations that spanned centuries. The resulting structure combines Romanesque, Gothic, and Baroque features.

Like most churches, St-Germain-des-Prés assumed a new function during the Revolution, due to the Jacobins' anticlericism. Made a state prison in 1674, it was seized by the people on June 30, 1789, providing them with a dress rehearsal for the storming of the Bastille. The church was then desanctified and did a brief stint as a saltpeter mill, which helped to further erode the already deteriorating structure. In 1794, 15 tons of gunpowder that had been stored in the abbey exploded; the ensuing fire devastated the church's collection of artwork and treasures, including much of its renowned monastic library. Baron Haussmann destroyed the the last remains of the deteriorating abbey walls and gates when he extended the rue de Rennes to the front of the church and created the **place St-Germain-des-Prés.** Yet the church has maintained an air of sanctity throughout and wears its battle scars well. The magnificent interior, painted in shades of terra cotta and deep green with gold, was restored in the 19th century. Astute wanderers can pick out a millenium's worth of clashing architectural detail: the Romanesque capitals atop some of the pillars, the hidden stonework in the side chapels, the medieval shrines, the 17th-century vaulting. In the second chapel on the right inside the church you'll find a stone marking the interred heart of Descartes and an altar dedicated to the victims of the September 1793 massacre, in which *sans-culottes* slaughtered 186 Parisians in the courtyard. Pick up one of the free maps of the church, with information in English on St-Germain's history and its artifacts. (Information office open Mon. 2:30-6:45pm, Tues.-Sat. 10:30am-noon and 2:30-6:45pm.) Come here for one of their frequent concerts. As in most medieval churches, built to accommodate an age without microphones, the acoustics are wonderful. (Ticket prices range from 60F to 160F. Church open daily 9am-7:30pm.)

Moving north from bd. St-Germain toward the Seine, you'll come upon some of the most tangled streets in central Paris. Haussmann retired before he could figure out a way to extend the rue de Rennes across the Seine to meet up with the rue de Louvre. Subsequent urban designers puzzled over this impassable quarter, seeking a plan to improve local traffic circulation. Before they could destroy the old streets, a preservationist aesthetic kicked in and, as a result, the neighborhood has been left as a largely unreconstructed maze. Don't even try to figure it out; instead, lose yourself in this *quartier* and amble down the rue de Seine, rue Mazarine, rue Bonaparte, and rue Dauphine, past art galleries of every stripe, displaying everything from modern mixed-media works to classic oil paintings. Specialty stores carry eclectic decorative arts, elegant home furnishings, and collections of books of every ilk, from parchment manuscripts to sexploitation comic books.

To see what local art students are up to, walk around the **Ecole Nationale Supérieure des Beaux Arts (ENSBA),** 14, rue Bonaparte (tel. 47 03 50 00; M. St-Germain-des-Prés), at quai Malaquais. France's most acclaimed art school, the *école* was founded by Napoleon in 1811 and soon became *the* strong-hold of French academic painting and sculpture. The current building for ENSBA was finished in 1838 in a gracious style much like that of the nearby **Institut de France.**

Just one block to the east on the *quais,* the **Palais de l' Institut de France,** pl. de l'Institut (M. Pont-Neuf), broods over the Seine beneath its famous *coupole,* the black- and gold-topped dome. This one-time school (1688-1793) and prison (1793-1805) was designed by Le Vau to lodge the college established in Cardinal Mazarin's will. The glorious building has housed the Institut de France since 1806. Founded in 1795, the *institut* was intended to be a storehouse for the nation's knowledge and a meeting place for France's greatest scholars. During the Restoration, appointment to the *institut* was more dependent on one's political position than one's talent, but since 1830 the process has been slightly more meritocratic.

One of the *institut*'s branches is the prestigious **Académie Française,** which, since its founding by Richelieu in 1635, has assumed the task of compiling the official French dictionary and served as guardian of the French language. Having already registered its disapproval of *le weekend, le parking,* and other "Franglais" nonsense, the Academy recently triumphed with the passing of a constitutional amendment affirming French as the country's official language. It is so difficult to become elected to this arcane society, limited to 40 members, that Moliére, Balzac, and Proust never made it. In 1981 the first woman, Marguerite Yourcenar, gained membership.

Next door, the **Hôtel des Monnaies,** once the mint for all French coins, still proudly displays its austere 17th-century façade to the heart of the Left Bank. Today it mints only honorary medals. You can still tour its foundry and its significant coin collection by entering the **Musée de la Monnaie de Paris** (see Museums). The **Pont des Arts,** the footbridge across from the *institut,* is celebrated by poets and artists for its delicate ironwork, its beautiful views of the Seine, and its spiritual locus at the heart of France's most prestigious Academy of Arts and Letters. Built as a toll bridge in 1803, the *pont* was unique on two counts: it was the first bridge to be made of iron, and it was for pedestrians only. On the day it opened, 65,000 Parisians paid to walk across it; today, it is less crowded and free, though still lovely. Come here at dusk to watch the sun go down against the silhouette of Paris's most famous monuments.

■■■ SEVENTH ARRONDISSEMENT: THE FAUBOURG ST-GERMAIN

Since the eighteenth century, the 7ème has stood its ground as the city's most elegant residential neighborhood. Home to the French National Assembly, countless foreign embassies, the Invalides, the Musée d'Orsay and the Eiffel Tower, this section of the Left Bank is a medley of France's diplomatic, architectural, and military achievements.

On some streets in the 7ème you might be the only one without a uniform, a gun, or a cellular phone; many policemen and soldiers guard the area's consulates and ministries. Once owned by Talleyrand, the **Hôtel Matignon,** at 57, rue de Varenne, is the official residence of the French Prime Minister. It cannot be visited without a personal invitation from Edouard Balladur. The nearby **Hôtel Biron,** at no. 77, was built by Gabriel in 1728. Under the state's aegis, it became an artists' *pension* in 1904. The sculptor Auguste Rodin rented a studio on its ground floor in 1908. When the Ministry of Education and Fine Arts evicted all tenants in 1910, Rodin offered to donate all of his works to make the *hôtel* an art museum—on the condition that he be permitted to spend his last years there. The Hôtel Biron now houses the **Musée Rodin** (see Museums).

Walk up rue de Bellechasse toward the Seine to arrive at the elegant **Hôtel de Salm,** built in 1786 by the architect Rousseau for the Prince de Salm-Kyrbourg. The prince, who actually didn't have enough money to pay for it, later returned it to the architect; he continued to live there as a tenant until decapitated in 1794, six days after the fall of Robespierre. The state raffled the *hôtel* the following year to a wealthy hairdresser named Lieuthraud, a charlatan who became known as Count Beauregard. In 1797, when Lieuthraud was jailed as a forger, the mansion was purchased by the Swedish ambassador and his wife, *salonnière* Mme. de Staël. Benjamin Constant, political theorist and novelist, frequented her world-famous salon. Purchased by Napoleon in 1804, the *hôtel*'s current name bears the mark of its most recent owner. Now called the **Palais de la Légion d'Honneur,** it houses the **Musée National de la Légion d'Honneur.** Though the museum's display of medals and other military honoraria may not spark the interest of many tourists, the 5F admission fee allows a look at the 18th- and 19th-century interiors. (The *hôtel* was renovated in 1878 to repair the damage done by arsonist *communards* seven years previous.) Two rooms and the façades facing rue de Lille and the Seine are original (see Museums.) Across the street stands the **Musée d'Orsay,** known for its architectural elegance and large collection of Impressionist paintings. Its glass and steel roof recalls to the building's former function as a train station (see Museums.)

At 75, rue de Lille, Montesquieu, Marivaux and others frequented the literary salon of Mme. de Tencin. Famous for her adventurous parties during the Regency, she once hosted a *"soirée d'Adam"* for which guests arrived dressed only in fig leaves. Continue down rue de Lille and turn right on rue du Bac. In the 18th century, this street marked the boundary between town and country. Now it is lined with specialty stores. Buy dessert at **Christian Constant** (no. 26) or at the nearby **Le Nôtre** (no. 44), a ubiquitous but terrific *pâtisserie* chain.

The 17th-century **Eglise St-Thomas-d'Aquin** (tel. 42 22 59 74), off rue du Bac on rue de Gribeauval, was originally dedicated to St. Dominique, only to be reconsecrated as a Temple of Peace during the Revolution. Built in the form of a Greek cross, the former Jesuit church's dome and 18th-century paintings are worth a look. (Church open Mon.-Sat. 9am-noon and 3-7pm, Sun. 9:30am-6:30pm.)

Just off to the left from rue du Bac at 55-57, rue de Grenelle, the **Fontaine des Quatres Saisons** (Fountain of Four Seasons) features a personified, seated version of the city of Paris near reclining figures of the Seine and the Marne. Bouchardon built the fountain 1739-1745 to provide water to this part of Paris year-round. Nearby at 202, bd. St-Germain, the poet Guillaume Apollinaire lived and died.

Follow bd. Raspail, turn left on rue de Babylone, and continue to its corner with rue de Monsieur. There stands **la Pagode**, a Japanese pagoda built in 1895 for M. Morin of the Bon Marché fortune. A gift to Morin's wife, it endures as a testament to conjugal love and to the 19th-century orientalist craze in France. When Mme. Morin left her husband for his colleague's son, the building became the scene of Sino-Japanese soirées during the pre-WWI years, a period of tension between the two countries (only to deepen with Japan's conquest of Manchuria). The Chinese Embassy,

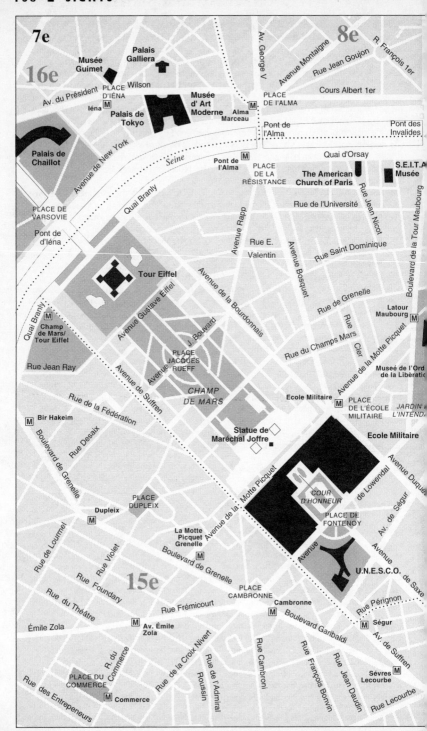

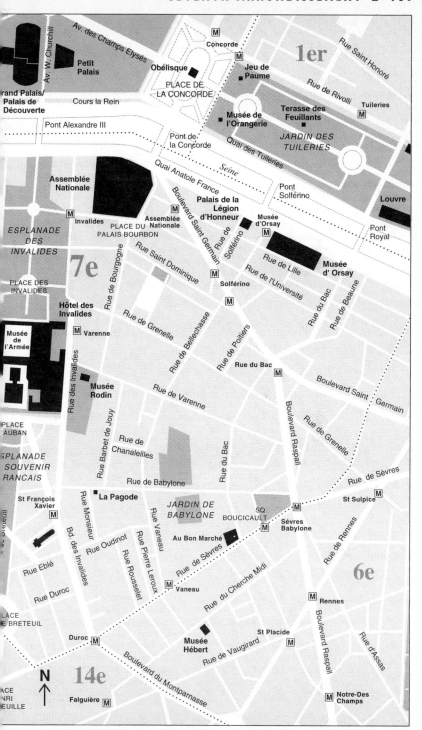

located nearby, thought of renting the elegant building but never did. In 1931, la Pagode opened its doors to the public, becoming a cinema and fashionable address where the likes of Gloria Swanson, silent screen star, were known to lift a glass. During the period of German occupation and accompanying film censorship, the theater closed. It reopened in 1945 in new resplendence. Today, preserved as a historic monument, it livens up the architectural tedium of ministries and *conseils,* and offers a range of excellent movies, old and new (see Entertainment—Cinema). Walk down rue Monsieur, turn left on rue Oudinot, and take rue Rousselet down to **rue de Sèvres.** Restaurants line the streets of this busy market street.

The **Palais Bourbon,** right across the Seine from the place de la Concorde, would probably not be recognized by its original occupants. Built in 1722 for the Duchess of Bourbon, daughter of Louis XIV and Mme. de Montespan, the palace was remodeled after 1750 to align with the place de la Concorde. Sold to the Prince of Condé in 1764, the building grew in size and ornateness under its new ownership. Napoleon erected the present Greek revival façade in 1807 to harmonize with that of the Madeleine (see Sights—8*ème*.) From 1940-44, the Germans occupied the palace. During the Liberation parts of it were damaged and many of the library's books were destroyed. Any tourist hoping for a closer look at the allegorical sculpture on the building's façade would need to scale the tall iron gates and sneak past the guards, as the **Assemblée Nationale** currently occupies the palace. Machine-gun-toting police stationed every few yards are ostensibly there to prevent a replay of a 1934 attempted coup, during which rioters stormed the building. French-speakers and Government majors might want to observe the Assembly in session. Foreigners should expect a one-hour security check before entering the chamber and will be required to present their passports. Appropriate dress is required. Foreign nationals interested in attending a session of the National Assembly must write for permission in advance to 33, quai d'Orsay 75007 Paris. (Sessions Oct.-Dec. and April-June, weekday afternoons.)

The security check does not apply to those who take guided tours of the assembly's chambers. Show up at 33, quai d'Orsay (tel. 40 63 63 08) on Saturday afternoon at 10am, 2pm, or 3pm for a free tour (in French, with pamphlet in English available). The tour includes a visit to the **Salon Delacroix** and to the library, both spectacularly painted by Eugène Delacroix. The library's holdings include the original transcripts of Jeanne d'Arc's trial. The tour continues to the assembly's chamber itself, called the **Salle de Séances.** The *Président du conseil* presides over the chamber from a throne-like chair decorated by Lemot and Michallon. Behind him, a framed tapestry of Raphael's *School of Athens* depicts the republic of philosopher-kings. Members of the political right and left sit to the right and left of the president's seat. Free tours are offered all year. The Kiosque de l'Assemblée Nationale, 4, rue Aristide-Briand (tel. 40 63 61 21) has information about the Assemblée Nationale, as well as the standard collection of souvenirs. (Open Mon.-Fri. 9:30am-7pm, Sat. 9:30am-5pm.)

The green, tree-lined **Esplanade des Invalides** runs from Pont Alexandre III, lined with gilded lampposts, to the gold-leaf dome of the **Hôtel des Invalides,** 2, av. de Tourville (M. Invalides). In 1670, Louis XIV decided to "construct a royal home, grand and spacious enough to receive all old or wounded officers and soldiers." Architect Libéral Bruand's building accepted its first wounded in 1674, and veterans still live in the Invalides today. Jules Hardouin-Mansart provided the final design for the **Eglise St-Louis,** the chapel within the Invalides complex. This church received Napoleon's body for funeral services in 1840, 19 years after the former emperor died in exile. His body was said to be perfectly preserved when exhumed from its original coffin before the service. Napoleon's ornate sarcophagus, now on display in the *hôtel,* wasn't completed for 20 more years. **Napoleon's tomb** (and the **Musée de l'Armée, Musée d'Histoire Contemporaine,** and **Musée de l'Ordre de Libération)** is housed within the Invalides museum complex (see Invalides Museums). Enter from either pl. des Invalides to the north or pl. Vauban and av. de Tourville to the south. Around the "back," to the left of the Tourville entrance, the **Jardin de** l'Intendant provides a shady, almost elegant place to rest on a bench. The ditch, lined with foreign cannons captured in various wars, used to be a moat, and still makes it impossible to leave by any but the official entrance.

SEITA (Société pour l'Exploitation Industrielle des Tabacs et Allumettes), at the intersection of quai d'Orsay with rue Surcouf, is France's tobacco lobby. The **Musée-Galerie de la SEITA** next door sponsors exhibits not necessarily related to cigarettes. The giftshop, however, sells posters, etc. of famous smokers in action.

The **American Church in Paris,** 65, quai d'Orsay (tel. 47 05 07 99), helps out English speakers in search of accommodations, jobs, counseling, cultural programs, et al. The appropriately named av. Bosquet (Thicket Avenue) borders an area to the east filled with restaurants, hotels, and food stores. The market at rue Cler can satisfy any and all culinary needs. Visit the **Musée des Egouts de Paris (Sewer Museum),** near pl. de la Résistance, to retrace the steps of the French Resistance or, alternately, of the Phantom of the Opera.

Of the **Tour Eiffel** (Eiffel Tower), Gustav Eiffel wrote in 1889: "France is the only country in the world with a 300m flagpole" (tel. 44 11 23 45; M. Bir-Hakeim). The tower's design, actually conceived by engineers Emile Nouguier and Maurice Koechlin (who worked for Eiffel's bridge company), was the winning entry in an 1885 contest. Judges chose the "Eiffel" design to be the centerpiece of the 1889 World's Fair, held to coincide with the French Revolution's centennial jubilee. Yet before construction had even begun, shockwaves of dismay reverberated through the city. In February of 1887, one month after builders broke ground on the Champ de Mars, French writers and artists published a scathing letter of protest in *Le Temps.* Writers Guy de Maupassant, Dumas *fils,* Charles Garnier (architect of the Opéra), and the composer Gounod joined countless others in condemning the construction "in the heart of our capital, of the useless and monstrous Eiffel Tower." After the building's completion, Maupassant ate lunch every day in the Eiffel Tower's ground-floor restaurant—the only place in Paris, he claimed, from which he couldn't see the Eiffel Tower. Other Parisians dismissed the tower as "American." Designed as the tallest structure in the world, Eiffel's tower was conceived as a monument to engineering and industry, to rival and surpass the Egyptian pyramids in size and notoriety.

Inaugurated March 31, 1889, it opened for visitors on May 15, 1889 to popular, if not critical, acclaim; nearly two million people ascended the tower during the fair. Numbers dwindled by comparison during the following decades. As time wore on and the twenty-year property lease approached expiration, Eiffel faced the imminent destruction of his masterpiece. The so-called Tower of Babel survived because of its importance as a communications tower, a function Eiffel had helped cultivate in the 1890s. The radio-telegraphic center on the top of the tower worked during World War I to intercept enemy messages. A handful of those decoded by the French resulted in the arrest and execution of Mata Hari.

With the 1937 World Exposition, the Eiffel Tower again became a showpiece, now the uncontested symbol of Paris. Eiffel himself walked humbly before it, remarking: "I ought to be jealous of that tower. She is more famous than I am." Renovations for the French Bicentennial have given it new sparkle. Since then, Parisians and tourists alike have reclaimed the monument. Sadly, the tower, now on everything from postcards to neckties and umbrellas, is sometimes shunned by tourists as either too "touristy" or too tacky. Don't miss out on one of the most satisfying experiences in Paris.

All those kitschy replicas don't even get the Tower's color right. It is a soft brown, not the metallic steel gray that most visitors anticipate. And despite the 18,000 pieces of iron, 2,500,000 rivets, and 9,100,000 kilograms of sheer weight that compose it, the girders appear light and spidery. This is especially true at night, when artfully placed spotlights make the tower a lacy hologram.

While at the Eiffel Tower, buy exorbitantly priced souvenirs in the stores, eat good food in pricey restaurants, or send mail with the "only-available-here" Eiffel Tower postmark. The cheapest way to ascend the tower is by walking up the first two floors (12F). The Cinemax, a fun and relaxing stop midway through the climb on the first floor, shows documentaries about the tower. Also take some time to read one of the posters chronicling the its history. If nothing else, they're an excuse to catch your breath and rest your legs. Visitors should, must, take the elevator to the third story. Tickets can be bought from the *caisse* or from the coin-operated dispenser. Enjoy the unparalleled view of the city from the top floor and consult posted, captioned aerial photographs to locate landmarks. Accompanying blurbs, in English, fill in the history. (Tower open daily July-Aug. 9am-midnight, including holidays. Sept.-June 9:30am-11pm. Elevator tariff to 1st floor 20F, 2nd floor 36F, 3rd floor 52F. Under 12 and over 60: 1st floor 10F, 2nd floor 18F, 3rd floor 25F. Under 4 free. Wheelchair-accessible.)

Across the river (and the Pont d'Iléna) from the Eiffel Tower is the **Trocadéro** and the **Palais de Chaillot.** Built for the 1937 World's Fair, the Palais de Chaillot's elegant, expansive terrace and gardens provide the city's best views of the tower. Save your pictures for here (see Sights—16$^{\grave{e}me}$.)

Though close to the 7$^{\grave{e}me}$'s military monuments and museums, the **Champ de Mars** (the Field of Mars) celebrates the god of war in name alone. This flower-embroidered carpet stretching from the Ecole Militaire to the Eiffel Tower is above all a well-equipped playground, with jungle gyms, monkey bars and wood trains along its southwestern edge. The park's name comes from its previous function as a drill ground for the adjacent Ecole Militaire. In 1780 Charles Montgolfier launched the first hydrogen balloon (with no basket attached) from here. During the Revolution the park witnessed an infamous civilian massacre and numerous political demonstrations. Here, at the 1793 Festival of the Supreme Being, Robespierre proclaimed the new Revolutionary religion. During the 19th and 20th centuries it served as fairgrounds for international expositions in 1889, 1900, and 1937. After the 1900 Exhibition, the municipal council considered parceling off the Champ de Mars for development. They concluded, as you will, that Paris needed all the open space it had.

Louis XV created the **Ecole Militaire** at the urging of his mistress, Mme. de Pompadour, who hoped to make educated officers of "poor gentlemen." Jacques-Ange Gabriel's building first accepted students in 1773, when lottery profits and a tax on playing cards financed the school's completion. In 1784, the 15-year-old Napoléon Buonaparte arrived from Corsica to enroll. A few weeks later he presented administrators with a comprehensive plan for the school's reorganization.

As the Ecole Militaire's architectural if not spiritual antithesis, **UNESCO (United Nations Educational, Scientific, and Cultural Organization)** (tel. 45 68 03 59; M. Ségur) occupies the Y-shaped building across the way at 7, pl. de Fontenoy. Established to foster science and culture throughout the world, the agency developed a reputation for waste, cronyism, and Marxist propaganda, prompting the U.S., the U.K., and Singapore to withdraw in 1984. In so doing, they withdrew 30% of the agency's budget. With Moscow no longer able to bankroll the group, UNESCO's director Federico Mayor Zaragoza hopes the United States will return to its fold. Roundly criticized by world diplomats, UNESCO seems to spend inordinate sums on its image. Decorating the building and its garden are ceramics by Miró and Artigas, an unnamed painting by Picasso, a Japanese garden, and an angel from the façade of a Nagasaki church destroyed by the A-bomb. UNESCO frequently mounts temporary exhibitions of photography as well as exhibits on international art, science, and culture—anything from Japanese wood-carving to Ugandan irrigation projects. The library is only open to approved specialists. The bookstore is open Mon.-Fri. 9am-1pm and 2-6pm. (Opening times vary for temporary exhibits. Free.)

■■■ EIGHTH ARRONDISSEMENT: THE CHAMPS-ELYSÉES

To the Arc de Triomphe de l'Etoile:
raise yourself all the way to the heavens, portal of victory
That the giant of our glory
Might pass without bending down.

—Victor Hugo

Almost as elegant as its neighbor to the southwest, the 16ème, the eighth is home to Haussmann's wide sidewalks and tree-lined *grands boulevards,* including the famous **avenue des Champs-Elysées.** Well-known salons and boutiques of *haute couture* pepper fashionable streets like rue du Faubourg St-Honoré. Embassies crowd around the Palais de l'Elysée, the state residence of the French president. Already attractive to the bourgeoisie of the early 19th century, the neighborhood took off with the construction of boulevards Haussmann, Malesherbes, Victor Hugo, Foch, Kléber, and the others that shoot out from the Arc de Triomphe in a star-like formation known as l'Etoile (the star). The whole area bustles, and it should; within a very few blocks, the 8ème provides the resources necessary to dine exquisitely, dress impeccably, and accessorize magnificently. Moreover, you can indulge your esoteric musical tastes, appease your sweet tooth, and buy the ticket for your winter flight to Rio with the greatest amount of ease (and money). Most importantly, the wide open spaces of the 8ème provide you with the chance to show it all off. But be forewarned. In the 8ème, you may feel underdressed and overwhelmed. This is the Paris you've seen in *Vogue* and in *Cosmo,* where the scarf is always Hermès, the watch is pure Cartier, and everyone has had a busy day at the boutique.

The **Arc de Triomphe** (tel. 43 80 31 31; M. Charles-de-Gaulle-Etoile), looming gloriously above the Champs-Elysées at place Charles de Gaulle, commemorates France's military victories as well as its long obsession with military history. The world's largest triumphal arch and an internationally recognized symbol of France, this behemoth was commissioned by Napoleon in 1806. When construction began, the Etoile marked the western entrance to the city through the *fermiers généraux* wall. Napoleon was exiled before the monument was completed, but Louis XVIII ordered resumption of work in 1823 and dedicated the arch to the war in Spain and to its commander, the Duc d'Angoulême. The Arc, designed by Chalgrin, was finally consecrated in 1836, 21 years after the defeat of the great army of *"Le Petit Corporal."* There was no consensus on what symbolic figures could cap the monument, and it has retained its simple unfinished form. The names of Napoleon's generals and battles are engraved inside; those generals underlined died in battle. The most famous of the Arc's allegorical sculpture groups depicting the military history of France is François Rude's *Departure of the Volunteers of 1792,* commonly known as *La Marseillaise,* to the right facing the arch from the Champs-Elysées.

Primarily, the Arc is a military symbol. As such, the horseshoe-shaped colossus has proved a magnet to various triumphal armies. The victorious Prussians marched through in 1871, inspiring the mortified Parisians to purify the ground with fire. On July 14, 1919, however, the Arc provided the backdrop for an Allied celebration parade headed by Maréchal Foch, whose memory is now honored by the boulevard that bears his name, stretching out from the west side of the Arc into the 16ème. In 1940, Parisians were brought to tears as the Nazis goose-stepped through the Arc and down the Champs-Elysées. After four years of Nazi occupation, France was liberated by British, American, and French troops who marched through the Arc on August 26, 1944 to the roaring cheers of thousands of grateful Parisians. The Tomb of the Unknown Soldier has rested under the Arc since November 11, 1920; the eternal flame is rekindled every evening at 6:30pm, when veterans and small children lay wreaths decorated with blue, white, and red. De Gaulle's famous cry for *Résistance* is inscribed on a brass plaque in the pavement under the Arc.

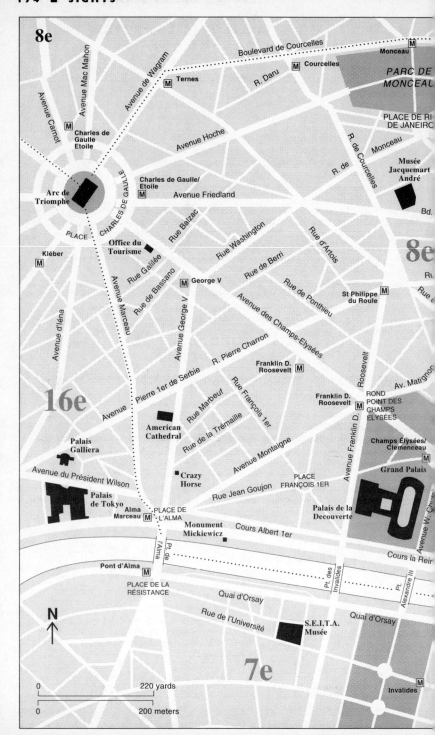

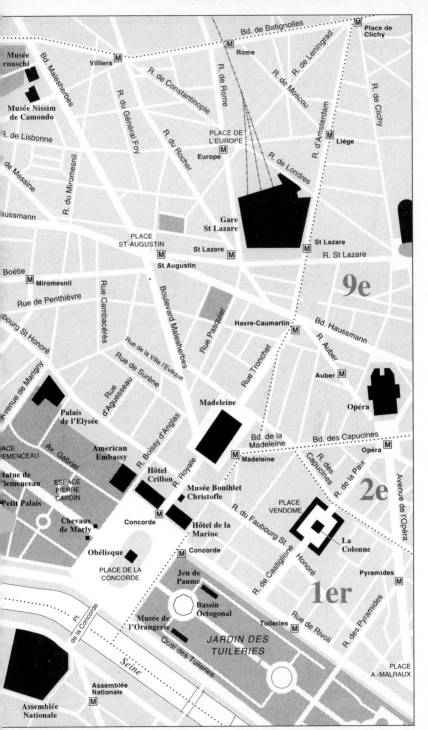

The Arc sits in the center of the **Etoile,** which in 1907 became the world's first traffic circle. Rather than risk an early death by crossing the traffic to reach the Arc, use the underpasses on the even-numbered sides of both the Champs-Elysées and av. de la Grande-Armée. Inside the Arc, climb 205 steps up a winding staircase to the *entresol* and then dig deep for the 29 more that take you to the *musée* or tackle the lines at the elevator for a muscle-pull-free ride. The museum recounts the Arc's architectural and ceremonial history in French, complete with drawings and appropriately tacky souvenirs. The real spectacle lies just 46 steps higher—the *terrasse* at the top of the Arc provides a terrific view of the gorgeous avenue Foch (see 16*ème*) and the sprawling city. (Observation deck open daily 9am-6pm. Admission 31F, students 18-25 and ages 60 and older 20F, ages 7-17 6F, under 7 free. Lockers underneath the Arc for 5F a day. Phones available. Expect lines even on weekdays and buy your ticket before going up to the ground level.)

The **avenue des Champs-Elysées** is the most famous of the twelve symmetrical avenues radiating from the huge rotary of place Charles de Gaulle; it may even be the most famous avenue in the world. In a popular children's song, French youth are taught that you can do all you want on the Champs-Elysées. While this may not be entirely true, no one can deny that this 10-lane wonder, flanked by exquisite cafés and luxury shops and crowned by the world's most famous arch, deserves its reputation. Le Nôtre planted trees here in 1667 to extend the Tuileries vista, completing the work begun under Marie d'Medicis in 1616. In 1709, the area was renamed the "Elysian Fields" because of the shade provided by the trees. During the 19th century, the Champs (as many Parisians call it) developed into a fashionable residential district. Mansions sprang up along its banks, then apartments and smart boutiques, making this strip of pavement the place to see and be seen in Paris. Balls, café-concerts, restaurants, and even circuses drew enormous crowds; the *bal Mabille* opened in 1840 at no. 51, and, at no. 25, in a somewhat more subdued setting, the charming hostess and spy Marquise de Païva entertained her famous guests.

Today, you can escape the crowds and watch the modern-day circus of tourists walk by while seated at **Fouquet's,** an outrageously expensive and famous café/restaurant near the Arc de Triomphe where French film stars hang out. Paris's answer to Hollywood's Sunset Strip, this stretch of the Champs-Elysées bears golden plaques with the names of favorite French recipients of the coveted César award (the French equivalent to the Oscar). Among those with names emblazoned here are Isabelle Adjani, Catherine Deneuve, and Louis Malle, the director of *My Dinner with André* and *Au Revoir Les Enfants,* and the husband of Candice Bergen. Street performers move in at night all along the Champs-Elysées, moving to an industrial beat. During the day, anyone can enjoy the potpourri of restaurants and overpriced stores, planted next to airlines and commercial offices.

Six big avenues radiate from the Rond Point des Champs-Elysées. Av. Montaigne runs southwest from the point and shelters the houses of *haute couture* of Christian Dior, Chanel (no. 42), Valentino (no. 17 and 19). St-Laurent, Nina Ricci, and Pierre Cardin (pl. François 1*er*) hold sway nearby. You may not be able to afford even the smallest bottle of Chanel, but it's fun to look. Nearby, 15, av. Montaigne is home of the **Théâtre des Champs-Elysées,** built by the Perret brothers in 1912. The three large *salles* still host performances, but the theater is best known for staging the first performance of Stravinsky's *Le Sacre du Printemps*. Around the corner from the *théâtre*, a long-time cabaret, the **Crazy Horse Saloon,** still entertains a mostly Parisian clientele.

Next to Cartier's (no. 51), at 49, rue Pierre Charron, stands Pershing Hall, a 113-year-old, five-story piece of America. Given to the U.S. federal government, the building has allegedly been used as a brothel, a brawling bar, a gambling house, and a black- market money exchange. Refurbished, it now provides office space for respectable businesses like Council Travel and CIEE.

At the foot of the Champs-Elysées, the **Grand Palais** and the **Petit Palais** face one another on av. Winston Churchill. Built for the 1900 World's Fair, both *palais* are prime examples of Art Nouveau architecture; the glass over steel and stone composition of the Grand Palais makes its top look like a giant greenhouse. The Petit and Grand Palais house exhibitions on architecture, painting, sculpture, and French history; the Grand Palais also houses the Palais de la Découverte (see Museums). Built at the same time as the palaces, the first stone of Pont Alexandre III was placed by the tsar's son, Nicholas II. It made a stir as the first bridge to cross the Seine in a single span. Today this is considered the most beautiful bridge across the Seine, providing a noble axis with the Invalides (see Sights—7ème). The statues on pilasters facing the Right Bank represent Medieval France and Modern France; facing the Left Bank, they show Renaissance France and France of the Belle Epoque.

The guards pacing around the house at the corner of avenue de Marigny and rue du Faubourg St-Honoré are protecting the **Palais de l'Elysée.** The palace was built in 1718 but was embellished to its present glory as the residence of the Marquis de Marigny, brother of Madame de Pompadour. During the Restoration, July Monarchy, and Second Empire, the Elysée was used to house royal guests. Since 1870, it has served as state residence of the French president. Socialist or not, President Mitterrand lives in style. Or ought to—in recent years Mitterand has been criticized by the French for living in his own residence instead of the grandiose state palace. Although entrance requires a personal invitation, the persistent visitor can catch a glimpse of the luscious gardens (M. Champs-Elysées-Clemenceau). The Union Jack flying overhead at no. 35, rue du Faubourg-St-Honoré marks the British embassy. At 2 av. Gabriel, an equally large building flies the Stars and Stripes.

The **place de la Concorde** (M. Concorde), Paris's largest and most infamous public square, forms the eastern terminus of the Champs-Elysées. Like many sights in Paris, this immense *place* was built from pride—constructed between 1757 and 1777 to provide a home for a monument to Louis XV. Fittingly, as punishment for this royal hubris, the vast area soon became the place de la Revolution, the site of the guillotine which severed 1,343 necks. On Sunday, January 21, 1793, Louis XVI was beheaded by guillotine on a site near where the Brest statue now stands. In 1993, hundreds of French (and the American ambassador) honored this event with flowers placed on the very spot. The celebrated heads of Louis XVI, Marie-Antoinette, Charlotte Corday (Marat's assassin), Lavoisier, Robespierre, and others rolled into baskets here and were held up to the cheering crowds who packed the pavement. After the Reign of Terror, the square was optimistically renamed place de la Concorde.

At the center of the place de la Concorde, the **Obélisque de Louxor** was one of those king-pleasing gifts offered by Mehemet Ali, Viceroy of Egypt, to Charles X in 1829. Getting the obelisk from Egypt to the center of Paris was no simple task; a canal to the Nile had to be dug, the monolith had to be transported by sea, and a special boat built to transport it up the Seine. Finally erected in 1836, Paris's oldest monument dates back to the 13th century BC and recalls the deeds of Ramses II. On July 14th, a marvelous fireworks display lights up the sky over the place de la Concorde. Every night, the obelisk, fountains, and turn-of-the-century cast-iron lamps are illuminated, creating a romantic glow from the *place's* otherwise dark and dismal past. Don't be surprised if you see a commercial being shot on location here—and why not? What better way to create demand for your favorite product?

Flanking the Champs-Elysées at the place de la Concorde stand the **Cheveaux de Marly** (Africans Mastering the Numidian Horses), 18th century creations of Guillaume Coustou who originally designed them for Marly, Louis XIV's château near Versailles. Although the originals are now in the Louvre to protect them from the devastating effects of city pollution, perfect replicas still boldly hold their places. Eight large statues representing the major French cities also grace the *place*; Juliette Drouet allegedly posed for the town of Strasbourg.

Directly north of the *place,* like two sentries guarding the gate to the Madeleine, stand the **Hôtel Crillon** (on your left) and the **Hôtel de la Marine** (on your right). Architect Jacques-Ange Gabriel built the impressive colonnaded façades between 1757 and 1770. Chateaubriand lived in the Hôtel Crillon between 1805 and 1807. On February 16, 1778, the Franco-American treaties were signed here, making

France the first European nation to recognize the independence of the U.S. Today it is one of the most expensive and elegant hotels in Paris. If you're dressed for the occasion, step inside and have an espresso in the plush salon to the accompaniment of soft chamber music. Coffee will run you 40F, but you'll be able to experience Parisian life in a different form. The businesses along rue Royale boast their own proud history. Christofle has been producing works in gold and crystal since 1830. (Call 49 33 43 00 to make an appointment to see their museum, or save yourself the hassle and just gawk at the store.) World-renowned Maxim's restaurant, 3, rue Royale, won't even allow you a peep into what was once Richelieu's home.

The **Madeleine,** formally called Eglise Ste-Marie-Madeleine (Mary Magdalene), is the commanding building ahead at the end of rue Royale. Screened for the present behind a construction barrier tastefully painted to resemble the façade, the church is nevertheless impressive.It was begun in 1764 at the command of Louis XV and modeled after a Greek temple. Construction was halted during the Revolution, when the Cult of Reason proposed making the generically monumental building into a bank, a theater, or a courthouse. Completed in 1842, the structure stands alone in the medley of Parisian churches, distinguished by its four ceiling domes, which light the interior in lieu of windows, 52 exterior Corinthian columns, and the lack of even one cross. An immense sculpture of the ascension of Mary Magdalene into Heaven adorns the altar (open Mon.-Sat. 7:30am-7pm, Sun. 7:30am-1:30pm and 3:30-7pm; occasional organ and chamber concerts, look for posters.) Marcel Proust spent most of his childhood at 9, bd. Malesherbes, which runs northwest from the place de la Madeleine.

At the end of the Madeleine's rue Royale, the high-fashion, and high-priced **rue du Faubourg St-Honoré** stretches out like a jeweled Cartier necklace. You could spend hours window-shopping at the lavish, colorfully outrageous, and oh-so French decorated windows of Hermès (no. 24), Yves St-Laurent, Guy Laroche, and others. You'll find no number 13, rue du Faubourg St-Honoré; the superstitious Empress Josephine banned the number during the reign of Napoleon.

Square Louis XVI, on rue Pasquier below bd. Haussmann, include the improbably large **Chapelle Expiatoire** and a park whose many benches make it a popular spot for lunch. The intriguing Chapelle holds monuments of Marie-Antoinette and Louis XVI. A cemetery, affiliated with the Madeleine, was opened on the site in 1722; during the Revolution victims of the guillotine, Louis and Marie among them, were dumped here. Although Louis XVIII had his brother's and sister-in-law's remains removed to St-Denis in 1815, Charlotte Corday (Marat's assassin) and Philippe-Egalité (Louis XVI's cousin, who voted for the king's death, only to be beheaded himself) are buried on either side of the staircase. Statues of the expiatory ex-king and queen, displaced crowns at their feet, stand inside the Chapelle. Their last letters are engraved in French on the statue bases. (Open April-Sept. 10am-6pm; Nov.-Jan. 10am-4pm; Oct. and Feb.-March 10am-5pm.)

A few blocks north squats the **Gare St-Lazare,** whose platforms and iron-vaulted canopy are not to be missed by train riders and fans of Monet and Emile Zola. To the north of the train station is the place de Dublin, the setting for Caillebotte's famous painting, *A Rainy Day in Paris,* which hangs in the Art Institute of Chicago.

The **Parc Monceau,** a bizarre preserve guarded by gold-tipped, wrought iron gates, borders the elegant bd. de Courcelles. Whereas the Jardin du Luxembourg emphasizes show over relaxation, the Parc Monceau serves as a pastoral setting for kids to play and parents to unwind in the shade—all in a series of false ruins and strange grottoes built in the best of the Romantic tradition. The painter Carmontelle designed the park for the duc d'Orléans; it was brought to its present form in 1862 by Haussmann. The Rotonde de Monceau is a remnant of the Farmers-General wall of the 1780s. Designed to enforce customs duties rather than to keep out invaders, the wall and its fortifications reflected their creator's tastes in ornament more than the latest advances in military engineering. An array of architectural follies—a pyramid, covered bridge, pagoda, Dutch windmills, and picturesque Roman ruins— make this one of Paris's most pleasant spots for a *déjeuner sur* bench. Here, as elsewhere in Paris parks, frolicking on the grass is forbidden. Unlike in most Parisian parks, however, this rule is not always strictly enforced. (Open 7am-10pm; Nov.-March 7am-8pm. Gates close 15min. earlier; M. Marceau.) For more release from Paris's architectural uniformity, skip down the rue Rembrandt to the place du Pérou, where a Chinese pagoda holds the Galerie C.T. Loo.

In the days of pre-revolutionary Russia, many Russian aristocrats owned vacation houses in France. Paris still retains a sizable Russian community. The onion-domed **Eglise Russe,** also known as **Cathédrale Alexandre-Nevski,** 12, rue Daru (tel. 42 01 10 23; M. Termes), built in 1860, is an Eastern Orthodox Church. The gold domes, spectacular from the outside, are equally beautiful on the inside; they were intricately painted by artists from St. Petersburg. (Services held Mon.-Sat. at 7am and 6pm, Sun. at 10am.)

■■■ NINTH ARRONDISSEMENT: OPÉRA

The ninth *arrondissement* goes by the name *"Opéra;"* the Opéra Garnier and the boulevards nearby form this area's core. The Opéra lies on the southernmost border of the 9ème, and this part of the *arrondissement* is definitely the most prosperous and the most visited by tourists. Along the boulevards des Capucines, des Italiens, and Montmartre, many pleasant restaurants serve mouth-watering delicacies and cater to the post-theater and post-cinema crowd. This area also contains quite a few major movie houses showing big American and European box office hits. Near the Opéra, many large banks and chic boutiques greet their affluent clientele. Perhaps the busiest site of the 9ème, however, is the American Express office, where hordes of tourists go each day to change their Traveler's Cheques commission-free.

Most tourists, willy-nilly, begin their tour with the Opéra Garnier. Emerging from the underground den of the Opéra *métro* station, feast your eyes on Charles Garnier's grandiose **Opéra** (tel. 40 17 33 33; 40 17 35 35 for recorded program and schedule information), built under Napoleon III in the showy eclecticism of the Second Empire. This is Haussmann's most extravagant creation: an outpouring of opulence and allegory, not actually opened until 1875, five years after the Empire's collapse. Towering high above the *grands boulevards* of the southern 9ème, the Opéra epitomizes both the Second Empire's obsession with canonized ostentation and its rootlessness; a mix of styles and odd details tie it to no formal tradition. Queried by the Empress Eugénie as to whether his building was in the style of Louis XIV, Louis XV, or Louis XVI, Garnier responded that his creation belonged to Napoleon III. The interior of the Opéra demonstrates the fabric of 19th-century bourgeois social life, with its grand staircase, enormous golden foyer, vestibule, and five-tiered auditorium—all designed so that the audience could watch each other as much as the action on stage.

Garnier's elaborate design beat out hundreds of competing plans in an 1861 competition, outshining even the entry of the "Pope of Architects," Viollet-le-Duc. At that time, Garnier was a virtual unknown; the Opéra made him famous. The magnificent and eclectic interior is adorned by Gobelin tapestries, gilded mosaics, a 1964 Chagall ceiling (with a whimsical, Chagallian view of Paris), and the six-ton chandelier, which fell on the audience in 1896. Since 1989, when the new Opéra de la Bastille was inaugurated, most operas occur at the newer hall and Garnier's opera is used mainly for ballets. Ballet these days tends to perform its own elegy, staging retrospectives on the work of 20th-century greats; summer 1993 featured the work of Balanchine and Jerome Robbins. In 1992, Rudolf Nureyev made his last public appearance here shortly before his death after a long battle with AIDS. Schedules for performances are available in the entrance hall at the opera (see Entertainment).

Visits cost a hefty 33F, 20F for ages 10-16, and they include all public parts of the theater, except for the auditorium on performance days. The library and museum hold documents about costumes and objects tracing the history of opera and dance.

They focus particularly on the *ballet russe,* Diaghilev's innovative troupe that liberated classical dance from fluffy Romanticism, and launched 20th-century experimentation with such works as Stravinsky's *Firebird.* To arrange for private tours, call 44 61 21 66 or 69. (The Opéra is open for visits Mon.-Sat. 10am-4:30pm. Library open Mon.-Sat. 10am-5pm. Tickets for the ballet start at 30F; for the opera 50F; for the movies 60F. Rush tickets at reduced prices available at the box office 15 min. before each performance. To reserve seats, call 7-14 days ahead at 47 42 53 71 noon-6pm.)

Directly across from the Opéra is the **Café de la Paix,** a famous café from the 19th century, catering to the after-theater crowd and anyone else who doesn't mind paying 30F for coffee (see Cafés). Rue de la Paix, originally called rue Napoléon, is the most valuable square on French Monopoly boards, and the street lives up to its reputation for luxury; Cartier is at no. 11. Behind the Opéra, at 9, rue Scribe, tourists line up at the American Express office; it's probably not worth a special trip. All around this area, change bureaus advertise "No commission." Unless you're trying to change traveler's checks already in francs, they aren't lying, and rates aren't bad. Of more historic interest, a bit farther down the bd. des Capucines, are the giant red glowing letters of the **Olympia** music hall, where Edith Piaf achieved her fame, along with Jacques Brel, Yves Montand, and many others. Popular artists still perform here, in a strongly nostalgic vein; check posters for concerts. Returning up bd. des Capucines, you will arrive at bd. des Italiens and bd. Montmartre. These three *grands boulevards* represent one of the busiest areas in the *quartier,* crowded with popular restaurant/cafés (pricey, but perfect for people-watching), cinemas, and shops. Thomas Jefferson, in Paris in the 1780s as the American ambassador, lived near what is now the intersection of bd. Haussmann and rue du Helder. At no. 10, bd. Montmartre stands the carnivalesque **Musée Grevin** (see Museums).

West from this area along bd. Haussmann, toward M. Chaussée d'Antin and Trinité, you'll find the largest clothes shopping area in Paris. Two of Paris's largest department stores, **Au Printemps** and **Galeries Lafayette,** are located on the bd. Haussmann, and the streets around here are littered with stores selling clothes and shoes (see Shopping). At the northern end of the rue de la Chaussée (M. Trinité), is the **Eglise de la Sainte-Trinité.** This church, built at the end of the 19th century in Italian Renaissance style, has beautiful, painted vaults. It is surrounded by a pleasant park with a fountain and tree-shaded benches. The quixotic **Musée Gustave Moreau** is also located in this area, up the rue de La Rochefoucauld (see Museums) in the painter's house and studio, on a quiet residential street.

A short walk west from here, on the place Kossuth, at M. Notre-Dame-de-Lorette, is the church **Notre-Dame-de-Lorette,** built in 1836 to "the glory of the Virgin Mary." This Neoclassical church is full of statues of the saints and frescoes of scenes from the life of Mary. The street of the same name, constructed in 1840, quickly became the site of low-rent apartments of ill repute, stomping ground for Emile Zola's Nana (whose name has made its way into French *argot*—slang for girl, on par with "chick"). The term *lorette* came to refer to the quarter's crop of young *demoiselles* of easy virtue—post-adolescent adventuresses who came to the city from the provinces, their reputations forever tarnished. The mere mention of Notre-Dame-de-Lorette made men look away and good girls blush. As home to illicit bars, hotels, and restaurants for a crowd which rented by the hour, the rue des Martyrs enjoyed an equally bad reputation. Now filled with fruit stands, cheese shops, and multi-ethnic *épiceries*, the street no longer advertises delicacies of a different ilk.Continuing up rue Notre-Dame-de-Lorette, you reach the square Alex Biscarre near the **place St-Georges,** a small park with very young children and stroller-pushing parents, complete with a sandbox.

North of the rue de Châteaudun is a quiet, mostly residential area with a large student population and many small, well-priced, ethnic restaurants. The streets are narrow and quiet, full of small shops, *tabacs*, little hotels and modest private residences. The **Musée Renan-Scheffer,** or Musée de la Vie Romantique, is up one of these charming narrow streets, the rue Chaptal, off the rue Fontaine (see

Museums). The interior courtyard and garden of the hou
layout of most of the residences on these streets. Farthe
18ème, is the area called **Pigalle,** which Marcel Prous
another Paris in the heart of Paris itself." It is now a Xan
laid on a tight budget. Once the hub of the lesbian life an
Moulin Rouge of Toulouse-Lautrec's saucy drawings, n
prostitution and sexploitation flicks. Tourists, especially
around here alone at night and should be wary of pickp
which in the words of Dimitri Karamazov, spans from t
9ème spans from the most chic to the most sordid.

■■■ TENTH ARRONDISSEMENT

"I live between two train stations, at the edge of a canal, in one of the *arrondisse-ments* of Paris most rich in prisons, hideouts, pleasures, and hospitals. It is a rather vague *arrondissement*...much like one of those animal-molecules that can both expand and be cut in half. Half-worm, half-butterfly, one never knows which is the head and which the tail, and it is permanently caught at the mid-point of creation, straddling flight on the one side, abjectly crawling on the other." So wrote a resident of the tenth *arrondissement* in the 1920s, in terms still accurate today. Far from the normal tourist route, and not the safest or most well-kept of areas, the tenth offers a few gems of its own to the adventurous soul. In the southern portion, along the fau-bourg St-Denis, a curious and bustling market area offers ethnic foods and spices. The rue de Paradis in the western section is home to some of the world's finest china and crystal. Travelers looking to stretch their legs on a layover at the Gare de l'Est or Nord should head for the tree-lined Canal St-Martin and relax in the shade of trees, away from the noise and bustle of downtown Paris. Still waters and moss-cov-ered drawbridges make this a pleasant jog close to the *gares*.

The **Gare du Nord** (M. Gare du Nord) is generally encountered out of necessity rather than curiosity, but it merits a look. Jacques-Ignace Hittorf created the enor-mous station in 1863, in the midst of the great re-building of Paris. The grandiose Neoclassical exterior is topped by statues representing the great cities of France. Inside, the platforms are covered by a vast *parapluie* (umbrella), as Napoleon III called the glass and steel heaven which creates the giant vault of the train station. Across from the station a fringe of *brasseries* and cafés caters to the thousands of travelers who go through here every day.

Facing away from the Gare du Nord and walking one block down the rue de Com-piègne takes you to the rue de Belzunce and the **Eglise St-Vincent de Paul,** a Neo-classical structure built in the early 19th century by architects Hittorf and Jean-Baptiste Lepère. The entrance, in the shape of a temple, is topped with a dramatic frieze sculpted of the Glorification of St. Vincent de Paul by Leboeuf-Nanteuil. (Church open to the public Mon.-Sat. 7:30am-noon and 2-7pm; Sun. 7:30am-12:30pm and 3:30-7:30pm. A mass with Gregorian chant Sun. at 9:30am.)

The **Marché St-Quentin,** 85, bd. de Magenta, is a massive, elegant construction of iron and glass, built in 1866. Inside you can find an enormous variety of goods, from flowers to fresh produce and skinned rabbits for your delectable *lapin à la mou-tarde d'Irène* (open Tues.-Sat. 8am-1pm and 3:30-7:30pm; Sun. 8am-1pm). From the Marché St-Quentin, cross bd. de Magenta and follow rue du 8 Mai 1945 until it arrives at the **Gare de l'Est.** Directly across from the train station, the place du 11 Nov. 1918 opens into the bd. de Strasbourg, a hopping thoroughfare, crowded with cafés, shops, and fruit stands.

Close by, the small **rue de Paradis** offers a quaint little area bordered by shops dis-playing fine china and crystal. The beautiful (and expensive) objects mark the road to the **Baccarat Co.** headquarters and the **Cristalleries Baccarat,** housed in an 18th-century building at 30-32, rue de Paradis (see Museums). Farther up the street, at 18, rue de Paradis, the art gallery **Le Monde de l'Art** displays remarkable tile murals and

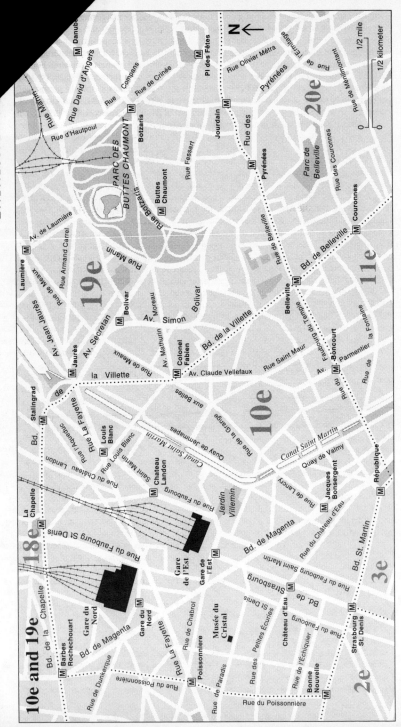

10e and 19e

N

1/2 mile

1/2 kilometer

19e

20e

Pl des Fêtes

Rue Olivier Métra

Rue de l'Ermitage

Rue de Ménilmontant

Rue de Crimée

Rue Compans

Rue David d'Angers

Rue Namm

Rue d'Hautpoul

PARC DES
BUTTES CHAUMONT

Botzaris

Buttes
Chaumont

Rue Fessart

Pyrénées

Jourdain

Rue des

Parc de
Belleville

Rue des Couronnes

Av. de Laumière

Av. de Laumière

Rue Armand Carrel

Laumière

Rue Manin

Bolivar

Av. Simon

Bolivar

Bd. de la Villette

Belleville

Bd. de Belleville

Couronnes

Rue de Belleville

11e

Av. Jean Jaurès

Rue de Meaux

Av. Secrétan

Jaurès

Av. Mathurin

Moreau

Colonel
Fabien

Rue de Meaux

Av. Claude Vellefaux

aux Belles

Rue Saint Maur

Rue de la Grange

Rue du Faubourg du Temple

Boncourt

Parmentier

Av. de

Rue de la Fontaine

la Villette

de

Bd. Stalingrad

Rue La Fayette

Louis
Blanc

Rue du Château Landon

Rue Louis Blanc

Saint Martin

Chateau
Landon

Canal Saint Martin

Quay de Jemmapes

Canal Saint Martin

Quay de Valmy

Jardin
Villemin

Rue de Lancry

Jacques
Bonsergent

10e

République

La
Chapelle

18e

Bd. de la Chapelle

Rue du Faubourg St Denis

Gare
de l'Est

Gare
de l'Est

Bd. de Magenta

Rue du Château d'Eau

Bd. St. Martin

3e

Barbès
Rochechouart

Gare
du Nord

Bd. de Magenta

Gare
du Nord

Rue de Chabrol

Poissonniere

Musée du
Cristal

Rue de Dunkerque

Rue La Fayette

Rue des Petites Écuries

St Denis

Château d'Eau

Bd. de
Strasbourg

Rue du Faubourg Saint Martin

Rue de Paradis

Rue de Poissonnière

Rue du Poissonnière

Rue de l'Échiquier

Rue du Faubourg

Bonne
Nouvelle

Strasbourg
St. Denis

2e

contemporary exhibits; it is housed in what was once the headquarters of the Boulanger china company (see Museums).

Going south on the **rue du Faubourg St-Denis,** you will walk through crowds of Parisians buying dinner ingredients in a very active market area. Individual stores, many owned by African, Arab, and Indian vendors, specialize in seafood, cheese, bread, or produce, rebuking supermarkets everywhere with the quality and selection they offer. **Passage Brady,** which intersects with bd. de Strasbourg and rue du Faubourg St-Martin, is lined with Indian and Pakistani stores that are stocked with exotic foodstuffs and prepared delicacies that the budget traveler can afford. At night it becomes a challenge to thread your way through the sea of tables, as Parisians and tourists enjoy a spicy meal outside. With intimate, fancy restaurants next to more rudimentary, honest establishments, the animated alley is a bold departure from the deserted commercial area of the lower bd. de Strasbourg.

At the end of rue Faubourg St-Denis, the majestic **Porte St-Denis** (M. Strasbourg/St-Denis) welcomes the visitor into the inner city. Built in 1672 to celebrate the victories of Louis XIV in the Rhineland and Flanders, it imitates the Arch of Titus in Rome. In the Middle Ages, this was the site of a gate in the city walls, but the present arch, characterized by André Breton as *très belle et très inutile* (very beautiful and quite useless) served only as a ceremonial marker and a royal entrance on the old road to St-Denis. On July 28, 1830, it was the scene of intense fighting; revolutionaries scrambled to the top of the old Bourbon icon and rained cobblestones on the monarchist troops below. At its side, two blocks down the bd. St-Denis, the **Porte St-Martin** is a smaller copy, built in 1674 to celebrate yet another victory. On the façade, look for Louis XIV represented as Hercules (nude, except for the wig).

The stretch from Porte St-Martin to place de la République, along rue René Boulanger and bd. St-Martin, served as a lively theater district in the 19th century and has recently begun to retrieve some of its former sparkle. Newly refurbished, the **Théâtre de la Renaissance,** with a sculpted façade of griffins and arabesques, has breathed new life into neighboring streets. A handful of mid-priced, fashionable establishments hail from this Bohemian enclave (see Bars and Restaurants).

Going east from here along the bd. St-Martin, you arrive at the **place de la République** (M. République), the meeting point of the tenth, the third and the eleventh *arrondissements.* This is a good place to avoid at night, when prostitutes and swindlers abound. In the center a monument to the Republic of France celebrates the victories of the 23 years of intermittent republican rule between 1789 and the monument's erection in 1880. The statue of *La République* by Morice stands on a base by Dalou, with bronze reliefs representing various revolutions in French history.

A bit farther east lies the **Canal St-Martin,** 4.5km long and connecting the Canal de l'Ourcq to the Seine. The canal has several locks, which can be traveled by boat on one of the **canauxrama** trips (see Sights—intro). You can also walk along the tree-lined banks. Again, be careful in this area after dark. East of the canal, follow rue Bichat to the entrance of **hôpital St-Louis,** one of the oldest hospitals in Paris. Built by Henri IV as a sanctuary/prison for victims of the plague, it was located across a marsh from the city, and downwind of both the smelly mess at Buttes-Chaumont (see 19ème) and a gallows. Its distance from any source of fresh water confirms that it was intended more to protect the city from contamination than to help the unfortunates inside. Today, hôpital St-Louis specializes in dermatology, and offers a peaceful Renaissance courtyard to those willing to brave any plague bacilli that might have survived the centuries.

Just north of hôpital St-Louis, in the area between the canal, rue des Ecluses St-Martin, rue Louis Blanc, and rue de la Grange aux Belles, once stood the **Montfaucon gallows**—famous for its hanging capacity of 60, an efficiency unrivalled until the invention of the guillotine several centuries later. In the early 14th century, the initial wooden structure was replaced by a two-story stone framework, designed by Pierre Rémy, treasurer to Charles IV. (Rémy had a chance to test his creation in 1328, when he was hanged with great pomp and circumstance.) By the 17th century, the Montfaucon gallows had fallen into disuse, and today only memories linger.

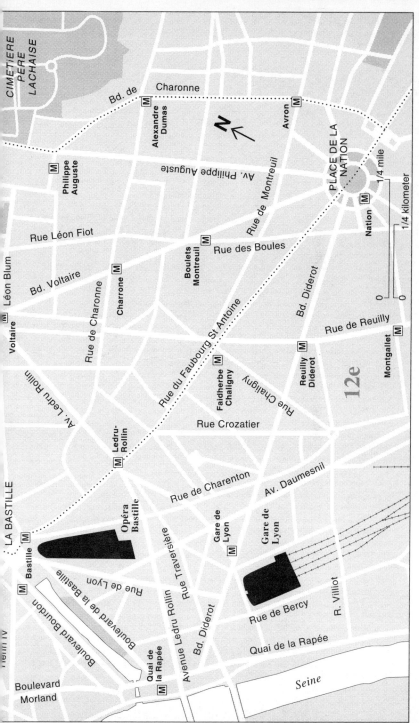

But in 1954, workers building the garage at 53, rue de la Grange aux Belles uncovered an eerie reminder of this area's former use: two of the original pillars, along with several human bones.

■■■ ELEVENTH ARRONDISSEMENT

Near the dressed-down, plexiglass opera house at **place de la Bastille** (M. Bastille) disgruntled shopkeepers stormed the Bastille prison on July 14, 1789. Long since demolished, the prison was originally commissioned by Charles V to safeguard the eastern entrance to Paris. A treasury vault under Henry IV, the fortress became a state prison under his successor Louis XIII; internment there, generally reserved for religious heretics and political undesirables, followed specific orders from the king. The man of the iron mask lived and died here at Louis XIV's request. In the last years of the Old Regime, however, the prison turned from draconian nightmare to deluxe hotel. Its titled inmates furnished their suites, brought their servants, and received guests. The Cardinal de Rohan held a dinner party for 20 in his cell. The prison itself provided fresh linen. Notable prisoners included Mirabeau, Voltaire, and the Marquis de Sade, one of the last seven prisoners to be held there. He left July 7, 1789, just a week before the prison's liberation.

When Revolutionary militants stormed the Bastille, they came for the prison's supply of gunpowder. After sacking the Invalides for weapons, they needed munitions. Surrounded by an armed rabble, too short on food to entertain a siege, and unsure of the loyalty of the Swiss mercenaries who defended the prison, the Bastille's governor surrendered. Soon after, while under armed escort to the Hôtel de Ville, the mob hacked off his head with a pocketknife and paraded it around on a pike.

In spite of the incident's gruesome details, the storming of the Bastille has come to symbolize the triumph of liberty over despotism. Its first annual anniversary was the cause for great celebration. Since the late 19th century, July 14th has been the official state holiday of the French Republic.

Demolition of the prison began the morrow of its capture and concluded in October 1792. Some of its stones were incorporated into the Pont de la Concorde. A commemorative pile can be found in square Henri Galli, a few blocks down bd. Henri IV from pl. de la Bastille. A certain Citizen Palloy, the main demolition contractor, used the stones to construct 83 models of the prison which he sent to the provinces as reminders of "the horror of despotism." Original stones also outline the prison's original location. (Shades of the Berlin Wall...)

The **Opéra Bastille,** a space-age conversation piece, is regularly the butt of jokes by passersby. Designed by Canadian architect Carlos Ott, the building is second only to Euro Disney in the minds of Parisians as an example of North American barbarism. It has further been described as a huge *toilette,* a version no doubt of the coin-operated facilities in the streets of Paris. Many complain that the acoustics of the hall leave much to be desired. Worse yet, the "people," for whom the opera was supposedly designed, can't afford to go there. Tours (20F, students 10F; 1-2 per day at 1 or 5pm) are the only way to see the interior unless you attend a performance. The schedule frequently changes. Call 40 01 19 17 for performance information; stop in the box office for a free brochure describing the season's events. (Discount tickets sold 15 min. in advance. Office open Aug. 26-July 19. See Entertainment—Opera for more information.)

In 1831, King Louis-Philippe laid the cornerstone for the **July Column,** located at the center of the *place.* It commemorates the Republicans who died in the Revolutions of 1789 and 1830, the latter of which brought Louis-Philippe to power. The column's vault contains the bodies of 504 martyrs of 1830, along with two mummified Egyptian pharaohs moved from the Louvre when they began to decompose.

The neighborhood behind the Opéra Bastille has eclipsed the Latin Quarter as the youthful, artistic center of Paris. This portion of the 11ème has become, like Montmartre, Montparnasse, and the *quartier latin* before it, the city's latest bohemia. Don't count on the BCBG glamor of the Left Bank; styles here change as quickly as new galleries open and close. Today's Beautiful People sport tattered miniskirts, bell-bottoms, and platform shoes.

Along the streets radiating from the *place* lived many of the Revolution's profiteers and victims. Nos. 157-161, rue de Charonne once housed the infamous Docteur Belhomme whose Maison de Retraite et de Santé sheltered condemned aristocrats and other notables with ready cash during the Terror (1792-1795). For 1000 *livres* a month, Dr. Belhomme would let a room in his sham sanatorium and certify his clients as too ill to brave the scaffold. Arrested himself after word got out, Dr. Belhomme holed up in a like establishment on the rue de Picpus (12ème). Thrown in jail for uncivicism under the Directory, he died peacefully at home at the age of 87.

Off rue de Charonne, **Eglise Ste-Marguerite** was built in 1627 to save parishioners in the village of Charonne the commute to St-Paul in the Marais (see Sights—4ème). The Chapelle des Ames du Purgatoire, added to the church in 1764 by architect Louis, is of particular note. The trompe l'oeil paintings are by Brunetti, the pietà behind the altar by Girardon. During the Revolution, Ste-Marguerite continued to act as a place of worship despite the sweep of anticlericism throughout the nation. Its vicar was among the first priests to get married. (Open daily 9am-noon, 5-7pm.)

Next to the church, **Cimetière Ste-Marguerite** is another stop on the Revolution's trail of blood and trivial pursuit. At least 73 victims of the guillotine from June 1794 fertilized these grounds. The most enigmatic headstone to be found here remains that of "the child dead in the dungeon of the Temple"—the headstone of Louis XVII, located near the outside wall of the Chapelle des Ames du Purgatoire Ornot. Nineteenth-century forensic tests confirmed that the body to be that of a boy 18-20, but his identity has never been conclusively proven. The stone reads, "L...XVII 1785-1795."

Head back on the rue de Charonne toward the Bastille and turn left on **rue de Lappe** for a showcase of 17th- and 18th-century quotidian life and architecture. In this heart of Bastille chic, the streets are lined with cafés, galleries, old passageways, and gardens. This is the 11ème at its most accessible and most charming. Michelet, the great 19th-century historian of the Revolution, lived at no. 49. His statue may be seen on the **Hôtel de Ville** (see Sights—4ème). Turn right from rue de Lappe onto **rue de la Roquette** for a glimpse of another 17th-century byway. The poet Verlaine lived at no. 17.

Farther east along la Roquette, past its intersection with the rue Voltaire, sits a park where a prison once stood. La Petite Roquette served as a prison for Parisians condemned to death until its demolition in 1899. A guillotine once rested upon five flat stones at the street's junction with rue de la Croix Faubin. In 1871, Communard soldiers shot numerous abbots and curés here.

■■■ TWELFTH ARRONDISSEMENT

Until joining Paris proper, the area east of pl. de la Bastille comprised the Faubourg (suburb) St-Antoine. Royal decree exempted this artisanal district from duties levied against residents of the wealthier, center city. Hard hit by food shortages in the late 18th century, *faubourg* residents spiritedly joined the Revolution's more radical contingents. Participating in both the 1830 and ill-fated 1848 Revolutions, the *faubourg* became known as the "red belt" around Paris. In the 20th century, the region has proved a bastion of both left- and right-leaning unrest. Residents numbered importantly among the pre-1944 resistance movement; plaques to this effect, conspicuously absent in central Paris, are sprinkled along the city's eastern fringe. On May 28, 1958, over 150,000 people marched to combat an attempted *coup d'état* by the armed forces, brought on by their anger at De Gaulle's policy in Algeria. In their pro-government march, *faubourg* residents followed what historian Jean Lacouture has called "the traditional left-wing route from the place de la Nation to the place de la République."

The 12ème, made up mostly of businesses and tree-lined boulevards, offers little to the sight-seer. One exception is the **Ministère des Finances (Ministry of Finances)**, 238, quai de Bercy. Until recently, the Finance Ministry shared space with the Louvre art museum. Mitterand commissioned the current Finance building when construction began on the Louvre's new pyramid. Chemetov and Huidobro's design yawns across the Seine—the only of Mitterrand's *grands projets* accessible by dinghy and parachute. Its flat top serves as a helicopter landing pad. Employees drive speedboats from here to the Assemblée Nationale (3 min.). Shiny and spiky, the building resembles an obsidian wafer cookie (in profile).

In the *arrondissement*'s southeastern corner, the radial **place de la Nation** (M. Nation) marks the boundary of the 12ème with the 11ème. Dalou's statue *Triomphe de la République* (1899) surveys the *place*, formerly known as the **place du Trône** because of a throne placed here in 1660, when Louis XIV married Marie-Thérèse. During the Revolution, the throne was replaced by a guillotine;1300 nobles were executed on this spot, and the square was renamed the **place du Trône-Renversé (Square of the Toppled Throne).** It became the **place de la Nation** on July 14, 1880. East of the *place*, twin tollhouses—part of Claude-Nicolas Ledoux's 18th-century city walls—flank the cours de Vincennes, a broad avenue leading to the Château de Vincennes and to the wooded park that surrounds it.

■■■ THIRTEENTH ARRONDISSEMENT

Although its battery of office towers offers little to the sightseer, the 13ème is a gem for gourmands. Come to explore Paris' **Chinatown,** located along av. de Choisy, or wander the tangled, countrified streets of the **Butte aux Cailles**, a pocket of artsy restaurants and bars. In the near future, the 13ème is likely to surface as an important axis of French intellectual and cultural life; it is the site of the new **Bibliothèque de France** (Library of France).

Until the 20th century, the 13ème was one of Paris' poorest, most squalid neighborhoods; Victor Hugo used parts of the 13ème as a setting for *Les Misérables*. Traversed by the **Bièvre,** a still stream clogged with industrial refuse, it was notoriously the city's worst-*smelling* district. Environmentalists eventually won their campaign to close its tanneries and paper factories. In 1910, the Bièvre was filled in. While no longer a health risk, the 13ème throws few bones to even the most dedicated sightseer. Among its highlights, however, is the **Manufacture des Gobelins,** 42, av. des Gobelins (tel. 43 37 12 60; M. Gobelins), a tapestry workshop over 300 years old. Masters and journeymen still employ 17th-century weaving techniques, and can spend a full year on one square meter of tapestry. In the mid-17th century, the Gobelins was a prison-like establishment, where whole families lived in poverty to produce what have become priceless artworks, displayed in the Cluny museum and châteaux near Paris (see Museums and Daytrips). Still an adjunct of the state, the factory receives commissions from French ministries and foreign embassies. Guided tours, the only way to get inside the factory, explain the intricacies of the weaving process. (Tours in French with free English-language handout, 90 min., Tues.-Thurs. 2 and 2:45pm, 35F, ages 7-24 25F.)

In the **place d'Italie,** filled with uniform-looking skyscrapers, stands the ultramodern **Gaumont** movie theater, home to the largest screen in France. Architect Kenso Tange's glass-paneled office building at no. 30 pl. d'Italie merits an elevator ride to the top if you can smooth-talk your way past the receptionist.

Further southwest, narrow streets wag through the **Butte aux Cailles** (quail knoll) district, one of the few old Parisian neighborhoods to escape the notice of both Picasso and Hemingway. (It did not, however, escape the notice of Pilâtre de

Rosier or of the Marquis d'Arlandes, who landed the world's first hot-air balloon here on Nov. 21, 1783.) It might not enjoy secluded status much longer, though; trendy, painterly Parisians have begun to frequent its bars. On weekends, the junction of Butte aux Cailles with rue des Cinq Diamants becomes quite animated.

Due south on rue Tolbiac stands the Romano-Byzantine **Eglise Sainte-Anne de la Maison Blanche,** built 1894-1912. Construction halted in 1898 due to lack of funds, but resumed after a grant from the Lombarts, a local family who owned a chocolate store on av. de Choisy. The front of the church is nicknamed *"la façade chocolat,"* in their honor. Although Ste-Anne's pointed twin towers and rose-shaped clock make it impressive from the outside, it is dark and plain inside, with heavy columns and small windows.

Chinatown, located east of Ste-Anne's on av. de Choisy and av. d'Ivry, is populated not only by myriad Chinese, Vietnamese, and Cambodians, but by hundreds of Asian restaurants and grocery stores as well. Like Chinatowns the world over, it offers delicious Asian cuisine for half the price of dinners elsewhere in the city.

Believe it or not, the panchromatic, Lego-like building in the southeast corner of the 13ème is a Salvation Army shelter, designed by Le Corbusier in 1931. The Princesse de Polignac, patron of the avant garde and friend to the architect, financed the project, named the **Cité de Refuge** (12, rue Cantagrel).

The 13ème is the site of the new **Bibliothèque de France (Library of France)**, scheduled to open its doors in the fall of 1996. The new complex will replace, in function if not in spirit, the old **Bibliothèque Nationale** (see Sights—2ème). Designed by architect Dominique Perrault, the new library is a 7-billion-franc endeavor encompassing 7.5 hectares along the Seine, across from the Ministry of Finance.(The Bibliothèque de France is just one piece of the 13ème's urban renewal puzzle; a new project called **ZAC (Zone d'Aménagement Concerte)** Seine-Rive Gauche provides for the construction of a university, five schools, a sports complex, a public garden, and a new metro line (Méteor)). Librarians' associations and ad-hoc committees of intellectuals (including Claude Lévi-Strauss) have written open letters to François Mitterrand arguing the inadequacy of Perrault's design. Critics warn that the four L-shaped towers, to serve as the library's depositories (and designed to look like open books from above), would be difficult for researchers who needed one book from the 15th story of tower A and another from the 16th story of tower B across the way. Others worry that light streaming through the clear, glass walls will damage rare volumes. Indeed, by the summer of 1994, the buildings were in large part constructed and quite transparent.

■■■ FOURTEENTH ARRONDISSEMENT: MONTPARNASSE

At first glance, the fourteenth *arrondissement* appears to have nothing more to offer the tourist than the much-acclaimed cafés along the bd. Montparnasse and the eight-level commercial center that serves as a base for the architecturally tragic Tour de Montparnasse. Deeper into the *arrondissement,* however, hidden sights abound. Still, quaint this *quartier* is not—you may have to save your search for post-card Paris for another day.

Montparnasse has served as a magnet for an impressive array of residents since the turn of the century. The first to arrive were Bretons, who had lost their livelihoods after failed harvests. Arriving en masse at the Gare de Montparnasse, they settled around the station so that they could cut a quick path home if the agricultural tide turned. Vestiges of Breton culture—*crêperies,* stores selling traditional Breton crafts and books, and even Breton cultural associations—remain strong in this area. Montparnasse then became a center for the artistic and political avant garde of art, marking a veritable golden age of Bohemia. Artists including Modigliani, Utrillo, Soutine, Chagall, and Léger migrated from the lamentably less hip Montmartre, forming

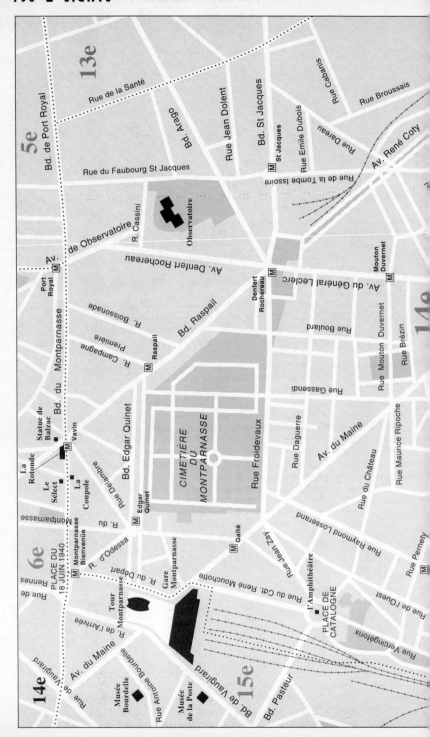

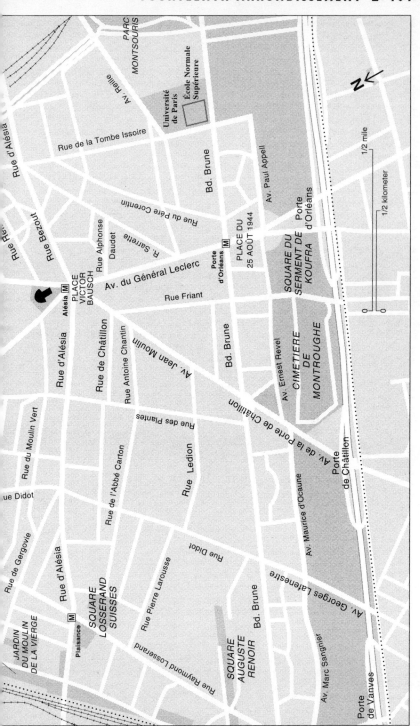

PARC MONTSOURIS

École Normale Supérieure

Université de Paris

Av. Reille

Rue de la Tombe Issoire

Rue d'Alésia

Rue Bezout

Rue Re...

Bd. Brune

Rue du Père Corentin

R. Sarrette

Rue Alphonse Daudet

Av. Paul Appell

Porte d'Orléans

PLACE DU 25 AOÛT 1944

Porte d'Orléans Ⓜ

Av. du Général Leclerc

PLACE VICTOR BAUSCH

Alésia Ⓜ

Rue Friant

SQUARE DU SERMENT DE KOUFRA

Rue d'Alésia

Rue de Châtillon

Rue Antoine Chantin

Av. Jean Moulin

Bd. Brune

Av. Ernest Revel

CIMETIERE DE MONTROUGHE

Rue du Moulin Vert

Rue des Plantes

Av. de la Porte de Châtillon

Rue Ledion

Porte de Châtillon

ue Didot

Rue de l'Abbé Carton

Av. Maurice d'Ocaune

Rue de Gergovie

Rue d'Alésia

Rue Pierre Larousse

Rue Didot

Av. Georges Lafenestre

JARDIN DU MOULIN DE LA VIERGE

Plaisance Ⓜ

SQUARE LOSSERAND SUISSES

Rue Raymond Losserand

SQUARE AUGUSTE RENOIR

Bd. Brune

Av. Marc Sangnier

Porte de Vanves

N

1/2 mile

1/2 kilometer

the base of the artistic movement called the Paris School. Political exiles, notably Lenin and Trotsky, spent evenings planning strategies over cognac in cafés.

After WWI, Montparnasse drew in other artists, especially Americans who wanted to escape Prohibition and profit from a favorable exchange rate. Man Ray transformed an apartment into a photolab; Calder worked on his first sculptures; Hemingway did some of his most serious writing and drinking; and Henry Miller created the shocking, steamy *Tropic of Cancer* at Seurat's villa with the encouragement of Anaïs Nin and Lawrence Durrell. It was all fun and games until the outbreak of the Spanish Civil War, then WWII, which put a final, resolute damper on the Bohemian community in Montparnasse. The *quartier* is now predominantly Parisian. Denfer-Rochereau, Plaisance, and Penerty remain unattractive and residential, and the Cité Universitaire is a French Animal House for the university set. The area around the *tour* teems with commercialism and caters to tourists.

Although officially in the 15ème, the **Tour de Montparnasse** merits a word of discussion as your eye is involuntarily, inexplicably drawn to it from any point in the 14ème. Yes, it is as tall and unattractive as you've heard—all 209m of it. Rising from the intersection of the 6ème, 14ème, and 15ème *arrondissements* like a rook in a game of urban renewal of monumental proportions, the *tour* casts a black pall on anything unlucky enough to fall in its shadow (see Sights—15ème.)

The **Cimetière Montparnasse,** 3, bd. Edgar Quinet (tel. 44 10 36 50; M. Edgar Quinet) is less than romantic. Shrouded by the shadow of the Tour Montparnasse, crisscrossed by avenues, too crowded with tombs for grass, and occupied by cats and chattering grounds keepers who appear to be doing their best not to disturb the final resting places of heaps of beer and mineral water bottles, the Cimetière Montparnasse is better left to the dead. Armed with a free *Index des Célébrités* (the detailed map available just left of the main entrance), determined sightseers thread their way through the unknown to pay their respects to writers like Guy de Maupassant, Samuel Beckett, Jean-Paul Sartre and Simone de Beauvoir (who share a grave), car manufacturer André Citroën, composer Camille Saint-Saëns, sculptor Ossip Zadkine, editor Pierre Larousse (of dictionary fame), artist Man Ray, newly arrived composer Serge Gainsbourg, , and loyal Frenchman Alfred Dreyfus. Don't miss the tomb of Charles Baudelaire who, in his *Fleurs du Mal*, six years before he died, greeted Death willingly: "O Death, old captain, it is time! Lift the anchor! We wish, so much this fire consumes our brains, to plunge into the abyss, Heaven or Hell, what matters? To the very edge of knowledge in order to find something *new!*" (Open Mon.-Fri. 7:30am-6pm, Sat. 8:30am-6pm, Sun. 9am-6pm; Nov. 6-March 15 closes 5:30pm. Free.) **Place Denfert-Rochereau** is presided over by a magnificent lion sculpted by **Bartholdi,** the creator of the Statue of Liberty.

Les Catacombs, 1, pl. Denfert-Rochereau (tel. 43 22 47 63; M. Denfert-Rochereau) are subterranean tunnels that were originally excavated to provide stone for building the city. By the 1770s, much of the Left Bank was in danger of caving in, and digging stopped. The former quarry was then converted to a mass grave, to relieve the unbearable stench emanating from cemeteries around Paris. Near the entrance to the ossuary reads the ominous caution, "Stop! Beyond Here Is the Empire of Death." Many have ignored the sign. In 1793, a Parisian got lost and was not found for nine years, at which point, he'd become, so to speak, one with the pile of bones. During World War II, this place was actually full of life—the resistance set up headquarters among these old and loyal Parisian bones.

The depths of the ossuary compose an underground city (note the "street" names on the walls), with bones for bricks and marrow for mortar. Navigate your way through femur-lined tunnels, complete with fibulas, and anchored by craniums. The ghoulish arrangement is tidy, practical, and often quite artistic. Beware the low ceilings and unidentifiable liquid seeping from the walls. Some rooms sport cheery sayings to make the journey more interesting—*"Pensez le matin que vous n'irez peut être pas jusques au soir et au soir que vous n'irez pas jusques au matin."* (Think each morning that you may not be alive in the evening, and each evening that you may not be alive in the morning.) The stacks of bones are often labeled, indicating which cemetery they came from, but they all look alike—who would notice if something were out of order? Bring a sweater, a flashlight, and a friend for support. Not recommended for the faint of heart or leg; the 85 steep steps you climb on the way out will provide you with a day's worth of exercise. Not wheelchair accessible. (Open Tues.-Fri. 2-4pm, Sat.-Sun. 9-11am and 2-4pm. Admission 27F, students 15F, under 6 free.)

Parc Montsouris offers a sunny return to the land of the living. Begun in 1867 by the Baron Haussmann, this park doubles as an arboretum, offering sanctuary to hundreds of rare and unusual trees, all well-labeled and cared for. An amazing variety of birds, ducks, and geese splash contentedly in the artificial lake at one end of the park. (The designer of this lake killed himself after the water mysteriously drained during the park's opening ceremony.) Sunbathers, children, and *clochards* are even allowed to stretch out on a 50m x 50m strip of grass along the street side of the lake. Don't give into the temptation to pet a lesser snow goose, Australian rajah shelduck, or fulvous whistling duck—all of these hiss a warning, then deliver a nasty bite.

Across the bd. Jourdan, thousands of students study, argue, and/or drink themselves silly in the **Cité Universitaire,** a 40-hectaredisplay case for students who've come from no less than 122 countries to no less than 30 dorms, two of them designed by Le Corbusier. The "vertical slab" called the **Pavilion Suisse** (1932) is adored by architects as a monument of his early career. With its *pilotis* (stilts) underneath and its garden on the roof, the building reflects the architect's dream of a vertical city, with life lived on several levels. During the German occupation, the roof garden housed a battery of anti-aircraft guns. Le Corbusier returned in 1959 with the **Maison du Brasil.** South and west of the dorms, the expansive greenery flaunts Parisian park customs, as hundreds of joggers, frisbee throwers, bikers, and boom-box players flout the "keep off" signs that ring the lawns.

North of the Parc Montsouris is the **Hôpital Ste-Anne,** 15, rue Cabanis, a psychiatric hospital with an interesting history. It first opened its doors to the nervous citizens of Paris in 1221 but did not begin to thrive until Louis XIV took the throne, when state funds, mostly earmarked for the imprisonment of "wanton girls and women," poured in. After a series of fires, the hospital went through several incarnations, including a dairy farm in the 18th century with a full complement of 140 cows and 700 pigs, before being finally restored to its original life as a clinic by Napoleon III in 1863. Although access to most of the buildings is restricted to the medical staff and patients (neither of which you really want to visit), a tour of the grounds affords a quick respite from the bustle of the streets (open daily 7am-9pm). In a bizarre, and perhaps planned, coincidence, all of the neighboring streets are named after artists like Camille Claudel and Vincent Van Gogh, many of whom were out of their minds.

■■■ FIFTEENTH ARRONDISSEMENT: TOUR MONTPARNASSE

Perhaps the best introduction to the 15ème is the metro ride that gets you there. Metro line 6 runs on an elevated track; board at Trocadéro and ride to the 15ème's central stop, **La Motte-Picquet-Grenelle.** From the metro car window there's a lovely view of the Seine, the Eiffel Tower, and the rooftops. A mostly residential quarter, this Parisian neighborhood has little in the way of sights. It does, however, present a charming picture of Parisian everyday life. The bd. de Grenelle stretches through most of the brighter cafés, stores, and specialty shops of the 15ème. The festive rue du Commerce overflows with flowershops, markets, and inexpensive houseware shops. For coffee and a front-row view of this vibrant Parisian neighborhood, get off at the La Motte-Picquet-Grenelle stop and relax at the **Café Bouquet de Grenelle** next door. Or take a walk through the colorful markets of the rue du Commerce. For more people-watching, pop out of the Convention *métro* stop, where perfect cafés occupy each corner of the intersection between rue de la Convention and rue de Vaugirard. If you're still interested in seeing the city's sights from afar, take the elevator to the top of the towering Tour Montparnasse.

The **Tour Montparnasse** (tel. 45 38 52 56; M. Montparnasse-Bienvenue) dominates the *quartier's* northeast corner. Standing 56 stories tall, this controversial building looks somewhat out of place amidst the older architecture of Montparnasse. Some argue that the *tour,* completed in 1973, is a slice of Manhattan inserted awkwardly in the middle of Paris. But the group of French architects who designed the tower believed that it would revolutionize the Paris skyline. It has, but not without the disapproval of many Parisians. Shortly after it was completed, the city of Paris passed an ordinance forbidding any further structures to be built within Paris proper, designating La Défense as the only possible home of future structures like the Tour Montparnasse. The *tour,* which houses a huge underground shopping mall and train station, used to hold the European record for the tallest office building. Take advantage of this fact by riding to the top, where a fabulous view of the unobstructed Paris skyline awaits (open daily 9:30am-11pm, Oct.-March 9:30am-10pm; admission 40F, students and seniors 32F, under 15 24F).

In front of the Tour Montparnasse, the **place du 18 juin** commemorates two important events from World War II. The name recalls the June 18, 1940 radio broadcast from London by General de Gaulle in which he called on his fellow citizens to resist the occupying Nazi forces and the Vichy collaborationist régime of Maréchal Pétain. And it was on this *place* that General Leclerc, the leader of the French forces, accepted the surrender of General von Choltitz, the Nazi commander of the Paris occupation, on August 25, 1944. It is due to his love of the city that the Tour Montparnasse is not Paris's only monument. Despite continual orders from Hitler to destroy Paris ("Is Paris burning?") and retreat, von Choltitz disobeyed, thus saving countless landmarks of Parisian history and architecture.

La Ruche, 52, rue Dantzig (M. Convention), is a round brick building designed as a wine pavilion by Gustave Eiffel for the exposition of 1900, a decade after its more famous sibling came into existence. During the early 1900s the building, whose name means "the beehive," was bought by the private charitable foundation La Ruche Seydoux, and used to house struggling artists (among them Chagall and Soutine). Today the foundation still gives artists grants, studios, and housing. The garden surrounding the building is studded with sculpture, the work of the house's residents. As La Ruche is a private foundation, visitors are asked to call ahead to gain entry to the garden, though some people just wander in when the gate is open.

L'Institut Pasteur, 28, rue du Dr. Roux (tel. 45 68 82 82 or 45 68 82 83 for museum information; M. Pasteur), founded by the French scientist Louis Pasteur in 1887, is now an international center for biochemical research, development, and treatment facilities. It was here that Pasteur, a champion of germ theory in the 17th century, developed his famous technique for purifying milk products. Today, some of the most interesting research on HIV is conducted here. In 1983, the *institut* gained notoriety for Dr. Luc Montaigner's isolation of HIV, the virus that causes AIDS. For years, Montaigner was embroiled in an international legal and scientific dispute with Dr. Robert Gallo of the American Centers for Disease Control over who had first isolated the HIV virus. Now less interested in such debates over "fame," Montaigner continues his work here on HIV.

The Institute houses an extensive museum on Pasteur and his work. The museum offers an exhaustive run-down of Pasteur's medical and artistic projects, a tour of his lab equipment and preserved living quarters, and a visit to the crypt which houses the scientist's corpse. Pasteur's son designed the symbolic fantasyland on the ceiling, a mosaic recalling Pasteur *père's* work with wine casks, rabid dogs, sheep, and of course, lots of happy cows. Tours are in French with photocopied English translations (open Mon.-Fri. 2-5pm; admission 15F, students 8F. Closed in August.). Should Pasteur's life spur you to perform some selfless act, a blood donation center is across the street.

Also in the 15ème is the surprisingly interesting **Musée de la Poste** (Postal Museum), and the **Musée Bourdelle,** a well-stocked collection of the works of the French sculptor Emile-Antoine Bourdelle (see Museums).

■■■ SIXTEENTH ARRONDISSEMENT

On January 1, 1860 the wealthy villages of Auteuil, Passy, and Chaillot banded together and joined Paris, forming the current 16ème *arrondissement*. More than a century later, the area's original aristocratic families continue to maintain their ground, making the 16ème a stronghold of conservative politics, fashion, and culture. Some members of the local nobility even prohibit their children from singing *La Marseillaise,* the anthem advanced by the Revolutionaries who beheaded their ancestors. In this sumptuous residential neighborhood, townhouses retire graciously from generally wide, quiet roads. Businesses, storefronts, and tackiness are at a minimum. Thoses buildings that are not private homes tend to be embassies, 64 of which reside here. And, if neither home nor embassy, then museum; about half of Paris' museums are located here. To do this *arrondissement* justice, you'll have to flip back and forth many times between these pages and our Museums section.

Enter by M. Porte Dauphine, one of the few surviving examples of Hector Guimard's Art Nouveau Paris metro stops recognizable by its twisted, spider-like, winged metal frame. To the west lies the Bois de Boulogne; to the east, the av. de Foch stretches to the Arc de Triomphe. One of Haussmann's finest creations, this avenue's expansive width (about 120m) accommodates stretches of lawn running up each of its sides and through its center. Ave. de Foch was for years the preferred carriage route of fashionable Parisians on their way to the Bois de Boulogne. The stately *hôtels* which line both sides of the street are some of the city's most expensive addresses.Those on the south side are more desirable: they get more sunlight. Stop at the **Musée d'Ennery** and the **Musée Arménien** as you walk down the avenue toward the Arc de Triomphe.

The **Arc de Triomphe** is the axis from which many of the 16ème's avenues radiate; following the commercial av. Marceau down to the Seine takes you past the **Eglise St-Pierre de Chaillot,** between rue de Chaillot and av. Pierre-1er de Serbie. This church, located at the former heart of the village of Auteuil, is a neo-Romanesque structure with brilliantly lit stained glass and a striking sculpture by Henri Bouchard over its front three arches. Stop in for information about foreign-language religious services around Paris. At the end of av. Marceau is the place de l'Alma and a life-size replica of the torch of the Statue of Liberty, one of several tributes in the neighborhood to France's most famous gift to the United States.

The **Palais de Tokyo,** to your left as you turn up av. du Président Wilson, houses the **Musée d'Art Moderne de la Ville de Paris** and numerous other exhibition halls. Built for the 1937 World Expo, the palace took its name from the adjacent quai de Tokyo. (After WWII, in which Japan fought as an Axis power, it was renamed the quai de New York.) The gardens of the Palais Galliera, across from the Palais de Tokyo, draw both young children and sculpture enthusiasts; inspect the three allegorical figures framed by Romanesque arches. The **Palais Galliera,** built for the Duchess of Galliera by Louis Ginain as a repository for Italian Baroque art, has never served that function. The collection went elsewhere and the Italianate structure, completed in 1892, now houses the four-room **Musée de Mode et Costume.** To enter the museum, follow either of the streets next to the garden to av. Pierre-1er de Serbie. Further down the avenue at pl. d'Iéna, the **Musée Guimet** contains a spectacular collection of Asian art.

Follow ave. de Président Wilson from pl. d'Iéna to pl. du Trocadéro et 11 Novembre (generally referred to as "Trocadéro"). The radical modernist structure located in the *place* is the **Palais de Chaillot,** a museum and entertainment complex that contains the **Musée du Cinéma Henri-Langlois,** the **Musée de l'Homme,** the

Musée de la Marine, and the **Musée National des Monuments Français** as well as the **Théâtre National de Chaillot** and the **Cinémathèque Française.** Built for the 1937 World Expo, Jacques Carlu's design features two curved wings built around a paved courtyard. Surveyed by the 7.5m-tall bronze Apollo, another Bouchard sculpture, the building's open-air centerpiece attracts tourists, vendors, roller-skating dancers, and political demonstrators; it also offers the best view in all of Paris of the nearby Eiffel Tower and Champ de Mars. The Palais Chaillot is actually the last of a series of buildings built on this site. Cathérine de' Medici had a château here, later transformed into a convent by Queen Henrietta of England. Napoleon razed the old château and planned to build a more lavish one on the same site for his son; construction came to a halt after Waterloo. In the 1820s, the duc d'Angoulême built a fortress-like memorial to his victory at Trocadéro in Spain—hence the present name. That in turn was replaced in 1878 by a supposed exemplar of "Islamic" architecture built for the World Expo. That too was demolished. Below the palace are the **Jardins du Trocadéro,** which extend to the Seine. The fountains lining the central avenues (aves. Gustave V de Suède and Albert 1er de Monaco) are particularly striking when lit up at night. After a day of sight-seeing, children might enjoy the carrousel in pl. de Varsovie (10F a ride).

Passy, the area immediately south and southwest of Trocadéro, was known historically for its restorative waters. The **Cimitière de Passy** runs along its northern walls. The tiny necropolis, shaded by a chesnut bower, contains the tombs of Claude Debussy, Gabriel Faure, and Edouard Manet. Ask the concierge at the cemetery entrance for directions to these or other grave sites.

Rue Benjamin Franklin commemorates the elder statesmen's one-time residence in Passy. It runs south from Trocadéro past the surprisingly fascinating **Musée Clemenceau,** located in Clemenceau's own home; the museum chronicles the former Prime Minister who, despite a lifetime of accomplishments, is most remembered as France's hard-line negotiator of the Versailles Treaty. Walk all the way down rue Benjamin Franklin to the **Maison de Balzac,** located on rue Raynouard. Balzac lived here while completing the last volumes of *La comédie humaine;* the museum will have little appeal to those unfamiliar with his work or biography. Further down rue Raynouard, between what is now av. du Colonel-Bonnet and rue Singer, Benjamin Franklin built France's first lightning rod.

As you pass the **Maison de Radio-France**—the unmistakeable, large, white, round building at the end of rue Raynouard—take rue de Boulainvilliers down to the miniature **Statue of Liberty** near the pont de Grenelle. Donated by a group of American expatriates in 1885, it moved to this spot for the 1889 World Expo.

The end of rue Raynouard marks the boundary of Passy with the town of **Auteuil.** A 17th-century meeting ground for men of letters like Racine, Molière, and Boileau, Auteuil currently assembles a startling array of old and new architectural styles, combining *hôtels particuliers* with Art Nouveau and Modernist residential buildings.

Follow rue La Fontaine (an extension of rue Raynouard) to Hector Guimard's famous **Castel Béranger** (1898), located at no. 14. The swooping arabesques of the *castel*'s balconies, staircases, and rooftops (called "noodle style" by one skeptical *hôtelier*) are this structure's distinctive Art Nouveau flourishes. The architect himself lived there briefly before decamping to another of his creations at 122, av. Mozart. At 40, rue La Fontaine, visit one of the churches or enjoy the beautiful gardens of the **l'Oeuvre des Orphelins Apprentis d'Auteuil (Society of Apprenticed Orphans).** The society was founded in 1866 to provide a home and future for local orphans, who now perform apprenticeships in 30 occupations (the Auteuil "campus" does printing) throughout France. Apprentice gardeners tend the grounds.

17th-century *hôtels particuliers* (large mansions with courtyards and grand entrances) cluster along rue d'Auteuil. No. 11bis is one splendid example; John Adams and his son John Quincy Adams lived at nos. 43-47. For a dramatically different cityscape, return to rue La Fontaine, walk up rue Pierre Guérin in the other direction, down rue de la Source and left on rue Raffet; pink stucco, black marble, and mosaic-covered townhouses adjoin more familiar-looking gray façades and iron

LET'S GO® TRAVEL

CATALOG

1995

E GIVE YOU THE WORLD... AT A DISCOUNT

scounted Flights, Eurail Passes,
avel Gear, Let's Go™ Series Guides,
stel Memberships... and more

t's Go Travel

vision of

rvard Student
encies, Inc.

**Bargains
to every
corner of
the world!**

Travel Gear

A   Let's Go T-Shirt..$10

100% combed cotton. Let's Go logo on front left chest. Four color printing on back. L and XL. Way cool.

B   Let's Go Supreme..........$175

Innovative hideaway suspension with parallel stay internal frame turns backpack into carry-on suitcase. Includes lumbar support pad, torso, and waist adjustment, leather trim, and detachable daypack. Waterproof Cordura nylon, lifetime gurantee, 4400 cu. in. Navy, Green, or Black.

C   Let's Go Backpack/Suitcase.....................$130

Hideaway suspension turns backpack into carry-on suitcase. Internal frame. Detachable daypack makes 3 bags in 1. Waterproof Cordura nylon, lifetime guarantee, 3750 cu. in. Navy, Green, or Black.

D   Let's Go Backcountry I..$210

Full size, slim profile expedition pack designed for the serious trekker. New Airflex suspension. X-frame pack with advanced composite tube suspension. Velcro height adjustment, side compression straps. Detachable hood converts into a fanny pack. Waterproof Cordura nylon, lifetime guarantee, main compartment 3375 cu. in., extends to 4875 cu. in.

E   Let's Go Backcountry II............................$240

Backcountry I's Big Brother. Magnum Helix Airflex Suspension. Deluxe bi-lam contoured shoulder harness. Adjustable sterm strap. Adjustable bi-lam Cordura waist belt. 5350 cubic inches. 7130 cubic inches extended. Not pictured.

800-5-LETSGO

Discounted Flights

Call Let's Go now for inexpensive airfare to points across the country and around the world.

EUROPE • SOUTH AMERICA • ASIA • THE CARRIBEAN • AUSTRALIA •

AFRICA

Eurail Passes

...urailpass (First Class)

...days......................................$498
...onth (30 days)....................$798
...onths (60 days)................$1098

Unlimited rail travel anywhere on Europe's 100,000 mile rail network. Accepted in 17 countries.

Eurail Flexipass (First Class)

A number of individual travel days to be used at your convenience within a two-month period.

Any 5 days in 2 months.............$348
Any 10 days in 2 months...........$560
Any 15 days in 2 months...........$740

...urail Youthpass (Second Class)

...days......................................$398
...onth (30 days)....................$578
...onths (60 days)....................$768

All the benefits of the Eurail Pass at a lower price. For those passengers under 26 on their first day of travel.

Eurail Youth Flexipass (Second Class)

Eurail Flexipass at a reduced rate for passengers under 26 on their first day of travel.

Any 5 days in 2 months.............$255
Any 10 days in 2 months...........$398
Any 15 days in 2 months...........$540

...uropass (First & Second Class)

...st Class starting at................$280
...ond Class starting at............$198
... more details......................CALL

Discounted fares for those passengers travelling in France, Germany, Italy, Spain and Switzerland.

Hostelling Essentials

Undercover Neckpouch............$9.95
Ripstop nylon with soft Cambrelle back. Three pockets. 6 x 7". Lifetime guarantee. Black or Tan.

Undercover Waistpouch.........$9.95
Ripstop nylon with soft Cambrelle back. Two pockets. 5 x 12" with adjustable waistband. Lifetime guarantee. Black or Tan.

H Sleepsack.................................$13.95
Required at all hostels. 18" pillow pocket. Washable poly/cotton. Durable. Compact.

I Hostelling International Card
Required by most international hostels. For U.S. residents only. Adults, $25. Under 18, $10.

J Int'l Youth Hostel Guide.......$10.95
Indispensable guide to prices, locations, and reservations for over 4000 hostels in Europe and the Mediterranean.

K ISIC, ITIC, IYTC..........$16, $16, $17
ID cards for students, teachers and those people under 26. Each offers many travel discounts.

800-5-LETSGO

Order Form

Please print or type — Incomplete applications will not be processed

Last Name	First Name	Date of Birth

Street *(We cannot ship to P.O. boxes)*		

City	State	Zip

Country	Citizenship	Date of Travel

( ) -		
Phone	School (if applicable)	

Item Code	Description, Size & Color	Quantity	Unit Price	Total Price
			SUBTOTAL:	

Domestic Shipping & Handling		Shipping and Handling (see box at left):	
Order Total:	Add:	Add $10 for RUSH, $20 for overnite:	
Up to $30.00	$4.00	MA Residents add 5% tax on books and gear:	
$30.01 to $100.00	$6.00		
Over $100.00	$7.00	**GRAND TOTAL:**	
Call for int'l or off-shore delivery			

MasterCard / VISA Order

CARDHOLDER NAME _____

CARD NUMBER _____

EXPIRATION DATE _____

Enclose check or money order payable to:
Harvard Student Agencies, Inc.
53A Church Street
Cambridge, MA 02138

Allow 2-3 weeks for delivery. Rush orders guaranteed within
one week of our receipt. Overnight orders sent via FedEx the same afternoon.

Missing a Let's Go Book from your collection?
Add one to any $50 order at 50% off the cover price!

Let's Go Travel
1-800-5-LETSGO

(617) 495-9649   Fax: (617) 496-8015
53A Church Street
Cambridge MA 02138

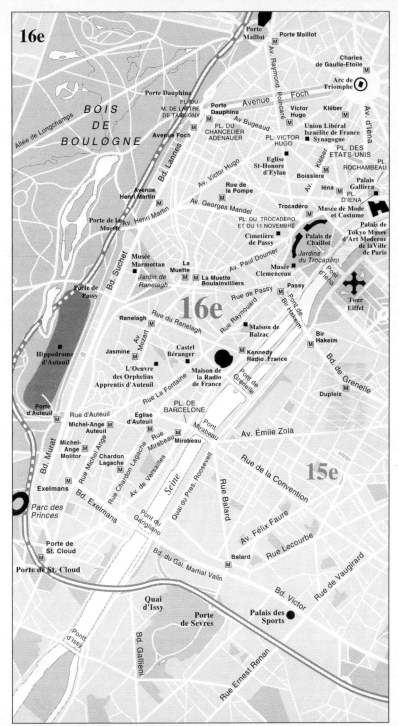

16e

BOIS
DE
BOULOGNE

Allée de Longchamps

Porte Dauphine

Porte
Maillot

Porte Maillot

Av. Raymond Poincaré

Charles
de Gaulle-Etoile

Arc de
Triomphe

PL. DU
M. DE LATTRE
DE TASSIGNY

Porte
Dauphine

Avenue   Foch

Av Bugeaud

Avenue Foch

Bd. Lannes

PL. DU
CHANCELIER
ADENAUER

Victor
Hugo

Kléber

Union Libéral
Israélite de France
Synagogue

Av. d'Iéna

PL. VICTOR
HUGO

PL. DES
ETATS-UNIS

Av. Victor Hugo

Avenue
Henri Martin

Rue de
la Pompe

Eglise
St-Honore
d'Eylau

Kléber

Boissiere

PL.
ROCHAMBEAU

Av.   Iéna

PL.
D'IENA

Palais
Galliera

Av. Georges Mandel

Trocadéro

Musée de Mode
et Costume

Porte de la
Muette

Av. Henri Martin

Bd. Suchet

PL. DU TROCADÉRO
ET DU 11 NOVEMBRE

Musée
Marmottan

Jardin de
Ranelagh

La
Muette

Cimetière
de Passy

Palais de
Chaillot

Jardins
du Trocadéro

Palais de
Tokyo Musée
d'Art Moderne
de la Ville
de Paris

Pont
d'Iéna

Porte de
Passy

La Muette
Boulainvilliers

Av. Paul Doumer

Musée
Clemenceau

Passy

Rue de Passy

Pont de
Bir Hakeim

Tour
Eiffel

16e

Ranelagh

Rue du Ranelagh

Rue Raynouard

Maison de
Balzac

Bir
Hakeim

Av. Mozart

Jasmine

Castel
Béranger

Kennedy
Radio .France

Bd. de Grenelle

Hippodrome
d'Auteuil

L'Oeuvre
des Orphelins
Apprentis d'Auteuil

Maison de
la Radio
de France

Pont de
Grenelle

Dupleix

Rue La Fontaine

Porte
d'Auteuil

Rue d'Auteuil

Michel-Ange
Auteuil

PL. DE
BARCELONE

Eglise
d'Auteuil

Rue
Mirabeau

Pont
Mirabeau

Mirabeau

Av. Émile Zola

Bd. Murat

Michel-
Ange
Molitor

Rue Michel Ange

Chardon
Lagache

Rue Chardon Lagache

Av. de Versailles

Rue de la Convention

15e

Exelmans

Bd. Exelmans

Seine

Quai du Pres. Roosevelt

Rue Balard

Parc des
Princes

Pont du
Gariglano

Av. Félix Faure

Rue Lecourbe

Porte de
St. Cloud

Porte de St. Cloud

Bd. du Gal. Martial Valin

Balard

Bd. Victor

Rue de Vaugirard

Quai
d'Issy

Porte
de Sevres

Palais des
Sports

Pont
d'Issy

Bd. Gallieni

Rue Ernest Renan

grillwork along this street. . Around the corner at 55, rue du Docteur-Blanche stand two Le Corbusier villas, completed in 1925. The **Villa La Roche** and **Villa Jeanneret** are white, stark, built around trees, and maintained by the **Fondation Le Corbusier.** The Villa La Roche is a museum whose interior is far more exciting than the simple exterior would suggest.

Bd. de Beauséjour is the continuation of bd. Montmorency as it approaches M. La Muette. Northwest of the metro once stood the Château de la Muette, where Louis XV entertained his mistresses. In 1783 Pilâtre de Rozier and the Marquis d'Arlandes became the first two humans to escape gravity, lifting off from the castle's lawn in a Montgolfier balloon; they landed 20 min. later in what is now the 13ème. Walk through the **Jardin de Ranelagh,** past playgrounds, benches, and an old-style carrousel. On the other side of the park, the **Musée Marmottan** displays an exquisite collection of Impressionist paintings and medieval illuminations.

■■■ SEVENTEENTH ARRONDISSEMENT

La Pauvre 17ème! The seventeenth is a hodgepodge, an entity that wouldn't exist were it not for the willful mix-and-match played by Haussmann when creating Paris' *arrondissements.* On its southern and southwestern edges, the 17ème borders the 8ème and the 16ème and, like them, feels like old money. Part and parcel of the conservatic wealth of the old towns of Neuilly and Passy, this corner of the *arrondissement* will remind of the side-streets off the Champs Elysées—no surprise, since it *is* just off the Champs Elysées. Relatively small geographical distances result in extreme personality difference here, as opposing neighborhoods meet; the region around the Arc de Triomphe epitomizes bourgeois respectability, while the corner based around the pl. Clichy is a continuation of pl. Pigalle (see Sights—9ème and 18ème) with a similar cast of prostitutes and heroin addicts.

The most interesting and safe sections of the 17ème are the eastern and southern slices. The lovely **place des Ternes,** on the border of the 8ème, has a number of lively cafés and a daily flower market that brings color to the drab 17ème. **Parc Monceau**, technically in the 8ème, provides an open space and a number of architectural marvels (see Sights—8ème). From *métro* station Monceau the nearest entrance to the gilded iron gates of the park is from the bd. de Courcelles. (Open 7am-10pm; Nov.-March 7am-8pm. Gates begin closing 15 min. earlier.)

Frankly, there isn't much else to see. While barricades were erected and novels written in the heart of the city, les Batignolles was, until the mid-19th century, little more than farmers' fields. If you happen to be staying in the area, though, don't miss the **Musée Jean-Jacques Henner,** 43, av. de Villiers, a museum dedicated to this late 19th-century painter (see Museums). Nearby, at 1, place Général Catroux, a building belonging to the **Banque de France** (tel. 42 27 78 14) dominates a small garden with its huge mosaic brickwork. Built in 1884 as the residence of the bank's regent, the house features gargoyle capitals leering from the façade and serpentine iron drainpipes which slither down the building's sides, spiraled by gold paint and ending with spitting fish as spouts. The interior, open to the public, contains a lobby with vaulted ceilings rising to impossible heights (open Mon.-Fri. 8:45am-noon and 1:45-3:30pm).

The enormous and ultra-modern **Palais des Congrès** stands at the very farthest western end of the 17ème and of Paris (M. Porte Maillot). The high-rising glass-towered shopping galleries and conference halls are used as a convention center year-round. For a free view of the sprawling Bois de Boulogne to the south, go up to the terraces on the fifth and seventh floors. The Palais also houses restaurants, a disco, and a cinema. The conference hall hosts conferences and music and theater performances, and is considered one of the most modern and acoustically effective performance spaces in Europe. (For more info on performances call 40 68 25 11.)

The **Cimetière des Batignolles** (tel. 47 37 25 44; M. Porte de Clichy), in the north-west corner of the 17ème, contains the graves of both André Breton and Paul Verlaine. Maps at the front can help you find them. Nearby, the less famous and somewhat comic, though touching, **Cimetière des Chiens** is the final resting spot of countless Parisians' beloved pets. Names like Fifi, Jean-Pierre, Jack, and Chérie mark small stones and tiny graves for all these beloved pups (open Wed.-Sun. 10am-noon and 3-5pm).

The far-ranging flavor of the 17ème is perhaps best explored through the vast repertoire of foods available in its marketplaces and specialty stores. Rue des Batignolles is considered the center of the **Village Batignolles,** a chic and quiet village of shops and residences near the place Félix-Lobligeois and the Eglise de Ste-Marie des Batignolles. Rue Lemercier has a daily covered market filled with meat, cheese, flowers, produce, and old bourgeois women who've shopped on this street since before World War II. Rue de la Jonquière (M. Guy Môquet), lined with shops and restaurants, forms the focus of an active North African community. And Cité des Fleurs boasts a row of exquisite private homes and gardens that wouldn't seem out of place in a novel by Balzac himself.

■ ■ ■ EIGHTEENTH ARRONDISSEMENT: MONTMARTRE

Built high above the rest of Paris on a steep *butte* (knoll), Montmartre gets its name from its ancient history of Roman occupation and Christian martyrdom. A bishop named Dionysus, now known as St. Denis, came to this hill to introduce Christianity to the Gauls. The unappreciative Romans hadn't heard about constructive criticism: they cut off his head in 272 A.D. Legend has it that he and two other martyred bishops then picked up their heads and carried them north to their final resting point, 7km away, where the Eglise St-Denis now stands (see Daytrips). The hill has borne the name **Montmartre** (hill of martyrs) ever since.

A rural area until surprisingly recently, the *butte* used to be covered with vineyards, wheat fields, windmills and gypsum mines. Located outside city limits until the 20th century, its picturesque beauty and low rents attracted notable bohemians like Gustave Charpentier, Toulouse-Lautrec, and Eric Satie, as well as performers and impresarios like "la Goulue" and Aristide Bruant. Toulouse-Lautrec, in particular, immortalized Montmartre through his paintings of life in disreputable nightspots like the **Moulin Rouge.** A generation later, just before WWI smashed its spotlights and destroyed its crops, the *butte* welcomed Picasso, Modigliani, Utrillo, and Apollinaire into its artistic circle. As years passed, Montmartre grew in reputation and diminished in rural charm. Where once were wheatfields, there rose city blocks. Now area residents and businessmen profitably maintain the last quaint traces of old Montmartre. The neighborhood's reputation for countrified bohemia is now, for the most part, little more than a pose. With this said, parts of the *butte* are charming, if touristed preserves of what Montmartre once was. You'll see windmills on top of restaurants, a few vineyards, and another generation of painted ladies, women in kick lines, and so on. The *butte* also provides a dramatic panorama of Parisian rooftops, of the musicians and peddlers who gather in front of Sacré-Coeur at night, and of the portrait artists of the adjacent pl. du Tertre. Together with the Montagne Ste-Geneviève (see 5ème), this is one of the two hills in Paris Baron Haussman's remaking of Paris left intact. At dusk, gas lamps trace the line of the steps up the hillside to the basilica.

One does not merely visit Montmartre; one climbs it. Enter this *quartier* at M. Barbès-Rochechouart, M. Anvers, M. Pigalle, M. Blanche, or M. Clichy, all along its southern boundary. The walk up rue Steinkerque from M. Anvers is either (a) a scene from the movie *Taxi Driver,* or (b) where you met your wife. At night, use M. Abbesses even if it makes for a more roundabout route. To ascend from M. Abbesses

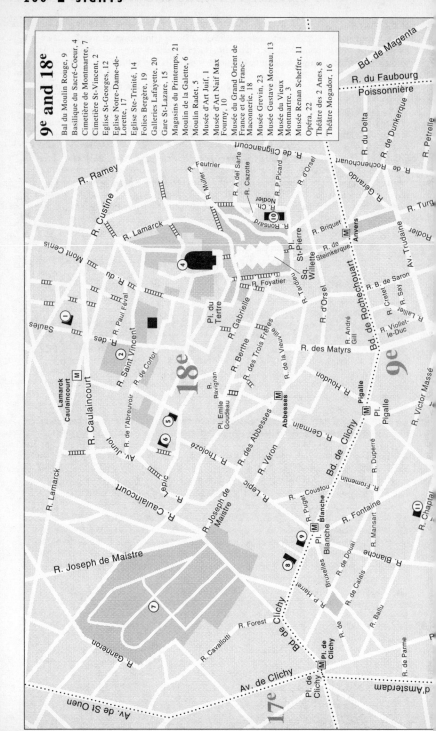

9e and 18e

Bal du Moulin Rouge, 9
Basilique du Sacré-Coeur, 4
Cimetière de Montmartre, 7
Cimetière St-Vincent, 2
Eglise St-Georges, 12
Eglise Notre-Dame-de-Lorette, 17
Eglise Ste-Trinité, 14
Folies Bergère, 19
Galleries Lafayette, 20
Gare St-Lazare, 15
Magasins du Printemps, 21
Moulin de la Galette, 6
Moulin Radet, 5
Musée d'Art Juif, 1
Musée d'Art Naïf Max Fourny, 10
Musée du Grand Orient de France et de la Franc-Maçonnerie, 18
Musée Grevin, 23
Musée Gustave Moreau, 13
Musée du Vieux Montmartre, 3
Musée Renan Scheffer, 11
Opéra, 22
Théâtre des 2 Anes, 8
Théâtre Mogador, 16

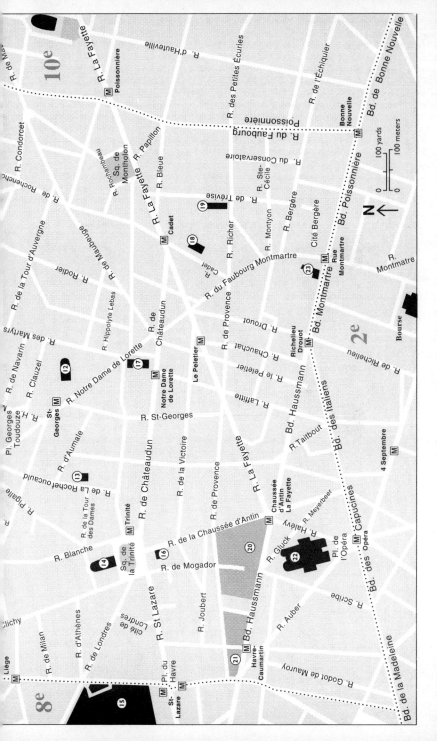

to Sacré Coeur, walk up rue Abbesses, turn right on rue Tholozé, and take rue Lepic through pl. Marcel Ayme to rue Norvins. Follow rue Caulaincourt for a very circuitous route up the hill. The stairs at rue de Mont- Cenis take you almost to the back yard of the basilica.

For the classic approach to Sacré-Coeur, climb up the switchbacked stairs leading up from square Willette (up the disreputable rue Steinkerque from M. Anvers). Though steep, the walk is not difficult. At night, crowds of students and tourists mingle in the square to play guitar, drink wine, and smoke whatever's handy. To the east of the square, **Musée d'Art Naïf Max Fourny** houses its neo-primitivist art collection in a 19th-century iron and glass market pavilion. For a less wearying ascent to the basilica, take the glass-covered funiculaire from the base of the rue Tardieu (from M. Anvers, walk up rue Steinkerque and take a left on rue Tardieu to the very top). This *funiculaire,* reminiscent of a ski lift or a San Francisco cable car, is operated by the metro service and can be used with a normal metro ticket (7F). In 45 seconds, you are miraculously whisked up an impressive 45 degree gradient. Turn around and watch how the city below comes almost immediately and spectacularly into sight.

However you choose to get there, the **Basilique du Sacré-Coeur (Basilica of the Sacred Heart),** 35, rue du Chevalier de la Barre (tel. 42 51 17 02; M. Anvers, Abbesses, or Château-Rouge), is inviting and odd, an exotic headdress or a white meringue, or the head the hill now (like a martyr) carries with it. In 1873, the Assemblée Nationale selected the birthplace of the Commune to build Sacré-Coeur "in witness of repentance and as a symbol of hope." Politician Eugène Spuller called it "a monument to civil war." The basilica was not completed until 1914, after a massive fundraising effort, and not consecrated until 1919. The style is pseudo-Romanesque-cum-Byzantine, a hybrid of onion domes and arches. Its white color sets it apart from the smoky grunge of most Parisian buildings. The church's bleached look is a quirk of the stone used to build it, which secretes white lime when wet. As a result, the parts of the building sheltered from rain are noticeably darker than more exposed ones. The mosaics in the basilica's interior are stunning, especially the ceiling depiction of Christ and the mural of the Passion found to the back of the altar. The gray plaque near the front entrance explains that, through divine intervention, the basilica was spared from destruction when the Germans bombed in 1943. While the building remained intact, its stained-glass windows were shattered and replaced after the war. Climb the 112m bell tower for the highest point in Paris and a view that stretches as far as 50km on clear days. The crypt is open (for a price) and contains a relic of what many believe is a piece of the sacred heart of Christ. (Basilica open daily 7am-11pm; free. Dome and crypt open daily 9am-7pm; in winter 9am-6pm. Admission to dome 15F, reduced tariff 8F; to crypt 10F, reduced tariff 5F.)

As you exit the basilica, turn right on the winding rue du Mont to arrive at **place du Tertre.** Crowded with cafés, restaurants, and portraitists, this is perhaps the city's loveliest spot for a coffee or a photograph. The painters here, often ambitious and skillful youngsters, run off souvenir Parisian landscapes in order to eat. At 21, place du Tertre, the **tourist office** (tel. 42 62 21 21) gives annotated maps (5F) and information about the area (open daily 10am-10pm; Oct.-April daily 10am-7pm). Around the corner, the **Musée Salvador Dalí** has a wonderful collection of the mustachio'd artist's lithographs and sculptures (see Museums).

Moving away from the crowded pl. du Tertre you'll find narrow, winding streets, hidden walled gardens and other whimsical remnants of the old bohemian-pastoral Montmartre. The last vineyard in Montmartre is on rue des Saules. Actually planted in 1933, the vineyard attempts to recreate the Montmartre that once was. At 22, rue des Saules is the **Lapin Agile,** Picasso's main haunt during his years here. In a zany satire of the painter's work, other regulars at the Lapin Agile borrowed the owner's donkey, tied a canvas to its back and a paintbrush to its tail, and produced their own painting. (Later exhibited as the work of an unknown Italian artist, the painting received favorable reviews and fetched a respectable sum when sold.) Overlooking the vineyard, at no. 12, rue Cortot, the **Musée du Vieux Montmartre** presents a scintillating history of the neighborhood, with in-depth information about Montmartre's bloody history during the Prussian siege of Paris (1870) and the short-lived Paris Commune (1871).

Walk down rue de l'Abreuvoir and left on rue Girardon to rue Lepic, which twists past **Moulin Radet,** one of the last remaining windmills on Montmartre. Further down is the **Moulin de la Galette,** depicted by Renoir during one of the frequent dances held there. Van Gogh lived at no. 54, rue Lepic. These days, restaurants, antique stores, and *boulangeries* crowd this corner of Montmartre along the rue des Abbesses, rue des Trois Frères, and rue Lepic. Tall iron gates hide the beautiful gardens of 18th-century townhouses. Follow rue Caulaincourt, below and parallel to rue Lepic, to the landscaped, secluded **Cimetière Montmartre,** 20 av. Rachel (tel. 43 87 64 24; M. La Fourche).Edgar Degas, Alexandre Dumas, Jacques Offenbach, Hector Berlioz, Nijinsky, and Stendhal are all buried here; Emile Zola used to be (his corpse was moved to the Panthéon in 1908). In 1871, this cemetery was the site of huge mass graves from the Siege and Commune (open Mon.-Fri. 8am-6pm, Sat. 8:30am-6pm, Sun. 8am-7pm; Nov. 6-Mar. 15 open until 5:30pm).

Along the bd. de Clichy and bd. de Rochechouart, you'll find many of the cabarets and nightclubs that were the definitive hangouts of the Belle Epoque: the **Moulin Rouge,** for example, immortalized by the paintings of Toulouse-Lautrec and the music of Offenbach. After World War I, Parisian bohemians relocated to the Left Bank; the area around pl. Pigalle (see 9ème) became just another seedy, red-light district. The Moulin Rouge, located at place Blanche, still offers its risqué revues, but at a ridiculously high price. At the turn of the century, Paris' (otherwise respectable) upper bourgeoisie came here to play at being bohemian; today, the crowd consists of (otherwise respectable) tourists out for an evening of sequins, tassles, and glitz (see Entertainment—Cabarets). Pl. Pigalle also has some discos, trendy nightspots for Parisian and foreign youth (see Entertainment—Discos). Other than that, it offers a somewhat uniform diet of peep-shows, prostitutes, and XXX movie theaters. During World War II, American servicemen appropriately called Pigalle "Pigalley." No one should walk around this area alone at night. Farther down bd. de Clichy, at the edge of the 17ème, the **place de Clichy** is filled with popular restaurants and cinemas, but is also a dangerous corner of Paris.

■■■ NINETEENTH ARRONDISSEMENT

The Parc de la Villette (see Museums) is the only major sight in the 19ème, a primarily working-class residential quarter. A host of recent emigrés from Africa, India, and East Asia have settled here, and it is common to see native dress in the streets, or unique combinations of traditional and Western styles. Gentrification a has nonetheless begun, especially around rue Mouzaia, where wealthy Parisians pay handsomely for houses with small gardens.

To the south, the **Parc des Buttes-Chaumont** (M. Buttes-Chaumont) is an engaging mix of man-made topography and transplanted vegetation. Before its construction in the 19th century, however, this area of Paris was an eyesore. From the 13th century until the Revolution it contained a gibbet, an iron cage filled with the rotting corpses of criminals and intended for public display. After the Revolution it was a garbage dump, then a dumping-ground for dead horses. After a stint as a commercial breeding-ground for worms (sold as bait), it became a gypsum quarry, the source of "plaster of Paris."

As a young man, Louis Napoleon lived exiled in England and for the rest of his life waxed nostalgic for Hyde Park. Once emperor, he added four public parks to the greater Parisian area: Bois de Boulogne, the Bois de Vincennes, the Parc Monsouris, and the Parc des Buttes-Chaumont.

Making a park out of this mess took four years and 1000 workers. In order for trees to grow, all of the soil had to be replaced. Furthermore, designer Adolphe Alphand ordered that the heavily quarried remains of a hill be built up with new rock, to create fake cliffs surrounding a lake. Workers made a fake waterfall and a fake cave with fake stalactites. A pioneering suspension bridge leads to a fake Roman temple on top of the mountain. From this little temple, you have a view of the whole park and of the skyscrapers that surround it. The park is well-policed at night (open 7am-11pm; Oct.-April 7am-9pm).

■■■ TWENTIETH ARRONDISSEMENT: BELLEVILLE AND MÉNILMONTANT

As Haussmann's rebuilding expelled many of Paris's workers from the central city, thousands migrated east to Belleville (the northern part of the *arrondissement)* and Ménilmontant (the southern). By the late Second Empire, the $20^{\grave{e}me}$ was known as a "red" *arrondissement,* solidly proletarian and radical. In January 1871, just before the lifting of the siege, members of Belleville's National Guard stormed a prison to demand the release of some leftist political leaders—an omen of the civil war to come. Some of the heaviest fighting during the suppression of the Commune took place in these streets, as the *communards* made desperate last stands on their home turf. Caught between the *Versaillais* troops to the west and the Prussian lines outside the city walls, the Commune fortified the Parc des Buttes-Chaumont and Père-Lachaise cemetery, but soon ran out of ammunition. On May 28, 1871, the *communards* abandoned their last barricade and surrendered.

After the Commune, the $20^{\grave{e}me}$ continued on as the fairly isolated home of those workers who survived the massacres. As historian Eugen Weber observed, "Many a workman's child grew to adolescence before World War I without getting out of Ménilmontant or Belleville." Today, locals freely admit that the only thing to see in the area is Père Lachaise. The neighborhood is fairly safe, but avoid the area around the Belleville metro stop at night.

The **Cimetière Père Lachaise,** bd. de Ménilmontant (tel. 43 70 70 33; M. Père-Lachaise), encloses the decaying remains of Balzac, Colette, Corot, Danton, David, Delacroix, La Fontaine, Haussmann, Molière, and Proust within its winding paths and elaborate sarcophagi. Nor is this, the most illustrious of Parisian cemeteries (named after Louis XIV's confessor), restricted to the French; foreigners inhumed here include Chopin, Jim Morrison, Gertrude Stein, and Oscar Wilde.

The land for Père Lachaise was bought in 1803 by Napoleon's government to create a "modern and hygienic necropolis" that would relieve the overcrowding of city cemeteries. At first, Parisians were reluctant to bury their dead in a site so far from the city. To increase the cemetery's popularity, Napoleon ordered that the remains of a few famous figures be dug up and reburied in Père Lachaise. Thus arrived the remains of Molière, La Fontaine, and several other pre-19th century figures. (Héloïse and Abélard are only rumored to lie here.)

Over one million people have been buried here. Yet there are only 100,000 tombs. The discrepancy is due to the practice of burying the poor in unmarked mass graves; in addition, old corpses are removed from the unmarked plots of the cemetery at regular intervals to make room for new generations of the dead. This process of digging up graves is necessary in a densely populated city like Paris. The 44 hectares of Père Lachaise are filled to bursting, so the government makes room by digging up any grave which has not been visited in a certain number of years. (In other words, if this likely event seems unattractive to the soon-to-be-dead, it's best to hire an official "mourner," much as wealthy patrons used to hire church choirs to sing their masses every year after their death.)

Père Lachaise Cemetery

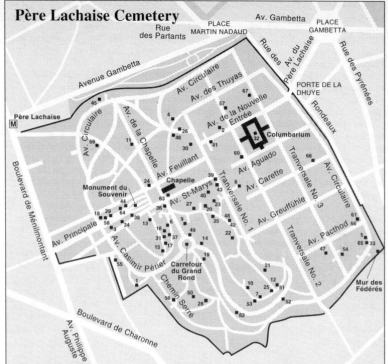

1 Abélard and Héloïse	**32** Isadora Duncan	**61** Gertrude Stein
2 Guillaume Apollinaire	**33** Paul Éluard	**62** Talleyrand
3 Arago	**34** Félix Faure	**63** Adolphe Thiers
4 Honoré de Balzac	**35** Joseph Gay-Lussac	**64** Général Thomas
5 Henri Barbusse	**36** Thédore Gericault	**65** Maurice Thorez
6 Vincenzo Bellini	**37** André Grétry	**66** Alice B. Toklas
7 Beaumarchais	**38** Baron Haussmann	**67** Général Trujillo
8 Sarah Bernhardt	**39** Jean Auguste Ingres	**68** Oscar Wilde
9 C. Bernard	**40** General Junot	
10 Anna Bibesco	**41** Allan Kardec	
11 Georges Bizet	**42** Jean La Fontaine	
12 Caroline Bonaparte	**43** René Lalique	
13 Eduoard Branly	**44** General Lecomte	
14 Jean Champollion	**25** Maréchal Lefebvre	
15 Gustave Charpentier	**25** Maréchal Masséna	
16 Luigi Cherubini	**45** Georges Méliès	
17 Frédéric Chopin	**46** Michelet	
18 Colette	**47** Modigliani	
19 Auguste Comte	**48** Molière	
20 Camille Corot	**49** Monge	
21 David d'Angers	**50** Jim Morrison	
22 Alphonse Daudet	**51** Prince Murat	
23 Honoré Daumier	**52** Nadar	
24 Jacques-Louis David	**53** Maréchal Ney	
25 Maréchal Davout	**54** Edith Piaf	
26 Eugène Delacroix	**55** Camille Pissarro	
27 Gustave Doré	**56** Francis Poulenc	
28 Ferdinand de Lesseps	**57** Marcel Proust	
29 Alfred de Musset	**58** Rossini	
30 Gérard de Nerval	**59** Georges Seurat	
31 Bernardin de St-Pierre	**60** Simone Signoret	

Père Lachaise is the antithesis of the church cemetery; a tribute to this world and not to the next, it's a 19th-century garden party for the dead.Many of the tombs in this landscaped grove try hard to remind visitors of the dead's many worldly accomplishments. The tomb of Géricault wears a bronzed reproduction of *The Raft of the Medusa*; on Chopin's tomb sits his muse Calliope with a lyre in her hand. Recognize Oscar Wilde's by the life-sized, streaking Egyptian figure atop it. The most visited grave is that of **Jim Morrison** (lead singer of The Doors). His fans' graffiti fills the cemetery. In summer, dozens of young people bring flowers, joints, beer, poetry, or general Doors paraphernalia to leave on his tomb. Some take hits, others photographs, but there's a rule against filming Morrison's grave.

How did Jim Morrison and Oscar Wilde end up here? Simply by dying in Paris. Anybody who was born in or who died in Paris has the right to burial in a Parisian cemetery. Because of overcrowding, however, city policy now requires a family to pay a hefty fee for a departed member to be inhumed in a popular cemetery like Père Lachaise. Cheaper, less desirable cemeteries are farther away from the city center. Still, if you're looking for a unique gift for that special someone, a gravesite near a path is only 38,395F, one away from a path only 23,595F. If these prices are beyond your reach, but you still want your remains to be near those of Jim Morrison, your family can rent shelf space for your cremated ashes in the columbarium: 50 years 9000F, 30 years 6000F, 10 years 2000F.

Remembered by inauspicious plaques in the columbarium are Isadora Duncan and Richard Wright, whose monument, hidden behind a stairwell, is hard to find. Fans of his will be disappointed. The columbarium, a landscape of memorials to the cremated, is located beyond the entrance from the place Gambetta. The plaques of Maria Callas and Max Ernst may also be found there. You won't be able to help noticing that many visitors to Père Lachaise have had love, rather than death, on their minds; it's been a popular rendezvous spot, and many happy congresses here are remembered by plenty of incongruous graffiti.

To direct your wanderings, buy a map (10F) of notable graves at any of the flower stores near each entrance to the cemetery.

Père Lachaise's other big pilgrimage site is the **Mur des Fédérés (Wall of the Federals).** Nobody actually hangs out at this small wall (found on the upper right hand corner of the map), but most French people have heard of it and will at least have had a look. In May 1871 a group of *communards* murdered the Archbishop of Paris, who had been taken hostage at the beginning of the Commune. They dragged his mutilated corpse to their stronghold in Père Lachaise, where they tossed it in a ditch. Four days later the victorious *Versaillais* found the body. In retaliation, they lined up 147 *Fédérés* against the eastern wall of the cemetery, shot them, and buried them on the spot. Ironically, Republican Adolphe Thiers shares the cemetery with them; he died of natural causes in 1877. Since 1871, the Mur des Fédérés has been a rallying point for the French Left, which recalls the massacre's anniversary every Pentecost. Near the wall, a number of monuments containing human remains from concentration camps commemorate the victims of the Nazis. (Père Lachaise is open Mon.-Fri. 8am-6pm, Sat. 8:30am-6pm, Sun. and holidays 9am-6pm; Nov.-Mar.15 Mon.-Fri. 8am-5:30pm, Sat., Sun., and holidays 9am-5:30pm. Last entrance 15min. before closing.)

■■■ BOIS DE BOULOGNE

An 846-hectare green canopy at the western edge of Paris, the Bois de Boulogne (M. Porte Maillot, Sablons, Pont de Neuilly, Porte Dauphine, or Porte d'Auteuil) is a popular place for walks, jogs, and picnics. Formerly a royal hunting ground, the Bois was given to the city of Paris by Napoleon III in 1852. The Emperor had become a dilettante landscape-architect during his exile in England and wanted Paris to have something comparable to Hyde Park. Acting on these instructions, Baron Haussmann filled in sand-pits, dug artificial lakes, and cut winding paths through thickly

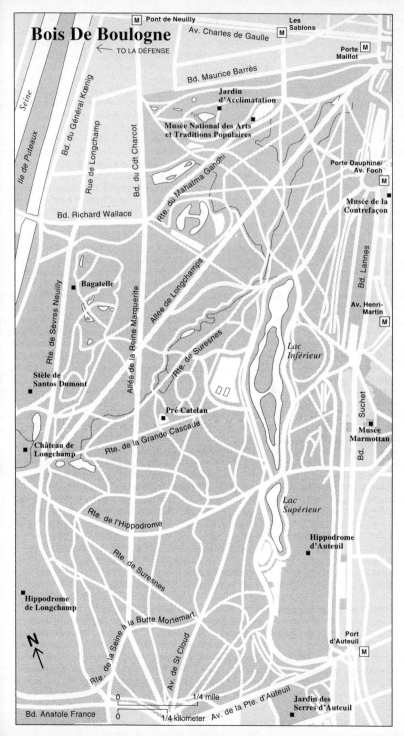

Bois De Boulogne

M Pont de Neuilly

Av. Charles de Gaulle

Les Sablons M

← TO LA DÉFENSE

Porte Maillot M

Bd. Maurice Barrès

Bd. du Général Koenig

Rue de Longchamp

Bd. du Cdt Charcot

Jardin d'Acclimatation ■

Musée National des Arts et Traditions Populaires ■

Rte. du Mahatma Gandhi

Seine

Ile de Puteaux

Porte Dauphine/ Av. Foch M

Bd. Richard Wallace

Musée de la Contrefaçon ■

Bagatelle ■

Allée de Longchamps

Bd. Lannes

Av. Henri-Martin M

Allée de la Reine Marguerite

Rte. de Sèvres Neuilly

Rte. de Suresnes

Lac Inférieur

Stèle de Santos Dumont ■

Suchet

Pré Catelan ■

Musée Marmottan ■

Bd.

Château de Longchamp ■

Rte. de la Grande Cascade

Lac Supérieur

Rte. de l'Hippodrome

Hippodrome d'Auteuil ■

Rte. de Suresnes

Hippodrome de Longchamp ■

Rte. de la Seine à la Butte Mortemart

Av. de St. Cloud

Port d'Auteuil M

N

Bd. Anatole France

0   1/4 mile

0   1/4 kilometer

Av. de la Pte. d'Auteuil

Jardin des Serres d'Auteuil ■

wooded areas. (This attempt to copy nature marked a break with the tradition of French formal gardens, rectilinear hedges and flowerbeds established by Le Nôtre.)

When Paris annexed Auteil in 1860, the park, though outside the city walls, became part of the 16ème. In 1871, it was the site of a massacre of *communards,* as General Gallifet executed the most politically, socially undesirable he could discern among the prisoners bound for Versailles. The hundreds he selected—men with gray hair, with watches, with "intelligent faces"—were shot that night. At the turn of the century, the park became a scenic, fashionable spot for carriage rides. Families of chic road weekly to the park, to spend their "Sunday afternoon in the country" eyeing the finery of their friends from back home.

The Bois de Boulogne contains several stadiums, the most famous of which are hippodromes **Longchamp** and **Auteuil.** During the Belle Epoque, the Grand Prix at Longchamp in June was one of the premier events of the social calendar. Also within the Bois, the **Parc des Princes** hosts soccer matches; the **Stade Roland Garros** is home of the French Open tennis tournament (see Sports). The Bois further consists of several separate parks, and boathouses that rent rowboats. You may also rent faster, more stylish, remote-control boats, from the classic tug to a replica of George Bush's "cigarette" boat.

There are some amusements, however, that the government has tried to discourage. Until a couple of years ago, the Bois by night was a bazaar of sex and drugs, where transvestite prostitutes would stand along the roads, and violent crime was quite common. Since 1991, however, the police have calmed things down considerably, closing the roads at night and stepping up patrols. Nonetheless, it's a bad idea to come here for a moonlight stroll. In 1991, a flood of newly liberated Eastern Europeans visiting Paris camped out in the park, in an odd imitation of the Cossacks who bivouacked here after Waterloo. The lawn-crashers have since been nudged out.

The **Jardin d'Acclimatation** (tel. 40 67 90 82), at the northern end of the Bois (M. Sablons), posts the thrill of a small zoo, a mini-golf course, a carousel, and kiddie motorcycle racetrack. Except for the bumper cars, you must be child-size to use these rides. This eclectic, old-fashioned spot for a family outing also offers pony rides and holds outdoor jazz concerts. (Park open Sept.-July daily 10am-6pm. Ticket office closes 5:15pm. Admission 10F, under 3 free. No dogs allowed; no bikes for kids over 6 years old).

Within the park, the **Musée en Herbe** (tel. 40 67 97 66) is a modern art museum designed for children. Youngsters learn about artists through puzzles and games. Previous shows have featured Chagall and Picasso. The museum also offers a studio workshop; kids made Chagallian kites there during the summer of 1994. (Museum open Sun.-Fri. 10am-6pm, Sat 2-6pm; 15F. Studio sessions during school term Wed. and Sun., during holidays daily. Participation 20F, 60-90 min.) Also within the garden is a participatory theater company for children (shows Oct.-July Wed. and Sat.-Sun.) and a puppet show (Wed., Sat.-Sun., and school holidays 3:15pm and 4:15pm). To get to the park from M. Porte Maillot, go to the big house marked l'Orée du Bois and follow the brown signs that point to the right of the building. Or you can go to the left of the building and take a cute, little train. (Trains run Wed., Sat.-Sun., and public holidays, daily during school vacations, every 10min., 1:30-6pm. 5F, under 3 free.)

Hear pins drop at the **Bowling de Paris** (tel. 40 67 94 00), near the rte. Mahatma Gandhi entrance of the Jardin d'Acclimatation (32F/ game; open 10-2am). On the edge of the garden, the **Musée National des Arts et Traditions Populaires** (tel. 44 17 60 00; M. Sablons) displays exhibits of tools and everyday artifacts illustrating French rural life before the Industrial Revolution. Enter from the Jardin or from rte. Mahatma Gandhi. (Museum open Wed.-Mon. 10am-5pm. 17F, under 25 and over 60 11F, Sun. 11F.)

Pré Catelan is a neatly manicured park supposedly named for a troubador who died in these woods. Arnault Catelan, who rode from Provence to Paris in order to deliver gifts to Philippe le Bel, hired a group of men to protect him on his journey. The men robbed and murdered him in the dead of night, believing that Arnault carried valuable parcels. In fact, Arnault carried only rare perfumes and essences. Authorities later captured the marauders, who, doused in scent, were easily identified. The huge purple beech tree on the park's central lawn is almost 200 years old. You can sit on the grass, except where there are *pelouse interdite* signs. Inside the Pré Catelan, the **Jardin de Shakespeare** (created 1952-53) features plants mentioned by the bard, grouped by play—there is a collection of Scottish highland vegetation in the *Macbeth* area, a Mediterranean section for *The Tempest,* etc. In the center, a lovely open-air theater, the **Théâtre de Verdure du Jardin Shakespeare** (tel. 42 76 47 72), gives popular performances of Shakespeare's plays (in French) in the summer, usually Sat. and Sun. at 4pm (see Entertainment—Theater). The park also hosts marionette shows for children (Mon.-Sat. at 3 and 4pm). Take the metro to Porte Maillot, then take bus #244 to Bagatelle-Pré-Catelan. (Pré Catelan open 10am-6pm. Jardin de Shakespeare open daily 3-30pm and 4:30-5pm; admission 3F, under 10 1F50.)

The **Parc de la Bagatelle** (tel. 40 67 97 00; same bus stop as Pré Catelan) was once a private estate within the Bois; Bagatelle did not become a public park until 1905. The Count of Artois, the future Charles X, built the little Château de la Bagatelle in 64 days in 1777 on a wager with Marie-Antoinette, his sister-in-law. The garden is famous for its June rose exhibition and for its water lilies, which the gardener added in tribute to Monet. It frequently plays host to art exhibits. Do *not* walk on the grass. They really care about this—enough to put up signs in English along with the normal *"pelouses interdites"* (stay off the grass). Guided French tours of the castle at 3, 4, and 5pm (25F) and of the castle and park at 4pm (35F) run from March 15 through October on weekends and public holidays. Meet at the castle. Call 40 71 75 23 to check these times. (Admission to park 6F, ages 6-10 3F. Open Jan. 16-31 9am-5:30pm; Feb. 1-15 and Oct. 16-Nov. 30 9am-6pm; Feb. 16-28 and Oct. 1-15 9am-6:30pm; March 1-15 and Sept. 8:30am-7pm; March 16-April 30 and Aug. 8:30am-7:30pm; May 1-15 8:30am-8pm; May 16-July 31 8:30am-8:30pm; Dec. 1-Jan. 15 9am-5pm. No, we don't know why they made it this complicated.)

The two **artificial lakes** stretching down the eastern edge of the Bois make for a delightful stroll. Come on a weekday to avoid the crowds; come on a weekend to watch them. The manicured islands of the **Lac Inférieur** (M. Porte Dauphine) can be reached by rented rowboat only. (Boathouses open late Feb.-early Nov. Mon.-Fri. 9am-6pm, Sat.-Sun. 9am-7pm. Daily and annual schedules depend on weather; in good weather they rent boats longer, in bad weather they close earlier. Rentals 43F per hr., 400F deposit; with insurance against damage to boat 50F per hr., 200F deposit.)

Dedicated horticulturists may want to stroll through the **Jardin des Serres d'Auteuil** (Greenhouse Garden), full of hothouse flowers and trees (open daily spring-summer 10am-6pm; autumn-winter 10am-5pm; admission 3F). Enter at 1, av. Gordon-Bennet, off bd. d'Auteuil (M. Porte d'Auteuil or Michel Ange Molitor). Free and prettier, though something of a make-out spot, is the neighboring **Jardin des Poètes.** Poems are attached to each flower bed: trip through Ronsard, Corneille, Racine, Baudelaire, and Apollinaire. Rodin's sculpture of Victor Hugo is partially obscured by a thicket. Those bored by preciosity and poems may attend **soccer** or **rugby** matches at the **Parc aux Princes,** one of several stadiums in the Porte d'Auteuil area.

Bicycles, a delightful way to get around the park, can be rented at two locations: across the street from the boathouse at the northern end of the Lac Inférieur and in front of the entrance to the Jardin d'Acclimatation. (Open Mon.-Fri. 1-6:30pm, Sat.-Sun. 9:30am-6pm; Sept.-June Wed. 1-6pm and Sat.-Sun. 9:30am-6pm. 29F per hr., passport or driver's license deposit.)

■■■ BOIS DE VINCENNES

Like the Bois de Boulogne, the Bois de Vincennes (M. Château de Vincennes or Porte Dorée) was once a royal hunting forest, walled in to keep the exotic game from escaping. Since it lay outside the city limits— and thus outside the reach of Parisian authorities— it was also a favorite ground for dueling. Alexandre Dumas, *père* was frustrated here in his duel with a literary collaborator who claimed to have written the *Tour de Nesle*. Dumas's pistol misfired, and the author had to content himself with using the experience as the basis for a scene in *The Corsican Brothers*. Along with its fellow *bois*, the Vincennes forest was given to Paris by Napoleon III, to be transformed into an English-style garden. Not surprisingly, Haussmann oversaw the planning of lakes and pathways. Annexed to a much poorer section of Paris than the Bois de Boulogne, Vincennes was never quite as fashionable or as formal. As one *fin-de-siècle* observer wrote, "At Vincennes, excursionists do not stand on ceremony, and if the weather is sultry, men may be seen lounging in their shirt sleeves, and taking, in other respects, an ease which the inhabitants of the boulevards, who resort to the Bois de Boulogne, would contemplate with horror." Today's *bois*, officially part of the 12ème, is not as swanky or as well-known as the Bois de Boulogne.

The **Parc Zoologique de Paris**, 53, av. de St-Maurice (tel. 44 75 20 10; M. Porte Dorée), on the other hand, is considered the best zoo in France. Unlike their brethren in the Jardin des Plantes, the animals strut around in relatively natural surroundings. While it's still disturbing to see waterbucks prance on hard, dry ground when the sign says their natural habitat is swampy, the zoo has been working hard to improve the animal's environment. The *phoques* (yes, it's pronounced just like you think it is)—seals—are fed with great spectacle daily at 4:30pm. Don't feed the animals. (Open Mon.-Sat. 9am-6pm, Sun. 9am-6:30pm; winter Mon.-Sat. 9am-5pm, Sun. 9am-5:30pm. Ticket office closes ½hr. before zoo. 40F; ages 4-16, students 16-25, and over 60 20F; under 4and disabled free. Wheelchair accessible. Train tour leaves from restaurant: 10F, under 10 8F.)

Joggers, cyclists, and park bench-sitters happily share the turf around **Lac Daumesnil.** There, people dare to sit on the grass. Discover the lake in a rented rowboat. (Boat rental May-Nov. 15 daily 10:30am-5:30pm. 1-2 people 45F/hr., 3-4 people 51F/hr., 50F deposit, plus tip.) Penetrate farther into the park for good running and cycling paths. The **Vélodrome Jacques Anquetil,** the **Hippodrome de Vincennes,** and many other sports facilities lie within the sizable *bois* (see Sports).

The **Château de Vincennes,** on the northern edge of the park, is called "the Versailles of the Middle Ages" (M. Château de Vincennes). French kings held court here as early as the 13th century. Although the Louvre was royalty's principal home, every French monarch from Charles V to Henri IV spent at least part of his time at Vincennes. Charles V built up a true medieval fortress on the site his ancestor Philippe-Auguste chose for a royal hunting residence. Henri III found it a useful refuge during the Wars of Religion, and Mazarin and the court found its defenses useful in the wake of the Fronde. Château lovers will recognize the hand of Louis Le Vau in the buildings farthest from the entry; the Queen's palace and the King's palace, built for Louis XIV, face each other across the courtyard, bounded by an arch-filled wall. In the 18th century, Vincennes became a a country-club prison for well-known enemies of the state. Mirabeau spent 3½ years here, killing time by writing lecherous letters to his (married) mistress. When Diderot was imprisoned in the château; Rousseau walked through the forest to visit him.

In the 19th century, the complex resumed its military functions, serving as fortress, arsenal, and artillery park. In 1917, the infamous Mata Hari, convicted of spying for the Germans, faced a firing squad within its walls. In 1940, the château served as headquarters for General Maurice Gamelin, Supreme Commander of French Land Forces. De Gaulle later criticized Gamelin for holing himself up in the *Thébaïde*—ivory tower—of Vincennes, without even a radio tower to connect him with the front. Today, the Services Historiques des Armées and other military-history institutes are headquartered at the château.

The 52m-high **donjon** (keep) was built between 1360 and 1370; it's a striking piece of medieval architecture and an impressive hideout for any king. The **Sainte-Chapelle** was founded as a church in 1379 but the building was not inaugurated

BOIS DE VINCENNES

Bois De Vincennes

N ←

Fontenny-sous Bois M

Nogent sur Marne M

Jardin Tropical

Av. de la Belle Gabrielle

École d'Horticulture

Joinville le Pont M

ARBORÉTUM

Av. de la Dame Blanche

Av. de Nogent

Lac des Minimes

Rte. Montmart

Rte. de la Ferme

Av. du Tremblay

Stade Pershing

Hippodrone

Fort de Vincennes

PARC FLORAL DE PARIS

Rte. de Pyramide

Rte. Saint Hubert

Rte. du Pesage

Château de Vincennes M

Château de Vincennes

Caserne

Stade Municipal de Vincennes

Rte. Bourbon

1/4 mile

1/4 kilometer

Rte. Dauphine

Rte. de la Demi Lune

Av. de Paris

Allée Royale

Rte. de la Tourelle

Rte. de la Tourelle

Rte. de la Tourelle

Av. Victor Hugo

Av. Daumesnil

Rue de la République

PARC ZOOLOGIQUE

Av. de Gravelle

Bd. Périphérique

Bd. Soult

Musée des Arts Africains et Océaniens

Lac Daumesnil

Centre Bouddhique

Porte Dorée M

Rue de Paris

until 1552. Dainty in its décor and especially beautiful in late afternoon, the Sainte-Chapelle is looking even better these days after restoration of the exterior. (Open daily 9:30am-7pm; Oct.-April 10am-5pm. Guided tours of the Sainte-Chapelle and *donjon* daily at 10:15am, 11am, 11;45am, 1:15pm, 2pm, 2:45pm, 3:30pm, 4:15pm, and 5:15pm are the only way to get inside, but these monuments, stripped down to their bare bones over the centuries, may be more impressive from the outside than from the inside. Tours are in French, with info sheets in English. 26F, students under 26 and seniors 17F.) Survey the archeological digs in the main courtyard. Wander around the ramparts, for a pleasant, if unexciting, view of the surrounding area. If you go on the appropriate day, drop by the **Musée des Chasseurs,** dedicated to the art of hunting (open Wed. 10am-5pm, Sat. 9am-3pm).

One of the gems of the Bois de Vincennes is the **Parc Floral de Paris,** esplanade du Château (tel. 43 43 92 95; M. Château de Vincennes), reached by walking down rue de la Pyramide from the castle. The park has miniature golf and all kinds of games (10 that cost, 60 that don't) for kids. Picnic areas, restaurants, and open-air concerts make it a center of summer entertainment (open daily 9:30am-8pm; shorter winter hours; admission 10F, children 5F).

■■■ LA DÉFENSE

Located just outside the city limits, La Défense is the comic-book city of the future come to life. As the skyscraper's rebuttal to Paris's *hôtels particuliers* and nostalgia for Henri IV, this office complex and beacon of the new world order makes first-time visitors feel like time travelers. Clustered around the Grande Arche (a 35-story office block in the shape of a hollowed cube), shops, galleries, trees, and a sprinkling of sculptures make the pedestrian esplanade a pleasant place for a stroll. The artwork to be found here—by such European notables as Miró, Calder, and César—are for the most part open-air sculptures built to harmonize with the techno theme park that surrounds them. Concrete, steel, and glass are the preferred working materials here for architects and sculptors alike.

La Défense is the current endpoint of the famous *axe historique de Paris* (the historical axis of Paris), also known as the *voie triomphale* (the triumphal way). This magnificent corridor began in 1664 as an extension of the path through the Tuileries garden, designed by Le Nôtre and lined by a gracious row of elms. Le Nôtre wasn't *trying* to make a road through Paris represent the march of history: he just wanted to make it easy for the court to get from the Louvre to the hunting-grounds of St-Germain-en-Laye. In 1772, the construction of the Pont de Neuilly extended the path across the Seine to a hill called the Montagne du Chante-Coq. Back in Paris, the route became more and more elaborate. In 1808, the Louvre end saw the completion of a little arch, the Arc de Triomphe du Carrousel, built to commemorate Napoleon's victories in 1805. Then in 1836, the larger Arc de Triomphe d'Etoile was completed, aligned perfectly with the Arc de Carrousel. Forty years later, planners selected Chante-Coq for a memorial to the defenders of Paris during the Siege of 1870. The resulting statue, called La Défense, gave the area its current name.

The proliferation of office towers in the area began in 1956, as part of a scheme to provide office space for Paris without drastically altering the city center. Not that this growth has been unregulated—since 1958, a government agency known as EPAD has directed the development of La Défense. (Today, La Défense boasts the sleeker-than-thou headquarters of 14 of France's top 20 corporations.) Originally the planners intended to limit buildings to certain heights and styles to create a unified complex. By the late 60s and early 70s, companies were allowed to build distinctive *gratte-ciels* (skyscrapers), "Manhattan-style." But this haphazard building threatened the grandeur of the *axe historique.* La Défense needed something more than a random assortment of office towers if it were to maintain the monumentality of the line stretching down the avenue Charles de Gaulle, the avenue de la Grand Armée, the avenue des Champs Elysées, and the place de la Concorde all the way to the Louvre.

LA DÉFENSE ■ 213

LA DÉFENSE

In 1969, I. M. Pei suggested the first plan for a monument to anchor the end of the axis. French Presidents Pompidou, Giscard d'Estaing, and Mitterrand all sponsored international contests for such a monument, though only Mitterrand acted on the results. Of 424 projects entered, four were presented anonymously to the president, who chose the plan of previously unknown Danish architect Otto von Spreckelsen for its "purity and strength." Spreckelsen backed out of the project before its completion, disheartened by red tape and by his own design, which he deemed a "monument without a soul." Others, however, have celebrated the arch as a "window to the world" whose slight asymmetry gives the empty cube a dash of humanity. Spreckelsen died of cancer in 1987 and never saw its completion.

The **Grande Arche de la Défense,** inaugurated on the French Republic's bicentennial, July 14, 1989, now towers over the metro/RER stop bearing its name. The roof of this unconventional office building covers 2.5 acres—Notre-Dame cathedral could fit in its hollow core. Its walls are covered with white marble that shines blindingly in sunlight. Most of all, its modern design blends into the centuries-old architectural context of the *axe historique,* though, unlike the smaller arches, this one is aligned 6 degrees off the axis. EPAD plans to extend the *axe historique* by developing the area behind the Grande Arche; most work should be done by 1995. As for I. M. Pei, who first proposed a monument at the west end of the *voie triomphale,* he was instead asked to redesign the eastern terminus—the courtyard of the Louvre.

As you approach the Grand Arche and walk around its perimeter, it shifts from a two-dimensional paper-cut-out arch to a three-dimensional cube. An unparalleled view and an entirely modernist aesthetic await at the top. But first go to the **Info Défense booth** (tel. 47 74 84 24), located near the arch in front of the CNIT building. Tickets for the roof are sold at a booth near the elevator shaft. (Open Sun.-Thurs. 9am-8pm, Fri.-Sat. 9am-9pm; roof closes 1 hr. after ticket office. Admission 32F, under 18 25F. Wheelchair accessible.)

Even if you don't want to go to the roof, it's worth climbing the steps of the big white cube and admiring the view of the Arc de Triomphe across the river. Notice, on your left, the odd shape of the **Bull Tower,** which looks as if it's had a piece cut out of it. As you walk down toward Paris, the **CNIT building** is on the left— at only 37 years of age, it's the oldest building in the complex. To the right sits the **Colline de l'Automobile** (tel. 46 92 46 00), a slick showcase for cars past and present. **L'Espace Marques** promotes itself as the "premier permanent auto display in the world." Resist the urge to test drive a Toyota, and head to the adjoining **Musée de l'Automobile**—of interest to anyone who needs a breather from the Minis and Fiats which clog the streets of central Paris. Car-related accessories and 110 vintage *voitures* are gathered here (open daily 10am-7pm; 45F, reduced 35F).

Just a few steps away to the right of L'Espace Marques, the globe-shaped hi-tech cinema **Dôme IMAX** (tel. 46 92 45 45) offers programs in-the-round which compensate for lack of plot, substance, or taste with their immediacy (see Entertainment—Cinema). Upstairs, the Spider cafeteria offers a good lunch deal at 50F, which includes quiche, salad, a *petit pain,* dessert, and coffee (open 10am-4pm).

Near here, plans are underway to construct the **Tour sans fin** (tower without end)—a 400m structure that will be Europe's highest skyscraper. The brightly colored sculpture at pl. de La Défense is by **Joan Miró,** and looks remarkably like one of his anthropomorphic paintings come to life. Across the *place,* **Alexander Calder's** linear, spidery red steel sculpture provides a fitting counterpart. Calder seems to have thought Miró's work resembled a popsicle: when he first saw a model of it, he asked, "Is that good to lick?"

Just past the little lawn in front of you is a white tube called the **galerie art 4** (tel. 46 98 94 98; open Wed.-Mon. noon-7pm; call to find out about temporary exhibits and tours of La Défense, in French only, 20F). To the right, on a high pedestal, is the bronze statue after which La Défense was named (formerly the area was known as Courbevoie). Louis-Ernest Barrias's statue beat 100 other proposals, including one by Auguste Rodin. It was moved while the district was constructed, then returned to its original place in 1983. The name "La Défense," by the way, has engendered some serious confusions: an urban-planning official whose title was "Managing Director of La Défense" was not allowed off a plane in Egypt, because that country did not welcome military personnel during wartime.

To the left of the brightly colored fountain behind the statue, the 1964 Esso building is being replaced by the Coeur-Défense complex, to be completed in 1995. Built in 1964, the Esso building came to be something of an embarrassment for the company, dwarfed as it was by the Fiat and Elf headquarters nearby. Esso executives, mortified that other businessmen had bigger towers, crawled off to Reuil in 1992. The planned Coeur-Défense will provide acres of office space and a modern art museum. A staircase in front of the construction site leads to another art gallery, the **Galerie de l'esplanade** (open for temporary exhibits daily noon-7pm). A tree-lined path takes you the rest of the way to the Esplanade de la Défense *métro* stop. The low buildings on either side are apartment blocks. At the end of the path, the stark steel lamps rising out of water are the work of the Greek artist Takis.

If you want to eat or shop in La Défense, the best place to go is the huge **4 Temps shopping center**—one of the largest shopping malls in Europe. Enter from the Grande Arche *métro* stop, from doors behind the Miró sculpture, or from next to the Colline de l'Automobile. The multilingual information desk on the first floor near the escalator to the *métro* distributes maps of the complex. (Shops open Mon.-Sat. 10am-8pm. Supermarkets—*hypermarchés*—open Mon.-Sat. 9am-10pm.)

To get to La Défense from Paris you can take the metro or RER. Older maps do not show the La Défense metro stop (it opened in 1992). The RER is faster, but the metro is cheaper; La Défense is zone 2 for the metro but zone 3 for the RER. If you do take the RER, buy the more expensive ticket before going through the turnstile. A normal metro ticket may get you into the RER station in Paris, but won't get you out at La Défense.

Museums

Since Charles de Gaulle appointed France's first Minister of Culture in 1956, thousands of hours and millions of francs have been spent shaking the dust off the reputation of the Parisian museum. Paris' national museums are multi-purpose, user-friendly machines shaped by public interest and state funds. Serving as forums for lectures, art films, concerts, and the occasional play, the museums here—most prominently the Louvre, Orsay, and Pompidou—broadcast Paris, past and present.

Catering to an international public, Paris' *grands musées* are mobbed, particularly in summer. Take advantage of evening hours and be forewarned: the Mona Lisa may be obscured by raised cameras and clamoring schoolchildren. If you tire of dangling from chandeliers for a better view, look for Paris' smaller museums, which display specialized collections often comparable in content to wings of their larger cousins. For listings of temporary exhibits, consult the bimonthly *Le Bulletin des Musées et Monuments Historiques,* available at the central tourist office at 127, av. des Champs-Elysées. *Paris Museums and Monuments* not only provides phone numbers, addresses, and hours, but also describes the museums (including wheelchair access) and lists them by *arrondissement. Pariscope* and *l'Officiel des Spectacles* also list museums with hours and temporary exhibits.

Frequent museum-goers may want to invest in a **Carte Musées et Monuments.** This pass covers admission to any of 65 museums in the Paris area *without waiting in line*—an important consideration in summer, when lines to museums can be more than half an hour long. The card is available at all major museums and metro stations (1 day 60F, 3 consecutive days 120F, 5 consecutive days 170F; for more information, call **Association InterMusées,** 25, rue du Renard, 4ème (tel. 44 78 45 81). It saves money only for die-hard museum goers who do not qualify for the omnipresent student, teacher, and senior discounts.

Larger museums often offer group tours in various languages. Prices are typically around 500F for a group of adults, 250F for students and seniors. (Seniors means 60 and over unless otherwise stated.) In the past few years, many of Paris' museums have turned their attention toward a national audience, foregoing regularly scheduled English-language tours for more extensive programs in French. This is particularly the case in smaller museums with major collections. Relatively inexpensive anglophone pamphlets can usually be found at bookstores within these museums.

Galleries are an art lover's quick fix when *en route* to the cinema or a bar. Pick up the indispensable *L'Officiel des Galleries* (35F), a reader-friendly monthly publication available at newsstands and *librairies* (bookstores) in chic areas of town and at the Pompidou bookstore. Inside you'll find comprehensive listings of temporary expositions at both museums and galleries throughout town.

Most of the city's 200 galleries specialize in one type of art, such as naive painting, modern sculpture, prints, or sketches of Parisian scenes. The eighth *arrondissement* is loaded with galleries of a more canonical sort; those near M. Franklin Roosevelt on the Champs-Elysées (av. Matignon, rue du Faubourg St-Honoré, and rue de Miromesnil) focus on Impressionism and post-Impressionism. Thanks to the new opera house, the Bastille area has become a haven for artists and galleries with an *épater-les-bourgeois* (shock-the-bourgeoisie) spin. The highest concentration of galleries is in the Marais; during a casual stroll through the third and fourth *arrondissements* (especially on Rue Quincampoix and Rue des Blancs-Manteaux) you're sure to pass several. The St-Germain-des-Prés (Rue de Seine) area also contains an assembly of small, enticing galleries. Walk right in and don't feel intimidated; you're not necessarily expected to buy. Most galleries are closed Sunday and Monday and are open until 7pm on other days. The galleries that require appointments are not appropriate for casual browsing.

)U LOUVRE

f a medieval castle, constructed by a team of French architects to
ourt, restructured by a 20th-century Socialist politician and a Chi-
hitect, and filled with priceless objects from the tombs of ancient
, the halls of Roman emperors, the studios of French painters, and
churches, the Louvre is an enormous intersection of time, space,
laries. And you thought museums were boring. Just think of how
many thousands of years (5000 years, to be specific), how many millions of lives,
and how many traditions are represented in the Louvre's building and collection.
Even the hordes of visitors add a final impressive touch; just imagine, you may be
the 53-millionth visitor to smile back at the Mona Lisa.

THE BUILDING

Construction of the Louvre began in 1200, and still isn't finished today. King Philippe-Auguste built the original structure to protect Paris while he was away on a crusade. In the 14th century, Charles V extended the city walls beyond what is now the
Jardin des Tuileries, thus stripping the Louvre of its defensive utility. Not one to let a
good castle go to waste, Charles converted the austere fortress into a residential château. Later monarchs avoided the narrow, dank, and rat-infested Louvre, preferring
more modern and more grandiose homes in Paris or on the banks of the Loire. In
1527, however, François I returned to the Louvre in an attempt to flatter the Parisian
bourgeoisie, whom he hoped to distract from their raised taxes. François razed
Charles' palace and commissioned Pierre Lescot to built a new royal palace in the
open style of the Renaissance. All that remains of the old Louvre are its foundations,
unearthed in the early stages of Mitterrand's renovations and displayed in an underground exhibit called "Le Louvre Mediéval" (admission included in museum ticket).

François I started work on the **Cour Carée** (Square Courtyard) in 1546. Except
for its west wall, finished by Louis XIII, the Cour owes its ponderous classicism to
Louis XIV, who hired a domestic trio—Le Vau, Le Brun, and Perrault— to transform
the Louvre into the grandest palace in Europe. Louis eventually abandoned the Louvre in favor of Versailles, and construction did not get past the Cour Carrée.
Through the passage in the Renaissance wing is the **Cour Napoléon,** a larger courtyard conceptualized by Catherine de' Medici and completed by Napoleon III over
200 years later. The two wings stretching into the distance were once connected by
the Palais des Tuileries, a royal residence begun in 1563 to grant Catherine privacy.
Henri IV completed the Tuileries and embarked on what he called the Grand
Design—a project to link the Louvre and the Tuileries with two large wings like the
ones you see today. He only built a fraction of the project before his death in 1610.

With the departure of the court to Versailles, the buildings around the Cour Carrée (the **Sully** wing) fell into disrepair, while indigent artists, prostitutes, and soldiers settled in much of the palace. In 1725, the Academy of Painting inaugurated
annual *salons* in the halls to show the work of its members. For over a century,
French painting would revolve around the *salons,* and, in 1793, the Revolution
made the exhibit permanent, thus creating the first Musée du Louvre.

The museum's fortune took a turn for the better when Napoleon I filled the Louvre with plundered art from all over continental Europe and Egypt. With his defeat
at Waterloo, however, most of this art had to be returned to the countries from
which it had been "borrowed." More durably, Napoleon built the **Arc de Triomphe
du Carrousel,** a copy of the Arch of Septimus Severus in Rome, to commemorate
his victories.

In 1857, Napoleon III finally instituted Henri IV's Grand Design, extending the
Louvre's two wings to the Tuileries palace. In order to give architectural unity to the
newly dubbed Cour Napoléon, Napoleon ordered his architects to redo the façades
of all the older buildings. As a result, the François I wing gained a new façade on its
west side but retained its original design on the Cour Carrée side. Only 14 years after
the completion of the Grand Design, the Tuileries palace was burned to the ground

by the Paris Commune. Ever since, the Louvre's two large wings **(Denon and Richelieu)** reach out to grasp only empty space.

The glass **pyramid** in the middle of the courtyard made its dazzling appearance in 1989. It was the most crucial step in Mitterrand's campaign to turn the Louvre into a museum that welcomes visitors instead of sending them away cursing the French. I.M. Pei, designer of the sleek Hancock Tower in Boston, came up with the idea of moving the museum's entrance to the center of the Cour Napoléon, on an underground level surmounted by a glass pyramid. At first, Pei's proposal met with intense disapproval, and many still lament its stark contrast with the courtyard's Baroque façades. Others consider Pei's pyramid a stroke of genius. An enlarged reception area facilitates welcoming services, and escalators provide ready access to each of the palace's wings. Equipped with a bookstore, a cafeteria, and even an auditorium, this **Halle Napoléon** glows in the sunlight streaming through the glass pyramid, cleaned (at great expense) by robots of its grime and pigeon droppings. Legend has it there are exactly 666 panes of glass on the Pyramid; we haven't counted.

Another pyramid, this one inverted, coifs the newly opened underground shopping center attached to the Hall Napoléon, called the Galerie Le Carrousel du Louvre. There is little for the average traveler in this pricey collection of shops and boutiques (exept maybe theVirgin Megastore). A Mastercard- and Visa-compatible ATM is located on the main floor. The mall is linked to an underground parking lot, and to M. Palais-Royal/Musée du Louvre (link open 8:15am-11pm). It is possible to reach the museum's entrance directly through this underground network.

THE MUSEUM

Because of the recent opening of the **Richelieu (north) wing,** by 1997, curators will have relocated 80% of the museum's collection. Until then, a few galleries will remain closed as paintings are rehung. All of this juggling means that no guidebook can give you an adequate walking tour of the museum. Be sure to pick up an updated map in the entrance hall or take one of the guided tours of the museum. Whatever your visiting pace, consider purchasing *The Guide for the Visitor in a Hurry* (15F), an English-language brochure available in the bookstore of the Hall Napoléon and at booths at the tops of escalators in each museum wing. Otherwise, make frequent use of the free info sheets found in gallery corners. Often overlooked by visitors, they provide intelligent commentary on nearby paintings.

Though best known for its European paintings, the Louvre contains seven departments and also exhibits the building's original medieval foundations on the underground level of the Sully wing. **Oriental Antiquities** has nothing to do with East Asia, and everything to do with Mesopotamia and ancient Iran. Its collection includes the world's oldest legal document, a basalt slab from the 18th century BCE on which is inscribed the code of King Hammurabi—the first written set of laws. The **Egyptian Antiquities** section is stocked with statues of jeweled cats and interesting tools, and keeps several mummies under wraps. **The Greek, Etruscan, and Roman Antiquities** department displays two of the museum's most famous pieces: the *Venus de Milo* and the *Winged Victory (Nike) of Samothrace.* A 2nd-century BC piece copied from a 4th-century BC statue, the *Venus de Milo's* harmonious proportions and sensuous curves became world-famous in the 19th century as the ideal of classical female beauty. *Winged Victory,* standing aloft atop a flight of stairs, was sculpted around 190 BC and represents Nike, Greek goddess of victory.

The **Sculpture** department picks up where the Romans left off, and runs until the 19th century. The undisputed stars of the collection are two of **Michelangelo's** *Slaves,* originally planned for the tomb of Pope Julius II. Michelangelo—a workaholic notorious for sleeping in his boots—said that he attempted to free each of his sculptures from the marble block in which it was imprisoned; his tormented *Slaves* are the physical embodiment of this sentiment.

Napoleon III's lavishly furnished apartments form part of the **Objets d'Art,** a collection of furniture, jewelry, and porcelain located in the Richelieu wing. The

THE MUSEUM

140,000 works, comprising the **Prints and Drawings Collection,** rotate through temporary exhibits held in the Pavillon de Flore.

Paintings

The Louvre's painting collection begins in the Middle Ages and stops in the early 19th century. The collection extends through the entire second floors of the Richelieu and Sully wings, and along the length of the first floor of the Denon wing.

Hieronymous Bosch's small *Ship of Fools,* hidden away in the **Flemish** art galleries, provides a surreal allegory of greed and folly. **Jan Van Eyck's** *Madonna of Chancellor Rolin* is one of the finest products of the late Gothic period—all three figures are rendered with the same attention to naturalistic detail. **Peter Paul Rubens'** many paneled *Medici Cycle* (1621-5), occupies its very own room. Returning from an exile imposed by her son, Louis XIII, Marie de' Medici hired Rubens to retell her personal history to the world (or at least to the treacherous French court).

French works stretch from the Sully end of the Richelieu wing through the entire Sully wing. In a circular room bordering the two wings, **Nicolas Poussin's** *Four Seasons* is the canonical work of French classicism; Poussin would be an important influence on Jacques-Louis David. Nearby portraits of Louis XIV and other notables show the Bourbon kings in high-heeled pumps, skirts, and earrings. The saccharine, adorable Rococo works of **Antoine Watteau, Jean-Honoré Fragonard,** and **François Boucher** delighted courtiers during the Regency and the subsequent reign of Louis XV. Eighteenth-century philosopher-writers like Diderot preferred the scenes of quotidian life by **Jean-Baptiste Greuze.** Greuze disgraced himself when he sought prestige by painting Romans. His clumsily drawn *Septimus Severus* (1769) made him the laughing-stock of the Academy.

Jacques-Louis David (1748-1825) was more successful. No matter how lost you get in the Louvre, you are unlikely to miss the wall-sized canvases of the greatest Neoclassical painter, in the northern first-floor corridor of the Denon wing, along with other large French works from the late 19th century. As a young man, David rejected the Rococo fluff of Boucher (his cousin and one-time instructor), seeking to illustrate moments of classical history in an austere fashion. In 1785, the young artist electrified Paris with the *Oath of the Horatii,* which shows three Roman brothers swearing loyalty to their father, each other, and most of all, the *patria.* Such paintings jibed perfectly with the republican ideals brewing on the eve of the Revolution.

When the Revolution did come, David headed for the thick of it as a prominent member of the Jacobin club. He served the regime with his art, arranging extravagant festivals and replacing the Romans of his earlier pictures with heroes of the Revolution. Arrested in Thermidor, during the Terror that followed the Revolution, he vowed to give up politics. The chastened David mostly gave himself to painting portraits, but he soon fell under the charismatic spell of General Bonaparte, a spell that would culminate in his colossal *Sacre* (Coronation), which depicts in detail the Corsican's self-crowning.

David's followers are well represented. **Antoine-Jean Gros'** portraits of the emperor are even more adoring; look for Napoleon curing a plague victim with a touch of the imperial hand. **Jean-Auguste Ingres,** one of David's students, abandoned his mentor's devotion to classical physiques in favor of a more sensuous line. **Théodore Géricault's** *Raft of the Medusa* (1819) used David's classical physiques and formal composition, but the story it tells is one of disaster and brutality, not moral heroism. After a French frigate ran aground, 150 of its passengers lashed together a raft. Over the next 13 days, the castaways on the raft fought each other with sabers, stole provisions, and, by the third day, resorted to cannibalism. Géricault spent eight months on the painting, keeping his head shaven so he wouldn't be tempted to leave the studio. **Eugène Delacroix** was one of the last French painters to successfully carry off a big canvas showing a heroic action; his *Liberty Leading the People* expresses the heroism of violent uprising. Louis-Philippe thought the painting so dangerous that he immediately bought it and kept it from view for the duration of his reign. Rather than imitating the severe colors and polished drafting of

David, Delacroix founded the Romantic School, with an emphasis on dramatic movement, flashy colors, and swirling lines.

The **Italian Renaissance** collection, in the southern part of the first floor of the Denon wing, is rivalled only by that of the Uffizi in Florence. For paragons of Renaissance portraiture, look to **Raphael's** *Portrait of Balthazar Castiglione* and **Titian's** *Man with a Glove,* a great influence upon Baroque portraitists. Titian's *Fête Champêtre* presents a quietly atmospheric feast of the Gods, later reinterpreted scandalously by Manet's *Déjeuner sur l'Herbe* (see Musée d'Orsay). **Veronese's** gigantic *Wedding Feast at Cana* occupies an entire wall. Recently it was accidentally dropped while being restored; the fall caused a meter-long tear in the canvas. The tear has since been repaired and the painting hangs again, showing off its stunning colors.

The most famous painting among the Italian Renaissance works is also the most famous in the world. **Leonardo da Vinci's Mona Lisa** (or *La Gioconda,* 1503), bought by François I to hang above his bath, smiles mysteriously at millions of guests each year. Actually, she's fortunate to be here at all. Louvre curators discovered her missing one morning in 1911. Guillaume Apollinaire warned his friend Pablo Picasso, who owned two statues stolen from the Louvre, that a search for the *Mona Lisa* might uncover the contraband sculptures. The pair panicked, and at midnight struck out into the darkness with the statues packed into a suitcase, intending to dump them in the Seine. Near the *quais* they suspected they were being followed and decided instead to leave the statues anonymously with a local newspaper. But the police soon tracked down and jailed Apollinaire as a suspect in the *Mona Lisa* heist. After two days of intense questioning, Apollinaire's resolve broke—the loyal friend accused Picasso of stealing the painting. In spite of this treachery, Picasso cleared his name with a convincing plea. Only through the efforts of local artists, who attested to the fine quality of Apollinaire's character, was the poet released. The *Mona Lisa* turned up two years later in the possession of a former Louvre employee, who had snuck it out of the museum under his overcoat, leaving behind only the frame and a fine impression of his left thumb. Unfortunately, the museum recorded only its employees' right thumbprints. The joyful, albeit embarrassed, museum directors returned the smiling lady to her proper place, where she now resides securely within a glass enclosure. Look at the *Mona Lisa*, but don't forget to look at her remarkable neighbors as well. Leonardo's *Virgin of the Rocks* is unquestionably one of his most beautiful paintings, illustrating the rocky landscapes and *sfumato* (smoky) technique for which he is famous.

PRACTICAL INFORMATION

Entrance to the Louvre (tel. 40 20 50 50; M. Palais-Royal/Musée du Louvre) is through the center pyramid, where an escalator descends into the **Hall Napoléon.** Tickets are sold in the Hall. If you are buying full-priced tickets, save time by using coins or a credit card in one of the automatic ticket machines. Pick up an updated map at the circular information desk in the center of the Hall Napoléon.

Visiting the Louvre's gargantuan collection warrants one rule of thumb: don't be too ambitious. Taking in the whole thing in one day is quite impossible. If you can't afford to spend more than one day here, at least take a couple of breaks; your ticket, valid all day, entitles you to leave the museum and come back. To avoid heat and crowds, visit on weekday afternoons or on Mon. and Wed. evenings, when the museum stays open until 9:30pm (only the Richelieu wing stays open Mon. night). Holders of a **Carte Musée** can skip the line by entering the Louvre from the Rivoli entrance (on the passage connecting the Cour Napoléon to the rue de Rivoli.)

There are three places to eat in the Hall Napoléon. Two cafés (sandwiches 25-35F) are located on the upper and main floors. A pricier restaurant is on the main floor. It's best to pack a lunch and picnic in the Louvre courtyard or in the Tuileries.

The Louvre is fully **wheelchair-accessible.** You may borrow a wheelchair for free at the central information desk (passport deposit). The Louvre has begun a series of **workshops for children** in English (selected Mon. and Fri. at 2 and 2:30pm; the information desk in the Hall Napoléon has more info). The **auditorium** in the Hall Napoléon hosts concerts (65-130F), films, lectures, and colloquia (all 25F). For information on lectures and colloquia, call 40 20 51 12. (For films and concerts, see Entertainment.) There is also a small theater in the hall with free one-hour films relating to the museum (every 90 min., from 11am). The **bookstore** sells a wide range of postcards and posters, as well as various guides (open Wed.-Mon. 9:30am-10pm).

Audio-guides, available at the top of both Denon and Sully escalators, describe museum highlights; recorded commentaries on selected works last from 30 seconds to 3 minutes (audio-guide rental 30F; deposit of driver's license, passport, or 500F). To operate these gadgets, enter the three-digit code listed on the sheet you've been handed. This will activate the voice of a friendly, older British gentleman.

English-language **guided tours** leave Mon. and Wed.-Sat. at 10am, 11:30am, 11:30am, 2pm, and 3:30pm (33F, ages 13-18 22F, under 13 free with museum ticket). Buy tickets for tours at the **accueil des groupes** in the Hall Napoléon. Call 40 20 52 09 for more information. You can only reserve spots for morning tours in the morning, for afternoon tours after 1:15pm. Tours fill up quickly. Temporary expositions are housed in the **Hall Napoléon,** the **Pavillon de Flore,** and the **Salle des Etats** (opens at 10am; additional admission 28F, under 18 free; ticket to both regular and temporary expositions 55F before 3pm, 33F after 3pm and on Sun.)

(Museum open Mon. and Wed. 9am-9:30pm and Thurs.-Sun. 9am-5:30pm. Last entry 45 min. before closing, but they start asking people to leave 30 min. before closing. Admission 40F before 3pm, 20F after 3pm and on Sun; free under 18 and for teachers with ITIC cards—see Essentials: Identification.)

■ MUSÉE D'ORSAY

Works by Monet, Degas, Pissarro, and others have established the **Musée d'Orsay,** 1, rue de Bellechasse, 7ème (tel. 40 49 48 14, recorded information tel. 45 49 11 11; RER Musée d'Orsay; M. Solférino), as the "impressionist museum," despite an equally illustrious collection of paintings and sculpture from before and after this period. Covering the period from 1848 to 1914, the museum showcases avant-garde iconoclasts of the 19th-century art world. Devoted to sculpture as well, the museum's collection includes reclining Napoleons and Rodin's *Gates of Hell.* Statues on modest pedestals displayed in the lower-level courtyard meet passing crowds at eye-level. In contrast to the aloof hallways of the Louvre, this is art at its most accessible.

The steel, glass, and stucco Musée d'Orsay is itself a period piece—a former train station built in time for the 1900 Universal Exposition. Victor Laloux's design marries elegance to industry. For several decades, it was the main departure point for southwest-bound trains, but newer trains were too long for its platforms and it closed in 1939. During World War II, the Gare d'Orsay served as the main French repatriation center, receiving thousands of concentration camp survivors.

The current museum has, since its opening in 1986, retained more than the ceiling of its former self. It features the traffic frenzy of any large *gare.* For all its size and complexity, however, Orsay may be the friendliest museum of its size that you'll ever encounter. It's crowded, it's noisy, but it is designed to help you. A specially marked escalator at the far end of the building even ascends to the Impressionist level. A slew of maps and English-language pamphlets covers the information desk, just past the ticket booths. The museum wants visitors to learn a little history, and many a guide book has been compiled for this purpose. The best one is the *Guide to the Musée d'Orsay* by Caroline Mathieu, the museum's curator—more than worth the 110F price. For 15F, you can buy the practical, if rushed, *Guide to the Visitor in a Hurry.* Multilingual **Audioguides** provide analyses of 30 masterpieces throughout the museum. The tape lasts 50 minutes, but you need at least 90 minutes to do the path (28F, driver's license or passport deposit; tapes must be returned by 6pm). (See below for information on guided tours.) Underneath the main staircase, the display "Ouverture sur l'Histoire" offers a historical look at the building through newspapers, photos, and posters.

In addition to the permanent collection, seven temporary exhibitions, called *dossiers,* are dispersed throughout the building.

GROUND FLOOR: FROM CLASSICISM TO PROTO-IMPRESSIONISM

Academic and eclectic painting from the Second Empire adorn the rooms along the right-hand side of the ground floor. *Venus at Paphos* (1852-3) shows the soft, rounded curves, and crisp lines that defined **Ingres'** "Classical" style. In the other corner, representing the "Romantic" school, Eugène Delacroix focused on brilliant colors, swift movement, and dramatic landscapes. More conventional artists—such as Alexandre **Cabanel** with his *Birth of Venus* (1863)—achieved great success by following in Ingres' footsteps. The result, to the eyes of contemporaries like Manet and Courbet, was not only artificial but utterly absurd.

The paintings by Jean-François Millet, Jean-Baptiste-Camille Corot, and Théodore Rousseau illustrate the spirit of the Barbizon school of painting, named for the village on the edge of the Fontainebleau forest to which they retreated in 1849.

Gustave Courbet began a school of Realist painting, rooted in socialist-utopian ideas. His monumental *Burial at Ornans,* displayed in the Salon of 1850-1851, fell flat. His equally grandiose *Allegory of an Artist's Studio* (1855) was refused by the Salon; in defiance Courbet set up a separate "Pavilion of Realism" outside the Salon grounds. The face at the far right is Baudelaire.

For the most controversial of paintings—and the artist whom many consider to be the first modern painter—look to **Edouard Manet.** His *Olympia* (1863) caused an uproarious scandal at the 1865 salon. Manet took the format of Titian's *Venus of Urbino* (1538), the standard for female nudes in Western art, and altered it according to the objective ideals of Realism. As his model, he used a high-salaried prostitute whose compact body, olive skin, and tied-back hair put her as far as possible from the classical standard of female beauty. Viewers objected to Olympia's fuzzy slippers and the ridiculously awake black cat (taking the place of the sleeping dog in Titian's painting). Caricatures of the painting covered the pages of Paris's newspapers and art journals while Manet was met with insults as he walked down the street. Whereas the *Venuses* of both Titian and Cabanel seem entirely passive and vulnerable to the spectator's gaze, *Olympia* stares boldly back, comfortable with her nudity, rebuffing the bourgeois observer who might, after all, be her next client. This was pornography, cried the critics, not art. (Sound familiar?) Manet himself was bewildered by the scandal. The ever-optimistic Baudelaire told him by way of support, "you are only the first in the decrepitude of your art."

UPPER LEVEL: IMPRESSIONISM AND POST-IMPRESSIONISM

Upstairs, the Impressionist celebration begins in earnest. The location is ideal; soft light, filtered through the glass ceiling, illuminates the paintings to highlight the colors and the spontaneity of brushstrokes without producing a glare off the canvases.

Manet's *Déjeuner sur l'Herbe* (Luncheon on the Grass, 1863) caused yet another brouhaha. Once again (actually, two years before *Olympia),* Manet took an icon of Western art, Titian's *Fête Champêtre* (see Louvre), and brought it scandalously into the everyday, contemporary world. *Why,* critics asked, were two perfectly respectable bourgeois gentlemen (the artist's brother and future brother-in-law) picnicking with a nude female? *Déjeuner* was refused by the official Salon and subsequently shown in the famous *"Salon des Refusés"* (Salon of the Rejected), where Manet and contemporary "rejected" artists showed their work independent of the Academy.

Paintings like **Claude Monet's** *Gare St-Lazare* (1877) and **Renoir's** *Le bal du Moulin de la Galette* (1876) capture modern-day Paris—the iron train stations, the huge, crowded boulevards, and balls. Paintings by Alfred Sisley, Camille Pissarro, and Berthe Morisot provide a tranquil expression of daily life, especially in the countryside around Paris. Monet indulged in an almost scientific endeavor to capture the changing effects of light, as in his stunning series on the Rouen cathedral (1892-3).

Edgar Degas represents an alternative side of Impressionism, focusing on lines, patterns, and simple human expressions. His sculptures and paintings of ballet dancers are set not on stage, but in rehearsal or backstage. The dancers in *La classe de danse* (1874) scratch their backs, massage their tense necks, and cross their arms while vaguely listening to the ballet master. Paintings like *l'Absinthe* highlight the loneliness and isolation of life in the city, especially among the female working class.

Pushing on through the museum and through history, you arrive at the Post-Impressionists. Everyone inevitably crowds around **Vincent Van Gogh's** tormented *Portrait of the Artist* (1889). The bold colors and distorted perspective of *The Room of Van Gogh at Arles* (1889) were planned "to be suggestive of repose or of sleep in general." The stunning *Doctor Paul Gachet* and *Eglise d'Auvers-sur-Oise* are two of the last works Van Gogh painted. Meanwhile, **Paul Cézanne** painted his famous still-lifes, portraits, and landscapes, experimenting with the soft colors and broken-down geometric planes that would open the door to cubism.

As you're leaving this area, don't miss the pastels displayed in a special, dim room. Inside, the strange creations of **Odilon Redon** represent a unique strain of mysticism among his more conventional contemporaries. His *Bouquet of Wildflowers* (1912) glows against the brown paper on which it is drawn.

Moving into the north wing, you arrive at the chaos of the late 19th-century avant-garde. Pointillists like **Paul Signac** and **Georges Seurat** strayed from their Impressionist beginnings to a theory of painting based on tiny dots—a proto-version of the TV-screen. **Henri de Toulouse-Lautrec** left his aristocratic family background behind to paint the dancers and prostitutes who alone accepted his physical deformity. **Paul Gauguin's** chef d'oeuvre, *La belle Angèle* (1889) sets the title figure—a Breton peasant woman—in a circle reminiscent of Japanese art.

MIDDLE LEVEL: BELLE EPOQUE AND ART NOUVEAU

After taking you through the ornate Neo-Rococo Salle des Fêtes, once the elegant ballroom of the Hôtel d'Orsay, the middle level displays late 19th-century sculpture, painting, and decorative arts. A display on Salon painting from 1880-1900 shows what was going on in the official world, while Impressionists were gaining their separate victories away from the Academy. (Most of the world's art museums display only the Impressionists and not their traditionalist rivals, depriving viewers of the chance to see why the Impressionists were so revolutionary.) Naturalism that carried an almost photographic realism, as in Jules Bastien-Lapage's *The Hay* (1877), was one of the most favored forms of art under the Third Republic.

Even if you're exhausted, don't miss a walk through the furniture, lamps, and general extravaganza of the whimsical Art Nouveau displays—an elegant exhibit of desks, vases, and sofas with wavy lines and arabesques which sought to give 'function' new prominence in design. Walk forward into the 20th century, with brilliantly colored works by the Nabis artists, as well as paintings by **Henri Matisse** (1861-1954) and **Gustav Klimt** (1862-1918). End your tour with the fascinating "Birth of Cinema" display.

PRACTICAL INFORMATION

The museum is least crowded on Thursday evenings when it is open late (until 9:45pm in summer) or early on Sunday mornings. For a break while you're inside, unwind in the **Café des Hauteurs,** situated artistically behind one of the train station's huge iron clocks. The adjoining balcony offers a beautiful view of the Seine and Right Bank and a concession stand with snacks. Climbing the stairs leads to the **Salle de consultation** (documentation room). Usually uncrowded, the *salle* has books about many of the featured artists and the official guide book on hand for consultation. Remarkable computer terminals provide on-line access to information about any artist or painting, complete with video replica. Downstairs, browse in the

bookstore, which offers reproductions, postcards, and every 19th-century art book imaginable (open Tues.-Wed. and Fri.-Sun. 9:30am-6:30pm; Thurs. 9:30am-9:30pm).

Don't miss a look at the **Restaurant du Palais d'Orsay** on the middle floor. A stylish artifact of the Belle Epoque designed by Gabriel Ferrier (1877-1914), the restaurant offers a view of the Seine, a gilt ceiling, and plenty of chandeliers. Despite appearances, you *can* afford to eat here. *Formule rapide* at 75F provides all-you-can-eat access to the bottomless buffet table and a dessert. (Open Tues.-Sun. 11:30am-2:30pm, Thurs. 7-9:30pm; open Tues.-Sun. as a *salon de thé* 3-5:30pm.)

Guided tours leave from the group reception (Tues.-Sat. 11:30am, Thurs. also at 7pm; in summer additional tour at 2pm; 90min.; 35F). Inquire at the information desk for all details. Tours, normally in French, are available in other languages when arranged in advance. The booklet *Nouvelles du Musée d'Orsay,* free at the information desk, gives details about current tours, conferences, concerts, and exhibits.

(Museum open June 20-Sept. 20 Tues.-Wed. and Fri.-Sun. 9am-6pm, Thurs. 9am-9:45pm; Sept. 21-June19 Tues.-Wed. and Fri.-Sat. 10am-6pm, Thurs. 10am-9:45pm, Sun. 9am-6pm. Last tickets sold 5:15pm, Thurs. 9pm. Admission 35F; ages 18-25, over 60, and all on Sun. 24F; under 18 free. Admission to both permanent collection and temporary exhibits 55F, reduced 38F. Wheelchair accessible.)

■ CENTRE POMPIDOU

Often called the Palais Beaubourg, the Centre National d'Art et de Culture Georges-Pompidou, 4ème (tel. 44 78 12 33; 42 77 11 12 for recorded information in French) has inspired architectural controversy ever since its inauguration in 1977 (M. Rambuteau, Hôtel-de-Ville, or Châtelet-Les Halles. Wheelchair access through the back on rue Beaubourg.) Chosen from 681 competing designs, Richard Rogers and Renzo Piano's shameless building-turned-inside-out bares its circulatory system to all. Piping and ventilation ducts in various colors run up, down, and sideways along the outside (blue for air, green for water, yellow for electricity, red for heating). Framing the building like a cage, huge steel bars support its weight.

The Centre Pompidou attracts more visitors per year than any other museum or monument in France—more than Versailles, and more than the Louvre and the Eiffel Tower combined. Popularity, unfortunately, has taken its architectural toll; renovations set for 1995 will better adapt the museum to its swarming crowds.

The **Musée National d'Art Moderne,** the center's main attraction, houses a rich selection of 20th-century art, from the Fauves and Cubists to Pop and Conceptual Art. The sun and the museum's own harsh track lighting create unappealing glares on some of the artwork. Check you lipstick and move on. This is a state museum, with all of the drawbacks. Curators may be able to fit everything, but not gracefully. Most of the works were contributed by the artists themselves or by their estates; Joan Mirô and Kandinsky's wife number among the museum's founding members.

The entrance to the museum is on the fourth floor, which features the work of seminal modernists Matisse, Dérain, Picasso, Magritte, Braque, and Kandinsky. Three terraces display sculptures by Miró, Tinguely, Ernst, and Calder. The lower level of the museum (which can only be reached by a small escalator from the floor above) houses works from 1960 to the present. In addition to the permanent collections of the Musée National d'Art Moderne, the Centre Pompidou has temporary display areas on the ground floor, the mezzanine and the fifth floor. Museum tours in French Mon. and Wed.-Fri. 4:30pm and 7pm; Sat. 11am, 4:30pm, and 7pm; Sun. 4:30pm. Tours in English Mon. and Wed.-Fri. at 3:30pm. The museum's two gift-shops sell posters and postcards (4-6F), as well as contemporary art journals and books in both French and English. (Museum open Mon. and Wed.-Fri. noon-10pm. Admission 30F, under 26 20F, under 18 free, Sat.-Sun. 10am-2pm free. Buy your ticket on the main floor, since they are not available at the museum entrance; note that tickets do not permit reentry.)

Displaying art is only one of the four functions of the Centre Pompidou. The **Salle Garance,** the Pompidou's cinema, hosts adventurous film series featuring little-known works from all corners of the globe (see Entertainment: Cinema). The **Bibliothèque Publique d'Information,** a free, non-circulating library, is open to anyone who walks in (entrance on the second floor). The **Centre de Création Industrielle (CCI),** studies the relationships between humans, architecture, and technology. Although the resources of the center are closed to the public, its gallery is open to visitors (admission 16F). Finally, the **Institut de la Recherche et de la Coordination Acoustique/Musique (IRCAM),** until recently directed by composer/conductor Pierre Boulez, is an institute of musical research housed next to the Stravinsky fountain (open Mon.-Fri. 9:30am-6pm). Concert repertories fall somewhere between out and way-out, including multi-media events combining film, theater, and contemporary music. Finally, the **atelier des enfants** caters to the very young, with multimedia programs aimed at expanding minds 6 to 12 years old.

While you're there, move up to the fifth floor for coffee or a meal, or simply for the great (free!) view. The Pompidou's restaurant and terraced *salon de thé* offer lunch menus for 58F and 120F respectively.

■ MUSÉE RODIN

The Musée Rodin, 77, rue de Varenne, 7ème (tel. 47 05 01 34; M. Varenne), located both inside and outside the elegant 18th-century Hôtel Biron (see Sights—7ème), highlights the work of France's greatest sculptor. During his lifetime, Auguste Rodin (1840-1917) was among the country's most controversial artists, classified by many as sculpture's Impressionist (Monet was a close friend and admirer). Today, almost all acknowledge him as the father of modern sculpture. Born in a working-class district of Paris, Rodin began study at the Petite Ecole, a trade school, of sorts, for technical drawing. He tried three times to get into the famous Ecole des Beaux-Arts, and failed each time. Frequenting the Louvre to study Classical sculpture, he later worked as an ornamental carver, eventually setting up a small studio of his own. His travels away from Paris allowed him to articulate a definitive, powerful style, completely unlike the flowery academic style then in vogue. One of his first major pieces, *The Age of Bronze* (1875), was so anatomically perfect that he was accused of molding it directly from the body.

The museum houses many of Rodin's better known sculptures in plaster, bronze, and marble, such as *The Hand of God* (1902), which depicts a rough-hewn hand holding a man and woman embracing, and *The Kiss* (1888-98) which portrays a woman kissing her seated lover. But don't just look at the famous sculptures. Take time to appreciate lesser-known but no less powerful pieces on the second floor.

Rodin's training in drawing is evident everywhere: as he said, "my sculpture is but drawing in three dimensions." On the first floor one room is dedicated to a rotating display of drawings and sketches/studies. In addition to temporary exhibits, the museum has several expressive works by Camille Claudel, Rodin's muse, collaborator, and lover. Her *Chatterers* shows a scene in which even the benches on which the figures are seated lean in to hear the gossip.

The *hôtel*'s expansive garden is a museum unto itself. Flowers, trees, and fountains frame outdoor sculptures. If you're short on time or money, consider paying the smaller admission fee for the grounds only. You won't miss the collection's stars: just inside the gates sits Rodin's most famous work, *The Thinker* (1880-1904).

Balzac (1891-1897), behind *The Thinker*, was commissioned in 1891 by the Société des Gens de Lettres, but a battle over Rodin's design and his inability to meet their deadlines raged for years. (At one point the Société demanded, rather ridiculously, that Rodin deliver the statue within 24 hours.) Unlike the portrait the Société expected, the finished product shows a dramatic, haunted artist with hollow eyes. The plasticity of the body and the distortion of the author's well-known face enraged countless artists and non-artists. Rodin cancelled the commission and kept the statue for himself, claiming proudly, "I have the formal wish to remain the sole owner of my work." Later in his life, he noted, "Nothing which I made satisfied me as much, because nothing had cost me as much; nothing else sums up so profoundly that which I believe to be the secret law of my art." On the other side of the garden, a cast of the stunning *Burghers of Calais* (1884-1895) somberly recreates a moment in the Hundred Years War. Beyond stands one version of Rodin's largest and most intricate sculpture, *The Gates of Hell* (1880-90) (another towers inside the Musée d'Orsay).

A small **café** is tucked away in a leafy and shaded part of the garden to the right as you enter the gardens behind the Hôtel Biron. The café, a superb place for lunch, offers an extensive salad bar (30F), desserts (7-20F), and a daily 50F *menu*.

Temporary exhibits are housed in the chapel (to your right as you enter). Entrance is included in the price of admission to the museum. (Museum open Tues.-Sun. 10am-5:45pm; Oct.-March Tues.-Sun. 10am-5pm. Last admission 30 min. before closing. Admission 26F; students, seniors, and under 18 17F; admission to park alone 4F. Cafeteria open same hours, but April-Oct. only.) Persons who are blind or visually-impaired may get permission to touch the sculptures, but they must obtain an okay before they begin their visit.

For more on Rodin and his sculpture, go out to the smaller **Musée Rodin,** 19, av. Auguste Rodin (tel. 45 34 13 09), in Meudon. The "country" house where Rodin spent the final years of his life now contains most of his minor works and the plaster models for *The Thinker, The Gates of Hell,* and his other major bronze casts. In the garden, *The Thinker* sits contemplatively above the tombs of Rodin and his wife, Rose Beurat, whom he married the year of her death—after 53 years of cohabitation. (Open Sat.-Sun. 1:30-6pm. Admission 9F, students 5F.) Take RER line C to Meudon-val-Fleury. Be sure to take a train that stops at all stations; some express trains zoom right by. When you exit the train station, take your first right, then your next right onto av. A. Rodin. The museum is on the left-hand side (15min. walk). Or take bus #192 (direction: Hôpital Percy). Ask the driver to let you off at the museum.

■ THE INVALIDES MUSEUMS

The Invalides complex guards a series of museums, revolving around French history and above all, France's martial glory (M. Invalides; also see Sights—7*ème*).

Lying under the massive gilded dome constructed by Jules Hardouin-Mansart is **Napoleon's Tomb.** Six chapels dedicated to different saints lie off the main room, sheltering the tombs of famous French Marshals. Finished in 1861, Napoleon's tomb actually consists of six concentric coffins, made of materials ranging from mahogany to lead. The tomb is placed on the lower level and viewed first from a round balcony above, forcing everyone who visits to bow down to the emperor even in his death. This delighted Adolf Hitler on his visit to Paris in 1940. Names of significant battles are engraved in the marble surrounding the coffins—note Waterloo's absence. Ten bas-reliefs recall the institutional reforms of law, education, and the like under Napoleon, who is depicted wearing that most typical of French attire: a toga and laurels. The Roi de Rome, Napoleon's son, is buried at his feet. Bring a 5F coin to the Tomb for a 5-minute recorded explanation in English. (Tomb open daily 10am-7pm; Oct.-March 10am-5pm; April-Dec. 10am-6pm. Admission 34F; students, seniors, and under 18 24F; under 7 free. Ticket, valid for 2 days, permits entry to the Musée de l'Armée, Musée des Plans-Relief, and the Musée de l'Ordre de La Libération.)

More war trophies are housed inside the **Musée de l'Armée** (tel. 44 42 37 72 or 44 42 37 64), which celebrates centuries of French military history. The museum is housed in two wings on opposite sides of the Invalides' cobblestoned main court-yard, the Cour d'Honneur. The East Wing houses war paraphernalia from the 17th, 18th, and 19th centuries and culminates in the First Empire exhibit on the second floor, with a special focus on Napoleon. The west side's 20th-century exhibits revolve around Charles de Gaulle. Electronic maps trace troop movements during the First and Second World Wars. The General's *képi* and letters join an elaborate model of one of the D-Day beaches. The incongruity of peppy martial music floating over numerous swastikas and pictures of work camps can be nauseating.

Escape by going upstairs to the temporary location of the **Musée des Plans-Reliefs** (tel. 45 51 95 05), a collection of a hundred models of fortified cities. Spanning the period from 1668 to 1870, the exhibit is one-of-a-kind, of interest to architects and urban planners. Most of the descriptions in the museum are in French. Pick up the English brochure (free) at the coat room on the ground floor of the East Wing. (Museum open daily 10am-6pm; Oct.-March 10am-5pm. Admission included in price for Napoleon's Tomb. No wheelchair access.)

Independent from its warring neighbors, but housed in a gallery off the Invalides' Cour d'Honneur, is the **Musée de l'Histoire Contemporaine** (tel. 44 42 54 91). M. et Mme. Henri Leblanc decided in 1914 to create a library and museum to hold documents about the history of the unfolding world war. The three-room museum mounts two temporary exhibits per year (March-June and Oct.-Dec.), using posters, magazines, pictures, and other documents from the library to probe recent history. Most of the posters and all of the labels are in French, but the visual nature of the exhibits helps transcend the language barrier, as does the enthusiasm of the staff. "Images et Colonies," an exhibition on the nature, discourse, and iconography of African representation and French colonialism from 1920 to Independence opened in October of 1993. An exhibit on the Dreyfus Affair will open in March of 1994. (Open March-June and Oct.-Dec. Tues.-Sat. 10am-1pm and 2-5:30pm, Sun. 2-5:30pm. Admission 20F, students and seniors 10F.)

One of the least celebrated but most worthwhile parts of the Invalides is the **Musée de l'Ordre de la Libération,** 51bis, bd. de Latour-Maubourg (tel. 47 05 04 10). Quiet and uncrowded, the museum tells the story of those who fought for the liberation of France. A diverse collection of Charles de Gaulle-related paraphernalia is complemented by tributes to the fighters of Free France. The staircase and upstairs gallery, dealing with deportation, present by far the most devastating message. *"N'oubliez jamais!"* (Never forget) cries the newspaper article next to the heartbreaking picture of a five-year-old girl in concentration camp uniform. The exhibit juxtaposes forbidden journals and prisoner drawings with camp uniforms and instruments of torture, in an attempt to capture the mental and physical horror endured by so many. Though the museum is housed in the Invalides complex, it is independent; you cannot gain access to it from the Cour d'Honneur, but must exit and walk around to the bd. de Latour-Maubourg (open same hours as the Musées de l'Armée and des Plans-Reliefs).

■ MUSÉE DE CLUNY

The **Hôtel de Cluny,** 6, pl. Paul-Painlevé, 5ème (tel. 43 25 62 00; M. Cluny-Sorbonne), not only houses one of the world's finest collections of medieval art, jewelry, and tapestries, but is itself a perfectly preserved medieval manor, built on top of Roman ruins. One of the three Roman baths in the Paris area, the *thermae* and their surroundings were purchased by the Abbot of Cluny, who then built his own residence upon them. Excavations begun after World War II unearthed what remains of the baths, which have since been re-incorporated into the layout of the building. Visitors may now pass through the flamboyant Gothic museum entry, replete with pointed arches and a cobblestone courtyard, into a time when Paris was not Paris but Lutèce, the Gallo-Roman city that emerged here in the first century AD. Most of the building actually dates from the 1480s and 90s, when it was built for the Order of Cluny, a religious order then led by the powerful Amboise family, whose fondness for Italian forms is evident in their home. In 1843 the state converted the *hôtel* into the National Museum of the Middle Ages.

The best-preserved room of this ancient health club is the *frigidarium*, where third-century Gauls gathered to take cold showers. First they worked out in the *palestre*, then took a hot bath in the *caldarium* and a cold one in the *frigidarium*. The shock of this transition was eased by a dip in the *tepidarium*, or lukewarm bath. Only the *frigidarium* and swimming pool remain intact and open to visitors (see room XII on the ground floor). Call the museum for details about guided tours of the hallways and rooms that comprise the rest of the *thermae*.

The museum houses one of Europe's most impressive collections of tapestries, most of which come from northern France and date from the 15th and 16th centuries. Particularly ornate are those of the *mille-fleurs* (thousand flower) variety, so named because of the incredible variety of plants and flowers that adorn the background . (This pattern may derive from the old practice of sprinkling flowers on the floor at festivals.) The masterpiece of the collection, a series of six panels entitled **La Dame et la Licorne** (The Lady and the Unicorn—all tapestries center upon a lady, a unicorn, and a lion), is generally considered to be the best surviving medieval tapestry series. Each of the first five represents one of the five senses. The purpose of the last one, *A mon seul désir,* has been a source of controversy throughout the 150 years of this series' public display. It pictures a lady holding a necklace near a box carried by her servant. Is she about to put the necklace on or to put it away? George Sand was the first to suggest that the tapestries had been woven as a gift of love. She believed them to be the present of a captured Muslim prince to his beloved. Scholars have traced them instead to Jean le Viste, a merchant whose coat of arms (three crescents) appears throughout the series. Nonetheless, many still believe that *A mon seul désir* was indeed a gift of love. Others hold with equal conviction that the tapestry shows the lady removing her necklace and locking it away, symbolically rejecting the material, sensual world of the previous five tapestries. In this interpretation, *"A mon seul désir"* would mean "by my own volition," indicating her wish to abandon the world of the senses and to retreat into spiritual hermeticism.

Downstairs, Room VI glows with colored light from its eye-level display of medieval stained glass, which includes some of the original windows that once adorned Ste-Chapelle, as well as a selection of those from the cathedrals at Rouen and St-Denis. Down the hall in Room VIII, the **Galerie des Rois** displays a set of 21 stone heads of Judean and Israelite kings, dating from 1210 to 1230. These heads (once attached to bodies) sat atop Notre-Dame's portals until 1793 when Revolutionaries, itching to decapitate royalty, mistook them for statues of French kings and severed them from their bodies. Discovered in a Parisian backyard in 1977, the heads still bear faint traces of their original paint. Upstairs an entire room (Room XVI) is devoted to medieval royal jewelry and crowns. The gold rush continues down the corridor with an enormously rare and valuable gold altarpiece from Basel, Switzerland (Room XIX).

Museum open Wed.-Mon. 9:15am-5:45pm. Admission 27F; under 25, over 60 and Sun. 18F; under 18 free. The museum also sponsors chamber music concerts performed on Renaissance and Baroque instruments. Concerts are held Fri. at 12:30pm and Sat. at 4pm—call ahead to confirm times. 52F (33F for students and seniors; 15F for those under 18) with admission to the museum. Evening concerts are also held; call FNAC (see Entertainment) or stop by the museum for a schedule. Tickets are 100F; 70F for students, senior citizens, and people with same-day Cluny Museum ticket stubs.

■ LA VILLETTE

La Villette, 19ème (M. Porte de la Villette or Porte de Pantin), is a highly successful urban renewal project in the northeastern corner of Paris that proves once and for all that the French have a talent for taking the scientific and making it approachable and fun. Its 55 hectares enclose a huge science museum, a landscaped park, an Omnimax cinema, a conservatory, an exhibition hall, and a concert arena. The area had previously been home to a nationalized meat market-*cum*-slaughterhouse compound that provided most of Paris' beef. With the advent of refrigerated transport in 1969, it became more economical to kill cattle in the countryside and deliver the meat directly to butchers; the government closed down the La Villette meat center in 1974. In 1979, plans began for the new, modern La Villette.

The **Cité des Sciences et de l'Industrie** (tel. 40 05 80 00) perches on the northern end of La Villette, next to the Porte de la Villette *métro* stop. Inaugurated in 1985, this establishment is dedicated to making science more accessible to lay people. The star attraction, located on the top two stories, is the **Explora** science museum: even when you know the scientific principles behind a particular display, you'll be surprised by the ingenious way it is presented. There are quite a few English translations throughout the museum. The Cité-Pass ticket allows you to enter the **planetarium** (2nd floor) as well as temporary exhibitions, the 3-D movies in the Cinéma Louis-Lumière (floor 0), and the modest aquarium (floor S2). Floor S1 houses the *médiathèque*—a multimedia, open-stack library with more than 300,000 scientific and technical works.

If you're traveling with children, you may wish to leave them in the care of the Cité's innovative **children's programs.** The Inventorium (for ages 3-6) costs 20F for a 90-minute session (free for 1 or 2 accompanying adults per family). The Cité des Enfants (ages 5-12) costs 20F for a 90-minute session (no adults admitted). They also offer hands-on classes that delve deeper into scientific concepts (90 min., 30F). All programs are in French, but because of their dependence on all the senses not just that of hearing, are suitable for kids of all languages. Or take the kids with you to the Explora museum; many exhibits will fascinate the whole family. The *vestiare* (level 0) rents strollers and wheelchairs; the entire Cité is wheelchair-accessible. To guide you around the Cité and La Géode (below), headsets with English commentaries on each major attraction (including the architecture) can be rented in the Cité on Level 0 for 15F (museum open Tues.-Sun. 10am-6pm; *Médiathèque* open Tues.-Sun. noon-8pm).

La Géode (tel. 36 68 29 30 for general info and reservations) the huge mirrored sphere mounted on a water basin in front of the Cité des Sciences, will remind you of an enormous extraterrestrial golf ball caught in a tiny water trap. The exterior is coated with 6433 polished stainless-steel triangles, which reflect every detail of their surroundings. Inside, Omnimax movies are shown on a 1000 square-meter hemispheric screen, "the largest in the world" (or so they say). Come here for exciting 3-D documentaries on such topics as Niagara Falls or volcanoes. (Showings Tues.-Sun. on the hour 10am-9pm. Also Mon. during French school holidays; last showing 6pm. Reserve tickets early; they sell out anywhere from 2 months to 3days ahead of time depending on the show.)

Between the Canal St-Denis and the west side of the Cité is a little marvel called the **Cinaxe** (tel. 42 09 34 00). Watch one of several 10-minute movies representing what you would see if you were in a Formula 1 car, in a rocket, or in an airplane flying low over mountains, while sophisticated hydraulic pumps jerk and spin the movie theater, so that you feel the curves and bumps as you see them. (Open Tues.-Sun. 11am-7pm; shows every 20min. Forbidden to those under 6; not recommended for pregnant women or people with heart disorders.)

A one-day "Cité-Pass" covers entrance to all exhibits of the museum, including the planetarium and the *Argonaute* (passes 45F, under 25 35F, under 7 free; tickets to *Argonaute* only 25F, ages 3-7 free). Buy tickets for Géode shows at the Géode entrance (55F, students and under 18 40F; no reduced-price tickets 1-6pm weekends or holidays. Cinaxe tickets 32F, students and under 18 29F; combined tickets: Géode, museum, and Cinaxe 119F, *tarif réduit* 104F; Géode and museum 90F, *tarif réduit* 75F); Géode and Cinaxe 84F, *tarif réduit* 69F).

At the opposite end of La Villette from the Cité des Sciences is the **Cité de la Musique** (tel. 44 84 45 00; M. Porte de Pantin). By January 1996 the whole project will be completed—featuring a concert hall, housing for music students, and a museum displaying 4500 musical instruments from the 16th century to the present. Free concerts and theatrical performances are given regularly.

The **Parc de la Villette** is a vast open area separating the two Cités, cut in the middle by the Canal de l'Ourcq and bordering the Canal St-Denis. Bernard Tschumi, the park's designer, rejected the 19th-century notion of a park as an oasis of nature, attempting instead to achieve a 20th-century urban park, "based on cultural

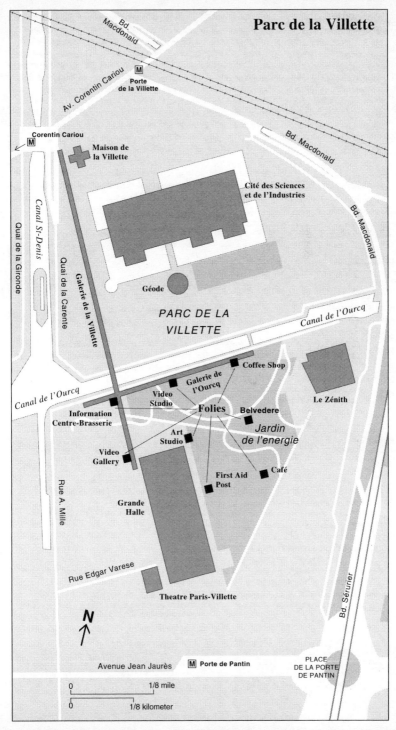

Parc de la Villette

invention, education, and entertainment." Unifying this space, a set of roughly cubical red metal structures form a grid of squares 120m x 120m. Known as *folies,* they serve a variety of purposes. One houses a fast-food restaurant, three are day-care centers, and one, right on Canal l'Ourcq, next to the Canal St-Denis, is an **information office** (open daily 10am-7pm). Also in the park, the steel-and-glass **Grande Halle** (tel. 40 03 75 75), constructed in 1867 as the La Villette beef building, has become a cultural Jack-of-All-Trades, with frequent plays, concerts, temporary exhibitions, and films. Next to the Canal de l'Ourcq is the **Zénith** (tel. 42 40 60 00 or 42 08 60 00), a concert hall whose high-tech acoustics and 6400-person capacity make it a favorite among such artists as Tina Turner, Ziggy Marley, and Sting.

Finally, the park encompasses a number of thematic **gardens,** which you are likely to miss unless you follow the winding path known as the *promenade cinématique* (the map in the information office helps). Of particular interest, the Mirror Garden uses an array of mirrors to create optical illusions, while the Garden of Childhood Fears takes you through a little wooded grove resonant with spooky sounds. At night the *promenade cinématique* is lit up, and makes for an interesting walk (reasonably safe, too, because the park has plenty of security guards).

■ OTHER MAJOR ART COLLECTIONS

Musée Marmottan, 2, rue Louis-Boilly, 16ème (tel. 42 24 07 02). M. La Muette. Collector Jules Marmottan purchased this hunting lodge in 1882. His son Paul, fascinated by the art of the Napoleonic era, bequeathed the building with his collection to the Académie des Beaux-Arts. Later, Michel Monet added 65 of his father's paintings, many from the later years at Giverny, to the museum's existing Impressionist collection. Altogether, the 100 Impressionist canvases include some stunning works, including Monet's *Impression: soleil levant (Impression: Sunrise).* Displayed in 1874 with eight other paintings, it led one critic to refer derisively to "those *impressionistes*", an epithet Monet and his colleagues enthusiastically embraced. Stolen in 1985, the painting was recently recovered in Corsica. The Wildenstein room of medieval illuminations is also beautiful. Open Tues.-Sun. 10am-5pm. 35F, *tarif réduit* 15F.

Musée National des Arts Asiatiques (Musée Guimet), 6, pl. d'Iéna, 16ème (tel. 47 23 61 65). M. Iéna. The largest collection of Asian art in the West and one of the best organized and most peaceful in the 16ème. Statues of Buddha, Jina, and Vishnu welcome visitors. Admire the detail of the 19th-century teak model of a Burmese monastery and the breadth of the Khmer art collection. *Midi l'Asie* (Asia Noon) is an informative lecture series (in French) focusing on aspects of Asian culture. Open Wed.-Mon. 9:45am-6pm. 27F, students, seniors, and Sun. 18F. Admission to temporary exhibits (35F; students, seniors, and Sun. 26F) grants admission to everything. Inquire about group visits, workshops, and concerts. A few steps away is the Musée Guimet's annex, the **Hôtel Heidelbach-Guimet,** 19, av. d'Iéna. The *hôtel,* surrounding a Japanese garden, contains Buddhist pieces from China and Japan, some 14 centuries old. Open same hours as Musée Guimet. Admission to one assures free entry to the other. Both museums are wheelchair-accessible, but call ahead.

Musée d'Art Moderne de la Ville de Paris, 11, av. du Président Wilson, 16ème (tel. 47 23 61 27). M. Iéna. One of the world's foremost collections of 20th-century art. Permanent exhibit includes works by Matisse (*The Dance*) and Picasso (*The Jester*) while temporary displays vary dramatically in topic and scope. Offers little in the way of explanatory documentation and, thus, may not be the best place for those unfamiliar with modern art. Nonetheless, a visit may proffer rewarding discoveries, whether your tastes lean to 7-foot pictures of Diana Ross or to Laurencin and Modigliani. Open Tues.-Fri. 10am-5:30pm, Sat.-Sun. 10am-7pm. Admission to permanent collection and exhibits 40F, reduced tariff 30F .

Musée de l'Orangerie, 1er (tel. 42 97 48 16). M. Concorde. A small collection of Impressionist paintings nestled in the southwest corner of the Tuileries. Though less spectacular than Orsay, this museum is also less crowded, so you can admire the Cézannes, Renoirs, Matisses, Picassos, and other greats in comfort. Claude

Monet's *Les Nymphéas* (The Water Lilies) occupies 2 rooms of the underground level. Each is paneled with 4 large curved murals that were created for these chambers. It was on the day of the Armistice that Monet decided to give to France, like a bouquet of flowers, these paintings of the lilies in his garden at Giverny. He spent the rest of his life working on them, finishing in the year of his death (1926). The museum also hosts temporary exhibitions. Open Wed.-Mon. 9:45am-5:15pm. 26F; ages 18-25, over 60, and Sun. 14F.

■ FROM ART AFRICAIN TO ZADKINE

Musée des Arts Africains et Océaniens, 293, av. Dumesnil, 12ème (tel. 43 43 14 54), on the western edge of the Bois de Vincennes. M. Porte Dorée. A stunning collection of several millennia of African and Pacific art. Highlights include the immense, breathtaking display of African statues and masks, and jewelry and wedding dresses from the Maghreb (Morocco, Tunisia, and Algeria). Built for the 1931 Colonial Exposition, the museum building still contains its original Eurocentric murals and friezes. Families and young school children crowd downstairs to the the tropical fish aquarium; the crocodile room is a perennial favorite. Open Mon. and Wed.-Fri. 10am-noon and 1:30-5:20pm, Sat.-Sun. 12:30-5:50pm. Last entry 30 min. before closing. Aquarium and temporary exhibits open Mon. and Wed.-Fri. 10am-noon and 1:30-5:20pm, Sat.-Sun. 10am-5:50pm. Admission to aquarium, permanent collection, and exhibits 27F, students and seniors 18F, under 18 free.

Musée des Arts Décoratifs, 107, rue de Rivoli, 1er (tel. 42 60 32 14). M. Palais-Royal. Enter through a side door of the Louvre building. Tapestries, china, paintings, and furniture from the late Middle Ages to the avant-garde fill 5 stories. Come here for the true meaning of "changing fashions." 25F, under 25 16F, under 5 free. Open Wed.-Sat. 12:30-6pm, Sun. noon-6pm.

Musée d'Art Juif, 42, rue des Saules, 18ème (tel. 42 57 84 15). M. Lamarck-Caulaincourt. Housed on the 3rd floor of the Jewish Center. Founded after the war, the collection includes objects used during Jewish rituals, pictures and models of synagogues, as well as an enormous model of Jerusalem. The library displays a variety of beautifully illustrated Jewish texts and a collection of works by popular artists from North Africa and Eastern Europe. Open Sun.-Thurs. 3-6pm. Closed on Jewish holidays. 30F, students and groups 20F, children 10F. Open Sept.-July.

Cristalleries Baccarat, 30-32, rue de Paradis, 10ème (tel. 47 70 64 30). M. Gare de l'Est. The impressive building, built under the Directory between 1798 and 1799, houses both the Baccarat crystal company headquarters and the Baccarat museum. Since its founding in 1764, Baccarat has become one of the most prestigious and expensive of crystal makers, patronized by kings, czars, and shahs. The museum houses an array of every imaginable crystal object, including a life-size chandelier-woman at the entrance. With exquisite vases, goblets, and sculptures reflected in mirrored tables, the display looks like an ice palace. Open Mon.-Fri. 9am-6pm and Sat. 10am-noon and 2pm-5pm. Free.

Maison de Balzac, 47, rue Raynouard, 16ème (tel. 42 24 56 38). M. Passy. If you don't have a shrine to Balzac yourself, you may not be interested in visiting this one. Honoré de Balzac (1799-1850), one of France's greatest novelists, lived in this house (1840-1847) while finishing *La comédie humaine.* Goods and chattel located here include the author's desk and a mural outlining the genealogy of every character in *La comédie humaine.* Without an audio-guide (15F) or textual guide (25F) don't even bother. Open Tues.-Sun. 10am-5:40pm. 17F50, students 9F, seniors free. Temporary exhibits vary in admission fee.

Musée Henri Bouchard, 25, rue de l'Yvette, 16ème (tel. 46 47 63 46). M. Jasmin. The cluttered workshop of Henri Bouchard (1875-1960), sculptor of the Palais de Chaillot's bronze Apollo, illustrates not only his range of media (copper, plaster, clay, stone) and subjects (monuments, religious decoration, portraits), but also the complexity of his technique. Temporary 3-month exhibits in the front hall. Bouchard's son (who speaks English) and daughter-in-law are knowledgable curators. On each month's first Sat. at 3pm, Mme. Bouchard guides a tour (free with admission). Open July-Sept. 15, Oct.-Dec. 15, Jan. 2-March 15, and April-June 15 Wed. and Sat. 2-5pm. 15F. Call about lectures on sculpting technique.

Musée Bourdelle, 18, rue Antoine Bourdelle, 15ème (tel. 45 48 67 27). M. Falguière. People who don't appreciate the raw aggressive style of Antoine Bourdelle (1861-1929) will become fans after spending the afternoon wandering his studio-turned-museum. Room after room packed with statues overwhelms the casual visitor with the sheer productivity and genius of the sculptor, a longtime friend and artistic contemporary of Rodin. Open Tues.-Sun. 10am-5:40pm. Last entry 5:15pm. Admission 17F50, students 9F.

Musée Nissim de Camondo, 63, rue Monceau, 8ème (tel. 45 63 26 32). M. Villiers or Monceau. This building tells the story not only of 18th-century decorative arts but also of a family that met tragedy. Comte Moïse de Camondo built this *hôtel particulier* from 1911-1914, on the model of the Petit Trianon at Versailles, to house his exquisite collection of 18th-century furniture, paintings, tapestries, and porcelain. Camondo's will left the house to the Union des Arts Décoratifs, dedicated to the memory of his son, Nissim, who died in aerial combat in 1917. The rest of the family died at Auschwitz. On a visit in 1990, Barbara Bush—overcome by the combination of Savonnerie carpets, Sèvres porcelain, and a ravishing 1780 mahogany roll-top desk—in a rare burst of strong language exclaimed, "Isn't this the darnedest place you ever saw?" Take one of the 45-min. audio-guides (25F, 35F for 2, available in English) or buy a 20F general brochure (more detailed guide 60F) to supplement the otherwise meager explanations. Open Wed.-Sun. 10am-noon and 2-5pm. 20F, students under 25 and seniors 14F.

Musée Carnavalet, 23, rue de Sévigné, 3ème (tel. 42 72 21 13). M. Chemin-Vert. Housed in a 16th-century *hôtel*, it traces Paris' history with prehistoric bones and stones, a series of paintings, and other memorabilia. The strength of the presentation lies in its collective impact as a display of the changing faces of Paris. The reconstructed Bijouterie Fouquet may be the star of the show for Art Nouveau junkies. French decorative art fans will also appreciate the period rooms. (For information on the museum's courtyard see Sights—3ème). The museum is popular with large groups of French schoolchildren and their teachers. Offers guided visits in French for a fee, Tues. and Sat. at 2:30pm. Pick up the schedule which includes all tours and workshops in the city's public museums at front desk. Large part of museum space is wheelchair accessible. Open Tues.-Sun. 10am-5:30pm. 25F, 19F for ages 19-25 and above 60, and teachers with suitable ID. Sun. free when temporary exhibits are isolated from main exhibition. Combined entrance fee and participation in guided tour 44F. Temporary exhibits cost extra.

Musée Cernuschi, 7, av. Velasquez, 8ème (tel. 45 63 50 75), outside the gates of Parc Monceau. M. Villiers or Monceau. A magnificent, charmingly personable collection of Asian art is housed in a villa that belonged to Henri Cernuschi (1820-1896), a financier of Milanese descent who took off on a trans-world tour after being "affected" by the Commune. Second to the Guimet as an Asian art museum, the Cernuschi nevertheless contains some very impressive pieces including an 18th-century Japanese 3-ton, 3.5m-high bronze Buddha. Wheelchair access. Open Tues.-Sun. 10am-5:40pm. Admission to permanent collection 17F50, reduced 9F.

Musée de la Chasse (Hunting Museum), 60, rue des Archives, 3ème (tel. 42 72 86 43). M. Rambuteau. Housed in the spacious, 17th-century Hôtel Guénégaud, professionally-stuffed animals (entire and in pieces) will attract only the most committed hunter or huntress. Highlights include the head of a 3-ton white rhino, a rearing polar bear, and a Gabonese bush pig. Portraits of Diana, pictured with dogs, and huntresses, by Brueghel, Rubens, Velcours, and Monet, help make light of the collection of animal trophies and weapons, like the crank-operated crossbow. Open Wed.-Mon. 10am-12:30pm and 1:30-5:30pm. 25F, students and seniors 12F50, children ages 5-16 5F. Permission to take photos 10F.

Musée du Cinéma Henri-Langlois, in the Palais de Chaillot, 16ème (tel. 45 53 74 39). M. Trocadéro. Traces the history of film from its beginnings with magic lanterns and shadow theaters. Chronological arrangement of sets, costumes, scripts, and posters. The museum may only be visited by guided tour (1 hr.) in French. Open Sept.-July Wed.-Sun. for tours at 10am, 11am, 2pm, 3pm, 4pm and 5pm. Tours canceled if fewer than 8 people. 25F.

Musée Clemenceau, 8, rue Benjamin-Franklin, 16ème (tel. 45 20 53 41), through a small courtyard. M. Passy. Journalist and statesman, Georges Clemenceau (1841-

1929) has been both revered and villified for nearly a century. The museum thoroughly documents his life: as journalist, when he published (and titled) Émile Zola's article *"J'accuse,"* and thus announced his anti-governmental stance during the Dreyfuss Affair; as mayor of Montmartre; as Prime Minister of France; as Président du Conseil; as Minister of War (1917-1920); as the much-criticized negotiator of the Versailles Treaty. The museum makes no attempt to gloss over Clemenceau's life. The assembled documents and clippings (among them scores of political cartoons, as often as not unfriendly) present a nuanced portrait of the man, not the hero. On the ground floor, Clemenceau's apartment has been left as it was when he died; even the calendars are all torn off at November 24, 1929. Pamphlet (in French and English) explains nearly all museum contents, like the painting done for Clemenceau by his friend Monet, and the withered bouquet of flowers given him by a soldier at the front. Open Sept.-July Tues., Thurs., Sat.-Sun., and holidays 2-5pm. 20F, students and seniors 15F.

Musée Cognacq-Jay, 8, rue Elzévir, 3ème (tel. 40 27 07 21). M. St-Paul, Chemin-Vert or Rambuteau. This collection of Enlightenment art, formerly owned by turn-of-the-century department store mogul Ernest Cognacq and his wife, Marie-Louise Jay, has passed to the hands of the city. Works by Watteau, Canaletto, Rembrandt, Greuze, and Fragonard. A showcase of the Old Regime as it would like to be remembered—as lute-strumming nobles at *fêtes galantes* and wind-blown coquettes. The museum occasionally hosts 18th-century plays (four short works of Fagon, Barthe, Forgeot and Colle programmed from Dec. 1, 1994-Feb. 28, 1995. Shows at 3:30pm and 8:30pm last 90 minutes. For matinees, admission 70F; for evening shows, 100F, students and seniors 80F). Open Tues.-Sun. 10am-5:40pm. Admission 17F50, 9F for students, seniors and teachers, under 18 free.

Musée de Contrefaçon (the Counterfeit Museum), 16, rue de la Faisanderie, 16ème (tel. 45 01 51 11). M. Porte Dauphine. "I can't see the difference. Can you see the difference? Is there a difference?" Direct these questions toward the display of bottles, logos, handbags, and their illegal counterfeits for about 2 min. Then ask: "Who cares?" The potentially novel, wacky display looks like a pile that "fell out of a truck". Open Mon. and Wed. 2-4:30pm, Fri. 9:30am-noon. Free.

La Fondation Le Corbusier, 10, square du Docteur-Blanche (tel. 42 88 41 53). M. Jasmin. Walk up rue de l'Yvette, take a left on rue du Docteur-Blanche and another left onto square du Docteur-Blanche. The foundation is located in the Villas La Roche and Jeanneret, designed—down to the smallest piece of furniture—by Le Corbusier. The Villa La Roche, commissioned by the young banker La Roche to house his collection of Cubist art, holds the museum, or rather, is the museum. It offers an exceptional glimpse of some of Le Corbusier's architectural trademarks: his use of light; his attempt to harmonize with the natural world; his preference for curved forms and for ramps over stairs. The building itself is without question the museum's most impressive artwork. The Villa Jeanneret next door holds the library and the foundation's offices. Pick up the excellent pamphlet guide. Open Sept.-July Mon.-Thurs. 10am-12:30pm, 1:30-6pm, Fri. 10am-12:30pm, 1:30-5pm. 15F, reduced tariff 10F.

Musée Salvador Dalí (Espace Montmartre), 11, rue Poulbot, 18ème (tel. 42 64 40 10). M. Anvers, Blanche, or Pigalle. Right off pl. du Tertre, this space dedicated to the "Phantasmic World of Salvador Dalì" is full of lithographs and sculptures by the Spanish surrealist, with scads of incarnations of the famous droopy clocks. The museum is laid out in "Surrealist surroundings", which amounts to wonderful spacing, interesting lighting and slightly ridiculous "space-music" in the background. Open daily 10am-6pm. 35F, students 25F.

Musée Delacroix, 6, rue Furstenberg, 6ème (tel. 43 54 04 87). M. St-Germain-des-Prés. Behind the Eglise St-Germain off rue de l'Abbaye. At the round courtyard, follow the sign to the *atelier Delacroix*; you'll pass through another small courtyard to get into the museum. Located in the artist's 3-room apartment and attached studio, this museum contains works spanning the duration of his career. Delacroix (1799-1863) was one of the leaders of French Romanticism, most famous for his painting *Liberty Leading the People*. A surprising number of sketches, watercolors, and engravings found here bely a kindler, gentler Delacroix than a visitor to the Louvre might expect. Also displays a few works by other artists (including two Manet watercolors). Open Tues.-Sat. 9:45am-5:15pm, last entry 4:45pm. 12F, ages 18-25 and over 60 8F, under 18 free.

Musée des Egouts de Paris (Museum of the Sewers of Paris), actually inside the sewers, at the corner of the quai d'Orsay and pl. de la Résistance, 7ème (tel. 47 05 10 29). M. Pont de l'Alma. This unique museum details the history of the city's fascinating subterranean avenues. In *Les Misérables,* Victor Hugo wrote, "Paris has beneath it another Paris, a Paris of sewers, which has its own streets, squares, lanes, arteries, and circulation." Actual *égoutiers* (sewer workers) lead tours year-round, held on demand whenever enough people are present (call ahead for guided tours). While the tours themselves are not gross, the smell can be overwhelming. Should the worst occur and you fall into the sewers (highly unlikely), follow the advice of *égoutiers* and close your mouth. Open Sat.-Wed. 11am-6pm; winter Sat.-Wed. 11am-5pm. Last ticket sold 1hr. before closing. 25F, students and under 10 20F. Closed for 3 weeks in Jan.

Musée d'Ennery, 59, av. Foch, 16ème (tel. 45 53 57 96). M. Porte Dauphine. Despite its name and the bust in its front hall, this museum is not the collection of Adolphe d'Ennery (1811-1899), a prolific but not-very-good French writer of the Second Empire. Instead, it is the collection of his wife, who scavenged the city's flea markets and antique shops for Orientalia during the 19th-century's Far East craze. Particularly amazing are the *netsuke* (Japanese miniatures originally used to tie pouches to kimonos), of which the museum has over 300 spectacular examples. Open Sept.-July Thurs., Sun., and holidays 2-6pm. On the 1st floor of the same building is the **Musée Arménien** (tel. 45 56 15 88), which displays Armenian jewelry, paintings, and religious decoration both past and present. Open Sept.-July Thurs., Sun., and holidays 2-5pm. Free.

Galerie d'Entomologie (Insect Museum), across the street from the Jardin des Plantes on 45, rue Buffon, 5ème. (tel. 40 79 34 00). M. Censier-Daubenton or Gare d'Austerlitz. Most of the 1-room gallery is dedicated to various specimens, in different colors and sizes, of beetles and butterflies. Among the gorgeous array of insects on display is a Peruvian butterfly with a striking resemblance to the *tricolore.* Open Wed.-Sat. and Mon. 2-5pm. 12F, students 8F.

Musée du Grand Orient de France et de la Franc-Maçonnerie, 16, rue Cadet, 9ème (tel. 45 23 20 92). M. Cadet. Housed in a masonic lodge, this 1-room museum tells the story of the masons from early Scottish brotherhood to their peak in the 18th and 19th centuries. Folksy captioning, hand-written in French, accompanies one-of-a-kind pamphlets, medals, portraits, and busts of renowned freemasons, including Voltaire and Talleyrand. The museum is housed in the Hôtel Cadet, built in 1852 and designed as the headquarters for French freemasonry. During World War II, Vichy officials used it to identify and persecute masons. Open Mon.-Sat. 2-6pm. Closed first 2 weeks in August. Free.

Grand Palais, 3, av. du Général Eisenhower, 8ème (tel. 44 13 17 17). M. Champs-Elysées-Clemenceau. Most of the building houses the Palais de la Découverte (see above), but the other 2 entrances lead the way to temporary exhibits. Call to see what's going on. Open, when an exhibit is there, Thurs.-Mon. 10am-8pm, Wed. 10am-10pm. Last entry 45 min. before closing. Admission varies with the exhibit, but anticipate something like 55F, students and Mon. 29F, under 13 free.

Musée Grévin, 10, bd. Montmartre, 9ème (tel. 42 46 13 26). M. Rue Montmartre. This wax museum can be entertaining if you don't mind over-enthusiastic French kids on field days or the disturbing stares of life-like figures. The super-ornate halls are filled with illustrious personages, present and past. Marie-Antoinette awaits her execution in the Conciergerie; the cannibals from Géricault's painting *The Raft of the Medusa* reach out for the rescue ship on the horizon. Open daily 1-7pm, last entry 6pm. 48F, ages 6-14 34F. The smaller subsidiary at level "-1" of the **Forum des Halles,** near the Porte Berger, 1er (tel. 40 26 28 50; M. Châtelet-Les Halles), presents a fascinating spectacle of Paris during the "Belle Epoque" (1885-1900). A terrific *son et lumière,* in French, recreates the turn of the century. If you're in a group, arrangements can be made to have the show in English. Open Mon.-Sat. 10:30am-6:45pm, Sun. and holidays 1-6:30pm. Ticket office closes 45 min. before museum. 42F, ages 6-14 32F, under 6 free.

Musée Jean-Jacques Henner, 43, av. Villiers, 17ème (tel. 47 63 42 73). M. Malesherbes. This small museum displays the paintings of Jean-Jacques Henner (1829-1903). Often in soft focus, his subjects are painted with luminous, bone-white skin; the technique is most haunting in his painting of St. Sebastian and his series of nymphs. On the ground floor are a number of portraits of his family and friends. Open Tues.-Sun. 10am-noon and 2-5pm. 14F, students 10F.

Musée de l'Histoire de France, 60, rue des Francs-Bourgeois, 3ème (tel. 40 27 60 96). M. Hôtel de Ville or Rambuteau. Housed in the Hôtel de Soubise, this museum overflows with important French documents—Napoleon's will, a letter by Jeanne d'Arc, and *the* Edict of Nantes. Labels are in French only. (For more information on content and history of the Hôtel Soubise, see Sights—*3ème arrondissement.*) Open Wed.-Mon. 1:45-5:45pm. 12F, students 8F.

Musée d'Histoire Naturelle, in the Jardin des Plantes, 5ème (tel. 40 79 30 00). M. Gare d'Austerlitz. A 3-building museum which covers three fields within the natural sciences. The **Gallery of Comparative Anatomy and Paleontology** houses a dinosaur exhibit, whose triumph is the 7m skeleton of an iguanodon. The rest of the gallery is devoted to more familiar, though equally large skeletons (like those of elephants and whales) and contains an unremarkable collection of fossils. Next door is the **Musée de Phanérogamie,** which focuses upon evolutionary life. The **Musée de Minéralogie,** surrounded by well-kept rose trellises, contains diamonds, rubies, and sapphires along with assorted *objets d'art* fashioned with them, including two Renaissance Florentine marble tables inlaid with lapis lazuli, amethyst, and other semi-precious stones. Downstairs are a collection of giant crystals and an exhibit addressing the practical uses of minerals. Open Mon. and Wed.-Fri. 10am-5pm, Sat. and Sun. 11am-6pm. 25F, students 15F.

Musée de l'Holographie, level "1" of the Forum des Halles, between porte Berger and porte Lescot, 1er (tel. 40 39 96 83). M. Châtelet-Les Halles. A small, moderately interesting set of holograms. A woman blows a kiss at you and winks as you walk by. Open Mon.-Sat. 10am-7pm, Sun. 1-7pm. 30F, students 25F.

Musée de l'Homme (Museum of Man), in the Palais de Chaillot, 16ème (tel. 44 05 72 72). M. Trocadéro. A painted cart from Sicily, a Turkish store, a band of Inuits....The museum's multi-media presentations cover civilizations and cultures worldwide, from prehistory to today. Renovations are currently underway, to be completed by summer 1995. Labels in French often accompany self-explanatory displays. 1994-1995 museum hosts *"Tous parents, tous différents,"* a special exhibit on human biological diversity. Open Wed.-Mon. 9:45am-5:15pm. 25F, reduced 15F, children under 6 and disabled persons free. Films Wed. and Sat. at 3pm and 4pm.

Maison de Victor Hugo, 6, pl. des Vosges, 4ème (tel. 42 72 10 16). M. Chemin Vert. A small museum dedicated to the "father of the French Romantics," housed in the building where he lived from 1832-1848. The museum offers an assortment of Hugo memorabilia, including his own expressionistic graphic art. Also features works by Rodin and Delacroix. Relics/icons attest to the cult of the poet that persisted long after his death. Francophones may read his elegant love letters. Open Tues.-Sun. 10am-5:15pm. 17F50, students 9F, under 18 free.

Musée Jacquemart-André, 158, bd. Haussmann, 8ème (tel. 42 89 04 91). M. St-Philippe-du-Roule. Works from the Italian Renaissance (Donatello, Della Robbia) and the French 18th century (Fragonard, Watteau) join pieces by Rembrandt and Rubens under Tiepolo's fresco. Collections belonged to the Jacquemart family and the *hôtel particulier* to 19th-century collector Edouard André (hence the name). Open Sept.-July Wed.-Sun. 1:30-5:30pm; closed holidays.10F.

Musée du Jeu de Paume, 1er (tel. 47 03 12 50). M. Concorde. The Jeu de Paume, in the northeast corner of the Tuileries, was originally constructed under Napoleon III as a court on which to play *jeu de paume*, an ancestor of tennis. In 1909, it was converted into a display area, mostly for art exhibits. When the Nazis took over Paris, they sent plundered art here, where much of it was labelled "degenerate" and burned. Between 1947 and 1986, the building housed an Impressionist collection which has been transferred to the Musée d'Orsay. Since June 1991, the museum has been a showcase for contemporary art. For exhibit info, call 42 60 69 69 (answering machine, in French), or just go there and take a look. Open, when exhibits are on, Tues. noon-9:30pm, Wed.-Fri. noon-7pm, Sat.-Sun. 10am-7pm. 35F, students 25F, under 13 free.

Musée National de la Légion d'Honneur et des Ordres de Chevalerie, 2, rue de Bellechasse, 7ème (tel. 45 55 95 16). M. Solférino. Housed in an 18th-century mansion built for Prince Frederick of Salm-Kyrbourg, this museum displays innumerable medals, ribbons, and dress costumes of the French Legion of Honor, created by Napoleon in 1802 to reward civilian and military virtue. Unless Jerome Bonaparte's wedding reception glass thrills you, consider admiring the architectue from across the street at the Musée d'Orsay. Open Tues.-Sun. 2-5pm. 20F, students and seniors 10F.

Musée de la Marine (Museum of the Navy), in the Palais de Chaillot, 16ème (tel. 45 53 31 70). M. Trocadéro. Engrossing display of model and real ships, of nautical rope, of paintings and of antique divers' suits. English-language brochure available at the ticket counter. Open Wed.-Mon. and holidays 10am-6pm. Last entry at 5:30pm. 35F, seniors 16F. No student discount.

Les Martyrs de Paris, porte du Louvre at the Forum des Halles, 1er (tel. 40 28 08 13). M. Les Halles. A macabre museum of torture, with a heavy emphasis on the medieval. Realistic waxwork shows people being branded, burned, and abused, while signs in English and French explain the historical details. Heavy Metal fans will be delighted to see a model of the "Iron Maiden" torture machine from Nuremberg Castle. All of it is most appropriate for the city that brought you the Bastille, the Guillotine, and the St. Bartholomew's Day Massacre. 43F, students 32F. Martyrs of Paris and Rock and Roll Hall of Fame 66F, students 48F, groups of more than 10 adults 48F per person. Open daily 10:30am-6:30pm.

Centre de la Mer et des Eaux, 195, rue St-Jacques, 5ème. (tel. 46 33 08 61). M. Luxembourg. Opened in 1993 after extensive renovations, this museum presents more than just the requisite tanks of corals and tropical fish. There is a "hands-on" learning area: push buttons and pull handles to educate yourself about fish disguises and algae life cycles. An entire room is entitled "The Mysterious Voyage of Eels." Films and exhibitions change. Be forewarned that all labels are in French and all chairs are designed for small-sized French students. Open Tues.-Fri. 10am-12:30pm and 1:15-5:30pm, Sat.-Sun. 10am-5:30pm. 25F, students 15F.

Musée Adam Mickiewicz, 6, quai d'Orléans, 4ème (tel. 43 54 35 61), on the Ile-St-Louis. M. Pont Marie. Ring the doorbell to enter, turn left at the courtyard, and climb stairs to the second floor. Located in the former home of famed Polish poet Adam Mickiewicz (1798-1835), the museum exhibits his belongings—including letters he received from Goethe and Victor Hugo, and a sketch by Delacroix on George Sand's letter-head. One room focuses on the life of Chopin, compatriot and friend of Mickiewicz. See first edition manuscripts by the composer, a few letters, and one of the three surviving copies of his death mask. The building also houses a Polish library. Open Thurs. 2-6pm. Visit only by guided tour, conducted by friendly, knowledgable staff volunteers. Tours begin at 2, 3, 4, and 5pm. Free.

Musée de la Monnaie de Paris, 11, quai de Conti, 6ème (tel. 40 46 55 33). M. Pont-Neuf. On the Left Bank between Pont Neuf and Pont des Arts. Housed in the Hôtel des Monnaies, once the mint of all money in France, this high-tech museum displays an impressive array of French coins from the 9th century to the present. Today, the *hôtel* manufactures medals of honor (some on sale on the ground floor). Tues. and Fri. at 2 and 2:45pm, a guided tour takes you past artisans at work. Most of the coins are on the 1st floor, all accompanied by small video or slide shows explaining their history (in French). Open Tues.-Sun. 1-6pm; Wed. until 9pm. 20F, students 15F, children under 16 free.

Musée de la Mode et du Costume (Museum of Fashion and Clothing), in the Palais Galliera, 10, av. Pierre 1er-de-Serbie, 16ème (tel. 47 20 85 23). M. Iéna. With over 12,000 ensembles in its possession and only four small display rooms, the museum has no choice but to rotate in temporary exhibitions showcasing fashions of the past 3 centuries. Open Tues.-Sun. 10am-5:40pm. Last entry at 5:15pm. 35F, students and seniors 25F.

Institut du Monde Arabe (Institute of the Arab World), 23, quai St-Bernard, 5ème (tel. 40 51 38 38). M. Jussieu. This newest and most architecturally innovative of Parisian museums opened in 1987 as a cooperative project between 27

Arab nations and the French government to promote education about Arab history, art, culture and language. The riverside façade is shaped like a boat, representing the migration of Arabs to France. Notable for its displays of Arabic rugs and ceramics, the museum assembles art from three Arab regions (Maghrib/Spain, the Near East, and the Middle East) from the 3rd through the 18th centuries. Level 4 is devoted entirely to contemporary Arab artists. An extensive library contains works of literature in Arabic, French, and English, as well as periodicals, all of which are open to the public. At night, the auditorum hosts Arab movies (subtitled in English and French; 30F, students 20F) and theater (free). Call for a schedule of events. On Level 9, a delightful cafeteria cooks up 3-course lunches (79F), including many Arabic specialties. Take your tray to the rooftop terrace outside for one of the best views of the Seine. Museum and library open Tues.-Sun 10am-6pm. Museum admission 25F, students 20F, under 12 free. 90-min guided tour of museum on Mon.-Fri.at 3pm and Sat.-Sun. at 2 and 4pm, 40F. Admission to temporary exhibits and permanent collection, 50F. Institute open Tues.-Sun. 10am-6pm. Cafeteria open Tues.-Sun. 11:30am-6pm.

Galerie Le Monde de l'Art, 18, rue de Paradis, 10ème (tel. 42 46 43 44). M. Gare de l'Est. The airy and light-filled interior of this gallery is decorated with tiled Art Nouveau landscapes and Portuguese frescoes, installed when the building served as headquarters for the Boulanger China Company. Upstairs is a private gallery with an exquisitely tiled floor and often inaccessibly contemporary art. Definitely a very cool place. And, unless you're planning to buy some artwork, it's free. Open Mon. 2-7pm, Tues.-Sat. 1-7pm.

Musée National des Monuments Français, 1, pl. du Trocadéro, in the Palais de Chaillot, 16ème (tel. 44 05 39 10). M. Trocadéro. Primarily a scholarly museum of doubtless appeal to artists, architects, and medievalists. Displays feature life-sized models of façades and tombs from churches all over France. The scant captioning is in French. Interested specialists should ask about the museum's documentation center. Open Wed.-Mon. 10am-6pm. 21F; students ages 18-25, seniors, and Sun. 14F. Call for info about frequent lectures.

Musée Gustave Moreau, 14, rue de La Rochefoucauld, 9ème (tel. 48 74 38 50). M. Trinité. This museum is a gem. Located in the house of the 19th-century symbolist painter Gustave Moreau, it contains thousands of his drawings and paintings. The house itself is charming, and the rooms are lined with works in all stages of completion, from sketches and half-painted canvases to fully complete works, including the celebrated painting of Salomé dancing before the severed head of John the Baptist. Open Mon. and Wed. 11am-5:15pm, Thurs.-Sun. 10am-12:45pm and 2-5:15pm. 17F; students, children, and Sun. 9F.

Musée Naïf Max Fourny (Halle St-Pierre), 2, rue Ronsard, 18ème (tel. 42 58 72 89). M. Anvers. Neo-Primitivist art in an iron and glass ex-marketplace. No artist is represented more than once. Participatory games are available for visitors ages 3-12. Open Tues.-Sat. 10am-10pm, Sun. and Mon. 10am-6pm. 22F, students 16F.

Palais de la Découverte (Palace of Discovery), in the Grand Palais, entrance on av. Franklin D. Roosevelt, 8ème (tel. 40 74 81 82 or 40 74 80 00). M. Franklin Roosevelt. More central, less flashy than the Cité des Sciences. Interactive exhibits run the gamut of scientific subjects and run it remarkably well. Kids will (and do) tear around at a manic pace to turn wheels that teach about complementary colors, press buttons that start comets on their celestial trajectories, spin on seats to investigate angular motion, and glare at all kinds of cleverly camouflaged creepy-crawlies. Open Tues.-Sat. 9:30am-6pm, Sun. 10am-7pm. 22F; students, seniors, and under 18 11F. Planetarium shows at least three times daily.

Palais de Tokyo, 13, av. du Président Wilson, 16ème (tel. 47 23 36 53). M. Iéna. Closed for renovations until the spring of 1996 when it will become the Palais de l'Image, an enormous film library.

Petit Palais (also called the Palais des Beaux-Arts de la Ville de Paris), av. Winston Churchill, 8ème (tel. 42 65 12 73). M. Champs-Elysées-Clemenceau. This decaying "palace" displays gems from ancient art through 19th- and 20th-century painting and sculpture. Each room in the permanent collection has a theme: 17th-century Flemish and Dutch paintings or canvases depicting the French Revolution. Houses Jean-Baptiste Carpeaux's *Young Fisher with the Shell;* Camille Claudel's bust of Rodin, Monet's *Sunset at Lavacourt,* as well as the occasional Rubens, Rembrandt, Cézanne, Pissarro, and Renoir. Wheelchair accessible by the door at 1, av. Dutuit—call ahead. Open Tues.-Sun. 10am-5:40pm. Admission to permanent collection 27F50, reduced 14F50. Admission to temporary exhibits roughly 40F, *tarif réduit* 30F. Conference visits (1-1½hr., in French and English), focusing on a special theme, are held in the afternoon.

Musée Picasso, 5, rue de Thorigny, 3ème (tel. 42 71 25 21). M. Chemin Vert. When the cubist Pablo Picasso died in 1973, his family opted to pay the French inheritance tax in artwork, which is how the French government came to own this collection. (The 17th-century Hôtel Salé, which houses the museum, never belonged to Picasso. See Sights—3ème.) Many works are of minor significance, but the collection as a whole is fascinating, thanks to the museum's well-paced and informative layout. Light fixtures by Giacometti illuminate the first rooms of a circuit that traces the artist's development. Alongside Picasso's pieces are works by artists who influenced him, including Braque, Cézanne, Miró, and anonymous African and Oceanian sculptors. In addition, photos of Picasso's friends—Marie Laurencin, Braque, and Cocteau among others—taken in his studio, provide a who's who of the early 20th-century avant-garde. A restriction on school groups after 1pm ensures more peaceful viewing. Well-stocked giftshop. Museum open Wed.-Mon. 9:30am-6pm, last entrance 5:15pm; Oct.-March 9:30am-5:30pm, last entrance 4:45pm. 33F, ages 18-25 and over 60, and Sun. 24F.

Musée des Collections Historiques de la Préfecture de la Police, 1bis, rue des Carmes, 2nd floor, 5ème (tel. 43 29 21 57). M. Maubert-Mutualité. Founded in 1909, this 1-room gallery is devoted to the preservation of police paraphernalia. Guarded by a group of life-sized wax *flics* (slang for cops), the cases protect wholly uninteresting writs and warrants, police awards, and metals. More interesting are the 2 cases of exotic weaponry. Displayed near the weapons is a Revolutionary-era guillotine, tied with a 15cm stuffed doll prepared to undergo the treatment. While the museum is mostly a favorite with retired officers visiting Paris from the provinces, it can be an amusing diversion for anyone, especially since free admission includes use of the impeccable restrooms and the thrill of getting buzzed into the building by the attending guards. Open Mon.-Fri. 9am-5pm, Sat. 10am-5pm. Free.

Musée de La Poste, 34, bd. de Vaugirard, 15ème (tel. 42 79 23 45). M. Montparnasse-Bienvenüe. Most impressive are several thousand stamps which adorn the walls of an entire floor. Also of note are various mailbox designs, including a high-concept hollow cannonball, which was stuffed with letters and then floated downstream to Parisians during the Prussian siege of 1870. Nascent bureaucrats thrill to a scale replica of a post office window; everyone else suffers mysterious waves of impatient anxiety. Open Mon.-Sat. 10am-6pm. 25F, students 19F.

Musée de la Maison de la Radio-France, 116, av. du Président Kennedy, 16ème (tel. 42 30 21 80). M. Passy or Mirabeau, RER (C) Av. du Pt. Kennedy/Maison de la Radio-France. Head for the Seine and enter through Door A of the big, white, round building. A whirlwind tour through the history of communications. The museum can be visited only by guided tour (in French), which hastily traces the advent of radio, of TV, and of the *maison* itself (with appropriate bias toward the French contribution to all three). Childhood radio-builders will enjoy this chance to inspect classic specimens. Open Mon.-Sat. Tours at 10:30am, 11:30am, 2:30pm, 3:30pm, and 4:30pm. 14F, students and seniors 7F.

Rock 'n Roll Hall of Fame, porte du Louvre of the Forum des Halles, 1er (tel. 40 28 08 13). M. Les Halles. The Hall is much less interesting than its neighbor the Martyrs of Paris. Wax dummies of stars like Madonna and the Beatles; video clips and piped-in music. If you think that can't be any more exciting than staying at home and watching MTV, well...you're right. Admission 40F, students 29F. Martyrs of Paris and Hall of Fame combined 66F, students 48F. Open daily 10:30am-6:30pm.

Musée Renan-Scheffer (also called **Musée de la Vie Romantique),** 16, rue Chaptal, 9ème (tel. 48 74 95 38). M. St-Georges. Housed in the former residence of 19th-century painter and *salonnier* Ary Scheffer, a friend of George Sand, the small museum displays busts, portraits, letters, and personal belongings (rings, locks of hair, a model of Franz Lizst's right hand) that recall Scheffer, Sand, and other *salonniers.* The house is lovely—with a garden and down a tree-lined lane—and never crowded. Open Tues.-Sun. 10am-5:40pm. 20F, students 10F.

Musée-Galerie de la SEITA (Société d'Exploitation Industrielle des Tabacs et Alumettes), 12, rue Surcouf, 7ème (tel. 45 56 60 17 or 45 56 60 18). M. Invalides or Latour-Maubourg. Owned and operated by the tobacco lobby, the museum tells the story of tobacco from Jean Nicot's 1561 presentation of its medicinal qualities to the court, through Napoleon's 1810 imposition of a state monopoly, and up to the present-day. Temporary exhibits are stylish and obliquely tobacco related. Paraguayan Baroque statuary on display summer 1995. Museum store sells postcards of celebrities lighting up (3F) and past exhibition posters (10F). Open Mon.-Sat. 11am-7pm. Free, usually: some exhibitions may require a fee (around 25F, 15F reduced tariff). Nice free bathrooms too.

Musée de la Serrure (Lock Museum), 1, rue de la Perle, 3ème (tel. 42 77 79 62). M. Chemin-Vert or St-Sébastien Froissart. Housed in the Hôtel Libéral-Bruant, this private museum holds an odd but mildly interesting collection of locks. Small rooms, all in the *cave*, display an assortment of padlocks, slide-bolts, hammers, clasps, and latches. Intriguing lion's head lock, circa 1780, clamps its upper mandible around the hands of those who insinuate false keys. Re-created blacksmith shop is worth a quick look. Open Sept.-July, Mon.-Fri. 2-5pm.20F.

Musée des Techniques, 292, rue St-Martin, 3ème (tel. 40 27 23 31). M. Réaumur-Sébastopol or Arts-et-Métiers. In 1794, French Revolutionaries created a national collection of new technology, housed in the 12th-century priory St-Martin-des-Champs. There you'll find Lavoisier's chemistry apparatus, Pascal's calculating machine, and early cameras, steam engines, wooden telescopes, and brass models of the solar system. The roomful of 18th-century automata is activated on the first Wed. of each month at 2:30pm. Major renovations have been undertaken for the 200th anniversary in 1994, to be completed in October. Open Tues.-Sun. 10am-5:30pm. 20F, Sun. 10F.

Musée du Vieux Montmartre, 12, rue Cortot, 18ème (tel. 46 06 61 11). M. Lamarck-Caulaincourt. A museum dedicated to the political, artistic, cultural, and religious past of the butte Montmartre. The beautiful 17th-century house, overlooking a pleasant garden and Montmartre's only vineyard, has been home to diverse artists, including one of Molière's actors, Renoir, and Utrillo. The museum's collection includes old maps, paintings, photographs, and a wooden model of the *quartier*. One room recreates a turn-of-the-century café owned by M. Buillot, complete with one of the few zinc bar counters left after the metal rationing during the Nazi Occupation. The documentation is in French and English (and in fact, is better in English). Open Tues.-Sun. 11am-6pm; register closes at 5:30pm. 25F, reduced tariff 15F.

Musée du Vin, rue des Eaux or 5-7, sq. Charles Dickens, 16ème (tel. 45 25 63 26). M. Passy. A free wine tasting follows the mildly entertaining tour of this former limestone quarry, now filled with wax models making, storing, judging, and drinking wine. Real connoisseurs will learn little or nothing. Others might get a kick out of the anecdotes. Display includes a wax model of Honoré de Balzac running through the quarry pursued by debtors, just as he did over a century ago. Remind the often forgetful guides to offer you a free tasting of red, rosé, or white. Tour in French, with info sheet available in English. Open daily noon-6pm. 29F, seniors 26F, students 23F.

Musée Zadkine, 100bis, rue d'Assas, 6ème (tel. 43 26 91 90). M. Notre-Dame-des-Champs or Vavin. Just south of the Jardin du Luxembourg. This reasonably-sized museum is the perfect antidote to Parisian aesthetic overload. Installed in 1982 in the house and studio where he worked from 1928 until his death, the museum highlights the work of master sculptor Ossip Zadkine (1890-1967). Zadkine's work spans the major developments in modern sculpture, moving from the extremes of Cubism to a renewed Classicism, and using a wide variety of mediums. Even if you don't want to pay the admission to the museum, a visit to the garden is both free and worthwhile; a good selection of the artist's most important works, including his two-faced *Woman with the Bird,* resides there and you can relax on the benches in peace while you contemplate his work. Open Tues.-Sun. 9:45am-5:30pm. 17F, students 9F50.

Entertainment

Paris teems with cabarets, discos, and smoky jazz clubs; with U.S. and European cinema; with avant-garde and traditional theater; with rock and classical concerts. Consult the two bibles of Paris entertainment: the magazine **Pariscope** (3F) and the **Officiel des Spectacles** (2F), both on sale weekly at any newsstand. Even if you don't understand French, you should be able to decipher the listings of times and locations. Or, contact **Info-Loisirs,** a recording that keeps tabs on what's on in Paris (English tel. 49 52 53 56; French tel. 49 52 53 55).

Paris is one of the world's premier jazz capitals, so big-name American artists make frequent stops here. The city also offers a mixed diet of West African music, Caribbean calypso, Latin American salsa, North African raï, and rap. Classical concerts play in both expensive concert halls and more affordable churches, especially during the summer. To get more information and to buy tickets for rock, jazz, or classical concerts, check out **FNAC Musique,** 24, bd. des Italiens, 9ème (tel. 48 01 02 03) or 1, rue de Charenton, 12ème (tel. 43 42 04 04).

Parisians are inveterate film-goers and are particularly keen on American classics; frequent English-language film series and annual festivals make Parisian cinema a popular, accessible, and affordable entertainment option for visitors and locals alike.

The famous Montmartre cabarets still pack in American businessmen for all-girl, topless revues. Other cabarets, such as the comedy-oriented *café-théâtres* and the music-oriented *chansonniers,* perpetuate the ambiance of 1930s Parisian cabarets, which helped launch the careers of Edith Piaf and Jacques Brel.

Keep in mind that the neighborhoods around popular night-spots are not always safe. The areas around Pigalle, Gare St-Lazare, and Beaubourg fill nightly with prostitutes and drug dealers. Also remember to keep an eye on the time in order to avoid expensive, late-night taxis; though the metro stops running at 1am, hop on a train at about 12:30am if you have to make a connection.

■■■ CINEMA

Paris is famous the world over for a movie scene that rivals—some say surpasses—that of New York. After all, cinema was invented here by the Lumière brothers, Auguste and Louis, and the first movie premiered at the Grand Café (14, bd. des Capucines) in 1895. At the time, Louis belittled his discovery as "an invention without a future." Needless to say, he was wrong.

Don't expect to find many megaplexes and greasy popcorn; film-going in Paris is an evening on the town. Cafés, bars, and restaurants cohabit with projector rooms in some of the city's smaller theaters, whose intimate rooms can have as few as twenty or thirty seats (almost always plush, roomy, and comfortable). The **Fête du Cinéma,** a three-day, all-day, city-wide celebration transforms Paris and its suburbs into a community of film fans young and old (see Festivals, in this chapter).

Proof of Paris' movie enthusiasm are the mile-long lines for anything from Robert Mitchum to Bambi. Beating the crowds requires some know-how. The two big theater chains—**Gaumont** and **UGC**—offer **cartes privilèges** for frequent customers. At 150F for five entries, the *carte Gaumont* allows bearers to skip past lines and reserve seats in advance. UGC offers a like deal: 120F for 4 entries, 180F for 6. Cards are active for two months, at all shows and franchise locations. Since these cards are a recent development, watch out for changes. In any case, don't worry, the Parisians are as confused as you are.

Catering to the city's enormous student population, Paris' cinemas offer a range of ticket discounts. On Mondays and Wednesdays prices drop about 10F. Check *Pariscope* for details—days and reductions vary with the theater. The confederation of independent cinemas, a bulwark of little-guys competing with Gaumont and UGC, offers reduced tickets for all on both days. In addition to students and seniors, *chô meurs* (the unemployed) get reduced rates; but you must be French to qualify.

The entertainment weeklies list show times and theaters. Film festivals are listed separately. The notation **v.o. (version originale)** after a non-French movie listing means that the film is being shown in its original language with French subtitles; watching an English-language film with French subtitles is a great way to pick up new (and sometimes very interesting) vocabulary. **v.f. (version française)** means that it has been dubbed—an increasingly rare and entirely avoidable phenomenon. If you're braving Paris' intermittent, summertime heat spells, make sure the movie theater is **climatisé (air-conditioned).**

While Hollywood studios have tended to option and remake French films (*Trois hommes et un couffin* became *Three Men and a Baby, Le retour de Martin Guerre* became *Sommersby,* and *La femme Nikita* became *Nikita*), Parisians celebrate U.S. exports as they find them. In the 1940s, French critics discovered Hollywood's thrillers and coined the phrase *film noir;* Jean-Paul Belmondo comically mimicked Bogart in Godard's *A bout de souffle* (*Breathless*). Clint Eastwood found a cult following in France long before he did in America; when he received his first Oscar in 1993, he thanked the French heartily. The Parc de la Villette, 19ème (tel. 40 28 40 33) hosts annual, genre film festivals in July and August. Previous themes have included westerns and road movies; call to find out what's in store for summer 1995.

Throughout the city, and particularly on the Left Bank, you'll find more old Hollywood movies—from Hitchcock to Lubitch—than you ever knew existed. Many American movies that never make it to the big American theaters are shown here; don't be surprised to find a "blockbuster" hit that never played in your home town. Even the stars here run a little counter to American tastes: Mickey Rourke is an icon, Rosanna Arquette a star, and Jerry Lewis the standard-bearer for good comedy. Feature films play in large theaters on the Champs-Elysées, and on boulevards St-Germain, Montparnasse, and St-Michel. Artsier flicks roll in the little theaters on the side streets of the Left Bank.

The **séance** (screening) begins with series of commercials and previews that roll for as much as a half hour. Don't be surprised if a soft-porn music video turns out to be a coffee ad. Also note the cigarette ads, which by law aren't allowed to show anyone smoking. Make sure you tip the person who points you to your seat (about 2F). An old law assuring service workers 12-15% inadvertently bypassed ushers and taxi drivers. Most foreigners are not aware they are expected to tip ushers and often encounter hostility when they fail to do so.

Many theaters in Paris specialize in *art-et-essai* programs featuring the great European auteurs, current independent film, and U.S. classics. **Art-et-essai** is the umbrella term for this particular mix of old and new, but always edifying, cinema.

The options below are some of the most interesting, most unusual, and most popular theaters in Paris.

Action Christine, 4, rue Christine, 6ème, off rue Dauphine (tel. 43 25 85 78). M. Odéon. Plays a variety of artsy films, American and otherwise. Admission 40F; reduced (for students, large families, on Mon. and Wed.) 30F. For 110F (plus a 30F fee at the first purchase), buy a pass good for 1 year that admits you to 6 movies. One of the 2 rooms is wheelchair-accessible; descend down a steep, twisting staircase to get to the other.

L'Arlequin, 76, rue de Rennes, 6ème (tel. 45 44 28 80). M. St-Sulpice. A revival *art-et-essai* cinema with occasional visits from European *auteurs* and first-run preview showings. Some films shown in *version originale,* while others are dubbed; check *Pariscope* to find out about your movie. Admission 43F, students 32F (Mon.-Fri. only), Mon. and Wed. 32F. Full price for all on festival opening nights. Buy tickets in advance. MC, V.

Centre Georges Pompidou, Salle Garance, rue St-Merri, 4ème (tel. 42 78 37 29). M. Rambuteau. Multi-cultural programming fills a gap in the U.S.-laden Parisian film scene. Past series have featured early Caucasian and Neapolitan cinema. Admission 27F, ages 18-25 20F.

Le Ciné-Beaubourg, 50, rue Rambuteau, 3ème (tel. 42 71 52 36; 36 68 69 23 for schedules and film descriptions). Six theaters screen talked-about first-run films. Cannes submissions and prize-winners run May-June. Films competing in Deauville festival screened in September. Additional repertory of cult favorites like *Blade Runner* and *Blue Velvet* changes weekly. All foreign films in v.o. Admission 43F, students 35F, before 1pm 31F50, Wed. 35F for all .

Cinémathèque, Française, at the Musée du Cinéma in the Palais de Chaillot, on av. Albert de Mun at av. Président Wilson, 16ème (tel. 47 04 24 24). M. Trocadéro. Enter through the Jardins du Trocadéro. Answering machine lists all shows. A must for serious film buffs. 1-2 films per day, many of them classics, near-classics, or soon-to-be classics. Foreign films almost always in v.o. Expect long lines. Open Tues.-Sun. Last show 9pm. Admission 25F.

Dôme IMAX, La Défense (tel. 46 92 45 45), to the right of L'Espace Marques. Programs in-the-round which compensate for lack of plot, substance, or taste with their immediacy; past features include *The Fires of Kuwait* and *In Space.* Admission (for 2 films) 55F during the day, 75F at night. Students 45F, 65F at night. Upstairs, the Spider cafeteria (open 10am-4pm) offers a good lunch deal at 50F.

L'Entrepôt, 7-9, rue Francis de Pressensé, 14ème (tel. 45 43 41 63). M. Pernety. Organizes a wide variety of week-long festivals, sometimes with director debates. Independent cinema with a global reach. Adjoining bookstore **Atmosphère** (tel. 45 42 29 26) offers a selection of technical manuals, picture books, and biographies of auteurs. Open Mon.-Sat. 2-8pm. Delightful bar/restaurant (tel. 45 40 60 70) at same address with secluded garden terrace. 58F menu at lunchtime. Beer 15-22F. Restaurant open Mon.-Sat. 12:30-11pm, Sun. 12:30-3pm. Bar open daily 2pm-1am. Two branches project high-quality independent, classic, and foreign films. **Les Trois Luxembourg,** 67, rue Monsieur-le-Prince, 6ème (tel. 46 33 97 77). M. Odéon. All films in v.o. Admission 38F, students 28F. **Le St-Germain-des-Prés,** 22, rue Guillaume Apollinaire, 6ème (tel. 42 22 87 23). M. St-Germain-des-Prés. A big, beautiful theater. Admission 40F, Reduced (for students, seniors, Mon., Wed., and at noon) 30F.

La Géode, 26, av. Corentin-Cariou, 19ème (tel. 36 68 29 30). M. Corentin-Cariou, in La Villette. Mostly scientific documentaries on a huge hemispherical screen. Shows daily on the hour 10am-9pm. Admission 55F, students Mon.-Fri. 40F. Reserve in advance. Wheelchair accessible.

Le Grand Rex, 1, bd. Poissonnière, 2ème (tel. 42 36 83 93). M. Bonne-Nouvelle. This 2800-seat behemoth is the largest theater in Paris. Visit to experience "privatized" viewing amid thousands. Mostly first-runs. Last show around 9:30pm. Admission 42F, students and Mon. 34F. A UGC affiliate.

Musée du Louvre, 1er (tel. 40 20 51 86, reservations 40 20 52 29). M. Palais Royal/Musée du Louvre. A perhaps unlikely venue for cutting-edge film series. Also hosts silent movies with live musical accompaniment. Movies 25F. Call 40 20 54 55 for schedule. Open Sept.-June.

La Pagode, 57bis, rue de Babylone, 7ème (tel. 47 05 12 15). M. St-François-Xavier. The intimate *salle japonaise,* with velvet seats and painted screens, helps make this Paris' most charming cinema. Specializing in contemporary films of the artsy-though-accessible ilk, the Pagode is a well-disguised outpost of Gaumont; the *carte Gaumont* works here. Admission 44F, students and Wed. 36F. 3-5 shows per day. Also visit the *salon de thé,* whose terrace spills into the Japanese garden. *Salon de thé* open Mon.-Sat. 4-9:45pm, Sun. and holidays 2-8pm.

Passage du Nord-Ouest, 13, rue du Faubourg Montmartre, 9ème (tel. 47 70 81 47). M. Rue Montmartre. A descent into cutting-edge multi-media productions. The chameleon-like *café-ciné-concert* adapts its interior to the mood of the festival. Also a concert space for jazz fusion, reggae, world music, and whatever else comes into town. Prices vary with the soirée. Film events 28-80F.

■■■ THEATER

Generally speaking, Parisian theatergoers will either be ushered into large, plush playhouses or crowded onto benches in the smallest of rooms. Intimate performance spaces like *café-théâtres* and *chansonniers* book anything from Vaudevillian comics to accordianists. National theaters, especially the Comédie Française, are stately venues with generally classical repertoires. The famed *grands guignols* (traditional puppet shows) are intended for children but likely to attract adults as well. Most theaters close for the month of August. *Pariscope* and *l'Officiel des Spectacles* provide complete listings of current shows.

Theater tickets can run as high as 200F, but reduced, student rates are nearly always available. In addition, a number of theaters sell rush tickets 30-45 min. before performances. Also try one of the following discount ticket box-offices.

Kiosque-Théâtre, 15, pl. de la Madeleine, 8ème. M. Madeleine. Far and away the best discount box office. Sells half-priced tickets the day of the show. Open Tues.-Sat. 12:30-8pm, Sun. 12:30-4pm. Also in metro stop Châtelet-les-Halles. Open Tues.-Sat. 12-5pm.

COPAR (Service des Activités Culturelles), 39, av. Georges Bernanos, 5ème (tel. 40 51 37 13). M. Port-Royal. Sells tickets at a large, student discount and publishes a monthly list of plays. Also sells discount concert tickets. Accepts any student ID. Open Sept.-July Mon.-Fri. 9am-4:15pm; July-Aug. Mon.-Fri. 9am-5pm. No credit cards.

Alpha FNAC: Spectacles, 136, rue de Rennes, 6ème (tel. 49 54 30 00). M. Montparnasse-Bienvenüe. Also at Forum des Halles, 1-7, rue Porte Lescot, 1er (M. Châtelet-Les Halles); 26-30, av. des Ternes, 17ème (tel. 44 09 18 00; M. Ternes); and 71, bd. St-Germain, 5ème (tel. 44 41 31 50). Tickets for theater and a variety of concerts and festivals. *Carte FNAC* (150F for 3 years, students 100F) holders receive 40% reduction. Open Mon.-Sat. 10am-7:30pm. MC, V.

Virgin Megastore, 52, av. des Champs-Elysées, 8ème (tel. 40 74 06 48 or 42 89 87 27). M. George V. Look for the ticket office below the first floor.

NATIONAL THEATERS

Four of France's five national theaters (add one in Strasbourg) are located in Paris. With the advantages of giant auditoriums, great acoustics, veteran acting troupes, and, in certain cases, centuries of prestige, they stage polished, extremely popular productions. Though modern works are occasionally staged, expect Molière, Racine, Goethe, and Shakespeare (all in French). Unless you're banking on last-minute rush tickets, make reservations 14 days in advance.

La Comédie Française: Salle Richelieu, 2, rue de Richelieu, 1er (tel. 40 15 00 15). M. Palais Royal. Founded by Molière, now the granddaddy of all French theaters. Guaranteed pomp and prestige, with red velvet and chandeliers. Expect wildly gesticulated slapstick farce in the much parodied *"style Comédie Française."* You don't need to speak French to understand the jokes. Will Reopen from renovations Jan. 1995. 892 seats. Open Sept. 15-July; usually no shows on Monday. Box office open daily 11am-6pm. Admission 25-165F, under 25 60F. Rush tickets (25F) available 45 min. before show; line up an hour in advance. The *comédiens français,* as actors here are known, also mount plays in the 330-seat **Théâtre du Vieux Colombier,** 21, rue du Vieux-Colombier, 6ème (tel. 44 39 87 00 and 44 39 87 01; recorded info tel. 36 68 01 50). M. St-Sulpice. 1995 repertory to include works by Marivaux and Racine. Tickets 130F; rush tickets 60F sold 45 min. before performances, available to students under 27 and others under 25.

Odéon Théâtre de l'Europe, 1, pl. Odéon, 6ème (tel. 44 41 36 36). M. Odéon. Eclectic programs run the gamut, from classics to avant-garde. 1042 seats. Also **Petit Odéon,** a much smaller, affiliate with 82 seats. Open Sept.-July. Box office open Mon.-Sat. 11am-6:30pm. Admission 50-165F for most shows, though some cost more; student rush tickets 60F, available 45 min. before the performance. Tickets for Petit Odéon 70F, students 50F. MC, V.

Théâtre National de Chaillot, in the Palais de Chaillot, pl. du Trocadéro, 16ème (tel. 47 27 81 15). M. Trocadéro. Plays and occasional concerts. 2 rooms, one with 1000 and the other with 400 seats. Handicapped-accessible; make arrangements. Box office open Mon.-Sat. 11am-7pm, Sun. 11am-5pm. Admission 150F, under 25 and over 60 110F. Student rush tickets 80F.

Théâtre Nationale de la Colline, 15, rue Malte-Brun, 20ème (tel. 44 62 52 52). M. Gambetta. Grand Théâtre, 760 seats. Also Petit Théâtre, 200 seats. Founded in 1988, this fledgling national theater features contemporary plays, both French and foreign. 1994-95 season for the Grand Théâtre includes works by Mrozek, de la Parra, Bowles and Weingarten; at the Petit Théâtre, works by Tilly, Brusati, Berkoff and Nieva. Both handicapped accessible; call ahead. Open Sept.-July. Box office open Tues.-Sat. 11am-8pm, Sun.-Mon. 11am-6pm. Admission 150F, under 26 and over 60 one ticket 110F, two 150F. Petit Théâtre offers a Wed. lunchtime show (100F) with a set meal (50F). Hosts modern classical music concerts (100F) one night a week Nov.-April.

PRIVATE THEATERS

Paris' private theaters, though less celebrated than their state-run counterparts, often stage outstanding productions. Yet in this realm of the weird and wonderful, risky performances sometimes misfire. Check the reviews in newspapers and entertainment weeklies before investing in a seat. Watch for schedules on the green, cylindrical *spectacles* notice boards posted throughout the city.

Athénée-Louis Jouvet, 4, sq. de l'Opéra, 9ème (tel. 47 42 67 27). M. Opéra or Auber. 687 seats. Hard-to-find, with an unremarkable exterior, but a magnificent 18th-century interior and outstanding classical productions. Open Oct.-May. Box office open Mon.-Sat. 11:30am-6pm. Admission 80-110F.

Experimental Theater Wing Studio, 14, rue Letellier, 15ème. M. Emile Zola. Six-year-old extension of New York University's theater program. Interesting and unusual productions in English. Prices vary with performance.

Jardin Shakespeare du Pré Catelan, in the center of the Bois de Boulogne, west of the Lac Inférieur (tel. 42 76 47 72). Take bus #244 from Porte Maillot. 500 seats. Summertime Shakespeare in French, set in a garden of plants mentioned by the bard. Tickets at the door or at FNAC. Shows usually Sat. 4pm and 6:15pm, Sun. 4pm. Buses stop running before late shows end, and walking in the large deserted Bois de Boulogne is dangerous even if you know your way out. Instead, take a taxi to Porte Maillot. Admission 60-100F.

Théâtre de la Huchette, 23, rue de la Huchette, 5ème (tel. 43 26 38 99). M. St-Michel. 100 seats. Tiny theater whose productions of Ionesco's *La cantatrice chauve* (The Bald Soprano) and *La leçon* (The Lesson) are still popular after 33 years. Shows Mon.-Sat. Box office open Mon.-Sat. 5-9pm. Admission 100F, students 70F; for both shows 160F, students 100F. No discounts Sat.

Théâtre Mogador, 25, rue de Mogador, 9ème (tel. 48 78 04 04). M. Trinité. With 1792 seats, one of the largest theaters in Paris. Grandiose comedies and musicals on a colossal stage. Frequent matinees Sat. 4pm. Open Sept.-May Tues.-Sat. Box office open daily 11am-7pm. Admission 160-260F, matinees 140-230F.

Théâtre Renaud-Barrault, 2bis, av. Franklin D. Roosevelt, 8ème (tel. 44 95 98 00). M. Franklin D. Roosevelt. 920 seats. Also **Petite Salle** (tel. 42 56 08 80). 150 seats. Large stage hosts outlandish musicals and comedies. Open Sept.-July. Box office open Tues.-Sat. 11am-6pm, Sun. noon-4pm. Admission 110-140F, students and seniors 100F. Petite salle 120F, reduced 60-90F.

Théâtre de la Ville, 2, pl. du Châtelet, 4ème (tel. 42 74 22 77). M. Châtelet. 1000 seats. Excellent productions of all ilks, including classical music concerts. Wheelchair-accessible. Open Sept.-June. Box office open Sun.-Mon. 11am-6pm; also open for telephone sales Mon.-Fri. 9am-8pm. Admission 70-120F, students 60-85F.

CAFÉ-THEÂTRES

Visit one of Paris' *café-théâtres* for an evening of word-play and social satire in mostly black-box theater settings. Expect low-budget, high-energy skits filled with political puns and double-entendres; in general, knowledge of French slang and politics is a must for audience members. One-wo/man shows are a mainstay.

Au Bec Fin, 6, rue Thérèse, 1er (tel. 42 96 29 35). M. Palais Royal. A tiny, 60-seat theater, usually with 2 different shows per night. Dinner and 1 show from 178F, Sat. 210F. Dinner and 2 shows from 300F. Shows at 7, 8:30, and 10:15pm. Auditions sometimes open to the public (45F). Admission 80F, students 65F; Mon.-Tues. admission 50F.

Café de la Gare, 41, rue du Temple, 4ème (tel. 42 78 52 51). M. Hôtel-de-Ville. Where the infamous Coluche got his start. Couched in the cobbled courtyard of the Centre de Danse du Marais, the Café de la Gare attracts an engaging, youthful crowd to bold performances ranging in comic flavor and cast size. Recent acts have included solo comics and a look-alike Addams Family. Reservations daily 3-7pm. Otherwise, come to the box office 30 minutes before the show. Most shows start at 8 and 9:15pm. Admission 80-100F, students 60F.

Petit Casino, 17, rue Chapon, 3ème (tel. 42 78 36 50). M. Arts-et-Métiers. Once a plumbing store, now a basement dinner-theater with a stage that's 4 paces wide. Self-serve smorgasborg of salads, charcuteries and desserts. Performances tend toward low comedy. Usually two shows per night. Reservations Tues.-Sun. 2-7pm. Dinner and 2 shows Tues.-Fri. and Sun. 120F, Sat. 220F. Last show 70F.

Le Point Virgule, 7, rue Ste-Croix-de-la-Bretonnerie, 4ème (tel. 42 78 67 03). M. Hôtel-de-Ville. As intimate and interactive as theater can be short of sitting on the stage. Capacity crowds of 140 sit shoulder-to-elbow on small benches. Shows generally feature one or two actors. Frequent slapstick acts ideal for non-French speakers. You may leave feeling the actor spent as much time watching you as you did her. Reservations suggested, accepted 24 hrs. Mon.-Fri. 2 shows 130F; 3 shows 150F. Admission 80F, students 65F. Open 5pm-midnight.

CHANSONNIERS

The *chansonnier* is the musical cousin of the *café-théâtre*. In the spirit of old Paris, audience members sing along to French folk songs. The better your French, the better the time you'll have. Come to belt out French classics you don't even know. Admission usually includes one drink.

Au Lapin Agile, 22, rue des Saules, 18ème (tel. 46 06 85 87). M. Lamarck-Coulaincourt. Picasso, Verlaine, Clemenceau, Renoir, Apollinaire, and Max Jacob hung out here during the heyday of Montmartre. Arrive early for a good seat. Usually crowded with tourists. Shows at 9:15pm. Admission and first drink 110F, students 80F. Subsequent drinks 25F. Open Tues.-Sun. 9pm-2am.

Caveau des Oubliettes, 11, rue St-Julien-le-Pauvre, 5ème (tel. 43 54 94 97). M. St-Michel. Located in what were once the bowels of the Petit-Châtelet Prison. The dark wood paneling and *"musée avec guillotine,"* together with old French folk songs, lend this place a medieval feel. Cover and first drink 140F, 100F with student ID. Open Mon.-Sat. 9pm-2am. V.

Caveau de la République, 1, bd. St-Martin, 3ème (tel. 42 78 44 45). M. République. A mostly Parisian crowd fills the 482 seats of this 90-year old venue for political satire. Shows string together 6 or 7 separate acts; the sequence is known as the *tour de champs* (tour of the field). Tickets sold 6 days in advance, 11am-6pm. Shows Tues.-Sat. 9pm, Sun. 3:30pm. Admission 170F; during the week, students and over 60 105F. MC, V.

Deux Anes, 100, bd. de Clichy, 18ème (tel. 46 06 10 26). M. Blanche. 300 seats. Shows Mon.-Sat. 9pm. Reservations by phone 11am-7pm, 2 weeks in advance. Admission 120F, students 95F. Open Sept.-June.

GUIGNOLS

Grand guignol is a traditional Parisian marionette theater aptly featuring the *guignol*, its classic stock character. These antic performances have long thrilled adults as well as children. Though the puppets speak French, you'll have no trouble understanding the slapstick, child-geared humor. Nearly all parks have *guignols;* check *Pariscope* for others that change location weekly.

Marionettes des Champs-Elysées, Rond Point de Champs-Elysées, 8ème (tel. 42 57 43 34), at the intersection of av. Matignon and Gabriel. M. Champs-Elysées-Clemenceau. The classic adventures of the *guignol* character. Wed. and Sat.-Sun. 3, 4, and 5pm. Admission 12F50.

Marionettes du Luxembourg, Jardin du Luxembourg, 6ème (tel. 43 26 46 47). M. Luxembourg or Notre-Dame-des-Champs. In the opinion of many smaller folk, the best thing about the Jardin du Luxembourg. This roofed-in theater plays the same children's classics it has since it opened in 1933: *Little Red Riding Hood, The Three Little Pigs,* and so on. Running time is about 45 min. Arrive 30 minutes early for good seats. Shows Wed. and Sat.-Sun. 3:15 and 4:15pm, Tues., Thurs., and Fri at variable times. Call ahead for time changes. Admission 21F.

Théâtre de la Petite Ourse, Jardin des Tuileries, 8ème (tel. 42 86 03 34). M. Tuileries or Concorde. A classic marionette show within walking distance of the Louvre. Call for times and titles. Admission 20F, children 15F. Wed. and Sat.-Sun. 3:30 and 4:30pm.

CABARETS

Contrary to popular tourist belief, Parisian cabarets (officially called *revues)* are not exclusively for foreigners. The big names—the Moulin Rouge and the Folies Bergère—are frequented by as many cameras as people, but some of the less-publicized cabarets lure Parisians as well; stampedes of well-hoofed locals unwind at the Crazy Horse after work. Although the complete dinner package is prohibitively expensive, you can often just watch from the bar.

Le Bal du Moulin Rouge, pl. Blanche, 9ème (tel. 46 06 00 19). M. Blanche. The most famous of them all, this *revue* celebrated its centennial in 1989. Unfortunately, tourists—of the money-burning-a-hole-in-their-pocket variety—have replaced Toulouse-Lautrec, who selected his artistic models from the performers on stage. Still, an impressive show with 100 dancers, singers, and castanet players. Opens at 8pm. Shows daily at 10pm and midnight. Reserve by phone 10am-7pm. Dinner and show from 670F. Show 465F.

Crazy Horse Saloon, 12, av. George V, 8ème (tel. 47 23 32 32). M. Alma-Marceau. More Parisians, fewer tourists; more flesh, less glamour. Crazy Horse just did some renovation and now has 380 seats. A pretty racy place. Dancers have names like Betty Buttocks and Funky Coconut. Shows daily at 9 and 11:15pm; arrive 30 min. early. Reserve by phone 11am-6pm. Bar 195F, under 26 130F. Tables from 290F (2 drinks included).

Les Folies-Bergère, 32, rue Richer, 9ème (tel. 42 46 77 11). M. Cadet or Rue Montmartre. Over 60 dancers and musicians in the music hall Manet immortalized with his the haunting work, *Bar aux Folies-Bergère.* 106 years running. Shows Tues.-Sun. at 9:15pm. Reservations at box office daily 11am-6pm or by phone 11am-6:30pm. Dinner and show 670F. Show 152-295F, July-Aug. Tues.-Thurs and Sun. 100-295F. Special under 25 discount Tues.-Thurs. and Sun. (120F).

Le Monocle, 60, bd. Edgar Quinet, 14ème (tel. 43 20 81 12). M. Edgar Quinet. This *cabaret féminin* (women's cabaret) caters to a sophisticated crowd. Transvestite revue starts at 9pm. Shows daily starting at 4pm.

■■■ MUSIC

CLASSICAL MUSIC, OPERA, AND DANCE

Paris toasts the classics under lamppost, spire, and chandelier. The city's squares, churches, and concert halls feature world-class performers from home and abroad. But visitors may find in France's cultural capital a giant with a limp, favoring classical music and opera in lieu of dance; the quality and quantity of classical repertoires here seem to follow the tastes of the city's patron, François Mitterrand. Acclaimed foreign and provincial dance companies swing into town to take up the slack; watch for posters and read *Pariscope*. Summer music and, to a lesser extent, dance festivals bring soloists from all over the world to locations near you. Connoisseurs will find the thick and indexed *Programme des Festivals* indispensable (free at *mairies* (town halls) and at the tourist office). Paris offers cheap tickets to high culture in great quantities, thanks to a socialism that peddles gentler arts to the masses. Beware, however, of rock-bottom prices. The Opéra Bastille suffers from an irremediable acoustical disease. And, while Balanchine may have said "see the music, hear the dance," you may not agree from the back row of the Opéra Garnier, Paris's ballet-only theater. Try to check a theater floor plan whenever possible. **ALPHA-FNAC,** 1-7, rue Pierre Lescot, Forum des Halles (tel. 40 41 40 00) is the popular booking agent (open Tues.-Sat. 10am-7:30pm, Mon. 1-7:30pm); call to find a FNAC near you. (See Festivals and Theater sections for details on annual events and rush tickets.)

IRCAM, Institut de la Recherche et de la Coordination Acoustique/Musique, Centre Pompidou, 1, pl. Igor-Stravinsky, 4ème (tel. 44 78 48 16; for reservations 44 84 44 72). M. Rambuteau or Hôtel-de-Ville. Contemporary compositions sometimes accompanied by "film" or "theater." If it's weird and legit, it's here. Stop by the office near the Stravinsky fountain for schedules. (See also Museums.)

Musée du Louvre, 1er (tel. 40 20 52 99 for information; 40 20 52 29 for reservations). M. Palais-Royal/Musée du Louvre. Classical music in a classy auditorium. Tickets for individual concerts 65-130F. Music-film combos 25F. Open Sept.-June.

Opéra de la Bastille, pl. de la Bastille, 11ème (tel. 43 43 96 96). M. Bastille. The Opéra de la Bastille staged its first performance on July 14, 1989, during the bicentennial jubilee. Hailed by some as the hall to bring opera to the masses, decried by others as offensive to every aesthetic sensibility, this huge theater features classic opera and ballet, often with a modern spin. The Bastille opera has acoustical problems, spread democratically throughout the theater, making this a bad place to go all-out for front row seats. Subtitles in English and French during impossible-to-understand lyrical performances. Tickets range from 50-560F. Call or write for a free brochure of the season's events. Tickets can be purchased: by writing and sending a check (foreigners can pay on arrival in Paris by presenting their letter of confirmation); by phone (tel. 44 73 13 00; open Mon.-Sat. 11am-6pm; by minitel (3615 code THEA then Opéra Bastille); or in person Mon.-Sat. 11am-6:30pm. Tickets go on sale, on site, 14 days in advance. Opera reserves the right to limit the number of tickets purchased. Reduced rush tickets for under 25, students, and over 65, often available 15 min. before show. Wheelchair access; call (tel. 44 73 13 73) to make arrangements at least 15 days in advance. MC, V.

Opéra Comique, 5, rue Favart, 2ème (tel. 42 86 88 83). M. Richelieu-Drouot. Operas on a lighter scale—from Rossini to Offenbach. Purchase tickets at the box office Mon.-Fri. 11am-6pm or reserve over the phone. Tickets 40-430F.

Opéra Garnier, pl. de l'Opéra, 9ème (tel. 40 17 35 35 for information, 47 42 53 71 for reservations). M. Opéra. The historic Opéra Garnier now hosts the Ballet de l'Opéra de Paris and visiting ballet troupes, as well as occasional operas and concerts by foreign companies and orchestras. Tickets available at the box office 2 weeks before each performance Mon.-Sat. 11am-6:30pm. Tickets 30-370F. MC, V.

Orchestre de Paris, in the Salle Pleyel, 252, rue du Faubourg St-Honoré, 8ème (tel. 45 43 96 96). M. Ternes. The internationally renowned orchestra delivers first-class performances under the baton of music director Semyon Bychkov. Season runs Sept.-May; call or stop by for concert calendar. Tickets 50-250F.

Théâtre des Champs-Elysées, 15, av. Montaigne, 8ème (tel. 49 52 50 50). M. Alma Marceau. Top international dance companies and orchestras. To play here is to "arrive" at the highbrow music scene. Buy tickets 3 weeks in advance. Box office open by telephone Mon.-Fri. 2-6pm; otherwise Tues.-Fri. 11am-7pm, Mon. and Sat. 11am-5pm. Tickets 40-500F.

Théâtre Musical de Paris, pl. du Châtelet, 1er (tel. 42 33 00 00). M. Châtelet. A superb 2300-seat theater normally reserved for guest orchestras and ballet companies. Magnificent acoustics. Call for a schedule. Tickets run 70-300F. MC, V.

Free concerts are often held in churches and parks, especially during summer festivals. These are extremely popular; get there early if you want to breathe. Check the entertainment weeklies and the Alpha FNAC offices for concert notices. **AlloConcerts'** 24-hr. hotline provides info in French on free open-air concerts in the parks (tel. 42 76 50 00). The **American Church in Paris,** 65, quai d'Orsay, 7ème (tel. 47 05 07 89; M. Invalides or Alma Marceau), sponsors free concerts (Oct.-June Sun. at 6pm). **Eglise St-Merri** is also known for its free concerts (Sat. at 9pm and Sun. at 4pm, except in Aug.); contact Accueil Musical St-Merri, 76, rue de la Verrerie, 4ème (tel. 42 76 93 93; M. Châtelet). Sunday concerts take place in the Jardin du Luxembourg band shell (tel. 42 37 20 00); show up early for a seat or prepare to stand. Infrequent concerts in the **Musée d'Orsay** are free with a museum ticket. The **Maison de la Radio-France** hosts concerts, both free and not. (See Entertainment—Literary Life).

Other churches, such as **Eglise St-Germain-des-Prés,** 3, pl. St-Germain-des-Prés, 6ème (M. St-Germain-des-Prés), **Eglise St-Eustache,** rue du Jour, 1er (M. Les Halles), and **Eglise St-Louis-en-l'Ile,** 19, rue St-Louis-en-l'Ile, 4ème (M. Pont Marie), stage frequent concerts that are somewhat expensive (70-100F for students), but feature fantastic acoustics and unbeatable atmosphere. For information about church concerts, call 43 29 68 68. Arrive 30-45 min. ahead to find a front-row seat. **Ste-Chapelle** hosts concerts a few times per week in summer (sometimes free on Sun.). Contact the box office at 4, bd. du Palais, 1er (tel. 46 61 55 41; M. Cité; open daily 1:30-5:30pm; admission 120-150F, students 80-100F).

■■■ JAZZ

Some critics mourn that Paris is not the jazz capital it once was. Even so, there are a healthy number of nightly gigs to choose from, ranging from French unknowns to big-name Americans on tour.

Aided by the sudden influx of American recordings into post-war France, Paris' status as a jazz hot-spot emerged in the late 1940s. Since then, French jazz musicians have themselves become fixtures on the international scene. Among them is pianist and native Parisian Michel Petrucciani, the apple of the city's eye. On the Paris scene, pianist Laurent de Wilde won France's Django Prize in 1993. Funk-groove leader and guitarist Hervé Krief is well loved by French crowds, as is the old-guard blues organist Eddy Louis. Right now in Paris, acid jazz and hip-hop fusion are popular; meanwhile 70s fusion has nearly disappeared.

Frequent summer festivals sponsor free or nearly free jazz concerts. The Fête du Marais often features free big-band jazz, while the Parc de la Villete hosts jazz orchestras with a Latin beat. In fall, the Jazz Festival of Paris comes to town as venues high and low open their doors to celebrity and up-and-coming artists (late Oct. to early Nov.) To participate in a jam session is to *faire le boeuf;* travelers should consider doing just that at Paris' **Fête de la Musique,** when streets and storefronts fill with amateur and professional, often ad-hoc ensembles (see Entertainment—Festivals).

Jazz Hot (45F) and *Jazz Magazine* (35F)—France's answers to *Downbeat* and *Metronome*—are both great sources of information, as is the hard-to-find, bimonthly *LYLO (Les Yeux, Les Oreilles).* If you can't find it in bars or FNACS, try the main office, 55, rue des Vinaigriers, 10ème (tel. 42 09 02 98). Also, read Pariscope.

New Morning, 7-9, rue des Petites-Ecuries, 10ème (tel. 45 23 51 41). M. Château d'Eau. 400-seat, former printing plant with the biggest American headliners in the city. Halfway between club and concert hall, it only feels cozy when it's packed; come for music, not ambiance. Sit in the lower front section or in the near wings for best acoustics. Good sound system, a grand piano, and a large stage. Attracts big names like Wynton Marsalis, Bobby McFerrin, and Betty Carter. All the greats have played here—from Chet Baker to Stan Getz and Miles Davis; Archie Shepp is a regular. Open Sept.-July 9:30pm; times vary. Admission 110-130F.

Au Duc des Lombards, 42, rue des Lombards, 1er (tel. 42 33 22 88). M. Châtelet. Murals of Duke Ellington and Coltrane swath the exterior of this principal member of the Lombard club threesome. The best French jazz, with only occassional American soloists. Dark, smoky, and packed with regulars. For Tuesday jam sessions, musicians skip 1st drink charge. One Tues. per month, the *Lombards sur Jazz* event offers all-night admission to all three Lombards clubs for 70F (drinks not included). Otherwise, 1st drink 60-110F. Open daily 7:30pm-4am. MC, V.

La Villa, in Hôtel La Villa, 29, rue Jacob, 6ème. M. St-Germain-des-Prés. Downstairs in a 4-star hotel, this exclusive and expensive new club can afford to fly American soloists here for week-long engagements with French rhythm sections. Short list of stars that have appeared here include Shirley Horn, Joe Lovano, Josh Redman, and Clifford Jordan. Bar serves cocktails with clever names like "Night and Day" and "Blue in Paris." 1st drink weekdays 120F, weekend 150F. Special musician price 60F. Open Mon.-Sat. 10pm-3am. MC,V.

Le Petit Journal Montparnasse, 13, rue du Commandant-Mouchotte, 14ème (tel. 43 21 56 70). M. Montparnasse-Bienvenüe. Look for the large animated neon sign of a horn player. An elegant club, popular with a well-to-do, older clientele. Very good piano and sound system at the service of best contemporary mainstream French jazz; 1994 saw Michel Legrand, Michel Petrucciani, Eddy Louiss. Obligatory first drink 100-160F. Open Mon.-Sat. 9pm-2am.

Caveau de la Huchette, 5, rue de la Huchette, 5ème (tel. 43 26 65 05). M. St-Michel. You probably haven't seen such enthusiastic jive dancing since junior high. Bebop dance lessons offered weekday evenings before club opens; call 42 71 09 09. Swing, blues, and boogie bands are suitable for dancing, though not always a thrill to hear. The *caves* are thrilling, though, with a gruesome history; they served as tribunal, prison, and execution rooms, used by by Danton, Marat, St-Just, and Robespierre during the Revolution. When the club moved into this space in the late 40s, they found 2 skeletons chained together. Two thumbs up for atmosphere. Crowded on weekends. Min. age 18. Cover Sun.-Thurs. 55F, students 50F. Fri.-Sat. cover 60F. Drinks from 35F. Open Sun.-Thurs. 10pm-2:30am, Fri. 9:30pm-3am, Sat. 9:30pm-4am.

Le Petit Journal St-Michel, 71, bd. St-Michel, 5ème (tel. 43 26 28 59). M. Luxembourg. A crowded but intimate establishment, where students mix with fortysomethings reminiscing about 1968. New Orleans bands and first-class performers play in this Parisian center of the "Old Style." Music played Sept.-July Mon.-Sat. 9:30pm-1:45am. Obligatory 1st drink 100F, 40F thereafter.

Le Petit Opportun, 15, rue des Lavandières-Ste-Opportune, 1er (tel. 42 36 01 36). M. Châtelet. A relaxed and unpolished pub, where you can hear some of the best modern jazz trios and quartets around, including a lot of American bands and soloists. The club is tiny (60 seats), and so popular that it ought to seat 500. Come early. Open Sept.-July Tues.-Sat. from 11pm; bar open until 3am. 1st drink 100F, 50F thereafter.

Le Baiser Salé, 58, rue des Lombards, 1er (tel. 42 33 37 71). M. Châtelet. Rounding out the Lombards club trio in style, this upper-floor club remains one of the few strongholds of 70s-style fusion. Intimate space feels like a student's garret, with murals of troglodytes playing fifes and guitars. African and Antillean Music also featured here; watch for 2-week African music festival in Jan. Concerts at 8:30pm and 10:30pm. Jam sessions Wed. 60F including drink, reduced musician price 30F. Thurs.-Tues. 1st drink 60-85F. Participates in "Lombards sur Jazz" (see **Le Duc des Lombards**).

Slow Club, 130, rue de Rivoli, 1er (tel. 42 33 84 30). M. Châtelet. Miles Davis' favorite jazz club in Paris. Big bands, traditional jazz, and Dixieland in a wonderful old-time setting. Expect dancing and a crowd in the 30s. Weekday cover 60F. Weekend cover from 75F. Women and students 5F less during the week. Drinks from 25F. Open Tues.-Thurs. 10pm-3am, Fri.-Sat. 10pm-4am.

Le Passage du Nord-Ouest, 13, rue du Faubourg Montmartre, 9ème (tel. 47 70 81 47). M. Rue Montmartre. This 4-year old *art-et-essai* space books jazz and world beats from Brazil to the Mississippi, Egypt to Cameroon. Times vary with the event; call or stop by for a program. Admission around 120F.

Le Sunset, 60, rue des Lombards, 1er (tel. 40 26 46 60). M. Châtelet. The most easy-going of the Lombards clubs; books lesser-known French musicians. The underground room resembles a metro, in its arched ceiling and walls, and in its acoustics; sit close. For Mon. jam sessions, 1st drink 58-78F; Tues.-Thurs. 78-98F; Fri.-Sat. 88-108F; Sun. 78-98F. Participates in "Lombards sur Jazz" (see Duc des Lombards). Open daily 10pm-dawn.

Jazz O'Brazil, 38, rue Mouffetard, 5ème (tel. 45 87 36 09). M. Monge. Excellent samba guitarists and new groups. Try the house drink *caitirissa* (lime juice and vodka). No cover. Drinks 60F. Open daily 9:30pm-2am

Café de la Plage, 59, rue de Charonne, 11ème (tel. 47 00 91 60). M. Bastille. A 2-tiered club for a very trendy Bastille crowd. Upstairs canned African, Latin, and mainstream jazz rhythms; downstairs acid jazz. *Cave* features mostly DJs, with some live music. Cover and first drink 90F; no cover Thurs. Upstairs open 8pm-2am. Downstairs 11pm-as long as you can stand.

■■■ DISCOS AND ROCK CLUBS

Paris is not Barcelona, Montréal, or Buenos Aires; you won't find entire streets filled with young people waiting and struggling to get into discos. Instead, the clubs are small, private, and nearly impossible to find out about, unless you're a native. The discos that are "in" (or even in business) change drastically from year to year; only a few have been popular since the 1960s. Many Parisian clubs are officially private, which means they have the right to pick and choose their clientele. The management can evaluate prospective customers through peepholes in the handle-less front doors. Parisians tend to dress up more than North Americans for a night on the town; haggard backpackers might be wise to try a bar instead.

In general, word of mouth is the best guide to the current scene. Some of the smaller places in the *quartier latin* admit almost anyone who is sufficiently decked out. To access one of the more exclusive places, you need to accompany a regular. Otherwise, plan to look good, don't publicize your foreignness, and be prepared to shell out a good amount of money. Many clubs reserve the right to refuse entry to unaccompanied men. Women often get a discount or get in free, but don't go alone unless you're looking for lots of amorous attention. Weekdays are cheaper and less crowded so you'll have a better chance of moving, but most of the action happens on weekends. **Les Bains** is still the best.

Les Bains, 7, rue du Bourg l'Abbé, 3ème (tel. 48 87 01 80). M. Réaumur-Sébastopol. Ultra-selective and ultra-expensive, but worth it—if you can get in past the fearless bouncers. The man formerly called Prince established its reputation with a surprise free concert a few years back. It used to be a public bath, visited at least once by Marcel Proust. More recently, Mike Tyson, Madonna, Roman Polanski and Jack Nicholson have stopped in. Lots of models and super-attractive people. Cover and 1st drink 140F, 2nd drink 100F. Open Tues.-Sun. 11:30pm-6am.

Le Balajo, 9, rue de Lappe, 11ème (tel. 47 00 07 87). M. Bastille. A youthful, energetic crowd assembles at this seasoned Parisian hang-out, once Edith Piaf's favorite venue. Founded in 1936 by Jo France—hence the name *Bal à Jo*. Cover and 1st drink 100F. Open Wed.-Sat. 11pm-5am.

La Casbah, 18-20, rue de la Forge Royale, 11ème (tel. 43 71 71 89). M. Faidherbe-Chaligny. This chic, whimsical dance lair mixes pop and Arabic music. Elegant, with a strict door policy. Cover 80F for women, 100F for men. Open daily 9pm-6am.

Flash Back, 18, rue des Quatre-Vents, 6ème (tel. 43 25 56 10). M. Odéon. Two levels of secluded lounges and a small mirrored dance floor with disco ball. On Tuesday retro-nights, DJ spins hits from the 70s and early 80s. Thursday night floor show features anything from Lola the Showgirl to fly dancers. Comfortable, easy atmosphere among Paris' beautiful youth. Cover 70F, Tues.-Thurs. women free. Drinks 70F. Open Tues.-Sat. 11pm-dawn.

Le Palace, 8, rue du Faubourg Montmartre, 9ème (tel. 42 46 10 87). M. Rue Montmartre. A funky disco, although its days as the hottest club in Paris have gone by.

If you hit a private party and still get in, the music and crowd can be very cool. Otherwise, the music is all too top-40. A mix of happy high school students wanting to "get together" and some older people wanting to get in on the action. Still, the place is huge (up to 2000 people per night), with multi-level dance floors, each with separate bars and different music. American cocktails and occasional rock concerts. Sun. features the Gay Tea Dance, a 15-year institution of the Parisian gay scene. Cover and 1 drink Tues.-Thurs. 100F, Fri.-Sat. 130F, Sun. 130F for men, women free. Subsequent drinks 60F. Open Tues.-Sun. 11:30pm-6am. The British owners also run **Le Central,** 102, av. des Champs-Elysées, 8ème (M. George V). With an older clientele and higher percentage of foreigners.

Le Queen, 102, av. des Champs-Elysées, 8ème (tel. 42 89 31 32). The closest Paris comes to the New York scene. Flashing purple on the Champs Elysées, it's easy to see but hard to get into. Transvestites dance on tables to excellent house music. Dress your most (insert adjective) and try to look nonchalant. Open daily.

Le Saint, 7, rue Saint-Séverin, 5ème (tel. 43 25 50 04). M. Saint-Michel. Plays a wide range of music, rap, soul, R&B, retro, reggae, and zouk. A small club filled with regulars who come to dance. Tues.-Thurs. Cover 60F, Fri. 70F, Sat. 80F. Drinks 15-50F. Open 11pm-6am.

Scala de Paris, 188bis, rue de Rivoli, 1er (tel. 42 61 64 00 and 42 60 45 64). M. Palais-Royal. Halfway between a disco and a rollercade; strings of lights and 2 disco balls hang above the central, two-story dance floor. Not as famous or trendy as other Parisian clubs, it's gaining ground as others decline. There is a smaller, third-floor dance floor as well. Mixes house and techno for an 18-24 crowd. Lots of foreigners. Cover Sun.-Thurs. 80F, women free, Fri. 80F, Sat. 90F. Additional drinks 45F. Open daily 10:30pm-dawn.

Le Tabou, 33, rue Dauphine, 6ème (tel. 43 25 66 33). M. Odéon. An older, very chic crowd of habitués make this club somewhat difficult to get into. Elegantly dressed pairs have a fighting chance. Music ranges from reggae to rock to house, depending upon the DJ. Reggae nights on Tuesday and Thursday. Cover and 1st drink Mon.-Thurs. 70F, Fri.-Sat. 80F. Drinks from 50F. Open daily 11pm-dawn.

For **folk music,** try the restaurant **Au Limonaire** (see Restaurants—12ème arrondissement). Also popular in France are clubs specializing in **Brazilian samba** and **African music:**

Chez Félix, 23, rue Mouffetard, 5ème (tel. 47 07 68 78). M. Monge. Eat upstairs and then descend for an evening of samba or lambada in the cave. Music 11pm-dawn. Cover and first drink 100F, subsequent drinks 70F. Open Sept.-July Tues.-Sat. 11pm-5am.

La Plantation, 45, rue Montpensier, 1er (tel. 49 27 06 21). M. Palais-Royal. Well-dressed, thirtysomething crowd comes to dance the night away to African, Antillean, and salsa rhythms. In decor, the club is mainly a dance floor. Things don't pick up until 2am. Cover and first drink 90F, subsequent drinks 50F. Open Tues.-Sun. 11pm-dawn. MC, V.

Le Tango, 13, rue au Maire, 3ème (tel. 42 72 17 78). M. Arts et Métiers. Crowd dances Friday and Saturday to Antillean, African, salsa, and zouk music. Regulars (ages 20-35) all know each other. Except for summer, every second Wednesday features a live groove-jazz funk band. Kind of square, red decor compensated for by cool art deco lamps and good sound. Cover Wed. 50F, Fri. 40F, Sat. and eves of holidays 60F. Drinks 25-40F, beer 35F. Open mid July-Sept. Fri., Sat. and eves of holidays 11pm-4am; Oct.-early July also open every second Wed. 11pm-4am.

■■■ BARS

Apart from booze and chairs, there is no common denominator to the Parisian bar scene. Let *arrondissement* reputations be your guide. Bars in the 5ème and 6ème often cater to anglophone students, while the Marais and Bastille—the chic quarters of the moment—host lively crowds of Paris' young, hip, and friendly. Draught beer is *bière pression; kir* is a mixture of white wine and *cassis*. The bartender is the *bar-*

man. As with cafés, expect two lists of prices for drinks; stand at the bar and pay less or sit and pay a few francs more for *ambiance.* Law dictates a price increase after 10pm, but no one really ventures out before this wee hour.

Le Petit Fer à Cheval, 30, rue Vieille-du-Temple, 4ème (tel. 42 72 47 47). M. Hôtel-de-Ville. A small bar and restaurant named from the horseshoe-shaped bar. Busy sidewalk terrace and small, intimate restaurant in the back make this a great place to meet with friends. Beer 16F. Cocktails 34-44F. Last call 1:30am. Limited chalkboard menu includes a salmon pasta dish (67F) and a warm *chèvre* salad called, appropriately, *le salade du petit fer à cheval* (56F). The denim-shirted waiters here are zany and fun. Open daily 9am-midnight, but often later.

La Perla, 26, rue François-Miron, 4ème (tel. 42 77 59 40). M. Hôtel-de-Ville. The best of the Parisian Tex-Mex rage, La Perla mixes a superb margarita (50F) and attracts laid-back, turned-out twentysomethings with money and time on their hands. Draught beer 20F, bottled 32F. Quesadillas 32-40F. Fajitas 48F. Open daily noon-2am.

Le Bar sans Nom, 49, rue de Lappe, 11ème (tel. 48 05 59 36). M. Bastille. There's nothing cooler than this bar—cavernous, deep crimson, and packed with the hippest of the hip. Beer 20F. Cocktails 44F. Open daily 10:30pm-2am.

Café de l'Industrie, 16, rue St-Sabin, 11ème (tel. 47 00 13 53). M. Bastille. They think it's a café; we think it's a bar. Garage-sale assemblage of odd chairs, alligator skins, and tassled lamps alongside contemporary art and people too hip to try. Quick service and huge drinks. Beer 16-27F. Cocktails 25-40F. Good selection of food: *tagliatella carbonara* 42F. Open Sun.-Fri. 11am-2am.

Café Oz, 184, rue St-Jacques, 5ème (tel. 43 54 30 48). M. Luxembourg. The crew at this newly opened café/bar swears it's "the only Australian thing in continental Europe." Boomerang-shaped ashtrays, Aussie knick-knacks fixed to the walls, and rustic wood furnishings. If you're nice to the guy behind the bar, he might even let you play the *didgeridoo,* the aboriginal wind instrument hanging above his head. Ever-changing menu includes fresh fruit juices, meat and vegetable pies, chocolate and banana cake, and daily specials. Bountiful and creative sandwiches 20-40F, meat and veggie pies 20F. Huge, ever-expanding beer selection: canned, bottled, and on draught 20-35F. Australian wine a little steep at 25-38F the glass. Cocktails 25F during the jazz cocktail hours, daily 6:30-8:30pm. Bar open daily 11am-1:30am.

La Chope des Artistes, 42, rue du Faubourg St-Martin, 10ème (tel. 42 02 86 76). M. Strasbourg St-Denis. Ochre-colored walls and chandelier frame a cozy piano bar. Theater-goers often head here for a cocktail (around 50F) and a musical evening, after 8pm. The young proprietor sets the tone; many an *artiste* while away the hours here. Open Tues.-Sat. 8am-2am.

L'Entrepot, 14, rue de Charonne, 11ème (tel. 48 06 57 04). M. Bastille. The real pool table draws a chic and yuppie crowd. Drinks from 50F. Open daily 7pm-2am. MC, V.

Finnegan's Wake, 9, rue des Boulangers, 5ème (tel. 46 34 23 65). M. Cardinal Lemoine. From the metro walk up rue des Boulangers to this boisterous Irish pub set in a renovated 14th-century wine cellar. Pours the best pints of Guinness in the city (18-32F), and hosts a variety of Irish cultural events during the school year. Call about poetry readings, jig, and Gaelic lessons. A Bloomsday extravaganza, of course. Open Mon.-Fri. 11am-12:30am, Sat.-Sun. 4pm-12:30am.

James Joyce Pub, 71, bd. Gouvion-St-Cyr, 17ème (tel. 44 09 70 32), near the Palais des Congrès. M. Porte Maillot. The James Joyce is one of Paris' three most lively Irish pubs (next to Kitty O'Shea's (tel. 40 15 00 30) and Finnegan's Wake). The mahogany bar and tall green barstools create a warm backdrop to the daily and nightly crowd of Irish, British, and American expatriates downing a pint. Run by a friendly Irish staff, the pub is full of James Joyce paraphernalia, including a number of letters and pages penned in his own hand. Live Irish music every Mon. beginning at 8:30pm. Lunch served noon-2:30pm; dinner from 7:30pm on. Open daily noon-1:30am.

Le Merle Moqueur, 11, rue de la Butte-aux-Cailles, 13ème (tel. 45 65 12 43). M. pl. d'Italie. Take rue Bobillot south until rue de la Butte-aux-Cailles branches right.

Psychedelic Beatles posters pepper the walls of this tiny, super-cheap bar (beer 12-30F; nothing over 50F). Order from the bartender. Comfortably alternative music like U2 and Bob Marley. Most customers head for the terrace; if you can't find a seat, join the crowds leaning against cars. Open daily 5pm-1:45am; Aug. Tues.-Sun. 5pm-1:45am. 50F minimum for credit cards. MC, V.

La Micro Brasserie, 106, rue de Richelieu, 2ème (tel. 42 96 55 31). M. Richelieu-Drouot. Possibly the best place for beer in Paris. You can choose from more than 60 kinds, but the best deals are on the beers they brew themselves. The Morgane should not be missed: slightly reddish, it is called in French a *bière rousse*. Also, try mussels and fries with your drinks (40F). You can visit the brewery downstairs Tues. and Thurs. 10am-8pm without paying extra. Before 10pm house beer is 12F at the bar or 13-14F at a table; after 10pm both beers go for 20F. Between 5 and 7:30pm, buy 1 beer and get 1 free. Open daily noon-midnight.

Polly Magoo, 13, rue St-Jacques, 5ème (tel. 46 33 33 64). M. St-Michel. Walk down quai St-Michel and turn right on rue St-Jacques. When the Violon Dingue closes at 2am, Polly's gets going. Super-friendly, lively crowd often bubbles over into the street. Beer on tap 10-24F. Open 1pm-5am.

Pub St-Germain-des-Prés, 17, rue de l'Ancienne Comédie, 6ème (tel. 43 29 38 70). M. Odéon. The place where they have to take you in, all night, every night. Perhaps the largest pub in Europe, this 9-room mammoth bar is a longtime favorite among American students looking for a good time. Parisians go elsewhere. About 100 types of whisky. Over 450 different types of bottled beer and 25 varieties on tap. At night beers and cocktails start at an outrageous 75F per bottle. Open 24 hrs. MC, V, AmEx.

Le Violon Dingue, 46, rue de la Montagne Ste-Geneviève, 5ème. M. Maubert-Mutualité. Reminiscent of a crowded frat party with American waiters and fast-flowing beer. Cable and widescreen TV make this a good bet for Super Bowl Sunday. Bottled beer starts at 25F, on tap 32F. Cocktails from 30F. Open daily 6pm-2am.

■■■ BISEXUAL, GAY, AND LESBIAN ENTERTAINMENT

While the bisexual, gay, and lesbian communities of Paris may not be as politically active as those in New York or San Francisco, the scene is far from closeted. This is Gay Paree, where Eartha Kitt is Queen Camp, where Jean-Paul Gaultier fits Madonna's bullet bras, and where everybody's had a rough day at the gym. Lesbians are less visible here, and much of the entertainment is more widely scattered across the city.

The indisputable center of gay life is still the Marais, known throughout gay and straight Paris as the *chic*-est part of the city. There, in the 3ème and the 4ème *arrondissements,* you will find gay and lesbian café/bars, intimate restaurants, a gay and lesbian bookstore, and occasional window displays of Gay-Pride-wear. As usual, it's helpful to dress well. Quieter gay and lesbian hangouts line the rue Vieille-du-Temple.

A word on the current *mode.* You will find very few men here with long hair, who wear earrings or other jewelry, or who cross-dress (except, of course, at the Gay Pride parade). Styles among women vary greatly, though there tend to be more lipstick lesbians than in many U.S. cities. For the most comprehensive listing of gay and lesbian restaurants, clubs, hotels, organizations, and services, consult Gai Pied's *Guide Gai 1995* (50F at any kiosk or *papeterie*). *Lesbia*'s ads are a good gauge of what's hot, or at least what's open (24F).

Le Bar Central, 33, rue Vieille-du-Temple, 4ème (tel. 48 87 99 33). M. Hôtel-de-Ville. On the ground floor of the Hôtel Central and located at the nerve center of Marais nightlife, this bar fully lives up to its name. A comfortable setting for everyone, especially men. At the Central's long mahogany bar regulars drink draught beer (15F), check out the boys, and eye the black marble torso tacked to the back wall. Open Sun.-Thurs. 2pm-1am, Fri.-Sat. 2pm-2am.

Le Café Majéstic, 34, rue Vieille-du-Temple, 4ème (tel. 42 74 61 61). M. Hôtel-de-Ville. A vibrant, eclectic young crowd of bisexual, gay, lesbian, and straight people converge under red and blue lights to show off and look around. Big and round rock/pop mix provides soundtrack for sometimes clothed, often buff Beautiful People. Drinks 16-46F. Open daily 9am-2am. MC, V, AmEx.

Le Champmeslé, 4, rue Chabanais, 2ème (tel. 42 96 85 20). M. Pyramides or Bourse. This intimate lesbian bar has comfortable couches, dim lighting, and a young and yuppie clientele. Cabaret show on Thurs. Come on the 15th of every month for the *soirée zodiaque;* if it's your birthday month, you get a free drink. No cover. Drinks 25-40F. Open Mon.-Sat. 6pm-2am, Sun. 5pm-2am. AmEx, MC, V.

Le Club, 14, rue St-Denis, 1er. M. Châtelet-Les Halles. Found in a less chic, but *très* gay area of Beaubourg, next to the Marais. A dark, subterranean, intimate place to dance. Bouncers only admit women and straight men if accompanied by a gay man, preferrably one they recognize. Wednesday is garage-techno night. Le Club is renowned for its Thurs. night theme parties. Cover (48F including 1st drink) Fri.-Sat. only. Drinks 32-50F. Open daily 11:30pm-dawn. MC, V.

Le New Monocle, 60, bd. Edgar Quinet, 14ème (tel. 43 20 81 12). M. Edgard Quinet. This lesbian bar has been around since the days of Gertrude Stein, Natalie Barney, and René Vivier. Its name comes from the fashionable monocles worn by cross-dressed lesbians in the 1930s, a style that George Brassaï captured in his 1930s photos of Paris, and that Romaine Brooks captured in her paintings of lesbian women of the era. Open Tues.-Sat. 11pm-6am.

Le Palace Gay Tea Dance, 8, rue Faubourg-Montmartre, 9ème (tel. 47 70 75 02). M. Rue Montmartre. A fabulous place to meet on Sunday afternoons. Here, Beautiful People nurse drinks and gossip about less swanky gay and lesbian establishments. Mostly techno music. Occasional male strip shows. Drinks 40-60F. Cover 40F before 6pm, 60F after 6pm. Men and women welcome. Open Sun. 5pm-2am.

Le Piano Show, 20, rue de la Verrerie, 4ème (tel. 42 72 23 81). M. Hôtel-de-Ville. Welcome to the lipstick-smacking world of drag. For over 10 years, this small restaurant-cabaret has been performing a drag cabaret that's sure to knock your pantyhose off! It may be a bit expensive, but divas cost and here's where you start payingóin sweat, tears, and hilarious laughter. Dinner consists of *rôti de veau brisé, filet de dinde,* and *banane brésilienne* (*brésilien* is a French insider's slang for gay, and *banane* denotes, well, you know). Dinner and show Sun.-Thurs. 8:45pm-11:30pm. 199F. Reservations required. MC, V.

Le Piano Zinc, 49, rue des Blancs Manteaux, 4ème (tel. 42 74 32 42). M. Rambuteau. According to some, *the* seasoned gay hangout in the Marais. The piano downstairs sparks campy homage performances to Judy, Liza, Eartha, Madonna, Bette, Grace Jones, and Edith Piaf. Xeroxed lyric sheets allow all to join in bar theme song: *"Moi je suis dingue dingue dingue du Piano Zinc."* First beer 35F, first mixed drink 45F. Subsequent drinks 19-42F. Piano Bar after 10:30pm. Open Tues.-Sat. 6pm-2am. MC, V, AmEx.

Le Palace Gay Tea Dance, 8, rue Faubourg-Montmartre, 9ème (tel. 47 70 75 02). M. Rue Montmartre. A fabulous place to meet on Sunday afternoons. Here, Beautiful People sip coffee and drinks and gossip about less swanky gay and lesbian establishments. Mostly techno music. Occasional male strip shows. Drinks 40-60F. Cover 40F before 6pm, 60F after 6pm. Men and women welcome. Open Sun. 5pm-2am.

Subway, 35, rue Ste-Croix-de-la-Bretonnerie, 4ème (tel. 42 77 41 10). M. Hôtel-de-Ville. New and in vogue, Subway is dark, cramped, loud, and probably the best bet for a 20something pick-up of any gay bar in the Marais. Beer 14-18F, mixed drinks 39-48F. Getting in can be a hassle, especially for women, even accompanied. Open daily 2:30pm-2am. No credit cards.

Le Swing, 42, rue Vieille-du-Temple, 4ème (tel. 42 72 16 94). M. Hôtel-de-Ville. A 50s retro-bar with a young, brill-creamed, male crowd. Drinks 11-40F. Open Mon.-Sat. noon-2am, Sun. 2pm-2am. MC, V.

Le Quetzal, 10, rue de la Verrerie, 4ème (tel. 48 87 99 07). M. Hôtel-de-Ville. Popular high-tech neon bar. Mostly thirtyish men who stand around the bar and play pinball while scoping. Beer 14F. Drinks 30-42F. Open Mon.-Fri. noon-2am, Sat.-Sun. 2pm-2am.

Le Privilège, 3, cité Bergère, 9ème (tel. 42 46 50 98). M. Rue Montmartre. This nightclub is the place to go for a glam all-female crowd; dance all night and into the morning, when the club becomes an after-hours joint for the boys from the KitKat upstairs. Selective door policy. Drinks 100F. Open Tues.-Wed. and Sun. 11pm-dawn, Fri.-Sat. 11pm-noon.

■■■ FESTIVALS AND OTHER SEASONAL EVENTS

At the slightest provocation, Parisians rush to the streets, drink, dance, and generally lose themselves in the spirit of the *fête* (festival) or *foire* (fair). The gatherings in Washington on July 4, in Times Square on New Year's Eve, on Parliament Hill on July 1, or in Auckland, pale before the many and varied multitude on hand for Bastille Day fireworks or the arrival of the New Year. The **Office de Tourisme,** 127, av. des Champs-Elysées, 8ème (tel. 47 23 61 72; M. Charles de Gaulle-Etoile), distributes the multilingual *Saisons de Paris 1995,* a booklet listing all the celebrations. The English information number (tel. 47 20 88 98 or 49 52 53 56) reports a weekly summary of current festivals. *Pariscope* lists festival events for the coming week. You can also get a listing of festivals from the **French National Tourist Office** (see Essentials).

Course des Garçons De Café, starts and finishes at Hôtel de Ville, 4ème (tel. 40 07 30 12). If you thought service was slow by necessity, let this race change your mind. Tuxedoed waiters sprint through the streets carrying a full bottle and glass on a tray. One day in mid-June.

Foire du Trône, Neuilly Lawn of the Bois de Vincennes. M. Porte Dorée. A gigantic amusement park. End of March-May. Open 2pm-midnight.

Festival de Musique de St-Denis (tel. 42 43 72 72). Late May-late June.

Festival de Paris, 38, rue des Blancs-Manteaux, 4ème (tel. 40 26 45 34). M. St-Paul. Great orchestras and choruses. Mid-May to late June. Admission 50-500F.

Festival de Versailles (tel. 30 21 20 20, ext. 234). Ballet, operas, concerts, and theater. Prices vary radically from one event to another. Late May-late June.

Les Trois Heures de Paris (tel. 49 77 06 40). A day-long regatta on the Seine on a Sun. in May. Races between pont d'Austerlitz and Ile St-Louis.

Festival de la Butte Montmartre, 14bis, rue Ste-Isaure, 18ème (tel. 42 62 46 22). M. Abbesses. Experimental drama, dance, and jazz in landmark sites throughout Montmartre, from mid-June to mid-July. For details, visit the Tourist Office of Montmartre at 21, pl. du Tertre.

La Grande Parade de Montmartre, 18ème (tel. 42 62 21 21). M. Abbesses. This newly inaugurated event is just what it sounds like—a big parade. Marching bands from across the world (11 in 1994) join with Montmartre locals and various costumed brigades (like the green Santa Clauses) to parade across the *butte.* A Scottish-Hindu bagpiping troupe and Little Rock marching band are among the acts scheduled to appear.

Fête du Cinéma, around June 28. Purchase one ticket at maximum price and receive a passport that admits to an unlimited number of movies for the duration of the 3-day festival at a cost of 10F each. Most cinemas in Paris participate, so choose your first film carefully; the maximum ticket price varies considerably from theater to theater. Look for posters or ask at cinemas in Paris for the specific dates.

Festival Chopin (tel. 40 67 97 00 or 45 00 22 19). 14 concerts and recitals held at the Orangerie de la Bagatelle in the Bois de Boulogne. Not all Chopin, but all piano music, arranged each year around a different aspect of the Polish Francophile's *oeuvre.* Many 2pm matinees. Mid-June to mid-July.

Festival Foire St-Germain (tel. 43 29 12 78). Antique fair in pl. St-Sulpice, concerts in the Mairie du 6ème. Both free. Mid-June to early July.

Festival du Marais, 68, rue François Miron, 4ème (tel. 45 23 18 25). M. St-Paul. Open-air classical music, theater, and exhibits animate the splendid courtyards and back yards of many of the beautiful *hôtels* of the district. Concerts held in the pl. des Vosges, at the Musée Cognacq-Jay, and elsewhere. Early June-early July.

Festival d'Orgue à St-Eustache (tel. 45 22 28 74). Organ concerts in the beautiful St-Eustache church. M. Châtelet-Les Halles. Tickets 70-120F, on sale at ARGOS, 34, rue de Laborde, 8ème (M. St-Augustin). Mid-June to early July.

Fête de la Musique (tel. 42 20 12 34). Also called *"faîtes de la musique"* (make music!), this June 21 solstice celebration gives everyone in the city the chance to make as much of a racket as possible; noise laws don't apply on this day. Closet musicians fill the streets, strumming everything from banjos, to ukeleles, to Russian balalaikas. La Villette holds major rock concerts. Partying in all open spaces: before you join that samba parade, put your wallet in a safe place. Free.

Fêtes du Pont Neuf (tel. 42 77 92 26). M. Pont Neuf. The bridge is opened for dancing, music, street artists, and minstrels. A weekend in late June.

Musique en Sorbonne, 47, rue des Ecoles, 5ème (tel. 42 62 71 71 for imformation and to audition). M. Maubert-Mutualité. Classical music. Late June-early July. Admission 60-140F.

Nuit de la St-Jean (tel. 45 08 55 25). For the Feast of St. John the Baptist, June 24. Magnificent fireworks at 11pm on the quai St-Bernard. For a spectacular, though bird's-eye view of the spectacle, stand in front of Sacré-Coeur. Call for verification of the location.

Bastille Day, July 14. *Vive la République* and pass the champagne. The day starts with the army parading down the Champs-Elysées and ends with fireworks. The parade is best seen on TV. The fireworks can be seen from any bridge on the Seine. Groups also gather in the 19ème *arrondissement*, where the hilly topography allows a view all the way to the Trocadéro. Traditional street dances are held on the eve at the tip of Ile St-Louis (the Communist Party always throws its gala there), the Hôtel de Ville, pl. de la Contrescarpe, and of course, pl. de la Bastille, where it all began. These so-called *Bals de Pompiers* (yes, firemen's balls) take place in front of every fire station in the city and are free of charge and crowded with jubilant French people. Dancing continues the next night. Unfortunately, the entire city also becomes a nightmarish combat zone of leering men cunningly tossing firecrackers under the feet of unsuspecting bystanders; avoid the metro and carry a fire extinguisher with you at all times.

End of the Tour de France, fourth Sun. in July. Expect a huge crowd along the banks of the Seine on the Right Bank. Join the riotous crowd in the cheering, you may never see calves this strong again in your life. In 1994, the last day's race took off from the Euro Disneyland so expect crowds there as well.

Musique d'Eté Au Marais (tel. 40 27 07 21). Classical music matinees held in the courtyards of Marais museums, including the Musée Cognacq-Jay, Musée de la Chasse, and Musée Carnavalet. Concert ticket includes museum entrance. Admission 110F, 80F under 25 and over 60. June-early Sept.

Festival d'Automne (tel. 42 96 12 27). Drama, ballet, expositions. Late Sept.-Dec.

Festival de l'Ile-de-France (tel. 47 39 28 26). Late Sept.-late Dec.

Festival du Cinéma en Plein Air, at Parc de la Villette. A temporary screen is set up, seats are arranged in the Prairie du Triangle, and Paris sits down for its version of a drive-in theater. Movies usually focus on one theme, although exceptions are made for certain cult classics defying notion of theme and category. Takes place from mid-July to mid-Aug., tickets 40F. All films shown in original version. Films at 10pm.

La Saison Musicale de L'Abbaye de Royaumont consists of weekend concerts fron mid-June to mid-Sept. The *abbaye* arranges for bus transportation from Paris. Tickets 50-100F. Tel. 34 68 05 50 for information and reservations.

Fête de l'Humanité, Parc de la Courneuve. Take the metro to Porte de la Villette and then one of the special buses. The annual fair of the French Communist Party—like nothing you've ever seen. Entertainers in recent years have included Charles Mingus, Marcel Marceau, the Bolshoi Ballet, and radical theater troupes. A cross between the Illinois State Fair and Woodstock; you don't have to be a Communist to enjoy it. 2nd or 3rd week of Sept.

Festival d'Art Sacré, 4, rue Jules-Cousin, 4ème. Sacred music by Radio France Philharmonic Orchestra and Choir of Cologne. Early Oct.-Dec.

Fête des Vendanges à Montmartre, rue Saules, 18ème (tel. 42 62 21 21). M. Lamarck-Caulaincourt. A celebration of the wine-grape harvest from Montmartre's own vineyards. Features costumed picking and tromping of the last vineyard's grapes. First Sat. in Oct.

Rallye Paris-Deauville (tel. 46 24 37 38). More than 100 vintage cars assemble at the Trocadéro fountains at 7am on a Friday in early October. A like display takes place in Deauville on Sunday.

Concours International de Danse de Paris (tel. 45 22 28 74 for information and auditions). Week-long dance competition in the first two weeks of Dec. at the Opéra Comique (tickets 70-180F).

Festival Internationale de la Guitare (tel. 45 23 18 25). Concerts in many Parisian churches. Mid-Nov. to mid-Dec.

Christmas Eve. At midnight Notre-Dame becomes what it only claims to be the rest of the year: the cathedral of the city of Paris.

New Year's Eve. Bd. St-Michel and the Champs-Elysées transform into pedestrian malls, much to the dismay of the cops, who still attempt to direct traffic. More of the brouhaha that you tried to avoid on the 14th of July.

■■■ SPORTS

PARTICIPATORY SPORTS

You might find it hard to believe while pounding the city's pavement, but Paris and its surroundings teem with indoor and outdoor sports opportunities. If you don't believe us, call the *Mairie de Paris'* sports hotline, **Allô-Sports** (tel. 42 76 54 54; open Mon.-Thurs. 10:30am-5pm, Fri. 10:30am-4:30pm). They also have an office called **l'Espace Information Jeunesse et Sports (Youth and Sports Information Center),** 25, bd. Bourdon, 4ème (tel. 40 45 90 00). M. Bastille. Many of the introductory courses offered by the city are for residents only, but if you're in town for an extended period, you may be able to talk your way into one. Also for residents, the city coordinates summer introductory courses for kids to a variety of sports. All such courses are offered in French only. The *Pariscope* (see Essentials—Publications) "Sports et Loisirs" section lists 10 pages of facilities, hours and prices for a variety of sports locations. *L'Officiel des Spectacles* has a less comprehensive list. Also see *Paris Pas Cher* for lists of affordable gyms geared toward the long-term visitor. Hostels, hotels, and student services at the Université de Paris may have suggestions for students.

Below is a grab-bag of recommended activities for the budget traveler. Sports facilities of all kinds form a ring around Paris, lining the inner and outer edges. While many house private clubs, specialized sports schools, or host pro events, some are open to the public.

Jogging: Joggers are becoming a very common sight in Paris, especially in some of the athletically-oriented parks. Road-running will be difficult in the center city; the 16ème is often quiet and residential enough to make a jog feasible on smaller roads. For the most part, in-city routes (even in the parks) will have lots of traffic, pollution, and people. Many joggers hop on the metro and head to one of Paris' outlying public parks. Keep in mind that running in unknown or deserted areas can be dangerous, especially as dark falls or if you're wearing a walkman.

Central Paris: The **Champs de Mars,** 7ème (M. Bir Hakeim), is a popular in-city jogging spot, with a 2.5km path around the outside.The leafy **Jardin du Luxembourg,** 6ème (M. Cluny-La Sorbonne), offers a 1.6km circuit. **Parc Monceau,** 8ème (M. Monceau), crawls with kids but remains serenely green; 1km loop.

Periphery: Parc des Buttes Chaumont, 19ème (M. Buttes Chaumont), offers labyrinthine paths that are great for hill-work. A swooping path (1.6km) rings the park. The **Bois de Boulogne,** 16ème, has 35km of trails. Maps can be found at regular intervals on the periphery of the park. A long path, marked in red and yellow, follows the periphery of the park. A shorter one, marked in blue and white, circles about half of it. Large crowds and numerous bicyclists make the

PARTICIPATORY SPORTS

shorter path tiresome. Some artificial lakes and a few stadiums are good running sights. Make sure to leave before dark and be forewarned about the utter lack of public restrooms. Less renowned, but no less runnable, is the **Bois de Vincennes,** 12ème. Begin at the northwest corner of the park at the medieval **Château de Vincennes** (M. Château de Vincennes). Peripheral path, marked in red and yellow on park maps, is 11km; inside path (marked in blue and white) is 8km. A map close to M. Château de Vincennes gives a sense of the park's roads. A lovely run through groves and clearings. Many joggers, mostly in-shape long-distance types. The park also contains a track open during the day.

Swimming: The Mairie de Paris has created a network of public-access pools. Opening hours vary, but all are open in summer (Mon. 2-7pm, Tues.-Sat. 7am-7:30pm, and Sun. 8am-5pm). Call Allô-Sports to have a copy of *Les Piscines à Paris* sent to you, or pick one up at a *mairie.* It lists hours and services available at each pool. A warning on swimming laps in France: lane lines are not marked. Be prepared for confusion. Entry to any **municipal pool** 10F, under 17, over 64, or those accompanying children but not swimming 5F. Ask about 1-yr. passes and youth discounts. Under 8 must be accompanied by an adult. Last entry 30 min. before closing; pools are cleared 15 min. before closing. Some pools have a *"nocturne,"* 1 or 2 nights a week, when they are open past 8pm. **Municipale concédée** pools grant public time to the municipality and thus are a bit more expensive. They include the large, well-lit **Piscine des Halles,** level -3 of the Les Halles complex, 1er (tel. 42 36 98 44). Open Tues. and Thurs.-Fri. 11:30am-10pm, Wed. 10am-7pm, Sat.-Sun. 9am-5pm. July-Aug., also open Mon. 11:30am-8pm. Last entry 45 min. before closing; pool cleared 30 min. before closing. Admission 22F50, under 16 17F50. Pass for 10 entries 205F, under 16 165F. Wheelchair accessible. Also the **Piscine Pontoise-Quartier Latin,** 19, rue de Pontoise, 5ème (tel. 43 54 06 23 or 43 54 82 45; M. Maubert-Mutualité), a snazzy pool with a counter-current machine (admission 20F, students 18F, under 16 16F).

Tennis: Serious players should bring their equipment; Paris boasts of 170 municipal tennis courts in 45 "tennis centers," each open to the individual player. Free introductory lessons offered to children. To use the municipal courts, apply for a free **Carte Paris Tennis,** which enables you to reserve space through minitel. Court reservation is crucial, especially in summer. Pick up an application at one of the tennis centers scattered throughout the city. Cards take 5 weeks to process. For municipal courts, rates are low (25F per hour).

Gyms and Fitness: Alésia Club, 143, rue d'Alésia, 14ème (tel. 45 42 91 05; M. Alésia), has a gym, sauna, and other facilities and will sell you a membership for the day (200F, Open Mon.-Fri. 11:30am-9pm, Sat. 11:30am-8pm and Sun. 2-8pm). If you feel the need of a beach, or perhaps just a sauna, jacuzzi, wavepool, and waterslide, find them at **Aquaboulevard,** 4, rue Louis Armand, 15ème (tel. 40 60 10 00; M. Balard or Porte de Versailles). Come early in the morning to avoid the crowds. (Open Sun.-Thurs. 9am-11pm, Fri.-Sat. 8am-midnight. Admission 68F for 4hr.; 75F on weekends. More facilities are available to club members: annual membership 1300F, classes supplement 125F per month.) Try the **Espace Vit'Halles,** 48, rue Rambuteau, 3ème (tel. 42 77 21 71), near Les Halles in place Beaubourg. Labelled "the American-style health club you've been looking for," Vit'Halles offers both long-term and short-term memberships (600F per month; open daily 10am-11pm).

Cycling: The city proper is not a good place for a leisurely afternoon pedal, but cyclists happily while away the hours in the **Bois de Vincennes,** 12ème, around Lac Daumesnil (M. Porte Dorée) or deeper into the woods. The **Bois de Boulogne,** 16ème, officially boasts of 8km of bike paths, but any cyclist can make up an original route among the innumerable trees. The **canal de l'Ourcq** passes through the Parc de la Villette, 30, av. Corentin Cariou, 19ème (M. Porte de la Villette), and has a bicycle path alongside. English-language mountain bike tours of the sights of Paris are available for the adventuresome. For more information on bike rental and cycling around the city, consult the Essentials section under Getting Around—Bicycle. Long-distance cyclists may want to try the 109km ride out to **Ferté Milon** in the province of Aisne. The real test, of course, is getting back. Also consider the **Forêt de Fontainebleau** (see Daytrips).

Roller Skating: Roller Blades have yet to catch on, but their lack is well compensated for by the skill, speed, and fearlessness of Paris' many roller skaters. The Jardins du Trocadéro in front of the Palais de Chaillot fills with motorless Evil Knievals. Rent skates at **La Main Jaune,** pl. de la Porte-de-Champerret, 17ème (tel. 47 63 26 47; M. Porte de Champerret). Open Wed. and Sat.-Sun. 2:30-7pm, Fri.-Sat. and holidays 10pm-dawn. Admission Wed., Sat. evening, and Sun. 40F, skate rental 10F; Fri. and Sat. night 70F, skate rental 15F.

Fishing: Contact the **Annicale des Pêcheurs de Neuilly, Levallois, et environs,** Base Halientique de la Jatte, 19, bd. de Levallois prolongé, 92000 Levallois-Perret (tel. 43 48 36 34). They'll fill you in on angling in the Bois de Boulogne.

Golf: Golf enthusiasts must reach deep into the suburbs for a real 18-hole game. Nevertheless, Paris contains a number of putting greens. Including club and ball rental, expect to pay about 100F. Try **Golf Club de l'Etoile,** 10, av. de la Grande Armée, 17ème (tel. 43 80 30 79) or **Aquagolf Ecole de Golf de Paris,** 26, rue Colonel Pierre Avie, 15ème (tel. 45 57 43 06). The **Académie de Golf de Paris,** 1, rue Camp Canadien, 92210 St-Cloud (tel. 47 71 39 22) is a further option.

Bowling: Bowling de Paris (tel. 40 67 94 00), in the Bois de Boulogne near the rte. Mahatma Gandhi entrance of the Jardin d'Acclimatation. Open daily 5pm-2am. Closed Mon. in Aug. Games Mon.-Fri. 20F, after 8pm 29F, Sat.-Sun. 30F. Obligatory bowling shoe rental 10F. After the park closes, you have to enter through the park's Mahatma Gandhi entrance, which remains open. Because the Bowling de Paris is inside the garden, you must also pay the garden's admisson fee. **Bowling International Stadium,** 66, av. d'Ivry, 13ème (tel. 45 86 55 52; M. Tolbiac) is a joint bowling alley and billiard hall. American billiards require a 100F deposit, a 5F supplementary fee, and cost 45F per hour (before 8:45PM) and 50F/hr (after 8:45PM). Bowling, in any of the 12 lanes, costs 19-32F depending on the time of day, the day of the week, and the kind of person you are (reduced prices for senior citizens and students); rent shoes for 7F a pair. Open daily noon-2am.

SPECTATOR SPORTS

If you think that Parisians are obsessed with only the very highest of high culture, think again. Parisians follow sports with fierce interest, reading between the lines of their own sports daily, *l'Equipe* (6F), as well as the sports section of other newspapers. Sports talk provides fodder for heated discussion on the metro and raucous play-by-play in bars; as for actually attending the real thing, it's almost a religious experience. Parisians' knowledge of sports is not limited to French and European teams—their fervor is of global proportions. Once again, Allo-Sports can tell you all you need to know. The **Palais Omnisports Paris Bercy,** 8, bd. de Bercy, 12ème (tel. 44 68 44 68; M. Bercy), hosts everything from opera and beach volleyball to figure skating and horse jumping beneath its radical, sod-covered roof. Ticket prices vary wildly according to the event.

Soccer: Soccer (called *"football"*), France's hands-down national sport, consumes Paris, especially during the big championships like the World Cup (*Le Mondial*), which will take place in the France in 1998. Join the Parisian multitudes in waiting to see where *les bleus* will go from here. The **Club de Football Paris St-Germain** (tel. 40 71 91 91) is Paris's own professional *football* team, splitting its time between road games and matches at the enormous **Parc des Princes** (box office tel. 44 26 45 45; M. Porte de St-Cloud), the city's premier outdoor stadium venue. The finals of the Coupe de France take place in early May; the Tournoi de Paris is in late July. Tickets to all events can be purchased at the Parc des Princes box office, 24, rue du Commandant-Guibaud, 16ème (M. Porte d'Auteuil), and go on sale anywhere from 2 days to 2 weeks in advance. Games on weekends and some weekday evenings. Prices 50-300F, depending on the seat and the event. Box office open 9am-6pm when selling tickets for an event; purchase tickets in advance by Mastercard or Visa. The Parc des Princes also hosts **rugby** matches, including the Tournoi des Cinq Nations (Feb.-March) and the final of the Championnat de France de Rugby in early June. Call the box office for details.

Cycling: Held in July, the **Tour de France** pits 200 of the world's best cyclists against the Alps, the elements, and each other for 21 gruelling stages. Call *l'Equipe* (tel. 40 93 21 92), one of the tour's sponsors, for information about the race's itinerary. Spectators turn out in droves along the way, stationed at bends in highways to cheer their favorite to victory. Parisians and tourists alike line the Champs-Elysées for the triumphal last stage, usually between noon and 6pm. Show up early and be prepared for a mob scene; you may see more on TV. The women's Tour de France leaves Paris in mid-Aug. near the Eiffel Tower. Call 43 57 02 94 for information. The **Grand Prix Cycliste de Paris** is an annual time trial competition held in June at the Vélodrome Jacques Anguetil, Bois de Vincennes, 12ème (tel. 43 68 01 27; tickets 50F, available on site).

Tennis: The *terre battue* (red clay) of the **Stade Roland Garros,** 2, av. Gordon Bennett, 16ème (M. Porte d'Auteuil), has ended more than one champion's quest for a Grand Slam. Two weeks each year (May 24-June 6 in 1993), **Les Internationaux de France de Tennis (The French Open)** welcomes the world's top players to Paris. Write to the **Fédération Française de Tennis,** located at the stadium, (tel. 47 43 48 00) in Oct. for information on tickets for the next spring's tournament. Also, ask your national tennis association; they sometimes have an extra supply of tickets.

Horse Racing: The numerous hippodromes in and around town host races of all kinds throughout the year. Far from seedy, an afternoon at the track is a family outing. The level of classiness climbs a notch or two for the season's championship races. **Hippodrome de Vincennes,** 2, rte. de la Ferme, in the Bois de Vincennes, 12ème (tel. 05 11 21 14). M. Château de Vincennes. A hike through the woods from the metro stop takes you to the home of Parisian harness racing since 1906. Prix d'Amérique (late Jan.), Prix de France (early Feb.), and Prix du Président de la République (late June). Tickets 15-30F, even for the big races. **Hippodrome d'Auteuil,** in the Bois de Boulogne, 16ème (tel. 45 27 12 24). M. Porte d'Auteuil. Steeplechases since 1873; the stands date from 1921. For the big races in June and July, shuttles run from the metro and RER stations. Open Sept.-Nov. and Feb.-June. Tickets about 25F during the week, 40F on Sun., 50F for major events. No reservations. **Hippodrome de Longchamp,** deeper in the Bois de Boulogne, 16ème (tel. 44 30 75 00). M. Porte d'Auteuil. On race days, shuttles run from nearby metro stops. Open Sept.-Oct. and April-June. Major event in fall season is the *Prix de l'Arche de Triomphe* , early October: to reserve seats, call 49 10 20 30. Same ticket prices as at Auteuil. **Hippodrome de Chantilly,** Chantilly (tel. (16) 44 57 02 54). For info see Daytrips.

Golf: The **Peugeot Open de France** (also called the French Open) attracts some of Europe's top golf players to the Paris area in late June. Tickets cost 50F per day and can be purchased by writing to the Société Promo-Golf, 4, rue Senton (tel. 47 72 28 10), 92150 Suresnes. Try to reserve two months in advance. To reach the course at Golf National de Guyancourt, 2, av. du Golf, 78280 Guyancourt, take the RER to Guyancourt and take a shuttle bus.

These people are only a third of the 150 students who bring you the *Let's Go* guides. With pen and notebook in hand, a few changes of underwear stuffed in our backpacks, and a budget as tight as yours, we visited every *pensione*, *palapa*, pizzeria, café, club, campground, or castle we could find to make sure you'll get the most out of *your* trip.

We've put the best of our discoveries into the book you're now holding. A brand-new edition of each guide hits the shelves every year, only months after it is researched, so you know you're getting the most reliable, up-to-date, and comprehensive information available.

But, as any seasoned traveler will tell you, the best discoveries are often those you make yourself. If you find something worth sharing, drop us a line. We're at Let's Go, Inc., 1 Story Street, Cambridge, MA 02138, USA (e-mail: letsgo@delphi.com).

H A P P Y   T R A V E L S !

Shopping

If you have to ask, you probably can't afford it. Most stores close on Sunday and some of the smaller ones close during lunch on weekdays. When you walk into a Paris boutique, many store owners will take that as a declaration of intent to buy. They will approach you immediately. If you want to browse, which they may not like, say: *"Merci. J'aimerais seulement regarder"* (Thank you, I'd just like to look). Do not be coerced into buying something you don't want, but don't be surprised at reactions ranging from disdain to hostility if you leave without making a purchase.

■■■ WINDOW SHOPPING

The most famous of Paris' clothing boutiques skirt the **rue du Faubourg St-Honoré,** which runs northwest through the 8*ème arrondissement*. This is the area of *haute couture* (custom made clothing and accessories). Gawk at the impeccably French scarves and bags at **Hermès** (no. 24), the outlandish solid knits at **Sonia Rykiel** (no. 70), the untouchables of all types at **Yves Saint Laurent** (no. 38), and the high fashion design of the Japanese **Ashida** (no. 34) The Pierre Balmain, Karl Lagerfeld, and Versace boutiques mingle nearby. (Pierre Cardin designs for Balmain; Karl Lagerfeld designs for Chanel.) Nearby, the streets projecting from **pl. des Victoires** (1*er* and 2*ème*) harbor lots more *maisons de couture*. Running southwest from the Rond Point des Champs-Elysées, **av. de Montaigne** shelters the houses of **Christian Dior** (no. 32), **Chanel** (no. 42), **Valentino** (no. 17-19), and **Nina Ricci** (no. 39). The name **Pierre Cardin,** seemingly omnipresent in Paris, appears on a regal house in place François 1*er*. The windows in **place Vendôme** and along **rue de la Paix** (north to the Opéra) glitter with the designs of **Cartier, Van Cleef & Arpels,** and other offerings from the city's jewelry overlords.

■■■ MAGASINS DE TROC

There are a number of places where you can buy designer labels at lower prices. A unique Parisian shopping phenomenon is the *magasin du troc*, a large store that resells clothes bought and returned at more expensive stores.

Réciproque, 16*ème* (tel. 47 04 30 28). M. Pompe. Different branches have different specialties: menswear at 101, rue de la Pompe; women's coats at 123, rue de la Pompe; leather accessories at 92, rue de la Pompe; women's clothing at 95, rue de la Pompe. Greatly discounted, though not inexpensive, designer clothing. Cheapest women's dresses 300-500F. Big names in ready-to-wear and couture are represented here. All branches open 10:30am-7pm.

Mouton à Cinq Pattes, 8-10-18, rue St-Placide, 6*ème* (tel. 45 48 86 26). M. Sèvres-Babylone. Also, 19, rue Grégoire de Tours, 6*ème* (tel. 43 29 73 56). M. Odéon. An eclectic storehouse of understated, reasonably cheap chic. Open Mon.-Fri. 10:30am-7:30pm, Sat. 10:30am-8pm. MC, V, AmEx.

Also try **Troc Mod**, 230, av. du Maine, 14*ème* (tel. 45 40 45 93; M. Alésia; open Sept.-July Tues.-Sat. 10am-7:30pm; Aug. Tues.-Sat. 11am-7:30pm) and **Troc'Eve,** 25, rue Violet, 15*ème* (tel. 45 79 38 36; M. Dupleix; open Tues.-Sat. 10am-7pm) for heavily discounted designer fashions. A number of other discount stores offer designer labels and stock at used, returned, or discount prices: **Cacharel Stock,** 114, rue d'Alésia, 14*ème* (tel. 45 42 53 04); **Stock Daniel Hechter,** 16, bd. de l'Hôpital, 5*ème* (tel. 47 07 88 44); **Stock Chevignon,** 122, rue d'Alésia, 14*ème* (tel. 45 43 40 25).

■■■ VINTAGE CLOTHING

Magic Circle, 25, rue Etienne Marcel, 1er (tel. 42 33 39 99). M. Etienne-Marcel. Two floors straight out of Twiggy's closet. Spunky retro 70s clothing for women, with an awe-inspiring shoe collection downstairs. High-heeled pink sneakers in evidence. Open Mon.-Sat. 11am-7:30pm. MC, V.

Occa-Locca, 23, rue des Dames, 17ème (tel. 42 93 96 46). M. pl. de Clichy. Clothing tacky and funky, retro and gross. Sequined, tassled dresses along with shoes, books, small furniture and bric-a-brac. Mon.-Fri. 10:30am-8pm, Sat. 4:30-8pm.

Orlando Curioso, 78, rue de Rennes, 6ème (tel. 42 22 28 66). M. St-Sulpice. A second-hand clothing store with everything from silver lamé to white peasant blouses. Crammed with racks of high-quality camp that can easily cross over to cutting-edge cool. Clothing 50-100F per item. Prices, written in soap on the windows, are by rack. Open Mon.-Sat. 11am-6pm.

■■■ DEPARTMENT STORES

The first department stores in Paris were also the first in the world, designed as glamorous showplaces for affordable, ready-to-wear goods. When visiting the city's grand old stores like Samaritaine and Bon Marché, keep your eyes peeled for their turn-of-the-century ornamented ceilings and decorative metal work. In recent years, Paris has responded to increased demand for *prêt-à-porter* with newer and bigger *grands magasins* (department stores), offering fabulous one-stop shopping. Shoppers there browse unhassled by the over-aggressive salespeople of Paris's boutiques. Sales staff in these stores remain behind the counter until you approach them.

At seasonal *soldes* (sales), prepare to elbow through mobs of hell-bent bargain hunters, practice your *"pardon"*s and *"excusez-moi"*s, and fight to the death for that last size or color. Also keep in mind that many *grands magasins* are mini-malls; you can often get your hair cut, mail a letter, do your grocery shopping, and have lunch, all without leaving the store.

Bon Marché, 3, rue de Sèvres, 7ème (tel. 45 49 21 22). M. Sèvres-Babylone. Paris' oldest department store and perhaps its best. As chic as Galeries Lafayette without the tourists and chaos. Designers of every cant, from Laura Ashley to Cachet. Travelers with children will enjoy the *Rentrée des Classes* (back to school) section, stocking children's supplies and toys from Tintin backpacks to model airplanes. Across the street is the **Grande Epicerie de Paris,** Bon Marché's gourmet food annex (see Groceries). Open Mon.-Sat. 8:30am-9pm. MC, V, AmEx.

Au Printemps, 64, bd. Haussmann, 9ème (tel. 42 82 50 00). M. Chaussée d'Antin. Also at 30, pl. d'Italie, 13ème (tel. 40 78 17 17). M. pl. d'Italie. 21-25, cours de Vincennes, 20ème (tel. 43 71 12 41). M. Porte de Vincennes. 10, pl. de la République, 11ème (tel. 43 55 39 09). M. République. Bills itself as "the most Parisian of all the department stores," but when you see the international clientèle you may wonder why. Merchandise on par with Galeries Lafayette. Anything you could possibly want (but not necessarily need) at typical (high) department store prices. You will also find more people than you could possibly want to see in a lifetime. Haussmann store open Mon.-Sat. 9:35am-7pm. Check with branches for slightly different opening and closing times. MC, V, AmEx.

BHV, 52, rue de Rivoli, 4ème (tel. 42 74 90 00). M. Hôtel-de-Ville. The initials stand for Bazar de l'Hôtel de Ville, logical enough for a department store across the street from the Hôtel de Ville. Heavy on housewares, electronic equipment, and luggage; light on trendy fashions. Less chic than Samaritaine. Open Mon.-Tues and Thurs.-Sat. 9:30am-7pm, Wed. 9:30am-10pm. MC, V, AmEx.

Galeries Lafayette, 40, bd. Haussmann, 9ème (tel. 42 82 34 56). M. Chaussée d'Antin. Also at 22, rue du Départ, 14ème (tel. 45 38 52 87). M. Montparnasse. Prices are high, but not outrageous. Keep your eye out for *soldes*. So many Americans come here that it was considered highly unsafe during the terrorist attacks of the mid-80s. Take the time to admire the ornate Belle Epoque dome in the main

building. Main store open Mon.-Sat. 9:30am-6:30pm. Rue du Départ branch open
Mon.-Sat. 9:45am-7:15pm. All major credit cards accepted.

Samaritaine, 19, rue de la Monnaie, 1er (tel. 40 41 20 20). M. Pont-Neuf, Châtelet-
Les-Halles, or Louvre. 4 large buildings between rue de Rivoli and the Seine, connected by tunnels. Not as chic as Galeries Lafayettes or Bon Marché, Samaritaine
tends more toward home furnishings than endless racks of designer clothing.
More French than Americans here. Building 2 has a beautiful ceiling with tur-
quoise and ivory ironwork and a peacock mosaic. Rooftop observation deck provides one of the best views of the city; take the elevator to the top floor and climb
the short, spiral staircase (see Sights, 1er). Open Mon.-Wed. 9:30am-7pm, Thurs.
9:30am-10pm, Fri.-Sat. 9:30am-7pm. MC, V, AmEx.

Tati, 11, pl. de la République, 3ème (tel. 48 87 72 81). M. République. 106, rue Faubourg du Temple, 11ème (tel. 43 57 92 80). M. Goncourt. 140, rue de Rennes, 6ème
(tel. 45 48 68 31). M. Montparnasse. 4, bd. de Rochechouart, 18ème (tel. 42 55 13
09). M. Anvers. The original bargain basement store (dresses 80-150F, T-shirts 15-
40F, nightgowns 40-60F). In the cheapest department store in Paris, meet may-
hem with an attitude; prepare to push through cramped displays and scavenge
bins for that elusive something. A good place for cheap clothes with nothing in
the way of designer clothing. Get your sales slip made out by one of the clerks (
who stand around for just that purpose) before heading to the cashier. Open
Tues.-Fri. 10am-7:15pm, Sat. 10am-7:30pm. MC, V.

■■■ BOOKS AND MAGAZINES

Books in Paris, in either English or French, are much more expensive than in North
America. New English-language books sell for about US$20 a novel (paperback).
Scope the banks of the Seine, where *bouquinistes* sell their wares, peddling treasures in all languages and at all prices. Otherwise try second-hand shops where
livres d'occasion (used books) go for 5-50F. Almost all bookstores will order books
for you, but the cost of mailing books from the U.S. can be apoplexy-inducing. Specialty bookshops also provide an excellent resource for information concerning specific ethnic groups in the city. The *Sunday New York Times* (75F) may be
purchased at W.H. Smith (see listing) and at a kiosk on rue Pierre Lescot, 1er, in front
of the east entrance to Les Halles.

Les Archives de la Presse, 51, rue des Archives, 3ème (tel. 42 72 63 93). Wide-
reaching collection of vintage magazines; politics, fashion, photography, and
music are strong suits. Some precious finds from the 50s. Old mags from 40F.
Open Tues.-Sat. 10am-7pm.

Brentano's, 37, av. de l'Opéra, 2ème (tel. 42 61 52 50). M. Opéra. An extensive
selection, especially of American literature, and a wide display of guidebooks.
Open Mon.-Sat. 10am-7pm.

Chantelivre, 13, rue de Sèvres, 7ème (tel. 45 48 87 90). M. Sèvres-Babylone. A
child's vision of a children's bookstore. Classics for the young (Puss-in-Boots) and
not so young (Dumas, Jack London). Some adult titles like *Parents en souffrance*
(Suffering Parents). Open Mon. 1-6:50 pm, Tues.-Sat. 10am-6:50pm. V.

Galignani, 224, rue de Rivoli, 1er (tel. 42 60 76 07; fax 42 86 09 31). M. Tuileries.
The marvelous, wood-paneled "first English bookshop established on the conti-
nent," (as the bookmarks declare). An wide selection of British books. Open
Mon.-Sat. 10am-7pm.

Gibert Jeune, 5, pl. St-Michel, 5ème (tel. 43 25 70 07), near the Seine. M. St-Michel.
The bookstore near bd. St-Michel, and also the place to go for French classics.
Lots of reduced books for the short-on-cash. The same variety of books and stationery abounds at the branch at 15bis, bd. St-Denis, 2ème (tel. 43 26 82 84). M. Strasbourg-St-Denis. The store at 27, quai St-Michel (tel. 43 54 57 32; M. St-Michel),
sells university texts.

Gibert Jeune VALEC, 7, rue Dupuytren, 6ème (tel. 46 33 43 19). M. Odéon. Right
across from original locale of Shakespeare and Co., Sylvia Beach's legendary
librairie. You'll find paperbacks in French (as well as a smattering of books in

English) at rock-bottom prices. Bins outside receive our applause: 5-10F. Books inside slightly more. Open Tues.-Sat. 10am-2pm and 3-7pm. MC, V.

La Librairie des Femmes, 74, rue de Seine, 6ème (tel. 43 29 50 75). M. Odéon. The onetime home of feminist collective MLF, this bookstore (and the press it supports) has lost much of its former radical edge. No longer geared exclusively toward feminism, it now stocks all literature by or about women. Open Mon.-Sat. 10am-7pm, sometimes closed late July-Aug.12:45-2pm. MC, V, AmEx.

Librairie Gallimard, 15, bd. Raspail, 7ème (tel. 45 48 24 84; fax 42 84 16 97). M. Rue du Bac. The main outlet of this famed publisher of French classics. A huge selection of pricey Gallimard books. Open Mon.-Sat. 10am-7pm.

Librairie Gourmande, 4, rue Dante, 5ème (tel. 43 54 37 27; fax 43 54 31 16). M. Maubert-Mutualité. Bookstore on the art of living *par excellence;* new and old volumes chronicle food and drink from Middle Ages to now. Some English-language titles. Books in remainder bins around 30F. Open daily 10am-7pm. Closed Christmas and New Year's Day. MC,V.

Librairies Ulysse, 26, rue St-Louis-en-l'Ile, 4ème (tel. 43 25 17 35). M. Pont-Marie. Specializes in travel books and antiquarian maps. Used and out-of-print books. Open Tues.-Sat. 2-8pm.

Librairie Un Regard Moderne, 10, rue Git-le-Coeur, 6ème (tel. 43 29 13 93). M. St-Michel. Underground comics (please, call them "graphic novels") rub shoulders with graphic maybe-not-art in a cramped, smoky room with books piled from floor to ceiling. Where you'll find that delightful piece of ultra-violence or arty-porn you've yearned for. Otherwise, crouch and flip through works by Douglas Coupland, Bill Watterson, and Jack Kerouac. Prices can be high. You can always just read it in the store. Mon.-Sat. 11am-8pm. MC, V.

Les Mots à la Bouche, 6, rue Ste-Croix-de-la-Bretonnerie, 4ème (tel. 42 78 88 30). M. St-Paul or Hôtel-de-Ville. Offers the most extensive collection of gay and lesbian literature of any bookstore in the city, including novels, essays, art criticism, and magazines in French, English, German, and Italian. Also a small selection of videos. A must-visit for those in search of an inside line on gay and lesbian nightlife and political and cultural events. Open Mon.-Sat. 11am-11pm. MC, V.

Presence Africaine, 25, rue des Ecoles, 5ème (tel. 43 54 15 88). M. Maubert-Mutualité. French-language texts from Antilles and Africa put out by publishing house of the same name (tel. 43 54 13 74). Children's books, scholarly texts, poetry, and more. Paperbacks 30-70F. Also a helpful resource for travelers seeking businesses which cater to black clientele. The proprietor keeps a stack of out-of-print guide books to Paris behind the desk. Open Mon.-Sat. 10am-7pm.

Shakespeare and Co., 37, rue de la Bûcherie, 5ème, across the Seine from Notre-Dame. M. St-Michel. Run by George Whitman (alleged great-grandson of Walt), this shop seeks to reproduce the atmosphere of Sylvia Beach's establishment at 8, rue Dupuytren and, later, at 12, rue de l'Odéon, an extraordinary gathering-place for expatriates in the 1920s. Beach published Joyce's *Ulysses* in 1922; avant-garde composer George Antheil wrote *Music for Pianos and Airplane Propellers* as her boarder. Shakespeare and Co.'s current location and proprietor have absolutely no official link to Sylvia Beach, George Antheil, James Joyce, or any other Lost Generation notables. The current store has, however, accumulated a quirky and wide-ranging selection of new and used books. Bins outside offer a mixed bag of bargains, including many French classics in English (30F). Profits support impoverished writers who live and work in this literary cooperative. The first *Let's Go* writer stayed at Shakespeare's; so did beatniks Allen Ginsberg and Lawrence Ferlinghetti. Open daily noon-midnight.

W.H. Smith, 248, rue de Rivoli, 1er (tel. 42 60 37 97; fax 42 96 83 71). M. Concorde. Find the latest publications from Britain and America here, including many scholarly works. Large selection of magazines, from *Lilith* to *Esquire. Sunday Times* available by Tuesday. Open Mon.-Sat. 9:30am-7pm. MC, V .

Tea and Tattered Pages, 24, rue Mayet, 6ème (tel. 40 65 94 35). M. Duroc. The place to go for second-hand English-language fiction, cookbooks, sci-fi, and much more. The crazy-quilt selection is subject to barter and trade; sell books at 3-5F a paperback and get a 10% discount on your next purchase. If what you want isn't what they've got, sign the wish list and you'll be called if and when it comes in.

Adjoining tea room serves rootbeer floats, brownies, and American coffee with free milk and free refill. Open daily 11am-7pm.

The Village Voice, 6, rue Princesse, 6ème (tel. 46 33 36 47). M. Mabillon. An English-language bookstore with a terrific sci-fi section and a decent collection of feminist literature, as well as (you guessed it) the *Village Voice*. Open Mon. 2-8pm, Tues.-Sat. 11am-8pm. MC, V, AmEx.

■■■ MUSIC

Highly taxed in France, CDs and cassettes are luxury goods here (CDs 100F or more). Used LPs (*disques d'occasion*) can be found at *marchés aux puces* (flea markets, see Markets). In general, you'll find larger selections of certain musical types (like French and African) than in North America. Dedicated collectors will jump for joy at finding European labels that never crossed the Atlantic. Each of the following "megastores" has helpful clerks, decent prices, and a huge selection.

B.P.M., 1, rue Keller, 11ème (tel. 40 21 02 88; fax 40 21 03 74). M. Bastille. Catering to your rave needs, this address serves as a clubhouse, information point, and music store for house and techno fans. Rare and expansive collection. Check posters in the window for upcoming raves. Open Mon.-Sat. noon-8pm.

Gibert Joseph, 26 bd. St-Michel, 6ème (tel. 44 41 88 88). M. Cluny-Sorbonne. Stocks new and used tapes, CDs, and LPs in the basement. Used CDs around 55F, LPs 20-200F, new tapes about 40F. Open Mon.-Sat. 9:30am-7:30pm. MC, V.

FNAC (Fédération Nationale des Achats de Cadres): Several branches. **Montparnasse,** 136, rue des Rennes, 6ème (tel. 49 54 30 00). M. Rennes. **Etoile,** 26-30, av. des Ternes, 17ème (tel. 44 09 18 00). M. Ternes. **Forum des Halles,** 1-7, rue Porte Lescot, 1er (tel. 40 41 40 00). M. Les Halles. **Italiens,** 24, boulevard des Italiens, 9ème (tel. 48 01 02 03). M. Opéra. Huge selection of tapes, CDs, and stereo equipment. The Les Halles branch contains a well-stocked shelf of books about music.The Italiens branch screens music videos all day in a public viewing room, no charge. Also a box office for concert and theater tickets (see Entertainment). Montparnasse store open Mon.-Sat. 10am-7pm. Etoile and Les Halles branches open Mon.-Sat. 10am-7:30pm. Italiens branch open Mon.-Sat. 10am-midnight.

Virgin Megastore, 52-60, av. des Champs-Elysées, 8ème (tel. 40 74 06 48). M. Franklin Roosevelt. This music mecca includes an affordable restaurant and countless headphones that let you listen to the latest hits. If it's been recorded, it's likely to be at Virgin. Beware of free listening stations; they can be hard on your pocketbook since they invariably have recordings you've never heard of, but find you can't live without. Open Mon.-Thurs. 10am-midnight, Fri.-Sat. 10am-1am.

■■■ ODDS AND ENDS

Paris is crawling with specialized boutiques selling imported and domestic knick-knacks and handicrafts. Budget travelers beware of impulse-buy items that leave you sleeping in the streets. At the same time, the city offers you a great opportunity to buy a unique souvenir or gift that will always remind you of Paris. We list some interesting stores with gift ideas that you might not have thought of before, but your most memorable purchases could well be from places that you discover yourself.

Clair de Rêve, 35, rue St-Louis-en-l'Ile, 4ème (tel. 43 29 81 06). M. Pont Marie. Come to admire, if not to buy, the spectacular, hand-painted marionettes displayed here. Open daily 2:30-5:30pm. MC, V, AmEx.

Curiosités et Jouets Anciens, 65, rue Laugier, 17ème (tel. 45 74 88 74). M. Porte Cmaperret. Small store selling antique toys and curiosities, especially old tin model trains and cars. Many are collector's items. Prices as high as you're willing to pay. 50-100F will get you an antique French matchbox car or an old children's book, either of which makes a portable, sturdy souvenir. Open Mon. 2:30pm, Tues.-Fri. 11am-12:30pm and 2:30-7pm, Sat 10:30am-12:30pm. MC, V, AmEx.

MARKETS

Françoise Cousseau, 52, rue St-André des Arts, 6ème (tel. 43 25 44 45). M. Odéon. Eclectic proprietor imports handbags, fabric, ceramics, jewelry, and exquisite glass bottles from South America, Indonesia, and Morocco. A fair share of European handicrafts as well. Open Mon. 3-7:30pm, Tues.-Sat. 12:30pm-7:30pm.

F. Martinez, Estampes Anciennes-Livres, 97, rue de Seine, 6ème (tel. 46 33 08 12). M. Odéon. A small store with prints from the 16th century to now. Engravings of Parisian monuments, as they were centuries ago, make great souvenirs. Smallest works 20F. Many rare, expensive finds. Open Mon.-Sat. 9:45am-6:20pm.

Pentagram', 15, rue Racine, 6ème (tel. 43 26 99 99), directly across from the Ecole de Médicine. M. Cluny-Sorbonne. Do you have child relatives? What about childish relatives? Select a kaleidoscope, puppet, or wooden toy for the folks back home. Variety of books and games for children and adults. The room upstairs exhibits contemporary art. Open Mon.3-7pm, Tues.-Sat. 10:30am-7pm. MC, V.

Pylones, 57, rue St-Louis-en-l'Ile, 4ème (tel. 46 34 05 02). M. Pont Marie. Also at 7, rue Tardieu, 18ème (tel. 46 06 37 00). M. Anvers. Sells colorful, gag souvenirs: wineglasses with matchbox cars for stems, a theme chess set made of Simpsons characters, umbrellas with plastic tulip handles, and the like. Prices start at 50F. Open daily 10:30am-7:30pm. MC, V.

Rouge et Noir, 26, rue Vavin, 6ème (tel. 43 26 05 77). M. Notre-Dame Des-Champs. Dice, chess boards, travel games, billiard equipment, and juggling tools. A sophisticated game shop. Prices vary, but start at 40-50F. And yes, they do have French Monopoly. Open Tues.-Sat. 10:30am-1:30pm and 2-7pm. MC, V, AmEx.

■■■ MARKETS

Paris' covered and uncovered markets often show the visitor a unique characteristic of daily life in the neighborhood. For a complete list of the locations and hours of Paris' 84 markets, ask for the brochure *Les Marchés de Paris* at the tourist office or at your local *mairie*. For food markets, see Groceries in the Food section.

Carreau du Temple, on the angle of rue Dupetit Thouars and rue de Picardie, 3ème. M. Temple. This structure of blue steel and glass is a neighborhood sports center in the afternoon and a clothes market in the morning. The market is especially strong in leather—coats, bags, and shoes—but also sells fur and other kinds of clothes. One of the last places in the capital where you can still bargain—usually you can get the price down by about 25%. Even if your French isn't up to bargaining, the starting prices are quite low. As in any public market, watch your wallets and pocketbooks. It gets crowded on weekends, so it's best to come during the week. Open Tues.-Fri. 9am-noon, Sat.-Sun. 9am-1pm.

Marché aux Fleurs (flowers), 4ème, on pl. Louis-Lépine just across from the M. Cité staircase. This permanent flower market, filling the plaza near the Palais de Justice with color and fragrance, should be a staple of any walk down the Seine, especially *à deux*. Open Mon.-Sat. 8am-7:30pm. On Sun., a bird market appears in its stead, featuring an unremarkable collection of goldfish, rabbits, gerbils, and pet food stalls. Parakeets 500F. Rabbits 100F. Goldfish 10F. Open 9am-5:30pm.

Marché Ternes, 8bis, rue Lebon, 17ème. M. Ternes. Walk west on av. des Ternes. Take a right on rue Perre Demours and a left on rue Lebon. The closed market doesn't look very market-ish. Glemaing new and metallic, it hosts a variety of meat, cheese, and produce stalls with decent quality and not-so-rock-bottom prices. Still, its more affordable than the markets next door. Open Tues.-Sat. 8am-1pm and 4-7:30pm, Sun. 8am-1pm.

Marché aux Timbres (stamps), on the Champs-Elysées at av. de Marigny. Thurs. and Sat.-Sun., during daylight hours.

Quai de Mégisserie, 1er. M. Pont-Neuf or Châtelet. Parisians used to call this 3-century old animal bazaar "the valley of misery." One of the few old, open-air markets that have remained in central Paris. Buy a turkey, pigeon, or rabbit, or come to browse. Waterfront shops sell all manner of strange pets. Cages spill out from the stores onto the sidewalk. Open daily until sunset.

PUCES DE ST-OUEN (ST-OUEN FLEA MARKET)

You'll find fleas and just about everything else at the **Puces de St-Ouen (St-Ouen Flea Market),** where spangled 1920s dresses comingle with antique armoires, used kitchen sinks, and con artists. The prices and quality of the merchandise vary as widely as the products, beginning at the dirt cheap, low-quality bargains found among the renegade stalls. At the other end of the spectrum, astronomically expensive, high-quality antique dealers use buzzers to ring in their preferred customers while keeping out the riff-raff. Antique itself, the market was formed during the Middle Ages, when merchants resold the cast-off clothing of aristocrats (crawling with the market's namesake insects) to peasant-folk on the edge of the city, and it has gradually developed into a highly structured, regular market alongside a wild, anything-goes street bazaar.

A rule of thumb for first-time visitors: bring as little money as possible, watch your wallet, and have something in mind before you go. There are no five dollar diamond rings here. If you find the maltese falcon mixed into a pile of schlock jewelry, the vendor probably planted it there. The one area, however, where peddlers seem not to know what they have is that of rare rock-and-roll recordings. If you know your stuff and have unlimited patience, this is the place—1960s and 70s garage bands, funk, and much more. The music stalls tend to have lots of records, slightly fewer CDs, and almost no cassettes. There is a stall just across from the restaurant Au Baryton (see below) with an extensive collection of blues. Best deals are cut on on rainy days. The market is least crowded before noon.

If you take the metro, you'll encounter the street bazaar first. The 15-minute walk to the official market is jammed with tiny **unofficial stalls.** Most of these sell flimsy new clothes at exorbitant prices, but the leather jacket stalls have some good buys (suede jackets for 275F). Don't be turned off by the raucous hurriedness of the stalls; once you pass through to the real market you'll be able to browse leisurely. Pickpockets love this crowded area, and Three Card Monte con artists positively proliferate (don't be pulled into the game by seeing someone win lots of money; they're part of the con, planted to attract suckers to the crooked game).

The **regular market** is comprised of six markets, located on rue des Rosiers and rue Jules Vallès. Note that street names belong to the marketplace itself and not the 18ème *arrondissement* in which it is found. Expect to get lost. Rare finds linger at the **Marché Malik** (new and used clothing), **Marché Vernaison** (antique bric-a-brac), and **Marché Paul Bert** (antique bric-a-brac). The remaining three—**Marché Biron** (used valuable tableware: crystal glasses, etc., plus some gold and silver jewelry), **Marché Dauphine** (expensive antique furniture stores), and **Marché Serpette** (expensive antique furniture stores) will help you plan what to buy when you're rich and famous. Wherever you shop, be prepared to bargain; sellers don't expect to get the starting price. (Market open Sat.-Mon. 7am-7:30pm.)

If you want to stop for lunch while at the flea market, try a steaming bowl of *moules marinière* with *frites,* the uncontested specialty of restaurants in the area. Two restaurants in particular stand out: **Chez Louisette,** 130, av. Michelet (tel. 40 12 10 14), inside the Marché Vernaison, allée no. 10, all the way at the back, where cigarette-puffing singers enliven the already boisterous atmosphere. It's an eclectically decorated restaurant with classic French café *chansons.* Unfortunately, the secret is out, and you'll hear as much English and German as French. (*Moules* 58F. Open Sat.-Mon. 12:30-6pm.) A younger, grungier, less-touristy clientele frequents **Au Baryton,** 50, av. Jules Vallès (tel. 40 12 02 74), outside the Marché Malik, where people slurp up the *Moules-Frites* combo for only 54F while taking in the free live blues and rock concerts. (Open Sat.-Mon. 8am-10pm. Live music 4:30-9pm.)

Other *marchés aux puces,* while less impressive, are also less crowded: **Vanves,** av. de la Porte-de-Vanves and av. Georges-Lafenestre, rue Marc Sanguier, 14ème, M. Porte de Vanves (open Sat.-Sun. 2-7:30pm); **Marché à la Ferraille,** rue Jean-Henri Fabre, 18ème, M. Clignancourt (open Sat.-Mon. 7am-7pm); **Montreuil,** av. de la Porte Montreuil, 20ème, M. Porte de Montreuil (open Sat.-Mon.7am-7:30pm).

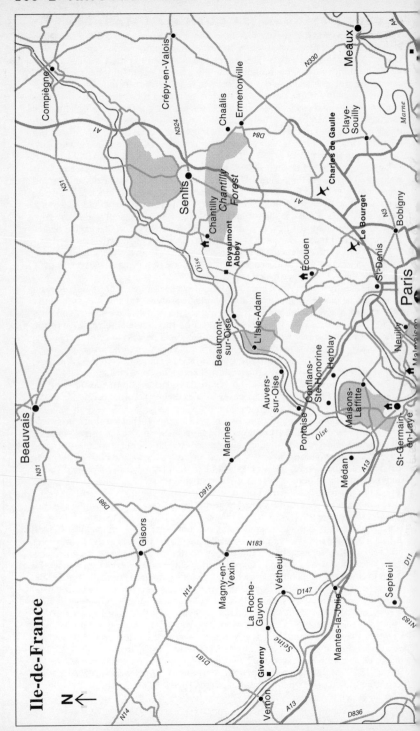

Ile-de-France

N←

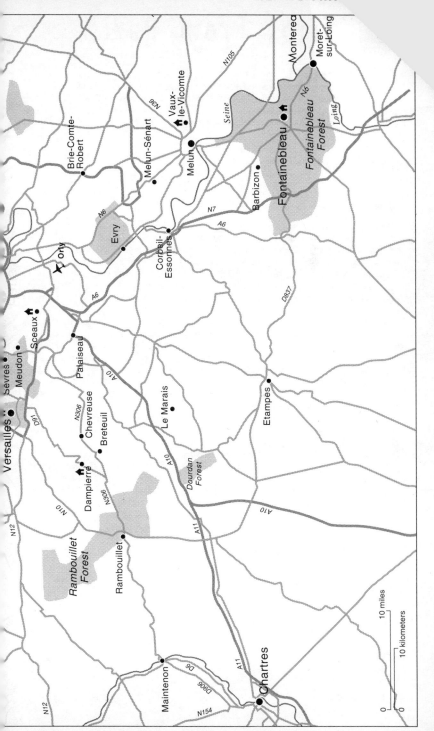

Montereau

Moret-sur-Loing

N105

N6

Loing

Seine

Fontainebleau

Fontainebleau Forest

Barbizon

Vaux-le-Vicomte

N36

Melun-Sénart

Melun

Brie-Comte-Robert

N6

Evry

N7

A6

Corbeil-Essonnes

D837

Orly

A6

Sceaux

Palaiseau

A10

Le Marais

Etampes

Versailles

Sèvres

Meudon

D91

N306

Chevreuse

Breteuil

A10

Dourdan Forest

Dampierre

N306

A11

A10

N10

Rambouillet Forest

Rambouillet

N12

10 miles

10 kilometers

Maintenon

D6

A11

Chartres

D906

N154

N12

0

0

rips From Paris

*e maître, I was indeed in Paris during the heat: it was truly "Tro
adopt the pronunciation of M. Amat, governor of the palace of
), and I sweated profusely. I was twice at Fontainebleau. And
nd time, following your advice, I saw the sands at Arbonne.*
—Gustave Flaubert to George Sand, 10 August 1868

DAY TRIPS

■■■ CHÂTEAUX

Although a château is literally a "castle," the magnificent structures that ring Paris
are by no means heavy defensive shields. Rather, they were built for 16th- and 17th-
century French aristocrats and kings as sometimes whimsical, always elaborate
retreats from the city. Surrounding the châteaux are formal French gardens with
fountains, trellised rose gardens, and a maze of rectilinear hedges stretching to forest groves. Teams of architects, sculptors, and landscape designers created these
compounds with money from the state treasury. The over-taxed peasantry footed
the bill.

Some helpful hints on château sight-seeing: in general, weekends are far busier
than weekdays, although Tuesdays (when most museums in Paris are closed) can
also be a bit hairy. On special occasions such as the fountain displays at Versailles on
Sundays, it may be worth braving the crowds. Keep on top of other special events—
son et lumière, classical music concerts, temporary exhibitions, and more—by reading the entertainment weeklies in Paris or by calling the châteaux directly. The main
tourist office in Paris may also be of some assistance regarding festivals and other
annual events. Beware of groups of schoolchildren on weekdays, although if you
understand French, you might get the benefit of their guided tour. The morning is
always a better time to arrive than the afternoon. Don't start a visit 45 minutes
before the château closes for lunch—the guards will rush you by locking the door
behind you each time you walk into a room. Please leave your cameras alone while
you're inside the building. Flash pictures are forbidden for a good reason: they
slowly fade and discolor furniture, paintings, curtains, tapestries, etc. Besides, unless
you're a professional with a tripod and lighting equipment, your pictures won't look
nearly as good as the postcards you can buy for less money than it would cost to
develop your film. Most of these sights are gargantuan in size and will not fit into the
view finder of the average camera—you'll only get bits and pieces anyway. Make a
real effort to take your time, look around you at both the big picture and the delightful details, and revel in the history of these spectacular residences, hunting lodges,
and summer homes.

■ VERSAILLES

Built by the "Sun King," Louis XIV, when he'd outgrown the Louvre, Versailles is
quite simply the world's most famous palace. The sprawling château—its Hall of
Mirrors, its oversized royal suites, its countless guestrooms, antechambers, and family portraits—stands as testament to the despotic playboy-king who lived, entertained, and governed on the grandest of scales.

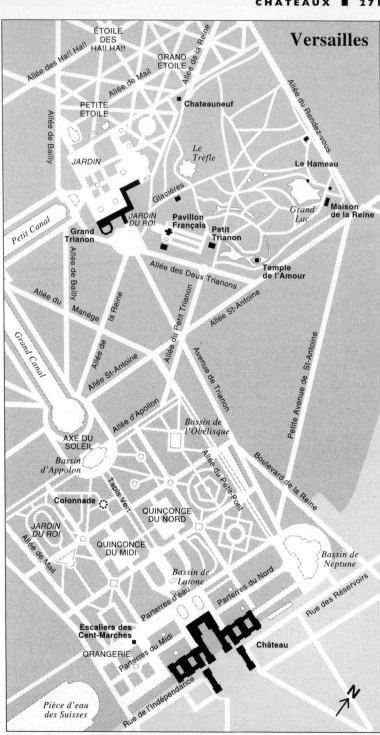

Versailles

ÉTOILE DES HA!! HA!!

GRAND ÉTOILE

Allée des Ha!! Ha!!

Allée de Mail

Allée de la Reine

Chateauneuf

Allée du Rendez-vous

PETITE ÉTOILE

Allée de Bailly

Le Trèfle

Le Hameau

JARDIN

Glacières

Grand Lac

Maison de la Reine

Petit Canal

JARDIN DU ROI

Pavillon Français

Petit Trianon

Grand Trianon

Allée de Bailly

Allée des Deux Trianons

Temple de l'Amour

Allée du Manège

Allée de la Reine

Allée du Petit Trianon

Grand Canal

Allée St-Antoine

Avenue de Trianon

Allée St-Antoine

Petite Avenue de St-Antoine

Allée d'Apollon

Bassin de l'Obélisque

AXE DU SOLEIL

Bassin d'Appolon

Allée du Petit-Pont

Boulevard de la Reine

Colonnade

Tapis Vert

QUINCONCE DU NORD

Bassin de Neptune

JARDIN DU ROI

QUINCONCE DU MIDI

Allée de Mail

Bassin de Latone

Parterres du Nord

Parterres d'eau

Rue des Réservoirs

Escaliers des Cent-Marches

Parterres du Midi

Château

ORANGERIE

Pièce d'eau des Suisses

Rue de l'Indépendance

HISTORY

A child during the aristocratic insurgency called the Fronde, Louis XIV is said to have entered his father's bedchamber one night to find (and frighten away) an assassin. Scared of conniving aristocrats for the rest of his life, Louis XIV fled Paris for the suburbs. Settling in the town of Versailles, Louis XIV turned his father's hunting lodge into a royal residence, built and decorated mainly by Le Vau, Le Brun, and Le Nôtre, the team stolen from Vaux-le-Vicomte. The court became the center of noble life where more than a thousand of France's greatest aristocrats vied for the king's favor. Busily attending to Louis XIV's wake-up *(levée)* and bed-going *(coucher)* rituals, they had little time for subversion. Louis XIV had successfully drawn the high nobility away from their fiefs and under his watchful eye. He outlawed duels at court, as a further precaution.

The château itself is a gilded lily of classical Baroque style. No one knows just how much it cost to build Versailles; Louis XIV himself burned the accounts so no one would ever find out. At the same time, life there was less luxurious than one might imagine—courtiers wearing rented swords urinated behind statues in the parlors, wine froze in the drafty dining rooms, and dressmakers invented the color *puce* (literally, "flea") to camouflage the insects crawling on the noblewomen. Although Louis XIV and his palace number among the few monarchical successes of 17th-century Europe, the kind of mass extortion that Versailles represents would spark the French Revolution a century later. On October 5, 1789, 15,000 fishwives and National Guardsmen marched out to the palace and brought the royal family back with them. Under the July monarchy, King Louis-Philippe established a museum here, dedicated to *toutes les gloires de la France* (all the glories of France). In so doing, he preserved the château against the wishes of most French people, who wanted Versailles demolished. In 1871 the château took the limelight once again, when Wilhelm of Prussia became Kaiser Wilhelm I of Germany in the Hall of Mirrors. That same year, as headquarters of the Thiers regime, Versailles sent an army against its old rival, Paris, then ruled by the Commune. In 1919, a vengeful France forced Germany to sign the ruinous Treaty of Versailles in the very room of its birth.

THE MAIN TOUR

When you arrive at the Versailles Rive Gauche RER train stop, exit the station and take a right. The elegant building on the right is the *mairie* of Versailles. Continue walking away from the train station the length of the *mairie*'s façade and turn left at the first huge intersection. Walk toward the now-visible, gilt-fenced outer courtyard of Versailles. An equestrian statue of a crimped, turned-out Louis XIV stands at the courtyard's center. Overlooking the courtyard is the terrace at which Molière's *Tartuffe* debuted. The clock on the pediment used to be set to the time of death of the previous king. Above what appears to be the main entrance is the balcony of the **king's bedroom,** at the center of the east-west axis along which the château and gardens are laid out. The placement of the room was no mistake; the Sun King's place was at the center of the château system, and he rose each morning, to great ritual, in the east.

Signs in the courtyard point you to Entrance A, B, C, or D. Most of Versailles' visitors enter at **entrance A,** located on the right-hand side in the north wing. (**entrance B** is for groups, **entrance C** leads to the King's Bedchamber, **entrance D** is where guided tours start, and **entrance H** is for visitors in wheelchairs.) Buy general admission tickets at entrance A (40F, ages 18-25, over 60, and Sun. 26F; the *carte musée* includes general admission to Versailles). General admission allows entrance to the following rooms the *grands appartements,* where the king and queen received the public; the War and Peace Drawing Rooms; the Galerie des Glaces (the famed Hall of Mirrors); the dauphin's and children's apartments. Note that the private suites of the king and queen may only be seen by guided tour. If you intend to take one, proceed directly to entrance D, purchase the regular admission ticket, and inquire about English-language guided visits. General admission tickets are also for sale at entrance C, as are tickets for the single tour that leaves from there.

The general admission ticket starts your visit in the **Musée de l'Histoire de France,** created in 1837 by Louis-Philippe to celebrate his country's glory. Along its textured walls hang portraits of men and women who shaped course of French history. The face of Louis XIV is everywhere; you may wonder if he spent his entire life sitting for portraits. Of particular interest are portraits by Philippe de Champaigne, preeminent court artist under Louis XIII. The 21 rooms, arranged in chronological order, try to construct an historical context from which to understand the château. The north wing ground floor, in Louis XIV's day, was a bustling open-air market where men bought wigs and women ribbons; now thronged with tourists, it has preserved the ambiance of its old self.

Each of the **drawing rooms** in the **State Apartments** is dedicated to a mythological god—Hercules, Mars, and the ever-present Apollo, among others. Although less brilliant than you would expect, the gilt wood is still splendid, fresh from the five-year, $70 million restoration that ended in 1989.

Framed by the **War and Peace Drawing Rooms** is the **Hall of Mirrors.** The hall was a somewhat gloomy passageway until Mansart added mirrors and doubled the light. Don't expect a wall of seamless mirrors—the Hall is a series of mirrored panels joined together and set in wooden frames. Each of these mirrors was the largest that 17th-century technology could produce; the ensemble represented an unbelievable extravagance. Although many of the mirrors are old and cloudy, little compares to the impact of standing at one end of the Hall and looking past the mirror-filled arches, gold figures, and many chandeliers. Le Brun's ceiling paintings tell the history of Louis XIV's heroism, culminating in the central piece entitled *The King Governs Alone.*

The **Queen's Bedchamber,** which saw the public births of 20 members of the royal family, is furnished year-round in its floral summer decor—not the darker plush red and black velvet used during 18th-century winters. A version of David's painting depicting Napoleon's self-coronation dominates the **Salle du Sacré** (also known as the Coronation Room), in which the king used to wash the feet of 13 poor children on Holy Thursday.

You can rent a **cassette guide** in English for 28F (with ID deposit of passport) at the information desk behind the ticket booths. While an audioguide may help compensate for the lack of explanatory signs in the château, be aware that the narration is not paced to the sequence of the rooms. An excellent printed guide is Daniel Meyer's 50F color-photo guide to the palace called *Versailles Tour of the Château, Gardens, and Trianon*, on sale at the gift desk. This 96-page book, written by Versailles' curator, has dazzling photos and detailed explanations of the countless paintings, rooms, antiques, gardens, and fountains of Versailles.

GUIDED TOURS

Consider starting your visit at **entrance D,** at the left-hand inside corner as you approach the palace (1-hr. tours 23F, ages 7-17 15F, under 7 free; 2-hr. tours 46F, ages 7-17 31F, under 7 free). Choose between seven tours of different parts of the château; only three are offered in English. One good bet is the whirlwind "best of Versailles" guided visit. Guided tours in sign language are available of the King's State Apartments, the Hall of Mirrors, and the Apartment of the Queen. Reservations must be made in advance with the Bureau d'Action Culturelle (tel. 30 84 76 18).

Consider taking the tour of the opera house, which leaves from entrances A and C. Completed at break-neck speed by 20,000 workmen in time for the wedding of Marie-Antoinette and the future Louis XVI, the opera took architect Jacques-Ange Gabriel 20 years to design. Often considered the world's most beautiful theater, the pink and blue oval room is a marvelous fake; though apparently marble or bronze, the restored opéra is actually made of wood, and with good reason; Gabriel wanted the hall to resound like a violin. The mirrored galleries reflect chandeliers and gilt archways, making the theater seem larger than it is. The room's splendor brought the Marie-Antoinette to breach royal etiquette on her wedding day; she took her eyes off the stage and ogled the decor. Many of Molière's plays premiered here, accompanied by the music of court composer Jean-Baptiste Lully. Lully's death is one of the oddest tales in music history. Before the advent of the conducting baton, leaders of musical ensembles used a long, pointed stick to keep time. During a performance celebrating Louis XIV's recovery from illness in 1687, Lully accidentally stabbed himself in the foot with his stick. He died later that year of gangrene.

Most of the other tours take you through seemingly empty, if historically important, rooms. The tour of **Louis XV's Apartments** showcases a small collection of furnishings, instruments, and tapestries, while providing a history of Versailles under that monarch. You can see the room where Mozart played on his youthful visits (at ages 7 and 22) to Versailles and learn the origin of the name of the *voyeuses* chair. The visit to **Marie-Antoinette's Apartments** does not trail through as many lavishly decorated rooms as you would think. Versailles was sacked during the Revolution and only a tiny portion of its original glory has been restored. Much of the tour is spent in rooms filled with portraits, learning the who's who for the Hapsburgs, Bourbons, and their ministers. The same is true of apartments belonging to Louis XV's daughters, Mme. de Pompadour, Mme. du Barry, and the dauphin and dauphine. True French Revolution buffs will, however, not want to miss the door and passageway through which the Marie-Antoinette fled to rejoin her king on October 6, 1789, when a crowd of bloodthirsty Parisians stormed her bedroom, demanding the head of the "Austrian whore."

The **King's Bedchamber** yields a look at the Sun-King's gold bed and balustrade, and more than a passing glance at Nocret's beautiful family portrait, featuring Louis XIV as Apollo and his brother, Philippe d'Orléans, as holder of the morning star. Philippe was the first after the morning chaplain to see the Sun King—Philippe was also kept in skirts until he was 18. (Tickets to the bedchamber tour, in French or in English, on audio-cassette or led by a guide, are sold at Entrance C.)

Longer tours go to the **Jardins et Bosquets (Gardens and Groves)** and to the **Petit Trianon and English Garden.** The two-hour Gardens and Groves tour, with considerable walking, provides the history of Le Nôtre's gardens and their countless fountains (June-Oct. Tues.-Sat. afternoon). Be advised, however, that the groves are rarely open for viewing, and the tour usually only visits the gardens. Guided visits to the **Petit Trianon** illuminate this favored hangout of Marie-Antoinette (July-Sept. 1-hr. tour at 11am. 2-hr. French-only tour 4pm). Both tours leave from the entrance to the Petit Trianon (June-Oct. Tues.-Sat., 46F, ages 7-17 31F, under 7 free).

THE GARDENS

Versailles gardens are breathtaking and enormous, perfectly scaled to the palace. Numerous artists—Le Brun, Mansart, Coysevox—executed statues and fountains here, but master gardener André Le Nôtre provided the master plan. Louis XIV, landscape enthusiast, wrote the first guide book to the gardens entitled the "Manner of presenting the gardens at Versailles." Start, as he suggests, on the terrace, pausing to study the layout of the gardens. During the summer, the grounds at Versailles have an overwhelming impression of green rare to this area of France. Even more rare are the wide paths and tall trees—you can feel quite alone, even with lots of people around. During the summer, the grounds are open until dusk. Come in the evening to see the immense château without people, like the empty stage of a grand opera.

To the left of the terrace, the **Parterre du Midi** graces the area in front of Mansart's **Orangerie,** once home to 2000 orange trees. The temperature inside never drops below 6°C (43°F). In the center of the terrace, the **Parterre d'Eau** boasts statues by the *ancien régime's* greatest sculptors. Below is one of the most extraordinary fountains, the **Bassin de Latone.** Latona, mother of Diana and Apollo, is seen shielding her children from the attack of peasants, whom Jupiter is turning into frogs. Part-human, part-frog figures belch water into the air when the fountains are turned on. The fountain can also be read as a thinly veiled political allegory—Latona as Anne d'Autriche, fleeing Paris and the Fronde with her children, Louis XIV (Apollo) and Philippe d'Orléans (Diana). Louis XIV appears as both victim (Apollo) and savior (Jupiter).

Past the *bassin* and to the left is the **Rockwork Grove,** built between 1681 and 1683. Once known as the ballroom because courtiers danced on the long-gone marble floor, the Grove shows off odiferous water cascading over shell-encrusted steps. The south gate of the grove leads to the magnificent **Bassin de Bacchus (or de l'Automne),** one of four seasonal fountains marking the intersection of pathways on either side of the main alley. The **Bassin du Miroir d'eau** spurts near the peaceful **Jardin du Roi** and the **Bassin de Saturne (or de l'Hiver),** sculpted as an old man. The **Colonnade** is a 32-column peristyle, decorated by sculptures and 28 white marble basins, in the center of which the king used to take light meals. The north gate to the Colonnade exits onto the **Tapis Vert (Green Carpet),** the central strip of grass linking the château to the much-photographed **Char d'Apollon (Chariot of Apollo).** Pulled by four prancing horses, Apollo/Sun God/Louis XIV rises out of dark water to enlighten the world.

On the north side of the garden is Marsy's incredible **Bassin d'Encelade.** One of the giants who tried to unseat Jupiter from Mount Olympus, Enceladus cries in agony under the weight of rocks that Jupiter has thrown to bury him. When the fountains are turned on, a 25m jet bursts from Enceladus' mouth. Flora reclines more peacefully on a bed of flowers in the **Bassin de Flore (or du Printemps),** while Ceres luxuriates in sheaves of wheat in the **Bassin de Cérès (or de l'Eté).**

The **Parterre du Nord,** full of flowers, lawns, and trees, overlooks some of the garden's most spectacular fountains. The **Allée d'Eau,** a fountain-lined walkway provides the best view of the **Bassin des Nymphes de Diane.** The path slopes toward the sculpted **Bassin du Dragon,** where a dying beast spurts water 27m into the air— the highest of any jet in the gardens. The culmination of any visit to the gardens is the **Bassin de Neptune,** the largest of the fountains. Ninety-nine jets of water attached to urns and seahorses surround a menacing Neptune. (Gardens open sunrise-sundown. Free; May-Sept. Sun. 20F.)

Beyond the **Petit Parc** of Le Nôtre's classical gardens stretch wilder, more natural woods and farmlands. The **Grand Canal,** a rectilinear pond beyond the Bassin d'Apollon. Rent a bike to the right (north) of the canal, just outside the garden gates, to appreciate Versailles' vast grandeur (35F/hr.). Forgo the unremarkeable *bateau-mouche* canal tour (25F, under 16 20F). If you're traveling with friends, rent a barque for 4 people at the boathouse to the right of the canal (60F/hr., open 10am-5:30pm).

THE TRIANONS AND MARIE-ANTOINETTE'S HAMEAU

Also within the grounds of Versailles are the two Trianons—"smaller" châteaux made of lavish pink, white, and black marble—and the **Petit Hameau,** an idyllic peasant village where Marie-Antoinette came to milk cows. Trianon was the name of the village the Sun King bought in 1668 in order to expand his estate. Built by Mansart, the single-story, marble-decorated **Grand Trianon** was intended as a meeker château in which, if need be, the king could reside alone with his family. Stripped of its furniture during the Revolution, the château was restored and inhabited by Napoleon and his second wife. Today important state meetings, including the one that passed the constitutional amendment for Maastricht, are held at the Grand Trianon, and Versailles briefly becomes the capital of France once again.

The **Petit Trianon,** built for Louis XV and Mme. de Pompadour by Gabriel, was presented to Marie-Antoinette by Louis XVI. Restoration has closed off all but four rooms to the public—their cozy feel may not be worth the price of admission. The English Garden, made for Marie-Antoinette, and the Grand Trianon gardens provide calm far from the madding crowds found closer to the château. Quainter still is the **Hameau** (the Queen's Hamlet), a collection of countrified, Norman cottages built for Marie-Antoinette. The young queen liked to play peasant here, to the dismay of the people who actually fit that description. The buildings are not open to the public, but they once contained drawing rooms of considerable, un-peasant-like elegance.

VERSAILLES

(Grand and Petit Trianons open Tues.-Sat. 10am-6:30pm; Oct.-April Tues.-Fri. 10am-12:30pm and 2-5:30pm, Sat.-Sun. 10am-5:30pm. Admission to the Grand Trianon 21F, reduced tariff 14F; to the Petit Trianon 12F, reduced tariff 8F. Combined ticket to the palace and Trianons 60F, reduced tariff 45F, purchase before 12:30pm.) Shuttle trams from the palace to the Trianons and the Hameau leave from behind the main château most of the day (round-trip 27F). The train does a 35-minute circuit that allows you to get off, tour the Trianons, and get back on another train. But the commentary on the gardens only repeats what is written on the pamphlet. Otherwise, the walk takes about 25 minutes.

SPECIAL EVENTS

On Sundays from May through September, come to see (and hear) the **Grandes Eaux Musicales,** when the fountains are in full operation. Aglitter with geysers, the park becomes the sensual feast it was designed to be. A slightly diminished version of this spectacle, called the *grande perspective,* runs 11:15-11:35am. Tour the 24 activated, musically accompanied fountains 3:30-5pm. A free pamphlet lays out a suggested walking path; don't bother with the more expensive 25F guide to the fountain; the same info appears in the Meyer *Guide to the Château and Gardens.* (Admission to park during *Grandes Eaux* 20F.)

The **Grande Fête de Nuit,** a musical and fireworks extravaganza, imitates the huge *fêtes* of Louis XIV. The garden at Versailles had to be finished in 1664 in time for one such party, the Fête of the Enchanted Isle, for which Molière wrote an up-to-the-minute *masque* (theatrical vignette). (*Fêtes* held at the Neptune Fountain July and Sept. Sat. nights rain-or-shine. 80 min. 60-185F, reduced rates for children. Call the tourist office at 39 59 36 22 for dates and ticket info.) Tickets go on sale at the tourist office and box offices within Paris. Doors open 1 hour before the show; enter at 2, bd. de la Reine.

The **Centre de Musique Baroque de Versailles,** 16, rue Ste-Victoire, gives concerts, equestrian shows, masques, dance performances, and theater presentations in period costume, many focusing on the 18th-century French court, music, and drama (May-early Sept. Sat. 5:30pm; tickets 50-180F). Musical Thursday concerts by the Maîtrise Nationale of Versailles are held in the Royal Chapel (Nov.-June 5:30pm; tickets 20F). For more information call 39 02 30 00 in Versailles; in Paris call 42 60 58 31 or 43 59 24 60.

Versailles offers two ongoing lecture series. The first (*Histoire du Château*) provides an in-depth historical look at various parts of the palace. The second (*Visites Approfondies*) provides for a scholarly treatment of themes, with lecture titles like "Court Costumes under the Old Regime," and "Their First Name was Adélaïde." There is much here for both the 18th-century French scholar and the lay Marie-Antoinette aficionado. (*"Histoire du Château"* 1-hr. lectures Sat. 10:30am and 2:30pm, admission 23F, under 17 15F. *"Visites approfondies"* Sat.-Sun. 2pm, 46F under 17 31F. Call 30 84 76 18 for more information.)

PRACTICAL INFORMATION

Visiting Versailles is a mammoth undertaking; you may want to take two days to do it. Arrive early in the morning to avoid the worst of the crowds. Versailles is most crowded on Sundays, when May-Sept. the fountains are turned on. In late June when the palace is swamped with French schoolchildren on field trips. (Château open Tues-Sun. 9am-6:30pm; Oct.-April 9am-5:30pm. Last admission 30 min. before closing. Gardens open 7am-sunset. General admission to the palace 40F; ages 18-25, over 60, and Sun. 26F; the **Carte Musée** includes admission to Versailles. For more information on the *carte,* see introduction to Museums.)

For more on Versailles, check out the **Ancienne Comédie Bookshop** in the *cour des Princes* next to the palace. Or call the **Office de Tourisme de Versailles,** Les Manèges, rue du Général de Gaulle (tel. 39 53 31 63), across from the train station, which has information about château events, other sights, lodging, and food. Food is both scarce and expensive at Versailles. There are two pricey restaurants: the **Caféteria** (tel. 39 50 58 62; open 9:30am-5pm) and **La Flotille** (tel. 39 51 41 58).

For lunch, exit the main gate of the château, turn left, and head for the row of blue parasols on the tree-lined landing just beyond the parked tour buses. There are three cafés there. The middle one has an outdoor sandwich counter with sandwich-drink combo for 35F.

The RER has direct and frequent train service between Paris and Versailles. Trains run from M. Invalides on RER Line C5 to the Versailles Rive Gauche station (every 15min., 35-40 min., 19F round-trip). From the Invalides metro stop, take trains with labels beginning with "V." Buy your RER ticket *before* going through the turnstile to the platform, even though your metro ticket will get you through these turnstiles; it will not get you through the RER turnstiles at Versailles.

■ FONTAINEBLEAU

What do the words "hunting lodge" mean to you? A log cabin, with a stuffed deer head, tucked away in the thick of the woods? A gun rack and a stone hearth? The men who commissioned and designed the Château de Fontainebleau had something else in mind; their efforts converged in this sprawling structure, deceptively simple when viewed from the main courtyard. Made from sandstone formed in the lush tangle of forest surrounding the château, Fontainebleau's warm yellow exterior, accented with red brick, hides the splendor and extravagance within. Not a bad place for a harried sovereign to get away from it all.

Like its name, believed to come from a certain Monsieur Bliaut who owned a local fountain, Fontainebleau is a composite of architectural and decorative styles. It has been a glorified hunting lodge for nearly 500 years, presenting a radically different architectural statement from the unity of Vaux-le-Vicomte and Versailles. Kings of France have lived on these grounds since the 12th century, when the exiled Thomas à Beckett consecrated Louis VII's manor chapel. In 1528, François I tore down and rebuilt the castle, to bring him closer to the "red and black furred animals" he so loved to hunt. Italian artists designed and decorated the palace, and their paintings, the *Mona Lisa* and the *Virgin in the Rocks* among them, filled his private collections. Subsequent kings had varying degrees of affection for the château, depending generally on their love for dead and dying furry animals. Most used their favorite designers to add at least one magnificent room, while some attached whole new wings. The château remained a happening place throughout. Louis XIII was born here in 1601, Louis XV was married here in 1725, and Louis XIV revoked the Edict of Nantes here in 1685. Fontainebleau was also the perfect place to welcome the Pope, who had come to crown Napoleon in 1804, and to imprison His Holiness between 1812 and 1814. Napoleon popped in to Fontainebleau frequently and it is presented as one of his main residences; in reality he only spent 194 days in the building whose eclectic blend of architecture led him to dub it *"La Maison des Siècles"* (the House of Centuries). **Cour des Adieux** was so named after serving as the scene of his dramatic farewell in 1814. Also known as the **White Horse Court,** it is used as the main entry to the château. Note the unique horseshoe-shaped stairway leading to the front door.

The **Grands Appartements,** the standard visitors' circuit, provides a lesson in the history of French architecture and decoration. Guides available in English will make the whole visit more meaningful: 15F will get you a pamphlet about the château and some of the gardens or one describing the Grands Appartements alone; 25F buys the glossy booklet with more complete descriptions. All labels in the rooms are in French. Dubreuil's **Gallery of Plates** tells the history of Fontainebleau on a remarkable series of porcelain plates, fashioned in Sèvres between 1838 and 1844. In the **Gallery of François I,** arguably the most famous room at Fontainebleau, muscular figures by Mannerist artist Il Rosso (known in French as Maître Roux) tell mythological tales of heroism and bravado, brilliantly illuminated by light flooding in from courtside windows. The **Ball Room's** magnificent octagonal ceiling, with complementary floor, reminds the visitor that much of Fontainebleau should be observed with a craned neck. The **King's Cabinet** (also known as the **Louis XIII Salon),** decorated under Henri IV, was the site of many an important meeting, as well as *le débotter,* the king's post-hunt boot removal. Gobelin tapestries and Savonnerie carpets line walls and floors throughout the palace—the four seasons, with floral hoops, are depicted on the wall of the **Empress's Antechamber.** Every Queen of France since the 17th century slept in the gold, green, and leafy **Queen's** (later Empress's) **Bed Chamber;** the gilded wood bed was built for Marie-Antoinette, who never used it. The *N* on the throne is another testament to Napoleon's enduring humility; the red and gold velvet meets in a crown above the throne. **Napoleon's Bed Chamber** boasts predictably fancy decor, but the **Emperor's Small Bed Chamber,** complete with camp bed, seems more in the style of a military man. In the **Emperor's Private Room,** known today as the **Abdication Chamber,** Napoleon signed his abdication in 1814. (Grands Appartements open Wed.-Mon. 9:30am-12:30pm and 2-5pm. Without break during July-Aug., closes 1hr. earlier the rest of the year. Last entry 11:30am and 4pm. Admission 31F; students, seniors, and Sun. 20F; under 18, teachers with ID, unemployed, and art students with ID free. 90-min. guided tours available in French and possibly English Wed. and Sat.-Sun. at 11am and 3pm, everyday during summer; 34F; students, seniors, and Sun. 21F. Call 60 71 50 700 for details.)

The same ticket admits you to the **Musée Napoléon,** a collection of paraphernalia including his tiny shoes, his toothbrush, his field tent, and his son's toys. Not to be missed are the gifts (don't you wish you had enemies like this?) from Carlos IV of Spain. (Same tel. and hrs. as Grands Appartements. Last entry 11:30am and 4pm.)

The **Petits Appartements,** private rooms of Napoleon and the Empress Josephine, are accessible only by guided tours and only on certain days. If you are desperate to see these rooms, call ahead. (Admission 12F, under 26 and over 60 8F. Call ahead for tour schedule. English-language tours available.) The **Musée Chinois de l'Impératrice Eugénie,** also in the château, offers a welcome respite from the sometimes crowded apartments upstairs. Reopened after restoration in 1991, these four rooms were remodeled in 1863 by the Empress to house the collection she herself called her *"Musée chinois"* (Chinese museum), a gathering of Far Eastern decorative art: porcelain, jade, and crystal. These pieces were brought to her after the 1860 Franco-English campaign in China and also by Siamese ambassadors received by Napoleon III in 1861. The rooms are quietly decorated in green and maroon and are among the few in the château that seem to have anything to do with real people living comfortably. (Open same hrs. as château. Last entry 11:30am and 4pm. Admission 12F; students, seniors, and Sun. 8F.)

Underkept and fairly unimpressive, the gardens at Fontainebleau still make for a pleasant stroll. Quieter and more refined are the **Jardin Anglais,** complete with rustic grotto and the famous Fontaine-belle-eau, and the **Jardin de Diane,** guarded by a statue of the huntress. (Gardens open daily sunrise-sunset. Jardin Anglais and de Diane open variably.) You can also cruise around the **Etang des Carpes** in a rented boat. (4-person max. per boat. Boat rental May 23-Aug. daily 10am-12:30pm and 2-7pm; Sept. Sat.-Sun. 2-6pm. 40F/½hr., 58F/hr; 50F deposit.)

The **Forêt de Fontainebleau** is a thickly wooded 20,000-hectare preserve with hiking trails and the famous sandstone rocks used for training alpine climbers. If you're going to be around for a while and are up for it, you too can learn how to climb. Bikes can be rented in town. Maps of hiking and bike trails are available at the tourist office. Fans of 19th-century art will recognize the thick hardwoods and sandstones made famous by Rousseau and Millet, painters of the Barbizon school.

In the town itself, the **Musée Napoléonien d'Art et d'Histoire Militaire,** 88, rue St-Honoré (tel. 64 22 49 80), grew out of Louis Prost's (creator and conservator of the museum) childhood fascination with Napoleon and things military. This is the place to go if you've seen Fontainebleau but, like France, didn't get enough of Napoleon the first time. (Open Tues.-Sat. 2-5pm. Last entrance 4:30pm. Admission 10F.)

Fontainebleau's **tourist office,** 31, pl. Napoléon (tel. 64 22 25 68), across from the **post office** and near the château, organizes tours of the village surrounding the château and can help you with accommodations. (Open Mon.-Sat. 9:30am-6:30pm; Sun. 10am-12:30pm; Oct.-May slightly shorter opening times.) A *petit train* (tel. 42 62 24 00) run by the tourist office, gives a 30-minute tour of the park, with multilingual commentary (Wed.-Mon. 10am-12:30pm and 2-6pm; 30F, children 15F). Hourly **trains** run to the town from the Gare de Lyon, *banlieue* level (45min., 74F round-trip). The château is a pleasant 20-minute walk or short bus ride. Take Car Vert A from the station (8F10). You can also rent a bike at the train station from **MBK** (tel. 64 22 36 14; fax 60 72 64 89). (For a basic model, , 40F/half-day, 60F/day. 3-speeds 30F/hr., 60F/half-day, 100F/day. Mountain bikes 40F per hour, 80F per half-day, 120F all day. Helmet rental 20F. Open daily 9am-7pm.)

NEAR FONTAINEBLEAU: BARBIZON

On the edge of the Fontainebleau forest blossoms the rustic village of **Barbizon,** a favorite of 19th-century French landscape painters. Théodore Rousseau, Jean-François Millet, and Jean-Baptiste Camille Corot were the key figures in the Barbizon School, living and working in this artistic haven in the mid-1800s. Influenced at once by the writings of Jean-Jacques Rousseau and the 17th-century Dutch landscapists, they were the spiritual and artistic predecessors of the Impressionists.

The **Musée Municipal de l'Atelier de Théodore Rousseau,** 55, rue Grande (tel. 60 66 22 38), showcases the work of the man who founded the Barbizon School and whose wooded scenes capture the dark beauty of the forest (open Wed.-Mon. 10:30am-12:30pm and 2-6pm; Oct.-March Wed.-Mon. 10:30am-12:30pm and 2-5pm; admission 15F). It is also the site of the town's **Office du Tourisme** (same hrs. as museum). The town's other museum, the **Maison et Atelier de Jean-François Millet,** 27, rue Grande (tel. 60 66 21 55), shifts focus to Millet, the best-known of the Barbizon masters, famous for his portrayal of the French peasantry as the great, the proud, the victimized, the simple, and the uncorrupted (open Wed.-Mon. 9:30am-12:30pm and 2-5:30pm; free). Galleries dedicated to the Barbizon School, as well as contemporary art, line the main drag, misnamed rue Grande. The tourist office at Fontainebleau sells a 5F map of Barbizon for the faint of heart (others may do without) and can provide a schedule for the *autocars verts* that connect the two towns (12F40 each way); it is wise, however, to check before you arrive as the schedule is highly erratic and scheduled buses are liable to pass you by. Biking to Barbizon is probably the cheapest and most reliable option for those without a car; otherwise, a taxi from the Melun or Fontainebleau train station is the most practical (if highly extravagant) option.

■ COMPIÈGNE

Tranquil Compiègne (pop. 45,000) has tripped through twelve centuries of diplomatic notoriety, without being much affected by it. The town emerged as a diplomatic capital in the 8th century, welcoming Frankish and Byzantine officials to the banks of the Oise. The English captured Jeanne d'Arc here in 1430 during a siege in yet another round of the Hundred Years' War. The armistice ending World War I was signed on November 11, 1918 in a forest clearing about 6km away; in 1940 Adolf Hitler forced the French to surrender at the same spot. Beech trees, landscaped grounds, and the 17th-century château make today's Compiègne a quaint town with a few skeletons hidden in the *armoire*; under the German occupation, Compiègne served as one of France's largest detention centers for Jews on their way to concentration camps farther east. It was from the train station in Compiègne that the "death train" to the concentration camps left—a train ride that ended in the death of more than half of its passengers. This dark period in the town's history is carefully neglected by most tour guides, and visitors can enjoy Compiègne's 17th-century château, three unusual museums, and web of hiking trails in peaceful ignorance. Remember that towns as well as people look gentler as they age. A walk through the compact center and proximate periphery will lead you past medieval spires, half-timbered façades, a decaying monasteries, and, more prominently, architectural remains from the Second Empire.

The **Musée National du Château de Compiègne** (tel. (16) 44 38 47 00), just beyond the Hôtel de Ville and behind the Eglise St-Jacques, is a souped-up version of the hunting lodge that served French kings since Charles IX. Compiègne later served Louis XIV as one of the three royal abodes, a folksy time-out from Versailles and Fontainebleau. Fond of its rustic appeal, Louis would quip, "I am lodged as king at Versailles, as gentleman at Fontainebleau, as peasant at Compiègne." With the original manor house too small for the royal entourage, ministers and servants stayed with villagers and at neighboring châteaux. Louis XV showed less of a taste for its humble charms and in 1751 started the building of a large palace; it forms the outline of what we see today.

In the 19th century Compiègne served as second home to Napoleon Bonaparte, and later as autumn residence for Second Empire pomp, circumstance, and guests. Napoleon III played emperor here before a rotating circle of distinguished friends. The château's interior bears the mark of his ostentatious tastes, an often consciencously opulent ensemble of nude nymphs and tapestried chairs.

The elite of Paris elite spent their days hunting at Compiègne in 16th-century costume and, according to some observers, felt ill at ease. As Théophile Gautier told the Goncourts, "everybody behaves very awkwardly: the whole atmosphere is one of embarrassment. They aren't used to it....The only people who are completely at their ease are the old servants, the remnants of dynastic varletry, handed down from Charles X and Louis-Philippe. They are the only people who look as if they knew what a court was like." Painted ceilings by Redouté, tapestries from Beauvais, and a *trompe l'oeil* bag of tricks—secret doors, baffling paintings with every appearance of carved marble, and the like—let alone the gardens make the château of Compiègne a period piece well worth the hour train ride from Paris. Resist any temptation to deface the rooms, lest the fate that befell Napoleon III's son Prince Eugène-Louis fall on you too. When the prince skipped his math lesson, Louis-Napoleon grounded the twelve-year old from a hunting expedition. In sulking rebellion, the young prince scrawled the day's date (October 14, 1868) on a marble table-top. When the emperor came home and discovered it, he made his son copy out 100 times (presumably not on the table), "I should not write on the imperial furniture."

Located next to the palace, the **Musée de la Voiture** (Carriage Museum; tel. 44 40 04 37) features 18th-, 19th-, and early 20th-century coaches and omnibuses, including those used by Napoleon I and III. Perhaps the most impressive set of wheels to be found in the Musée de la Voiture is that of an anonymous 19th-century charlatan and traveling dentist, a surrey with a fringe on top painted with lions, horned beasts, and harpies. Though initially engaging, gazing at coach after *calèche* rapidly loses it appeal, and is probably not worth more than a 5-min. visit. The Chateau de Compiègne, including the Grands Appartements and Musée de la Voiture, may only be visited by guided tour in French, every 15 min., Wed.-Mon. 9:15am-6:15pm, last entry 5:30pm; Oct.-March Wed.-Mon. 9:15am-4:30pm, last entry 3:45pm. Admission to palace and museums 31F; students, seniors, and Sun. 20F. The palace and Musée de la Voiture are accessible by wheelchair; please call ahead.

No visit to the palace is complete without a tour of the grounds designed at Napoleon's request in 1811. These gardens are in the process of being restored to their original state; they should be finished in 1996. Meandering walkways, shade trees, and English-style, natural-looking flower beds are perfect for a picnic or tryst. And while, officially, the *grande pelouse* (great lawn) is forbidden territory, the tolerant grounds crew don't seem to notice. Just beyond this vast expanse of manicured grass lies the untamed **Forêt de Compiègne,** a more adventurous setting for a bike ride or hike. Check with the tourist office for details about hunting season.

Six km into the forest is the **Clairière de l'Armistice** (Armistice Clearing). The Ludendorff Offensive of 1918 put Compiègne on the front line between the French and German forces, so it was here that the Supreme Commander of the Allies,

Maréchal Foch, brought his railway carriage for the signing of the Armistice in November. In June 20, 1940, Hitler ordered that the leader of France's delegation of surrender be driven all the way from Tours so he could be presented with the German terms for peace in the very same railway carriage, in the very same clearing. Hitler himself arrived and sneered at the monument to French victory, showing, in the words of eyewitness William Shirer, his "burning contempt for this place now and all that it has stood for in the 22 years since it witnessed the humbling of the German Empire." After the capitulation was signed two days later, Hitler destroyed the monument and took the railway carriage to Berlin as a trophy. It was destroyed there by Allied bombing; a sturdy replica is now berthed here in a small **museum** (tel. 44 40 09 27) with a simple monument (open Wed.-Mon. 9am-12:30pm and 2-6:30pm; Oct.16-March Wed.-Mon. 9am-noon and 2-5:30pm; admission 3F). To get there, it is possible to walk or ride a bike next to the road, but not advised, as the shoulder is not adequate. The safest bet is to take a taxi (about 35F one way).

The **Musée de la Figurine Historique,** in the annex of the Hôtel de Ville (tel. 44 40 72 55), contains a charming collection of toy kings, soldiers, and commoners reenacting highlights of French history, impressive in the detail of costume, but absorbing to the layperson for no more than fifteen minutes. The highlight is a staged battle of Waterloo (open Tues.-Sun. 9am-noon and 2-6pm; Nov.-Feb. 9am-noon and 2-5pm; admission 12F, students and seniors 6F, under 18 free on Wed.).

To begin your visit, head to the **tourist office** (tel. 44 40 01 00), in the Hôtel de Ville, which provides maps (furnished with a friendly and compact one-hour walking tour of historic monuments) and info on music festivals, bike rentals, and forest hiking trails. To get to the office from the train station, walk straight across the parking lot, take a right along the canal, and then take the next left across the bridge. Keep going along this street, and l'Hôtel de Ville appears soon enough on the left. (Open Easter-Oct. Mon.-Tues. and Thurs.-Fri. 9am-noon and 1:45-6pm, Wed. and Sat. 9am-noon and 1:30-6pm, Sun. 9:30am-12:30pm and 2:30-5:30pm.)

Highlights of the walking tour include the **Musée Vivenel** (tel. 44 40 72 54), with strong collections of Greek vases, regional archaeology, and *objets d'art* from the Renaissance. (Admission 12F, reduced 6F; open Tues.-Sat. 9am-noon and 2-6pm; sun. 2-6pm.) There is an impressive stained glass of Jeanne d'Arc taking communion in **l'Eglise St-Jacques** on May 23, 1430, the same day she was captured by the English, in that very church, located one block further along the street that brings you to l'Hôtel de Ville. For those who decide to stay overnight, there is a **Crédit Mutuel** across the street from St-Jacques that runs on the **Cirrus** network.

The town is easily accessible by **train** from Paris' Gare du Nord (1hr., 132F round-trip). The train station is across the river from the center of town. To reach the center, cross place de la Gare in front of the station, turn right, and then turn left onto the bridge. If you decide to take the late train back to Paris (or miss the one around 7pm), there is a charming street called rue des Lombards (easily found on the map of the walking tour) that features a number of reasonably priced restaurants. The lower part of this winding street is pedestrian, and the terraces provide views of the few medieval buildings that survive in this part of the village. Two eateries of mention are **La Lombardine,** featuring cuisine similar to a *salon de thé,* with daily *plats* at 52F and full salads for 42F (open Mon.-Thurs. noon-3pm, Fri-Sat. noon-3pm and 7-10:45pm); and **La Calabraise** a family pizza joint, where individual pizzas go for 40-47F (open Mon. 6:30-10:45pm, Tues.-Sat. 11:30am-1:45pm and 6:30-10:45pm).

■ VAUX-LE-VICOMTE

Some might consider **Vaux-le-Vicomte** a mere hut compared to Versailles in terms of size and opulence. But as Le Vau, Le Brun, and Le Nôtre's first masterpiece, it is in many ways the more coherent creation and the place most likely to be called a home. Nicolas Fouquet, Louis XIV's Minister of Finance, assembled the team of architect, artist, and landscaper to build Vaux for him between 1656 and 1661. In so doing, he financed the creation of a new standard of country château, in a uniquely

French, Neoclassical Baroque style. To show off his new pad, Fouquet threw a *fête* to end all *fêtes* on August 17, 1661. Louis XIV and Anne d'Autriche were but two of the witnesses to a sensual orgy that provided poetry by La Fontaine, a new ballet by Molière, and concluded in a fireworks extravaganza featuring the King and Queen's coat of arms and pyrotechnic squirrels (Fouquet's symbol).

The celebration of Fouquet's impeccable grace, sophistication, and culture—he was surrounded by a circle of the finest artists and intellectuals—did not last long. Furious at being upstaged by his first minister, the young Louis ordered Fouquet arrested. Three weeks later at Nantes, d'Artagnan, the captain of the Musketeers immortalized by Dumas, arrested the hapless man for speculation. Behind Fouquet's downfall were hidden causes. Colbert, another minister, had been turning the monarch against Fouquet for years; Fouquet's ill-advised expression of affection for Mme. de Lavallière, beloved of the king, didn't help matters either. And someone, even the man who had kept the French treasury solvent by raising funds against his own fortune, needed to be the fall guy for the state's abysmal financial condition. In a trial that lasted for three years, the judges in Fouquet's case voted narrowly for banishment over death; Louis XIV overturned the judgment in favor of life imprisonment. Pignerol, a dreary citadel, housed the fallen minister until his death in 1680, leading some to speculate he was the famous man in the iron mask. Louis did appreciate Fouquet's tastes; soon after the minister's arrest, the King confiscated many of Vaux's finest objects and hired the same trio—Le Vau, Le Brun, and Le Nôtre—to take their crafts to Versailles. Everything at Vaux-le-Vicomte has been orchestrated to create an impressive whole. The designers integrated painting and sculpture, architecture and décor, building and garden to please the viewer with ideal forms and harmony and impress one with man's ability to govern and tame nature through symmetry and invention.

THE CHATEAU

The château itself (tel. 60 66 97 09) recalls both the grandeur of a Roman past, with its rusticated columns, and a French fort, complete with squat walls and moat. Walk over the moat, invisible from the road, and appreciate Le Vau's sense of symmetry and his use of water to set off the building. With the Spanish war ended, Fouquet's entrance sends the message that peace unites art and prosperity. Although the tour begins to your left, upon entering, peek up at the dome in the Oval Room ahead and then out to the gardens. Vaux was designed to draw people inside, contain them within the cupola, and expel them into the seemingly infinite space of the gardens.

A thorough pamphlet, available in English, guides the visit to the château. For more detail and a brilliantly colored souvenir, buy the glossy guide in the gift shop (40F). Notice the ornate scripted Fs all round the château, and keep an eye out for the ever-present squirrel, Fouquet's industrious symbol, and for the tower with three battlements, his second wife's crest. The **Minister's Bedchamber** may lead you to wonder who the real monarch was in this kingdom. The opulent red and gold bed stands under an allegorical ceiling in which Apollo bears the lights of the world. (One begins to understand why he was arrested.) **Mme. Fouquet's Closet** once had walls lined with small mirrors, the decorative forerunner of Versailles' Hall of Mirrors. Le Brun's portrait of Fouquet, whose penetrating look overrides his general appearance of humility, hangs over the fireplace. Tear your eyes away from the beautiful 1877 billiard table in the **Square Room** to admire the exquisite beams of the Louis XIII-style ceiling. The vivid colors and engaging expressions of the nine muses in the **Room of the Muses** make this one of Le Brun's finest decorative schemes. Le Brun planned to crown the **Oval Room** (or Grand Salon) with a fresco entitled *The Palace of the Sun,* but Fouquet's arrest halted all activity. The tapestries once bore Fouquet's squirrel, but Colbert seized them and replaced the rodents with his own adders. The ornate **King's Bedchamber** (the balustrade gives it away) boasts an orgy of stucco, cherubs, and lions fluttering around the centerpiece of *Time Bearing Truth Heavenward.*

THE GARDENS

Vaux-le-Vicomte presented André Le Nôtre with his first opportunity to create an entire formal garden. Three villages, a small château, and many trees were destroyed to open up space, though countless trees were later replanted to draw the all-important contrast between order and wilderness. Even a river was rerouted to provide the desired effect. With Vaux, Le Nôtre gave birth to a truly French style of garden—shrubs were trimmed, lawns shaved, bushes sculpted, and pools of water strategically placed to produce a kind of embroidered tapestry exuding classical harmony.

Start by considering the impressive panorama from the steps behind the château. The garden seems perfectly symmetrical and the grottoes appear to be directly behind the large pool of water. Closer inspection reveals otherwise. The right-hand *parterre* was a flowerbed in its original incarnation, but today is dominated by a statue of Diana. Its matching green area on the left side is actually wider and sunken. The **Pool of the Crown,** named for the gold crown at its center, is the most ornate of the garden pools. The **Round Pool** and its surrounding 17th-century statues mark an important intersection: to the left, down the east walkway, are the **Water Gates,** likely backdrop for Molière's performance of *The Annoyances* before Louis XIV. The **Water Mirror,** farther down the central walkway, was designed to reflect the château perfectly, but you may have some trouble positioning yourself to enjoy the effect. The Mirror also hides the sunken canal, known as **La Poêle** (the Frying Pan), fed by the Anqueuil River. Although somewhat smelly and scum-covered today, the canal is a reminder that Fouquet made his fortune in shipping. Climb to the **Farnese Hercules** (the vanishing point when you look out from the castle), and survey the land and imposing château before you. The old stables today house a carriage museum, **Les Equipages.** Magnificent carriages of all kinds come complete with piped-in music, dressed-up party-goers, and liveried footmen. Picnicking in the gardens is prohibited, but the restaurant **L'Ecureuil** (squirrel) on the castle grounds provides good salads (35-40F) and cooked meat and vegetables (54-58F).

Vaux is exquisite; getting there is exquisite torture, which may explain the absence of crowds. Your best and cheapest option, if traveling with other people, is to rent a car. Take Autoroute A4 or A6 from Paris and exit at Val-Maubée or Melun, respectively. Head toward Meaux on N36 and follow the signs. Or take the train to Melun, a fairly large center on the SNCF *banlieue* line (every 15-30 min. from Gare de Lyon, 45 min., 62F round-trip). Unfortunately, the station is a smug 6km from the château. You can take a bike on the train free of charge, but riding on the undivided highway without shoulder next to big trucks is not advisable. It might be worth it to splurge and take a taxi. The 6km ride will cost you at least 66F one way (pick one up at the train station; call 64 52 51 50 from Vaux). Fit troopers might not mind the 70- to 90-minute hike for at least one part of the trip though they should be prepared to jump off the highway and into the grass at any minute. The effort may pay off most handsomely on Saturday evenings from May to October (8:30-11pm) when the candle-lit château may remind you of a wedding cake. The fountains in Le Nôtre's gardens are turned on from 3 to 6pm every second and last Saturday of the month from April to October. The **tourist office,** 2, av. Gallieni (tel. 64 37 11 31), by the train station in Melun, can help you with accommodations, sight-seeing opportunities, and give you a free map—essential for those planning to walk (open Tues.-Sat. 10am-noon and 2-6pm). If the tourist office is closed, however, do not fear. While the highway is perilous, the directions are relatively simple: just follow Avenue de Thiers through its many name-changes to highway 36 (direction Meaux) and follow signs to Vaux-Le-Vicomte.

(Château open June-Aug. Mon.-Sat. 10am-1pm and 2-6pm, Sun. and holidays 10am-6pm; visits by appointment the rest of the year, call for more information. *Equipages* open same hrs., but remain open during lunch and 30min. after the château closes. Gardens open same hrs. as the *equipages,* except Sun., when they are open an additional 30min. Admission 56F, students with ID and under 16 46F, under 6 free. Estate open May-Oct. Sat. 8:30-11pm for candlelit evenings. Admission 75F, students with ID and under 16 65F. Admission to gardens 45F.)

■ CHANTILLY

Chantilly says a lot about unreality. The faux-Renaissance castle, built in the late 19th century, looms above a carefully-tended "natural" landscape, while a play village recalls the idealized view of peasant-life depicted by a medieval artist. The whole scene testifies to an aristocracy a bit removed from the real world. Fittingly, during World War I, French commander-in-chief Général Joffre established his headquarters here, whence he plotted grand strategy in blithe and happy ignorance of the magnitude of the slaughter taking place on the front.

Set in the magnificent gardens Le Nôtre sculpted from the surrounding forest, the **Château de Chantilly** drapes elegantly over its serene gardens, lakes, and canals. A Roman citizen named Cantilius built his villa here, leaving his name and a tradition of high property values. A succession of medieval lords constructed elaborate fortifications, but the château did not come into its own until the Grand Condé, cousin of Louis XIV, brought Le Nôtre to create the gardens and, eventually, commissioned the Grand Château. His château was razed during the Revolution; the present building is a reproduction built in the 1870s by its owner at that time, the Duc d'Aumale, fifth son of Louis-Philippe. As you approach, the dramatic Renaissance façade, lush greenery, and extravagant entrance hall, whet your appetite for something truly remarkable.

Inside, the château houses the **Musée Condé** (tel. 44 57 08 00), crowded with the duke's private collection of elegant furniture and dusty paintings. For the castle's most sumptuous experience, head to the wood-paneled library, which displays medieval miniatures, a Gutenberg Bible, and a facsimile of the museum's most famous possession, the **Très Riches Heures du Duc de Berry,** a 15th-century manuscript showing the French peasantry and aristocracy engaged in the labors of the different months. The **Salle de Gardes** displays two Van Dyck paintings, along with a Roman mosaic of *The Rape of Europa* that was just the thing to hang over the duc d'Aumale's mantel. The galleries contain paintings by Raphael, Titian, Poussin, Gros, Corot, Delacroix, and Ingres—an impressive collection, but so crowded that it's hard to appreciate individual works. Think well before you pay the hefty 35F (25F *tarif réduit*) admission fee. For the dedicated royalist, it may be worth it, just to see the museum's collection of chairs taken from **Marie-Antoinette's** dressing room in Versailles.

Even if you skip the museum, consider taking a 15F wander through the **gardens,** the château's main attraction. For another 6F you can buy a map of the gardens with a suggested walking tour; free wandering, however, will lead you on a delightfully aimless tour of discovery. The central expanse, directly in front of the château, is in a typical French formal style, with neat rows of carefully pruned trees and calm statues overlooking geometrically shaped pools. To the right, hidden within a forest, the lovely "English" garden attempts to recreate the forms of nature, rendered more picturesque by the human element. Here, paths meander through woods and round pools where lone swans float along. Windows carved out in the foliage allow you to see fountains in the formal garden. You'll also find a play village, the inspiration for Marie-Antoinette's infamous hamlet at Versailles. Elsewhere, a statue of Cupid encased in a lovely gazebo reigns over the "Island of Love" with Dionysian ardor. (Château open Wed.-Mon. 10am-6pm; Nov.-Feb. Mon.-Fri. 10:30am-12:45pm and 2-5pm, and Sat.-Sun. 10:30am-5:30pm. Admission 35F, reduced 25F; to grounds 15F.)

The approach to the castle passes the **Grandes Ecuries,** immense stables that housed 240 horses and hundreds of hunting dogs from 1719 until the Revolution. The stables were originally ordained by Louis-Henri Bourbon, who hoped to live in them when reincarnated as a horse. These stables now house the **Musée Vivant du Cheval** (tel. 44 57 13 13 or 44 57 40 40), a huge museum dealing with all things equine: on display are saddles, horseshoes, merry-go-rounds, and horse postcards and sculptures. The horses themselves are here only for your viewing pleasure—no touching, no riding. The museum also puts on magnificent horse-training demonstrations (in French), a must-see for all horse lovers. (Museum open April-Oct. Mon.

and Wed.-Fri. 10:30am-6:30pm, Sat.-Sun. 10:30am-7pm; May-June also Tues. 10:30am-5:30pm; July-Aug. also Tues. 2-5:30pm; open Nov.-Mar. Mon. and Wed.-Fri. 2-4:30pm, Sat.-Sun. 10:30am-5:30pm. Horse shows May-June 11:30am, 3:30pm, and 5:15pm; July-Aug. 3:30pm and 5:15pm; Nov.-Mar. Mon. and Wed.-Fri. 3:30pm, Sat.-Sun. 11:30am, 3:30pm and 5:15pm. Admission to museum and show 45F, students and seniors 35F. Special show Sun. 4pm. Admission 1-4:30pm 50F.) Two of France's premier horse races are held here in June—the **Prix de Diane** and the **Prix du Jockey Club. Polo at the Hippodrome**, in mid-September, is free to the public (matches at 11am, 12:30pm, 2pm, 3:15pm, and 4:30pm).

The **tourist office** is stabled at 23, av. du Mal Joffre (tel. 44 57 08 58; open Mon. and Wed.-Sat. 9am-12:30pm and 2:15-5:30pm., Sun. 10am-2pm. April-Sept., also open Tues. 10am-noon). **Trains** run to Chantilly from Paris's Gare du Nord (35min., 72F round-trip). Call ahead for the schedule: many trains to Chantilly run only on weekends. To reach the château from the station, take the shuttle bus (6F, ask at the station for times), or walk down rue des Otages and turn left in front of the tourist office (2km). Rent **bikes** at **Cycle Aventure Chantilly** (tel. 44 57 73 72), located across from the château.

NEAR CHANTILLY: SENLIS

Tiny **Senlis**, a 10-minute bus ride from Chantilly, basks in the ineffable glory of being the quaintest and best-preserved village in the Ile-de-France. Its cobblestone streets, friendly residents, and intimate atmosphere are the closest you'll get to the France of storybooks. The **Cathédrale de Notre-Dame**, begun in 1191, is a prime example of early Gothic architecture. Its Grand Portal influenced the designs of Chartres and Notre-Dame in Paris. Across the *place* from Notre-Dame, the **Eglise St-Frambourg**, founded around 900 by the merciful Queen Adélaïde, also deserves a quick look. Reconstructed in 1177 by Louis VII and ransacked during the Revolution, this beauty found its most recent savior in the great pianist Girogy Cziffra, who restored the church as an international music center, now called, appropriately, the Fondation Cziffra. Enter the park next to the tourist office to reach the **Château Royal**, a hunting lodge for monarchs from Charlemagne to Henri IV, now converted to a hunting museum. The remains of Gallo-Roman fortifications, with 31 towers, surround the town (open April-Sept. Thurs.-Mon. 10am-noon and 2-6pm, Wed. 2-6pm; admission 15F, reduced 10F). The old town is a network of medieval alleyways winding up and down cobblestone hills between several of the original gates. Senlis's **tourist office,** pl. du Parvis Notre-Dame (tel. (16) 44 53 06 40), has information on concerts and exhibitions (open March-Nov. Mon. and Wed.-Fri. 2-6pm, Sat.-Sun. 10am-noon and 2-6pm). Erratic SNCF buses meet most trains to Chantilly for the 10-minute ride to Senlis (14F one-way; railpasses valid).

■ CHÂTEAUX DE MALMAISON AND DE BOIS-PREAU

Pack lunch and travel to the **Château de Malmaison**, 1, av. du Château (tel. 47 49 20 07), for a trip backstage the Napoleon and Josephine affair. Bought with borrowed funds in 1799 on the eve of Napoleon's rise to power, the château served as a love nest for the newlyweds, later to become Josephine's own Elba after their marriage was annulled in 1809. The house itself was built in 1622 on the site of a former leper colony—thus its name *"Mal-Maison"* (house of sickness).

Part temple to Napoleon, part temple to Nature, Malmaison is a mélange of his and hers; the restored Empire interiors combine *trompe l'oeil* marble and sarcophagus-inspired armchairs with a smattering of Romantic landscape paintings, many of the château itself. Private and public apartments feature paintings of the emperor by David, Greuze, Gros, and others. Josephine furnished them in the height of the Empire style: chairs with Egyptian motifs, square tables, short, tentlike beds. Especially interesting is Napoleon's study, decorated to look like a tent, reminiscent of council-rooms on a Napoleonic campaign. The museum at Malmaison is more about the Napoleon we never knew, following him off the battlefield and into the boudoir. Curators appear to have emptied the contents of his overnight bag; view his toothbrush, tweezers, and the handkerchief he carried at Toulon, behind glass.

The house itself overflows with Josephine memorabilia: her jewels, her shoes, her colossal dress bills, her harp, her perfumes (together, of course, with souvenirs of *"le petit corporal,"* including his death mask and the bed on which he died). Josephine's suite attests to her passion for the groomed outdoors. She preferred the modestly sized, sunny bedroom to the lavish one she had for show; at a corner of the house, its two walls of windows look out on the Malmaison grounds.

Left by Napoleon for a Habsburg after she failed to produce an heir, Josephine lived out her remaining years here, cultivating her gardens in plush seclusion. A devotee of the natural sciences, she consulted botanists worldwide about her gardens and collected exotic animals; camels, zebras, and kangaroos once walked these grounds. Josephine, née Rose—she changed her name to please her husband—devoted much attention to the rose gardens which now surround the château. In sharp contrast to the Mondrian/Rubic's cube surfaces of the Tuileries, these English style plantings are as much worth the trip as Malmaison itself. On vine and bush, hundreds of varieties bloom in the early summer months. On these grounds is also a memorial to Eugène-Louis-Jean-Joseph Bonaparte, the Prince Imperial, son of Napoleon III.

The **Ancienne Roseraie,** to the left as you enter the château, is a restful place to sit, contemplating the ends of this illustrious pair. Pierre-Joseph Redouté's roses were painted from the flowers in Josephine's gardens; some of his drawings are in Malmaison's collection.

Those unfamiliar with Napoleon's empire should visit the **Château de Bois-Preau,** located through the sizeable park up the path from Malmaison. It contains a museum *cum* shrine to the emperor. The ground floor summarizes Napoleon's life and then traces changing views of him since his death. Several copies of his death mask are here, as is an interesting collection of Russian toys created for the centennial anniversary of Napoleon's failed attempt to take Moscow. The second floor is devoted to Napoleon's death on St-Helena. Filled with models and sketches of the house, grounds, and his death-chamber, it also displays selected articles of clothing (boxer shorts, footsy pajamas) and from his toilette. Also pay a visit to the adjoining park of. It's one of the few in the Paris area where you can walk on the grass. (Château open Wed.-Mon. 10am-noon and 1-5pm. Admission to both chateaux 27F; students, seniors and Sun. 18F. The park of Bois-Preaux open 10am-7pm; Oct.-March Wed.-Mon. 10am-5:30pm; April Wed.-Mon. 10am-7pm; free.)

To get there, do not take the bus or metro to Rueil-Malmaison, which is quite far from the museum. Instead take the RER or metro to the Grande Arche de la Défense and change to bus #258 (ticket 6F50.) The RER stop is in zone 3 while the metro stop is in zone 2, meaning that you need an extra ticket if you take the RER. The bus stop "Bois-Preau" goes to Bois-Preau; the stop "Château" takes you to Malmaison.

■ ST-GERMAIN-EN-LAYE

A chic little hamlet with a château, boutiques, and a sizeable park, St-Germain-en-Layeit may be less noteworthy now than it once was. Louis VI le Gros built the first castle here in the 12th century, near the site where his ancestor Robert the Pious had constructed a monastery dedicated to St-Germain. Rebuilt by Charles V after destruction during the Hundred Years' War, the castle took on its present appearance in 1548 under François I. Lover of all things Italian, François I ordered his architects Chabiges and Delormé to construct a Renaissance palace—the current *château vieux*—on the foundations of the old church and castle. Henri IV added the *château neuf,* Louis XIII made it his home, and in 1638, his son, the future Louis XIV was born there. The Sun King retreated to St-Germain during the Fronde and while waiting for Versailles to be finished. Even after the court moved to Versailles, St-Germain was used for important ceremonial occasions. An impressive list of names graced these two châteaux—among them Colbert, Mme. de Sévigné, Rousseau, Molière, and Lully (the last two wrote plays and poems performed at the châteaux). James II of England died here in exile in 1701. But the 18th century was not kind to the estate. The *château neuf* was torn down; during the Revolution, the Empire, and the July Monarchy, St-Germain was alternately used as a prison, a cavalry school, and a military prison. The Austro-Hungarian Empire was formally dismantled here in 1919. In 1955, the independence of Morocco was here agreed.

Napoleon III decided to make the castle into a museum of antiquity. Today, the **Musée des Antiquités Nationals** (tel. 34 51 53 65) claims to have the richest collection of its kind in the world. At first, the display looks a bit like someone's pet rock collection, but the work gets more sophisticated as you move through the eras (100,000 BC to the 8th century AD), and by the time you get to the Iron Age, you can believe these relics were made by the ancestors of the French artists we know and love. The highlight may be the ancient tombs complete with dirt, bones, and burial loot. Despite the lack of explanation, the museum might interest the curious, well-informed viewer. The less-adept should call in advance for a schedule of guided tours. (Open Wed.-Mon. 9am-5:15pm. Admission 21F; students, seniors, and Sun. 14F. Wheelchair accessible.) If used tools don't thrill you, wander along the **garden terrace** (open daily 8am-10pm), designed by the omnipresent Le Nôtre. His gardens were destroyed along with the *châteaux neuf* at the end of the 18th century; the terrace survived. While lacking the extraordinary orchestration of Versailles, the gardens and nearby forest make for a pleasant stroll and panoramic view of Western Paris and *banlieue*. A map of forest trails is available from the tourist office.

Across from the château stands the **Eglise St-Germain**, consecrated in 1827 on the site of the 11th-century priory that gave St-Germain its name. The modern white pillars and piped-in religious music give the church a Southern evangelical atmosphere, but the 14th-century stone statue of **Notre-Dame-de-Bon-Retour** is one of the most venerated images in St-Germain. The statue was called Our Lady of the Safe Return because it was found buried deep underground when they dug the foundations for the church in 1775. (Church open daily 8:30am-noon and 2-7pm.)

Spend an afternoon at the two-room museum of the **Maison Claude Debussy,** 38, rue Au Pain (tel. 34 51 05 12), the Impressionist composer's birthplace. An autographed copy of *Prélude à l'après-midi d'un faune* (a work which was later interpreted in a ballet by Nijinsky) and a revealing survey he completed for a young girl—he wrote Hamlet down as his hero in fiction—are among the eclectic array of documents and pictures about the man who said, "I want to dare to be myself and to suffer for my truth." According to evidence in the museum, he also caused suffering to those close to him—he was quite a philanderer and twice drove his first wife Lilly to the brink of suicide. (Open Tues.-Sat. 2-6pm. Free.)

The **Musée Départemental du Prieuré,** 2bis, rue Maurcie-Denis (tel. 39 73 77 87), is dedicated to the works of painter Maurice Denis (1870-1943), the Symbolists, and the Nabis. Built in 1678 for the Marquise de Montespand and used as a hospital, *Le Prieuré* (The Priory) was purchased by Denis in 1914. He decorated the chapel with his interpretation of the Beatitudes. Today, you can visit his house and workshop and see the work of such artists as Vuillard, Bonnard, and Moret who, like Denis, received Gauguin's challenge to "risk everything." (Open Wed.-Fri. 10am-5:30pm, Sat.-Sun. and holidays 10am-6:30pm. Admission 25F, students 15F, children under 12 free.) Linger in the peaceful garden or at the *salon de thé*.

Eat at any of a number of places. **Le Collignon,** 7, rue Collignon (tel. 34 51 48 56), is cheap, close to the center and serves French fare on a shaded terrasse (68F *menu;* open Tues.-Sat. noon-3pm and 7-11pm, Sun. noon-3pm). The **Office Municipal de Tourisme,** Maison Claude Debussy, 38, rue Au Pain (tel. 34 51 05 12), provides lists of restaurants and hotels, and a map in English (open Mon.-Sat. 9am-12:30pm and 2:15-6:30pm; June-Sept. also open Sun. 10am-1pm).

You can rent a bike from the Bicyclub de France at the Parking de la Piscine. (March-Nov. Sat.-Sun. and holidays 9am-7pm; 5-speed bikes 25F/hr., 100F/day.

1500F deposit. Mountain bikes 40F/hr., 150F/day. 2000F deposit.) Inquire at the tourist office for more details.

St-Germain is 45 minutes from downtown Paris by RER Line A1 (11F there, 14F50 back).

■ SCEAUX

The peaceful, upscale suburb of **Sceaux**, 10km south of Paris, is one of the most fashionable places to live outside of Paris itself. Three hundred years ago, Sceaux was home to Colbert, Louis XIV's finance minister. His resplendent mansion, built by Claude Perrault, was expanded and embellished by his son, then sold to the Duc du Maine whose wife turned it into a much sought-after literary salon where such greats as Voltaire enjoyed spending time. During the Revolution, the château was confiscated, then later abandoned and destroyed during the first years of the 19th century. Only Le Nôtre's gracious gardens remain. In the 19th century, the Duc de Trévise inherited this property and built the charming (if more humble) **Château de Sceaux** (RER: Bourg-la-Reine or Parc de Sceaux), which now houses the **Musée de l'Ile de France** (tel. 46 61 06 71), dedicated to the *haute culture* and *traditions folkloriques* of the region surrounding Paris. Unlike the hulking, imposing, often tasteless structures that dot the landscape around France, this château is small (relatively), elegant, and inviting. To one side dips the **Grande Cascade** (with 20th-century additions by Rodin) which spills into Le Nôtre's graceful Octagon pool. Slightly to the southwest is a long stretch of the tree-lined grand canal. In front of the château is an immense lawn—the **Plaine des Quatres Statues.** You may have to hunt for these four; they are dwarfed by the expanse of green that precedes them. You'll know you're not in Paris anymore when you lie on the grass without a green-clad *gardien* whistling at you and yelling *"pelouse interdite."* (Museum open Wed.-Mon. 10am-6pm; off-season until 5pm. Admission 20F, students and seniors 12F. Park open daily 7am-9:30pm. Shorter hours off-season. Free.)

If you take the RER to Parc de Sceaux, the park is to the west. If you get off at Bourg-la-Reine, walk straight ahead out of the *gare,* past the Mairie, take a right on av. du Général LeClerc, then a right onto the shady Allée d'Honneur. The park entrance is straight ahead.

■■■ CHURCHES & CATHEDRALS

While most people think of demonic gargoyles, dank corners, dark medieval architecture, and the horrors of the Inquisition, the cathedrals of Paris and the Ile de France can offer some of the brightest moments of your stay. The great majority date from the Gothic era of the middle ages, whose great architectural achievement was using flying buttresses to remove the weight of the roof from the walls and enable stone to be replaced by scores of delicate windows. The dark gray interiors of Notre-Dame, Chartres, Beauvais, and St-Denis serve only as a somber contrast to the explosions of color that burst from the cathedrals' intricate rose windows and other masterpieces of stained glass. Despite the ravages of the Hundred Years' War, nine centuries of weather, political upheaval and war, including the Revolution and the bombs of two world wars, these ornate structures still stand as a testimony to human faith, architecture, and yes, technology. Most were built during the Gothic period of the Middle Ages by thousands of skilled sculptors, artisans, stone masons, iron smiths, and hard laborers who worked without the help of complex machinery or electricity to build some of the most beautiful buildings in to world.

The word "cathedral" literally means the "place of the cathedra," which is the Archbishop or Cardinal's seat (roughly equivalent in symbolic weight to a throne). A cathedral serves as the mother church for an archdiocese, a geographical county within the Roman Catholic Church. Cathedrals from the Middle Ages are most often built in the form of a cross that is rounded at one end: the vertical section of the cross is called the nave, the horizontal section is called the transept, and the tip of the rounded part is the apse. From the transept to the apse is the choir, where you find the altar; if the cathedral is still functioning as a place of worship, you probably won't be allowed into the choir area. The ambulatory is the passageway that goes around the far end of the choir, and is usually open to the public instead. Running up both sides of the seating area in the nave are aisles (the pedestrain areas that you will walk up) ; jutting off of the aisles and the ambulatory are usually chapels, which are small rooms devoted to specific saints and intended for prayer, This might seem like a lot of complex terminology, but as you visit a few churches (especially if you can see a floorplan), the labels will start to make sense. Aside from these basic similarities, cathedrals can be as architecturally diverse as museums and palaces. Some, like Notre-Dame, feature elegant and massive flying buttresses; others show off tall bell towers or have several ambulatories wrapping around each other like a rainbow. Still others, like St-Denis, serve as the burial ground for royalty, saints, and other well-known national figures.

Cathedrals can be a welcome break from the hot sun and the stressful bustle of busy Paris streets. They're also always open on Sundays, but realize that although it is considered perfectly acceptable to take pictures and comment to your friends about the interior, you are still visiting a place of religious worship. Be respectful of silent prayer areas and schedules for mass. For the most radiant view of the rose windows and stained glass, visit in the mid-morning or in the mid-afternoon when the sun is at its most direct slant. Check the bulletin boards at the back of the cathedral for information on concerts (choral, orchestral, and organ) and events (such as plays or opera performances), many of which are free or inexpensive. Don't be alarmed if some cathedrals charge a small admission fee. They use this money for much needed restorations and upkeep, and the fee, if any, is never more than 12-15F. Indeed, even if nothing is formally charged, there are often collection boxes for the upkeep of the church, and you might consider donating a few francs.

■ SAINT-DENIS

The home of the famed **Basilique St-Denis,** the burial place of France's kings and queens, this town is named after the missionary bishop Denis. According to legend, Denis was beheaded by the Romans in Montmartre in 250 AD and walked north carrying his head until he reached the town and was buried here in a plowed field. Today, St-Denis (M. St-Denis-Basilique) is a working-class town with a large and vibrant population of West and North African immigrants.

Ever since 768, the Basilica has been home to the remains of almost all of the kings and queens of France, whose funerary monuments form a progression from medieval simplicity to Renaissance extravagance. As importantly, its delicate 12th-century ambulatory (the cloistered passageway encircling the choir at the church's east end) is *the* first example of Gothic architecture in all of Europe. Toward the year 475, a little church was built to honor St. Denis' grave. About two centuries later, King Pepin destroyed that church to make way for a larger one, perhaps because he wanted to be buried there—he was, in 768. Vestiges of both of these early churches can be seen in today's crypt. Other early Frankish kings followed Pepin's lead, and at the end of the 10th century the church became the official necropolis of French royalty.

In 1136 Abbot Suger began the rebuilding of the basilica in a revolutionary style that would open its hallowed area to the "light of the divine." Suger was dissatisfied with dark and heavy Romanesque interiors, with their small windows and forests of thick columns. Instead, he brought together already-known architectural elements to create an unprecedented openness in the suddenly spacious nave. In the final Gothic creation, function melded with aesthetic form—the vaulted arches of the nave, essential to the cathedral's effect of verticality and weightlessness, funneled the weight of the roof into a few points, supported with long, narrow columns and flying buttresses outside. Freed from the burden of supporting the roof, the walls could be pierced with the huge stained-glass windows that became the style's trademark, and could even disappear completely in some places. The chapels around the first ambulatory have no walls at all between them, creating a second ambulatory that gracefully encircles the first.

In an age before skyscrapers and neon lights, the stained glass and human-dwarfing nave must have seemed miraculous. The height and spaciousness is indeed awe-inspiring; yet at the same time, there is a heaviness about the pillars that mark the construction as early gothic. The flamboyance would come later: Suger's contemporaries were flabbergasted and quickly worked to outdo him with their own cathedrals, building ever more intricate interiors, larger stained-glass windows, loftier vaults, and higher towers—the age of the Cathedral was born.

Suger himself died in 1151, well before most of his basilica had been rebuilt. His successors altered his plans, but did not stray from the Gothic pattern he had set. They created an unusually wide transept, complete with magnificent rose windows. The extra space was needed to accommodate the ever-growing number of dead monarchs. In 1593, underneath the newly spacious nave, Henri IV converted to Catholicism with his famous statement: *"Paris vaut bien une messe"* (Paris is well worth a mass). In 1610, he was buried here with the rest of France's Catholic kings. St-Denis' royal connection brought upon it the wrath of the Revolution. Most of the tombs were desecrated or destroyed, and the remains of the Bourbon family were thrown into a ditch. With the restoration of the monarchy in 1815, Louis XVIII ordered that the necropolis be reestablished. Louis XVI and Marie-Antoinette were buried here with great pomp. The remains of the other Bourbons were dug out of their ditch and placed in an ossuary inside the crypt. Tombs that had survived the Revolution were returned from the National Museum of Monuments (see Sights—*6ème arrondissement)*, where they had been displayed. Louis also added funerary monuments once located within churches that had been completely demolished by Revolutionary marauders.

Wreaking further destruction, Revolutionaries smashed the church's stained glass, upon which many of the windows at Chartes were modelled. Virtually all of St-Denis' original windows have been replaced, most during the 19th century when the church was restored. In the back of the ambulatory, however, you can still find some of the original 12th-century windows. Look closely and you can discern something other than the biblical tales: the Abbot Suger ensured his immortality by having pictures of himself put into the windows. Hence, the bottom panes of each of the aforementioned have a small monk piously praying, with his name written above him in case you couldn't recognize him. Admission to the necropolis includes a pair of headphones with a recorded tour (available in English). The headphones don't come with a tape recorder, but pick up infrared signals from a number of "islands." This whiz-bang technology makes for an enjoyable visit. Don't miss the little room on the left side of the church (outside the necropolis area). It contains the splendid funerary garments of the royal family. (Basilica open daily 10am-7pm; Oct.-April 10am-5pm. Admission 26F, seniors and students 17F, under 18 7F. Ticket booth closes ½hr. before the basilica. Guided tours in French daily at 10:30am, 11:30am, 3pm, 3:45pm, 4:30pm. Free organ concerts Sun. 11:15am.)

For a bite to eat before you head back to Paris, try one of the reasonably priced restaurants that cluster around the park in front of the basilica. There is also a market between rue Auguste-Blanqui and rue Jule-Joffrin. To reach it, walk straight out the front door of the cathedral, take a right at pl. Jean Jaurès, and continue one block up rue Pierre Dupont.

The helpful **tourist office,** at 1, rue de la République, (tel. 42 43 33 55) has lots of information on the cathedral and the town of St-Denis , including maps (open Mon.-Sat. 9:30am-12:30pm and 2-6:30pm, Sun. 10am-12:30pm and 2-6:30pm). Also worth a visit is the **Musée d'Art et d'Histoire,** 22bis, rue Gabriel-Péri (tel. 42 43 05 10). From the basilica, walk down rue de la Légion-d'Honneur, take a right fon rue Franciade, and then a left on rue Gabriel-Péri. The museum itself is housed in what was the Carmelite convent where Madame Louise, beloved daughter of Louis XV, lived most of her life. It now contains an archaeological history of St-Denis as well as a history of the convent, with the apothecary and Mme. Louise's cell both recreated. (Open Mon.-Sat. 10am-5:30pm, Sun. 2-6:30. Admission 20F; students, seniors, and Sundays 10F.) The tourist office also provides information on the museums of St-Denis and the annual **Festival de St-Denis** (tel. 42 43 77 72) which brings world-class orchestras and musicians, such as conductors Seiji Ozawa and Charles Dutoit and the Orchestre National de France, to the basilica in June.

■ CHARTRES

THE CATHEDRAL

The **Cathédrale de Chartres** survives today as one of the most sublime creations of the Middle Ages. The existing structure is the fifth to occupy this site—three different churches stood here before the year 1000. In 876, Charlemagne's grandson, Charles the Bald, made a gift to Chartres of the *Sancta Camisia,* the cloth believed to have been worn by Mary when she gave birth to Christ. Pilgrims have been flocking to the cathedral ever since to see the sacred relic and benefit from its supernatural powers. In 911 its magic was confirmed when the citizens of Chartres, under attack from Vikings, placed the relic on view at the top of the city wall. The infidels ran away; their leader Rollin converted to Christianity and became the first duke of Normandy.

The cathedral became a foremost center of learning, led by the brilliant Fulbert who arrived in 990 and supervised the building of the fourth church, a fine Romanesque cathedral. Disaster struck in 1194 when the third fire in 200 years burned all but the crypts, the west tower, and the Royal Portal. When they discovered that Mary's relic (hidden in the crypt by three loyal priests who stayed with it, sweating out the fire) had emerged unsinged, the villagers took it as a sign of not only Mary's love but her desire for a more worthy cathedral. Clerics took advantage of the miracle to solicit funds on a grand scale and building proceeded at a furious pace: most of the cathedral was completed by 1223 and consecrated in 1260. The stained-glass windows soon gained fame for their clarity and beauty, as did the magnificent sculptures adorning each of the main portals. Since then, in a series of miracles as great as the survival of the *Sancta Camisia* in 1194, the Cathédrale de Chartres has emerged intact from Protestant iconoclasm, the clergy's decision to "modernize" in the 18th century, the Revolution's attempt to turn it into a Temple of Reason, and two world wars.

Few cathedrals rival Chartres in size and majesty. A masterpiece of finely crafted detail, the cathedral will appeal to the aesthete in anyone. Imagine yourself a 12th-century farmer who set down the hand plow for a day of sculpture and stained glass. While the cathedral remains a showcase for the massive, the tall, and the glorious, its minute detail is equally worthy of attention. At the time it was built, Chartres served as a stage for cutting-edge contemporary artisanry. Sculpture and stained glass here tell the story of Christ, set in medieval castles and lordly dress. (Perhaps as remote to modern visitors as a fig leaf or a hairshirt, this is the rough equivalent of Jesus in the Trump Tower.) On the other hand, in the slouching figure of sloth or the tunicked and tempted St. Anthony, 13th-century visitors might have recognized themselves.

The cathedral is an extraordinary fusion of Romanesque and Gothic architectural elements. Built in a record-breaking 29 years (compared to 163 years for Notre-Dame de Paris) the cathedral stands as one of the most harmonious of medieval buildings. The famous twin-steepled silhouette is visible from miles around, rising up above the flat wheat fields that surround it. The flying buttresses, connected to the vaulting inside, fulfill both a functional and aesthetic role: they take the weight of the roof away from the walls (allowing the wall to open to the magnificent stained glass) and provide an elegant outside expression of the cathedral's interior structure. Towering over the surrounding town, the cathedral is a powerful embodiment of a time when the Church controlled every aspect of daily life, and the tallest buildings in existence were its cathedrals. The exterior of the church is marked by three lovely entrances. The famous 12th-century statues of the Royal Portal present an assembly of Old Testament figures at the height of late Romanesque sculpture. Those in the central bay, attributed to the "Master of Chartres," are especially beautiful: their elongated figures have a stillness and elegance that invites the visitor to leave the material world behind as they enter the divine space of the cathedral.

The 13th-century North and South Porch, representing the life of Mary and Christ triumphant, are highly expressive examples of Gothic sculpture. That of John the Baptist on the North Porch sadly examines the disc he holds; decorated with a lamb and cross, it symbolically foretells of the coming of Christ and the imminence of his own death. In the left bay, the figures of Mary and Elizabeth turn to greet each other, telling the story of the Visitation. They resemble two nuns, chatting privately during mass. Inside, the life of Mary is further elaborated in the beautiful Renaissance choir screen, begun by Jehan de Beauce in 1514 and finished in the 18th century, which tells Mary's story from birth, through the life of Christ, to death and ascension.

Most of the glass dates from the 13th century and was preserved through both World Wars by town authorities, who dismantled over 3000 square meters and stored then piece by piece until the end of hostilities. The merchant sponsors of each window are shown in the lower panels, providing a valuable record of daily life during the 13th century. The famous "Blue Virgin" window, an object of pilgrimage and one of the few pieces of 12th-century glass to survive the fire, is visible at the first window of the choir, on the right. The window has four panels with a large picture of the virgin mary dressed in blue (hence its name), holding Christ on her lap; the other panes of glass were 13th-century additions. The façade holds the rest of the 12th century glass: on the right is the tree of Jesse and on the left is the passion and reincarnation of Christ. The center window is the incarnation, which shows the life of Christ from the annunciation to the ride into Jerusalem. Mary is given the place of honor at the top of the window, flanked by kneeling angels. Bring binoculars if you can; many of the stories told by the stained glass are barely visible with the naked eye.

World-renowned tour guide Malcolm Miller, an authority on Gothic architecture, has brought the cathedral to life for English-speaking visitors for the past 35 years. Miller composes each tour individually to explain the cathedral's history and symbolism. Miller knows everything about the religion and daily routine that the windows depict. His presentation is intelligent, witty, and enjoyable for all ages—the only complaint is that he tells too much to remember, and often talks quickly. Consider taking notes to help you when you're on your own in the cathedral. He provides countless details about the church: on any given day, he might discuss the labyrinth on the floor, which provided a path for the penitent pilgrim to follow on hands and knees, or the slope of the floor, which permitted the cathedral to be washed—particularly necessary because of pilgrims billetted on its floor every night. If you can, take both of his tours. They are worth it, and Miller is careful to discuss different aspects of the cathedral depending on how many repeat visitors he has and what days (or years) they took his tours. Indeed, no two of his visits are alike and all are fascinating fun. You may want to invest in a 29-35F guide as well. (1¼ hr. tours April-Jan. Mon.-Sat. noon and 2:45pm. Admission 30F, students 20F. Avoid Sat. and Tues.—busy days in the high season. Private tours available on request: tel. 37 28 15 58; fax 37 28 33 03.)

The sacred relic is now on display in the cathedral's **treasury,** at the east end, along with other significant garments and objects from the building's history. (Open Mon.-Sat. 10am-noon and 2-6pm, Sun. and holidays 2-6pm; Oct. 16-March 15 Mon.-Sat. 10am-noon and 2:30-4:30pm, Sun. and holidays 2-5pm. Free.) Climb the north tower, **Tour Jehan-de-Beauce,** named after its architect and completed in 1513, for a magnificent view of the cathedral roof, the flying buttresses, and the city below. The tower itself is a wonderful example of flamboyant Gothic, a late medieval style named after the flame-like nature of its decoration. Built to replace a wooden steeple which continuously burned down, it provides a fascinating counterpart to its more sedate neighbor (and predecessor by three centuries), the octagonal steeple built just before the 1194 fire. (Open April-Sept. Mon.-Fri. 9:30-11:30am and 2-5:30pm, Sat. 9:30-11:30am and 2-4:30pm, Sun. 2-4:30pm; Nov.-Feb. Mon.-Sat. 10-11:30am and 2-4pm, Sun. 2-4pm. Admission 20F; students, big families, and seniors 13F; under 6 free.)

Parts of Chartres' **crypt,** one of the largest in Western Christendom, date back to the 9th century. You can only enter the subterranean crypt as part of a tour that leaves from *La Crypte,* the store opposite the cathedral's south ____

____ 37 21 56 33 for info) is in French ____

____ of the 16th-century ____ ront of the cathedral (while they hid the relic). ____ the ethereal forms of statues from the Royal Portal, copied and transferred to the crypt after severe weathering had almost erased their features. (30 min. tours daily at 11am (except Wed.), 2:15pm, 3:30pm, 4:30pm, and in summer 5:15pm. Admission 10F.)

The cathedral is open daily in summer from 7:30am to 7:30pm and in winter from 7:30am to 7pm. No casual visits are allowed Saturdays from 5:45pm to 7pm or Sundays from 9:15am to 11am because of religious services. If you want the true Chartres experience, however, try attending one of these services. Call the tourist office (see below) for information on concerts in the cathedral, as well as the annual student pilgrimage in late May and other festivals throughout the year.

THE TOWN

Rightly called a *ville d'art* (artistic city), Chartres celebrates the medieval crafts showcased in its cathedral. In addition to the workshops and galleries, the downtown area is itself a vision to behold. The charming *vieille ville* (old town) has the cobblestone staircases, gabled roofs, half-timbered houses, and iron lamps of a village with quite a lot of history. Old streets are named for the trades once practiced there; rue de la Poissonerie, for example, was home to the fishmonger. Charming stone bridges cross the Eure River. Although the town is surrounded by flat wheat fields, Chartres is built on a hill, and some of the best views of the cathedral are found by walking down the well-marked tourist circuit. Maps are available from the tourist office (see below).

Le Musée des Beaux-Arts (Museum of Fine Arts), 29, cloître Notre-Dame (tel. 37 36 41 39), next door to the cathedral, resides in the former Episcopal Palace. Built mainly in the 17th and 18th centuries on the site occupied by bishops since the 11th century, the palace houses a rich collection of painting, sculpture, and furniture. Zurbaran, Holbein, and Vlaminck all figure prominently, as do local scenes and medieval wood polychrome statues from the 13th century on. (Open Wed.-Mon. 10am-6pm; Nov.-March 10am-noon and 2-6pm. Admission 10F, students and seniors 5F. For temporary exhibits 20F, students and seniors 10F.)

La Galerie du Vitrail (Gallery of Stained Glass), 17, rue du Cloître Notre-Dame (tel. 37 36 10 03), provides information on the cathedral's stained glass and showcases and sells contemporary pieces. Films (8-25 min.) on the history and production of stained glass and on Chartres in the Middle Ages are shown free upon request in English, French, or German (open Tues.-Sun. 9:45am-7pm; Nov.-March Tues.-Sat. 9:45am-1pm and 2-6:30pm). The **Centre International du Vitrail,** 5, rue du Cardinal Pie (tel. 37 21 65 72), hosts temporary exhibitions on stained glass, both historical and contemporary. The 12th-century barn in which it is housed was once used to store wine and grains received by the clergy from surrounding farmers. Note the 14th-century wood rafters and the 12th-century vaulting downstairs (open 9:30am-6:30pm; Nov.-March 9:30am-12:30pm and 1:30-6pm). Anticipate a stylistic, topical range from 16th-century flat-faced supplicants to late 20th-century machine dreams, with an emphasis on Art Nouveau and Art Deco. The **Maison de l'Archéologie,** 16, rue Saint-Pierre (tel. 37 30 99 38), is a tiny museum with temporary displays of the resident archaelogists' research in and around Chartes (open daily 2-6pm; Oct. May Wed. and Sun. 2-6pm; admission 5F, students and seniors free). **Eglise St-Aignan,** on rue des Greniers, was rebuilt in the 16th century, but boasts feudal origins. The Romanesque **Eglise St-André** sits on a street by the same name overlooking the banks of the Eure River. Fires have ravaged it, but the church has been a part of Chartres since the 12th century. During the 16th and 17th centuries, its gallery was extended to cross the river; one of the arches on which it was supported is still visible. **Eglise St-Pierre** on the place St-Pierre is a delicate Gothic, 13th-century masterpiece. Once the church of the Benedictine monastery of St-Père-en-Vallée, St-Pierre was renamed during the French Revolution when the monastery was disestablished. (All churches open in season daily 9am-7pm; Oct.-June 10am-5pm.)

Well worth the 20-min. walk across the river (which offers the best view of the cathedral), up rue St-Barthelémy and down rue du Repos past the cemetery is the **Maison Picassiette,** 22, rue du Repos (tel. 37 34 10 78). From 1928 until his death in 1964, Raymond Isidore decorated his house and garden with mosaics made from broken china and colored glass. Beginning with the kitchen, the former graveyard groundskeeper worked with abandon and no preconceived plan, filling courtyards and building shrines, reconstituting Paris and Chartres on wall, planter, and rooftop. Stroll around and enjoy the mosaics of plants, animals, people, cathedrals and panoramas decorating every stationary object on the grounds. Don't miss the Eiffel tower plant holder in the garden; another room has France's most famous churches on its walls. Mosaic flowers on the walls and near the ceilings are juxtaposed with real flowers, blooming in the garden and the planters so that Isadore's wish could be fulfilled. "I hope that peple will leaves here also wanting to live among flowers and within beauty. I'm trying to find a way for men to escape their misery," he said in a 1962 interview. The visit isn't long, but it is magical. (Open April-Oct. Wed.-Mon. 10am-noon and 2-6pm. Call during off-season to arrange a visit; admission 10F, students 5F.)

Recent history also looms large in Chartres; filled with streets with names like bd. de la Résistance, the town harbors a monument to **Jean Moulin,** the famous resistance hero who worked closely with de Gaulle. *Préfet* of Chartres before World War II, Moulin attempted suicide rather than be forced by the Nazis to sign a document maintaining that French troops had commited atrocities. Tortured and then killed by the Gestapo in 1943, he was eventually buried in the Panthéon. To get to the monument, walk from the Cathédrale down rue Cheval Blanc until it turns into rue Jean Moulin; the monument will be on your right.

PRACTICAL INFORMATION

The **tourist office** (tel. 37 21 50 00), opposite the cathedral's main entrance, helps find accommodations in and near Chartres (10F fee). They also have a list of restaurants, brochures, and an excellent map with a walking tour marked. For 35F, one or two people can use a headphone guide (in English, French, or German) to see the old city. (Tour lasts 1½-2 hr. and is worth it. Available daily, but must be returned while the office is open.) The tourist office staff speaks excellent English, as well as other languages. (Open Mon.-Fri. 9:30am-6:45pm, Sat. 9:30am-6pm, Sun. 9:30am-12:30pm and 2:30-5:30pm; March-May and Oct. Mon-Fri. 9:30am-6pm, Sat. 9:30am-5pm, Sun. 10:30am-1pm; Nov.-Feb. Mon-Fri. 9:30am-6pm.)

For **food,** try sandwich or *brasserie* fare in rue de Cygne or place Marceau, open-air pedestrian areas with musicians and great atmosphere. **La Passacaille**, 30, rue Ste-Même (tel. 37 21 52 10), offers salads (20-40F) and filling pizza (28-53F) in tasteful surroundings; 63F and 78F *menus* (open June-Aug. daily 11:30am-10:30pm; around mealtimes rest of the year). **Le Pélage,** place Châtelet (tel. 37 36 07 49), serves ample portions of standard meat and potatoes fare. *Menus* from 59F (open Mon.-Sat. noon-2pm and 7-11:30pm).

Chartres is accessible by frequent **trains** from Gare Montparnasse (1hr., round-trip 132F. In Paris call 45 82 50 50 for info; in Chartres call 37 28 50 50). Roughly one train per hour during the summer, but many trains run only on certain days occasions—call ahead.

...ray, its literary ...m the train station down rue de Chartres. ...ap is a pilgrim's necessity, with Swann's way, the Guermante's way, and other fondly remembered promenades clearly marked. Visit **Maison de Tante Léonie,** 4, rue Docteur Léonie (tel. 37 24 30 97), the home of Proust's invalid aunt who "had gradually declined to leave, first Combray, then her bedroom, and finally her bed." Proust mementos displayed here may be only seen by guided tour (Tues.-Sun. at 2:30, 3:30, and 5:30pm—times subject to change; call ahead to verify and to ferret out foreign-language tours on weekday mornings; admission 25F). **Trains** to Illiers leave from Chartres irregularly, around midday and early evening. Pick up a schedule before you begin your trip; trains vary with the days of the week and with holidays. The ride costs 50F round-trip.

■BEAUVAIS

Originally known as Caesaromagus—Caesar's market—Beauvais was an important Gallo-Roman settlement until Germanic invasions destroyed it in the 3rd century AD. Heavy bombing during World War II destroyed many of the town's medieval buildings. Among the few still in evidence is the Gothic Cathédrale St-Pierre, whose structural flaws have caused its various parts to self-destruct. In the oldest extant portion of Beauvais, located north of the cathedral's ambulatory, fragments of the old Roman wall still stand.

During its boom in the 12th century, the town rebuilt its cathedral in the trendy Gothic style. The mammoth **Cathédrale Saint-Pierre** on rue St-Pierre looks just as it did several centuries ago—huge and incomplete. Its Gothic chancel, the tallest in the world, is the product of architectural ambition pushed beyond reason and engineering principle. Built between 1225 and 1275, it collapsed dramatically in 1284. After every effort to restore it, most notably in the 16th century, the spire disobligingly toppled. Construction of the nave never began; the slate-covered wooden panel that blocks the opening from the transept has been "temporarily" in place for 400 years. Because of the building's enormous size, however, the casual visitor might not notice its state of incompleteness; for a better look, examine one of the aerial-view postcards for sale inside the cathedral. Consider buying the pricey but excellent 35F guide, available in English.

Bordering the cathedral's grassy cloister is the **Basse-Oeuvre,** the ruins of a 10th-century Carolingian church that once stood here. The cathedral also vaunts a one-of-a-kind, 90,000-piece **astronomical clock,** crafted in 1865-1868 by Louis-Auguste Vérité. For details on its construction and operation, attend the 25-min. *son et lumière* (sound and light show). Renovations currently under way, to continue for another 5-7 years, will attempt to prop up what is left of the cathedral; parts may be closed to visitors. (*Son et lumière* about the clock daily at 11:40am, 3:40pm, 4:40pm and 5:40pm, except when masses are held. Admission 15F, children 5F. Cathedral open daily 9am-12:15pm and 2-6:15pm; in winter 9am-12:15pm and 2-5:15pm. Call Association "Espaces" at (16) 44 48 11 60 for further info about the church or the clock.)

Beauvais' three museums display medieval paintings, sculptures, ceramics, and tapestries. The **Musée Departemental de l'Oise,** 1, rue du Musée (tel. (16) 44 06 37 37) is located in the former palace of the Bishop de Nesle. The building dates from the 12th, 14th, and 16th centuries. The bishop commissioned the twin **Tours de Nesle,** to either side of the main entrance, after a local peasant uprising; the new fortifications were intended to keep out the commoners. The museum assembles local painting, furniture, and sculpture dating from the 16th century onward, plus a few fossils. The presidence it gives to regional artists is not always deserved. Nonetheless, occasional gems do surface, like Nabi painter Maurice Denis' seven canvas *l'Age d'Or* series (1912). Descend to the museum's basement for a look at Greco-Roman tombs and coins unearthed in nearby excavations. A wan and tragic "Head of Christ," from the old Eglise St-Sauveur, is exhibited on the first floor. Renovations currently underway will continue through the summer of 1995; while the museum will remain open, some display rooms will be closed. Call before visiting. (Open Wed.-Mon. 10am-noon and 2-6pm. Admission 16F; students, ages 18-25, and over 65 8F; under 18, free; Wed. free.)

On the other side of the cathedral, across from the ruins, the **Galerie Nationale de la Tapisserie** (tel. (16) 44 05 14 28), rue St-Pierre, pays homage to the Gobelins tapestry factory built here in 1664. Exhibits change frequently and may feature medieval or modern-day designs. The Gobelins factory itself is depicted in the *"King Visiting the Gobelins Factory"* tapestry (1673-1680), which features the Sun King, Colbert, Charles Le Brun—both the designer of the work and the first director of the factory—and countless weavers scrambling to look occupied. Gallo-Roman ramparts and a tower dating from the late 3rd and early 4th centuries jut into the gallery's basement. (Open Tues.-Sun. 9:30-11:30am and 2-6pm; Oct.-March Tues.-Sun. 10-11:30am and 2:30-4:30pm. Last entry 1 hr. before closing. Admission 21F; students, seniors, and under 18 13F.)

The **Manufacture Nationale de la Tapisserie,** 24, rue Henri Brispot (tel. (16) 44 05 14 28), spent 49 years in exile from Beauvais during and following World War II. Visitors may tour the tapestry workshop and watch its staff of weavers in action. Craftsmen here follow centuries-old techniques. (Open Tues.-Thurs. 2-4pm. Admission 19F; students, seniors, and under 18 10F. You must pay separately for the *manufacture* and the *galerie*.)

The **tourist office,** 1, rue Beauregard (tel. (16) 44 45 08 18), near the cathedral, offers countless brochures on the surrounding area, a list of hotels and restaurants, and an invaluable map of the town. (Open Tues.-Sat. 9:30am-7pm, Sun.-Mon. and holidays 10am-1pm and 2-6pm; in winter closed Sun.) On the last weekend in June (June 24-25 in 1995), the **Fête de Jeanne Hachette** celebrates the bravery of Jeanne Hachette, who led residents of Beauvais to fight the onslaught of Charles the Bold's Burgundian army in 1672. The *fête* is a mock-medieval event, with a medieval crafts market in the central square. Nearly all participants, including vendors, appear in tunics and gowns. Beauvais residents act as wandering troubadors, giving impromptu concerts of medieval tunes. The festival features numerous parades all weekend, most notably Sat. at 8pm and Sun. at 3pm. Locals reenact Jeanne Hachette's battle with the Burgundians on pl. Jeanne Hachette; ask for details at the tourist office.

Year-round, the **place Jeanne Hachette** brims with cafés, *brasseries,* restaurants, and bakeries. The nearby **place des Halles** hosts an all-day market Wed. and Sat. Roughly 12 trains leave daily for Beauvais from Paris' Gare du Nord, *grandes lignes* platform (75-90 min., express, Paris-Beauvais, 120F round-trip). For more info, call the Beauvais train station (tel. (16) 44 21 50 50). To reach the cathedral, follow bd. du Général de Gaulle straight out of the train station, pass the garden, and take your second left onto rue des Jacobins.

hosts seminars and conferences for scholars on topics from Gregorian Chant to monastic writings.

Founded by St-Louis (King Louis IX of France) in 1228 and completed in 1235, the *abbaye* was devoted to the order of Cîteaux (Cisterian Order). The king provided the plentiful funds necessary to establish the monastery, and brought learned and devoted men to dedicate their lives to prayer and scholarship within the *abbaye's* walls; the king's brother, three of his sons, and two of his grandsons studied here.

The monks of the Abbaye de Royaumont were divided into two vocations: those who dedicated their lives to a mere 10 hours of daily prayer, called *Réligieux de Coeur*, and those who dedicated their time and energy to scholarship and script-copying. St-Louis invited one of the most celebrated medieval monk-scholars in Europe, Vincent de Beauvais, to lecture on his work, the *Speculum Majus*, an encyclopedia of world leaders, historical figures, and scholars. It was the very first *Who's Who* and, at several thousand pages, was one of the most comprehensive—a prime example of the high quality of European medieval monastic scholarship. Since the *abbaye's* church was demolished by revolutionaries in 1791, the monastery has been used alternately as a prison, hospital, and a seat of local government.

Inside the *abbaye* you can tour the refectory, where the monks ate in silence while a designated reader recited scripture. In the *anciennes cuisines* (old kitchens), the beautiful 14th-century statue of the Vierge de Royaumont stood (and still stands), watching over the monks who prepared the meals. Visitors can also see the *palais abbatial*, the abbot's formal residence, designed by Louis Le Masson. (Abbaye open daily 10am-12:45pm and 2-6pm, all day Sun.; in winter daily 10am-12:45pm and 2pm-sundown. Admission 20F; students, scholars, and over 60 14F. Free tours on weekends only.) For more information or a schedule of concerts (held weekends June-Sept.), seminars, or conferences, call 30 35 88 90 or write to the Fondation Royaumont. Come for a weekend of rest in the abbey's rooms, where you can sleep in considerably more comfort than the monks who once occupied the same spartan cells.

To get to the Abbaye de Royaumont from Paris, take the Paris-Nord-Luzarches line from the Gare du Nord line and get off at the Gare de Viarmes (several trains daily, 40min., 46F; call 30 35 30 16 for train schedules). Once you get to Viarmes, avoid the temptation to take a taxi, each way will cost you 65F. Instead, enjoy an invigorating 3km hike down D909, following signs to the abbey. The abbey provides transportation to and from concerts for a reasonable fee if you can't bear the walk.

■ ■ ■ EURO DISNEY® RESORT

It's a small, small world and Disney® seems hell-bent on making it even smaller. When Euro Disneyland® opened on April 12, 1992, Peter Pan, Mickey Mouse, Cinderella, and Snow White were met with the jeers of French intellectuals and the popular press. Regardless, the park is an an exciting place to spend a day, even for the budget traveler; every show, attraction, and ride is included in the admission price, as is the chance to see Europeans get off their high horses and sway to Michael Jackson's "Captain Eo." Cash-strapped tourists should consider visiting the park at night; Euro Disney® Resort has started offering a discounted admission after 5pm (150F).

The Euro Disney® Resort's designers (called "Imagineers") and staff (called "Cast Members") have created a resort which celebrates imagination, childhood, fantasy, creativity, technology, and fun. The fanfare of publicists tout Euro Disney® Resort as a vast entertainment and resort center, the largest on the continent, covering an area one-fifth the size of Paris. But though Disney may eventually develop its 600 hectares, the current theme park doesn't even rank the size of an *arrondissement*. From the gate it takes only ten minutes to walk to the farthest point inside the park, nothing like the vast reaches of Florida's Disneyworld—a fact which Imagineers have attempted to disguise by designing the park as a veritable maze. On the other hand, this Disney park is the most technologically advanced yet, and the special effects on some rides are enough to knock your Reeboks off.

Despite the whines of Euro Disney® Resort's early critics , the park has been a hit, and Disney has had to close the ticket windows repeatedly for hours at a time to keep lines down during the summer. Try to get there on a weekday—Tuesdays and Thursdays are the least crowded. Otherwise, expect to spend most of your time fighting to keep your place in line, rather than having fun. Masses of people practice the French national custom of line-cutting, as whole families duck under barriers and worm their way up front. To make things worse, devious architecture hides the true length of the lines. A line just emerging from a building may be just the tail end of a 90-minute wait inside. The crowds thin out toward 5pm, when parents start crying to go home, reducing the wait in line to as little as 15 minutes. Saving the bigger rides for the evening is probably the best way to go, and considering that the park closes at midnight during the summer, you'll still have plenty of time to do all your favorite rides several times over.

ORIENTATION AND PRACTICAL INFORMATION

Everything in the Euro Disney® Resort is in English and French. The staff is extremely helpful, and the detailed guide called the *Euro Disneyland® Guest Guidebook,* which you'll receive when you enter the park, has information on everything from restaurants, to attractions, to bathrooms, to first aid.

Tickets: Instead of selling tickets, Euro Disneyland® Park issues *Passeports,* available at the 50 windows located on the ground floor of the Disneyland Hotel. You can also buy *Passeports* at the Paris tourist office on the Champs-Elysées (see Paris—Once There). Pursue this option if you plan on coming out on a weekend day, so you won't risk wasting a couple of hours while the windows remain closed due to the crowds. Admission 250F, under 12 175F. Open daily 9am-11pm. Hours subject to change during the winter when snow and sleet can make your experience less than satisfactory. Discount ticket for 150F if you arrive after 5pm.

Restaurants: Pick up a restaurant guide at City Hall or consult your *Euro Disneyland® Guest Guidebook*. Restaurants are classified by the type of service: sit-down, cafeteria or snack bars. For a sit-down, 3-course *menu,* expect to pay 80-150F, on average. Cafeteria meals run 40-50F for simpler *menus* (i.e. hamburger, french fries and a soft drink). Snacks from stands located all over the park cost 15-22F. The elegant but pricey **Auberge de Cendrillon** (Cinderella's cottage) in Fantasyland features mouth-watering salmon, tender veal, and chocolate *gâteaux à la sauce anglaise*. For less expensive fare head for the very British fish and chips at **Toad Hall Restaurant**, the frontier grub and saloon show at **Lucky Nugget Saloon**, or the burgers at Discoveryland's **Café Hyperion**. The **Lucky Nugget Saloon** offers what is perhaps the best value in the whole park. 80F buys a 4-course meal with buffalo wings, a bowl of chili, a hot beef sandwich and a brownie. Most restaurants also offer special *menus* for children at reduced prices.

Hotels: The resort has six hotels, each designed on a particular theme celebrating a region of the United States. The **Sequoia Lodge** is surrounded by sequoia trees imported from California, the **Hotel Santa Fe** is modelled on the adobes of New Mexico, and the **Hotel Cheyenne** is built to look like a frontier town. A group of

house
center of the park
ways of getting there. For more
U.K. tel. (071) 753 29 00, or in the U.S. tel. (407) W-DISNEY (934-7639). If you
can't find room at the Disney hotels of feel like staying away from the bustle of
rides and roaming street-performers, a good alternative is the bed and breakfast
Bellevue (tel. 64 07 11 05; fax 64 07 19 27), located in Neufmoutiers-en-Brie. The
B&B is located in the restored wing of an ancient farmhouse. There are five 2-
story rooms, all with the capacity to lodge up to 4 people. All rooms have private
bathrooms and color TV. One-person 200F, two 230F, three 310F or four people
400F. While the B&B is 15km from Euro Disney®, the proprietor will drive people
to and from the closest RER station if necessary. He also provides maps of the
area, which describe hikes through the adjacent forest. Cash only, try to reserve a
few weeks in advance.

NIGHTLIFE

Separate from Euro Disney® and free to enter is **Festival Disney,** a street filled with
bars and game rooms where people roam about wearing cowboy hats and clutching
beers (average prices 20-35F per bottle or glass). Festival Disney also contains a
number of restaurants with more sophisticated fare and post-modern architecture.
Behind the raucous fun of Festival Disney lies Lake Disney, surrounded by the hotels
of the resort. If you're planning on staying late be sure to check out the **Manhattan
Jazz Club** at the Hotel New York, a fascimile of a New York jazz club that has been
getting serious attention for bringing some of the best young jazz acts to Euro Dis-
ney® (nightly 9pm-midnight).

SIGHTS AND ACTIVITIES

For the wildest rides, look for those accorded the greatest warnings. While "may
frighten certain young children" might sound promising, it only means that the ride
is dark and things pop out at you. Warnings directed at pregnant women and people
with chronic heart problems are the hallmarks of the more exciting rides. The park
can be divided into five areas. **Main Street,** the first area you'll pass through after
the gate, is home to City Hall and the highest concentration of stores. The **Château
de la Belle au Bois Dormant (Sleeping Beauty's Castle)** contains one stupen-
dous high-tech smoke-breathing dragon in the dungeon, and a shop where you can
buy the crown jewels for a paltry 3200F. It makes one heck of a landmark. Exiting
out the back of the château, you fall into **Fantasyland.** Although the rides are tame,
Peter Pan's Flight, and **It's a Small World** merit a spin; **Alice's Curious Labyrinth** is a hedge maze, replete with squirting fountains and a bong-smoking
caterpillar.

Off to the left, **Adventureland** awaits both the intrepid explorer and the weary
parent with a mix of themes from so-called adventurous regions: the Middle East,
West Africa, and the Caribbean. **Pirates of the Cambeau** presents 15 minutes of
frighteningly life-like corsairs and a fantastic water-dungeon set. Be warned: the line
outside is only a fraction of the total wait. The brand-new ride, **Indiana Jones and
the Temple of Doom,** features the first 360° loop on a Disney ride. Unfortunately,
the ride last only three minutes and the loop is miniscule. Instead mosey over to
rough and ready **Frontierland** where **Thunder Mesa,** a towering sunset-colored
reproduction of a New Mexican desert mesa, hosts the park's most breathtaking
ride, **Big Thunder Mountain.** At high noon, the line is almost as deadly as the ride,
but the marvelous robot llamas and donkeys that border the track, and the bumpy
trip itself, are superb. Set apart on a scraggly hill, the creaky **Phantom Manor** is the
park's classic haunted house. While the Haunted Mansion at Disneyland in Florida is

a huge scary fortress, the architecture had to be changed in Europe, where fortresses and châteaux are common; this haunted Manor is based instead on the Victorian mansion in the film *Psycho.*

In addition to the rides, Disney also puts on three daily special events: a **Disney Character Parade** with myriad elaborate floats; the **Main Street Electrical parade** (for the best view of the parades stand to the left at the top of Main Street near the pseudo-rotary—that's where the special effects on the floats are timed to go off); and a fantastic **fireworks** show, set against the background of the château.

GETTING THERE

The easiest way to get to the Euro Disney® Resort is by taking the **RER** A4 from Paris. Get on at either M. Gare de Lyon or Châtelet-Les Halles and take the train (direction: "Marne-la-Vallée") to the last stop, "Marne-la-Vallée/Chessy." Before boarding the train, check the illuminated electric boards hanging above the platform to make sure there's a light next to the Marne-la-Vallée stop; otherwise the train won't end up there (every 30min., 50min., 70F round-trip). The last train to Paris leaves Disney at 12:22am, but you may have trouble getting the metro at the other end. By **car,** take the A4 highway from Paris and get off at exit 14, marked "Parc Euro Disneyland," about a 30-minute drive from the city. You can park for 40F in any one of the 11,000 spaces in the parking lot. **Euro Disney® Buses** make the rounds between the terminals of both Orly and Roissy/Charles de Gaulle airports and the bus station near the Marne-la-Vallée RER (every 45-60 min., 40min., 75F, 6:45am-10pm).

■■■ GARDENS

■ GIVERNY

Halfway between Rouen and Paris, Giverny is certainly charming; otherwise, arch-Impressionist Claude Monet wouldn't have settled here in 1883. Nor would he have painted, almost obsessively, the grounds, views, and famous water lilies; nor would his painterly friends have come here to set up their easels beside his. As Monet's fortune increased, so did his house and garden: Monet himself created them with enormous horticultural energy and skill.

Now his house is the **Musée Claude Monet** (tel. 32 51 28 21). The gardens were reconstructed from eyewitness reports and historical documents, now looking (as far as scholars know) as they did to the painter himself. The waterlilies float serenely on the pond; the Japanese bridge and the trailing weeping willows look like—well, like Monets; the turkeys' coloring harmonizes (however gawkily) with the pink, crushed-brick façade of the house; and it takes scores of contemporary gardeners to give the grounds' floral palette the color and variety of their master's brushstrokes. Less various—but, sadly, just as numerous—are the tourists. Though the seven-year-old soccer players and very tall amateur postcard-photographers can't rob Giverny of beauty, but they can steals its romance and tranquility. Nonetheless, the house is lovely; displayed within are many of Monet's personal belongings, including his impressive collection of 18th- and 19th-century Japanese prints and his deathbed. View the garden from the second floor. (House and garden open April-Oct. Tues.-Sun. 10am-6pm. 35F, students with cards 25F. Gardens only 25F. Arrive early; the line quickly becomes a 2-hr. wait.)

About 100m down rue Claude Monet is the **Musée Américan Giverny** (tel. 32 51 94 65), a recent addition to impressionist Giverny which purports to show American art in comparision and in contrast to the European stuff. Though mostly a collection of paintings by little-known, second-rate Monet hangers-on, it has a small room of Whistlers, a few Singer-Sargent sketches, and some touching Mary Cassatts. Inanely high entrance fees should keep all but the most devoted out. (Open April-Oct. Tues.-Sun. 10am-6pm; 30F, students 20F.)

Another 100m further is a truer treasure. The **Musée Baudy** (tel. 32 21 10 03), is in the old Hôtel Baudy, which lodged most of these Monet hangers-on at some point or other, as well as Monet himself (before he bought his house), and many of his close friends (Renoir, Pissarro, Clemenceau, and so on). Go with some time to spare. The gardens, while lacking the familiar vistas of Monet's own property, are serenely wonderful. Up a small hill, the tangled greenery and winding paths open to a small, shady fountain. A courtyard there offers a Breathtaking View of the Normandy Countryside. Mainly a rose garden, the grounds are best seen in June. The hotel itself houses a contemporary art gallery of works by local artists. (Museum open April-Oct. Tues.-Sun. 10am-6pm; 25F, students 15F.)

To eat in Giverny, click your heels three times and repeat "I want a budget restaurant." Mostly, restaurants are priced high for tourists. Most of the museum staff eats at **La Bonne Étable,** 9, rue de Falaise (tel. 32 51 66 32), rather than any of the closer restaurants. To get there, walk out the door from the museum, take a right, and walk down rue Claude Monet 300m until it intersects the larger road; there you should see signs to your left. Sandwiches cost 15-22F, salads 35-40F, desserts 12-22F, and 68F offers appetizer, main meal, and dessert. (Open Tues.-Fri. and Sun. noon-3:30pm, Sat. nonn-3:30pm and 7-10pm.) In Vernon itself are more options. At bright and floral **Pizza del Teatro**, 34, rue d'Albufers (tel. 32 21 35 49), appetizers are 36-46F and pizzas are 36-58F (open daily noon-3pm and 7-11pm).

400,000 tourists a year require Giverny and its lilies to be easily accessible by public transportation. **Trains** run from Paris to Vernon several times a day (every 2hr., 45min., from Gare St-Lazare, 62F each way). The train station of **Vernon** is across the river and a 6km hike from the museum. To get to Giverny, rent a bike from the station (55F per day, 1000F deposit), or take a bus from the front of the station (2-3 per day each way; 10min.; 10F, round-trip 16F). Taxis await outside the train station and cost about 60-65F in each direction ; if you can share a cab, or if you are with a party of four, the convenience of the ride might outweigh its slight increase in price. The hour-plus walk to or from Giverny is calming. Talk to the tourist office to find a map or walk back from Giverny to Vernon: the highway is unpleasant to follow, but the pedestrian path can be tricky to find. Consider a climb up the valley into the **Forêt de Vernon,** alongside Giverny, to see some of the beautiful poppy-covered countryside. The Vernon **tourist office,** 36, rue Carnot (tel. 32 51 39 60), distributes maps of hiking trails in the area (open Mon. 2:30-6:30pm, Tues.-Sat. 9:30am-nooon and 2:30-6:30pm). Frequent signs lead the way from the Vernon station to the tourist office and to Giverny. Finally, the **Musée de Vernon,** 12, rue du Pont (tel. 32 21 28 09), exhibits an eclectic but interesting collection. Besides the predictable local colorists (only one is a Monet), this museum displays archaeological relics found near Vernon. (Open Tues.-Sun. 2-6pm; 15F, students free.)

■ AUVERS-SUR-OISE

> *I am entirely absorbed by these plains of wheat on a vast expanse of hills like an ocean of tender yellow, pale green, and soft mauve, with a piece of worked (farmed) land dotted with clusters of potato vines in bloom, and all this under a blue sky tinted with shades of white, pink, and violet.*
> —Vincent Van Gogh, 1890

Auvers-sur-Oise, 30km north-west of Paris, is known as a birthplace of Impressionism; color-and-light enthusiasts dropped in to sample the sunlight and contours of thatched cottages and wheat fields (as in "Wheat Field with Crows"). Pre-Impressionist painter **Charles-François Daubigny** (1817-1878) fashioned a floating studio out of a boat so he could paint views from the middle of the river. He built a studio for himself here in 1864 and invited a number of famous painters to stay with hime, including Cézanne and Pissarro. His home, the **Atelier de Daubigny,** 61, rue Daubigny (tel. 34 48 03 03), is open to the public (Open April-Sept Tues-Sun. 10am-noon and 2-6pm. Museum open Fri.-Sun. 2-6pm, 20F, under 25 and over 50 15F.)

Docteur Gachet (1828-1909) was instrumental in placing Auvers on the artistic map; a doctor, painter, and patron, he supported painters like **Vincent Van Gogh** in Auvers. Gachet's own work is on display at the Musée d'Orsay. On May 20, 1890, Van Gogh accepted Gachet's invitation and moved to Auvers-sur-Oise, where he rented a room at the **Auberge Ravaux,** known today as the **Maison de Van Gogh** (at 52, av. du Général de Gaulle). The Maison was under renovation in summer 1993; the completion date is yet unknown. During his 70 days here, Van Gogh produced more than 60 sketches, *études*, and paintings, including the famous painting of *Auvers'Eglise de l'Assumption,* which now hangs in the Musée d'Orsay. On the night of July 29, 1890, the 37-year-old Van Gogh shot himself in the fields of Auvers; he died at the *auberge* two days later, attended by his close friend Dr. Gachet, and his much loved younger brother Théo, who died six months later. Both brothers are buried in the **Cimetière d'Auvers** on rue Daubigny. Vincent's grave lies next to his brother's grave against the far wall of the cemetery. From here, there's a lovely view of the church that Van Gogh immortalized.

The **Office de Tourisme d'Auvers-sur-Oise** (tel. 30 36 10 06), in the Manoir des Colombières, is in the parc Van Gogh, rue de la Sansonne (open Mon.-Fri. 9am-noon and 2-6pm, Sat.-Sun. 10am-noon and 2-6pm; 1½-hr. tours of Auvers on selected days at 3pm). Take the train from the Gare St-Lazare or the Gare du Nord to Pontoise, then switch to the Creil line to the Gare d'Auvers-sur-Oise (several trains/day, 1hr., 42F).

■ ST-CLOUD

The town of **St-Cloud**, 3km southwest of Paris, harbors a beautiful park, the former site of a château. Framed by orderly hedges and trimmed with rectangular beds of more than 30 varieties of flowers and 30 types of rosebushes, the multi-terraced park marches its way down the hillside, stretching almost all the way to the Seine below. By consulting horticultural guides of the 19th century, modern-day gardeners have painstakingly reconstructed the floral arrangements in the fashion of the court of Napoleon III during his stays at St-Cloud.

The **Château de St-Cloud** was the scene of the assassination of Henri III in 1589 and Napoleon's coup d'état in 1799, when troops loyal to the rising general invaded the chambers of the legislature in session there. In 1870 marauding Prussians burned the château; nothing remains but Le Nôtre's magnificent park. To orient yourself, consult the large marble slab in the center of the park. A map of the grounds in 1811, the slab shows clearly the parts of the original park that still remain, the parts that were destroyed, and the exact location of the château. To the left of the park gates, the **Musée Historique** offers drawings, paintings, and a short film tracing the history of the château. (Grounds open daily 7am-9pm. Museum open Wed. and Sat.-Sun. 2-5:30pm. Free. Maps of the park sold for 25F.)

To get to St-Cloud, take the *métro*, bus #72 from the Hôtel de Ville, or bus #52 from Madeleine to "Boulogne-Pt. de St-Cloud." There you can either take a local bus across the Pont de St-Cloud or walk (15min.) across. After you cross the river, the park is to your left, the town is straight ahead and up; look for the spire of Eglise St-Cloud. For someting on a more human scale, drop by the **Espace Departmental Albert Kahn,** 14, rue du Port (tel. 46 04 52 80), on the way from the metro station to the park. This museum consists of a beautiful 7-part garden showcase of planting styles from around the world. (Open Tues.-Sun. 11am-7pm, Oct.-April. Museum and gardens close one hour earlier. Entrance 20F, reduced 12F. No picnic, but a lovely tea salon serves up salads and other light meals for a reasonable prices.)

WEEKENDS AWAY FROM PARIS

> By all which it appears, quoth I, having read it over, a little too rapidly,
> that if a man sets out in post-chaise from Paris—he must go on travelling
> in one, all the days of his life—or pay for it.
> —Laurence Stern,Tristram Shandy

It's easy to forget that there's more to France than Paris and the Ile de France. The provinces, officially defined as the rest of the country, is where most of French history was played out, where most French landmarks are set, and— face it—where most of the French live. Foray into the Pays de la Loire (a mere 1 hour away) or into Normandy (2 hours away) for a glimpse at the France of châteaux, wars, and beaches.

■■■ PAYS DE LA LOIRE

The châteaux along the Loire, France's longest river, range from grim medieval fortresses to elegant Renaissance houses transfixed, like Narcissus, by pools that reflect their beauty. The surprisingly sordid history of many of these dignified mansions presents a mixed bag of mischief, genius, promiscuity, and profligacy. If the châteaux's true stories fail to mesmerize, their fairy-tale loveliness never fails to enchant.

Most of the châteaux were built in the 16th and 17th centuries, when French monarchs left Paris and ruled from the countryside around Tours so they could squeeze in hunting excursions between official state decrees. Some structures, however, remain from the days before the region belonged to the French crown. Henry II and Richard the Lionhearted, both English royalty, mobilized two of the oldest communities, Chinon and Beaugency, to defend the region from the Capetian monarchs of the 12th century. The English and the French played hot potato with the Loire until Joan of Arc helped win it for the French in the Hundred Years War (1337-1453). In the 15th century, under the Valois kings, the French monarchy acquired the region in a flux of martial and marital activity. The châteaux accumulated works of the finest Italian masters, fostering an opulence never before imagined.

GETTING AROUND

The excellent hostels in Blois, Chinon, Tours, and Angers are comfortable bases for châteaux exploration. The Paris-Austerlitz train station serves Blois, Tours, and Angers directly. Chinon and Chenonceaux can be reached by train from Tours and Chambord is accessible by bus (in summer) or bike from Blois. You may want to consider renting a car in Blois to visit Chambord, since a group of four can generally undercut tour bus prices by doing so. Bikes are for rent in almost every Loire town, often for under 50F per day. *Michelin's* road map of the region will steer you away from truck-laden highways and onto delightful country roads.

■ BLOIS

The small town of Blois maintains an air of quiet dignity. Its château (tel. 54 78 06 62) perches majestically on a hillside in the middle of town. Home to French monarchs Louis XII and François I in the late 15th and early 16th centuries, its power during the Renaissance was comparable to that of Versailles in subsequent ages.

The octagonal spiral staircase, built by François I's crew, juts out into the courtyard whose once-crumbling façades now glisten as the result of a massive restoration project. Stone salamanders wriggle on the staircase, symbols of the immortality of François I; legends held that the salamander is the only animal that fire cannot harm. Start with the Aile François I (François's wing), fronted by a grand, ornamental staircase connecting several fine Renaissance rooms. The basement of this wing houses the **Musée Archéologique's** piles of neolithic axe blades and other artifacts.

The Loire Valley and Poitou-Charentes

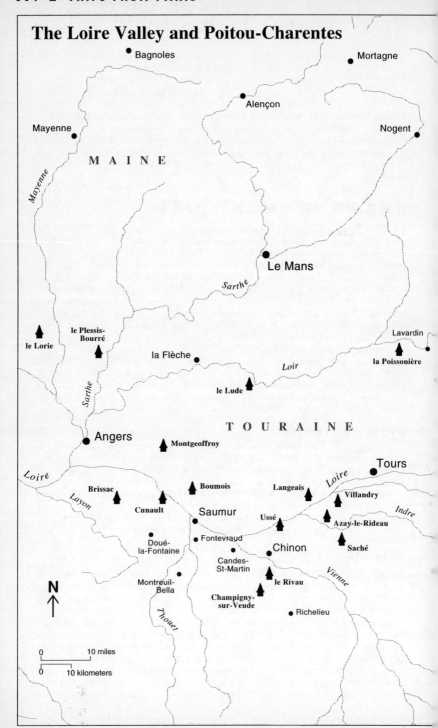

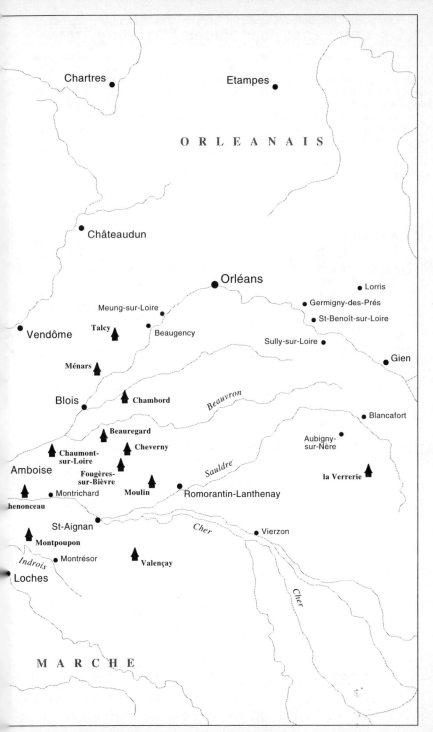

Continue into the **Salle des Etats,** the only part of the château surviving from the 13th century, and try to count the yellow *fleur-de-lis* which adorn the royal blue ceiling and walls of the room. (Open daily 9am-6pm; Nov.-March 9am-noon and 2-5pm. Admission 30F, students under 25 15F. Call ahead for tours in French or English.) The château also presents a *son et lumière* every evening June-Sept. at 10:30pm (in French). (Admission 60F; ages 5-15 and over 65 30F.)

Trains from Paris to Blois take 1 hr. (117F). From Blois, you can catch trains to Tours (1hr., 49F) and Angers (3hr., 108F). Contact the station (tel. 54 78 50 50) for schedules. **Banks** and **ATMs** are scattered everywhere in Blois' *centre ville,* especially near the Loire, along rue Denis Papin and around pl. de la Résistance. The **tourist office,** 3, av. Jean Laigret (tel. 54 74 06 49 or 54 78 23 21) supplies maps and info. You can stay overnight at the **hostel (HI),** 18, rue de l'Hôtel Pasquier (tel. 54 78 27 21), 7½km outside Blois in Les Grouets. From the tourist office, follow rue Porte Côte, bear right onto rue Denis Papin down to the river, and take bus #4 (direction: Les Grouets) to "Eglise des Grouets" (last bus at 7:30pm, 6F; buses do not run on Sun.). The hostel is about an hour's hike from town. (Members 40F, non-members 60F. Summer reservations highly recommended. Open March-Nov. 15.)

■ CHAMBORD

The largest and most extravagant of the Loire châteaux, Chambord overwhelms. Incredibly massive and unbelievably ornate, it was constructed as the royal hunting retreat of the immensely egotistical François I. The result is mind boggling: 440 rooms with 365 fireplaces (one for every day of the year), decorated with 700 of the trademark stone salamanders. The resulting hundreds of chimneys, along with decorative turrets and spires, create a stone forest on the rooftop terrace.

At the heart of the symmetrical château rises a spectacular double-helix staircase, perhaps designed by Leonardo da Vinci. The château was a favorite *auberge* of Louis XIV, who diverted the river Cosson and planted the magnificent kilometer-long, tree-lined avenue approaching the château. Today, the sprawling grounds cover over 5000 hectares—1200 of which are open to the public—forming a game preserve surrounded by a 2.5m high wall. (Open daily 9:30am-6:15pm; Sept.-June 9:30am-12:15pm and 2-5:15pm. Admission 33F, students 22F.)

To get to Chambord from Paris, take a **train** to Blois (1 hr.) then catch a **bus** at the *gare routière,* 2, route Victor Hugo (tel. 54 78 15 66). Buses run Mon.-Sat. from mid-June to mid-Sept. Take the **Transports Loir-et-Cher (TLC)** bus, circuit #1 (65F, students 50F.) Alternatively, you could **rent a bike** in Blois from **Cycles Le Blond,** 44, Levée des Tuileries (off rue Denis Papin) and 17, rue du Sanitas (tel. 54 74 30 13). Start the 15km trek by crossing the Loire in Blois and riding to the roundabout 1km down av. Wilson. The châteaux and towns are well-marked along the roads. Direct any additional questions to the Blois **tourist office** (info above) or the one in Chambord (tel. 54 20 34 86; open April to mid-Oct.), which **exchanges currency** (20F fee). You can stay overnight at Blois' **hostel** (info above). Campers can trek from the château to **Camping Huisseau-sur-Cosson,** 6, rue de Châtillon (tel. 54 20 35 26), about 5km southwest of Chambord on D33. (35F for two people, tent and showers included. Open April-Sept.)

■ CHENONCEAU

Sheltered by an ancient forest 35km east of Tours, the graceful **Chenonceau** (tel. 47 23 90 07) cultivates an intimacy with its natural surroundings that resists even the most ferocious of crowds. Originally commissioned by Thomas Bohier, tax collector under Charles VIII, Louis XII, and François I, Chenonceau was nevertheless largely designed by women: wives, mistresses, or queens. Today, Chenonceau, with its sublime symmetrical gardens, arched bridge, and two-story gallery spanning the Cher River, is well-preserved inside and out. Its unique charm will move even the most jaded castle-goer. (Open daily March 16-Sept. 15 9am-7pm; call for closing times during the off-season. 40F, students and children 25F.) From late-June-Sept., Chenonceau hosts a *son et lumière* at 10:15pm. (Show 40F, students 25F.)

The village of Chenonceaux is 214km from Paris (2 hrs.) and 34km from Tours (25 min.) by car on the A10. Take a **train** from Paris to Tours (2¼hr., 190F; TGV 1hr, 200F plus reservation); from the Tours station (tel. 47 20 50 50) catch a train to the village (3 per day, Sun. 1 per day, ¾hr., 32F). The station is 2km from the château. Follow the mob up the road from the station, left onto rue Bretonneau, and then left again onto rue du Château. **Les Rapides de Touraine** (tel. 47 46 06 60 in Tours) runs buses from Tours via Amboise (3 per day, ½hr., 24F) to Chenonceaux (1hr., 36F) and stops at the château gates.

For 62F, you can spend the night at the **HI hostel** in Tours, av. d'Arsonval, Parc de Grandmont (tel. 47 25 14 45), 4km from the station in a park by the freeway. From the station, take bus #1 (direction: Joue Blotterie, 6F) or bus #6 (direction: Chambray, 6F) from stop on right side of av. de Grammont, 30m down from pl. Jean Jaurès (last bus at 8:15pm). Or, you can **camp** a few blocks from the hostel (tel. 47 23 90 13; 15F per person, 10F per tent. Open April 15-Sept.).

For more information about Tours and Chenonceau, including guided château excursion lists, contact Tours' **tourist office,** rue Bernard Palissy (tel. 47 05 58 08). For **currency exchange,** go to **Crédit Agricole,** diagonally across (to the right) from the train station.

■ CHINON

Henry II Plantagenet, Richard the Lionhearted, Philippe Auguste, Saint Louis, Charles VII, Joan of Arc, the Templars, and Cesare Borgia, among many others, slept here: the château itself is in ruins, but this does not detract from its historical significance or its incredible panoramic view of the Vienne (a tributary of the Loire). One has only to take the excellent tour (offered in French, German and English) and explore the old walls and towers to imagine the past magnificence of the place. As ruins go, these are great ones. (Open Feb.-Nov. daily 9am-6pm. 25F, students 17F.)

Chinon, also known for its red wine, is home to the amusing **Musée Animé du Vin et de la Tonnellerie,** 12, rue Voltaire (tel. 47 93 25 63). The museum illustrates the wine-making process from grape-crushing to barrel-making. The 15- to 20-minute tour, which includes a glass of Chinon wine, ends with the doubtful exhortation "drink always and never die." (Open April-Sept. Fri.-Wed. 10am-12:30pm and 2-7pm. 20F, student 16F.)

From Paris, take a train to Tours (info under Chambord) and catch a connection to Chinon (1hr., 45F). The station is across the Vienne, near the youth hostel (20 min. from town). The **tourist office,** 12, rue Voltaire (tel. 47 93 17 85), off pl. Général de Gaulle, can change money when banks are closed. **Banks** with **ATMs** are scattered around pl. Général de Gaulle. The **HI hostel,** rue Descartes (tel. 47 93 10 48), is located along the quai Jeanne d'Arc. (Lockout 10am-6pm. 43F. Sheets 15F. Reserve in summer.)

■ ANGERS

From behind the massive, imposing walls of their château in Angers, the Dukes of Anjou ruled over the surrounding territory as well as a small island to the northwest of France. The château and its walls remain stunningly well-preserved. It may not be the prettiest château in the Loire Valley, but it is probably one of the quirkiest. Most of the buildings on the inside were constructed during the 15th-century reign of Anjou's last and greatest duke, René le Bon, who not only commanded an empire that included Sicily, Piedmont, and Lorraine, but also found the time to pen several novels and dozens of poems. The structure boasts 17 towers and a 900m long, 15m high wall surrounding the perimeter. Instead of a moat, visitors look down over the wall to see a colorful garden populated with deer. Take a deep breath and climb to the top of the northernmost tower for a spectacular view of the city.

Inside lies the 104m-long **Tapisserie de l'Apocalypse,** considered to be the largest woven masterpiece in the world. Testimony to the power of sibling rivalry, the tapestry was ordered by Louis I, Duke of Anjou, to show his brother, Charles V, that he was his equal. Its apocalyptic and prophetic scenes feature multi-headed lions and serpents and mysterious symbols. (Tours in French of the spartan royal lodgings leave from the château's chapel every ½hr. 10am-noon and 2-6pm. Château open 9am-7pm; Sept.-April 9:30am-12:30pm, and 2-6pm. Admission 32F, students 20F.)

Angers is connected to Paris by **train** (2¾hr., 192F). To reach the château, go straight out of the train station onto rue de la Gare. Turn right at the pl. de la Visitation onto rue Talot. A left onto bd. du Roi-René leads to the château's doorstep at pl. Kennedy. The **tourist office** will be directly on your right, facing the château (tel. 41 23 51 11). The enormous **HI hostel,** Foyer des Jeunes Travailleurs, is on rue Darwin (tel. 41 72 00 20). Take bus #8 (direction: Beaucouzé) to "CFA." If you miss the last bus at 7:20pm, you can take #1 to "Bull" until about 8pm; the tourist office can give you a bus map. (Hostel 48F per night, non-members 65F.) **Currency exchange** is available at the Angers post office, 1, rue Franklin Roosevelt, and at the tourist office (20F fee) when the banks are closed.

■■■ NORMANDY

Normandy, whose jagged coastline, gently sloping valleys, and elaborate cathedrals inspired the Impressionists, has had a tumultuous history. The territory was seized by Vikings in the 9th century, and in 911 the French king acknowledged the independence of the Norsemen (Normans). From the 10th to the 13th century, the Normans created a string of mammoth ornate cathedrals. Their most impressive achievement, however, was the conquest in 1066 of a certain small island to the northwest. William the Conqueror's defeat of England was celebrated by a magnificent tapestry that still hangs in the Norman town of Bayeux.

During the Hundred Years War, the English had their revenge; they invaded and overpowered fierce Norman resistance. English troops, led by the Duke of Bedford and aided by French traitors, succeeded in capturing Jeanne d'Arc after a great victory on September 8, 1430. Charged with heresy and sorcery, Jeanne was confined to Rouen's Tour Jeanne d'Arc (which still stands today) and condemned to be burned at the stake. Although the British were eventually overthrown, they left their mark on the customs, crafts, and cuisine of the area. The British did not attempt another invasion until D-Day, June 6, 1944, when they returned with American and Canadian allies to wrest Normandy from German occupation. The moving beaches near Bayeux, where the Allies landed, still bear scars from the attack.

GETTING AROUND

Rouen, Deauville, Trouville, and Bayeux are all accessible by train from Paris. A bus covers the last leg of the trip to Mont-St-Michel. Within Normandy, only major towns, such as Lille, Le Havre, and Caen, are connected by rail; buses fill in the gaps between smaller towns. Since many memorable spots lie off main roads, a bike or car helps for extended touring.

■ ROUEN

Best known as the city where Joan of Arc was burned and Emma Bovary was bored, Rouen (pop. 400,000) makes a great weekend trip from Paris. It had its two centuries of fame from the 10th to the 12th centuries, when it bloomed into a veritable flower garden of Gothic architecture, as befitted the capital of the Norman empire. Modern Rouen has been marred by war and pollution, yet amidst the destruction there is reconstruction. Through its excellent museums, beautiful churches, and splendid architecture, Rouen holds out the promise of its rebirth.

To get to the center of town from the station, take rue Jeanne d'Arc for several blocks. A left onto cobblestoned **rue du Gros Horloge** leads to pl. de la Cathédrale

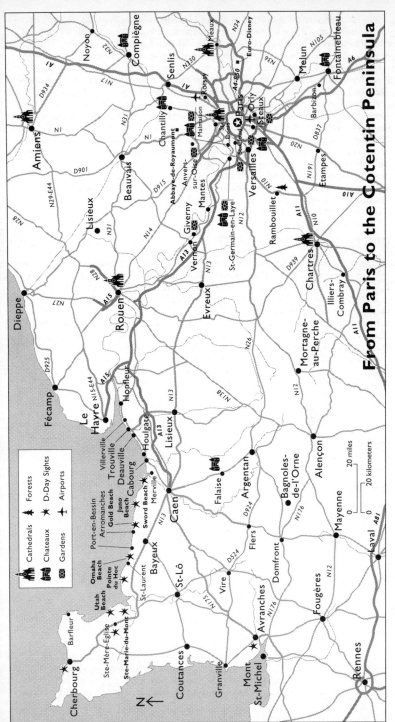

NORMANDY

From Paris to the Cotentin Peninsula

Cathedrals   Forests

Chateaux   D-Day Sights

Gardens   Airports

20 miles

0   20 kilometers

and the tourist office (the shopping district); a right leads to **pl. du Vieux Marché** (the food district). The **tourist office** is at 25, pl. de la Cathédrale (tel. 35 71 41 77). The **HI hostel,** 118, bd. de l'Europe (tel. 35 72 06 45), is across the river 5km from the station. (55F; Lockout 10am-5pm.) Call the **train station** (tel. 35 98 50 50) for info on trains to Paris (1¼hr., 97F).

A walking tour of Rouen easily covers the city's hotspots. The **Tour Jeanne d'Arc,** near the station on rue du Donjon, is the last remaining tower of the château which confined Joan of Arc (open Wed.-Mon. 10am-noon and 2-5:30pm; admission 6F, students free). A block up rue Jeanne d'Arc is the **Musée des Beaux-Arts,** sq. Verdrel (tel. 35 71 28 40). The excellent museum has works by Rouen's native artists as well as other European masters. (Open Thurs.-Mon. 10am-noon and 2-6pm, Wed. 2-6pm. Admission 20F, students free.) The impressive **Musée des Antiquités** is at 198, rue Beauvoisine (tel. 35 98 55 10). The **Cathédrale de Notre-Dame,** rue de la République, was built between the 12th and 16th centuries and incorporates nearly every intermediate style of Gothic architecture. Parts of the façade are disappointingly dingy, but renovations are in progress. (Open Mon. 9am-noon and 2-7pm, Tues.-Sat. 7:30am-noon and 2-7pm, Sun. 7:30am-6pm.) Other noteworthy churches are the **Eglise Jeanne d'Arc,** rue Jeanne d'Arc; the **Eglise St-Marcoul,** pl. Barthélémy; and the **Eglise St-Ouen,** pl. Général de Gaulle.

■ DEAUVILLE AND TROUVILLE

South of Honfleur, sophisticated Deauville and Trouville attract an international elite to their broad, gorgeous beaches, grand casinos, and famous racetracks. Exclusive shops are all the rage; Deauville's inhabitants are lucky enough to have a Hermès boutique less than 100m from the beach. In the ongoing rivalry between the twin cities, avant-garde Deauville lures with its world-famous annual yearling auctions whilst the more traditional Trouville entices with winding cobblestone streets and the genially-crafted altars and stained-glass windows of **Eglise Bon Secours**.

Ask one of the **tourist offices** for town maps and for info on races (July-Aug., race admission Mon.-Sat. 25F, Sun. 35F), polo games, and yearling auctions (throughout the year). **Deauville's** is at pl. de la Mairie (tel. 31 88 21 43). Cut diagonally left on rue Désire-Le-Hoc from the train station. To get to **Trouville's** tourist office, 22-36, bd. F. Moureaux (tel. 31 88 36 19), take a right over the pont de Belges from the train station and turn left onto bd. F. Moureaux. (Open Mon.-Sat. 9:30am-12:30pm and 2-7pm, Sun. 10am-4pm; Sept.-June Mon.-Sat. 9:30am-noon and 2-6pm, Sun. 10:30am-12:30pm.) **Trains** (tel. 31 88 28 80) run to and from Paris (2½hr., 138F).

Rooms here are expensive. Try **L'Orchidée,** 184, av. de la République (tel. 31 98 40 03), left of the station in Deauville. (Singles and doubles with shower 105-260F, off-season from 160F. Extra bed 85F. Breakfast 25F.) In Trouville, **La Petite Chaumière,** 23, rue Docteur Couturier (tel. 31 88 10 92) has a 165F demi-pension in old but adequate rooms. Turn right just before the end of bd. Fernand Maureaux onto rue Victor Hugo and left before the church. Those who plan ahead can reserve space at Trouville's **Camping Hamel,** 55, rue des Soeurs de l'Hôpital (tel. 31 88 15 56). Follow rue d'Agnesseau and rue d'Estimauville from the *place* at the foot of the bridge. (11F per person, 5F50 per tent or car. Open April-Sept.)

■ BAYEUX AND THE D-DAY BEACHES

Bayeux (pop. 17,000) is famous for its tapestry, an 11th-century linen embroidery nearly a soccer field long, depicting the Norman invasion of Britain in 1066. The beautifully preserved city basks in the prosperity of the rich surrounding farms and its burgeoning tourist trade. Bayeux is also a convenient base for exploring the landing beaches of the allied invasion of Normandy on D-Day, 1944.

Bayeux's **tourist office,** pont St-Jean (tel. 31 92 16 26), exchanges currency and is about ten minutes from the town center. Turn left onto the highway (bd. Sadi-Carnot) and then right, following the signs to the *centre ville.* Once there, continue up rue Larcher until it hits **rue St-Martin,** Bayeux's commercial avenue. On your right, at **rue St-Jean,** begins the pedestrian zone. **Trains** (tel. 31 83 50 50) run to and from Paris (2½hr., 161F). Bayeux's **HI hostel** is at 39, rue du Général de Dais (tel. 31 92 15 22); follow the signs for "Family Home" or "Auberge de Jeunesse" from the train station (85F, non-members 95F).

The celebrated **Tapisserie de Bayeux** is presented in the **Centre Guillaume le Conquérant,** a renovated seminary on rue de Nesmond (tel. 31 92 05 48; open daily 9am-7pm; Sept. 16-Oct. 15 and March 16-April 30 9am-12:30pm and 2-6:30pm; Oct. 16-March 15 9:30am-12:30pm and 2-6pm. Admission 30F, students 13F.) The **Musée de la Bataille de Normandie,** bd. Fabian Ware (tel. 31 92 93 41), vividly recounts the events of June-August 1944. (Open daily 9am-7pm; Jan.-March 15 and Oct. 16-Dec. 10am-12:30pm and 2-6pm; March 16-May and Sept.-Oct. 15 9:30am-12:30pm and 2-6:30pm. Admission 24F, students 11F.)

Memories of World War II are inseperable from the beaches near Bayeux, now known as the **D-Day Beaches** and code-named Utah, Omaha, Gold, Juno, and Sword. On June 6, 1944, over 1,000,000 Allied soldiers climbed from the English Channel onto these beaches—the first step in an incredible invasion of the Continent, most of which was occupied by the Nazis. Highlights of the beaches include the American and Canadian **cemetaries** and **Arromanches,** a small town at the center of **Gold Beach** where the British built Port Winston to harbor Allied supplies. The town's **Musée du Débarquement** (tel. 31 22 34 31) is worth a visit. **Bus Verts** (tel. 31 92 02 92 in Bayeux) serves the area from Bayeux (bus #70; Mon.-Sat. 3 per day, ½hr., 15F). For a guided tour, call **Normandy Tours** (tel. 31 92 10 70) or **Bus Fly** (tel. 31 22 00 08) in Bayeux. For more info, contact Bayeux's tourist office.

■■■ MONT-ST-MICHEL

Even if you've seen a hundred photos of this fortified island, your heart will flutter when you first glimpse Mont-St-Michel. Rising abruptly out of a huge expanse of sea, its dazzling abbey is visible for kilometers in every direction. Gray stone roofs, spires, and walls make a charmingly erratic climb up and around the sides of the island, which is dramatically lit at night. The island first came into existence in the 7th century, when a gigantic wave swamped the forest of Sissy, isolating the Mont from the mainland. In 708, the archangel St. Michel appeared in the dreams of the Bishop of Avranches, instructing him to build a place of worship on the barren and rocky island north of Pontorson.

The only break in the Mont's outer wall is the **Porte de l'Avancée.** Inside, the **tourist office** lies immediately to the left (tel. 33 60 14 30); to the right, the **Porte du Boulevard** and **Porte du Roy** open onto the town's major thoroughfare, **Grande Rue.** All hotels, restaurants, and sights are on this spiraling street, but sneak off via several inconspicuous stairwells and archways to explore Mont-St-Michel's less-visited corners. The **abbey** (tel. 33 60 14 14) is the departure point for all of the one-hour tours. (Open daily 9:30am-6pm; Sept. 16-Nov. 10 and Feb. 15-May 14 9:30-11:45am and 1:45-5pm; Nov. 12-Feb. 15 daily 9:30-11:45am and 1:45-4:15pm. Tours in English daily at 10am, 11am, noon, 1:30pm, 2:30pm, 3:30pm, 4:30pm, and 5:30pm. Tours in French every ½hr. Admission 36F, ages 18-25 and over 60 23F, under 18 27F, Sun. ½-price.) **La Merveille,** an intricate 13th-century cloister housing the monastery, encloses a seemingly endless web of passageways and chambers. Escape down the ramparts and into the abbey garden, where you can reflect upon the soaring stone buttresses that wrap around the entire island and the coastline of Normandy and Brittany. Avoid the asphyxiating crowds on the main street, descending to the **Porte du Bavole** via the ramparts. Do not wander off too far on the sand at any time; the bay's tides are the highest in Europe, shifting every six hours or so.

The nearest budget accommodations are in Pontorson, easily accessible by bus. Try the **Centre Duguesclin (HI),** rue Général Patton (tel. 33 60 18 65; 41F). To get to the Mont from Paris, take a **train** (tel. 33 60 00 35) to **Pontorson** (change at Rennes, 4hr., 235F plus 36-90F TGV supplement). For **bus** schedules from Pontorson to the Mont, call STN at 33 60 00 35.

Appendices

■■■ TIME ZONES

France is one hour ahead of Greenwich Mean Time (Britain and Ireland), six hours ahead of New York and Toronto, and nine hours ahead of California and Vancouver. France is one hour behind most of South Africa, including Johannesburg, seven hours behind Perth, and nine hours behind Sydney.

■■■ WEIGHTS AND MEASURES

1 millimeter (mm) = 0.04 inch	1 inch = 25mm
1 meter (m) = 1.09 yards	1 yard = 0.92m
1 kilometer (km) = 0.62 mile	1 mile = 1.61km
1 gram (g) = 0.04 ounce	1 ounce = 25g
1 liter = 1.06 quarts	1 quart = 0.94 liter

To convert from °C to °F, multiply by 1.8 and add 32.
To convert from °F to °C, subtract 32 and multiply by 5/9.

°C	35	30	25	20	15	10	5	0	-5	-10
°F	95	86	75	68	59	50	41	32	23	14

■■■ GLOSSARY

Here you will find a compilation of some of the French terms *Let's Go* has used, along with their pronouncitions. The gender of the noun is either indicated in parentheses or by the article (feminine, *la;* masculine, *le*). The glossary is followed by some phrases you might find helpful. The listed words or phrases which use the article "le" ("luh"), "la" ("lah"), "les" ("lay") indicate the pronounciation of the noun only. Eu and eue (pronounced the same) have a pronounciation in between the English "ew" and "uh." In this guide we have used "uh" to indicate this sound.

l'abbaye (f.)	abbey	lah-BAY
l'allée (f.)	lane, avenue	lah-LAY
l'abri (m.)	shelter	lah-BREE
l'aller et retour	round-trip	lah-LAY ay ruh-TOOR
l'arc (m.)	arch	LAHR
les arènes (f.)	arena	ah-REHN
l'auberge (f.)	inn, tavern	loh-BEHRZH
la banlieue	suburbs	bahn-LEEH
la basse ville	lower town	bahs VEEL
la bastide	walled town	bahs-TEED
le beffroi	tower	behf-WAH
la bibliothèque	library	bihb-lee-oh-TECK
le billet	ticket	bee -YAY
le bois	forest	BWAH
la calanque	cove	cah-LAHNK
le cap	cape, foreland	KAHP
la cathédrale	cathedral	kah-tay-DRAHL
la cave	cellar	KAHV

le centre ville	center	SAHN-truh VEEL
la chambre	room	SHAHM-bruh
la chambre d'hôte	rural bed and breakfast	SHAHM-bruh DOHT
la chapelle	chapel	shah-PEHL
le château	castle	shah-TOH
le cimetière	cemetery	see-meh-TYAYR
la cité	walled city	see-TAY
le cloître	cloister	KLWAH-truh
la côte	coast	KOHT
cours	tree-lined walk	KOOR
le couvent	convent	koo-VON
la croisière	cruise	kwahz-YAYR
la croix	cross	KWAH
le cru	wineyard, vintage	KRU
la dégustation	tasting	day-GOOS-tah-SYOHN
donjon	dungeon	dohn-ZHON
la douane	customs	DWAHN
l'école (f.)	school	lay-KOHL
l'église (f.)	church	lay-GLEEZ
l'escalier (m.)	stairway	lehs-kahl-YAY
le faubourg	quarter	foh-BOOR
la fête	celebration	FEHT
la foire	fair	FWAHR
la fontaine	fountain	fohn-TEHN
la forêt	forest	foh-RAY
la gare	station	GAHR
la gare routière	station	GAHR root-YAYR
le gîte rural	rural bed and breakfast	ZHEET roo-RAHL
la halle	market hall, covered market	LAHL
la haute ville	upper town	OHT VEEL
l'horloge (f.)	clock	lohr-LOHZH
l'hôtel (particulier) (m.)	mansion (town house)	loh-TEL(pahr-tee-cool-YAY)
l'hôtel de ville (m.)	town hall	loh-TEHL duh VEEL
l'île (f.)	island	LEEL
la mairie	seat	meh-REE
le marché	market	mahr-SHAY
la montagne	mountain	mohn-TAHN
le mur	wall	MYUR
le palais	palace	pah-LAY
le parc	park	PAHR
la place	square	PLAHS
la plage	beach	PLAHZH
le pont	bridge	POHN
le quartier	section (of town)	kahr-TYAY
la randonnée	hike	rahn-duh-NAY
la rue	street	RU
le salon	drawing or living room	sah-LOHN
le sentier	path, lane	sehn-TYAY
le téléphérique	cable car	tay-lay-fay-REECK
les thermes (m.)	hot springs	TEHRM
la tour	tower	TOOR
la vallée	valley	vah-LAY

HELPFUL PHRASES

| la vendange | grape harvest | vahn-DANZH |
| la vieille ville | old town | VYAY VEEL |

■■■ HELPFUL PHRASES

please	*s'il vous plaît*	see voo PLAY
thank you	*merci*	mehr-SEE
hello	*bonjour*	bohn-ZHOOR
good evening	*bonsoir*	bohn-SWAHR
How are you?	*Comment allez-vous?*	KOH-mehn TAH-lay VOO
I am well.	*Je vais bien.*	ZHUH VAY BYEHN
goodbye	*au revoir*	OH ruh-VWAHR
Excuse me.	*Excusez-moi.*	ehks-KOO-ZAY MWAH
Do you speak English?	*Parlez-vous anglais?*	PAHR-lay VOO zahn-GLAY
I don't understand.	*Je ne comprends pas.*	ZHUH NUH kohm-PRAHN pah
How much	*combien*	kohm-BYEHN
I'm sorry.	*Je suis désolé.*	ZHUH SWEE day-soh-LAY
who	*qui*	KEE
what?	*Comment?*	koh-MOH
how	*comment*	koh-MOH
why	*pourquoi*	poor-KWAH
when	*quand*	KAHN
What is it?	*Qu'est-ce que c'est?*	KEHS-kuh SAY
I would like	*Je voudrais*	ZHUH voo-DRAY
I need	*J'ai besoin de*	ZHAY buhz-WAN DUH
I want	*Je veux*	ZHUH VUH
I don't want	*Je ne veux pas*	ZHUH NUH VUH PAH
to rent	*louer*	loo-AY
The bill, please.	*L'addition, s'ilvous plaît.*	lah-dees-YOHN, SEE VOO PLAY
Where is/are	*Où est/sont*	OO AY/SOHN
the bathroom?	*les toilettes.*	twa-LET
the police	*la police*	po-LEES
to the right	*à droite*	ah DWAHT
to the left	*à gauche*	ah GOHSH
up	*en haut*	ahn OH
down	*en bas*	ahn BAH
straight ahead	*tout droit*	TOO DWAHT
a room	*une chambre*	oon SHAHM-bruh
double room	*une chambrepour deux*	oon SHAHM-bruh POOR DEUH
single room	*une chambre simple*	oon SHAHM-bruh SAYM-pluh
with	*avec*	ah-VECK
without	*sans*	SAHN
a shower	*une douche*	oon DOOSH
breakfast	*le petit déjeuner*	puh-TEE day-jhuh-NAY
lunch	*le déjeuner*	day-jhuh-NAY
dinner	*le dîner*	dee-NAY
shower included	*douche comprise*	DOOSH kohm-PREE
included	*compris*	kohm-PREE

■■■ NUMBERS

one	un	twenty	vingt
two	deux	thirty	trente
three	trois	forty	quarante
four	quatre	fifty	cinquante
five	cinq	sixty	soixante
six	six	seventy	soixante-dix
seven	sept	eighty	quatre-vingt
eight	huit	ninety	quatre-vingt-dix
nine	neuf	one hundred	cent
ten	dix		

■■■ MENU READER

agneau	lamb	frais	fresh
bar	sea bass	fraise	strawberry
beurre	butter	frites	french fries
bien cuit	well done	fromage	cheese
bière	beer	gâteau	cake
bifteck	steak	glace	ice cream
blanc de volaille	breast of chicken	grenouille	frog (legs)
bleu	very rare	haricot vert	green bean
boeuf	beef	jambon	ham
boissons	drinks	lait	milk
brioche	buttery bread, almost like pastry	lapin	rabbit
		légume	vegetable
canard	duck	magret de canard	breast of duck
champignon	mushroom	mille feuille	"thousand-layered" pastry; a Napoleon
Chantilly	whipped cream with sugar		
chaud	hot	nature	plain
chèvre	goat cheese	oeuf	egg
choix	choice	oignon	onion
citron	lemon	pain	bread
confit de canard	duck or goose preserved in its own fat	petit déjeuner	breakfast
		poisson	fish
côte	rib or chop	pomme	apple
crème fraîche	fresh heavy cream	pomme de terre	potato
croque-monsieur	toasted, open-faced ham and cheese sandwich	potage	soup
		poulet	chicken
		salade verte	green salad
crudités	raw vegetables, usually with dressing	saucisson	large dried sausage
		saumon	salmon
déjeuner	lunch	tartare	chopped raw meat topped with a raw egg
dîner	dinner		
échalote	shallot	tarte tatin	caramelized, upside-down apple pie
entrée	first course (appetizer)		
escargot	snail	viande	meat
foie gras	liver of a fattened goose	vin	wine

Index

★ FREE T-SHIRT ★

JUST ANSWER THE QUESTIONS ON THE FOLLOWING PAGES AND MAIL THEM TO:

Attn: Let's Go Survey
St. Martin's Press
175 Fifth Avenue
New York, NY 10010

WE'LL SEND THE FIRST 1,500 RESPONDENTS A LET'S GO T-SHIRT!

(Make sure we can read your address.)

■ LET'S GO 1995 READER ■
QUESTIONNAIRE

1) Name _____

2) Address _____

3) Are you: female   male

4) How old are you?   under 17   17-23   24-30   31-40   41-55   over 55

5) Are you (circle all that apply):   in high school   in college   in grad school
employed   retired   between jobs

6) What is your personal yearly income?
Under $15,000 $15,000 - $25,000 $26,000 - $35,000 $36,000 - $50,000
$51,000 - $75,000 $76,000 - $100,000   over $100,000   not applicable

7) How often do you normally travel
with a guidebook?
This is my first trip
Less than once a year
Once a year
Twice a year
Three times a year or more

8) Which *Let's Go* guide(s) did you buy
for your trip?
_____
_____

9) Have you used *Let's Go* before?
Yes   No

10) How did you first hear about
Let's Go? (Choose one)
Friend or fellow traveler
Recommended by store clerk
Display in bookstore
Ad in newspaper/magazine
Review or article in
newspaper/magazine
Radio

11) Why did you choose *Let's Go*?
(Choose up to three)
Updated every year
Reputation
Easier to find in stores
Better price
"Budget" focus
Writing style
Attitude
Better organization
More comprehensive
Reliability
Better Design/Layout
Candor
Other _____
_____
_____

12) Which of the following guides have
you used, if any?
Frommer's $-a-Day
Fodor's Affordable Guides
Rough Guides/Real Guides
Berkeley Guides/On the Loose
Lonely Planet
None of the above

13) Is *Let's Go* the best guidebook?
Yes
No (which is?) _____
Haven't used other guides

14) When did you buy this book?
Jan   Feb   Mar   Apr   May   Jun
Jul   Aug   Sep   Oct   Nov   Dec

15) When did you travel with this
book? (Circle all that apply)
Jan   Feb   Mar   Apr   May   Jun
Jul   Aug   Sep   Oct   Nov   Dec

16) How long was your stay in
Paris?
less than 1 week   1-3 weeks
1-3 months   4-12 months

17) How many travel companions did
you have?   0 1 2 3 4 over 4

18) Roughly how much did you spend
per day in Paris?
$0-15 $51-70
$16-30 $71-100
$31-50 $101-150
over $150

19) What was the purpose of your trip?
(Circle all that apply)

Pleasure	Business
Work/internship	Volunteer
Study	

20) What were the main attractions of your trip? (Circle top three)
Sightseeing
New culture
Learning Language
Meeting locals
Camping/Hiking
Sports/Recreation
Nightlife/Entertainment
Meeting other travelers
Hanging Out
Food
Shopping
Adventure/Getting off the beaten path

21) How reliable/useful are the following features of *Let's Go*?
v = very, u = usually, s = sometimes
n = never, ? = didn't use

Accommodations	v u s n ?
Camping	v u s n ?
Food	v u s n ?
Entertainment	v u s n ?
Sights	v u s n ?
Maps	v u s n ?
Practical Info	v u s n ?
Directions	v u s n ?
"Essentials"	v u s n ?
Cultural Intros	v u s n ?

22) On the list above, please circle the top 3 features you used the most.

23) Would you use *Let's Go* again?
Yes
No (why not?) _____
_____

24) Do you generally buy a phrasebook when you visit a foreign destination?
Yes   No

25) Do you generally buy a separate map when you visit a foreign city?
Yes   No

26) Which of the following destinations are you planning to visit as a tourist in the next five years?
(Circle all that apply)

Australasia

Australia	Japan
New Zealand	China
Indonesia	Hong Kong

Vietnam	India
Malaysia	Nepal
Singapore	

Europe And Middle East

Middle East	Switzerland
Israel	Austria
Egypt	Berlin
Africa	Russia
Turkey	Poland
Greece	Czech/Slovak
Scandinavia	Rep.
Portugal	Hungary
Spain	Baltic States

The Americas

Caribbean	The Midwest
Central America	Chicago
Costa Rica	The Southwest
South America	Texas
Ecuador	Arizona
Brazil	Colorado
Venezuela	Los Angeles
Colombia	San Francisco
U.S. Nat'l Parks	Seattle
Rocky Mtns.	Hawaii
The South	Alaska
New Orleans	Canada
Florida	British Columbia
Mid-Atlantic	Montreal/
States	Quebec
Boston/New	Maritime
England	Provinces

27) Where did you stay in Paris?

Hostel	Hotel
Apartment	Friend's home
Student housing	Campground

28) What other countries did you visit on your trip? _____
_____

29) Which of these do you own?
(Circle all that apply)

| Computer | CD-Rom |
| Modem | On-line Service |

Mail this to:
Attn: Let's Go Survey
St. Martin's Press
175 Fifth Avenue
New York, NY 10010

Thanks For Your Help!

Paris Metro

• The stations Liège and Rennes are closed after 8pm and on Sundays and holidays.

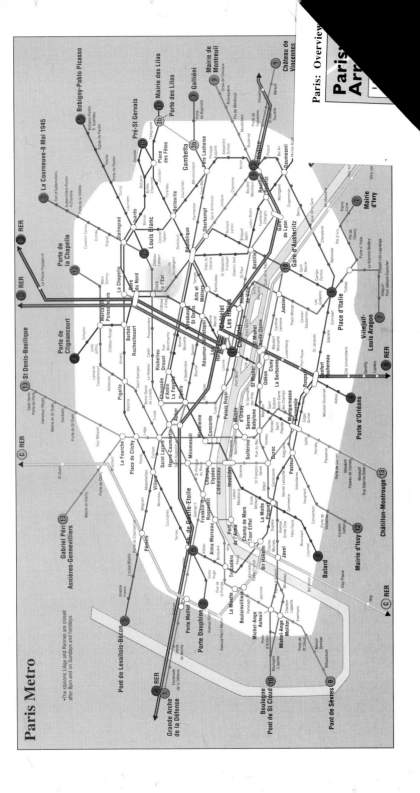

. Overview and
ondissements

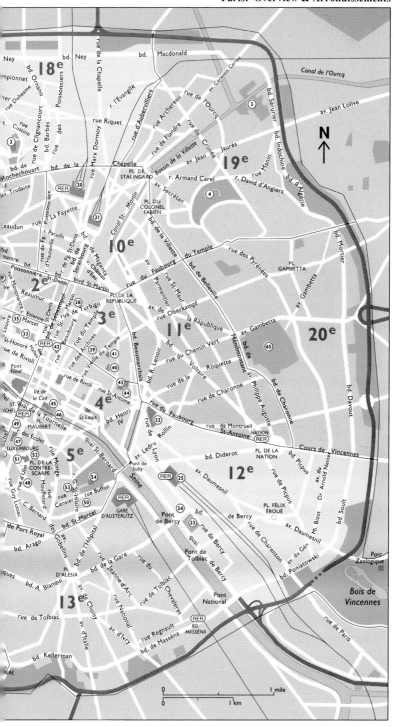

Paris: 1er and 2e

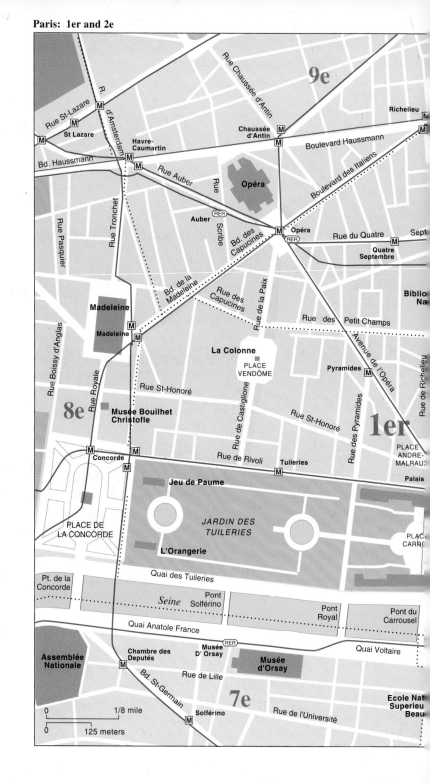

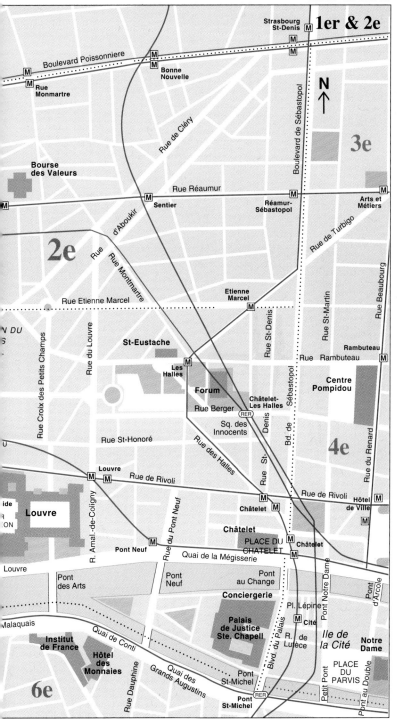

1er & 2e

Strasbourg
St-Denis

Boulevard Poissonniere

Bonne
Nouvelle

Rue
Monmartre

N

3e

Rue de Cléry

Bourse
des Valeurs

Rue Réaumur

Boulevard de Sébastopol

Sentier

Réaumur-
Sébastopol

Arts et
Métiers

2e

Rue d'Aboukir

Rue

Rue Montmartre

Rue de Turbigo

Rue Beaubourg

Rue Etienne Marcel

Etienne
Marcel

N DU
S

Rue Croix des Petits Champs

Rue du Louvre

St-Eustache

Les
Halles

Rue St-Denis

Rue St-Martin

Rambuteau

Rue Rambuteau

Forum

Centre
Pompidou

Rue Berger

Châtelet-
Les Halles

RER

Sq. des
Innocents

Rue St-Honoré

Rue des Halles

Rue St-Denis

Bd. de Sébastopol

4e

Rue du Renard

U

Louvre

Rue de Rivoli

Rue de Rivoli

ide
R
ON

Louvre

Châtelet

Hôtel
de Ville

R. Amal.-de-Coligny

Pont Neuf

Rue du Pont Neuf

Châtelet

Louvre

Pont
des Arts

Quai de la Mégisserie

PLACE DU
CHÂTELET

Châtelet

Pont
Neuf

Pont
au Change

Pont Notre Dame

Pont
d'Arcole

Malaquais

Conciergerie

Pl. Lépine

Quai de Conti

Palais
de Justice
Ste. Chapell

Cité

Ile de
la Cité

Notre
Dame

Institut
de France

Hôtel
des
Monnaies

Blvd. du Palais

R. de
Lutèce

PLACE
DU
PARVIS

Rue Dauphine

Quai des Grands Augustins

Pont
St-Michel

Petit Pont

Pont au Double

6e

Pont
St-Michel

RER

Paris: 5e and 6e

Palais du Louvre

Pont Neuf

Châtelet

Quai du Louvre

1er

Pont des Arts

Pont Neuf

Pont au Change

Concigerie

Conciergerie

Cité

Ste-Chapelle

Hô Di

Pont du Carrousel

Quai Malaquais

Quai de Conti

Pont St-Michel

Ile de la Cité

Rue de la Cité

Ecole Nationale Supérieure des Beaux Arts

R. Bonaparte

Institut de France

Hôtel des Monnaies

Quai des Grands Augustins

Pont St-Michel

Rue St-Jaques

Rue des Sts-Pères

Rue Jacob

Rue de Seine

Rue Mazarine

Rue Dauphine

St-Michel

Pl. St-Michel

R. de l'Abbaye

St-Germain Des Prés

Rue St-André des Arts

Rue Danton

Rue St-Jaques

PLACE ST-GERMAIN-DES-PRÉS

Bd. St-Germain

St-Germain des Prés

Mabillon

Bd. St-Germain

Odéon

Musée du Cluny

7e

R. du Four

Rue de l'Odéon

Rue Racine

Boulevard

Sorbonne

R. de Sèvres

R. du Vieux Colombier

R. du Saint Sulpice

Rue de Tournon

St-Michel

PLACE DE LA SORBONNE

R. du Cherche Midi

PLACE ST-SULPICE

St-Sulpice

PLACE DE L'ODÉON

Rue Soufflot

St-Sulpice

R. d'Assas

R. de Rennes

Palais du Luxembourg

Luxembourg

Bd. Raspail

R. de Vaugirard

6e

Rue Gay-Lu

Rennes

JARDIN DU LUXEMBOURG

St Placide

Rue du Montparnasse

Notre-Dame des Champs

Rue d'Assas

Boulevard St-Michel

Montparnasse Bienvenüe

Rue Vavin

Rue Notre-Dame des Champs

Avenue de la Observatoire

Vavin

Boulevard du Montparnasse

Port Royal

R. du Depart

14e

Boulevard Raspail

Edgar Quinet

Boulevard Edgar Quinet

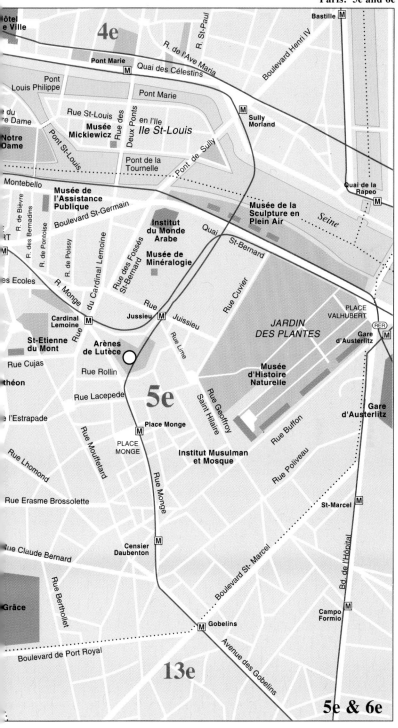

4e

Hôtel
de Ville

Bastille Ⓜ

R. St-Paul

R. de l'Ave Maria

Boulevard Henri IV

Pont Marie Ⓜ

Quai des Célestins

Pont
Louis Philippe

Pont Marie

Rue St-Louis

Rue des
Deux Ponts

en l'Ile
Ile St-Louis

Ⓜ
Sully
Morland

e du
e Dame

Pont St-Louis

**Musée
Mickiewicz**

Notre
Dame

Pont de la
Tournelle

Pont de Sully

Quai de la
Rapeo

Ⓜ

Montebello

**Musée de
l'Assistance
Publique**

R. de Bièvre

R. des Bernardins

R. de Pontoise

R. de Poissy

Boulevard St-Germain

Rue des Fossés
St-Bernard

**Institut
du Monde
Arabe**

Quai

**Musée de la
Sculpture en
Plein Air**

Seine

St-Bernard

RT

R. du Cardinal Lemoine

R. Monge

**Musée de
Minéralogie**

Rue Cuvier

PLACE
VALHUBERT

es Ecoles

Rue

Jussieu Ⓜ

Juissieu

**JARDIN
DES PLANTES**

RER

Gare
d'Austerlitz

Ⓜ

Cardinal
Lemoine Ⓜ

**St-Etienne
du Mont**

Rue

Rue Lime

Arènes
de Lutèce

○

Musée
d'Histoire
Naturelle

Gare
d'Austerlitz

Rue Cujas

Rue Rollin

héon

Rue Lacepede

5e

Rue Geoffroy
Saint Hilaire

Rue Buffon

e l'Estrapade

Rue Mouffetard

Place Monge

Ⓜ

Rue Lhomond

PLACE
MONGE

**Institut Musulman
et Mosque**

Rue Poliveau

Rue Monge

St-Marcel Ⓜ

Rue Erasme Brossolette

Censier
Daubenton Ⓜ

ue Claude Bernard

Rue Bertholet

Boulevard St- Marcel

Bd. de l'Hôpital

Campo
Formio

Ⓜ

Grâce

Ⓜ Gobelins

Boulevard de Port Royal

13e

Avenue des Gobelins

5e & 6e

Paris: RER

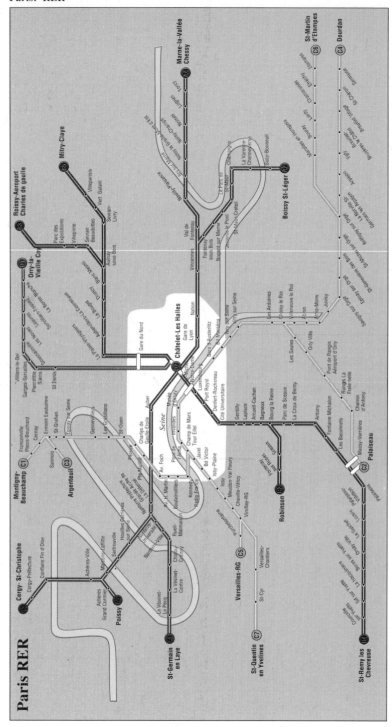

Paris RER